The Point of Pittsburgh

To Rita
In solidarity!

Charlie McCollester

The Point of Pittsburgh

Production and Struggle at the Forks of the Ohio

BY

CHARLES MCCOLLESTER

ILLUSTRATIONS BY

BILL YUND

People's Pittsburgh 250 Edition

BATTLE OF HOMESTEAD FOUNDATION
PITTSBURGH, PENNSYLVANIA
2008

Published: 2008
                              Pittsburgh, Pennsylvania, U.S.A,
                              Battle of Homestead Foundation

Copyright: © 2008, Charles McCollester
Illustrations: © 2008, Bill Yund

ISBN: 978-0-9818894-0-5   *(cloth)*
                              978-0-9818894-1-2 *(softcover)*
                              All rights reserved.

                              People's Pittsburgh 250 Edition
                              Point of Pittsburgh Book Project
                              P. O. Box 60104
                              Pittsburgh, PA 15211

Typesetting: **Steel Valley Printers**
Layout/Design: **Lloyd Cunningham**
                              Jim Hohman

Cover Design: **Bill Yund**

Printing: **Allegheny Commercial Printing**
                              Pittsburgh, Pennsylvania

For Information or Sales: **Steel Valley Printers, Inc.**
                              107 East Eighth Avenue
                              Homestead, Pennsylvania 15120
                              U. S. A.

                              412-461-5650
                              412-461-5653 *(fax)*

To my father, Sumner, who imparted a work ethic along with a love of geography, maps, stamps and travel, and especially to my mother, Margaret, who passed along her love of books, her passion for politics and social justice, her love of people and sympathy for the poor.

To all the people who lived at the Forks of the Ohio, past and present, near and far, especially those yet to come. As native peoples who once lived here said: "Think of the coming generations of our families, think of our grandchildren and of those yet unborn, whose faces are coming from beneath the ground."*

*Source and full quote, p. 21

Contents

Contents

Chapter Illustrations
by
Bill Yund

Chapter One: **Land and Waters**
From earliest times, Mother Earth favored this region, with layers of coal, oil and minerals that would bless inhabitants to come. The Grandfathers of Earth's mountains rose up, later to be tamed by the glaciers and worn smooth by the ages. We still owe Mother Earth.

Chapter Two: **Natives at the Forks: 12,000 BC —1740**
The earliest humans loved and respected this place so provident and welcoming. In the 1700s, at the great outcropping of rocks below the forks of the rivers (later to be McKees Rocks), family and social life flourished, rich flood plains nourished abundant crops, homes were built, children played and burial mounds testified to spiritual needs. The only enemies were other humans...

Chapter Three: **Invasion and Resistance: 1741-1790**
European values were of doubtful worth to the region, but its lush resources were a value never lost on Europeans. French appetites were modest compared to English hunger for power and wealth. Disputes brought bitter blood, with innocents caught between.

Chapter Four: **Gateway to the Heartland: 1791-1850**
Keelboats made paths of the rivers. On the Monongahela, travelers arrived - and passed through - the region, inspired by a brighter future. A wealth of resources nourished Pittsburgh's embryonic industry.

Chapter Five: **Civil War and Industrial Might: 1851-1875**
Pittsburghers of all stripes took non-violent action to stop shipment of Pittsburgh-made artillery to the South prior to the Civil War. The sons of Pittsburgh were not to die by products of Pittsburgh's manufacturing skills.

Chapter Six: **Domination and Resistance: 1876-1894**
"Violence is justified where justice is absent" seemed to be the thinking when robber barons, with the collusion of government, left working people with few viable alternatives. Riots and mayhem made the point, but justice was often truly blind and resolution slow to come.

Chapter Seven: **The Triumph of Capital: 1895-1909**
A Morewood miner's mother wails her grief at her last view of a son murdered by company deputies. Her sorrow and anguish is representative of family and community grief resulting from irresponsible and inadequate safety regulations of the time, as well as suppression.

Chapter Eight: The Americanization of Labor: 1910-1919
Fannie Sellins, widow, mother and union organizer, meets strikebreakers from the deep South to convince them not to take the jobs to which they've traveled so far. Some join the picket lines. She was murdered by company goons soon after.

Chapter Nine: Mellon Rule and capital's Crash: 1920-1932
Each family in its respective living space; one of elegance and comfort, with a transfer of knowledge and privilege that promises more of the same to the younger generation. The other is squalor, overcrowding and indignity, as signified by the lack of privacy. Here is a heritage whose only sure promise is hard work and danger.

Chapter Ten: Labor's Rise: 1933-1940
At J&L Steel's Aliquippa Works, employees strike to counter the company's defiance of court orders. Workers overturned a supply truck masquerading as a mail truck as it tried to enter the plant with food for strikebreakers.

Chapter Eleven: Victory and Division: 1941-1949
Out of the mines, mills and workshops of the Pittsburgh region poured phenomenal tonnages of coal, steel, glass, machinery, ships, railroad equipment, processed food, guns and ammunition for the war effort. Allegheny County sent over 190,000 soldiers to war and yet with the help of women workers, retirees and overtime, the area recorded record levels of production. After World War II, the cold war and political reaction bitterly divided the labor movement over the issue of Communism.

Chapter Twelve: Flowering of the Mill Town: 1950-1960
River valleys, full circle. Life is good. Children play, homes are being built "up the hill", local resources provide food, clothing and shelter. Spirituality is evident in a wide variety of churches. Social and family life thrive. Again, a young couple looks to the horizon - still promising, but now more complex and foreboding.

Foreword

Of the making of many books there is no end. This phrase from Ecclesiastes 12:12 certainly is true of histories of Pittsburgh. So, why another one?

Because there still has been lacking a history that includes a focus on *all* of the story of labor's role in a leading industrial center in the United States, indeed in the entire world. There have been numerous able accounts of the pivotal Homestead Strike in 1892; of Pittsburgh's giant industries themselves, such as Kenneth Warren's book on Big Steel; and of the collapse of heavy-industry of the 1980s as chronicled by John Hoerr and William Serrin—not to mention biographies of leading figures such as Andrew Carnegie, Henry Clay Frick, and George Westinghouse.

But in "The Point of Pittsburgh," author Charles McCollester goes beyond merely a narrow-based history of labor or of organized labor. He covers the history of Pittsburgh as a whole, with the story of labor crucially imbedded.

Especially valuable is the fact that Dr. McCollester approaches the subject from various personal vantage points. The first is as an academic, both as a labor historian and as director of the Pennsylvania Center for the Study of Labor Relations at Indiana University of Pennsylvania.

Further, he writes from a factory worker background, both as a skilled craftsman and as a labor union steward. During his college years he worked in manufacturing, retail and truck jobs to help finance his education at Boston College and at the University of Louvain, Belgium, where in 1968 he achieved a successful doctoral defense (magna cum laude) from its Institut Superieur de Philosophie.

But more significant was his role at the Union Switch & Signal Co. in Swissvale, PA. Hired in 1978 as a milling machine operator, McCollester after two terms as a United Electrical Workers' (UE) steward in the machine shop was elected Chief Steward of the entire plant following a bitter six-month strike (1981-82). As chief union officer, he witnessed firsthand the slow, painful dismantlement and then shutdown of a notable, century-old manufacturing establishment. At that point, he became a key activist in the so-called Mon Valley Insurgency, serving as an organizer of the Tri-State Conference on Steel and then officer of the grassroots-organized Steel Valley Authority.

This move was in keeping with McCollester's life of activism on numerous fronts, stemming from his Roman Catholic roots. That included the civil rights movement, where he participated in a Freedom Ride in the Eastern Shore of Maryland and the March on Washington, 1963. Following his graduate studies, he worked for six months as head branch librarian in an African-American ghetto neighborhood in Gary, Indiana. He also was active in the anti-Vietnam War movement. In recent years, he has called attention to the "other side" of the white settlement of the Ohio Valley region with lectures for the Pennsylvania Humanities Commonwealth Speakers Program on the subject, "Native American Resistance to the European Invasion of Western Pennsylvania," a topic addressed in "The Point of Pittsburgh."

McCollester also has had extensive experience abroad to add to his American scope. The bulk of his doctoral research at Louvain University for his dissertation, "Emanuel Levinas and Modern Jewish Thought," occurred in Paris, and during a six-month period in Israel, both on an Israeli kibbutz (Yasur in Galilee) and at the Hebrew University Library in Jerusalem. He spent the summer of 1970 hitchhiking through Mexico, followed by two years of travel in Africa which resulted in writings on the African independence struggle.

His connection with Indiana University of Pennsylvania commenced in 1986, where he held successive posts until his appointment in 1999 as director of the Pennsylvania Center for the Study of Labor Relations. In 1999 and 2000, he organized and taught in the IUP Summer in Poland program at Adam Mickiewicz University in Poznan, Poland. He also conducted research/consultation work in Sweden, Haiti, and Nicaragua.

McCollester's stature has been recognized within the profession with his election to two terms as president of the Pennsylvania Labor History Society. During the dismantling of the Homestead Works for the development of the Waterfront Mall, he worked with others to form the Battle of the Homestead Foundation to save the historic Pump House, the center in 1892 of worker resistance to the employer-hired Pinkerton strike-breakers. He has served as president of the organization.

All of this wealth of personal experience has contributed to the broad expanse of "The Point of Pittsburgh," keeping it from being a one-sided "catching up" story emphasizing only the labor viewpoint. Moreover, for the reader, academic or otherwise, the "garment" contains many touches of "embroidery," anecdotes and "insider" stories of important events, as well as appraisals of significant labor and management figures, whether little known or notable.

Speaking personally, I covered much of the same general Pittsburgh terrain in my book, "Front-Page Pittsburgh: Two Hundred Years of the Post-Gazette." But in reading the McCollester manuscript, I was impressed with the many facts and stories—especially on labor—that I had not uncovered in my research.

His book will be an invaluable resource in the future not only for historians but for general readers seeking a wider view of Pittsburgh's remarkable, tangled story.

Clarke M. Thomas
Pittsburgh Post-Gazette, Senior Editor *(retired)*
Author of three books on Pittsburgh history

Acknowledgments

My history has been composed to be an everlasting possession,
not the show-piece of an hour.
Thucydides, *The History of the Peloponnesian War I:22*

This history of Pittsburgh is a collective effort. Many deserve thanks. First, my wife Linda who provided a loving home dedicated to raising our five talented children, Karl (wife Lauren, children: Hadley and Seamus), Rebecca (husband Brian, son Hayden), Sarah, Matthew and Maria, all far-flung members of the Steeler Nation post-industrial diaspora which provides much of the inspiration to tell this story. Second, I am blessed with a close family: my brother Dave (his wife Kris, children Aaron, Dan and Kerry), and my sister Mary (her son Jorge). The determination and tenacity of my sister Mary has provided me a life-long model of personal courage.

I am especially grateful to the group of like-minded Pittsburgh friends who have supported these efforts: the members of the Battle of Homestead Foundation Board, a creation of the Wednesday morning labor history breakfast group that has met weekly for nearly 20 years, and which agreed to provide the vehicle for the publication of this Peoples Pittsburgh 250 Edition; as well as the devoted members of the Pennsylvania Labor History Society, which has been dedicated to the remembrance and celebration of workers' struggles and achievements for three decades. I am deeply appreciative for several very knowledgeable commentators and editors: Clarke Thomas, John Hoerr, Bill Serrin and Staughton Lynd. They read and commented on the text as it took shape. I am equally grateful to subsequent readers and editors, who provided a fresh, yet practiced eye on the text as it finalized: Millie Beik, Peter Oresick, Melanie Archangelo and Cindy Spielman. I have been the beneficiary of very useful information or suggestions on particular sections from Bill Yund, Russ Gibbons, Chris Mark, Joel Sabadasz, Doug McGregor, Anne Madarasz, Irwin Marcus, Jim Dougherty, Elizabeth Ricketts, Jim Watta, Eric Marchbein, Dave Demarest, Lynne Squilla, Laurence Glasco, Jim English, Steffi Domike, Howard Scott, Father Jack O'Malley, Jim Hohman, John and Linda Asmonga, Ken Wolensky, Cal Schuchman, Molly Rush, Tony Slomkoski, Dennis Seese, John Harper, Chris Moore, David Rosenberg, Jim Kunz, Pat McMahon. Mike Laquattra, Jr. and Pat Cassidy.

Mike Stout, Rosemary Trump and Russ Gibbons provided corrections, suggestions, as well as sustained enthusiasm, support and promotion for the project. Longtime collaborator, Mike Stout, wrote an amazing series of songs based on characters and events in the book. Lloyd Cunningham at the Steel Valley Printers provided layout, good-humored advice and a lot of work. Final proof-reading was done by a group including Kathleen Werner, Russ Gibbons, Raymond Martin, Stephanie Stout, Chuck Martoni, Rick Allison, Jim Catano, Susie Piotrowski, Lloyd Cunningham and Mike Stout. Gregg Mowry and Stephanie Stout are helping with distribution; Lynne Squilla and Bernie Lynch with promotion and marketing. Jim Hohman advised on book design. Rosemary Trump spearheaded the fundraising efforts. Peter Oresick has been a knowledgeable advisor concerning publication during the endgame.

Teaching Pittsburgh history to senior undergrads and labor history to graduate students at Indiana University of Pennsylvania helped me develop a narrative voice for this rich and complex story. Over the years, graduate assistants at IUP facilitated research and assisted in the organization of the book. Robin Donald, Christina Smith, John Lepley, Maggie Bloomgren, and especially Megan Butterbaugh down the stretch, helped with citations, bibliography, formatting and indexing. A grant from the Pennsylvania Historical and Museum Commission helped with research and the development of teaching materials based on the book compiled by my graduate assistant, Brandon Schmitt. PHMC historian Ken Wolensky provided advice, encouragement and documents. I am grateful for the always knowledgeable assistance from David Grinnell and for conversations with Anne Madarasz about glass and sports, at the Heinz History Center. The Carnegie Libraries in Mt. Washington and Oakland, especially the Western Pennsylvania Room, were indispensable. The University of Pittsburgh microfilm collection was useful. The Hunt Library staff at Carnegie Mellon University was helpful concerning an enquiry.

While books and writings formed the building blocks of the story, thirty plus years experience in the union movement as a steward in Local 57 of the Hotel and Restaurant Union, as chief steward of UE 610 at Union Switch & Signal, as a representative of temporary faculty at IUP, and as a labor educator involved with the entire range of labor organizations of Pennsylvania provided me insight and appreciation for workers' organizations, their trials and aspirations. The staff of the Pennsylvania Center for the Study of Labor Relations at Indiana University of Pennsylvania (IUP), Jim Watta and especially Cindy Spielman provided constant support and encouragement.

I am deeply grateful for the financial assistance from unions and individuals through The Point of Pittsburgh Book Project Committee that made this People's Pittsburgh 250th Anniversary Edition possible and printed by a union printer in Pittsburgh. Committee Co-Chairs are: Scott Malley, Ironworkers Local 3; Mike Dunleavy, IBEW Local 5; Leo Gerard and Jim English, United Steelworkers; James Kunz, Operating Engineers Local 66; Paul Quarantillo, Laborers District Council of Western Pennsylvania; Cynthia Spielman, Pennsylvania Center for the Study of Labor Relations, IUP. I appreciate the organizational support of Jack Shea, Allegheny County Labor Council, as well as Bill George and Rick Bloomingdale of the Pennsylvania AFL-CIO. The entire Book Project Committee is listed in the book along with a list of the Operating and Advisory Boards of the Battle of Homestead Foundation. I am humbled by the support from organized labor, since central to the story of Pittsburgh is the struggle of workers, their resistance to injustice rooted in social solidarity and concerted activity. I am even more humbled by the personal contributions of the many friends who are supporters of this project.

When my wife and I arrived in Pittsburgh, in July of 1973, we fell in love with the place and its people. Five children born and raised here gave us roots. The decade I spent prior to our arrival, studying and hitch-hiking in Europe, Africa, the Middle East and Mexico provided a certain perspective and sense of proportion. In the mid-1970s, I sketched my first outline for a history of the city. The dozen years spent working in restaurants, construction sites, and machine shops introduced me to the city's rich working-class life. Those years, especially the seven-plus years working as a machinist, operating milling machines and metal lathes, gave me a profound appreciation for the skill and work ethic of a culture that was in the process of being brutally pulverized – with the human dust scattered to the four winds. When my blue collar career was illegally terminated in 1986 in the course of the closing of the Union Switch & Signal plant in Swissvale, Pennsylvania, I was invited to join the staff of the Pennsylvania Center for the Study of Labor Relations at Indiana University of Pennsylvania by its Director Martin Morand. He, with fellow faculty members Jim Byers and Don McPherson, was instrumental in providing me an opportunity to move into a half-time teaching position in the graduate program of Industrial and Labor Relations. My first class at IUP was a senior synthesis course I developed called "Pittsburgh."

While this book was in germination for thirty years, it took three years of concentrated effort to write it. In the fall of 2005, I left with a car full of seven boxes of books and files relevant to Pittsburgh prior to 1870. With a one semester sabbatical from IUP, I arrived at my cousin John Pohl and his wife Helen's house on Jordan Bay just north of Shelburne, Nova Scotia. The nine weeks I spent alone there gave me the impetus that carried the project through to completion. Inspiration came from David Montgomery's American Labor History classes that I audited at Pitt in 1973-1974 (missing only one class in two semesters for the birth of my eldest son); from Alice Hoffman, my kind Quaker mentor and guide; and especially Staughton and Alice Lynd, always for me the gold standard of patient, non-violent intellectual service to workers and the poor. I benefited greatly from my more than twenty-year friendship with Monsignor Charles Owen Rice, his reflections on the city's history, recitations of poetry and great stories. My co-worker, Bill Yund, supplied his striking art to illustrate the book's chapters and devised maps to help the reader follow the story. He passed on any interesting book or article he stumbled on, and provided a steady supply of good natured advice with the best sense of humor I ever encountered.

This work celebrates the aspirations of the people of Pittsburgh, through two hundred of the city's two-hundred-and-fifty year history. There remains much yet to be told. There is much left out. Hopefully mistakes and at least some of the most glaring omissions can be rectified in a later national edition. Pittsburgh's story continues here at the Forks of the Ohio and extends out to the post-industrial refugees spread out around the country and beyond. God willing, another book dealing with the fifty years from 1960 to 2010 might yet emerge, but it will be a different sort of book. The story of the last half-century lies largely unwritten in the hearts and memories of the living. It resides beneath the "terrible towel" of memory.

May this book help present and future generations comprehend what Pittsburgh stands for, its meaning in the history of the nation. Just as the achievements and contributions of workers are often overlooked, Pittsburgh's significance is little noted in the telling of the country's story. *The Point of Pittsburgh* asserts that what happened *in* this city and *to* this city reveals a great deal about what this country was and what it has become.

On the Feast of John the Baptist,
A voice crying in the wilderness,

Charles J. McCollester
June 24, 2008

Chapter One
Land and Waters

All cities are shaped by land and water, few more emphatically than Pittsburgh. The site gained strategic importance from the rivers that joined to open a gateway to the American West. Its economic advantage derived from its position at the eastern headwaters of the vast Mississippi — Ohio — Missouri river system and on the northwestern edge of the rich Appalachian bituminous coal beds. Over the course of time, geography profoundly shaped the history of the area; but, in more recent times, humans have in turn drastically impacted the region's land, air and waters.

Beds of Coal

Three hundred million years ago, more than a hundred million years before the age of the dinosaur, the central interior of what is now North America was covered by a vast, but shallow, inland sea. Along the borders of this sea were broad areas of bogs and swamps where thick vegetation flourished in shallow waters and along the floodplains of rivers. Thick accumulations of organic material stretched along the western edge of lands that were rising and folding to the east due to the birth pangs of what became the Appalachian Mountains. Border zones were alternately submerged and then exposed by fluctuations in sea levels or by mountain-building activity, leaving characteristic layers of sediment. When the seas advanced, marine limestone beds formed from the proliferation of shellfish that thrived during those periods when the warm, inland sea covered the land. When the sea retreated, shale and sandstone were deposited by rivers from the erosion of higher ground to the east. Along this coastal plain, extensive forests and swampy lowlands flourished, creating vast peat beds. The most typical geologic formations of this age lie in the state that gave its name to the forty-million year Pennsylvanian Period. The Pennsylvanian coal beds, enormous storehouses of energy preserved in the highly compressed remains of intense vegetation growth, also provide an important source of natural gas in Pennsylvania in the form of coal bed methane.[1]

Luxuriant vegetation accompanied the advance and retreat of the inland sea. Coal strata in the Pittsburgh region are inter-bedded with both marine and brackish water rocks, as well as rocks derived from soils, river sand and mud. With the cyclic oscillation of the advancing and retreating seas, limestone layers often formed above western and central Pennsylvania coal seams. As the shallow seas advanced over the great bogs, the shells and bones of billions and billions of sea animals covered the thick, dark remains of the luxuriant swamp. Conversely, as the sea receded or the land uplifted, new swamps formed. As silt and mud washed down from rising eastern elevations, shale or sandstone "caps," responsible for many roof falls causing miners' death or injury, were formed over the thick layers of fossilized vegetation.

Known as the "coal age," the Pennsylvanian Period exhibits a fossil flora unlike any before or since. Giant relatives of modern ferns were the most common plants; horsetails, or Calamites, 30 feet tall abounded; scaly trees grew to heights of 100 feet; the forerunners of the modern conifers reached 50 feet. The density of the vegetal growth was a function of temperature and humidity, which in turn were influenced by Pennsylvania's geographic position. Pennsylvania was situated about five degrees south of the equator during the Pennsylvanian Period, so had a climate similar to the present day Amazon River basin. Mud and sand covered the thick layers of fallen vegetation, preventing oxidation and decay. Unfortunately, in light of environmental concerns raised in the late 20th Century, most of the western Pennsylvania coals include sulfur as an impurity. Swamps bordering inland saltwater seas were brackish due to sulfur-depositing bacteria, more prevalent in sea water than in fresh.[2]

Extraordinary insects proliferated and reached gigantic proportions. Cockroaches, spiders, scorpions and centipedes were prolific while dragonflies attained wingspans of two feet. More than a dozen insects exceeded four inches and three types were over a foot long. Cockroaches, virtually identical to the present type, existed in such incalculable numbers that the period has been called the "Age of Cockroaches." Amphibians and reptiles were also emerging onto the scene.[3]

The coalfields of the Pennsylvanian Period in the United States exceed 250,000 square miles, considerably larger than any other continent. During this same period, however, the great coalfields of Great Britain (Wales and Yorkshire), France (the Saar basin), Germany (the Ruhr), Belgium (the Meuse), Poland (Silesia) and Russia (the Donetz basin) were created. Eighty percent of the world's coal derives from this geologic period. The extensive anthracite coal regions of eastern Pennsylvania are also a product of the same period as the bituminous fields of central and western Pennsylvania. In the east, however, the immense forces unleashed by the collision of continents about 250 million years ago created coal fields of a dramatically different type. Anthracite coal is harder and closer to pure carbon than bituminous, because the folding of the sedimentary strata caused greater pressures and higher temperatures on the deposits, not because of greater antiquity. The tilting and folding of the anthracite beds during the Alleghenian orogeny (literally "mountain birth") explain the steep angles and convoluted strata that make them difficult to mine by machine.[4]

Coal was the foundation of Pittsburgh's wealth and the basis of its industrial development. Coal makes Pittsburgh a part of a region and a work culture shared by miners, as well as by coke, iron, steel and glass workers in the furnace industries whose fuel the miners' labor supplied. The bituminous beds of the Pennsylvanian Period underlie the Appalachian Plateau from southwestern Pennsylvania to Alabama. Historically, Pennsylvania, West Virginia, Ohio, Kentucky and Alabama were the major producers of coal from these beds. There are up to 60 separate beds of which 10 are thick enough to be commercially mined. Three seams of coal, the Redstone, the Pittsburgh, and the Upper Freeport, have been extensively mined in Allegheny County. The most important by far is the renowned "Pittsburgh seam." The 6,000 square miles of this seam in Pennsylvania, Ohio, West Virginia and Maryland contained an estimated 22 billion tons of coal. This seam, a great economic resource, has proven to be one of the greatest storehouses of energy on the earth rivaling the Saudi Arabian oil fields.

Of consistent thickness (6-12 feet) and high quality, the Pittsburgh coal seam exists at or near the surface in several areas of the city. In the Hill District and in a few patches north of the Allegheny

River, the coal was exposed at the surface. There is no significant amount of Pittsburgh coal north of the Allegheny, however. South of the Monongahela River, from a line three quarters of the way up the face of Mt. Washington, overlooking the Forks from the south at a height of approximately 300 feet above the rivers, the coal seam slopes gently downward in a more or less continuous layer toward Washington and Greene Counties in the southwest corner of the state. There, in 2006, the seam is still being vigorously exploited at a depth of between 500-600 feet. The seam passes under the Monongahela near Elizabeth, so the northern, downstream sections of the seam were easily accessible by drift mines advanced from the river valley where the coal could be directly loaded onto boats.

The Pittsburgh seam was crossed by the builders of Braddock's road and noted by James Kenny, a young Quaker traveler in 1758 near Brownsville. Discovered at Fort Pitt, allegedly by a Welshman in the service of the British army staring up at the ridge across the Monongahela, it was first mentioned by Colonel Hugh Mercer in a report to Colonel Henry Bouquet in 1759. "Excellent coal and limestone, contiguous to each other, have been lately discovered within a mile of the Monongahela, almost opposite to Pittsburgh."[5] In Allegheny County, it is estimated that the Pittsburgh seam alone produced nearly 1.3 billion tons of coal until it ceased being mined around 1990.

Another consequence of Pittsburgh's position on the site of a former saltwater sea is the presence of brine (salt water) in shallow sandstones. Extremely important to the early settlers, salt was produced at Saw Mill Run on the Ohio just below the Point, but especially along the Allegheny near Tarentum and its tributary, the Kiskiminetas at Saltsburg. While its production faded in importance in the mid-1800s as cheaper sources of salt became available, the drilling of brine wells and the development of drilling technology led to the striking of oil wells and, eventually, natural gas wells, and these changed the course of history. Pennsylvanian sedimentary deposits are an important source of petroleum and natural gas, and until 1925 were the country's major commercial producers. Since then, the exploitation of oil and gas deposits around the world and the creation of global energy markets have moved production elsewhere. [6]

Coarse sandstone used primarily for foundations and retaining walls was the main local stone used in construction. Local limestones were burned in kilns to produce lime for agriculture, or were used as flux in early steel making. Clay and shale were extensively quarried within the city limits to produce building bricks. One clay bed in particular, called the Pittsburgh red beds, which are responsible for most of Pittsburgh's landslide problems, still produces a good quality red brick in the Harmarville area. Most of the buildings constructed before 1900 are of this local red brick. Higher quality firebrick as well as yellow housing and paving brick were made from clays obtained from Kittanning, the Beaver Valley and Ohio, north and west of Pittsburgh. Iron deposits exist only in small quantities, but these native sources in central Pennsylvania, southeast of Pittsburgh along Chestnut Ridge, and in the counties north of Pittsburgh, were historically important as local charcoal-fed furnaces nurtured the early iron-working industry. They were eventually displaced as sources of supply and by the 1880s the bulk of the ore that fed the rapidly expanding local steel industry came from Lake Superior's Mesabi Iron Range.

Rising Mountains

A second geologic event that imprinted the Pittsburgh area with its peculiar character is the Alleghenian orogeny that created the Appalachian Mountains. Beginning in the Pennsylvanian period and continuing through the 30 million year-long Permian Period that followed, tremendous geologic forces of plate tectonics created a unified landmass called Pangaea that included all the continents of the world. Later, during the early part of the Triassic Period, the same forces split Pangaea asunder, giving rise to the separate continents of Europe, Africa and Asia to the east and the Americas to the west. During the Alleghenian orogeny, powerful compressive forces pushed against the thick sedimentary deposits in eastern Pennsylvania that in some areas reached seven or eight miles in depth. Over a period of 20 million years, these sediments were pushed to the northwest in gigantic folds and faults, forming mountains whose peaks were probably higher than the present-day Rocky Mountains. This dramatic geological happening created the long mountain ridges, like the striations of a washboard, which separated the western region of Pennsylvania from the eastern seaboard. The mountains provided the basis for the ancient northwestward-flowing drainage system that characterized western Pennsylvania until the coming of the Ice Age glaciers.

Pittsburgh presents a rugged, mountainous aspect. Going up or down is as much a constant of life as going right or left; but geologically speaking, the most western of the ridges of the Appalachians, the nearest mountain, is Chestnut Ridge thirty to forty miles east of the City of Pittsburgh. The strata underlying the forks of the Ohio is quite horizontal because the rocks were not put under as much mountain-building stress as the rocks in central Pennsylvania. Western Pennsylvania is considered a plateau because it was originally a flat tableland. As streams cut down through this plateau, they created the convoluted terrain we see today. Pittsburgh is a city of gorges and valleys, hills and ridges, hollows and runs. In some places, almost canyon-like valleys resulted, such as Panther Hollow in Oakland. High cliffs along the Allegheny at Troy Hill, Millvale and Verona, the cliff-like face of Mount Washington across the Monongahela from downtown, and the West End overlook along the Ohio give the three rivers their dramatic aspect.[7]

The Monongahela meanders north to Pittsburgh on an ancient path that once flowed all the way to where Lake Erie is today via today's Ohio, Beaver, and Mahoning river valleys. In the lost language of those natives who inhabited the region prior to 1650, the name is said to mean "muddy river with falling banks." This very old river snakes along toward the forks of the Ohio in a succession of generous curves that left broad flood plains on the insides of the curves. In these flat alluvial meadows, both natives and pioneers formed settlements and grew crops on the rich bottomlands. Later, these same flats provided space to invading factories and mill towns.[8]

Shifting Rivers

The original pattern of deepening canyons formed by ancient northwestward-flowing rivers such as the Monongahela was radically transformed by a third major, and much more recent, geologic event – the advent of the Ice Age. Successive Ice Ages, the first beginning more than one million years ago and the last ending as recently as 15,000 years ago, had a profound impact on the land. In Western Pennsylvania, a line from Ellwood City northeast to Slippery Rock through Warren, approximately parallel with the course of today's Allegheny River, marks the southeastern most advance of the ice pack. Aside from the scraping and leveling of the terrain north and west of Pittsburgh that created moraines and lakes, the effect of the glaciers on the direction and configuration of the rivers was dramatic.

The ancient streams that flowed out of the Appalachian Mountains toward the ancestral Lake Erie basin were blocked and dammed by the growth and advance of the vast continent-sized glaciers similar to that which today covers Greenland. Rivers that once flowed northwest now overflowed the hills that divided them and eroded new channels southwest into the headwaters of what is now the Ohio River basin. As ice blocked the northward flow, the river eroded the drainage divide and began flowing westward along the southern edge of the glacial ice to the Mississippi. The Monongahela and Allegheny became tributaries of an Ohio that drained into the Mississippi. The present-day Allegheny was three separate rivers. The Lower Allegheny followed the course of the Clarion River down the present river bed to its junction with the Monongahela. The two sections of the Middle and Upper Allegheny flowed north into the ancestral Erie basin. As the mass of ice blocked the northward flow of the two northern segments, they reversed course and joined the Lower Allegheny to form the present-day stream. The Beaver River, once a large and important north-flowing stream, was dammed by ice and forced to reverse its flow by the glacial advance. Impounded melt water pouring out of a glacier-created lake reversed Slippery Rock Creek and created the gorge at McConnell's Mill. The site of Pittsburgh emerged as the clear ice blue waters of the vigorous and youthful Allegheny intercepted the ancient riverbed of the meandering Monongahela and turned it toward the heart of a continent.[9]

The backing up of the Monongahela and Allegheny rivers and their tributaries during successive Ice Ages did more than radically reorient the river drainage. Over the centuries, when the northward flow of water was blocked by thick sheets of ice, rivers backed up, causing lakes to form in the valleys. River valleys were widened and their floors were covered by thick layers of debris. Sedimentation during these periods, followed by erosion when the ice plug melted, caused the formation of stepped benches along the riverbeds where native villages and settler towns later found such hospitable locations.[10] That astute observer, Hugh Henry Brackenridge, Pittsburgh's first author and founder of what became the University of Pittsburgh, described the stepped banks created by the subsequent damming and releasing of the rivers' flow.[11]

> The town of Pittsburgh, as at present built, stands chiefly on what is called the Third Bank; that is the third rising of ground above the Allegheny water. For there is the first bank which confines the river at the present time; and about three hundred feet removed is a second like the falling of a garden; then a third, at the distance of about three hundred yards; and lastly a fourth bank, all of easy inclination, and parallel with the Allegheny River. These banks would seem to have been the margin of the river which gradually changed its course, and has been thrown from one descent to another, to the present bed where it lies. In digging wells, the kind of stones are found which we observe in the Allegheny current, worn smooth by the attrition of the water. Shells also intermixed with these are thrown out.[12]

The wells Brackenridge mentions penetrated into another creation of the glacial period, the mythical "fourth river" at the Point. Below and much wider than the rivers, this aquifer made of sand, gravel and clay deposited by the Allegheny and Ohio rivers during and after the Ice Age, runs, at a depth of 50-70 feet, under much of the lower North Side and about one-third of the Golden Triangle. It is presently tapped to provide cool water for air conditioners in downtown buildings and to feed the large fountain at Point State Park. The glacial character of the Allegheny is also revealed in its *sharp, flinty* sand that proved very useful for the establishment of the early plate glass industry which employed it to create the glass and to grind plates of glass after rolling.[13]

Another consequence of the glacial blockage was a shift in the river channel of the Mon. The original Monongahela floodplain survives as a terrace some 200 feet above the present river level and forms the relatively flat area in Pittsburgh's East End, where some of Pittsburgh's prime residential areas are found. The Cathedral of Learning, the University of Pittsburgh's signature tower, sits on nearly forty feet of sand, gravel and clay deposited by the ancient Monongahela. This level plain underlies the business and residential areas of Braddock, Rankin, Swissvale, Edgewood, Shadyside, Point Breeze, East Liberty, Bloomfield and Oakland -the last two of these city neighborhoods separated by the deep gorge that represents the old river bed's lower reaches before meeting today's Allegheny above the Point. In the 19th Century, this ancient river bed provided the route for the Pennsylvania Railroad's entry into the city from the east. In the late 20th Century, it provides the path for an express busway from the eastern suburbs to downtown.[14]

Pittsburgh reveals itself as a town of ridges and valleys. Its scarred visage, its rugged and convoluted terrain, reveals the power of water and ice on ancient layers of rock over time.

Notes: Chapter One

[1]Henry Leighton. "Useful Minerals of the Pittsburgh Region." *Geology of Pittsburgh and Environs*, (Pittsburgh, 1915); Carl Dunbar, Historical Geology (New York: John Wiley & Sons, 1949), 249-78; W.R. Wagner and W.S. Lytle, *Geology of Pennsylvania's Oil and Gas* (Harrisburg: Commonwealth of Pennsylvania Department of Environmental Resources, 1968).

[2]William Spackman and Alan Davis, "Origin, Characteristics and Properties of Pennsylvania Coal, *"Pennsylvania Coal: Resources, Technology, and Utilization* (Harrisburg: The Pennsylvania Academy of Science Publication, 1983).

[3]Dunbar, *Historical Geology,* 272; Leighton, Geology of Pittsburgh and Environs, 55-69.

[4]Dunbar, *Historical Geology*, 260; Spackman and Davis, Pennsylvania Coal, 13-15.

[5]Howard Eavenson, *The Pittsburgh Coal Bed – Its Early History and Development* (New York: Transactions of the American Institute of Mining and Metallurgical Engineers, Coal Division, 1938), 7-8.

[6]Addison Cate and Louis Heyman, "Regional Geological Setting of Western Pennsylvania," Chapter 5 in *Geology of the Pittsburgh Area*, ed. W. Wagner (Harrisburg, Pennsylvania Geological Survey, 1970).

[7]Frank C. Harper, *Pittsburgh of Today: Its Resources and People* (Pittsburgh: The American Historical Society, 1931), 1: 4-5; Cate and Heyman, Geology of the Pittsburgh Area, 3.

[8]James Norris, "The Monongahela River," *Western Pennsylvania Historical Magazine* (July 1923), 135-7.

[9]John A. Harper, "Of Ice and Waters Flowing: The Formation of Pittsburgh's Three Rivers," *Pennsylvania Geology* (Fall/Winter, 1997), 28(1): 2-5.

[10]Cate and Heyman, *Geology of the Pittsburgh Area*, 5; John A. Harper, "Of Ice and Waters Flowing," 5-6.

[11]Cate and Heyman, *Pittsburgh Area Geology*, 5; John A. Harper, "Of Ice and Waters Flowing," 5-6; John A. Harper, "Lake Monongahela: Anatomy of an Immense Ice Age Pond," *Pennsylvania Geology* (Spring, 2002), v.32, no.3-4. provides a detailed description of the forming of the terraces.

[12]Earl R. Schmidt and D.B. Schmidt, eds., *Pittsburgh Regional Ecology* (Pittsburgh: Vulcan Press, 1971).

[13]Trevor Hadley, "Deep Waters Run Still," *Pittsburgh Magazine* (March 1989), 34-6.

[14]O.E. Jennings, "When Pittsburgh Was a Lake," *Carnegie Magazine* (1959), 49; John A. Harper, "Of Ice and Waters Flowing,"7-8.

Chapter Two

Natives at the Forks

12,000 BC – 1740 AD

When the first small bands of humans advanced along the edge of the retreating ice cap into what is today southwestern Pennsylvania, they were confronted by a pristine and magnificent natural setting. Crystal waters teemed with fish, vast forests spread over the ridges and stretched along the river banks, an enormous diversity of wild animals were sustained in this environment, including a number of fierce predators that competed with men for prey. Above, the skies were clear, but full, traversed by enormous flocks of birds with great diversity among the feathered tribe. The small groups of humans, hunting and gathering in tight-knit communities, were far from dominant in the scene; but people adapted and slowly found an expanding niche in the thick web of life. Over time, the hand and mind of man transformed this scene dramatically.

From Ancient Times

History, the written record of human affairs, is a reflection of literate societies, social classes and individuals. Those who write tell the tale. Pittsburgh's *history* begins with the arrival of the Europeans a little more than 250 years ago. However, the historical record reflects less than two percent of the human story of the region. One of the oldest carbon-dated human settlements in all of North America is located at Meadowcroft near Washington, Pennsylvania, only 50 miles south of Pittsburgh. The deepest levels of that dig produced radiocarbon dates from 12,000-13,000 BC demonstrating 15,000 years of continuous human habitation in the region. By the time of the earliest levels, the glaciers had retreated to present-day Erie. The ancient arrival of paleo-Indian peoples across the glacial bridge to North America was contemporaneous with the beginnings of human habitation in northern Europe as the Ice Age glaciers receded. Hunter/gatherer peoples from Asia followed the southern edge of the Laurentide glacial mass across Canada to Western Pennsylvania. New genetic studies have pushed the proposed dates for the arrival of *homo sapiens* into North America back to twenty thousand years ago or more.[1]

The Meadowcroft Rock Shelter is an overhanging sandstone ledge that protects an area of about 300 square feet. The twelve feet of materials excavated below it contains evidence of human activity from all four major cultural stages now recognized in North American archeology: the Paleo-Indian, the Archaic, the Woodland and the Historic. The shelter served primarily as a temporary hunting, gathering and food-processing center for prehistoric cultures. Meticulous excavations recovered more than 400,000 specimens of animal remains with mammals the most abundant. Deer and elk were eaten through the entire time span. No mammoth remains were discovered; however, a fossil of a peccary (an extinct prehistoric pig) constituted the first record in eastern North America of a predatory relation between early man and an extinct animal.[2]

Meadowcroft's layered bones and charred fire pits contain another indicator of the impact of the man's arrival. The human invasion was humble and tenuous in its beginnings, but would in time harness rivers, flatten hills and radically alter the total lived environment. Meadowcroft uncovered copious evidence of the presence of the passenger pigeon, probably hunted by youngsters around the hunting camp. Arguably the most abundant bird that ever lived on earth, it disappeared over a couple of generations at the end of the 19th Century. Naturalist John Muir wrote: "I have seen flocks streaming south in the fall so large that they were flowing over from horizon to horizon in an almost continuous stream all day long, at a rate of forty or fifty miles an hour like a mighty river in the sky, widening, contracting, descending like falls and cataracts, and rising suddenly here and there in huge ragged masses like high splashing spray." The birds fed on the nuts of the oaks, beeches and especially chestnut trees. As the great forests fell to the axe, the food supplies for the bird diminished. Between 1860 and 1890, systematic hunting to provide cheap food for the immigrant hordes flooding into the eastern cities, led to the bird's extinction. While native peoples hunted the birds during their mass migrations with clubs, nets and arrows, a shotgun could kill thirty to forty birds with a single shot. The bird had completely disappeared from the wild by 1900.[3]

Humans appeared on the scene in extended family groups of fifty or more, moving when necessary for hunting or gathering. They raised the young and transmitted the teachings of the ancestors, hunted all sizes of game with finely crafted stone points, roasted meat and wore hides, wove vegetal fibers for mats, roofs and baskets, and collected edible nuts, seeds and fruits. Some eight thousand years ago, they began living within defined family territories, hunting, trapping, fishing, gathering berries, herbs and roots, and establishing more permanent villages. Five thousand years ago, evidence suggests they began to exploit extensive beds of mussels and other shellfish. Three thousand years ago, in the Ohio Valley, soil was first broken by the hoe, marking the beginnings of agriculture that conferred greater permanence and fostered the expansion of some villages to towns. By the beginning of the Christian Era, Indian life from the St. Lawrence River southward was becoming increasingly sedentary. People were making pottery, hunting with the bow and arrow, growing and using tobacco, and developing ever more elaborate religious and cultural traditions.[4]

Women were very important economically and politically. As producer and reproducer, the woman was the core of an economy of survival in a decentralized village structure where the men hunted, fished and protected the periphery while the women raised the children, tended the fields of beans, corn and squash, and fabricated much of the clothing, as well as weaving baskets and making pottery (tasks often shared with men). The study of human prehistory has been dominated by the study of spear points and arrowheads, male technologies that endure in stone. Women's technologies were often of fiber and clay. Her story, the female side of the human epic, has yet to be fully credited.[5]

Western Pennsylvania was influenced by two important town cultures that flourished in southern Ohio: the Adena 500 BC-100 AD and the Hopewell 100 BC-500 AD. The Adena culture was marked by the erection of large circular burial mounds as well as such complex and apparently religious creations as the Serpent Mound. The Adena culture seems to have been superseded and absorbed gradually by a culturally distinct Hopewell culture that continued, however, many of their traditions. Hopewellian culture also produced extensive ceremonial centers of a distinctive style with large flat-topped pyramids and complex avenues, earthen rectangles and octagons. Highly developed in Ohio, this culture spread over much of the Midwest and is characterized by evidence of long-distance trade, so that Gulf coast conch shells are found in Wisconsin. Lake Superior copper was traded far to the south and Ohio flint is found over much of eastern North America.[6]

The farthest eastern mound with Adena characteristics is in McKees Rocks, a few miles downstream from Pittsburgh on the Ohio. The first archeological dig undertaken by the Carnegie Museum excavated the mound and recorded evidence of 33 burials and 747 artifacts including pottery, shells, as well as worked antler, bone, chert and stone. During the 1896 excavation, a local paper described the central grave: "With this skeleton were found 517 beads…, five excellent perforators, one bone scraper, two flakers, one gorget or amulet, one tomahawk, one tusk in a copper sheath, and several other instruments." The human remains are still in storage at a Carnegie museum annex.[7]

Early white settlers remarked on the existence of 'old forts' which clearly predated and were apparently unrelated to the natives who fought the early settlers so ferociously for control of the region. These old forts were built after 500 AD following the collapse of the Hopewell, at the time of the Fort Ancient culture, up until the establishment of Monongahela villages around 1000 AD. The fortified sites of Ohio and Pennsylvania may have marked the final disintegration of the mound builders societies under pressure from the gradual influx of Algonquin and Iroquoian invaders. [8] The early settlers identified these constructions as forts and, like most whites who examined the mounds of Ohio, they judged these earthworks to be the work of some earlier more advanced people, "a race more intelligent, or of a people of different habits of life."

> These remains of embankments, or "old forts," are numerous in Fayette County. That they are very ancient is shown by many facts. The Indians, known to us, could give no satisfactory account of when, how, or by whom they were erected or for what purpose save for defense. While the trees of the surrounding forests were chiefly oak, the growths upon and within the lines of the old forts [were] generally of large black walnut, wild cherry, and sometimes locust. We have examined some which indicated an age of from three to five hundred years….[9]

Contemplate for a moment the kind of world being described where young walnuts, cherries and locust trees might be distinguished from the surrounding ancient oaks by their relative youth of 300-500 years of age! The oldest tree in Pennsylvania today is about three hundred years old and trees of more than two hundred years in age are rare. Prior to the metal axe and saw that delivered trees into the hands of man, the great forests of Western Pennsylvania supported a rich variety of plant, animal, reptile and bird life typical of old-growth forests. Bears, panthers, mountain lions, wolves, elk, deer and other mammals were plentiful and as well-adapted to the natural terrain as man. Man and woman kind's great advantage over the other species, or "nations," as Native Americans often expressed it, was in the ability to build communities and extend communication and loyalties across great distances. With language and symbolic representation, humans developed a talent for concerted activity. Indeed, concerted activity has proved to be a defining characteristic of the Pittsburgh region and is a central theme of the present book.

Compared to Eurasia, the Americas were poorly served in both the availability of key cereal grains and draft animals. The lack of horses, oxen, and mules placed major restrictions on large-scale cultivation. Fields were tilled by hand-held tools and seeds were planted individually, not broadcast as in European plowed fields. Rather than field monoculture as practiced in Europe, most new world fields more resembled mixed gardens of many crops planted together. While the dearth of draft animals restricted agriculture and transportation, the absence of animals (except the ubiquitous dog and in Peru, the llama) suitable for domestication such as cows, pigs, chickens, etc. meant that Natives lacked a wide range of resistances to species-crossing diseases like influenza and small pox, common to agricultural societies in Eurasia. Furthermore, their agriculture was limited by the fact that only one of the dozen major food grains, corn, is native to the Americas. Prior to the slow movement of corn northward from Mexico, cultivated crops such as squash, sunflower, sumpweed and goosefoot were grown in the native gardens for their edible seeds that were a tenth the size of wheat or barley. A new variety of corn, adapted to northeast America's short summers, was not successfully cultivated until around 900 AD; the arrival of beans around 1100 AD completed the transfer of Mexico's agricultural trinity of corn, beans and squash. [10]

As northeastern farming intensified, more densely populated towns developed along the Mississippi River and its tributaries. At the very moment when Native American agriculture in the Northeast achieved a level of agricultural productivity sufficient for urban development, European diseases ravaged the populations.

Beaver Wars and White Disease

When the French and English penetrated today's Pennsylvania from the east, south, and north in the 17th Century, there were six main groups of native peoples living there. Additional native groups around the Great Lakes region, principally the Ottawa, Miami, Potowatomie, Ojibway and Wyandots, also played a major role in Western Pennsylvania, primarily as allies of the French. The three main indigenous groups, the Lenne Lenape, or Delaware as the whites called them, the related Shawnee, and the Iroquois with their Mingo dependents, continued to be factors until the final defeat of the natives in the region in 1794. The remaining three Indian nations, Susquehannocks, Erie and the Monongahela people, who occupied the region around the forks of the Ohio, were broken and destroyed as communities in the 1640-80 period, as a result of the fierce competition for control of the fur trade. Trade opened the door to vital European weapons and goods, as well as to the ravages of unknown plagues that spread invisibly, sometimes well in advance of the traders themselves.

The Susquehannocks lived along the Susquehanna River basin in central Pennsylvania. They are the best recorded of the three Pennsylvania groups that were swept away by the expansion of the Iroquois. They had early contact with the Virginia colonists at Jamestown and Captain John Smith left extensive descriptions of them:

> (The) Susquehannocks came to us with skins, bows, arrows, targets (shields), beads, swords, and tobacco pipes for presents. Such great and well proportioned men are seldom seen, for they seemed like giants to the English...(yet) of honest and simple disposition... Their language it may well befit their proportions, sounding from them, as a voice in a vault. Their attire is the skins of bears and wolves...One had the head of a wolf hanging in a chain for a jewel, his tobacco pipe three quarters of a yard long, prettily carved with a bird, a deer, or some such devise at the great end, sufficient to beat out one's brains.... They can make (muster) near(ly) 600 able men, and are palisaded in their towns to defend themselves....[11]

The Susquehannocks, members of the Iroquoian linguistic group like the Huron, viewed the Five Nations of the Iroquois as bitter enemies. They were a warlike and organized people who lived in well-defended towns. They were caught, however, in a vise between white settlers from Virginia and Maryland and the Iroquois to the north, whose advanced governmental forms, military organization and key strategic position between the French and English colonies made them the most powerful Native political entity in the Northeast for more than two hundred years. At first the Susquehannocks with the assistance of the Marylanders held their own; but the combination of constant war, white treachery and smallpox weakened them until they were crushed and dispersed in 1675. A remnant, adopted by their Iroquois conquerors, settled near Lancaster where they became Christianized and known as the Conestoga. In the wake of Pontiac's uprising in 1763, these peaceful Indians were attacked, many killed, and the remainder driven off their land by white vigilantes from Paxton, outside present-day Harrisburg.[12]

The Beaver Wars stemmed from the economic and political dilemma of the tribes situated just beyond the coast as European settlement began. On one hand they recognized the superiority of European goods and quickly became dependent on them, especially the rifle, hatchet and iron traps, for their survival. While they feared and often hated the whites, they eagerly established relationships with traders because they desperately needed their wares to survive. Alexis De Toqueville, astute observer that he was, described the dynamic of the natives' dilemma:

> The Europeans introduced among the savages of North America firearms, ardent spirits, and iron; they taught them to exchange for manufactured stuffs the rough garments that previously satisfied their untutored simplicity. Having acquired new tastes, without the arts by which they could be gratified, the Indians were obliged to have recourse to the workmanship of the Whites; but in return for their productions the savage had nothing to offer except the rich furs that abounded in his woods...While the wants of the natives were thus increasing, their resources continued to diminish.[13]

The only marketable commodity the natives could offer a technologically advanced mercantilist economy was furs. The seemingly insatiable hunger of a rapidly growing international market for skins and pelts pitted one tribe against another for control of land and the harvesting of pelts that might provide the means to resist for a time the unrelenting pressure of the alien invasion. A strategic but vulnerable position, a formidable political and military organization, an imperative need to control the fur trade in order to obtain guns or be overrun and destroyed, led to the aggressive expansion of Iroquois power at the expense of their weaker neighbors. As wars and disease thinned native ranks, they launched "mourning wars" designed to replace fallen warriors and lost family members with captives. Internecine wars made it difficult for native tribes to unite against the white invaders, although strong pan-native sentiments at times swept through the tribes. The Delaware prophet Neolin, preaching native unity and collective purification through a return to traditional religion, helped inspire Pontiac's "conspiracy," a movement that ultimately culminated in Tecumseh's efforts at coordinated resistance to white expansion under Shawnee leadership.[14]

Driven by desperation more than malevolence, the eruption of the Iroquois in the 1640s and 50s brought down the mighty Huron of Canada, wiped out a half-dozen weaker tribes including the Monongahela, and threatened the very survival of French Canada, especially Montreal, which endured serious attacks. In the late 1630s, a smallpox epidemic hit the Iroquois, and by 1640 the beaver was virtually exterminated in their territory. The French with their Huron allies were extending their control over the rich fur trade of the Great Lakes. The Iroquoian assaults constituted a war for national survival aiming to replenish their declining population and extend vital hunting grounds. The Huron themselves were in deep disarray in the 1630s when their population dropped from thirty to ten thousand as a result of smallpox and drought. The French arrival, contemporaneous with the appearance of the epidemics, marked an economic and ideological challenge as well. The missionaries effectively served as the public relations arm of the fur traders. The arrival of Recollect Franciscans at Quebec in 1615 began "the great missionary drive of the Counter-Reformation French clergy to persuade the nomadic hunters of the continent to change their entire way of life, abandon their ancient customs, values, religious beliefs, and live according to the precepts of a sophisticated European religion ill-adapted to their temperament and their needs."[15] Traditionalists among the Huron blamed the presence of Catholic missionaries and the abandonment of ancient religious rituals for the plagues that assaulted them. The progress of Christianity in their midst deeply divided the Huron at the moment when their very existence was put in question by the Iroquois offensive that began in 1649.[16]

The background of the Beaver Wars was a devastating and relentless slaughter of the animals that threw the Indian economy and spirituality fatally out of balance. Over-hunting directly threatened the Indian's existence by undermining the economic base of their society. Furthermore, Native American spirituality recognized a kinship with all living things and natural forces. Traditional hunting was accompanied by taboos and rituals based on a conviction that animals could communicate and had spirits. Natives were careful to offer spiritual reparation for killing, since they saw the beaver, the fox, and the bear as nations among whom they had to live, whose souls they had to keep at rest, and whose strength they might need to draw upon. An Englishman living among the Ojibwa of the Great Lakes described the following scene: "The bear being dead, all my assistants approached, and all, but more particularly my old (adopted Ojibwa) mother...took her head in their hands' stroking and kissing it several times; begging a thousand pardons for taking away her life: not to lay the fault upon them, since it were truly an Englishman who had put her to death." The Ojibwa however immediately butchered the animal for a feast, setting however the beast's head adorned with ornaments on a scaffold in the lodge with a plug of tobacco placed near the snout.[17]

The lethal combination of firearms with an insatiable and addictive international market fueled a constant state of war between Indian tribes, upsetting ancient equilibriums and relationships. An anecdote recounted by Moravian missionary John Heckewelder illustrates the spiritual alliances that could exist between men and animals:

> I found also that the Indians...paid great respect to the rattlesnake, whom they called their *grandfather,* and would on no account destroy him. One day, as I was walking with an elderly Indian on the banks of the Muskingum, I saw a large rattle-snake lying across the path, which I was going to kill. The Indian immediately forbade my doing so; "for," said he, "the rattle-snake is grandfather to the Indians, and is placed here on purpose to guard us, and to give us notice of impending danger by his rattle, which is the same as if he were to tell us 'look about!'. Now," added he, "if we were to kill one of those, the others would know it, and the whole race would rise upon us and bite us. I observed to him that the white people were not afraid of this; for they killed all the rattle-snakes that they met with. On this he enquired whether any white man had been bitten by these animals, and of course I answered in the affirmative. "No wonder, then!" replied he, "you have yourselves to blame for that! You did as much as declaring war against them...They are a very dangerous enemy; take care you do not irritate them in *our* country; they and their grandchildren are on good terms, and neither will hurt the other."[18]

The Erie, like the Susquehannocks, were an Iroquoian-speaking people who were decimated by the Iroquois in the 1650s. They lived along the southern shore of Lake Erie until their villages were destroyed and their populations dispersed. The Monongahela people, whose villages resembled the Delaware, lived in communities spread across the upper Ohio, Beaver, Monongahela, Youghiogheny, Allegheny, and Kiskeminetas river valleys.[19] They may have been responsible for some of the "old forts" noted by early white settlers of the region. They disappeared completely as an entity during the Beaver Wars, a direct casualty of the eruption of the Iroquois, but probably also weakened by epidemics. Remnants of Erie, Monongahela and others broken by the Iroquois were subsequently organized under Iroquois governance as Mingos. The "half-kings" like Tanaghrisson or Shikkellamy who played such important roles in the historical period were basically pro-consuls, governors of a conquered province, overseers of conquered peoples.

George Washington investigated but rejected the spine-like bluff overlooking the Ohio at McKees Rocks as a possible site for a fort commanding the forks of the Ohio in 1753. The trader George Mercer described the remains of an Indian fortification and called it "a very fine Situation for a Fort....There has been an Indian Fort there some years ago. The ditch is now to be seen. Here the Indians always fled upon an alarm, as it was reckoned the strongest Fort they had. Several thousands have lost their lives in the attack of it, but it has never yet been taken." The location may well have served as a final defensive refuge for Monongahela Indians under attack by Iroquois a century prior to Washington's visit. [20]

Native Americans had no acquired immunity against many European diseases. Measles, smallpox, influenza and tuberculosis traveled along well-established trade routes and raiding paths and sometimes ravaged Indian tribes before they had ever directly encountered a European. Great epidemics are believed to have destroyed communities, depopulated whole regions, and vastly decreased the native population everywhere in the unexplored interior of the continent. These early pandemics are believed to have run their course prior to 1600 AD."[21] It is estimated that the population of Mexico dropped from more than 25 million to about 1 million in the first century after the Spanish arrival. A very small percentage of these deaths were by the sword. It has been estimated that one out of four of New England's original inhabitants died from warfare during the first century after the arrival of the Pilgrims, while nearly three out of four died of foreign disease.[22]

Pandemics undermined the Native Americans' ability to resist conquest, and they threw the Indian's spiritual world into disruption as they sought to find a religious answer for their afflictions. "Throughout the Americas, diseases introduced with Europeans spread from tribe to tribe far in advance of the Europeans themselves killing an estimated 95% of the Pre-Columbian Native American population. The most populous and highly organized native societies of North America, the Mississippian chiefdoms, disappeared in that way between 1492 and the late 1600s, even before the Europeans themselves made their first settlement on the Mississippi."[23]

Lenne Lenape and Shawnee

The "historic period," when European witnesses documented the Indian presence and power in Southwestern Pennsylvania, stretches from 1740-1794. Aside from a small remnant of the Cornplanter Seneca living along the Allegheny River near the New York State line, Pennsylvania expelled her native peoples by 1794. During this "frontier" period, three large tribes, the Lenne Lenape, the Shawnee and the Iroquois, played important ongoing roles.

The Lenne Lenape saw themselves as the "original people," and other Algonquin peoples called them "grandfather." "There at the edge of the water where the land ends...the fog over the earth was plentiful....All of them said they would go together to the land there...it would be good to live on the other side of the water." The Walem Olum, a Delaware pictographic record of purportedly great antiquity, seems to provide the remnant of a folk memory of a vast migration across the frozen Bering straits and down through Canada into the Mississippi watershed. Pushing steadily until stopped by the Atlantic coast, they were also known as the Wabanaki or sunrise people. At the time of the arrival of the Swedes, Dutch and English off their shores, the Lenne Lenape were a peaceful, loosely organized village society based on agriculture, seafood and hunting. According to their accounts, they crossed the Mississippi in a vast migration of tribes into the land of the Allegewi or Tallegewi, a name preserved in the name of the river called Allegheny, possibly a native name for the people of the Hopewell/Adena cultures who had lived in developed towns with impressive religious and mortuary structures.[24]

In their account, the Lenni Lenape negotiated safe passageway through the Allegewi territory; but when the Allegewi saw that the Lenape numbered in the thousands, they attacked them. Many bitter battles ensued. The Iroquois, who were also migrating eastward, but separately to the north, joined in alliance with the Lenape on condition they would share in the conquered territories. When the Iroquois joined in the battle, the Allegewi were defeated and fled south down the Mississippi. The Iroquois then moved across the southern shores of the Great Lakes and settled in New York. The Lenape also migrated to the east and ultimately settled the rich rivers and bays of the area where today Pennsylvania, Delaware and New Jersey meet. The Lenape prospered and multiplied. Several related tribes sprang from the parent including the Mohican to the north in the lower Hudson River valley and the Nanticoke to the south in Virginia.[25]

A deep enmity developed between the Lenape and the Iroquois. Long warfare between them contributed to the founding of the Iroquois League or Five Nations. However, with the arrival of the Europeans, all native peoples were subject to new and existence-threatening pressures. Early on, the Iroquois entered into protracted war with the French for control of the St. Lawrence Valley and the western fur trade of the Great Lakes and beyond. Champlain's use of firearms against the Iroquois on behalf of the Huron had bloody consequences for both French and Huron. The Delaware, on the other hand, established relatively amicable relations with English Quakers led by William Penn, and with the small Swedish settlements on their coast. According to a friend of the Lenape, Moravian missionary John Heckewelder, whose account was published in 1819, the Iroquois, encouraged in their intrigue by the Dutch at New Amsterdam, came to the Lenape with a portentous proposal. They proposed that the Lenape "abstain from the use of arms, and assume the station of mediators and umpires among their warlike neighbors...to be made women....As men they had once been dreaded; as women they would be respected and honored, none would be so daring or so base as to attack or insult them; as women they would have the right to interfere in all the quarrels of other nations, and to stop or prevent the effusion of Indian blood. They entreated them, therefore, to become the woman in name and, in fact to lay down their arms and all the insignia of warriors, to devote themselves to agriculture and other pacific employments, and thus become the means of preserving peace and harmony among the nations."[26]

Another Moravian missionary, David Zeisberger, described the Iroquois proposal to the Delaware in words that make an assumption about the role of women in society that stands in contrast to the position of females in the Europe of the time. The delegate of the Six Nations said:

It is not profitable that all the nations should be at war with each other, for this would at length ruin the whole Indian race. They had, therefore, contrived a remedy by which this evil might be prevented while there was still opportunity to do so. One nation should become the woman. She should be placed in the midst, while the other nations, who make war, should be the man and live around the woman. No one should touch or hurt the woman, and if any one did say so, they would immediately say to him, "Why do you beat the woman?" Then all the men should fall upon him who has beaten her. The woman should not go to war but endeavor to keep peace with all. Therefore, if the men that surround her should beat each other and the war be carried on with violence, the woman should have the right of addressing them, "Ye men, what are ye about; why do ye beat each other? We are almost afraid. Consider that your wives and children must perish unless you desist." The men should then hear and obey the woman. [27]

Delaware acceptance of the peacemaker role, this "subjugation" would have dire consequences. While the feminization of the Lenne Lenape was honorable within the native context - for women were politically and economically powerful in Iroquois and Lenape communities alike - to the European mind, the Lenape's female role meant they were subservient and most important could not hold property. This proved a convenient device that served both English and Iroquois interests, as the Iroquois asserted the right to unilaterally cede Delaware land through treaties with the English. During much of the 18th Century, while constant colonist pressure pushed the Delaware villages ever westward across the Alleghenies, the cession of Delaware land was ratified by a succession of treaties between English and Iroquois.

The Lenape, or Delaware as they were referred to by the whites, enjoyed harmonious relations with William Penn and his Quakers. Perhaps these early years of peaceful relations with the whites made them all the more vulnerable as white power grew, and the competition between English and French increased. In 1683, William Penn described the Delaware:

> In Liberality they excel, nothing is too good for their friend; give them a fine Gun, Coat, or other thing, it may pass twenty hands, before it sticks; light of Heart, strong Affections, but soon spent; the most merry Creatures that live, Feast and Dance perpetually; they never have much, nor want much: Wealth circulateth like the Blood, all parts partake; and though none shall want what another hath, yet exact observers of Property. Some Kings have sold, others presented me with several parcels of Land; the Pay or the Presents were not hoarded by the particular Owners... We sweat and toil to live; their pleasure feeds them, I mean, their Hunting, Fishing and Fowling, and this Table is spread everywhere; they eat twice a day, Morning and Evening; their Seats and Table are the Ground. [28]

As described by Paul Wallace in his *Indians of Pennsylvania*, the structure of the native economy gave men and women distinct functions but equality of status:

> The man because of his greater physical strength and his freedom from the burden of child rearing and nursing, attended to the more strenuous and dangerous duties. He cleared the land, felled the trees (by girdling them and then hacking them down with his stone ax), built and repaired the house. He made the fish dam, attached the "fish basket," and gathered the catch. At certain seasons of the year he went out hunting to provide food and clothing for the family. He made canoes, war clubs, bows, and arrows. He went to war to defend his home. But he left the management

of the house to his wife and the chief matron of her lineage, and he listened to the advice of these women in matters of peace and war.

The Delaware woman was far from being a slave. She had a relatively higher, more respected position in the community than her sister in Europe. She was complete mistress in her home. She owned the house, its equipment, and the fields attached to it. In case of divorce, she kept the children....Her duties were commensurate with her privileges, and she bore her responsibilities without complaining. She nursed the children, made the pottery, tanned the hides, dressed the game her husband brought, kept the fire burning, made the bread, provided her husband and family with two good meals a day, and kept a kettle of soup on the fire for possible visitors. She gathered the firewood, fetched the water, and made clothing for herself and the family. She plowed the ground, planted the corn, cultivated it, gathered it, and ground it into flour or meal...she was unsurpassed as a cook. Her two meals a day were prepared with a nicety that astonished the Europeans.[29]

The gravest misunderstandings and conflicts between European and Native American were over land. While tribes defended territories including settlements and hunting grounds, neither the land nor its produce was subject to individual ownership or control. The earth was prior, the mother, the source of all life, herself alive. While the European sought possession of natural resources to exploit and transform them, the native American regarded the self and nature as one: a continuum of spirit, or life or power that some called manitou. As long as a person kept a proper place in the scheme of things, the supernatural beings who controlled the natural environment would aid and protect that person.[30]

William Penn made a conscientious effort to purchase all land from the Delaware despite holding title to it from the king of England. He also attempted to deal with conflicting and overlapping claims exhibiting sensitivity to the fact that the Indians had a very different sense of property. Subsequent authorities in Pennsylvania had less scruples and were also faced with a rising tide of immigration that exerted continuous pressure on any treaty agreement. The most notorious example of the sale of Indian land was the "walking purchase" of 1737. A conflict arose about the meaning of a sale of land to William Penn that was to extend as far as a man could travel in a day and a half. To settle the claim, the sons of William Penn hired three men to "walk" on a line that had been previously marked and cleared. One of the men managed to cover fifty-five miles in eighteen hours.[31]

These and other devices pushed the Lenape north into the Wyoming and west into the Susquehanna Valley where they joined other groups of native refugees. Lenape began moving into the Pittsburgh area in the 1720s where they founded Shannopin's town within the present city limits. Situated in the Lawrenceville neighborhood, along the Allegheny River between 27th and 30th streets, the village was given the name of its chief and founder. The village declined and was probably abandoned in 1758 with the conquest of Fort Duquesne and the founding of Pittsburgh. It last appeared as a name on a map in 1775. In 1861, while factory foundations were being excavated to meet the needs of a different war, workers discovered extensive burial grounds:[32]

Within the last few weeks quite a number of human skeletons, some of them in a tolerably fair state of preservation, have been dug up from the old Indian burial ground in the Ninth Ward....At a point here near the river bank, two skeletons were discovered, one of which appeared to be of an Indian Chief, and the other that of a young girl, who perhaps was the dead warrior's daughter....On each of her arms were two silver bracelets and suspended from her neck was a silver crucifix. At the time of her internment, clothing must have been covered by tiny silver bells, as some three or four hundred altogether of these with a large number of beads strung upon what appeared to be sadler's silk, was discovered in the grave. She had also a very rich ring on one of her fingers and wore earrings of enormous size.[33]

The Shawnees were refugees, a race of wanderers. Native to south-central Ohio, a large segment of them were pushed out of Ohio by Iroquois attacks in the 1630s. Some bands entered into Tennessee, Georgia and the Carolinas while others migrated north along the mountains into Pennsylvania around 1700. By 1725, one large segment of the tribe had moved into central and eastern Pennsylvania with the permission of the Iroquois who were concerned with building a buffer zone of Indian refugees against the growing pressure of the white settlers. An Algonquin people related to the Delaware, whom they called "grandfather," the Shawnee settled beside the Lenape, and many moved with them during the 1730s into the Allegheny and Ohio Valleys. The Shawnees were fierce and respected warriors, used to fighting on the run and contemptuous of the whites and distrustful of the Iroquois. Since their far-flung diaspora brought them into contact with both southern and northern tribes, they became natural leaders in pan-tribal efforts to mount concerted native resistance to the white invasions. Shawnee boys were physically hardened and taught to be self-reliant. When they had reached an appropriate age, they were trained to take a daily jump into the river - even in winter when they had to break the ice to get in. At about the age of ten, a boy underwent a test of endurance. He was sent into the woods with bow and arrows and told not to return until he had something to eat. Before he was sent out, his face was blackened with charcoal, a sign to all he met that he was on his test and was not to be helped.[34]

The Shawnee often adopted women and children taken captive in war, but could be ferocious in their treatment of opposing soldiers, practicing torture and sometimes eating the flesh of their enemies to give them strength. As with most Native Americans, they were generally respectful toward women, though they did massacre women and children in retaliation for incidents that sometimes bore no relation to the victims, as did, of course, the whites. They sided with the French during both the French and Indian War and Pontiac's Rebellion. Cornstalk, one of their greatest chiefs, resided in the early 1740s in Chartier's Old Town (Tarentum), fought with the French, and led native forces against the Virginians at the battle of Point Pleasant in 1774. Their most renowned chief, Tecumseh, attempted to unite all the major groupings of native peoples east of the Mississippi against expanding white power in 1812.

The League of the Iroquois

The Iroquois Confederacy, centered in the Finger Lakes region of central New York State, had a profound influence on the early history of Western Pennsylvania. Living as they did at the headwaters of the Susquehanna basin, as well as at the top of the Allegheny-Ohio watershed, they could rapidly descend in light, fast, birch-bark canoes with devastating effect on their enemies to the south. Their geographic position between the French fur trading settlements along the St. Lawrence River and, initially the Dutch traders of New Amsterdam, then the English of New York after 1674, gave them an important strategic position between competing European powers. In the late 1600s, they had to move their villages and towns southward away from the shores of Lake Ontario, where they were subject to French attacks by boat. For more than 150 years, they used their placement: first to expand their power, and then to survive long after other indigenous peoples were exterminated or pushed west. They are the primary northeastern woodland Indian people retaining an important though drastically reduced degree of political and cultural sovereignty to this day.

The Iroquois developed a sophisticated political organization that united five nations in a powerful confederacy, balancing a substantial degree of internal autonomy with a high level of external coordination. The Iroquois called themselves the people of the longhouse, describing both their dwelling places (long, bark-covered structures with multiple families living along a central corridor) and their political organization. The Mohawk were the keepers of the Eastern door and as such had the closest contact with the English. The Seneca, or keepers of the Western door, settled in the area between the Genesee and the headwaters of the Allegheny having the most direct impact on Western Pennsylvania and most extensive contacts with the French. At the center of the Longhouse were the Onondaga, or keepers of the Council fire, beside them were the "younger brothers," the Oneida and Cayuga. In the early 18th Century a related refugee tribe, the Tuscaroras, was admitted to the League as a sixth member. In Pennsylvania, remnants of conquered peoples lived under Iroquois rule as Mingos, while independent remnants of tribes decimated by Iroquois attacks reorganized in the lake regions as Wyandots.

Like other native peoples, the Iroquois distinguished themselves from Europeans by the power exercised by their women. Women had equal authority with the men in council and women elders appointed the successors to male chiefs when they died. Since important decisions, particularly matters of war and peace, required consensus, women were powerful political forces. They could start "mourning wars" by demanding captives to replace fallen family members, and they could rescue captives by claiming them for their family. The native attitude toward the land was intertwined with their attitude toward women who were akin to the earth in their fertility and also were the primary cultivators. South of the Great Lakes, female agricultural work provided approximately half of the people's diet.

> Mother Earth and the Corn Mother were female supernaturals who controlled the fertility of the garden; they were women's deities, and the natural forces they controlled could only be exploited by women... Women's status and importance reflected in part her economic importance to the society in which she lived; where women are not economically productive and where they are treated primarily as ornaments, they quickly descend to the status of slaves; where they play major roles in food production and contribute proportionately to their society, their status can surpass those of men... The Indian women held a more privileged and equal position in her society than women do in any European or American society today... Many white women who had been taken captive in warfare and who had become members of Indian communities refused to be ransomed; they would not return to the drudgery and subordination accorded women in colonial society".[35]

The female farmers of the Seneca nation alone raised as much as a million bushels of corn each year, with cultivated cornfields stretching for miles near towns and scattered clearings planted in the woods:

> Armed with crude wooden hoes and digging sticks, they swarmed over the fields in gay, chattering work bees, proceeding from field to field to hoe, to plant, to weed and to harvest. An individual woman might, if she wished, "own" a patch of corn, or an apple or peach orchard; but there was little reason for insisting on private tenure: the work was more happily done communally, and in the absence of a regular market, a surplus was of little personal advantage, especially if the winter were hard and the other families needed

corn. In such circumstances hoarding only led to hard feelings and strained relations as well as the possibility of future difficulty in getting corn for oneself and one's family. All land was national land...(and) there was little reason to bother about individual ownership of real estate anyway; there was plenty of land. Economic security for both men and women lay in the proper recognition of one's obligation to family, clan, community, and nation, and in the efficient and cooperative performance on team activities, such as working bees, war parties, and diplomatic missions.[36]

The Great League of the Iroquois, operated as a confederacy of independent "nations" welded into a powerful unified force when faced with questions of war or peace. Certainly the league's structure influenced the thinking of Thomas Jefferson, and especially Benjamin Franklin, as they helped design the governmental organization of the United States of America, since no appropriate model existed among the monarchies of Europe.[37] Even more fundamentally, a Native American philosophy that asserts the profound inter-relatedness of humans, the earth and all living things has taken on a renewed relevance and even urgency as mankind faces an earthly environment that is profoundly stressed by population growth, pollution and over-development. The strength of the Iroquois lay in their ability to unite disparate interests around a common goal. Dekanawidah, with Hiawatha one of the founders of the great peace, who brought together the bitterly fratricidal five nations centuries before the American Revolution, left words about peace and leadership, the generations, and the land, that speak across the centuries:

> We bind ourselves together, by taking hold of each other's hands so firmly and forming a circle so strong that if a tree should fall on it, it could not shake or break it, so that our people and grandchildren shall remain in the circle in security, peace and happiness... Be of strong mind, O chiefs!...Carry no anger and hold no grudges. Think not of yourselves, O chiefs, nor of your own generation. Think of the continuing generations of our families, think of our grandchildren and of those yet unborn, whose faces are coming from beneath the ground.[38]

Chapter 2 Notes

[1] Herbert Klein, "The Current Debate About the Origins of the Paleoindians of America, "*Journal of Social History* (2003); J.M. Adovasio and Jake Page, *The First Americans: In Pursuit of Archaeology's Greatest Mystery* (New York: Random House, Inc., 2002), 147-188. Adovasio's proof of the antiquity of human presence in Western Pennsylvania marks a very important moment in the region's Native American history. Initially, controversy over the antiquity of the site raged despite the meticulous methodology employed there. See the chapter "Melee Over Meadowcroft."

[2] Barbara Palowitch, "The Meadowcroft Dig, "*Carnegie Magazine* (1977).

[3] John Gilday, "The Pigeons of Meadowcroft, "*Carnegie Magazine* (1977); Clive Pointing, *A Green History of the World*, (New York: Penguin Books, 1992), 168-170.

[4] William J. Mayer-Oakes, *Prehistory of the Upper Ohio Valley: An Introductory Archeological Study* (Pittsburgh: Annals of Carnegie Museum, 1995), 34:7-25. James Fitting, "Regional Cultural Development, 300 B.C. to A.D. 1000," *Handbook of North American Indians*, (Washington, D.C.: Smithsonian Institute, 1978), v.15:14-57. The figure of 50 members as the minimum for a viable hunter-gatherer group comes from Adovasio, p. 256. Detailed descriptions of these developments can be found in the four essays collected under the heading "General Prehistory" in the Handbook of North American Indians.

[5] Adovasio and Page, *The First Americans*, 286-290. Much of this entertaining book concerns the author's struggle against the predominant Clovis point, big game hunter theory of human migration into the Americas. His discussion of "gender myopia" is p. 286-290.

[6] Fitting, *Handbook of North American Indians*, 44-57; Roger Kennedy, *Hidden Cities: The Discovery and Loss of North American Civilization* (New York: Penguin Books, 1994). An interesting discussion of the role the evidence of these civilizations produced on Albert Gallatin, George Washington and especially Thomas Jefferson, along with a discussion of the possible meaning behind these mysterious constructions is in *Hidden Cities: The Discovery and Loss of North American Civilization.*

[7] Mayer-Oakes, *Prehistory of the Upper Ohio Valley*; Don Dragoo, *Mounds for the Dead* (Pittsburgh: Annals of the Carnegie Museum, 1963). This study contains a description and photos of virtually all the artifacts dug at the site that are in possession of the Museum. A later publication, *Mounds for the Dead*, has an excellent picture of the mound as it looked with the trees removed at the start of the 1897 excavation.

[8] Mayer-Oakes, *Prehistory of the Upper Ohio Valley*, 25; Susan Woodward and Jerry McDonald, *Indian Mounds of the Middle Ohio Valley: A Guide to Adena and Hopewell Sites* (Blackburg: The McDonald & Woodward Publishing Company, 1986).

[9] James Veech, *The Monongahela of Old: Historical Sketches of South-Western Pennsylvania to the Year 1800* (Pittsburgh: Private Distribution, (1892), 17-18.

[10] Jared Diamond, "The Arrow of Disease, "*Discover*" (October 1992), 128, 151.

[11] John Lankford, ed., *Captain John Smith's America* (New York, Harper, 1967), 9.

[12] Paul A. Wallace, *Indians of Pennsylvania* (Harrisburg: The Pennsylvania Historical and Museum Commission, 1975) 95-103, 152-3. An account of the Paxton boy's massacre of the Conestoga is on p. 152-3.

[13] Alexis De Tocqueville, "America Visited," *Democracy In America*, ed. Edith I. Coombs (New York, Book League of America, 1900), 1:192.

[14] Fred Anderson, *The Crucible of War: The Seven Years' War and the Fate of an Empire in British North* (New York: Vintage, 2000), 13-16; Gregory Evans Dowd, *A Spiritual Resistance: The North American Indian Struggle for Unity 1745-1815* (Baltimore and London: The John Hopkins University Press, 1991).

[15] W.J. Eccles, *The Canadian Frontier* (Albuquerque: University of New Mexico Press, 1983), 26-28.

[16] George Hunt, *The Wars of the Iroquois: A Study of Intertribal Trade Relations* (Madison: The University of Wisconsin Press, 1960), 84; Francis Jennings, *The Ambiguous Iroquois Empire* (New York: W.W. Norton & Company, 1984), 84-112.

[17] Calvin Martin, *Keepers of the Game: Indian-Animal Relationships and the Fur Trade* (Los Angeles: University of California Pess, 1978), 80.

[18] Paul A. Wallace, ed., *The Travels of John Heckewelder in Frontier America* (Pittsburgh: University of Pittsburgh Press, 1985), 50-51.

[19] Wallace, *The Travels of John Heckewelder in Frontier America*, 3-15.

[20] William Butler, "The Archeology of McKees Rocks Late Prehistoric Village Site." *Pennsylvania Archeologist*, Date

[21] John Witthoft, *The American Indian as Hunter* (Harrisburg: Pennsylvania Historical and Museum Commission, 1990), 42; Dowd, *A Spirited Resistance*, 24.

[22] John Witthoft, *The American Indian as Hunter*, 42; Dowd, *A Spirited Resistance*, 24, 42; Charles Mann, "1491," *The Atlantic Monthly*, March, 2002, v. 289:3:41-53

[23] Jared Diamond, *Guns, Germs, and Steel: The Fates of Human Societies-* (New York and London: W.W. Norton & Company, 1999), 78.

[24] C.A. Weslager, *The Delaware Indians: A History* (New Brunswick: Rutgers University Press, 1996), 78-80.; Herbert Kraft, *The Lenape: Archaeology, History, and Ethnography* (Newark: New Jersey Historical Society, 1986), 4-7. A skeptical view of the authenticity of the Walam Olum can be found in Herbert C. Kraft's *The Lenape: Archeology, History and Ethnogaphy.*

[25] John Heckewelder, *History, Manners, and Customs of the Indian Nations Who Once Inhabited Pennsylvania and the Neighboring States*, (New York: Arno Press, 1971), 47-70.

[26] Heckewelder, *History, Manners, and Customs of the Indian Nations Who Once Inhabited Pennsylvania and the Neighboring States,* 56, 58.

[27] David Zeisberger, *David Zeisberger's History of the Northern American Indians* (Lewisburg: Wennawoods Publishing, 1999), 34-5.

[28] Paul Wallace, *Indians of Pennsylvania,* 17.

[29] Paul Wallace, *Indians of Pennsylvania,* 31.

[30] Witthoft, *The American Indian as Hunter,* 1-7.

[31] Kraft, *The Lenape,* 227-8.

[32] Joseph Borkowski, "Historical Background," *Miscellaneous History of Lawrenceville* (Pittsburgh, Lawrenceville Historical Society, 1989), 4-6.

[33] *Pittsburgh Post-Gazette,* November 1, 1861.

[34] Wallace, *Indians of Pennsylvania,* 119.

[35] Witthoft, *The American Indian as Hunter,* 5.

[36] Anthony F.C. Wallace, *The Death and Rebirth of the Seneca* (New York: Vintage Books, 1972). 24.

[37] Bruce E. Johansen, *Forgotten Founders: How the American Indian Helped Shape Democracy* (Boston: The Harvard Common Press, 1982).

[38] Johansen, *Forgotten Founders,* 42.

Chapter Three

Invasion and Resistance

1741-1790

When Europeans landed on the coast of what is now the United States, they found indigenous peoples, but no great cities to conquer or treasure to plunder as in Mexico and Peru. As John Smith of Jamestown Colony, Virginia, indicated, the land was incredibly rich and needed only hard labor. "Here are no hard landlords to rack us with high rents, or extorting fines, nor tedious pleas in law to consume us with their many year disputation for justice...here every man may be master of his own labor...and if he have nothing but his hands, he may set up his trade and by industry grow quickly rich."[1] Without iron or steel to fabricate axes to cut the primeval forest, or plough deeply Mother Earth, or provide the weapons to build empires, native peoples adapted their economic strategies around a mix of growing, gathering, fishing and hunting, with both fixed and migratory communities. As a consequence of frequent movement inside a territory and strong communal traditions, nature was viewed as a resource, not as property to be dissected, bought and sold.

Geopolitics and Dominion

The consciousness of the English and Scots-Irish settlers was molded by the Protestant reformation and the mercantile capitalism that emerged symbiotically in the 17th Century. The French retained more of the baggage of medieval Catholicism and feudal economic organizations. Both had a European attitude toward the land formed by the twin strains of Hebrew and Greek thought. In Genesis, God gives man dominion over the earth. "Be fertile and multiply; fill the earth and subdue it. Have dominion over the fish of the sea, the birds of the air, and all the living things that move on the earth" (Gen. 1:28). This viewpoint was hardened and extended by the economic expressions of Protestantism that emphasized personal acquisition and ethical individualism. Rejection of Catholic corporativism with its hierarchy of ranks and functions in the name of a philosophy of individual liberty and private property helped propel the spirit of entrepreneurial adventure toward the conquest of new worlds. As a general rule, the Protestant carried the Bible for his own use, for the savages he carried a gun. For most, if not all, neither law nor salvation extended beyond the line of settlement where darkness and savagery ruled. The extension of dominion was the Lord's work.

The logic of possession and occupation drove the English to be more concerned with boundaries and property lines than they were about exploration. "Profiting more from fields than furs and divided by conflicting claims between various companies and charters…(the English) placed more importance on surveying boundary lines than on exploring the land….Thomas Jefferson's 'Plan for Western Government' draws lines across unfamiliar land with no regard for the rivers and the mountains that will affect settlement and to which government should be adapted." It was as if once the land was symbolically possessed through such a survey, actual settlement could wait. And "the work of such a survey…in driving such a line straight across the land, effectively discouraged exploration because it was a far more difficult matter of travel than following the path of least resistance, a river."[2]

The ancient Greeks were sailors and tradesmen, more than farmers; and their philosophies were woven of calculations and measurements. They were weavers of fine distinctions and rational deliberations. In their sun-drenched Mediterranean home, they were lovers of the light of reason. By the 18th Century, Europe was under the spell of the rationalism of the Greeks. Progress in science and technology provided distinct military and economic advantage to the Europeans as they entered the Appalachian hinterland. The Europeans who first penetrated into the valleys of the Monongahela and Allegheny were neither philosophers nor theologians, though some toted the scriptures of the Great God Jehovah. Most of the earliest frontiersmen were merchants calculating profit margins between the cost of the trade goods they dispensed (glass beads, pots, cloth, alcohol, guns, iron hatchets and traps) and the cash value to be obtained with the skins of the myriad animal species supplied by the native hunter; pelts for which the European seemed, in Native American eyes, to have an inexplicable and inexhaustible appetite.

Close behind the adventurers and traders came the land hungry peasants who lived in Europe under aristocratic overlords where they could only hunt by poaching, or farm by the sufferance of their betters. They very well understood what dominion meant because they had long been subject to it. In 1700, the common peasant lived in a world completely owned by other people with no rights to firewood, game, recreation or farmland. Deprived of the dominion over the land and its creatures that the word of God assured them was theirs, they were mightily determined to achieve land ownership unfettered either by royal prerogatives or prior aboriginal claims. Nowhere in the world was a more absolute claim to unrestricted, individual, private property asserted as in America. God-given dominion and rational calculation marked the American attitude toward the land and its fruits. [3]

There were four primary entries into the heartland of North America. First, the northern entry to the continent, Hudson Bay, controlled by the English who established fur trading posts there in the 1660s, was of limited use for settlement or military invasion because of extreme weather conditions. Second, the St. Lawrence River offered the easiest access to the Great Lakes and from there into the great Ohio-Missouri-Mississippi basin. Except for the rapids at Lachine, upstream from Montreal, the St. Lawrence was navigable its whole length. Furthermore, the ancient Native American canoe route that began at the site of Montreal and stretched along the Ottawa River to within easy portage of the Georgian Bay of Lake Huron greatly shortened the voyage to Lake Superior and Lake Michigan. Third, the Hudson River, opened to trade first by the Dutch and then the English, offered an alternative route to the Great Lakes. However, the mighty Iroquois stood astride the route from the Hudson to the Mohawk River through Oneida Lake to Lake Ontario. They permitted the British to build trading posts and short-term forts to defend against French attacks, but they tightly controlled traffic across their land until they were defeated by the American forces during the American Revolution. Finally, the Mississippi River offered a southern route into the interior. During the course of complex political maneuvering over the issue of succession to the Spanish throne, the French took over Spanish claims and in 1700 established a colony in Louisiana.

French control of the two best entries into the North American heartland, the Mississippi and St. Lawrence Rivers, allowed them to rapidly penetrate the interior. With outposts and forts along the Mississippi-Illinois-Great Lakes trade routes, they threatened to enclose and block the westward expansion of the English colonies. While the French had the superior geographic position, their meager colonial population meant that they were spread extremely thin. A relative handful of French officials, fur traders, and priests sought to hold the allegiance of the western Native American nations and maintain possession of the interior of North America when traders from the English colonies began to move into the Allegheny-Ohio watershed. Early development of the Great Lakes-Mississippi linkage meant the geo-political importance of the forks of the Ohio was not clearly understood until the 1740s when English colonists began to spill over the Allegheny plateau into the Ohio country in significant numbers. At that point, the French military and fur trade routes collided with the relentlessly expanding Anglo-American land settlement frontier. [4]

The Scottish rebellions and the clearing of the Highlands for wool production meant England had a surplus population of people experienced in war and the hard-scrabble struggle for survival. The displaced peasantry of the British Isles had a deep hunger for land ownership. Religious upheaval in Ireland, Scotland, England, Germany, the Netherlands and France provided a large number of groups seeking asylum. The English kings with their German roots were inclined to use the new agriculturally suitable lands in the New World to resettle these and other groups to their advantage. The English-speaking colonies advanced behind a "line of settlement" created by the axe and the plow. Forests were cut, crops planted, roads built, saw and grain mills constructed. Indigenous peoples were pushed out or annihilated as an obstacle to progress. These agricultural communities made a slow but steady and permanent advance into the interior. One hundred thirty years of English settlements along the Atlantic produced at most a two hundred fifty mile advance into the interior from the coast. Compared to New France, the English colonies were densely populated. By the time of the French and Indian War, settlers in the English colonies numbered approximately one million. Largely Protestant, the settlers brought a strong sense of individual rights, a reliance on personal conscience, and were little restrained by any institutional church. England's greatest asset in its dealings with the natives was the superiority and cheapness of its trade goods. Ultimately, the population advantage of its colonies and England's naval superiority proved decisive.

France, on the other hand, exploited its geographical advantage. Through the Great Lakes and connecting rivers, the French penetrated quickly to the interior. They reached the Rockies at virtually the same time as the English were crossing the Alleghenies. The French, who only numbered 50,000 at the time of the great struggle for control of the continent's interior, needed the Native Americans as military allies and commercial partners, depending on them as their source of furs. Less industrialized than the British, the French had less of a surplus population to channel into their colonies. Quebec, in any case, was less suited for agriculture than Pennsylvania or Virginia because of climate and limited arable land.

The French depended on the Indians commercially and relied on them politically to offset the English superiority in numbers. The "coureurs des bois" lived like Indians and often intermarried with them. The French spoke Indian languages and their priests made heroic efforts to convert the Indians to Catholicism; this effort, however, often compounded the natives' spiritual alienation. In fact, it was France's better relations with the natives and better understanding of wilderness realities that constituted their primary advantage. The French claimed that Robert de La Salle, crossing Seneca territory, descended the Allegheny in 1669 and continued down the Ohio to the falls at Louisville, thereby becoming the first

European to see the Forks of the Ohio. Evidence for the claim was weak and contested by the English. LaSalle did discover the mouth of the Ohio at the Mississippi in 1682 and claimed all waters that entered into it for France. Frenchmen certainly entered the Allegheny-Ohio watershed in the early 18th Century, and small exploratory expeditions descended the rivers in 1729 and 1739. Scattered traders including the French, James LeTort and James Chartier; Scots, like John Frazier; and others including Anthony Sadowski, a Pole in the employ of Pennsylvania, penetrated the watershed of "La Belle Riviere" by the 1740s.[5]

In the early 18th Century, France and England were engaged in a centuries-old struggle for dominance that was now taking on global proportions. Called in Europe "The War of the Austrian Succession" (1740-1748) and the "Seven Years War" (1756-1763), the latter has come down to us as the "French and Indian War." These conflicts grew out of fierce competition to control the rich markets of India and South Asia, the cruel slave trade from Africa, and the sugar trade of the Caribbean. Meanwhile, across the lakes, rivers and woods of the eastern woodlands of North America, a mighty conflict raged.

A Half-King, a Queen and a Future President

While French and British empires contested for control of the Forks, English colonial and imperial interests frequently diverged, and, even among its colonial forces, loyalties were divided between Pennsylvania and Virginia. In 1748, the Ohio Company, formed by London and Virginia land speculators, was granted one-half million acres on the Upper Ohio by the British Crown. The name "Ohio" was a corruption of the Seneca "Ho-he-yu" or "beautiful river" which the French translated as "La Belle Riviere." Its ancient name Allegewi was eventually retained for its northern fork, the Allegheny, which was the faster flowing river and considered by the Iroquois, who descended its cold, blue-green waters in their swift canoes, the source of the Ohio. The Ohio Company contracted to build a fort. Its agent Christopher Gist, on the first of two trips to the region, determined that their initial outpost should be built at the Forks of the Ohio itself. Gist was one of a growing number of traders who penetrated into the Ohio Valley in the 1740s and 1750s whose guns and iron goods were eagerly sought by the natives. John Frazier had already been operating in the Monongahela Valley for a decade or more. The Ohio Company's claim to the region conflicted with the prior but undelineated claims of the descendants of William Penn. This lack of clarity inaugurated 50 years of competition between Virginia and Pennsylvania for control of the Ohio's headwaters.

The royal charter granted to William Penn and his descendants defined its western frontier as five degrees of longitude due west from Pennsylvania's border with Maryland at the Delaware River. Aside from the Iroquois, who actually controlled most of Western Pennsylvania as a hunting preserve and settlement area for dependent peoples for over a century, both France and Virginia contested this title. England's claim to the land was linked to the recognition by France in the treaty of Utrecht in 1713 of English suzerainty over the Iroquois, who themselves claimed the Forks of the Ohio and regulated the native groups that lived there. However, the French rather dubiously contended that their explorers had claimed the entire Ohio watershed before the Iroquois conquest of the original inhabitants. On the ground, French traders like the French-Shawnee Peter Chartiers were effective French agents among recent refugees from colonial land expropriation like the Shawnee and Lenape, fueling their resentment against both the Iroquois and the English settlers.[6]

William Penn treated the Lenape fairly and justly; under the influence of the Quakers, Pennsylvania adopted a policy of non-violence toward their native neighbors. Unfortunately, the enlightened policies of the Quakers were the exception as the stream of European settlers steadily increased during an era of intense imperial competition for strategic control. Without a militia, Pennsylvania was poorly equipped to stop illegal settlement of Indian lands or to contest the claims of its rivals. However, Pennsylvania was the first English colony to undertake a formal diplomatic mission to the forks of the Ohio through the person of a German from Wurtenberg, Conrad Weiser, a talented negotiator who understood native politics and tribal relations. He advised the Philadelphia provincial Council to support the Iroquois colonists in the Ohio Valley in their offer to take up arms against the French. Weiser traveled in May of 1745 to the Iroquois Great Council of the Six Nations at Onondaga to condemn the activities of the French half-breed Peter Chartier in the Ohio country. Laying a belt of wampum before the council, he appealed to them to compel the Shawnees to make restitution of goods and prisoners. "The Shawnee are in your Power and so is Peter Chartier, who is turned from a subject of the king to a Rebel against him." The Iroquois replied: "We look upon what has happened to your Traders as an open Breach of Peace on the side of the French against us and the Blow that is given as if it were given to our head." They sent a delegation to Canada to make inquiries about the matter.[7]

The French understood the threat that potential English control of the Ohio posed to their Great Lakes-Mississippi fur trade routes. In 1749, an expedition of some 25 French, 180 Canadian and 50 Indian allies under the command of Celeron de Blainville set out via Fort Niagara for the Chautauqua portage from whence they attained the Allegheny. Near Warren, Pennsylvania., the expedition buried the first of a series of lead plates that claimed the "river Ohio, and all those which fall into it, and of all the territories on both sides as far as the source of the said rivers." Stopping at Indian villages along the river, he warned them against dealing or trading with the English. These activities had little effect on the English traders, however, who continued to find willing customers along the Ohio.[8]

While priests seeking the salvation of souls often followed close on the heals of the French voyagers, traders like Christopher Gist and George Croghan were advance men for Virginia land speculators. For two years, Gist surveyed the Ohio Valley and reported on the fertile land and rich forests. In 1752, he and Croghan convened a treaty conference at Logstown on the Ohio fifteen miles below the Forks with the Iroquois appointed pro-consul or "Half-King" Tanaghrisson, who maintained uneasy control over restive Lenape, Shawnee and Mingo populations, many of whom were refugees from white expansion. Tanaghrisson, a Catawba captive raised by the Seneca, represented the Iroquois claim to sovereignty established a century before in the Beaver Wars eradication of the Monongahela. He needed the English presence to counteract the growing French influence among his charges. The Virginians needed him because the British alliance with the Iroquois provided the legal basis for their ambitions in the valley. Tanaghrisson agreed to the proposed fort at the Forks.[9]

The English cause had another important asset in the area, the 70 year-old Seneca, Queen Aliquippa, who was steadfastly loyal to Pennsylvania. Her treatment at the hands of historians has generally been worse than that accorded her by a stream of French and English visitors from both Pennsylvania and Virginia, who felt obligated to pay homage to her as representative of Iroquois sovereignty and friend of Pennsylvania. As a young woman, she had reportedly visited William Penn in New Castle, Delaware in the autumn of 1701 before his final parting from Pennsylvania. Conrad Weiser twice met with Aliquippa in 1748 while visiting the Forks to secure a treaty with the western tribes for Pennsylvania. "We dined in a Seneka Town, where an old Seneka Woman Reigns with great Authority. We dined at her House & they all used us very well." She later came down to Logstown and asked Weiser for "a cask of powder and some small shot to enable her to send out the Indian boys to kill turkeys & other fowls for her, whilst the men are gone to war against the French, that they might not be starved."[10]

Celeron, commander of the French expedition, wrote of his 1749 visit: "I re-embarked and visited the village which is called the Written Rock. The Iroquois inhabit this place, and it is an old woman of this nation who governs it. She regards herself as sovereign. She is entirely devoted to the English." This location was almost certainly McKees Rocks where the ancient Adena burial site rose undisturbed at the crown of the rocky bluff, marked with pictographic symbols, which protected the rich bottom-lands just downriver from the outlet of Chartiers Creek. It was there in 1752 that the Virginia Commissioners visited Aliquippa's Town "with colors flying" on their canoes in procession from Shannopin's town to Logstown. They were saluted with the discharge of guns at Aliquippa's town "and the compliment was returned from the canoes....The company then went on shore to wait on the Queen, who welcomed them and presented them with a string of Wampum, to clear their way to Logstown. She presented them also with a fine dish of fish to carry with them, and had some victuals set, which they all ate of. The Commissioners then presented the Queen with a brass kettle, tobacco and some other trifles and took their leave."[11]

Only a few months later, however, a major English trading post at the mouth of the Miami on the Ohio established by the Irishman George Croghan, a Pennsylvanian trader in league with Ohio Company land speculators, was overrun and destroyed by French-allied Indians under the leadership of mixed-blood, French-Ottawa, Charles Langlade. In 1753, the Governor-General of Canada, the Marquis Duquesne, initiated the invasion of the Ohio country. A French expeditionary force of more than two thousand soldiers established a string of forts, Presqu'ile, Le Boeuf and Venango, connected by road or rivers that established their military presence on the upper Allegheny.[12]

The Iroquois, alarmed at the growth of French power at their "western door," appealed again to both Pennsylvania and Virginia to build a "strong house" at the forks of the Ohio. A young and ambitious George Washington, envoy of Governor Dinwiddie of Virginia, was sent to observe the French activities and carry a warning on behalf of English interests. In November of 1753, Washington stopped at the gunsmith/trader John Frazier's cabin at the mouth of Turtle Creek. Frazier had been one of the earliest whites to penetrate the Monongahela Valley where his services to the natives and fair dealing gave him a measure of protection.[13] Washington borrowed a canoe to carry his gear to the forks of the Ohio while he proceeded there on horseback:

> As I got down before the canoe, I spent some time viewing the rivers and the land in the fork, which I think extremely well situated for a fort; as it has the absolute command of both rivers. The land at the point is 20 or 25 feet above the common surface of the water; and a considerable bottom of flat, well timbered land all around it convenient for building. The rivers are each a quarter of a mile or more across, and run here very nearly at right angles; Allegheny, bearing northeast; and Monongahela, southeast. The former of these two is very rapid and swift running water, the other deep and still, without any perceptible fall.[14]

After stopping at the McKees Rocks site to invite the formidable Delaware warrior Shingas to council at Logstown, he compared the site's rocky bluff to the Point as a possible location for a fort and judged it "greatly inferior" and more expensive to construct. Shingas earned a formidable reputation among those who resisted the European invasion. John Heckewelder wrote of him: "He was a bloody warrior, cruel in his treatment, relentless his fury. His person was small, but in point of courage and activity, savage prowess, he was said to have never been exceeded by anyone."[15] He proceeded with Shingas to Logstown where he met with the Half-King, Tanaghrisson, who recounted the message he delivered to the French just prior to Washington's visit:

> Fathers, we kindled a fire a long time ago, at a place called Montreal, where we desired you to stay, and not to come and intrude upon our land. I now desire you may dispatch to that place; for be it known to you, fathers, that this is our land, not yours.... If you had come in a peaceable manner, like our brothers the English, we should not have been against your trading with us, as they do; but to come, fathers, and build great houses upon our land, and take it by force is what we cannot submit to. Fathers, both you and the English are white, we live in a country between; therefore the land belongs to neither one nor the other: But the Great Being above allowed it to be a place of residence for us.[16]

According to Tanaghrisson, the French commander replied: "I am not afraid of flies or mosquitos, for Indians are such as those; I tell you, down that River I will go, and I will build upon it, according to my command." Washington traveled with Tanaghrisson and a wary young Seneca warrior named Guyasuta to Venango where he met with the French commander. Over wine and dinner, the French revealed their intent. "They told me that it was their absolute design to take possession of the Ohio, and by G-d they would do it: for that, although they were sensible that the English could raise two men for their one, yet they knew that their motions were too slow and dilatory to prevent any undertaking of theirs."[17]

Returning in late December in the company of his guide, Christopher Gist, Washington was shot at by an Indian north of the Allegheny and then was nearly drowned crossing the river just upstream from Shanoppin's town:

> There was no way for getting us over but on a raft, which we set about, with but one poor hatchet, and finished just after sun setting. This was one whole day's work: we next got it launched, then went on board it and set off; but before we were halfway over, we jammed in the ice, in such a manner that we expected every moment our raft to sink and ourselves to perish. I put out my setting pole to try to stop the raft that the ice might pass by, when the rapidity of the stream threw it with so much violence against the pole, that it jerked me into 10 feet of water; but I fortunately saved myself by catching hold of one of the raft logs. Notwithstanding all our efforts, we could not get to either shore, but were obliged, as we were near an island, to quit our raft and make to it.
>
> The cold was so extremely severe, that Mr. Gist had all his fingers, and some of his toes, frozen, and the water was shut up so hard, that we found no difficulty in getting off the ice in the morning....[18]

Cold, exhausted and wet, Gist and Washington made their way to Frazier's cabin at the mouth of Turtle Creek. There Washington learned that Queen Aliquippa was offended because he had gone to see the French without first coming to see her. In the final days of 1753, Washington "went up three miles to the mouth of the Youghiogheny River to visit Queen Aliquippa, who had expressed great concern that we passed her in going to the Fort. I made her a present of a match-coat and a bottle of rum, which the latter was thought much the better present of the two."[19] In January, returning to Virginia he encountered Captain William Trent on his way to the Forks with about forty men to erect fortifications. Trent began building the first European outpost at the Forks of the Ohio, which he named Fort Prince George, on February 17, 1754.

On the evening of April 16, a French force of around 1000 French, Canadian and Native allies swept down on the little English garrison which surrendered without resistance. The next day, a Sunday, witnessed the first Christian religious service, a mass dedicated to Our Lady of the Beautiful River, by Fr. Denys Baron, a Recollect Franciscan. His register includes a record of internments and baptisms (including a twelve year old Delaware girl who died two days later, a two-month old Irish girl who had been captured by the Shawnees, and a ninety-two year old Iroquois chief). By summer, 1,400 troops occupied a sturdy log fort they called Duquesne, after the Governor-General of New France. In May, George Washington led a force of 150 men toward the Forks when he was alerted to the approach of a French scouting party of 32 men led by the nobleman Jumonville. With a force of 40, plus a contingent of Mingo led by Tanaghrisson, Washington launched a surprise attack as the French were awaking in which Jumonville and nine others were slain. While tensions had been steadily building between the French and English, they were not formally at war. This impetuous act of the young Virginian lieutenant-colonel precipitated the Seven Years War. [20]

Washington's army was reinforced to 350 and he fell back upon a modest fortification, christened "Fort Necessity," that he had constructed in the middle of the "Great Meadow". On June 1, Queen Aliquippa arrived from her last encampment on the Monongahela with 30 families. There, on July 4, 1754, surrounded by 900 French and Indians in a poorly constructed fortification in an open field, Washington surrendered after a day-long punishment in the pouring rain. He retreated to Virginia, allowed by the French to retain arms and colors, but only after having signed a document of capitulation in French that admitted to the "assassination" of Jumonville. Washington denied that he understood what he was signing; and while his men certainly precipitated the attack, the actual coup de grace to Jumonville was delivered by the Half-King Tanaghrisson. Certainly, the native leader understood better than anyone that the line of French forts along the Allegheny cut the Iroquois from vital western hunting grounds and that the resulting white encirclement would strangle the Iroquois Confederacy. War between the European powers was the Confederacy's best hope. Further, many of the natives accompanying the French at the Great Meadows victory were Delaware, Shawnee and Mingo who saw the French incursion as a way to slip free of Iroquois hegemony. Tanaghrisson and Aliquippa fled east with their remaining followers to George Croghan's place at Aughwick where the Seneca Queen died shortly thereafter. [21]

The Battle of the Monongahela

The British government responded to the loss of the Forks by sending two regular army regiments to Virginia under the command of General Edward Braddock of the Coldstream Guards. Braddock was an arrogant man who made little effort to disguise his contempt for Americans both red and white. Benjamin Franklin, who helped the general obtain wagons and supplies, wrote of him: "This general was, I think, a brave man, and might probably have made a good figure in some European war. But he had too much self-confidence, too high of an opinion of the validity of regular troops, too mean a one of both Americans and Indians."[22]

While the Delaware and Shawnee were moving into the French orbit because of anger over the Iroquois cession of their lands between the Susquehanna and the Allegheny to the English at the treaty of Albany in 1754, the Iroquois were finding it increasingly difficult to help Braddock. When asked what rights the Indians would have in an Ohio Valley ruled by the British, he contemptuously told a delegation of Delaware, Shawnee and Mingo led by the Delaware Shingas, and Scarouady, Tanaghrisson's successor as representative of the Iroquois, that "the English should inhabit and inherit the land." The few Iroquois scouts who remained with Braddock deserted him on the way to Fort Duquesne when the son of the new Half-King Scarouady was accidentally slain by British troops. Scarouady, also known as Monakatooka, said after the battle: "He (Braddock) is now dead, but he was a bad man when he was alive; he looked on us as dogs, and would never hear anything that was said to him."[23]

Still, the General commanded the largest and best-equipped European army to penetrate into the American interior. His force numbered about thirteen hundred in the attack column, English regulars with Colonial troops, scouts, teamsters with light supplies and most of the artillery. The heavy baggage, the sick and the wagon train, including most of the women, wives and camp-followers, were left behind with Colonel Thomas Dunbar. An estimated fifty women, however, accompanied the attack column, as did a retinue of servants that included free blacks and slaves. The column advanced upon a weakened French garrison that sent a force out to meet Braddock numbering little more than a hundred French soldiers with another hundred Canadian militia. However, the French were accompanied by a significant collection of native allies (primarily Ottawa, Wyandot and Pottawatomie, with some Shawnee, a few Delaware and Mingo) for a total fighting force of about 800. These native bands were convinced to join the battle against the steep odds by the oratory of the French leaders Pierre de Contrecoeur, Daniel de Beaujeau and Charles Langlade on the eve and morn of battle. The natives included the Delaware warrior Shingas, perhaps Guyasuta, and possibly the great Ottawa leader, Pontiac himself. Besides Washington and Braddock, British forces included Thomas Gage, who would command British troops at Bunker Hill; Horatio Gates, who as an American general accepted Burgoyne's surrender at Saratoga; Hugh Mercer, who died as an American general at the Battle of Princeton; and a young teamster named Daniel Boone.[24]

On July 8, 1755, Braddock's army camped between the Youghiogheny and Turtle Creek on the east side of the Monongahela. Fearing ambush in the steep Turtle Creek Valley, Braddock broke camp around 3 a.m. on the morning of July 9th, crossed the shallow, slack Monongahela, marching downstream to a point just below the mouth of Turtle Creek where the army forded the river a second time and formed a resplendent line of march in the early-afternoon with drums beating, fifes playing and colors flying. Barely two miles from the crossing, the column collided with the French force and in the opening volley the French commander Beaujeau was slain. At this point, it seemed that the larger, better-armed British force was on the verge of an easy victory.

The Indians, however, divided and ran along both flanks of the English in a running "half-moon" attack. From their positions on the tree-shrouded hills to the British right and along the high muddy banks of the river to their left came a murderous fire. The force of the Indian pincer attack threw Braddock's advance guard into confusion and panic. In their retreat, they collided with the main body's advance. The mounted officers were early targets and heavy losses among them increased the confusion. Washington alone was unscathed with horses shot beneath him and bullets piercing his clothes. Remaining officers, including Braddock, tried to reform their lines, but these open field tactics only exposed the troops to the deadly fire of the Indians. Very quickly, the American colonials, many of whom had experience of forest warfare, tried to take cover, but were berated as cowards by their British officers.[25]

This internal conflict between the American troops and the stubborn Braddock was epitomized in the claim that, in fact, Braddock was slain by his own men. Allegedly, the general beat a Virginia soldier about the head with his sword for taking cover, and then he was shot by the man's brother. Although several claimants would later emerge, the most credible account gave the honor to "Old

Tom Fossit," a backwoodsman and tavern owner who was also among the party who disinterred Braddock's body in 1812. On that occasion, he was reported to have delivered the following memorable diatribe:

> We was cowards, was we, because we knowed better than to fight Injuns like you red-backed ijits across the ocean is used to fight; because we wouldn't stand up rubbin shoulders like a passel o' sheep and let the red-skins make sieves outen us!...And them boys-th'ole Virginny Blues-you made them git from behint th'trees and get kilt; and them others you cussed...and cut down with a sabre, my own pore brother, Joe, amongst 'em! Why, ef I hadn't stopped ye with a shot, ye'd had us all massacred and scalped."[26]

James Smith, an 18 year-old road-builder from Pennsylvania captured by the Caughnawagas, a northern branch of the Mohawks allied with the French, was being held at Fort Duquesne on the evening of Braddock's defeat.

> A runner had just arrived who said Braddock would certainly be defeated. The Indians and the French had surrounded him and were concealed behind trees and in gullies, and kept a constant fire upon the English, who were falling in heaps. If they did not take to the river and make their escape, the runner said there would not be one man left before sundown. Sometime after this I heard a number of scalp halloos and saw a company of Indians and French coming in. They had a great many bloody scalps, grenadiers' caps, British canteens, bayonets, etc., with them....After that another company came in which appeared to be about one hundred and chiefly Indians. It seemed to me that almost every one of this company was carrying scalps. After this came another company with a number of wagon horses and also a great number of scalps. Those that were coming in and those that had arrived kept up a constant firing of small arms and also the great guns of the fort. This was accompanied with the most hideous shouts and yells from all quarters, so that it appeared to me as if all hell was breaking loose.
>
> About sundown I beheld a small party coming in with about a dozen prisoners, stripped naked, with their hands tied behind their backs and faces and part of their bodies blacked. These prisoners they burned to death on the bank of the Allegheny River opposite the fort.[27]

Smith estimated that only seven Indians and four French were killed in battle while the British force left more than four hundred bodies on the field and many died in flight. The estimated total of over six-hundred of the British force killed makes the Battle of the Monongahela the second greatest Native American victory in American history.[28] Beaujeu, who rallied the Indians and led the French attack only to be killed in the opening volley, was buried with full military honors in the French Cemetery of the Blessed Virgin of the Beautiful River next to an existing native burial mound. The arrogant Braddock was buried in the middle of the road bearing his name with his defeated army's wagons driven over his grave to disguise its placement.[29]

While half the army escaped in panic back toward Virginia, others faced captivity. Just before the battle, Smith, a non-combatant road builder, had successfully run the gauntlet of his captors and his life had been spared. Removed from Fort Duquesne and unaware that he was to be adopted, Smith expected the worst.

> At that time I knew nothing of their mode of adoption, and had seen them put to death all that they had taken. As I never could find that they saved a man alive at Braddock's

defeat, I did not doubt that they were about to put me to death in some cruel manner. The old chief, holding me by the hand, made a long speech very loud, and handed me to three young squaws. They led me by the hand down the bank into the river until the water was up to our middle.

The squaws made signs to me to plunge myself in the water. I did not understand them. I thought the result of the council was I should be drowned, and these young ladies were the executioners. All three took violent hold of me. For some time I opposed them with all my might, which occasioned loud laughter among the multitude on the bank of the river. At length one of the squaws resorted to speaking a little English (for I believe they began to be afraid of me) and said, "No hurt you!" At this I gave myself up to their ladyships, who were as good as their word. Though they plunged me under water and washed and rubbed me severely, I could not say they hurt me much. These young women then led me up to the council house, where some of the tribe were ready with new clothes for me. They gave me a new ruffled shirt, which I put on, a pair of leggings done off with ribbons and beads, porcupine quills and red hair - also a tinsel-laced cloak. They again painted my head and face with various colors, and tied a bunch of red feathers to one of the locks they had left on the crown of my head....They seated me on a bearskin and gave me a pipe, tomahawk, and polecat-skin punch which contained tobacco and dry sumac leaves....When I was seated, the Indians came in dressed and painted in their grandest manner. They took their seats and for a considerable time there was a profound silence. Everyone was smoking, but not a word was spoken among them. Finally one of the chiefs made a speech which was delivered to me by an interpreter. "My son, you are now flesh of our flesh and bone of our bone. By the ceremony which was performed this day, every drop of white blood was washed out of your veins. You are taken into the Caughnawaga nation and initiated into a warlike tribe. You are adopted into a great family and now received with great solemnity in the place of a great man. You are one of us by an old strong law and custom."[30]

Smith was one of the rare lucky ones. After Braddock's defeat, the frontier was swept clean of English settlers nearly to the Susquehanna. The sound of the war whoop and the tomahawk spread blood and terror across the entire frontier. The Delaware warrior Shingas led many of the attacks. Pennsylvania attempted a forceful response when Colonel John Armstrong led a raid of 300 men against the Delaware chief Captain Jacobs. On September 8, 1756, he attacked the Delaware village at Kittanning where numerous Indian raids had originated, including the sack of Fort Granville where 25 adults and a number of children had been captured. Armstrong's forces set fire to some thirty dwellings and killed Captain Jacobs, a leader at the burning of Fort Granville and McCord's Fort, and at the defeat of militia at Sideling Hill. Only seven prisoners were freed however. A small force that Armstrong had left at a base camp on the high ground as he approached the Indian town was overcome with 17 men killed and 19 men taken prisoner, the expedition's horses stolen, their baggage and blankets spread over a hill that became memorialized as Blanket Hill. While the fight was a relative standoff, the expedition was declared a great victory in an attempt to rebuild settler morale.[31]

In his official report, Colonel Armstrong described the burning of Captain Jacobs's house. "As the fire began to approach, and the smoke grew thick, one of the Indian fellows to show his manhood began to sing. A squaw in the same house, at the same time, was heard to cry and make a noise, but for so doing was severely rebuked by the men; but by and by, the fire being too hot for them, two Indian fellows and a squaw sprung out and made for the cornfield, who were immediately shot down by our people; then surrounding the houses, it was thought Captain Jacobs tumbled himself out...at which he was shot – our prisoners...say they are perfectly assured of his scalp, as no other Indians there wore their hair in the same manner. They also say they know his squaw's scalp by a peculiar bob....With the roof of Captain Jacob's house, where the powder blew up, was thrown the leg and thighs of an Indian, with a child of three or four years old, such a height, that they appeared as nothing, and fell into an adjacent cornfield."[32]

The Forbes Expedition and Pontiac's Conspiracy

In June 1758, General Forbes, assisted by the capable Swiss mercenary officer Bouquet, began his march on Fort Duquesne with a force of nearly 7,000 including 1,200 regular army soldiers. Despite the urgings of Washington and other Virginians, eager to protect their financial interests in Virginia land claims, Forbes did not cut south from Philadelphia to use Braddock's Road. Instead, he built a more direct route that opened the west to Pennsylvania, thereby strengthening its claim to the headwaters of the Ohio. As he advanced, he built a string of fortified supply depots including Bedford and Ligonier. By mid-July 1758, the fall of Louisbourg, the great French fortress guarding the St. Lawrence from Cape Breton Island, tightened the strangulation of the French lifeline to the mother country. The drying up of French military supplies and trade goods increased the disaffection of tribes such as the Delaware and Shawnee. In August, a Moravian missionary Frederick Post made two daring diplomatic journeys to the Forks to try to woo the Delaware away from the French and reaffirm their old alliance with Pennsylvania. Post, having married a Delaware woman, was loved and trusted by the Delaware; when she died, he married a second. He met with the key Delaware leaders including Shingas and King Beaver under the guns of Fort Duquesne. He reported agreements reached at the treaty of Easton in October 1758, when the Iroquois and Delaware were assured possession of the lands west of the mountains if they allowed the English to pass unmolested to fight the French.[33]

Increasingly ill, Forbes grew anxious as the laborious task of fort and road building slowed his army's advance. While Bouquet was with the advance guard at Loyalhanna, he allowed Major James Grant to reconnoiter Fort Duquesne in force to gauge the strength of enemy garrison. Grant, possessed by dreams of glory, thought he could take the fort by surprise. On September 14, 1758, he divided his force of 800 into 4 parts, positioned on and to the sides of the knoll that overlooked the Point, which in time became the site of city and county government. Aroused by the Scotsman's bagpipes, the French and Indians, lying in wait, swarmed out toward him from the fort, enveloping his troops and killing 270 men while Major Grant himself was captured. The French and Indians only recorded eight fatalities. Guyasuta, who had accompanied Washington to Venango some years before, led the attack. The survivors fled in panic back to Ligonier.[34]

This setback led Forbes to consider wintering at Ligonier. A major raid by French and Indians on Fort Ligonier failed to take the fort, but succeeded in capturing 200 British horses and livestock quartered out along the Loyalhanna. George Washington and George Mercer were each given several hundred men to pursue the raiders. In the advancing twilight, the two British forces collided and opened fire. Thirty-eight men and two officers were killed, and Washington later wrote that this friendly fire incident was his closest brush with death in a long military career. However, credible information from an escaped prisoner about the weakened state of the French garrison with the return of native allies to their villages to prepare for winter made Forbes decide to push forward in late November. He advanced on the Forks of the Ohio with 2,000 soldiers. While crossing the Turtle Creek Valley, his army heard explosions of gunpowder as the remaining French garrison of 300 men burned and deserted one of the most strategic spots in North America. The advance guard reached the smoldering remains of Fort Duquesne on the evening of November 24, 1758; and the following day, the British army occupied the Forks of the Ohio. In homage to William Pitt, the energetic British minister who was vigorously pursuing the war against France, Forbes named his new post Pittsburgh in a letter to William Pitt dated November 27, and issued a formal proclamation to that effect on December 1. In the following summer of 1759, the erection of Ft. Pitt, an impressive brick and earthen structure that overlooked and dwarfed the site of Ft. Duquesne, was begun under General John Stanwix and completed in 1761.[35]

After the fall of Louisbourg and Ft. Duquesne, the military situation deteriorated rapidly for the French. On September 13, 1759, Quebec, the capital of New France, fell to a determined assault. Montreal capitulated the following summer. The French collapse left their Indian allies confused and anxious at the same time that it reduced the political importance to England of their longtime Iroquois allies. Following the fall of Quebec, the French network of forts and trading posts in the Great Lakes-Illinois interior was slowly and reluctantly turned over to the English. With relatively few troops, the English had to occupy and govern a vast area filled with natives who had recently been at war with them. Detroit, Michilimackinac, St. Joseph, Sandusky, and Green Bay were secured with thin garrisons. Without French competition, the English traders felt free to cheat the natives flagrantly and did. The British suspended traditional goodwill gift-giving and began building roads.[36]

Stripped of their French allies and increasingly resentful toward the English, a broad movement of religious revivalism gained adherence in many native communities. One of the most important of the native prophets was a Delaware named Neolin. He had received a vision of the Master of Life who called Indians to a rejection of their evil ways and dependence on whites. He taught that the native's spiritual power could be regained through a withdrawal from trade and the abandonment of European goods, especially rum, accompanied by a renewal of traditional values and rituals. Ritual purification could be achieved through the drinking of an herbal emetic that induced vomiting, by singing, dancing, prayer and cathartic weeping. Land encroachments by whites, the decline of game, and the plagues of small pox, influenza and other diseases were the result not of white power, but of native faithlessness and misdeeds.[37]

In 1763, an Indian warrior and leader arose among the western tribes with the ambition to unite them against the English settlers before they achieved a secure footing in the interior. Influenced by the teachings of Neolin, Pontiac, an Ottawa from near Detroit, united the Great Lakes tribes of the Chippewa, Pottawatomie, Ottawa and Wyandot as well as many Shawnee and Delaware with a vision of a concerted, far-flung attack on British outposts. Pontiac had been a longtime ally of the French, personal friend of Governor-General Montcalm, and a native leader at the battle for Quebec. His uprising was labeled a conspiracy because it was not the usual spontaneous and defensive native uprising triggered by repeated violations of land or treaty rights, but a well-planned, coordinated offensive that used deception and stratagems to surprise the British garrisons.[38]

The former French outposts at Presqu'ile, Le Boeuf and Venango were overwhelmed and an attack was made on Ft. Ligonier. Panic spread as far as Carlisle as settlers stampeded toward the forts. The Ft. Pitt garrison had about 300 soldiers with perhaps another 250 refugees sheltered within its rather formidable walls. The Swiss commandant Ecuyer burned all the cabins outside the walls and gathered surrounding families into the fort. Refugees arrived with tales of massacre and horror. On June 22 and again on July 26, the Indians mounted assaults on the fort that were fairly easily repulsed. In the course of these attacks, the British gave Indian negotiators blankets infected by smallpox during a truce conference at the fort. Bouquet wrote the commander of English troops Sir Jeffery Amherst that he planned "to extirpate that Vermin from a Country they have forfeited, and with it all claims to the Rights of Humanity." Amherst replied that all prisoners should "immediately be put to death, their extirpation being the only security for our future safety." He suggested carrying smallpox to the natives "by means of blankets, as well as to try every other method that can serve to extirpate this execrable race."[39]

Meanwhile, Colonel Bouquet raised a force of 500 men in Carlisle to march to the relief of Fort Ligonier and Fort Pitt. Troops were difficult to recruit since few wanted to leave their families to venture forth against such a fearsome foe. Bouquet reached Ligonier on August 2. He set out with 350 pack-horses for Fort Pitt. Ahead lay the dangerous Turtle Creek Valley. He planned to camp at Bushy Run and then march through the valley at night to avoid ambush. Before he could make camp, however, the Indians attacked his troops in a running half-moon attack almost precipitating the same panic that had led to the dissolution of Braddock's forces. Bouquet, however, had his troops retreat in good order and take cover at the top of a hill. While the number of attackers (primarily Shawnee and Delaware) was approximately equal to his troops, Bouquet's 450 men were exhausted and frustrated by the *attack and fade before counterattack* tactics of the native warriors. The Indians were wearing Bouquet's troops down, but neither commander nor troops panicked. After a night of great anxiety, Bouquet employed a classic maneuver (used by Hannibal against the Romans at the battle of Cannae in Italy). Allowing one side of his square to retreat, drawing the triumphant natives into his center, he sent his two retreating companies around the side of the hill to fall upon the Indians' right flank capped by a ferocious bayonet charge by his Highlander Scots regiment. Several days later, Bouquet entered Ft. Pitt and the Indian military challenge to European control of the Forks of the Ohio was effectively over. The fort at Detroit also withstood Pontiac's sustained siege. Native warriors, expert at forest fighting and guerilla tactics, were not used to the tactics of siege warfare on fortified sites.[40]

In 1764, Bouquet marched from Fort Pitt into the Ohio country with 1,000 troops forcing the Shawnee and the Delaware to sue for peace and agree to deliver up more than 200 captives. On May 10, the Shawnee, beating drums and singing songs of peace, crossed the Allegheny to Fort Pitt. Observers were astonished by the deep mutual affection displayed between captives and their captors. Some had to be forced to return to white society. "In some cases it was found necessary to deliver the captives bound to Bouquet. The Indians had become greatly attached to these captives and had adopted them into their families. They shed torrents of tears when they were compelled to give them up." There were of course other voices whose tales of horror and murder spread the desire for revenge, stimulating the recruitment of soldiers for the Indian wars to follow and acting as a moral justification for continued expansion.[41]

While the natives' defeat at Bushy Run proved to be the turning point in terms of military control over the Forks, it would be 30 years before Pittsburgh would be completely secure from Indian attack. Confirmed by treaty at Fort Pitt in 1765, the new borderline separating the native and colonist was the Allegheny-Ohio River. Pittsburgh remained a frontier town. At the treaty meeting, Guyasuta was a major spokesman denouncing the end of traditional gift-giving and the high prices of goods provided by the English. Attempts by Croghan to move guns, knives and other goods to the natives at the Forks were forcefully resisted at Sideling Hill by local militia led by Colonel James Smith, the former captive at Fort Duquesne. At the treaty of Fort Stanwix in New York, the Penns paid $10,000 for native lands west of the

Susquehanna. Settlers flooded into the Monongahela Valley, with some compensation paid to displaced natives at the 1768 Fort Pitt Council.

Seeds of Rebellion

Fort Pitt fell into disrepair, and the British seemed eager to facilitate its demise as a spirit of rebellion began to simmer in the colonies. In 1772, the fort was sold off to William Thompson and Alexander Ross. By 1792, the great fort was razed and building materials were sold to townsfolk who used them to build private homes and shops. Only the Fort's blockhouse has survived to the present. Virginians renewed their claims to the territory, especially the counties south of the Mon and Ohio. On the heels of Pontiac's defeat, surveyors James Mason and Jeremiah Dixon, hired by Pennsylvania and Maryland to define their border, worked their painstaking way for nearly four years from December 1763 to September of 1767 two hundred and thirty three miles from the Delaware to the Monongahela. They were determined to press on and establish Pennsylvania's western border a full five degrees of longitude according to the terms of Penn's royal charter. As they reached the major north-south Catawba trail at Dunkard's Creek, Shawnee and Delaware blocked their passage. Some fifteen years of political rivalry between Virginia and Pennsylvania increased tensions before they were ultimately resolved in 1782 when Pennsylvania gained uncontested control of the Forks while Virginia retained a slice of territory along the east shore of the Ohio that became known as the "panhandle."[42]

Overshadowing native and white conflict in the 1770s was the growing tension between England and its colonies. Pittsburgh became a nest of intrigue as pro-and anti-British groups were active, while simultaneously both Virginia and Pennsylvania had their partisans on hand. George Washington visited Pittsburgh in 1770 and met with Dr. John Connolly at Semple's Tavern on his way to examine his extensive local land interests. Washington continued on down the Ohio where he encountered his old adversary Guyasuta and held a long meeting with him.[43] Connolly was interested in extending Virginia's control over the Forks in violation of the treaty of 1763. Turmoil on the border provided rich grounds for intrigue. Brutal killings and atrocities between whites and natives helped spur fear and racial hatred. Logan, the Mingo chief and son of the important Iroquois leader Shikellamy, was famous as a peacemaker and friend of whites. He returned home to find that Daniel Greathouse with 20 men had lured some of Logan's family to a tavern where, following a marksmanship contest, the natives were murdered once their guns were emptied. A sister of Logan's was shot down trying to escape, but successfully pleaded for the life of her child fathered by Colonel John Gibson. Gibson's own life had been saved through adoption by an aged Shawnee squaw and the Delaware prophet Neolin after his capture in Pontiac's war. In all, ten members of Logan's band were killed. Logan believed Captain Michael Cresap was the leader of the band and wrote him a letter using gunpowder for ink. It began: "What did you kill my people on Yellow Creek for?"[44]

Logan's revenge was swift and ferocious. He spared Pennsylvanians, but with a small band of a dozen warriors launched a series of raids against Virginians on the west bank of the Monongahela Valley. His attacks provoked the evacuation of an estimated one thousand settlers from the west side of the Monongahela. First killed was William Spicer, his wife and six of his eight children in Greene County; and by the time Logan's thirst for revenge was slaked, an estimated thirty settlers were dead, including sixteen by the hand of Logan himself.[45] Finally, he delivered his famous speech to John Gibson, his nephew's father, who transcribed it word for word. It was compared by Jefferson in his *Notes on Virginia* to the finest oratory of the Greeks and Romans and for a hundred years was recited by children in American schools.

> I appeal to any white man to say if he ever entered Logan's cabin hungry, and I gave him not meat; if he came cold or naked, I gave him not clothing.

> During the course of the last long and bloody war, Logan remained in his tent, an advocate for peace. Nay such was my love for the whites, that those of my country pointed at me as they passed, and said, 'Logan is a friend of the white man.' I even thought to live with you, but for the injuries of one man, Colonel Cresap, the last spring, in cold blood, and unprovoked, cut off all the relatives of Logan; not sparing my women and children. There runs not a drop of my blood in the veins of any human creature. This called on me for revenge. I have sought it. I have killed many. I have fully glutted my vengeance. For my country, I rejoice at the beams of peace. Yet do not harbor the thought that mine is the joy of fear. Logan never felt fear. He will not turn on his heel to save his life. Who is there to mourn for Logan? Not one.[46]

In response to the killings, Virginia Governor Dunmore launched a retaliatory invasion of the Ohio country with 3,000 troops that fought to a costly victory against the Shawnee led by Cornstalk at Point Pleasant, West Virginia. As the revolutionary crisis came to a head, the British rallied most of the Iroquois, except the Oneida, to their cause. Hatred for the Virginians pushed the Shawnee and Delaware toward the English. Most of the interracial bloodshed shifted to northern Pennsylvania, especially the Wyoming Valley in the northeast and along the Allegheny Valley frontier. The Shawnee and Delaware opposed troops from either the British at Fort Detroit or Americans at Fort Pitt crossing their Ohio country to attack one another.

One consequence of Lord Dunmore's war was the political coup engineered by Connolly, who arrived at Pittsburgh with a commission from Lord Dunmore to rule in Virginia's name. Fort Pitt became Fort Dunmore and Connelly began recruiting a Virginia militia. Alarmed, the Pennsylvanians at their county seat, Hannastown in Westmoreland County, summoned Connelly and arrested him; but he subsequently appeared at his trial with 150 of his militia "with drawn swords and firelocks at the ready and took possession of the courthouse." He proceeded to arrest the Westmoreland justices and sent them to confinement in Virginia. These contentious activities aroused the concern of the new Continental Congress, and a communication signed by Thomas Jefferson, Patrick Henry and Benjamin Franklin among others urged restraint on both sides. "Our joint and urgent request to you is that all animosities which have heretofore subsisted among you as inhabitants of distinct colonies may now give place to generous and concurring efforts for the preservation of every thing that can make our common Country dear to us." The rising temper of the times was fanning a new sentiment of American patriotism that demanded unity. Officers of Dunmore's army, on return from their costly victory at Point Pleasant, declared: "As the love of Liberty, and attachment to the real interests and just rights of America outweigh every other consideration, we resolve that we will exert every power within us for the defense of American liberty and for the support of her just rights and privileges...."[47]

In September and October of 1775, with revolutionary forces appointed by the Second Continental Congress in charge of Pittsburgh, which was the headquarters of the Continental Army in the west, an important conference was convened with the Iroquois, Delaware and Shawnee. The treaty signed there marked the first agreement between the fledgling American nation and Native Americans. The Americans sought a guarantee of neutrality by the Indian nations during the revolutionary war that was looming. Affirming the 1768 Treaty of Lancaster, white settlement was recognized in Kentucky, but the lands north of the Ohio were to remain Indian forever. Divisions were revealed among the natives, however, as the Delaware, who had suffered much abuse from both Iroquois and the Virginians, asserted their rights to a section of the Ohio country, refusing further submission to the Iroquois' land claims or sovereignty. The Delaware chief White Eyes announced to both Iroquois and Americans that the Delaware would henceforth speak for themselves:

> You say…that you had conquered me, that you had cut off my legs – had put a petticoat on me, giving me a hoe and a cornpounder in my hands saying; "now woman! Your business henceforward shall be to plant and to hoe corn, and pound the same for bread, for us men and warriors!" – Look…at my legs! If, as you say, you had cut them off, they have grown again to their proper size! – The petticoat I have thrown away, and have put on my proper dress! – The corn hoe and pounder I have exchanged for these firearms, and I declare that I am a man![48]

Not everyone at Fort Pitt proved to be a supporter of the American cause. Loyalist sympathies were strong in some families, ethnic groups, and regions. Alexander McKee, Indian agent in charge of the commissary at Fort Pitt, and Simon Girty, with his two brothers a captive of the Indians as a child, left quietly for Detroit and the British cause in 1778, having initially served the Americans. Both men had strong ties to native peoples and understood the Americans were now the prime threat to the natives' survival. Theodore Roosevelt noted that the American Revolution in the east was "a struggle for independence," but in the west, it was "a war of conquest." Simon Girty became the most reviled of Americans, a traitor to his country and his race who, according to the testimony of Dr. Knight, laughed at the torture of his friend Colonel Crawford. In fact, there is extensive evidence of Girty's assistance to many white captives, including the great frontiersman Simon Kenton.[49]

Girty, however, served as the arch-traitor in the pantheon of the colonists until supplanted in that role by Benedict Arnold. In a world where superior technology, wealth and a belief in God's selection provided colonists with certainty in their right to displace native peoples, ignore ancient land claims, and even exterminate or enslave alien races with impunity, Girty, and others who tried to straddle the two worlds of indigenous resistance and imperial expansion, appears as a modern figure. He moved as easily among various Indian nations, as among Americans, French and British. Girty and his family have deep Pittsburgh connections. He was released from Shawnee captivity at Fort Pitt, many members of his family were buried here, and the family name is memorialized in Girty's Run that empties into the Allegheny near Pittsburgh, as well as other local place names.[50]

In the spring of 1778, Captain David Rodgers was ordered by the Virginia Governor to take an expedition to New Orleans to purchase badly needed gunpowder for the Revolutionary forces. With 40 Virginians from the Monongahela region, Captain Rodgers made a successful trip; but, upon their return, they were ambushed along the Ohio by a band of Shawnee assisted by Simon Girty. Most of the force including its captain was killed, and the Indians got the precious cargo. Colonel Broadhead's campaign up the Allegheny in the summer of 1779, while General Sullivan invaded the Iroquois heartland from the east with a larger force, was the major military action from Pittsburgh during the American Revolution. With 600 men, Broadhead scattered a small force led by the redoubtable Guyasuta and then proceeded to destroy cornfields and burn villages including 130 longhouses. With most of the Iroquois warriors fighting on another front, he encountered little serious resistance and returned without a single casualty. The Iroquois were broken as a military force, their fields and homes destroyed, with only enclaves surviving and many fleeing to Canada. Raids and isolated murders happened all around Pittsburgh. In Greene County, a woman named Experience Bozarth killed three Indians with an axe inside her cabin in defense of her children.[51]

The most famous Indian hunter was Captain Samuel Brady, who swore vengeance on the race after his brother and father were slain by natives. He was renowned as a fearless tracker who rescued captives and killed raiders with his band of rangers. He tracked, shot and scalped his younger brother's slayer, the Delaware warrior Bald Eagle. He escaped captors several times. Once, he avoided being burnt alive at the stake by breaking his bonds, shoving a squaw and her baby (in one version just the baby) into the fire intended for him, and escaping in the confusion. His most famous exploit was his 25-foot leap over the Cuyahoga River gorge to elude capture. Dressed in Indian garb, he rescued Jennie Stoops and her child captured near Crafton on Chartier's Creek. Late in his career, Brady was tried for killing the wrong Indians after a raid; and Guyasuta, who respected his warrior prowess, testified in his defense.[52]

While the revolutionary war ended with the surrender of Lord Cornwallis at Yorktown, Indian troubles in the neighborhood of Fort Pitt actually increased. The spirit of retaliation and vengeance was deeply ingrained on both sides. In 1782, one hundred and sixty volunteers under the command of John Williamson, in retaliation for a number of murderous raids in the Monongahela Valley by Great Lakes' Indians, descended on the peaceful Moravian Delaware settlement at Gnadenhutten in Ohio where it was charged some of the Wyandot raiders had been sheltered. The peaceful town offered no resistance; but when a woman was seen to be wearing a dress owned by one of the white female victims that she subsequently admitted was given to her by a raider, many demanded the entire town be executed rather than brought to Fort Pitt for examination of their individual guilt or innocence. A vote was taken, and it was overwhelming with only 16 voting against the collective death sentence. The Christian Delaware spent the night praying and singing hymns. On March 8, 1782, the sentences were carried out:

> The Indian men were led two by two to the cooper shop, where they were beaten to death by mallets and hatchets. The women and children were led into the church and there slaughtered. Many of them died with prayers on their lips, while others met their death by chanting songs. Altogether forty men, twenty women and thirty-four children were inhumanly butchered. Many of the children were brained in their wretched mother's arms. One of the murderers after having broken the skulls of fourteen of the Christian Delawares, with a cooper's mallet, handed the blood-stained mallet to a companion with the remark: "My arm fails me, go on with the work. I think I have done pretty well."[53]

This outrage provoked the gruesome torture of the captured Colonel Crawford, described in meticulous detail by fellow captive Dr. Knight. His famous account begins: "About the latter end of the month of March or the beginning of April, of the present year 1782, the western Indians began to make incursions upon the frontiers of Ohio, Washington, Youghiogheny and Westmoreland counties...." Crawford's disastrous expedition was in response to the increased native raids following the Gnadenhutten outrage. Four hundred and eighty horsemen, primarily Virginia settlers from Washington County, assembled to march on Sandusky against the hostile Wyandot and Shawnee, the source of most of the attacks on their settlements, while the mostly peaceful Delaware villages closest to the whites were taking the brunt of the retaliation. They elected William Crawford their commander by five votes over David Williamson, the commander at Gnadenhutten. Following a couple of days of fighting near Sandusky against a Wyandot – Shawnee force of lesser size, the American forces panicked and broke.[54]

Crawford was captured by the Delaware during the scattered retreat, but Williamson kept the rear guard intact and returned to Pennsylvania with 300 men. "In the hope of escaping such a dreadful fate as death at the stake, Colonel Crawford asked that his old friend, the Delaware chief, Wingenund, might be sent for…. Wingenund reluctantly advised the Colonel it was beyond his power to save him…. Failing to capture the hated Williamson, they determined Crawford must pay the penalty. Then Wingenund burst into tears and turned aside that he might not witness the torture of his friend."[55] Simon Girty, who was fighting with the British and Indian forces at the Battle of the Sandusky, also tried several times to intercede for his friend Crawford's life, including proposing an escape attempt, but refused to shoot Crawford when he appealed to Girty to end his misery, because he feared the natives would turn on him. [56]

Native fury delivered a major blow on July 13, 1782, when Guyasuta and Sayenqueraghta, principle Seneca war chief, led a military expedition of 100 Seneca and 60 Canadian rangers across the Allegheny to strike Hannastown, the seat of Westmoreland County that still included Pittsburgh. The 60 inhabitants fled to the fort while the town was burned to the ground, cattle killed, and horses scattered. More than a dozen were killed in the surrounding area, but the only casualty at the blockhouse was "a maiden of sixteen summers named Margaret Shaw, who received a bullet in her breast while exposed before a hole in one of the gates as she was rescuing a child, who had toddled out to danger." Hannastown would not rise from the ashes. The county seat of Westmoreland was relocated to Greensburg in 1787 on the new road from Bedford to Pittsburgh. The following year, on September 24, 1788, Allegheny County was established by an act of the legislature.[57]

With the crushing of the League of the Iroquois and their formal submission at the 1784 Treaty of Fort Stanwix, there only remained the legal subjugation of the remnant tribes of eastern Ohio. At Fort McIntosh near the mouth of the Beaver River, just west of Pittsburgh on the Ohio, Delaware, Wyandot, Chippewa and Ottawa representatives were informed by the American delegates of their powerlessness vis-à-vis the absorption of their lands by the United States. Their traditional ally, France, was allied with the United States; the peace treaty concluded with Great Britain had ceded all lands south of the Great Lakes; and the subjugation of the Iroquois meant the end of any recognition of the League's claims or protection. The Americans declared the "claim and title of each particular tribe" were without consequence, "because we claim the country by conquest." The natives were further informed that "in pursuance of the humane and liberal views of Congress," they could hunt in the ceded land until whites came there to settle.[58]

Military action continued its bloody way west. In 1790, General Harmar's expedition was defeated with the loss of 250. In 1791, in the worst defeat of an American army by natives, with higher casualties than any inflicted on Washington's army by the British in any single Revolutionary war battle, Westmoreland County native General St. Clair's force of 1400 was ripped apart and nearly annihilated by a roughly equal force of Miami, Shawnee, Delaware and Wyandot, plus a few Canadians with Simon Girty and Alexander McKee assisting. It was only with the campaign of General "Mad Anthony" Wayne that the Shawnee and their allies were finally defeated. Wayne came to Pittsburgh in June 1792 bearing the weight of Washington's injunction "that another defeat would be irredeemably ruinous to the reputation of the government."[59]

Wayne erected Fort Fayette as a supply depot a short way up the Allegheny from the former site of Fort Pitt, and in December his force of 5,000 men called "The Legion of the United States" was moved to a beautiful plain on the Ohio very near to the former site of Logstown that became known as Legionville. There, Wayne drilled and conducted mock battles to prepare his troops to counteract shifting Indian battlefield tactics. Seneca chiefs Guyasuta and Cornplanter, by then reconciled to American rule, visited Wayne there before his march west. In 1793, he advanced into western Ohio Indian country and established Fort Recovery at the site of St. Clair's defeat and Fort Wayne at the site of Harmar's debacle. He clashed with 2,000 Indians and Canadians at the site of a tornado's swath through the woods, and at the Battle of Fallen Timbers the Americans won a decisive victory.

Following the American triumph, an officer under Wayne named Kearney came upon an elderly Indian sitting on a log at the battlefield waving a white handkerchief. The old man named Maiden Foot said he'd "been a warrior all his life and desired henceforth to live in peace with all mankind." His handkerchief bore in black letters the name Mary Means, the maiden name of Kearney's wife. The Indian had met then eleven-year-old Mary at Fort Ligonier before Pontiac's revolt. He was charmed by her and gave her a gift of beads. Months later in the uprising he helped Mary and her mother escape from captivity and as remembrance he kept her handkerchief in his medicine pouch for thirty-one years, surviving campaigns against Bouquet, St. Clair and Wayne. Kearney took the Indian home to his wife. There, "Mrs. Kearney and the Indian immediately recognized each other…. Maiden Foot now explained that shortly before he met Mary Means, he had lost a sister about her age and size, and that the giving of the string of beads to her was in effect adopting her as his sister." He was taken into the Kearney home where he died four years later. Upon his gravestone in Cincinnati they inscribed: "In memory of Maiden Foot, an Indian Chief of the 18th Century, who died a Civilian and a Christian."

Lying in the heart of downtown Pittsburgh, the Trinity burial ground between the Episcopal and the Presbyterian churches is the city's oldest cemetery. Once an Indian burial mound and the probable site of the French cemetery of the Assumption of the Blessed Virgin Mary of the Beautiful River, where the French captain Beaujeu was carried in pomp with full military honors after Braddock's defeat, it contains the graves of many of the founding families of Pittsburgh. There in a corner against the Anglican Episcopal Church a stone is inscribed:

MIO-QUA-COO-NA-CAW

or Red Pole

Principal village chief of the Shawanese Nation

Died at Pittsburgh the 28th of January 1797

Lamented by the United States

Lying in the only marked grave in Pittsburgh of a native from the era of the conquest, Red Pole was the adoptive brother of Blue Jacket, one of the great military leaders of the Shawnee. Not far away in the same burial ground lay the remains (later relocated) of John Gibson, son-in-law of Logan, who transcribed for posterity the chief's powerful lament.[60]

The Forks of the Ohio was an important crucible of white and red race relations. Torture and terrorism became major defensive weapons of the native; genocidal attacks without regard for guilt or innocence became the common operation of whites. What is also true, but less remembered, however, is that many whites and many natives transcended the tragic divide that separated them, warned each others' communities of attack, fought each others' battles, protected each others' free passage, moved to spare prisoners, and tried to reach a peaceful accommodation. Peacemakers on both sides sometimes paid for their efforts with their lives. But the relentless motor of European immigration and constant advances in technology and weaponry drove the American juggernaut westward and the native peoples before them.

Notes Chapter 3

[1]John Lankford, ed., *Captain John Smith's America* (New York: Harper, 1967), 128-9.

[2]Gordon Sayre, *Les Sauvages Americans: Representations of Native Americans in French and English Colonial Literature* (Chapel Hill: North Carolina Press, 1997). This book does a great service by contrasting the differing attitudes of the two European invaders into Western Pennsylvania. Sayre cites Wayne Franklin, *Discoverers, Explorers, Settlers*, "The gridwork principle won out."

[3]John Witthoft, *The American Indian as Hunter* (Harrisburg: Pennsylvania Historical Museum and Commission, 1990), 1.

[4]W.J. Eccles, *The Canadian Frontier* (Albuquerque: University of New Mexico Press, 1983), 130, 156.

[5]Felix Fellner, "Early Catholicity in Western Pennsylvania," *Catholic Pittsburgh's One Hundred Years* (Chicago: Loyola University Press, 1943). A bronze plaque on the Allegheny County Courthouse placed by the Central Council of Polish Organizations commemorates Sadowski's trip to Logstown and establishment of a trading post at Kittanning in 1729; Dillie Steinmet, "Early History and Pioneer Settlements of Braddock's Field," *The Unwritten History of Braddock's Field (Pennsylvania)*, (Bowie: Heritage Books Inc., 1999).

[6]Andrew Gallup, ed., *The Celeron Expedition to the Ohio Country: The Reports of Pierre-Joseph Celoron and Father Bonnechamps* (Bowie, Maryland: Heritage Books, 1997), VII; Paul A. Wallace, *Conrad Weiser: Friend of Colonist and Mohawk* (Lewisburg: Wennawoods Publishing, 1996), 184, 209, 218.

[7]Wallace, *Conrad Weiser*, 221-2.

[8]Donald H. Kent, *The French Invasion of Western Pennsylvania 1753* (Harrisburg: Pennsylvania Historical Museum and Commission, 1981), 7-9.

[9]Fred Anderson, *The Crucible of War: The Seven Years' War and the Fate of Empire in British North* (New York: Vintage, 2000), 25-30.

[10]Wallace, *Conrad Weiser*, 66, 169. Aliquippa does not even get a mention in Fred Anderson's *Crucible of War*.

[11]C. Hale Sipe, *The Indian Chiefs of Pennsylvania* (Lewisburg: Wennawoods Publishing, 1995) 255. Wampum belts were long, wide belts painstakingly assembled from ocean shells with highly symbolic designs normally in black and white. They were important instruments of diplomacy that could call for peace or war.

[12]Bob Bearer, *Leading by Example: Partisan Fighters & Leaders of New France* (Westminster: Heritage Books, Inc., 2002), I:43-54. This provides a French view of Pickawillamy and Langlade's role in Braddock's defeat.

[13]Randolph C. Downes, *Council Fires on the Upper Ohio: A Narrative of Indian Affairs in the Upper Ohio Valley until 1795* (Pittsburgh: University of Pittsburgh Press, 1968), 58-62.

[14]Frank C. Harper, *Pittsburgh of Today: Its Resources and People* (New York: The American Historical Society, Inc., 1931), 1:35.

[15]C. Hale Sipe, *The Indian Chiefs of Pennsylvania*, (Lewisburg, Pennsylvania: Wennawood Publishing, 1995), 287.

[16]George Washington, *The Journal of Major George Washington* (Williamsburg: The Colonial Williamsburg Foundation, 1959), 7-8.

[17]Washington, *The Journal of Major George Washington*, 8.; Washington, *The Journal of Major George Washington*, 41.

[18]Washington, *The Journal of Major George Washington*, 47.

[19]Washington, *The Journal of Major George Washington*, 22.

[20]A.A. Lambing, *Register of Fort Duquesne, 1754-1756* (Pittsburgh, The Catholic Historical Society of Western Pennsylvania, 1954); Anderson, *Crucible of War*, 5-6, 50-59.

[21]On October 26, 2003 a state historical marker was dedicated to Queen Aliquippa on the site of her last encampment on a strategic stretch of level ground above the Monongahela two miles below its confluence with the Youghioghenny; Anderson, *Crucible of War*, 5-7, 62-5. The central role of the Half-King is critical to the mitigation of Washington's responsibility and is found on p. 5-7. The account of the Fort Necessity battle is on p. 62-5.

[22]Anderson, *Crucible of War*, 56.

[23]Paul E. Kopperman, *Braddock at the Monongahela* (Pittsburgh, University of Pittsburgh Press, 2003), 10, 99.

[24]Robert C. Alberts, "Braddock's Alumni" *American Heritage*, (February, 1961); Paul A. Wallace, *Daniel Boone in Pennsylvania* (Harrisburg: PHMC, 1987).

[25]Leroy V. Eid, "A Kind of Running Fight: Indian Battlefields Tactics in the Eighteenth Century," *The Western Pennsylvania Historical Magazine* (April 1988), 147-71.

[26]Kopperman, *Braddock at the Monongahela*, 139.

[27]James Smith, "Prisoner of the Caughnawagas, "*Captured by the Indians*," ed. Frederick Drimmer (New York: Dover Publications, 1985), 30.

[28]Only St. Clair's disastrous campaign against the Shawnee exceeds it, while Custer's defeat at the Little Big Horn cost less than half of Braddock's fatalities.

[29]Frank Cassell, "The Last Days of General Braddock: The March through Westmoreland and Allegheny Counties," *Westmoreland History* (September 2002); Stephen Quinon, "The Old Indian Burying Ground," *Western Pennsylvania Historical Magazine* (October 1920), 203-6

[30]Smith, *Captured by the Indians*, 31-32.

[31]Matthew C. Ward, *Breaking the Back Country: The Seven Years' War in Virginia and Pennsylvania, 1754-1765* (Pittsburgh: University of Pittsburgh Press, 2003), 106-7.; James P. Myers, "Pennsylvania's Awakening: The Kittanning Raid of 1756," *Pennsylvania History* (1999), 399-420.

[32]T.J. Chapman, *The French in the Allegheny Valley* (Cleveland: W.W. Williams, 1887), 79-80.

[33]Sipe, *Indian Chiefs of Pennsylvania*, 295-7; Anderson, *Crucible of War,* 270-2.

[34]Sipe, *Indian Chiefs of Pennsylvania*, 372-3

[35]Fred Anderson, ed., *George Washington Remembers: Reflections on the French and Indian War* (New York; Rowman & Littlefield Publishers, 2004), p. 23; Anderson, *Crucible of War*, 282; Walter O'Meara, *Guns at the Fork* (Pittsburgh: University of Pittsburgh Press, 1979), 198-215.

[36]Downes, *Council Fires on the Upper Ohio,* 93-122.

[37]Gregory Evans Dowd, *A Spirited Resistance: The North American Indian Struggle for Unity, 1745-1815* (Baltimore and London: the John Hopkins University Press, 1991), 32-37.

[38]Dowd, *A Spirited Resistance*, 117-121, 225

[39]Solon J. Buck and Elizabeth Hawthorn Buck, *The Planting of Civilization in Western Pennsylvania* (Pittsburgh: University of Pittsburgh Press, 1979), 103-6.; Anderson, *Crucible of War,* 542.; Sipe, *Indian Chiefs of Pennsylvania*, 389.

[40]Don Daudelin, "Numbers and Tactics at Bushy Run," *Western Pennsylvania Historical Magazine* (1985), 68, 153-179.

[41]Sipe, *The Indian Chiefs of Pennsylvania*, 391.; Downes, *Council Fires on the Upper Ohio,* 122.

[42]William Garbarino, Jr., *Along the Monongahela* (Midway: Midway Publishing, 2000), 43-4. I am indebted to Douglas MacGregor, archivist at the Fort Pitt Museum, for information on the timeframe of the Fort's demise, as well as many other suggestions in this chapter.

[43] On October 25, 2006, a statue commemorating this encounter between Washington and Guyasuta was dedicated on Mt. Washington, overlooking the city of Pittsburgh.

[44]Sipe, *Indian Chiefs of Pennsylvania*, 440-7.

[45]Garbarino, Jr., *Along the Monongahela: A History of the Early Events Along the Monongahela and its Tributaries*, 50-53.

[46]The speech and most of the information on Logan is taken from Sipe, *Indian Wars of Pennsylvania* (Harrisburg: The Telegraph Press, 1929), 490-501. Greathouse had been a member of Cresap's command. Though Cresap steadfastly denied taking part in the killings, Logan blamed him.

[47]Edward G. Williams, *Fort Pitt and the Revolution on the Western Frontier* (Pittsburgh: Historical Society of Western Pennsylvania, 1978), 2-35.

[48]Downes, *Council Fires on the Upper Ohio*, 184-185.

[49]Daniel K. Richter, *Facing East from Indian Country* (Cambridge: Harvard University Press, 2003), 190; David G. Colwell, "The Causes and Accuracy of the Reputation of Simon Girty in American History," *Pittsburgh History* (Spring 1994). This article makes a persuasive case for a re-examination of the history of Girty.

[50]I am indebted to Eric Marchbein for his reflections on Simon Girty conveyed to me in a letter. "Girty was important because, far from being the bloodthirsty caricature created by his adversaries, he reveals a rare glimpse of humanity in a brutal and violent epoch."

[51]Sipe, *Indian Chiefs of Pennsylvania*, 493-4; Sipe, *The Indian Wars of Pennsylvania*, 584-6.

[52]Sipe, *Indian Wars of Pennsylvania*, 572-82. Marie McClure, *Captain Sam Brady, Indian Scout* (Beaver: Beaver Area Heritage Foundation, 1971).

[53]McClure, *Captain Sam Brady, Indian Scout*; Sipe, *The Indian Chiefs of Pennsylvania*, 650.

[54]John Knight, "'The Narrative of Dr. Knight," in Archibald Loudon, *Loudon's Indian Narratives,* (Lewisburg, Pennsylvania: Wennawinds Publishing, 1996), 1-15; Parker B. Brown, "The Historical Accuracy of the Captivity Narrative of Doctor John Knight," *Western Pennsylvania Historical Magazine,* (January, 1987), 53-67.

[55]Sipe, *The Indian Wars of Pennsylvania*, 661.

[56]Allan W. Eckert, *That Dark and Bloody River* (New York: Bantam Books, 1995), 386-393. Contains a vivid imaginative recreation of Girty's dilemma.

[57]Sipe, *The Indian Wars of Pennsylvania*, 666; James B. Richardson, "Who Were Those Guys? The Destruction of Hanna's Town, Part II," *Western Pennsylvania History*, Fall 2007, 27-35.

[58]Downes, *Council Fires on the Upper Ohio*, 293-295.

[59]Downes, *Council Fires on the Upper Ohio,* 710.

[60]Charles W. Dahlinger, "A Place of Great Historic Interest: Pittsburgh's First Burying Ground," *Western Pennsylvania Historical Magazine* (October 1919), 205-11.; Quinon, *Western Pennsylvania Historical Magazine,* 201-10.

Chapter Four

Gateway to the Heartland

The point between the Forks of the Ohio is shaped like an arrowhead pointed west. During its early history, Pittsburgh was, in fact, the primary American entry to the vast Mississippi River basin unbroken by mountain barriers for more than a thousand miles from the Alleghenies to the Rocky Mountains; a city that looked west, outfitting armies, expeditions, and generations of westward-bound pioneer settlers. Down the broad Ohio opened the heartland of a continent - "in addition to the imposing grandeur of its vast extent...an immense region of animal and vegetable life in all their endless varieties." Down the Ohio, "the Beautiful River," a highway to the heartland of a continent for generations of pioneer families, seemingly limitless opportunity beckoned.[1]

River Life

hree rivers meet at the forks. To the north, the Allegheny, uninterrupted by falls, was navigable most of the 200 miles to its headwaters in the Seneca country of New York. To the south, the Monongahela, navigable in season for 150 miles, tapped the trade and travel of northern Virginia. Like two great arms, the rivers gathered in goods and travelers across a broad front and funneled them toward the busy little town at the confluence of the rivers. From that point, their combined flow created the Ohio. Zadok Cramer, publisher of an annual *Pittsburgh Almanack* full of weather information, planting tips and health advice, wrote a famous guide to river travel on the "Monongahela, Allegheny, Ohio and Mississippi" that was one of the first books published in Pittsburgh.[1] His seventh edition in 1811 described the three rivers in the following manner:

> The Monongahela, after it enters Pennsylvania, runs through a rich and well-settled country. Its waters when high are colored with the washy disposition of clay-loam land, of which is borne down with its current a thick sediment. Its banks are generally firm, bearing large and stately trees of the button-wood, hickory, white and black oak, walnut, sugar maple, beech, and cedar, and these afford a good supply of logs for the numerous saw-mills erected at and near the mouths of the creeks emptying into the river....
> Few rivers and perhaps none excel the Allegheny for the transparency of its water, or the beauty of its bottom, having a fine gravely bed, clear of rocks and uninterrupted by falls. Its surface is unbroken, and its mean velocity is about 2 1/2 miles an hour;

when high runs at the rate of 4 miles an hour, being a little more rapid in its course than the Monongahela. Its waters in some instances have proved medicinal; and the fish caught in it are allowed to be superior than the Monongahela. The junction of the Allegheny and Monongahela Rivers form the Ohio and this discharges itself into the Mississippi...about 1,188 computed miles from Pittsburgh.... The Ohio has been described, as "beyond all competition, the most beautiful river in the universe, whether we consider it for its meandering course through an immense region of forests, for its clean and elegant banks, which afford innumerable delightful situations for cities, villages, and improved farms: or for those many other advantages, which truly entitle it to the name originally given it by the French of 'La Belle Riviere', that is, 'the Beautiful or Fair River.'" This description was penned several years since, and it has not generally been thought an exaggerated one. Now the immense forests recede, cultivation smiles along its banks, towns every here and there decorate its shores, and it is not extravagant to suppose that the day is not very far distant when its whole margin will form one continuous village.[3]

Accounts from this time speak with wonder about the prodigious dimensions of plant and animal life. In 1788, a visitor to Pittsburgh, Colonel John May, recorded in his journal about the fishing he observed at the foot of what would become known as Mt. Washington, where boys brought him two perch weighing over forty pounds together and he saw a sturgeon four and one-half feet long. Cramer recorded several huge sycamores 16 feet across, reported on one 60 feet in circumference and another where 12 mounted men were able to fit in the tree's hollow center![4] Cramer also provided valuable information about the physical remnants of the native peoples that had lived in the area for thousands of years. He recognized the great antiquity of many of these artifacts and pondered the meaning of the extinction of their creators:

> On the Monongahela old fortifications are frequently discovered, as vestiges of a people of whom time has kept no other record, and of whose character the present race of man can form but a feint idea; for like that mammoth, they have left nothing behind them but evident marks of their once having possession of the country, and having been well acquainted with the arts of war, and perhaps as well as those of peace, if we may judge from the quantity and quality of pottery and many other articles of household convenience....all showing the work of indigenous artists. Curious carvings on rocks are to be seen on many parts of the Monongahela. At the mouth of Ten Mile Creek, above Redstone; there are many; some bearing the shape of a man's foot, a horse's foot, a hand, head, a turkey, a fish, birds, beasts, etc., all apparently carved by a people having more tools than our Indians can be supposed to have had in those early periods of time....I have sometimes thought the discoveries of time may yet prove them older than the earliest histories we have of the world.[5]

As the fear of Indian attack receded, the character of Pittsburgh changed from a frontier military outpost to a bustling commercial emporium. The difficulty of access over mountain roads to the cities of the east only accentuated the town's importance, since the western settler looked to Pittsburgh for provision rather than to Philadelphia or other eastern towns. Shielded from eastern competition by the washboard ridges of the Allegheny Mountains, connected with a vast continental interior filling up with agricultural and commercial settlements that hungered for a wide range of useful products, the Forks of the Ohio was a natural setting for the growth of commerce and industry.

As racial tensions with natives began to fade from the public consciousness, the issue of Negro slavery began to increasingly concern southwestern Pennsylvania. As early as 1688, a petition by Quakers and Mennonites urged the abolition of slavery in Pennsylvania. In 1775, the Society for the Abolition of Slavery was founded in Philadelphia, and the following year the Meeting of Friends disowned any slaveholders in their midst. On February 29, 1780, the Pennsylvania Assembly passed the first abolition law in the country. It provided that no child born from that point in Pennsylvania should be a slave, but those children of Negroes or mixed race born of a slave mother might be held in servitude until the age of twenty-eight.[6] Perhaps the first historical record of an African at the Forks is found in a deposition of Peter Tostee and George Croghan forwarded to Conrad Weiser in 1745. It recounted the seizure by Peter Chartier of thousands of skins and "a Negro man of his" (Tostee). Chartier was encountered near the Forks among a large band of seven or eight hundred natives including women and children migrating down the Ohio. In 1755, Braddock had black road builders and teamsters in his army and three years later General Forbes had 50 blacks serving similar functions in the army that secured control of the Forks and founded Pittsburgh. As the Virginians moved into the contested area west of the Monongahela and south of the Ohio, some of them brought their slaves. Pennsylvania's abolition of slavery provided, therefore, one more point of contention with the Virginians.[7]

Land Issues

In 1781, an ambitious and well-educated Princeton lawyer and journalist, Hugh Henry Brackenridge, came to town. By 1784, Pittsburgh was beginning to take shape. Colonel George Woods and Thomas Vickroy surveyed a "Triangle for the Penns" that established the basis for real estate transactions. Most of the Point had been considered a Manor under direct ownership of the Penn family who had, however, lost title to it owing to their loyalty to England during the revolution. Ferries were established across all three rivers and a state road was started to connect to the east. Aided by Brackenridge, who helped acquire its press and wrote regularly for it, *The Gazette*, the first newspaper west of the Alleghenies, was founded by two twenty-one year old printers, John Scull and Joseph Hall, in 1786. Brackenridge was also the guiding hand behind the charter granted in the same year to the Pittsburgh Academy, an institution of learning based on the classics, which became Western University and eventually the University of Pittsburgh. The same year, a postal service and a library were established. The following year, the Penns granted lots to the Episcopal, Presbyterian and Lutheran churches, and the town of Allegheny was surveyed and laid out on the north side of the river. Through the efforts of Brackenridge, the General Assembly created Allegheny County in 1788. This marked considerable institutional progress for a town that only had a population of 394 in the first U.S. Census in 1790.[8]

Brackenridge defended an Indian, Mamachtaga, in a case notable as the first courtroom trial of an Indian rather than the usual summary judgment and execution of natives judged guilty of some offense. The native had killed two whites in a drunken rage on Killbuck's Island, the notorious "Smoky Island" across the Allegheny from Fort Pitt where prisoners from Braddock's army had been tortured to death. The native, despite several opportunities, did not flee, admitted the murders, and was hanged; but, awaiting trial, he had been permitted to go into the woods and gather roots used to cure the fever of his jailor's daughter. Brackenridge's account of the whole bizarre affair is one of his finest writings. He had little respect for the natives' collective rights, however. Later in his career as a judge, he wrote an opinion that justified the taking of native land "for their not being a man…for what distinguishes an Indian from a wild beast…who lives upon his prey and cultivates little or no soil? …A savage cannot be said to have an absolute right to the soil he occupies, since he does not occupy it in a way that contributes to the civilization of man; for a close population and the scarcity of soil to a certain extent, are necessary to the improvement of the species. Arts and manufactures are the offspring of a close cohabitation, science also and all those endowments which elevate human nature." Consistently, he argued that black slaves who do cultivate land should be set free and in fact resettled "in that country forfeited by the native Indians in consequence of their hostilities toward us." [9]

The contentious land dispute between Pennsylvania and Virginia was finally settled in 1779 in Pennsylvania's favor as the Mason-Dixon line was extended west a full five degrees of longitude, with the western border drawn due north to Lake Erie. Control of the Forks fell to Pennsylvania, but Virginia's land titles were validated as the price of settlement. Thus was secured the extensive local land holdings of Virginians like George Washington. Another contentious issue arose since the delineation of the western border with Ohio coincided with the defeat of the Iroquois and the abrogation of their treaty rights over lands north and west of the Allegheny River to the Ohio border. Pennsylvania found itself with extensive holdings of land where some natives still lived, but now without title. Pennsylvania soldiers who served in the Revolutionary armies between 1777 and 1781 had been paid in bills of credit from both the state and the Continental Congress. This paper depreciated to the point where it was nearly worthless. In 1781, the Pennsylvania legislature issued certificates to soldiers for land good for up to the value of three-fourths of what was owed them.

The problem was that these "depreciation certificates" had also been used to pay Philadelphia merchants for supplies during the war, and so they held a vast amount of them. Furthermore, soldiers who had no assets sold them at a fraction of face value to merchants and distillers. When the Indian Treaty of 1794 formally ceded the northwest section of the state, the legislature had a system ready whereby wealthy land speculators from the east were able to grab the prime land.

The first sale was held in Philadelphia in November 1785, and out of a total of 720,000 acres of depreciation lands, 316,950 were sold at an average price of twenty-eight cents an acre. All the choice land from the rivers to the Butler County line and north along the Allegheny to the limits of the district were sold on this day, and the buyers were almost exclusively members of the political cabal and their speculative partners….Head and shoulders above all the land jobbers stood Robert Morris, once banker to the Revolution and senator from this state during Washington's administration….At one time he owned over a million acres in this state as well as vast acreages in others. In Butler County he had inchoate title to 90,000 acres and almost as much in Allegheny. [10]

Revolutionary soldiers, many of whom had already come to the area as squatters in anticipation of receiving land, were now faced with land agents charging exorbitant prices who refused to compensate the squatters for clearing and improvements done on the land. A separate conflict, also with roots in governmental indebtedness, was developing south of Pittsburgh in the Monongahela Valley. With the surrender of Lord Cornwallis' army and the end of the American Revolutionary War in 1781, the new nation was saddled with a huge national debt and a weak central government. The debt was both external and internal, to foreign countries (especially France and Holland) as well as to domestic bankers and ordinary soldiers who had served their country without pay. Under Washington's Secretary of the Treasury, Alexander Hamilton, bonds issued by a central National Bank of the United States covered the nation's debts. Payment of these bonds in Hamilton's view required tariffs on foreign imports and the imposition of the first federal tax, an excise charge on all distilled spirits that, conveniently for the rich, targeted commerce rather than wealth in land or money. Westerners favored a land tax that would tax eastern estates more heavily and force eastern speculators to sell off their large western land holdings. Hamilton's new tax on alcohol spared wealthy Easterners, but directly impacted the economy of Western Pennsylvania more than any region of the new nation.

A Spirited Rebellion

Western Pennsylvania was being transformed from a hunting ground to a subsistence agricultural economy. Scotch Irish settlers fanned out across the countryside clearing forests for crops, building roads and establishing villages. These new settlers had to carry or purchase basic manufactured goods like rifles, plows, horseshoes, knives, axes, nails, bottles, plates, cook pots, and textiles from east of the mountains. Many also found themselves having to purchase title from speculators for land they had lived on and improved for years without holding clear legal title. Western agricultural products - with one single exception - were not competitive in the East because of the high cost of transportation over the mountains. That exception was rye whiskey. Monongahela Rye established itself as a potent beverage and a highly marketable product. While a horse could only haul four bushels of grain over the mountains, the same horse could carry the equivalent of 24 bushels of grain in liquid form as alcohol, which was then readily convertible to money for the purchase of vital manufactured goods. There was also a growing whiskey export trade down the Ohio to the new settlements in the west. Hamilton's excise tax struck at the heart of the rural economy of Western Pennsylvania since it absorbed the distiller's margin of profit. Without the distiller, the farmer had no market for his grain in a sparsely populated rural economy. Moreover, the tax reminded the European peasant of highly unpleasant levies and taxes they thought were left behind them in the "old country."[11]

To enforce the new tax, John Neville, a former officer under George Washington and commander at Fort Pitt, was chosen as inspector. Tax collectors received a salary plus a bounty of one percent of all the taxes collected. Protest meetings against the tax were held in Washington, Pennsylvania, and Pittsburgh in the summer and fall of 1792. Tax collectors were seized, tarred and feathered. A spirit of rebellion swept the countryside, coming to a head in 1794. Farmers were feeling the pinch as large distillers, like General Neville himself, increased production to drive out the small farm-based distiller. Warnings against compliance with the law were signed by "Tom the Tinker," referring to the practice of "mending the stills" by rifle shot of those paying the hated tax.[12] Democratic societies inspired by the French Revolution sprang up in many locations, while liberty poles were erected with inscriptions such as: "an equal tax, and no excise," and "united we stand and divided we fall." President Washington, knowing full well the independent spirit of the region and seeing the enthusiasm for a revolution that might threaten property rights, was concerned. When a conference of notables in Pittsburgh including Brackenridge and Albert Gallatin called for treating the federal tax collectors with "that contempt they deserve," Washington warned them to "desist from all unlawful combinations and proceedings whatsoever, having for object or intending to obstruct the operation of the laws."[13]

When General Neville visited a small distiller in Allegheny County named William Oliver to serve papers closing his still for failure to pay the tax, an angry band of farmers gathered and fired on the General and his assistant. Neville fled to his Bower Hill plantation south of the Monongahela. At dawn on July 16, 1794, forty farmers surrounded his house. Neville was confrontational, opening fire first and mortally wounding Oliver Miller. A two-day siege ensued. A small troop of about a dozen federal troops managed to join Neville after the first day. One of the most respected of the insurgents, Revolutionary War veteran, Major James McFarlane, was shot and killed believing a truce had been called. On the second day, a crowd of around five hundred farmers stormed and burnt the house. Neville had fled during the night and the crowd allowed the federal soldiers to leave the site unscathed.

On July 23, a meeting of the insurgents at Mingo Creek was marked by heated debate and argument over tactics and the direction of the revolt. At the gathering, Hugh Henry Brackenridge artfully preached moderation to an aroused assembly. He warned that their attack on federal troops had placed them in rebellion against the government. "What has been done might be morally right, but it was legally wrong. In construction of law it was high treason. It was a case within the power of the President to call out the militia." He went on to focus on "the want of power to support what was done: the small basis on which they had to stand, a small part of a small country, not even the whole country west of the mountains with them, unprovided at the same time with arms, ammunition and resources of war."[14]

The leader of the radicals, David Bradford, dreamed grandly of secession and a Western Empire. Others wanted a 'Westsylvania' as a fourteenth state. Bradford put out a call to all the area's militia to gather at Braddock's Field for a march on Pittsburgh. More than five thousand men gathered, but under the influence of Brackenridge, Albert Gallatin, and other moderates, they conducted a peaceful march. Brackenridge wrote: "A revolution did not suit me nor any man else that had anything to lose or was in a way of making something….no man could calculate the consequence of putting the mass in motion with arms in their hands." Brackenridge urged the town to prepare for the invasion by putting out food and quantities of whiskey to welcome the rebel army along the wharf where boats would help ferry them across the Monongahela so they could return home. He personally demonstrated to the nearly two thousand mounted rebels that the river could be forded on horseback.[15]

President Washington declared western Pennsylvania to be in a state of insurrection. Stating that "the very existence of law and the fundamental principles of social order are materially involved," he dispatched 12,000 troops toward Pittsburgh. Brackenridge correctly predicted Washington's response. The President understood this revolt was more serious than earlier Indian or British attacks. "He will see that here the vitals are affected, whereas there the attack was upon the extremities." Resistance melted away before this determined show of force. Terror seized the countryside as soldiers rounded up selected insurgents. "Men were dragged out of their beds at two o'clock in the morning, not suffered to dress themselves but in an unfinished manner obliged to march, some of them without putting on their shoes…dragged out of their beds amidst the cries of children and the tears of mothers…driven before a troop of horses at a trot through muddy roads…impounded in a pen on the wet soil; the guards baying at them and asking them how they would like to be hanged, some offering a dollar for the privilege of shooting at them;…next day impounded in a waste house and detained there five days." Brackenridge asked: "Was this the way to quell the insurrection? Was this the way to make good citizens?" A loyalty oath was imposed on the Westerners and twenty men were taken to Philadelphia for trial. The federal government had weathered the first direct challenge to its authority from its own citizens.[16]

Brackenridge was subjected to intense interrogation by none other than Alexander Hamilton himself who came to Pittsburgh and transcribed his testimony in two long sessions. He explained his actions in a continuous narrative, asking his inquisitor dramatically whether he was not comparable to Richard the

Second who confronted the "mob of 100,000 men assembled on Blackheath? The young prince addressed them, put himself at their head, and said, 'What do you want, Gentlemen? I will lead you'." Hamilton, convinced by Brackenridge's explanations, pronounced him safe from official prosecution. "You will not be troubled even by a simple inquisition by the judge; what may be due to yourself with the public is another question."[17]

The Whiskey Rebellion marked the first time a president used federal troops to quell internal political opposition. Washington's action asserted the primacy of federal over state law and defined the act of treason. "The Rebellion resulted in the first arrests and trials for treason in the federal courts. These trials established the precedent that armed opposition to the execution of a United States statute was equal to 'levying war' against the United States and thus was within the constitutional definition of treason." The suppression of the rebellion strengthened the hand of the conservative counter-revolutionaries on the state and national levels for whom property rights trumped personal liberties. It contributed to the hardening of the Federalists, the "Friends of Order," and anti-Federalist forces, the "Friends of Liberty," into a two-party division that would endure and that in 1800 would bring Jefferson and Gallatin to power. In Pittsburgh, the Jeffersonian forces, supported by Brackenridge, started a new paper, *The Tree of Liberty,* to challenge the Federalist *Gazette.* Brackenridge survived to be named a Justice of the Pennsylvania Supreme Court when Jefferson's Democrats came to power. [18]

Despite the rebellion's suppression, agricultural production and rural development steadily advanced. The Pittsburgh region became increasingly self-sufficient as the generations unfolded and the farms advanced in fertility and productivity. Dr. Benjamin Rush in 1786 described three generations of farming from the rough early pioneer who cleared the land and supplemented meager agriculture with hunting and fishing to the third generation or owner who invests deeply in the cultivation of the soil and the propagation of livestock and thereby enjoys the bounty of the land and the flowering of community. The first generation was nearly all Scotch-Irish; but many of these grew restless when the neighborhood began to fill up, and they moved west, often several times in a lifetime. Those Scotch-Irish who stayed, however, often became political and business leaders. Often the man who took over the farm as the second or the third owner of the land was a German farmer. These Amish, Dunkards or Brethren farmers were steady, hard-working, law abiding men, who "in proportion as he increases in wealth, he values the protection of laws: hence he punctually pays his taxes toward the support of the government. Schools and churches likewise, as the means of promoting order and happiness in society, derive due support from him: for benevolence and public spirit...are the natural offspring of affluence and independence."[19]

Commerce and Exploration

In many American cities the founding families formed an elite based on land ownership that allowed them to form a regional ruling class that remained relatively stable for generations. In the case of Pittsburgh's founding families, the early arrivals often did become substantial landowners. As the town evolved into a major urban manufacturing and commercial center, however, the value of these properties came not from agricultural production but from their value as real estate. The major family fortunes in Pittsburgh were built on commercial, financial and manufacturing investments. "The agricultural hinterland was important in supplying the needs of Pittsburgh, but even this did not yield profits comparable to those realized by southern planters. The immense increase in population in the 19th Century would render these lands, and especially those holdings close to burgeoning Pittsburgh, quite valuable. By then, however, the profits from sales would be divided among the numerous descendants of the family founders."[20]

By the 1780s, Pittsburgh was connected intermittently by float boats to New Orleans and several attempts were made to obtain powder from the Spanish during the American Revolution. In 1789, after the Revolutionary War and the receding of the Indian threat along the Ohio, James Wilkinson took a large flotilla of 25 boats armed with light swivel cannons and 150 men to New Orleans. Trade expanded rapidly after that, providing an outlet for western goods, especially grain, whiskey and tobacco. Large boatyards operated at Brownsville (Redstone), Elizabeth, and Pittsburgh. A trip down the river could be a harrowing experience. In the seven years following the Revolution, possibly 1,500 whites died from Indian attacks on the Ohio or in the Kentucky Territory. Boats on the Ohio were subject to attack, especially from the Shawnee, as they passed between the Indian Territory on the north bank and the war zone of Kentucky to the south. Despite these losses, Kentucky had a population of about 75,000 in 1790 and most of these had come down the Monongahela and Ohio from Virginia and Western Pennsylvania. The abolition of slavery and the securing of Pennsylvania control over Western Pennsylvania pushed many Virginia settlers on to Kentucky.[21]

Pittsburgh's position at the Ohio's headwaters destined it to become a boat builder during the next two centuries. The light birch bark canoe used by the northern tribes was the most advanced craft designed by the Native American. Since the birch was a northern tree, the natives of Pennsylvania made their canoes from the less satisfactory elm bark or fashioned large dugouts which were less maneuverable and more difficult to portage or power upstream. Dugouts might be fifty feet long and five feet wide holding thirty men. Sometimes two were joined for more cargo space. Dangerously hard to control, rafts were commonly used by settlers to haul a family with their worldly possessions. The bateau was a French lake boat with around twenty oarsmen. These boats were gradually modified for river use by adding a built-in keel. These keelboats came to be built forty to eighty feet in length, with pointed ends, seven to eight feet wide at the beam, often with a covered shelter or cabin. They navigated small rivers and could return upstream from New Orleans. Barges or flatboats were wider, heavier, flatter boats, up to twenty feet wide, one hundred twenty feet long, steered by a rudder. Flatboats made one-way trips down the river. After their cargoes were sold, they were dismantled and sold as building material. They were notoriously difficult to control in strong river currents. It is estimated that a third of these boats perished en route during the flatboat era.[22]

In 1803, Meriwether Lewis, under commission from Thomas Jefferson to explore the Missouri and find a passageway to the Pacific Ocean, came to Pittsburgh to construct a keelboat and obtain smaller pirogues or large canoes for his expedition. A year earlier in Haiti, a 30,000 man expeditionary force sent by Napoleon against the army of rebel slaves led by Toussaint Louverture was soundly defeated by a combination of military leadership, the ferocious determination of the rebellious slaves, and tropical diseases that severely weakened the French force. The loss of Haiti as a base of operations to colonize Louisiana led Napoleon to offer a surprised American envoy the purchase of the extensive French rights west of the Mississippi, including the critical port of New Orleans. Prior to this, freedom of navigation had been continually restricted by the Spanish who claimed New Orleans and the entire west bank of the Mississippi until its cession to the French. Assigned to assess these new lands, Lewis's mission was to meet up with Clark in Louisville and proceed deep into Indian country surveying, exploring and establishing the American claim on the ground.

Lewis's famous journal of the expedition opens with the following: "Left Pittsburgh this day at 11 ock (sic) with a party of 11 hands 7 of which are soldiers, a pilot and three young men on trial they having proposed to go with me throughout the voyage." Lewis's stay in Pittsburgh was not a happy one since he was very extremely anxious to leave, but repeated delays by the builder of the keelboat detained him. In a letter to President Jefferson, he expressed his extreme dissatisfaction: "I am by no means sanguine, nor do I believe from the progress he makes that she will be ready before the 5th of August. I visit him every day, and endeavor by every means in my power to hasten the completion of the work." Despite the pressure, the expedition did not depart until August 31. While stopping at Brunot's Island, three miles below the Point, a demonstration of Lewis's air gun staged for some local dignitaries nearly turned tragic as the gun was mishandled and a female observer was grazed across the temple, bleeding profusely. Despite Lewis's unhappiness with his Pittsburgh sojourn, the keelboat proved to be a sturdy and an invaluable vehicle for the expedition. [23]

A frequent visitor to Pittsburgh about this time with considerably less than imperial interests was John Chapman, who became legendary as Johnny Appleseed. While Chapman was certainly a real person, his myth has proven to be a very marketable and expansive commodity. One charming version has John arriving in Pittsburgh in the midst of the Whiskey Rebellion, living on the top of Grant's Hill (much later with the hill removed, the site of the City-County Building), working in a local shipyard, tending the remaining apple trees of the King's Orchard outside the ruins of Fort Pitt, and providing "a way-station for the stranger in want." According to this version, it was in Pittsburgh that Chapman discovered his calling to be Johnny Appleseed.[24]

The reality was probably somewhat more prosaic. Born in 1774 in Massachusetts, Chapman, as a young man in his mid-twenties, made his way across northern Pennsylvania to the northern Allegheny Valley near Franklin. There he appears several times in local records and began his life's vocation of propagating the useful apple which could be eaten raw or cooked, made into sweet or hard cider for drinking, and into vinegar for preservation. He came periodically to Pittsburgh visiting large cider presses to collect seeds. R. I. Curtis wrote a credible first-hand reminiscence of Chapman and Pittsburgh in 1859. Curtis claimed to have known Chapman as a child of eight or nine. "He was very fond of children and would talk to me a great deal, telling me of the hardships he had endured of his adventures and hair-breadth escapes by flood and field." One story was that he'd lived through a winter eating nothing but butternuts; another local tale had him floating down the Allegheny on a spring ice floe. Curtis remembered him clearing little patches along French Creek "where he thought at a future day apple trees would be wanted; then, in the fall, repair to Allegheny County, Pennsylvania, and wash out of the pomace at cider mills a bushel or two of seeds, and return with them on his shoulder, plant them at the proper time, enclose the spot with a brush fence, and pay some attention to the cultivation. He never secured title to the land for his nurseries. He never grafted any."[25]

With what an early biographer described as "the thick bark of queerness on him," Chapman was "a man with no fixed address his entire adult life…who preferred to spend his nights out of doors: one winter he set up house in a hollowed-out sycamore stump outside Defiance, Ohio, where he operated a pair of nurseries. A vegetarian on the frontier, he deemed it a cruelty to ride a horse or chop down a tree; he once punished his own foot for squashing a worm by throwing away its shoe. He liked best the company of Indians and children – and rumors trailed him to the effect that he'd once been engaged to marry a ten-year-old girl, who'd broken his heart." Johnny Appleseed evolved into a powerful symbol of those who give of themselves for the betterment of those around them with no expectation of earthly reward. His mystical religious beliefs as a missionary of the Church of

New Jerusalem were inspired by Emmanuel Swedenborg who wrote: "Man is first introduced into the innocence of childhood, which consists of knowing what is true and good from the Lord only and not from himself, and in desiring and seeking truth only because it is truth, and good only because it is good." John Chapman's eccentricities, his acceptance of native peoples and the natural order, plus his life-long mission of uncompensated benevolence, have all combined to make him a profoundly attractive figure subject to almost endless reinterpretation, a truly mythical archetype. Recently, the historian of food and agriculture, Michael Pollan, has interpreted Johnny Appleseed as a pantheistic figure, a spiritual bridge-builder. Johnny Appleseed lived all his life along the border between the natives and the white settlers. With his horny, gnarled bare feet planted firmly in the earth, he was someone who was able to dissolve the rigid boundaries between nature and culture, especially between the whites and the native peoples. One of the few whites who could pass freely back and forth unarmed through the borderlands, he warned both races about impending attacks by the other.[26]

Johnny Appleseed, an "American Dionysus," who brought the ecstatic consolations of hard cider to the frontier cabin, was also a harbinger of botanical invasions that over time would prove both benign and destructive.

> Everyone knows that the settlement of the West depended on the rifle and the ax, yet the seed was no less instrumental in guaranteeing Europeans' success in the New World....The Europeans brought with them to the frontier a kind of portable ecosystem that allowed them to recreate their accustomed way of life – the grasses their livestock needed to thrive, herbs to keep themselves healthy, Old World fruits and vegetables to make life comfortable. This biological settlement of the West often went on beneath the notice of the settlers themselves, who brought along weed seeds in the feed bags of their horses, and microbes in their blood and gut. (None of these introductions passed beneath the notice of the Native Americans, however.) John Chapman, by planting his millions of seeds, simply went about this work more methodically than most.[27]

John Chapman's life story stands in sharp contrast to another legendary character from the same period, Mike Fink, the river boatman. The keelboat era was a brief but wild and romanticized period on the rivers. Boating involved hard backbreaking labor, but singing, fighting, and drinking were some of the occupational compensations before reaching the ladies of Louisville, St. Louis, Natchez or New Orleans. The most notorious of them all was Mike Fink, the archetype of the swashbuckling pirate entrepreneur. Born near Pittsburgh in 1780, he represented the brawny, boastful, hardworking, hard-fighting quasi-criminal that so dominates American frontier legend. "One of his favorite amusements was to make his woman place a tin cup on her head or between her knees, and then to shoot at it from a distance of thirty yards or so.... Another exploit of which he liked to boast occurred while he was hunting. He was about to take aim at a deer when he saw an Indian doing the same. Mike shifted his gun, and the instant the Indian shot the deer, Mike bagged the Indian." Mike Fink died as he lived. After a quarrel with a partner over a native woman, he shot one of his closest friends as they amused themselves by shooting tin cups off each other's heads. When he bragged later to another long-time associate that he had done it on purpose, the man shot Fink and killed him.[28]

In 1792, a seagoing vessel, the "Monongahela Experiment," was built on the Monongahela and floated to New Orleans. A number of Pittsburgh ships sailed to Philadelphia and New York in this manner. They were row galleys of 30 oars and 2 masts. In 1801, a Pittsburgh-constructed vessel crossed the Atlantic and arrived in Italy. In 1803, two large merchant ships were built. The largest, the "Pittsburgh," carried 170 tons. They had to be floated on the spring floods to make it through the dangerous rapids at Louisville. In 1811, the first steamboat constructed on western waters, the "New Orleans," passed astonished keelboat men as it steamed downriver at an impressive eight miles an hour. By 1819, there were 191 steamboats operating on the western waters. In 1820, technical improvements to the steamboats, moving the boiler up on deck, allowing them to be constructed flatter with less draft, spelled the end of the keelboats. By 1830, the steamboat was the undisputed leader on the river trade. A few keelboats kept operating on the tributaries; but by the 1840s, the keelboat age was over. In 1850, there were nearly 3,000 steamboats operating in the Mississippi River system. While the steamboat improved a traveler's chance of arriving at his destination safely, since an estimated one-third of keelboats and flatboats were lost to the river, river travel was still a problematic affair. Between 1840 and 1846, over 225 steamboats were lost on the western waters. In addition to currents and snags that threatened all boat traffic, the steamboat was subject to fires and explosions. Despite the risks, the rivers were instrumental in the city's advancement. Pittsburgh served as both the transfer center for east-west trade and the head of Ohio River navigation. New Orleans provided the city's primary access to world markets [29]

The steamboat "New Orleans" was launched from Pittsburgh in March, 1811. While leaving Louisville, the boat experienced the first major shock of the New Madrid earthquakes, but continued its way down river to the Mississippi where passengers witnessed the devastation first hand. Three major quakes struck between December 16, 1811 and February 7, 1812 and were accompanied by more than a thousand major and minor tremors. In the quake's impact zone, stretching along the Mississippi from its confluence with the Ohio 150 miles to Memphis, Tennessee, spectacular changes occurred to the landscape and river bed as some sections were violently uplifted and other sections depressed. Oil and gas were released from fractured strata. Both animals and humans were in a state of constant terror and uncertainty. Thought to be among the worst seismic events in recorded American history, it cracked chimneys and masonry walls in Pittsburgh. The earthquakes followed close upon a spectacular comet that hung in the sky from September to January. These heavenly and earthly signs fueled the last great desperate Native American political uprising and religious revival in the old Northwest Territory inspired by the great Shawnee warrior Tecumseh and his prophet brother, Tenskwatawa, that was blunted at the battle of Tippecanoe. Tecumseh was widely believed to have predicted the quake which he interpreted as a sign of spiritual anger and warning: "The Great Spirit is angry with our enemies; he speaks in thunder, and the earth swallows up villages, and drinks up the Mississippi. The great waters will cover the lowlands; their corn cannot grow; and the Great Spirit will sweep those who escape to the hills from the earth with his terrible breath."[30]

Growth of Manufacturing

The increasing sophistication of Pittsburgh manufacturing is evidenced by the rapid adoption of coal-fired steam power. Besides the expanding steamboat construction business, a steam flourmill, steam rolling and slitting mills, and a steam engine works were all operating by 1812. In 1819, the Union Rolling Mill, the most advanced steam mill in the nation, capable of rolling angle iron, and a steam-driven cotton mill were established on opposite sides of the Allegheny. A small and short-lived furnace had been constructed in today's Shadyside neighborhood of Pittsburgh by George

Anshutz in 1793 to make cannon balls for Wayne's Expedition; but in 1804, the Pittsburgh Foundry (predecessor to Mackintosh-Hemphill) was opened and the town quickly established itself as a production center for nails, tools, agricultural and military supplies.[31] Iron had to be imported into the area in pig form from charcoal-fired iron furnaces constructed along Chestnut Ridge to the south and east.

The War of 1812 stimulated production of cordage and war materials. Pittsburgh carpenters were heavily recruited to go to Erie to help build Commodore Perry's fleet that challenged the British for control of Lake Erie. Authorized by Congress to supply munitions to "large and important sections of exposed inland and maritime frontier," construction of the Allegheny Arsenal began in 1814 in Lawrenceville. William Barclay Foster founded Lawrenceville on the broad flood plain along the southern shore of the Allegheny River just outside Pittsburgh that same year. Some of the Arsenal's original designs were by Benjamin Henry Latrobe, designer of the U.S. Capitol and one of the greatest early American architects.[32] Foster, a prosperous merchant, and Captain Abram Woolley, the Arsenal's first commander, organized arms shipments to General Andrew Jackson in Louisiana. The first shipments were made by keelboats and barges, but the new Brownsville-constructed steamboat Enterprize was requisitioned to get emergency supplies of "cannon-balls, gun-carriages, smith's tools, boxes of harnesses, etc." to Jackson. The shipment arrived in New Orleans the day after Jackson's victory there.[33]

The forests immediately surrounding Pittsburgh were logged out early to provide fuel, construction and boat building material. Seemingly limitless coal fed seemingly insatiable consumption. "During the first three decades of the 19th Century, blacksmith shops, brickyards, glass factories, and iron and textile mills using coal sounded a hum of industry which someday would grow into a roar to be heard in every part of the union.... She (Pittsburgh) struck her roots deep into one of the greatest coal beds of the world. She attracted the iron from the furnaces of the surrounding ore-rich Somerset, Westmoreland and Fayette. These products supplied the needs of transients who would soon form the permanent population of the west and remain consumers of Pittsburgh's goods." While coal powered the machines that shaped and cut the iron, its high sulfur content made it unsuitable without coking off the impurities for iron making. Abundant timber on the mountain slopes near the ore sources meant that charcoal, though expensive, remained the dominant fuel in iron making until 1860. It took substantial hard labor to cut, haul and char the nearly 200 bushels of charcoal needed to produce a single ton of iron. Timber, in fact, became less and less available for use by steamboats all along the rivers, so coal from Pittsburgh spread all along the Ohio-Kentucky shores and down the Mississippi as a major fuel for home and industry.[34]

The proliferation of furnaces and coal-fired engines and mills gave Pittsburgh its sooty, sulfurous and smoky aspect that appalled many a visitor and shortened the lives of workers and residents. The city was defensive about its dark and dreary image and even touted the healthful effects of its blackened skies. "The smoke of bituminous coal is anti-miasmatic. It is sulphurous and antiseptic, hence it is, perhaps, that no putrid disease has ever been known to spread in the place. Strangers with weak lungs, for a while, find their coughs aggravated by the smoke; but nevertheless, asthmatic patients have found relief in breathing it....The abundance, cheapness, and consequent general and even profuse use of the best fuel, is certainly one of the great causes of our superior healthfulness. The low fevers so prevalent in the large cities, among the poor, during a hard winter, and the ague so common in wet seasons, in the eastern counties of the state, where wood is scarce, are here in a great degree avoided by the universal practice of keeping coal fires late in the spring, and early in the autumn, and indeed in all seasons when the weather is damp or inclement." [35]

James O'Hara and Isaac Craig established the first factory in Pittsburgh in partnership with William Eichbaum, a Westphalian glasscutter. Their glassworks was built in 1797 at the base of Coal Hill opposite the Point; by 1812 there were a half-dozen glass factories or "houses"; by 1837 fifteen; and by 1865 there were forty-five houses in and around the town. Pittsburgh remained an important production center for glass well into the 20th Century. Glass was not easily transported over the Allegheny Mountains, so regional producers found a ready and steadily growing market for the window glass and bottles produced by their furnaces. An American officer during the Revolution, James O'Hara, was named the quartermaster at Fort Pitt in 1781 and the quartermaster general for the U.S. Army in 1792. His extensive travel and trading interests made him acutely aware of the high price fetched by glass in the Ohio country. Swiss settler Albert Gallatin, while occupying a seat in the U.S. Congress, opened a glass works with German craftsmen in New Geneva, Fayette County, on the Monongahela. The enterprise struggled at first prompting Gallatin to confess: "The fact is, I am not well calculated to make money – I care but little about it, for I want but little for myself, and my mind pursues other objects with more pleasure than mere business." Despite his lack of personal interest in money, his skill in public finance and administration led Jefferson to name him the Secretary of the Treasury in 1801. [36]

The most famous of Pittsburgh's glass companies, Bakewells, was founded in 1808 and was the first to manufacture flint glass. Bakewell's beautiful quality leaded-glass tableware, including decanters, goblets, wine glasses, lamps, cream jugs, and egg cups, established itself as among the finest in the country. The company produced cut glass tableware for Presidents Madison, Monroe and Jackson and presented two cut-glass vases to the Marquis de Lafayette during his tour. [37]

Strikes and Conspiracies

As the city and its industries grew, tensions began to appear between owners and investors on one hand and workers on the other. The first Pittsburgh strike was in 1804 by the cordwainers, or shoemakers, followed in 1806 by the tailors. The cordwainers' strike was to establish an accepted price for the making of coarse shoes (75 cents), fine shoes (80 cents), long boots ($2.00), etc., and a raise in the board paid to apprentices from $1.50 to 2.50 per week. [38] In 1809, the cordwainers organized a society and appointed a "tramping committee" to inspect shops and wages. A rise in the cost of living, brought on by the War of 1812, led to a series of strikes of journeymen against the master cordwainers. An indictment was brought that members of the union "being workmen and journeymen in the art, mystery and occupation of cordwainers, did unlawfully, perniciously and deceitfully, designing and intending to form and unite themselves into an unlawful society and combination for the purpose of unjustly and iniquitously raising the price of their wages and the wages of all journeymen cordwainers…(and) assemble and meet together; and being so assembled and met together…unjustly and corruptly conspire, combine, confederate and agree together…and did wholly absent and withdraw themselves from employment of many master cordwainers in said (Pittsburgh) borough…to the great injury, damage and oppression of the good people of said borough." [39]

The cordwainers were found guilty and fined one dollar, but an important precedent was set. Conspiracy charges based on English Common Law, defining conspiracy as two or more men joining to harm a third or the public, meant workers could not legally unite to obtain benefits unobtainable by them as individuals. This and other similar cases concerning shoemakers, tailors, and printers were key battlegrounds for those asserting the maintenance of English Common Law (Federalists) versus those who argued that the revolution had swept away English Common Law (Jeffersonians). The Pittsburgh case was particularly important because in earlier conspiracy cases in Philadelphia and New York, labor combinations had involved violence or threats. There were no violent acts or threats in the Pittsburgh case; it was the act of talking together, of forming an organization, and of acting concertedly that constituted the crime. The defense argued the application of such law reflected "the absurd and tyrannical policy of the British government, in relation to the poor and labouring classes of the community. It is a policy, incompatible with the existence of freedom, and prostrates every right, which distinguishes the citizen and the slave. It may subserve the interests of the capitalist and the employer, but grinds to the earth a numerous class of people, from whose toil their wealth is obtained."[40]

While conspiracy charges continued to plague unions through much of the 19th Century, unions of skilled workers continued to develop. Early unions were local and craft-based. Skilled workers worked in small shops and often did not come into contact with other trades. Specific trades or crafts developed close bonds of mutual loyalty and solidarity, however, that made owners accommodate and negotiate with their workers. As in British shops, there were handshake agreements abided to by both sides. Efforts were aimed at setting minimum wages for craft skills, establishing closed shops, excluding scabs, choosing walking delegates or tramping committees to enforce work rules and standards, establishing "traveling cards" so workers could have their journeyman's status recognized by similar organizations in other cities. The movement for the ten-hour day in Pennsylvania was spearheaded by the Mechanics Union of Trade Associations, whose organization in 1827 in Philadelphia is considered the beginning of the American labor movement. For the first time, a labor organization rose above the protection or advancement of a particular trade or craft and articulated the needs of workers as a class. The association demanded shorter working hours so that workers could have sufficient time for self-improvement and the cultivation of the mind through a labor press, libraries and forums. "The real object of this association is to avert, if possible, the desolating evils which must inevitably arise from a depreciation of the intrinsic value of human labor; to raise the mechanical and productive classes to that condition of true independence and equality which their practical skill and ingenuity, their immense utility to the nation and their growing intelligence are beginning imperiously to demand."[41]

Considered the first central labor council, this form of organization, designed to provide mutual assistance between organizations and promote public policy favorable to workers, was copied during the following decade in more than a dozen cities including Pittsburgh in 1836. In that year, 14 trade unions came together to form the Pittsburgh Trades Union sending a delegate to a Convention of Trades Unions in Philadelphia. "At a Fourth of July picnic held by the Pittsburgh Trades Unions in 1836, a speaker called attention to the growth of classes in the country, and to the accumulation of great wealth as the cause of this. Such growth, he said, corrupted legislatures, gave security to monopolists, and perverted the judiciary. The remedy he declared was the ballot box."[42] In a rapidly growing economy, the central labor council remained weak in Pittsburgh for most of the 19th Century because the relative scarcity of skilled labor meant that workers and craft organizations were able to leverage higher wages without a strong central organization. Moreover, later in the century, it would prove increasingly difficult to elaborate common political strategies between craft and industrial workers.

A Working Men's Party was founded in Pittsburgh in 1830; but, unlike Philadelphia's working-class organization of the same name, it was "the work of professional politicians whose only interest in the working man was to garner his vote." Made up of prominent businessmen and industrialists, its platform espoused protectionism and public works. Despite its title, at no time in its short existence did it attract workers. The concern for protection against foreign competition, especially British manufactured goods, was shared by workers and owners, and would be a major political issue for the rest of the century. People remembered that the town had flourished during the War of 1812, "for so long as foreign commerce was depressed, so long our manufacturers succeeded."[43]

Famous Visitors

Pittsburgh in the 1820s was economically threatened by the building of the National Road from Baltimore to Wheeling and the diversion of many immigrants' Conestoga wagons around the town. Plank roads were quickly built from Harrisburg to Pittsburgh to compete, but eventually the coming of the railroad reduced the National Road's importance. Many famous travelers made their way to the forks of the Ohio. President James Monroe visited the town in 1817, but a more feted guest was General La Fayette, hero of the American Revolution, who stopped in Braddock on his farewell "Guest of a Nation" tour on May 28, 1825.[44] In 1838, the old Indian fighter, William Henry Harrison, wrote a letter of thanks to Harmar Denny, former congressman from Pittsburgh, for his efforts in getting the National Democratic Anti-Masonic Convention to nominate Harrison as a candidate for president. A year later, the Whigs, meeting in Harrisburg, nominated the hero of Tippecanoe as their candidate.

> Huge processions paraded through cities and towns, containing wagons on which were log cabins and men drinking cider, and Indians in war paint and feathers. In Pittsburgh on February 11, 1840, an immense meeting was held in the old Court House in the Diamond, in advocacy of Harrison's election, at which Harmar Denny presided. Harrison was triumphantly elected, receiving the largest majority in the electoral college ever given to a candidate for president. His reception in Pittsburgh, while on his way to Washington to be inaugurated, was the greatest ovation given to any man...[45]

Unfortunately for the tough Indian fighter, the nemesis of Tecumseh, his presidency was the shortest in American history, as he died shortly after taking office.

In 1824, the great American naturalist and artist, James Audubon, came to town staying with his wife's family, the glass-making Bakewells. There, he painted his famous and poignant painting of a pair of the ill-fated passenger pigeons. "He depicted the birds billing – that is courting by sharing regurgitated food – a behavior borrowed from the method pigeons use to feed their young. The birds perched on separate branches, the female above and the pink and blue-gray male below, the male's head curved back sinuously to receive the female's offering." He collected the specimens he used as models on the Allegheny near where Rachel Carson would be born a century later. He had once witnessed a huge flock of the birds in 1813 that he estimated at over a billion birds in such numbers that they darkened the sky for many hours. Within a century, the bird had disappeared from the wild.[46]

In 1834, the Pennsylvania Canal system was completed at state expense using primarily Irish labor gangs. This short-lived but extraordinary system included railroad segments, canals, and ten inclined planes to get over the Alleghenies, ending with a wooden aqueduct that crossed the Allegheny

River to Pittsburgh from the north side of the river. The day the Pittsburgh terminal opened, November 10, 1829, was described as "a day of more enthusiastic feeling than Pittsburgh ever witnessed…. Five minutes before the appointed hour, the water touched the Pittsburgh shore. In half an hour the canal was filled to the tunnel, and three packet boats crossed in fine style, hailed by ten thousand spectators, and under a salute of 105 guns from the artillery." As if the system were not complicated enough, the city fathers decided to have the canal tunnel more than eight hundred feet through Grant's Hill, descending several locks to the banks of the Monongahela. When after fourteen years of use, the original wooden aqueduct began to leak and show serious structural weakness, John Roebling was hired to use his new wire cable to help support the heavy load. This was perhaps the first application of the wire cable suspension idea to an aqueduct. The deck of the aqueduct supported a wooden trough carrying a 15 foot wide stream of water 4 foot deep, plus boats and freight. It was constructed largely of oak and white pine. An idea of the grandeur of the local forest products then available can be had from the dimensions of the construction lumber: foundation timbers for lock construction were 34 feet long and 12 inches thick; traverse beams supporting the aqueduct were 27 feet long, 16 inches thick, and 6 inches wide. These monster beams were spaced in pairs every 4 feet across a total length of more than 1,100 feet![47]

The canal was severely impacted by the completion of the Pennsylvania Railroad's line from Pittsburgh to Philadelphia in 1852. It limped along until 1857, when its failure brought down the Bank of Pennsylvania that had financed the effort. Charles Dickens rode on the system in 1842 and remarked on the environmental devastation caused by the clearing of the great forests.

> The eye was pained to see the stumps of great trees thickly strewn in every field of wheat, and seldom to lose the eternal swamp and dull morass, with hundreds of rotten trunks and twisted branches steeped in its unwholesome water. It was quite sad and oppressive to come upon great tracks where settlers had been burning down the trees and where their wounded bodies lay about like those of murdered creatures, while here and there some charred and blackened giant reared aloft two withered arms, and seemed to call down curses on his foes…. On the Monday evening, furnace fires and clanking hammers on the banks of the canal warned us that we approached the termination of this part of the journey…Pittsburgh is like Birmingham in England; at least, its townspeople say so. Setting aside the streets, the shops, the houses, wagons, factories, public buildings, and population, perhaps it may be. It certainly has a great quantity of smoke hanging about it, and is famous for its ironworks.[48]

In January 1852, Pittsburgh was visited by the celebrated leader of the failed Hungarian Revolution of 1848-1849. He was warmly received by all classes as a champion of democracy. The workers of Pittsburgh responded generously, especially at one workplace, the Pittsburgh Alkali Works in Birmingham (South Side), where German workers gave him a full week's wages in solidarity with Hungary's struggle. The upper-class Reception Committee, headed by General William Larimer, bitterly disappointed the Hungarian patriot guest, however, when it presented him with an inflated bill for all the local festivities. Kossuth's secretary commented on the demand of payment for the committee's expenses, including extravagant meals for its local members. "Kossuth was asked to pay for all this, using the funds he had collected for the liberation of our oppressed and poor Hungary; with the money that came from workers who had deprived themselves of food to be able to help us!"[49]

Change as well as smoke was in the air. An all-iron steamboat, the "Valley Forge," was produced in 1839, and to the general public's astonishment it did not sink. In the 1820s, Bakewell's became one of the pioneers of glass pressing technology, leading to major production efficiencies and greatly expanded output of tableware. "The advantage of pressing was speed and standardization: exact copies of the same object could be turned out by a pressing crew at a faster rate and each piece would look markedly alike." Telegraphic communication was inaugurated in 1846, and the first message was to President Polk indicating the second Pennsylvania regiment was ready to leave for the Mexican War. The *Pittsburgh Post* first printed telegraphic dispatches under a column entitled: "Received by Lightning, Printed by Steam." The Pennsylvania Railroad was opened for Pittsburgh to Philadelphia traffic in 1852, cutting the time of travel between the two cities from three days to fifteen hours. This qualitative improvement positioned Pittsburgh for its great leap forward as an industrial center during and after the Civil War. Between 1820 and 1860, the city grew from 10,000 to 130,000 in population. Iron and metalworking led the list of industries, but by 1860 one hundred separate industries and four hundred manufacturing establishments were identified. [50]

Fire and Foreign War

Paradoxically, a devastating fire provided a timely opportunity to modernize and rebuild the city's infrastructure and building stock. The great Pittsburgh fire of 1845, like that of the more famous Chicago blaze, was credited to the carelessness of an unnamed and perhaps apocryphal washer woman doing laundry. The spring had been dry. The day was clear and the breeze was steady from the west. Reportedly the initial fire was allowed to burn while the town's new-fangled hand driven pump engine was summoned. But when the machine was attached to the fireplug, there was only a weak, sickly stream of muddy water since the city reservoir on Grant's Hill was depleted. The winds increased and the fire raged out of control for seven hours as the flames marched eastward along the Monongahela Wharf, consuming the heart of the business and warehouse district. A third of the city's buildings representing two-thirds of its financial value were destroyed. Nine hundred and eighty-two buildings were burned including the mayor's office; the Monongahela House and other hotels; the Baptist, Third Presbyterian and Bethel African Methodist churches; Western University; the Custom House; and the covered wooden Monongahela Bridge. Steamboats were moved downstream to save them, affording whatever passengers on board with a spectacular view of the conflagration. Amazingly, considering the extent of the blaze, only two fatalities were recorded. [51]

The wealthiest part of the town had been consumed. Thieveries were reported. More than 2,000 families were homeless. While damage was estimated to reach eight million dollars, relief came in from eighteen states, as did investment capital from the east. The city quickly responded "until every shoulder in the city was pushing the effort to rebuild and to reconstruct, and soon results began to manifest themselves in the reappearance of new structures in spots all over the burnt district. These were better and more serviceable buildings, and it was not long until many losers were persuaded that they were gainers by the fire. A spirit of greater confidence in themselves and in the future of their city was born of misfortune, and every new building, public and private, that was put up within a year, many of them in a very few months, was a distinct expression of confidence in the city and its prospects." A contemporary account asserted: "The absence of despair and sullenness and a disposition of the afflicted to aid one another extended to all classes." One of those who saw another sort of opportunity was Thomas Mellon who "took advantage of the rebuilding boom and put his money into offices and homes. In 1846 alone, he had constructed eighteen rental units." [52]

Controversy raged when initial plans showed that the proposed replacement for the wooden Smithfield Street Bridge was to be built low above the river in order to impede commerce from Brownsville, Elizabeth and other points upriver. Finally, John Roebling, an engineer from nearby Saxonburg, constructed a revolutionary structure, the world's first suspension bridge employing braided wire cables for support. Roebling had left Prussia for political reasons and first employed his wire rope on the aqueduct carrying the Pennsylvania Canal across the Allegheny. He would go on to build a spectacular suspension bridge above the gorge of the Niagara River and then design the Brooklyn Bridge, one of the greatest bridges of all time. He also built a lovely bridge over the Allegheny in 1859 that, like his Smithfield Bridge, was torn down to make a wider deck to accommodate increased traffic and streetcars. [53]

In 1845, the Mexican War divided Pittsburgh. The Democratic *Pittsburgh Post* supported the annexation of Texas and were jubilant as American armies invaded Mexico itself. *The Gazette* and the Whigs opposed the war because it would lead to the extension of slavery. However, once war was declared and the troops were marching, "men vied with each other in their cry of 'Our Country right or wrong' and rushed into the army over every barrier set up by their late arguments. The nation was seized by a military madness, and in the furor, the cause of the slave went to the wall...." A dozen special light boats were constructed in Pittsburgh for army service on the Rio Grande and special orders included 500 wagons and 100,000 horseshoes. "On the wharf could be seen at almost any time, wagons, boats and cannon and other equipment manufactured here and in neighboring cities, to be shipped to the armies." Three Pittsburgh companies, the Duquesne Greys, the Jackson Blues, and the Irish Greens, fought in the campaign, some all the way to Mexico City. "The ranks of the Pittsburgh companies were sadly depleted for many of the men had died at Vera Cruz, Jalapa, Perrote and Pueblo....When the news arrived in Pittsburgh that the soldiers were coming home, a meeting of the citizens was held to make arrangements for their reception....Both regiments were received at the wharf by immense crowds of citizens, with the ringing of bells, firing of cannon and every demonstration of enthusiastic patriotism and joy." [54]

Not everyone shared the enthusiasm for war. Jane Grey Swisshelm, one of the great journalists of Pittsburgh, wrote regularly for the abolitionist paper, *The Spirit of Liberty,* about the imperialist ambitions behind the war which she saw as a means to extend slavery. "This great nation was engaged in the pusillanimous work of beating poor little Mexico – a giant whipping a cripple. Every man who went to the war, or induced others to go, I held as a principal in the whole list of crimes of which slavery was the synonym." Pittsburgh would hear a good deal more from Jane Grey Swisshelm. [55]

Cotton Mill Girls Revolt

Textile manufacturing found a place in Pittsburgh because there were mechanics and machinists who could construct the steam-powered looms, but also because shippers needed cargo to haul back to Pittsburgh on their return upriver. Boats heavily laden with manufactured goods including iron, hardware, whiskey, porter, glassware, coal and salt needed paying up-river freight to defray the cost of the round trip. Primary return bulk commodities were cotton and tobacco, and consumer goods like sugar, coffee, and pork from the southern river ports that were bulky, but light for the return upstream. These imports fostered the "stogie" and the textile industry in Pittsburgh, both targeting working class consumers. Pittsburgh's first cotton factory was founded in 1803, and, by 1847, there were seven factories in Allegheny City employing more than 1,500 workers, mostly young women and girls. These mills were geared primarily to the regional market and relied on access to cheap raw cotton from downriver. Technologically, the mills lagged behind the New England mills and declined rapidly during the Civil War as the cotton supply contracted. However, labor troubles were also blamed for the loss of this industry.[56]

Cotton mills in Pennsylvania and Massachusetts were prime employers of female and child labor. Machines set the pace, and workers were reduced to "hands" feeding relentless and unforgiving machines. Unlike most male labor organized around craft traditions, the cotton factories were highly capitalized, relatively low skill workplaces that demanded high utilization (long hours of work) and repetitive dexterity for which women were considered particularly endowed. Factory work marked a complete break with the agricultural rhythms and seasonal fluctuations of farm work, as well as the traditions and codes of established crafts. Because mass production techniques were pioneered in textile manufacturing, it was women workers who launched the first industrial strikes in Pittsburgh.

Labor turmoil in the cotton mills began in 1843 around agitation for the ten-hour day and was triggered by a reduction in wages. The female marchers of 1843 shocked believers in female decorum by parading through the streets with a banner inscribed with the Whig campaign slogan of 1840: "Two dollars a day and Roast Beef."[57] Agitation reached its peak in 1845 as 1,500 women textile workers struck for the ten-hour day. They were working 72 hours/week at $2.50/week. They were described as the "prettiest girls and bone and sinew of Allegheny City and Pittsburgh." The strike was marked by the forceful entry into several establishments by the strikers and their supporters with the ejection of scabs. Despite or because of the militancy, public opinion was against the women, the strike was lost. A reporter from the Pittsburgh *Journal* gave an eyewitness report:

> They were now in full force. A whole legion of men and boys accompanied them as auxiliaries, to be used in case they were required. Thus prepared, flushed with conquest...they marched to the scene of the great struggle - the Battle of Blackstock's Factory. On their arrival, they saluted the enemy with three shouts of defiance and a universal flourish of sticks and bonnets. After a minute or two spent in reconnoiter, they moved forward in a solid column of attack, on the ...pine gate of the yard. In a moment the gate was forced open. But the defenders were determined on a heroic defense, and the assailants were thrown back and the gate again closed. Both parties now took time for breath, and opened negotiations. The factory girls demanded the instant expulsion of the girls at work. The people inside obstinately refused the terms, and both parties again prepared to decide the matter by the uncertain chances of the field.... The garrison made a stubborn resistance - but what could you expect from pine boards? The gate gave way - "hurra! hurra!" - and in a moment the yard was filled, the fortress was taken by storm, and the garrison were prisoners of war.
>
> We are informed that the manufacturers have expressed a great deal of dissatisfaction with reference to the conduct of the Police on Monday during the disturbances. It seems to us that this is unjust. It was utterly impossible for any ordinary police force to have maintained order. There were hundreds of the male friends of the operatives standing round - ready to interfere whenever it should become necessary.... "Let 'em hit one of those gals if they dare, and we'll fetch them out of their boots!" said a grim double-fisted fellow on our right, while they were breaking open Blackstock's.[58]

This and other agitation led to a ten-hour law being passed in Pennsylvania in 1847. Manufacturers insisted they could not compete with the mills of New England where workers worked 12-14 hours a day. The law stated: "That the labor performed during a period of (10) hours, on any secular day in all cotton, woolen, silk paper, bagging and flax factories shall be considered a legal days labor, and hereafter no minor or adult engaged in any such factories, shall be holden or required to work more than 10 hours on any secular day or 60 hours in any secular week; and that after the 4th of July, of present year, no minor shall be admitted as a worker under the age of twelve years in any cotton, woolen, silk or flax factory." However, the statute contained a loophole that allowed workers, or a minor's parent or guardian, to sign an individual contract waiving the worker's right to the ten-hour protection. In July 1848, the owners locked workers out of the mills and the signing of such a personal contract became a de facto condition of employment. Wages remained an issue. The male labor rate for much of the 19th Century was $1.00 a day. The bulk of women in the cotton mills made $2.50 a week. For an entire month the mills lay idle and workers were without pay. When the textile mill owners attempted to reopen the Penn factory with a reduced force on July 31, a riot ensued.[59]

Those operatives entering the factory at 5 a.m. had to run a gauntlet of hisses and calls of "white slaves" from a couple of hundred strikers and sympathizers. All morning the crowd and the tension built. Stones were thrown at the building, and spindles were thrown back. By mid-morning, the crowd was estimated at 1,500. A small boy slipped through a hole in the fence, tried to open the gate and was seized by the manager and taken to his office, setting off rumors through the crowd that he was being abused. In an attempt to back off the menacing crowd, the manager had his engineer open a steam valve onto the yard, burning some strikers, including a young girl. The women, led by "a young Kentucky girl of unusual beauty who won notoriety as "The Unknown," took action.[60]

> The fury of the rioters then broke loose, and an attack was made on the fence, both in the rear of the building on Isabella Street and on the river front. The fence soon gave way, when the crowd rushed into the yard and commenced an attack upon the doors with axes and poles. One of the doors soon yielded to the blows of the infuriated Amazons, and the rioters carried the factory by storm. All the other doors were immediately thrown open, and the building was soon filled with the rioters…Through the exertions of some men who had influence with the attacking party, a line was formed, and the hands who had been at work were permitted to pass out amidst the shouts, and jeers, and scoffs of the rioters.[61]

A week later, the owners attempted to run the machinery with management, but only lasted five hours prompting the worker-friendly *Pittsburgh Post* to derisively term it the "five-hour system." The management steadfastly refused to negotiate with the workers' representatives who apparently were male and not cotton mill employees. However, "a beautiful, dark-eyed, pale, well-built Kentucky girl with long flowing tresses, identified only as 'the unknown' was one of the most ardent defenders of the ten-hour system. This young lady attended all the meetings of the operatives and was said to have a strange control over the girls, directing their movements, yet not indulging in any illegal acts herself." At the end of August, one of the mills agreed to the ten-hour day with a reduction in pay, and gradually the girls returned when a compromise was reached whereby the ten-hour day was established, but wages were reduced ten to sixteen percent. This was at least a partial victory for the women who failed, however, to establish the right to representation. [62]

The trial turned into a major legal battle with the majority of mill owners supporting a vigorous prosecution team including Edwin Stanton, who would become Lincoln's Secretary of War, and

Thomas Bingham, an abolitionist congressman who became a founder of the Republican Party. Thirteen of the rioters were tried, among them five pretty young women, the remainder male supporters of the women who had been involved in the violence. The defense failed to raise any substantive issues about worker's rights to organize, or how many hours young women or anybody should be forced to work each day. Judge Patton's charge to the jury left little room to find the defendants innocent and was such a concise exposition of the prosecution's argument that the manufacturers printed the Judge's charge as an introduction to a pamphlet on the riots. All thirteen of the defendants were convicted, but it is uncertain whether any but one served time. In a precedent that would cost it dearly after the 1877 railroad riot, Allegheny County was held to be responsible for damages done by the mob. [63]

The Cotton Mill Riots highlighted the role of female labor militancy. Women achieved by their actions a sort of equality with men. Indeed, the presiding judge strongly affirmed the prosecution's argument: "That females should be peaceful and law-abiding, and when they engage in mob violence against their own sex, they lose all title to consideration or pity." He elaborated: "They enjoy our respect as long as their conduct is consistent with the delicacy and modesty of the female character. But when...they play the part of ringleaders of a destructive mob and are guilty of acts that would disgrace the greatest ruffians of the opposite sex – they forfeit all claim to any peculiar degree of respect."[64] As the male-dominated steel industry became the prime terrain for labor conflict, women's roles changed. Women play an important role in virtually every prolonged labor conflict because without family backing a strike cannot be sustained. In a surprising number of instances, however, women in the Pittsburgh region played a leadership or highly active and public role in labor disputes.

Another example of female militancy came a little more than a year later during the Rolling Mill Riots of 1850. The local iron industry was in a crisis as Congress in 1846 reduced tariffs from a range of 49% to 109% to an across-the-board rate of 30% on iron imported primarily from England. Lower tariffs, higher American wages and overproduction in England combined to send a flood of cheap English iron into the market. The owners announced that they were reducing the rates paid to puddlers and boilers on a ton of iron by 25%. A strike of up to 1,500 ironworkers began on January 1, idling a dozen establishments. Workers were deeply caught up with the idea that they should form an association to start and run their own mill and thereby be masters of their own destiny. They were in touch with workers in Cincinnati and Sharon, Pennsylvania where similar efforts were underway. In February the owners began to aggressively recruit puddlers from Philadelphia where wage rates were substantially lower. When confronted by striking Pittsburghers, more than three-fourths of the replacements returned home. The ironworkers organized several peaceful marches through downtown with music and banners to appeal to public sympathy. [65]

As more replacements trickled in, tensions increased. On March 1, a group of nearly one hundred women gathered at one of the mills that had restarted and invaded the mill, driving off the scabs using sticks, stones and lumps of coal as weapons. They went on to a second mill where they were met by the populist and nativist Mayor Joe Barker, who got them to disperse. On March 2, a much larger crowd of women, children and men marched on a third mill and after a more violent struggle than the previous day, broke into it, chasing the replacements out and beating some. The strike sputtered out and two men received eighteen months sentences and five women thirty days in jail. Some of the union men went to Sharon to work in a worker cooperative that managed to survive five years. The dream of overcoming the labor vs. capital divide would endure however.

Anti-Immigrant and Anti-Slavery

The revolutions of 1848 in Europe had a widespread impact over Europe as democratic nationalist revolutions failed in France, Germany, Austria, and Italy. The Irish had been emigrating steadily from the 1820s, but the terrible potato famine of the mid-1840s in Ireland sent a massive wave of humanity toward America. By 1860, fifty percent of Pittsburghers were immigrants. Many of the new Irish, German and Italian immigrants who arrived in the 1840s and 50s were Catholics. While the first recorded European religious service at the Forks was a Catholic mass at Fort Duquesne in 1754, Pittsburgh was dominated by Protestants, especially Presbyterians, Episcopalians, Methodists and Lutherans. The first Catholic Church, St. Patrick's, had been established in 1811 outside the downtown district in what is today the Strip. In 1843, Michael O'Connor, a native of Cork who had received his doctorate in Theology in Rome, was assigned to create the new diocese of Pittsburgh. He established a diocese with 16 priests and 33 churches to serve an estimated 45,000 Catholics. He vigorously supported the institution of Catholic schools, initially run by the Sisters of Charity; strongly backed the temperance movement, founded a seminary and built orphanages; and with a group of zealous laymen founded a diocesan newspaper, the *Pittsburgh Catholic.* Responding to the growth and the poverty of the immigrant population, the first hospital in Pittsburgh was established by Mother Francis Xavier Warde. She was the leader of a group of six nuns dispatched to Pittsburgh by the Sisters of Mercy, a charitable order founded in Ireland in 1831. On January 1, 1847, Mercy Hospital opened its doors in a temporary location and moved to its present site the following year. The first Protestant hospital, eventually known as Passavant, was opened in 1849; Western Pennsylvania Hospital began operation in 1853. Growing Catholic power was expressed by the towers of St. Paul's Cathedral (begun in 1853) on Grant Street and St. Philomena's imposing spire in the Strip District (1846).[66]

The swelling immigrant population provoked an anti-Catholic political reaction in Pittsburgh, though it did not reach the level of violence that occurred at this time in Philadelphia. The decline of the Whigs and the increasing identification of the Democrats with slavery led to a political vacuum that was filled by a "Know-nothing" candidate. Joseph Barker was a well-known character in Pittsburgh. His preaching against Catholicism led first to his arrest and then his election from jail to the honorable office of Mayor of Pittsburgh. A man of native ability, but "very ignorant and bigoted – he himself stated that he had never been to school in his life – he conceived a violent prejudice against his fellow citizens of the Catholic faith, and spent much of his time on Market Street and Penn Avenue inveighing in loud, offensive, and often obscene language against the priests and members of that religion. He even assailed clergymen of other denominations because they would not join with him in his crusade. This conduct was tolerated for many months. At length the authorities interfered and Barker was arrested and indicted."[67]

At his trial, presided over by the same Judge Patton who had sentenced the cotton mill rioters, the judge asserted forcibly that jailing Barker was in no way an act of religious persecution.

> Whatever you may say or think of that large portion of your fellow-citizens whom you have made the principal, but not the exclusive object of your indecent assaults, the forbearance and patience they have shown during that long reign of outrage, injustice and oppression, reflect great credit on them and the creed they profess. They had a right to expect relief from the public authorities long before it came. But they are not the only parties affected by the result of this prosecution; the peace and welfare of all

parties, all men concerned for peace, the morals and reputation of our city began to raise their hands in astonishment that such things had been so long tolerated in a Christian Community.[68]

Barker had his supporters among the masses, however, and the decline of the two traditional parties allowed him to be elected mayor from jail without being the nominee of any party. Pennsylvania Governor Johnston pardoned him, and Judge Patton was summoned by city council to swear in the new mayor. While Barker only lasted a year in office, he managed to act upon his prejudices by issuing an order for the arrest of the Catholic Bishop O'Connor on the charge of maintaining a nuisance because of the linkage of a sewer from Mercy Hospital to a city sewer.[69]

While women were gaining visibility in labor struggles, an extraordinary Pittsburgh woman, Jane Grey Swisshelm, was pioneering in journalism, leading the struggle of women for equal rights under the law, and becoming a major figure in the national movement to abolish slavery. Born in 1815 in a log cabin in the heart of Pittsburgh across from the Trinity burial ground, she moved at an early age with her family to Wilkinsburg. At the age of 12, while returning from school in Braddock's Field, her wagon was caught in a flood, and she was rescued by a 16 year-old boy whom she later married in 1836. It was a rocky marriage almost from the start as religious differences, a domineering mother-in-law, and Jane's own superior intelligence and energy engendered constant conflict.[70] In 1838, the couple moved to Louisville, Kentucky, and it took precious little time for her to not like what she saw.

> I wondered what had happened that so many men were off work in the middle of the forenoon. Who or what they could be, these fellows in shining black broadcloth, each with a stovepipe hat on the side of his head, his thumbs in the armholes of a satin vest, displaying a wonderful glimmer of gold chain and diamond stud, balancing himself first on his heels and then on his toes, as he rolled a cigar from one side to the other? How did they come to be standing around on corners and doorsteps by the hundred, like crows on a cornfield fence?….It was some time before I learned that this was the advance guard of a great army of women-whippers, which stretched away back to the Atlantic, and then around the shores of the Gulf of Mexico, and that they were out on duty as a staring brigade, whose business it was to insult every woman who ventured on the street without a male protector, by a stare so lascivious as could not be imagined on American free soil. I learned that they all lived, in whole or in part, by the sale of their own children, and the labor of their mothers extorted by the lash. I came to know one hoary-haired veteran, whose entire support came from the natural increase and wages of nineteen women, one of whom, a girl of eighteen, lived with him in a fashionable boarding house, waited on him at table, slept in his room, and of whose yearly wages one hundred and seventy-five dollars were credited on his board bill.[71]

After being threatened for trying to start a school for Negro children, Jane returned to Pittsburgh over her husband's objection - to be with her dying mother. When James refused to sign the papers so that she could receive her mother's money, she was furious and launched a campaign to win the right for women to keep their own property. Her efforts were crowned with success initially when a progressive Pennsylvania Married Woman's Property Law of 1848 was passed by the legislature. "It continued in the married woman the property owned by them at marriage or afterward acquired, as fully as if they were unmarried." However, in a series of opinions from 1853 to 1858, conservative Pennsylvania

Supreme Court Judge George Woodward struck down most aspects of the law. He wrote: "In just so far as you sever the material interests of husband and wife, you destroy the sympathies which constitute the oneness of the relation, and degrade the divine institution into mere concubinage....The flames which litigation would kindle on the domestic hearth would consume in an instant the conjugal bond, and bring on a new era indeed – an era of universal discord, of unchastity, of bastardy, of dissoluteness, of violence, cruelty and murders."[72]

Swisshelm began her journalistic career writing regular letters to *The Pittsburgh Commercial Gazette*, where the editor praised the woman who "dips her pen in liquid Gold." After the failure of *The Spirit of Liberty*, she launched her own paper, *The Saturday Visitor*, which reached thousands of readers in every state and territory, as well as Canada and England. With the motto *Speak unto the people of Israel that they go forward*, the appearance of an anti-slavery political paper run by a woman wielding a sharp pen caused consternation among the universally male editors who accused her of wanting to steal their pantaloons! The outrage was of course most keenly expressed by the pro-slavery press. Swisshelm characterized reaction to her paper: "...no sooner did the American eagle catch site of it, than he swooned and fell off his perch. Democratic roosters straightened out their necks and ran screaming with terror. Whig coons scampered up trees and barked furiously. The world was falling....A woman had started a political paper." When a paper ran an attack headlined: "She's a man all but the pantaloons," Swisshelm replied with a rhyme.

> Perhaps you have been busy, horsewhipping Sal or Lizzie,
> Stealing some poor man's baby, selling his mother, may-be.
> You say – and you are witty – That I – and 'tis a pity –
> Of manhood lack but the dress; but you lack manliness,
> A body clean and new, a soul within it too.
> Nature must change her plan ere you can be a man.[73]

While labor's struggle and women's rights were issues that were coming to the fore in the 1840s, the deepening conflict over slavery and its extension would prove to be the issue that would dominate the politics of the next decade as the nation slid toward civil war. Pittsburgh was already a hotbed of abolitionist sentiment, but its geographic position and its industrial power made it the crucible of union feeling and resolve. By 1850, Pittsburgh had grown in fifty years from a small outpost into an important commercial and manufacturing center of 46,000 and had already established itself as the Iron City. Over 5,500 workers in its foundries and mills transformed 60,000 tons of pig iron into cast and wrought iron products of all descriptions from steam engines to tacks. Its cotton mills employed over 1,500 and its glass factories over 600 workers. Thousands of specialized craftsmen made a wide range of useful products as well as providing the repairs and services needed to make and move things. Pittsburgh's trade area was expanding with steady improvements in transportation. Steamboats, canals, railroads, better roads, and the telegraph made Pittsburgh the hub of an expanding commercial wheel.[74] The busy city at the Forks of the Ohio was prepared to play a significant role in the great struggle over slave labor that was looming on the nation's horizon.

Notes Chapter 4

[1] Joseph Doddridge, *Notes on the Settlement and Indian Wars,* ed. Special Collectors (Parsons: McClain Printing Company, 1912), 21.

[2] Catherine Elizabeth Reiser, *Pittsburgh's Commercial Development 1800-1850,* (Harrisburg: Pennsylvania Historical and Museum Commission, 1951), 1-2; Len Barcousky, "Pittsburgh Almanack Mixes Practical, Poetic," *Pittsburgh Post-Gazette,* February 10, 2008.

[3] Zadok Cramer, *The Navigator 1811: The Ohio River Collection,* ed. Benjamin F. Klein (Cincinnati: Young and Klein, Inc., 1979), VII. Cramer does not provide the source for his quote about the Ohio. The description of the sycamores is on p. 30.

[4] Solon J. Buck and Elizabeth Hawthorn Buck, *The Planting of Civilization in Western Pennsylvania* (Pittsburgh: University of Pittsburgh Press, 1979), 11.

[5] Cramer, *The Navigator 1811,* 16.

[6] Wyland F. Dunaway, *A History of Pennsylvania* (New York: Prentice-Hall, 1950) 2:185-6.

[7] Paul A. Wallace, *Conrad Weiser: Friend of Colonist and Mohawk* (Lewisburg: Wennawood Publishing, 1996). Deposition of Peter Tostee, James Dinnen and George Croghan, May 14, 1745, document in possession of the American Philosophical Society, Philadelphia, PA. This deposition is quoted in *Conrad Weiser: Friend of Colonist and Mohawk,* Paul A. Wallace, but without the section mentioning the seizure of Tostee's Negro.

[8] Clarke M. Thomas, *Front Page Pittsburgh: Two Hundred Years of the Post Gazette* (Pittsburgh: University of Pittsburgh Press, 2005), 3-7; Robert I. Vexler, *Pittsburgh: A Chronological & Documentary History, 1682-1976* (New York: Oceana Publications, 1977); Mel Seidenberg, Lois Mulkearn and James W. Hess, "Two Hundred Years of Pittsburgh History: A Chronology of Events Complied," *Pittsburgh, the Story of an American City* (Garden City: Doubleday & Company, Inc., 1964); Stefan Lorant, *Pittsburgh: The Story of an American City* (Garden City: Doubleday & Company, Inc., 1964). Lorant's book is an indispensable reference and the only single volume account of the city's history. His profusely illustrated, Euro-centric and upper-class interpretation provides a model that requires no duplication.

[9] Judge Hugh Henry Brackenridge, "The Trial of Mamachtaga, a Delaware Indian, the First Person Convicted of Murder West of the Allegheny Mountains, and Was Hanged for His Crime," *Western Pennsylvania Historical Magazine* (January 1918); Hugh Henry Brackenridge, *Famous Men & Women of Pittsburgh* (Pittsburgh: Pittsburgh History & Landmarks Foundation, 1981); Hugh Henry Brackenridge, "Thoughts on the Enfranchisement of the Negroes," *A Hugh Henry Brackenridge Reader, 1770-1815,* ed. Daniel Marder (Pittsburgh: University of Pittsburgh Press, 1970). Judgment rendered in "Thompson v. Johnston" quoted in Charles C. Ahrensberg Brackenridge 1970, p. 103-4.

[10] Francis R. Harbison, *Flood Tides Along the Allegheny* (Pittsburgh: Francis R. Harbison, 1941), 52-3.

[11] Jerry A. Clouse, *The Whiskey Rebellion: Southwestern Pennsylvania's Frontier People Test the American Constitution* (Harrisburg: Pennsylvania Historical and Museum Commission, 2000), 9-12.

[12] Thomas, *Front Page Pittsburgh,* 23; "Tom the Tinker," probably John Holcroft, a leading rebel, printed broadside sheets and placed a threatening ad in the Pittsburgh Gazette: "This is fair warning, traitors take care for my hammer is up and my ladel [sic] is hot…"

[13] Leland D. Baldwin, *Whiskey Rebels: The Story of a Frontier Uprising* (Pittsburgh: University of Pittsburgh Press, 1976), 86.

[14] Brackenridge, *A Hugh Henry Brackenridge Reader,* 277-8.

[15] Brackenridge, *A Hugh Henry Brackenridge Reader,* 282, 287.

[16] Brackenridge, *A Hugh Henry Brackenridge Reader,* 306, 340.

[17] Brackenridge, *A Hugh Henry Brackenridge Reader,* 345.

[18] Thomas P. Slaughter, *The Whiskey Rebellion: Frontier Epilogue to the American Revolution* (New York: Oxford University Press, 1986), 222-8.

[19] Benjamin Rush, "A Letter from a Citizen of Pennsylvania," in *Pen Pictures of Early Western Pennsylvania,* ed. John W. Harpster Pittsburgh: University of Pittsburgh Press, 1938), 200.

[20] Joseph F. Rishel, *Founding Families of Pittsburgh: The Evolution of a Regional Elite, 1760-1910* (Pittsburgh: University of Pittsburgh Press, 1990), 43. An interesting fact mentioned by Rishel for residents of Mt. Washington like the author, is that Samuel Dilworth, a family founder, made considerable money selling off extensive holdings south of the city to the Boggs family between 1796 and 1799.

[21] W. Espy Albig, "Early Development of Transportation on the Monongahela River," *Western Pennsylvania Historical Magazine* (April 1919).

[22] Leland D. Baldwin, *The Keelboat Age on Western Waters,* (Pittsburgh: University of Pittsburgh Press, 1980), 39-55; Reiser, *Pittsburgh's Commercial Development 1800-1850,* 32-3.

[23] Gary E. Moulton, *Journals of the Lewis and Clark Expedition* (Lincoln: University of Nebraska Press, 1987), II: 65; Donald Jackson, *Letters of the Lewis and Clark Expedition* (Champaign: University of Illinois Press, 1979), I: 112.

[24] E. John Long, "Johnny Appleseed in Pittsburgh," *The Western Pennsylvania Historical Magazine,* 1930, 13: 256-260.

[25]Robert Price, *Johnny Appleseed: Man and Myth* (Bloomington: Indiana University Press, 1954); Carolee K. Michener, *Franklin: A Place in History* (Franklin: Franklin Bicentennial Committee, 1995), 20-21; Michael Pollan, *The Botany of Desire* (New York: Random House, 2001), 3-50.

[26]Pollan, *The Botany of Desire,* 29-30, 36-39; Emanuel Swedenborg, *Heaven and Its Wonders and Hell: Things I Heard and Seen* (London: Swedenborg Society, 1966), 185. This work was originally printed in London in 1758. Johnny Appleseed was said to tear a page from Swedenborg's writings and leave it with frontier farmers after planting his apple seeds. There is a lovely Swedenborgian church still operating in Pittsburgh in Point Breeze.

[27]Pollan, *The Botany of Desire,* 42.

[28]Baldwin, *The Keelboat Age on Western Waters*, 112-114.

[29]Reiser, *Pittsburgh's Commercial Development: 1800-1850,* 29-36.

[30]James Penick, Jr., "...I will stamp on the ground with my foot and shake down every house...", *American Heritage*, v. XXVII (December, 1975), 82-87.

[31]In the mid-1970s, the author was interviewed for a machinist job at Mackintosh-Hemphill's plant near the 10th Street bridge in Pittsburgh's South Side. The manager bragged about providing cannon balls for the War of 1812.

[32]Arthur B. Fox, *Pittsburgh: During the American Civil War, 1860-1865* (Chicora: Mechling Bookbindery, 2002), 99.

[33]Max Rosenberg, *The Building of Perry's Fleet on Lake Erie, 1812-1813* (Harrisburg: Pennsylvania Historical and Museum Commission, 1974), 33.; Alfred A. Mass, "Brownsville's Steamboat Enterprise and Pittsburgh's Supply of General Jackson's Army," *Pittsburgh History* (Spring 1994), 22-8.

[34]Fredrick Moore Binder, *Coal Age Empire: Pennsylvania Coal and its Utilization to 1860,* (Harrisburg: Pennsylvania Historical and Museum Commission, 1974), 42, 76.

[35]Samuel Jones, *Pittsburgh: In the Year 1826* (New York: Arno Press, 1970), 31-2.

[36]Walter Walters, Jr., *Albert Gallatin: Jeffersonian, Financier and Diplomat* (Pittsburgh: University of Pittsburgh Press, 1969), 136-9.; Leland D. Baldwin, *Pittsburgh: The Story of a City, 1750-1865* (Pittsburgh: University of Pittsburgh Press, 1970), 146-9.; Anne Madarasz, *Shattering Notions* (Pittsburgh: Historical Society of Western Pennsylvania, 1988), 3-5, 20.

[37]Walters, *Albert Gallatin*; Baldwin, *Pittsburgh: The Story of a City*; Madarasz, *Shattering Notions*, 114.

[38]Laurence A. Glasco, ed., *The WPA History of the Negro in Pittsburgh* (Pittsburgh: University of Pittsburgh Press, 2004), 70.

[39]Glasco, *The WPA History of the Negro in Pittsburgh*, 70; John R. Commons and others, eds., A *Documentary History of American Industrial Society* (New York: Russell & Russell, 1958), 18-19.

[40]Commons, *A Documentary History of American Industrial Society*, 62.

[41]Philip Taft, *Organized Labor in American History* (New York: Harper & Row, 1964), 15; In 2004, a Pennsylvania State Historical Marker proposed by the author was dedicated to mark the creation of the Mechanics Union of Trade Associations in Philadelphia.

[42]Glasco, *The WPA History of the Negro in Pittsburgh*, 79.

[43]William A. Sullivan, "The Pittsburgh Working Men's Party," *The Western Pennsylvania Historical Magazine* (September 1951), 151-61; Jones, Pittsburgh, 49.

[44]*The Unwritten History of Braddock's Field* (Pennsylvania) (Bowie: Heritage Books, Inc., 1999), 316.

[45]"Letters from William Henry Harrison" (unsigned), *Western Pennsylvania Historical Magazine* (1918), I:145.

[46]Richard Rhodes, "John James Audubon: America's Rare Bird," *Smithsonian* (December 2004), 230; Clive Pointing, *A Green History of the World,* (New York: Penguin Books, 1992) 168-170; Audubon's painting of the Passenger Pigeon in Pittsburgh in 1824 was confirmed to me by Charlotte Tancin and Angela Todd of the Hunt Institute for Botanical Documentation at Carnegie Mellon University and Charles E. Aston of the University of Pittsburgh in response to a query; see Richard Rhodes, *John James Audubon: The Making of an American,* (New York: Alfred Knopf, 2004) and Susanne M. Low, *A Guide to Audubon's Birds of America....,* (New Haven: William Reese Company & Donald Heald, 2002).

[47]William H. Shank, *The Amazing Pennsylvania Canals,* (170th Anniversary Edition) (York: American Canal and Transportation Center, 2001).; Robert D. Ilisevich and Carl Burkett, Jr., "The Canal Through Pittsburgh: Its Development and Physical Character," *Western Pennsylvania Historical Magazine* (1985), 351-371.

[48]Charles Dickens, *American Notes: A Journey* (New York: International Publishing Corporation, 1985), 152-4.

[49] Steven B. Vardy, "Louis Kossuth: A Celebrated, Disillusioned Hungarian Revolutionary's Visit to Pittsburgh in 1852," *Western Pennsylvania History,* Spring 2008, 20-28.

[50]Madarasz, *Shattering Notions,* 43; Mel Seidenberg, Lois Mulkearn and James W. Hess, "Two Hundred Years of Pittsburgh's History," in Stefan Lorant, *Pittsburgh: The Story of an American City,* (Lenox Massachusetts: Authors Edition, Inc. 1980), 601-602.

[51]Baldwin, *Pittsburgh,* 228-9.

[52]Frank C. Harper, *Pittsburgh of Today: Its Resources and People.* (New York: The American Historical Society, 1931), 1: 232-3; Burton Hersh, *The Mellon Family: A Fortune in History* (New York: William Morrow and Company, 1978), 40.

[53]*Brownsville Herald*, May 24, 1845, June 10, 1845; Walter C. Kidney, *Pittsburgh's Bridges: Architecture and Engineering* (Pittsburgh: Pittsburgh History and Landmarks Foundation, 1999), 54, 113, 144.

[54]Thomas, *Front Page Pittsburgh*, 63-5; Jane Grey Swisshelm, *Half a Century*, (Chicago: Jansen, McClurg & Company, 1880), 91; Morton E. Stearns, "Pittsburgh in the Mexican War," *Historical Society of Western Pennsylvania* (October 1924), 341.

[55]Jane Grey Swisshelm, *Half a Century*, 93.

[56]Reiser, *Pittsburgh's Commercial Development, 1800-1850*, 47; Monte A. Calvert, "The Allegheny City Cotton Mill Riot of 1848," *The Western Pennsylvania Historical Magazine*, (April 1963), 97-8.

[57]Calvert, "The Allegheny City Cotton Mill Riot of 1848," 97-8; Baldwin, *Pittsburgh*, 226. None of the Pittsburgh sources in my possession deal with the 1845 altercation for which Foner provides so eloquent a description below, based on three citations from two sources: *Young America* (October 18 and Nov. 15, 1845) with Blackstock's Battle description from The Pittsburgh Journal, and the *New York Tribune*.

[58]Philip S. Foner, *History of the Labor Movement in the United States* (New York: International Publishers, 1962), 1: 208.

[59]Calvert, "The Allegheny City Cotton Mill Riot of 1848"; "An Act to limit the hours of labor, and to prevent the employment, in factories, of children under twelve years of age," *Laws of the General Assembly of the Commonwealth of Pennsylvania Passed at the Session of 1848*, (Harrisburg, Pa: J.M.G. Lescure, 1848), 278-279; Thomas, *Front-Page Pittsburgh*, 69-72.

[60]Baldwin, *Pittsburgh*, 266-7.

[61]*Pittsburgh Daily Gazette*, August 1, 1848.

[62]Calvert, "The Allegheny City Cotton Mill Riot of 1848," 114.

[63]Calvert, "The Allegheny City Cotton Mill Riot of 1848," 128-32

[64]*The Factory Riots in Allegheny City: Judge Patton's* Charge (Pamphlet printed by six of seven Allegheny City cotton manufacturers, HSWP archives, 1849), 13-14.

[65]James Linaberger, "The Rolling Mill Riots of 1850," *The Western Pennsylvania Historical Magazine* (January 1964), 1-10.

[66]Paul E. Campbell, "The First Bishop of Pittsburgh," *Catholic Pittsburgh's One Hundred Years*, (Chicago: Loyola University Press, 1943), 25-37.; Walter C. Kidney, *Landmark Architecture of Allegheny County* (Pittsburgh: Pittsburgh History and Landmark Foundation, 1999).

[67]Harper, *Pittsburgh of Today*, 235.

[68]Harper, *Pittsburgh of Today*, 235.

[69]Harper, *Pittsburgh of Today*, 236.

[70]Sylvia D. Hoffert, *Jane Grey Swisshelm: An Unconventional Life, 1815-1884*, (Chapel Hill: The University of North Carolina Press, 2004), 33-59.

[71]Swisshelm, *Half a Century*, 52-3.

[72]Charles W. Dahlinger, "The Dawn of the Women's Movement," *The Western Pennsylvania Historical Magazine* (1918), 82; Hoffert, *Jane Grey Swisshelm*, 61-77.

[73]Glasco, *The WPA History of the Negro in Pittsburgh*, 159-162. I am grateful for Larry Glasco's suggestion to include Swisshelm's caustic poem.

[74]Reiser, *Pittsburgh's Commercial Development 1800-1850*, 191-3.

Chapter Five

Civil War and Industrial Might

1851-1875

Pittsburgh and its region in the second half of the 19ᵗʰ Century became a muscular center of innovation and spawned important technical advances leading to the creation of modern industry, advances that catapulted the United States onto the world stage as a major power. The city's strategic position, expanding rail network, supply of skilled workers, and deepening reservoir of raw labor power, positioned it for dramatic growth at the very moment when an epic civil conflict challenged its capacity to mass produce the implements of modern war, the artillery and shells, as well as the extensive industrial infrastructure including railroads and bridges that were transforming the nature of military supply and logistics. The city's rapidly growing power and accumulated wealth failed to solve and, in fact, exacerbated the deepening class divide that had been dramatically revealed in the labor riots of the 1840s. In the following decade, however, the impending crisis over the institution and extension of slavery overshadowed other issues. In Pittsburgh, animosity toward slavery in general and the fugitive slave law in particular was shared by many whites, but the core of organized resistance to the institution arose out of the free black community.

Anti-Slavery Organization

Pittsburgh had a small but significant population of blacks who were becoming increasingly well organized and militant in their opposition to slavery. Negro road builders had accompanied both the Braddock and Forbes expeditions. From 159 slaves and 12 free blacks in 1790, the Negro population grew to 3,431 by 1850 clustered in two separate enclaves: Haiti or Hayti in the lower Hill and Arthurville in the upper Hill. These native-born Pittsburgh blacks ranked fourth in numbers behind native-born whites, Irish and German immigrants, but were more numerous than immigrant Scots, English or Welsh.[1] With white allies like Jane Grey Swisshelm and Charles Avery, a dedicated group of black activists became leaders in the abolitionist cause and spearheaded resistance to the despised Fugitive Slave Law of 1850. Charles Avery, a cotton mill owner, pharmacist, and Methodist minister, was a wealthy man. He contributed substantial sums to the abolitionist cause and founded a school for Negroes in Allegheny City that became known as Avery College.

The father of the black liberation struggle in Pittsburgh was John Vashon, whose father was a French officer and his mother a mulatto. Vashon fought in the War of 1812 as a seaman. After running a tavern in Carlisle, he came to Pittsburgh in 1829, where he opened a barbershop and a public bath that accommodated both ladies and gentlemen. Allied with the Reverend Lewis Woodson, Vashon was a great organizer of educational and political activity through the African Education Society (1832) and the Anti-Slavery Society of Pittsburgh that was founded in his house in 1833. His son George Boyer Vashon became a living testament to his father's insistence on the importance of education. A prodigy who excelled in ancient and modern languages, he became the first black graduate of Oberlin College; and after being rejected for admission to the Allegheny County bar because of his race, he stood successfully for the bar exam before the justices of the New York Supreme Court and became the first Negro admitted to the New York bar. After two and a half years in Haiti teaching at the College Faustin, he returned to Syracuse, New York, in 1850 where he taught college and contributed to Frederick Douglass' paper, the *North Star*.[2]

In 1837, the calling of a Pennsylvania constitutional convention brought to a head the issue of the right of suffrage for free citizens of color. While free blacks had enjoyed the franchise in many counties including Allegheny, they had been excluded from voting in Philadelphia and some other counties by the use of a poll tax and other mechanisms. In Pittsburgh, an extraordinary document, the *Memorial of the Free Citizens of Color in Pittsburgh and its Vicinity Relative to the Right of Suffrage*, was addressed to the convention. Signed by the Vashons, father and son, and 77 others, and perhaps written by Lewis Woodson, who was secretary for the committee, it included a description of the black community's deep feelings on the issue.

> It has been deemed both at home and abroad, a matter of just sarcasm, that, whilst the Declaration of Independence boasts of the universal equality of men, in many of the States, one half of the community is the absolute property of the other subject to the despotic will, nay to the passion, caprice, and cruelty of the master....The danger under which some of our sister states is now trembling is, that they hold within their bosom a population cut off from social rights, and looking with sullen discontent or eager hostility all around them. In Pennsylvania, the colored man, under her liberal and enlightened policy, has been taught to feel that he has an interest in common with the white man in sustaining her free institutions. He has felt that he shared in the blessing of her condition; and it has been his pride to show by his conduct as a citizen, that he is not unworthy of having been restored to the rights of humanity.[3]

On January 20, 1838, a Pennsylvania constitutional convention voted to amend the state constitution and restrict voting rights to white males. In the statewide count, the revised constitution passed by 113,971 to 112,759, though rejected by a majority of voters in Allegheny County. Until the passage of the Fourteenth Amendment in 1870, black citizens were denied the vote in Pennsylvania.[4]

The pre-Civil War period was a time of great enthusiasm for learning and moral elevation among all classes of people. Dozens of newspapers sprang up and cultural activities blossomed. In anticipation of slavery's abolition, white philanthropists supported various colonization schemes to return blacks to Africa, give them land taken from Indians, or colonize Central America - all offered as possible solutions to the potential presence of a huge population released from bondage. Blacks themselves were divided on colonization. Most rejected it as a distraction from the struggle against slavery and racial prejudice, but there was unanimity around the need for education and political organization. Religious organizations and some newspapers began to take increasingly strong stands for abolition, among them Pittsburgh's leading paper, *The Daily Gazette*.

A protege of Vashon's, the brilliant and energetic Martin Delany, came to Pittsburgh in 1831 at the age of 19. Five years later, he was selected as a Pittsburgh delegate to conventions in Philadelphia and New York. Like Vashon, he initially opposed the colonization schemes of conservatives despite a deep pride in his African ancestry. Vashon had written in *The Liberator* in 1832: "Why establish a Society for the purpose of inducing the African to forsake this soil which he has enriched with his labor and watered with his tears: which the violence and rapacity of Europe and America have made his native land?"[5] Five years later, Delany wrote:

> Our common country is the United States. Here we were born, here raised and educated; here are the scenes of childhood; the pleasant associations of our school going days; the loved enjoyments of our domestic and fireside relations, and the sacred graves of departed fathers and mothers; and from here we will not be driven by any policy that may scheme against us. We are Americans, having birthright citizenship – natural claims upon the country – claims common to all others of our fellow citizens – natural rights which may by virtue of unjust laws be obstructed, but can never be annulled.[6]

His great achievement in Pittsburgh was the founding of the first Black newspaper west of the Alleghenies, *The Mystery*, which carried on its masthead the saying, "Hereditary bondsmen! Know ye not who would be free, themselves must strike the first blow!" With agents in nine states and extensive outlets in Western Pennsylvania and Ohio, the paper carried Delany's editorial creed: "I have determined never to be guided by the frivolous rules of formality, but by principle, suggested by conscience, and guided by the light of reason. I love advice; I'll seek counsel, but detest dictation."[7] Deeply proud and cognizant of the African roots of both his father's and mother's sides, he fathered seven children and gave them names rich in historic meaning – among them a son Toussaint L'Ouverture and a daughter Ethiopia. When finances forced his paper to close in 1848, he joined Frederick Douglass as co-editor of *The North Star*. Reflecting on this man "of most defiant blackness," Douglass said: "I thank God for making me a man simply, but Delany always thanks him for making him a *black man*." Frank A. Rollin, an early biographer, wrote of Delany that Africa, in "her past and future glory became entwined around every fiber of his being; and to the work of replacing her among the powers of the earth, and exalting her scattered descendants on this continent, he has devoted himself wholly, with an earnestness to which the personal sacrifices made by him through life bear witness."[8]

The Reverend Lewis Woodson came to Pittsburgh around 1830 and took over "Mother Bethel," the oldest Black church west of the Alleghenies founded in 1815 in the heart of town at Smithfield and Water Streets. This institution, the barbershop and baths run by Vashon nearby, and John Peck's Oyster House in Market Square, constituted a nexus of community resistance to slavery. In close proximity to the Monongahela House, Pittsburgh's most prestigious hotel with a black wait and house staff numbering 300, a network was formed that led to numerous slave "snatchings" as public resistance grew to the increased activity of owners and bounty hunters tracking escaped property. A complex network of way stations and conductors that became known as the "underground railroad" conveyed escapees from routes that came up from Uniontown and little Washington and then north toward Erie, northeast through the town of Indiana toward New York, or northwest into Ohio.[9]

In 1845 in a case that attracted national attention, a young boy, Anthony Hollingsworth, was seized in Indiana, Pennsylvania, by Virginia bounty hunters. A crowd of anti-slavery citizens intervened and the case was put before a local judge. On a petition of *habeas corpus* from Dr. Robert Mitchell, a prominent local abolitionist, the judge ruled that Anthony should be freed since the slave catchers had not been able to produce a copy of the Virginia Constitution proving that slavery was indeed legal there![10] In another case, John Vashon thwarted the first seizure of a slave in Pittsburgh by paying two hundred dollars to free a boy that was working for him as an apprentice barber. In the 1840s, Pittsburgh blacks founded the Philanthropic Society that acted as "the defensive arm of the community," supporting slave snatching and providing key networks for the underground railroad. Martin Delany was the organization's secretary for many years. In one year, the society helped 269 persons escape to Canada.[11]

The passage of the Fugitive Slave Law, September 18, 1850, was the catalyst that drove many in Pittsburgh to overt acts of resistance. Within a week of its passage, hundreds of escaped blacks living in Pittsburgh began leaving in squads for Canada. "The Negroes were well-armed with rifles, revolvers and knives. Each company had a captain, and before starting all made a firm resolve to die rather than be taken back into slavery."[12] Ten days after the law's passage, a "tremendous concourse" of "colored people and their friends" was held in Pittsburgh to hear an eloquent address by Charles Avery denouncing a law that suspended both the right of *habeas corpus* and trial by jury. Another speaker asserted: "We should not allow ourselves to be turned from men into slave-catchers." Two days later on September 30, 1850, a massive protest meeting was held in the Allegheny City market-house attended by Allegheny City Mayor Hugh Fleming. Martin Delany spoke and made no secret of his intention to resist.[13]

> Honorable Mayor, whatever ideas of liberty I may have, have been received from reading the lives of your revolutionary fathers. I have herein learned that a man has a right to defend his castle with his life, even unto the taking of life. Sir, my house is my castle; in that castle are none but my wife and my children, as free as the angels of heavens, and whose liberty is as sacred as the pillars of God. If any man approaches that house in search of a slave, I care not who he may be, whether constable, or sheriff, magistrate, or even judge of the Supreme Court, nay, let it be he who sanctioned this act to become law (President Fillmore) surrounded by his cabinet as bodyguard, with the Declaration of Independence waving above his head as his banner, and the constitution of his country upon his breast as his shield, if he crosses the threshold of my door, and I do not lay him a lifeless corpse at my feet, I hope the grave may refuse my body a resting place and righteous Heaven my spirit a home. Oh No! He cannot enter my house and we both live.[14]

Having received medical training from several of Pittsburgh's finest white doctors, Delany was admitted to Harvard for medicine, but the hostility of white students forced his expulsion. He returned to Pittsburgh in 1851 and published the treatise that conferred upon him the title "father of Black nationalism." *The Condition, Elevation, Emigration, and Destiny of the Colored People of the United States, Politically Considered* was a declaration of racial pride and a call for emigration out of the United States. Delany moved his family to Canada, where he wrote the bulk of the most significant black novel of the period, *Blake or the Huts of America*. Written as a counterpoint to Harriet Beecher Stowe's depiction of the meek, long-suffering Christian mulatto, Uncle Tom, Delany's hero, a pure black West Indian from Jamaica, aspires to foment a revolt of slaves in the southern United States by leading a revolutionary rising in Cuba. He conferred several times with John Brown prior to his raid on Harper's Ferry and helped Brown convene an anti-slavery convention in Canada on May 8, 1858. When the Harper's Ferry raid transpired, Delany was leading a Niger Valley Exploring Party to present day Nigeria where in 1859 he negotiated land from the king of Abeokuta for a settlement. By the time he returned to the United States, the Civil War was placing the issue of slavery squarely on the nation's agenda, and Delany threw himself into the recruitment of Black soldiers. On February 8, 1865, Delany met with President Lincoln to urge him to form an army of black men under black commanders. Lincoln referred Delany to Secretary of War Edwin Stanton with the instruction: "Do not fail to have an interview with this extraordinary and intelligent black man." Shortly thereafter, Delany was commissioned a major, the first black officer in the U.S. Army.[15]

The first trial in Pittsburgh concerning the fugitive slave law occurred in 1851 when, after a judgment in favor of the owner, a slave named Woodson was taken to a boat under guard as several hundred hostile people tried to block his way. A clerk of the United States Court, together with citizens in Beaver where Woodson had lived, preached and worked as a "thrifty mechanic," raised sufficient money to eventually purchase the man's freedom. In 1855, several attempts were made to free a colored nurse owned by Leonard Boyd. Boyd, fearing the loss of his property, tried to leave town by boat. "On the way to the landing, desperate attempts at rescue were again made; but upon the presentation of arms by the police, the rescuers were driven back and the slave was placed safely in the boat. During the progress of the last attempt, severe struggling and riot occurred." The Democratic *Post* added: "The character of this city should not be stained, nor its business injured by negro mobs. Its business has suffered severely enough from other causes within the last year, without adding the curse and disgrace of negro riot. We hope that the next riot of this kind will be met with plenty of well charged revolvers in ready and resolute hands."[16]

In 1850, Jane Grey Swisshelm, itching to use her sharp pen in the battle against slavery, contacted Horace Greeley of the powerful *New York Tribune* and offered her services as a columnist. He accepted and she became the first woman reporter to be given a place in the reporter's gallery in Congress. She did not last long, as her biting and sarcastic writing won her notoriety and earned her the hostility of the powerful. She loved the excitement of the great issues and the distinction and respect she was gaining. However, her anger at the great Daniel Webster, whose ambitions for the presidency led him to make increasing compromise with advocates of Southern slavery, pushed her to write a damning column for the *Visiter* that thwarted Webster's political ambitions and forced her to leave Washington. She described the situation in her autobiography:

> Darkest of dark omens for the slave, in that dark day, was the defalcation of Daniel Webster. He whose eloquence had secured in name the great Northwest to freedom, and who had so long been dreaded by the slave-power, had laid his crown in the dust; had counseled the people of the North to conquer their prejudices against catching slaves, and by his vote would open every sanctuary to the bloodhound. The prestige of his great name and the power of his great intellect was turned over to slavery, and the friends of freedom deplored and trembled for the result.... In the nation's capital lived some of our most prominent statesmen in open concubinage with negresses, adding to their income by the sale of their own children, while one could neither go out nor stay without meeting indisputable testimony of the truth of Thomas Jefferson's statement: "The best blood of Virginia runs in the blood of her slaves." But the case which interested me most was a family of eight mulattoes, bearing the image and superscription of the great New England statesman, who paid the rent and the grocery bills of their mother as regularly as he did those of his wife. I wondered and began to look at and inquire about him,

and soon discovered that his whole panoply of moral power was a shell – that his life was full of rottenness.[17]

Know-Nothings and Republicans

The collapse of the Whig party in the election of 1852, when the Democrats gained the presidency and control of both houses of Congress, initiated an intense political realignment in search of a formula that might break the Democrat's absolute control of the national government. Though triumphant, the Democratic Party was itself an odd combination of a Southern party wholly subservient to slave interests and a northern party that asserted its friendship for the immigrant and the worker. The anti-Democrats, for their part, had to unite the nativist, anti-Catholic, skilled workers, with the business community who opposed the extension of slavery for economic reasons, in an alliance with the hard-core abolitionists who were absolutely determined to destroy slavery as an institution. While the new Republican Party succeeded in achieving victory only eight years from its conception in Pittsburgh and four years from its founding convention there, determining the balance of interests within the party worked itself out only gradually through political struggle.

While Ripon, Wisconsin and Jackson, Michigan have rival claims, a meeting in Pittsburgh, a few weeks after the 1852 electoral debacle, of manufacturers, business and professional leaders including the editors of the *Pittsburgh Daily Gazette* and the *Pittsburgh Commercial Journal*, wrestled with the task of reconciling the competing interests of nativists, Whigs, Anti-Masons, Free Soilers, Know-Nothings, anti-slavery Democrats, and Abolitionists. Meeting in the grocery store of David Herbst in the crowded business district along the Monongahela, "the men sat upon nail kegs, boxes, flour barrels, the counters, or clustered around the warm stove. All shades of political opinion were represented… Among them were a number who were active in politics. Their object was to formulate a basis for a new political party upon which all factions opposed to the pro-slavery Democracy might unite for the accomplishment of its overthrow."[18]

Bitter argument ensued over the new party's name until Charles Naylor proposed a solution: "Our country is a great Republic; why not name the new party Republican, without prefix or suffix." Naylor was an activist in the Native American Party and had played a major role in the anti-Catholic riots of 1844 in Philadelphia where several Catholic churches and two convent schools had been burned and many people killed. While anti-Catholicism was shared by most in the coalition, the anti-foreign aspects of the various nativist factions alienated the important Protestant German and Protestant Irish voters who tended to vote Democratic when foreigners were attacked. All present, however, opposed the extension of papal power into the United States since they believed "the Catholic Church was inherently incompatible with civil and religious liberties of America. Reprinting Catholic newspaper articles and documents, David White (editor of the *Pittsburgh Daily Gazette*) charged that Catholics were disloyal to the Constitution, threatened freedom of thought in America, and more important, admittedly hated Protestants. Expanding Romanism, warned White, spawned drinking and lawlessness on Sundays and endangered Christianity and morality in America."[19]

The Catholic Church in Pittsburgh added fuel to the nativist fire when it attacked the public school system. "Archbishop Hughes and Bishop O'Connor had first complained that Catholic children were being corrupted and driven from their parents' faith in public schools because of bible reading and other practices. Bishop O'Connor then asserted that it was unfair to tax Catholics to support such schools, and demanded a separate school fund for Catholics to support an independent system of parochial schools....Anti-Catholic editors charged that this war on the school system originated in Rome and was part of a papal conspiracy to destroy the freedom of thought and love of liberty in America." When the papal envoy, Gaetano Bedini, visited Pittsburgh in December 1853, "a mob jostled him roughly." Even the visit of the Hungarian democrat Louis Kossuth to Pittsburgh to seek financial and political support for the Hungarian Republic aroused suspicions about the loyalty of immigrants.[20]

In 1855, when St. Paul's Cathedral was dedicated at its prominent downtown location on Grant Street, the fiercely Protestant Jane Grey Swisshelm reported on the ceremony. She was appalled by the rituals and the pomp. She decried the Catholic bishop's sermon that "dwelt entirely on the importance of forms and the beauty of the building....No allusion to inner life, or nobler life, or any duties to God and man, except believing in these forms. Of the small matter of salvation from sin, he said not a word." The editor of the *Pittsburgh Catholic* shot back with equal insensitivity: "If this woman has a husband, and her tongue is like her pen, the unfortunate fellow deserves to be pitied."[21]

The flood of new immigrants into the United States from Ireland and Germany reached a record level of 114,371 in 1845, and then the flow accelerated until it reached a pre-Civil War high of 427,833 immigrants per year to the United States in 1854. By 1850, Pittsburgh was one-third foreign-born, and a high percentage of them were men of working age. The rift between the growing Catholic working class and the abolitionist Republicans certainly existed on the ground where blacks and immigrants competed for jobs, but it was exacerbated by the Republican - Democratic split over class and race. This was demonstrated at the 1850 anti-Fugitive Slave Law meeting in Allegheny. When the Democratic Workingman's candidate attempted to compare wage slavery with chattel slavery, he was shouted down. Jane Grey Swisshelm barely mentions the struggles of the cotton mill girls in her *Visiter* articles of the period, which is not surprising given her close alliance with Charles Avery, abolitionist and cotton mill owner. These racial and class tensions would be sharply intensified, of course, as the war dragged on. While blacks initially were not allowed to be in combat roles despite the eagerness of many among them to fight against slavery, the immigrants, in particular the Irish, were forcibly drafted at the same time that wealthier elements of society were able to pay a bounty and escape military service.[22]

On February 22, 1856, Washington's Birthday, the founding convention of the Republican Party was held in Lafayette Hall in Pittsburgh. Philadelphia was selected as the site for a national convention to choose a candidate for president, and a National Executive Committee was formed. In June, John C. Fremont was selected as nominee for president on a free soil platform. While the Democrat nominee from Pennsylvania, James Buchanan, convincingly won the state and the presidency, the Republicans downplayed sympathy for the plight of the Negro and defined their struggle as a sectional one devoted to the cause of capitalism and free labor. The *Gazette* asserted: "So far this contest being for the Negro race, as is falsely asserted by the Buchaniers (sic), it is emphatically for the rights of the free whites of the country against the encroachments of the aristocracy – the slave owners."[23]

There were, however, among skilled workers especially, those who were attracted to the new Republican Party because they saw the Democrats increasingly in thrall to the slave-holding aristocracy. In 1856, an *Address of the Workingmen of Pittsburgh to the Fellow Workingmen of Pennsylvania* that was issued in the name of 25,000 iron molders, textile workers, coal miners, carpenters, printers, masons and other skilled mechanics, said: "In another section of our country exists an...aristocracy owning labor.... Labor is servitude and freedom is only compatible with mastership. They despise us 'Greasy Mechanics,' 'Filthy Operatives,' and 'small Farmers doing their own drudgery' and 'unfit to associate with a Southern gentleman's body servant' – and being gentlemen no doubt believe what they say. The political power of that section is in their hands, from the ignorant and depressed conditions of our fellow workmen there – the 'poor whites' as they call them. These aristocrats desire to extend this system (slavery) over all the Territories of the nation. To extend it over the Territories is to give them supreme power over the government and they will extend it over us."[24]

Harmony and Depravity

William Coventry Wall introduced the Pittsburgh public to landscape painting. On one hand, he chronicled a pristine Pittsburgh region of clear streams and clean skies that was disappearing before his eyes; on the other, he documented the birth of an industrial landscape that was fundamentally transforming the relationship between man and nature. Born in Oxford, England, in 1810, he probably learned the painter's craft from his father. In Pittsburgh, he ran a business manufacturing mounted looking glass and picture frames, as well as selling canvas, brushes, varnish, etc. for artists. He earned great popularity after his series of paintings chronicling the devastation wrought by the 1845 fire. In them the post-fire panorama is laid out: a view of the ruins as seen from Grant's Hill down toward the Forks; burnt remains of the wooden, covered bridge at Smithfield Street, with steamboats drawn up along the smoldering bank of the Monongahela; the ruins of Bakewell's glass factory; the forest of blackened stone and brick chimneys standing like sentinels over the deserted city. Wall produced numerous landscapes that he displayed to admiring pedestrian crowds in the window of his shop. His masterpiece "Evening of Braddock's Defeat, July 9, 1755," shows native warriors returning to a Fort Duquesne nestled in the Forks, brandishing the trophies and booty of war. Across the whole right half of the painting, looking north and west across the Allegheny, a magnificent summer sunset bathes the pristine, primordial landscape. The scene marks a fundamental historical transition from the state of nature to the landscape of commerce and industry, whose poignancy was certainly not lost on the observers of Wall's day. In the century following the momentous historical events depicted, everything in the painting was gone or drastically altered: Native Americans, the British, the French, and nature itself. [25]

Born in 1826, Pittsburgh native Stephen Foster became the best-known American songwriter of the 19th Century. The son of William Barclay Foster of Lawrenceville, he demonstrated his genius early in life with *Oh Susanna!* Published when he was barely twenty, the song became the theme of the "Forty-Niners" of the California gold rush. He wrote over two hundred tunes, two of which, *My Old Kentucky Home* and *Old Folks at Home* were adopted as state songs by Kentucky and Florida respectively. He composed songs for the Christy Minstrels, the most famous singing group of his day, which spread his music all over the country. His personal and business affairs were unhappy however, and he turned increasingly to drink and died in 1863 at the age of thirty-seven in New York City during the Civil War. He wrote the haunting *Beautiful Dreamer* in the summer before he died.[26]

Another major Pittsburgh cultural figure of the period, David Blythe, led a tragic and alcoholic life, but unlike Stephen Foster who created images of sweetness and sentimentality out of his suffering, Blythe created unadorned scenes of Pittsburgh and Western Pennsylvania daily life that have an edge to them. Born into poverty, he began as a wood carver, contributing a statue fashioned from poplar that adorned the dome of the Fayette County Courthouse in Uniontown. Before coming to Pittsburgh, he toured the countryside exhibiting panorama paintings of Western Pennsylvania history. When he settled in Pittsburgh in 1856, he began his best work which resembled European contemporaries Daumier,

Hogarth or Goya in its fascination with violence and poverty, not at all the optimistic view that dominated American painting of the period. "In the haunts of the respectable ...and in the respectable themselves he found only pompous hypocrisy, but for the beggars, drunkards, and thieves his heart warmed with pity." Street urchins picking pockets or stealing alcohol from a barrel with a straw, the artist himself getting evicted from his studio, a mule rearing back from a haughty lady in a hoop skirt, these were his subjects. In perhaps his greatest work, *Courtroom Scene*, "a ranting, demonic prosecutor points a bony finger at a meek and utterly resigned defendant, the attention of the judge wanders, and a jury of slack-jawed rabble can hardly stay awake."[27]

Another artist from this time and place left as a child and eventually achieved international recognition. On May 22, 1844, Mary Cassatt was born in Allegheny City of French Huguenot and Dutch ancestors. In 1846, her father Robert was elected mayor of Allegheny and later served as Select Council President. When Mary was five, the family moved to Philadelphia, and two years later, the whole family went on a four-year sojourn in France and Germany. Her older brother, Alexander, would become the president of the Pennsylvania Railroad. The family settled in West Chester, west of Philadelphia, in 1855. In 1866, Mary went to Paris and launched an artistic career. In 1877 she joined the Impressionist group of painters at the invitation of Edgar Degas, who became a friend and mentor. She lived most of her life in France, generally painting maternal scenes and portraits, several notable ones being purchased by the Mellons for the National Gallery. While often touted as a great Pittsburgher, it is difficult to discern any enduring Pittsburgh influence on her life or work.[28]

City of Iron and Oil

The 1850s saw the establishment of the main trunk railroad lines east and west out of Pittsburgh, with a proliferation of shorter regional connections spreading out from the city as well. In 1851, a rail link was opened to Cleveland. In 1854 the completion of the Pennsylvania Railroad's mountain division created a direct rail link between Philadelphia and Pittsburgh, cutting the time for travel between the cities from three days to as little as thirteen hours for the fastest trains. Two years later, the Pittsburgh, Fort Wayne and Chicago opened its line through to Chicago from Allegheny. By 1857 a rail bridge was completed across the Allegheny River linking the two systems. This improvement proved a mixed blessing, however, since it destroyed the city's function as a trans-shipment center and displaced many established businesses. "The trunk lines took goods directly through the city to points beyond and thus ruined the business of those merchants and draymen that transferred goods between riverboats and railroads or between one railroad in Allegheny City and the other in Pittsburgh."[29]

Resentment began to develop in Pittsburgh business circles against the Pennsylvania Railroad's use of its immense lobbying power in the state legislature to gain governmental subsidies and to thwart the Baltimore and Ohio from creating a competitive connection from the east. "The Ohio and Pennsylvania, which monopolized shipments west, and the Pennsylvania, the only through line to the east, charged different rates for long hauls and short hauls and thus discriminated against Pittsburgh. For example, goods could be shipped more cheaply between Chicago or Cincinnati and New York than between Pittsburgh and Philadelphia over the Pennsylvania....Because of the lower transportation costs, western merchants bought manufactured products in New York and Philadelphia which they had formerly purchased in Pittsburgh. Competition from the East even increased in Pittsburgh itself."[30]

Pittsburgh was continuing to develop industrially, however. In 1853, Benjamin F. Jones with John Lauth and Samuel Kier built the American Iron Works, a complex of puddling furnaces and rolling mills on the south bank of the Monongahela upstream from the existing concentration of glass factories. The first tin-plated iron was achieved in 1858. By 1859 there were 31 puddling furnaces operating on the South Side. There, Lauth developed and patented the process of cold-rolling iron and steel to produce a shinier, smoother surface. The same year, James Laughlin, an organizer of First National Bank of Pittsburgh, began building the Eliza furnace and a battery of beehive coke ovens across the river on its north shore. In 1861 the two facilities merged into what would become known as Jones & Laughlin Steel (J&L). The Eliza furnace was the second blast furnace to become operational in the city; since, in 1859, the Clinton blast furnace on the south bank of the Monongahela opposite the Point was successfully "blown in" using Connellsville coke as fuel. The Clinton furnace thus became the first iron-producing facility in the city since the short-lived Anshutz furnace of 1794 in Shadyside. The success of the new furnaces helped assure the dominance of Connellsville coke that became the "benchmark against which all other cokes were measured." The furnaces came on line just as Civil War-driven demand accelerated.[31]

Both labor and management were organizing. B. F. Jones was the driving managerial force behind the growth of the J&L mills. He pioneered "vertical integration," linking blast furnace and puddling operations, helping to organize the Pittsburgh and Lake Erie Railroad to secure iron ore for his furnaces, and purchasing Connellsville coal properties to control fuel costs. He was also an innovator in labor relations, developing the "sliding scale," which Carnegie would subsequently make famous. This attempt to associate workers in common cause with management linked wage rates to fluctuations in the selling price of the metal produced. The panic of 1857 had forced wage reductions in the iron industry and prompted the founding of the Sons of Vulcan in Pittsburgh, the first organization of puddlers in the iron industry. The name of the organization evoked the almost mythical quality of the trade. James J. Davis wrote about the puddler's trade in his youth. "Those early iron workers learned to puddle forge iron and make it into wrought iron which is tough and leathery and cannot be broken by a blow. This process was handed down from father to son, and in the course of time came to my father and so to me. None of us went to school and learned the chemistry of it from books. We learned the trick by doing it, standing with our faces in the scorching heat while our hands puddle the metal in its glaring bath." In 1865, after a strike, B. F. Jones signed the first labor contract in the iron industry with the Sons of Vulcan. As the post-Civil War economic downturn deepened, manufacturers locked out the union for six months at the beginning of 1867, but finally signed an agreement that included the sliding scale but with the higher minimum base desired by the union.[32]

Labor was organizing on several fronts. An Iron City Industrial Congress was organized in 1849. In 1852, in Pittsburgh, the printers formed their first national union, the National Typographical Union. Pittsburgh's printers, who had organized in 1833, were chartered as Typographical Union Local #7 in the national organization. In 1897 all the various printing locals united in the Allied Printing Trades Council. Teachers organized into the Pennsylvania State Teachers Association at a meeting in Pittsburgh the same year, and the first public high school was opened in 1855. The National Union of Iron Molders was founded in 1859 in Philadelphia by William Sylvis, who spent a great deal of time in Pittsburgh. Sylvis became a major spokesman for the cause of labor unity, and the philosophy expressed in the preamble to the Iron Molders' constitution summarized the aspirations of many working people for some countervailing power to balance the burgeoning power of capital. "In union there is strength and in the formation of a national organization, embracing every molder in the country, a union founded upon a basis as broad as the land in which we live, lies our only hope. Single-handed we can accomplish nothing, but united there is no power of wrong that we cannot openly defy."[33]

Perhaps no event in these years impacted history more than the discovery and development of petroleum 75 miles north of Pittsburgh. The oil struck by Colonel Edwin Drake at Titusville on August 29, 1859, was the culmination of a decade of efforts by Samuel Kier, an energetic businessman and entrepreneur. Involved in coal mines, an iron furnace with B. F. Jones, a fire-brick and pottery factory, he was also boring salt wells near Tarentum, northeast of Pittsburgh, along the Allegheny River. Like other salt manufacturers, he initially perceived the slick, slimy, foul smelling liquid floating on the brine only as a nuisance. Oil was known and even exploited by the native peoples, who used it as a medicine, especially for joints and arthritis. Early oil prospectors encountered extensive ancient wells in Pennsylvania, Kentucky and Ohio. "Their origin has never been determined, but it is known that they antedated the Seneca and other Indian tribes of those regions, and they are believed to be the work of that mysterious race which built the great mounds of Ohio and other Midwestern states and operated the ancient copper mines of Lake Superior."[34]

First marketed in Pittsburgh in the 1790s, it was widely sold as Seneca Oil and used in the early 19th Century as "a sovereign remedy for several complaints." When Kier's wife became ill in 1848, her physician prescribed liberal doses of it. Kier immediately recognized that it was similar to the stuff that he was encountering in his salt wells and had it chemically analyzed. Finding that it was indeed the same substance, he began marketing it aggressively throughout the northeast. "Petroleum or Rock Oil – Celebrated for its Wonderful Curative Powers – A Natural Remedy!" Selling the substance in little medicine bottles, however, hardly even used the oil he was producing in a single 400 foot deep salt well. There had been attempts to burn it as a fuel or illuminant, but this usage was rejected because of its thick smoke and foul odor.[35]

In a house in downtown Pittsburgh, on Seventh Avenue near Grant Street, Kier began distilling the crude petroleum, creating the first American refinery. He was able to solve the smoke problem and produced lamps that could produce a good clear light. His lamp still gave off a horrible odor, however, a problem that would be solved a few years later by A. C. Ferris "treating it with caustic soda, and agitating it with sulfuric acid, processes that were still further improved in later years." Demand for the Ferris' illuminant, called kerosene, began to rise, but supply was still limited. To solve this problem, the Pennsylvania Rock Oil Company was formed in 1855. After many false starts, one of the investors, Edwin Drake, was dispatched to Titusville where property had been purchased. There, he hired William Smith, a blacksmith and tool-maker who had worked with Kier in Tarentum, to bore for oil. Smith described the moment: "While I was drilling I felt the jars stop working. I knew there was a crevice from this and I let out until the jars struck again. It was within a half hour after that time that I got oil out of the well…I called Drake's attention to it. He said: 'What does that mean?' I said, 'That's your fortune coming.'"[36]

Subsequently, dozens, then hundreds, and ultimately thousands of wells were drilled in the region, and refineries began producing primarily kerosene, but also benzene, naphtha, lubricating oil, paraffin and a "virtually useless liquid called gasoline."[37] The great oil rush began in earnest in 1863 when the most profitable strike in Pennsylvania history, the Noble well, returned almost five million dollars on an investment of four thousand dollars.

The well puffed and blowed, and the earth about it fairly trembled with agitation. No one dared to approach it, even within the circuit of the falling spray of oil and water. The little ravine near the derrick soon filled up with the great volume of oil rattling and foaming up through the two-and-a-half inch tubing. Mr. Noble offered fifty dollars each, to any three men who would enter the derrick and attach his ingenious device for conducting oil into tanks. The men stripped to the buff, and entered the derrick. The spray, oil and water hid them completely from view, and nearly drowned them before they could complete their task. At the end of an hour, or a little less, they had made the connection and returned to the outer world.[38]

Pittsburgh Mobilizes for the Union

Pennsylvania and Pittsburgh played a major role in the critical 1860 election. The Democrats were deeply split as their star candidate, Stephen A. Douglass, who might attract sufficient Northern voters to maintain Democratic control of the presidency, was unacceptable to many Southerners. The Democrats' April convention in Charleston, South Carolina, triggered walkouts by Alabama and several other slave states. Fifty-seven ballots provided no winner, and the party was forced to convene a second convention in Baltimore in June. There the split became formalized when the convention selected Douglass after the withdrawal of the southern delegates, who chose John C. Breckinridge as their candidate.

For the Republicans, Pennsylvania was critical, and an internal rivalry between Senator Simon Cameron, who had presidential ambitions, and Andrew Curtin, who wanted to be governor, literally determined the course of American history. Curtin enjoyed strong support in Allegheny County and proved to be the more skillful politician. At the Republican convention in Chicago, Curtin and his allies worked to undermine Cameron. After perfunctory support of Cameron as Pennsylvania's favorite son on the initial ballot, Curtin managed to swing forty-eight of fifty-four delegate votes to Lincoln on the second ballot, giving him the lead over William Seward. On the third ballot, Lincoln emerged triumphant. Curtin followed this coup by a personal victory in the October gubernatorial race with the Republicans sweeping both houses of the legislature. Campaigning on the need for a protective tariff and support for a homestead act to provide federal land to family farmers, while vigorously attacking Democratic candidates as corrupt prisoners of the slavocracy, too beholden to immigrants and Catholics, the Republicans established themselves as Pennsylvania's governing party after decades of Democratic dominance. The *Gazette* defined the issue over slavery in the following terms: "The real and true issue between the two great parties which underlies all the struggle and strife is whether the power of government shall be exerted to protect free white labor or black slave labor."[39]

After Curtin's convincing victory, *The Daily Post*, under the editorial line "White Men to the Rescue!" could only respond with racist invective:

Here on the threshold of a Republican triumph – in the sable shadow of an incoming administration composed of men who "love the Abolitionists" and deify Fred Douglass and John Brown – we declare our "prejudice" in favor of the white race, and our regret that they must yield to African sway. We know we are stiff-necked – we admit with all becoming humility, our shortness of vision, and our invincible aversion to unpleasant odors – but still, we repeat, and we shall steadily maintain it in the presence of rack, or cord, or guillotine, that we prefer white people with straight hair, to black people with twisted wool....We are opposed to Negro suffrage and amalgamation, and we are not in favor of Negro immigration into our state from any quarter whatsoever. What arrangements the South may make for a black population, we have nothing to do, we prefer that States where African slavery does not exist should be preserved to and for white men.[40]

Abraham Lincoln's victory on November 6, 1860, triggered a chain of events that included the secession of eleven southern states before Lincoln took office on March 4, 1861, and culminated in the attack on Fort Sumter, April 12-13, only 40 days into his presidency. In the four month interregnum between his election and inauguration, political struggle steadily intensified. In December, President Buchanan's Secretary of War, John Floyd, ordered 124 large cannon of various calibers to be shipped from Pittsburgh's Arsenal to coastal forts being constructed at Biloxi, Mississippi, and Galveston, Texas.[41] Appointed commander of the Allegheny Arsenal in 1857, Major John Symington was from Delaware and widely believed to have Southern sympathies, since his son joined the Confederate army and his daughter scandalized a church service in Lawrenceville by wearing a Confederate rosette. The protests of Pittsburgh citizens mounted. Meetings were held, resolutions passed, and angry letters written to the President. People were active in the streets. On December 24, 1860, massive demonstrations by thousands of citizens physically blocked the movement of 100 artillery pieces from the Arsenal to the Monongahela wharf without serious violence.[42]

The *Pittsburgh Gazette* thundered: "The hearts of this people was stirred to the utmost indignation yesterday upon learning that Secretary Floyd of the War Department had ordered most of the cannon at the U.S. Arsenal, here, to the extent of one hundred or more, to be shipped to New Orleans and Galveston.... These facts go to show conclusively the treasonable purpose of this administration. Every Northern Arsenal has been stripped of arms and ordnance and every Southern Arsenal crammed full...." Mass meetings on the 27th and 30th heard calls for the rule of law, but voices were also raised for armed resistance to the movement of ordnance to the south. The presidential orders were countermanded on January 2 and Symington returned the guns to the Arsenal. Pittsburghers' mass action marked the first act of Northern resistance to Southern secession.[43]

The swelling of patriotic sentiment on behalf of the preservation of the union found another outlet when Abraham Lincoln stopped and spent the night in Pittsburgh, February 14, 1861, in the course of his slow political march to Washington for the inauguration. More than ten thousand Pittsburghers waited for hours in the cold rain for his delayed train to arrive in Allegheny City. Once there, Lincoln proceeded by carriage across the Allegheny River to the Monongahela House. He made remarks inside to dignitaries and then to the crowd from a balcony both that evening and again the next morning. In appreciation for his ten thousand-vote margin in Allegheny County, Lincoln stated: "I have great regard for Allegheny County. It is the banner county of the state, if not the entire union." The following morning, as promised, he spoke about something "of peculiar interest to Pennsylvania." His statement that "labor being the true standard of value...a tariff should be arranged as to foster and protect the interests of all sections – the iron of Pennsylvania, the corn of Indiana, the reapers of Chicago" was met with "enthusiastic demonstrations and cries of 'that's the doctrine.'"[44]

The assault on Fort Sumter provoked an outpouring of enlistments and military activity in Pittsburgh. A Committee of Public Safety and a Home Guard were organized. The entire town with its diversity of productive capacities turned its considerable energies to the manufacturing of war supplies and the transportation of troops and supplies. "For quite the entire period of the war,

Pittsburgh was literally a camp and an arsenal. Her foundries, her rolling mills, her tanneries, her harness factories, her clothing manufactories, her wagon factories, her production of shot and shell…infantry and cavalry accoutrements…but few hours of the day or night were without the passage of guns or troops, or was the roll of the drum silent…her streets were literally a war path."[45]

Arsenal of the Union

Troops moved east along the Pennsylvania Rail Line to Harrisburg and on to the battlefields of Virginia. Other units boarded boats to take them down the Ohio and Mississippi to Shiloh and Vicksburg, or to campaigns in Kentucky and Tennessee. Major encampments were set up in the Strip District, Hulton Station, Braddock's Field, Shadyside, Allegheny, East Liberty, Wilkinsburg and four separate sites in Oakland.[46] "Soldiers were everywhere, crowding the theaters and hotels, some gallantly escorting demure, crinolined young belles, others quarreling drunkenly in pothouses. Every steamboat that landed at the wharf had its quota of sick, wounded, furloughed, or discharged boys in blue; even the freight trains sometimes had soldiers swarming on the tops of the cars."[47]

The city's wartime industry surged, causing labor shortages, high wages, and higher inflation. The demands of military recruitment and war production, plus the rapid growth of petroleum refining in the city (employing around 800 workers), certainly put pressure on the local economy. The decline of the textile industry because of the contraction of southern cotton supply and the shrinking of the glass industry during the war helped to some degree. "During the Civil War, there were 26 rolling mills in the city of Pittsburgh alone, with approximately 3,000 employees, producing 100,000 tons of rolled and bar iron, sheet iron and nails. The 33 foundries and machine shops employed another 1,625 workers and consumed 34,000 tons of metal annually in production of finished products. In addition, Pittsburgh contained 90 puddling furnaces, 130 heating furnaces, 260 mill machines, 8 boiler yards, and 23 glasshouses." Pittsburgh remained a major shipbuilding location employing 5,000 men producing over 750 steamboats, barges, ferry, keel and flatboats during the war. Its shipyards fabricated heavily armed ram-boats, monitors and iron-clad ships for the battles to control the Mississippi and provided iron plate, turrets and naval machinery to other ship-building locations.[48]

Many men who would become renowned in the development of the steel industry began their rise to prominence during the war. Andrew and Thomas Carnegie expanded operations in Millvale and then moved across the Allegheny River to Bayardstown where they built an enormous rolling operation fed by 38 puddling furnaces. Andrew and Anton Kloman, involved in the production of gun carriages, also moved from Millvale across the Allegheny to Lawrenceville where they joined with Carnegie in development of his Union Iron Mills. A young 23 year-old Henry Oliver became a partner and chief salesman in a South Side plant manufacturing bolts, nuts and other hardware.[49]

Pittsburgh's most important producer of military equipment was the Fort Pitt Foundry, where 60% of the heavy guns for the Union armies were made. Its achievements in casting large guns made it world famous. "There is probably no single establishment in the United States that attracted so much public attention during the war as the foundry….Distinguished military and naval officers from England, France, Spain, Russia, Sweden, Denmark, Prussia, Sardinia and Austria, who had come from Europe to observe the operations of our armies in the field, or to note the progress of the war and the manner of conducting it, came from Washington City for the special purpose of examining the works, and of witnessing the casting of the monster cannon."[50]

From the beginning of 1861 to the end of 1865, Fort Pitt Foundry produced over 2,281 pieces of artillery for both the army and the navy. Most had bore sizes ranging from 8 to 15 inches, but six monster 20-inch Rodman guns were produced that could throw a thousand pound ball five miles. Over 20,000 rounds of shot and shell for these heavy cannons were also produced there. Captain Thomas Jackson Rodman was associated with the Lawrenceville Arsenal for most of the twenty years that preceded the war and was keenly aware of the Fort Pitt Foundry capabilities. He was noted for major advances in artillery construction, including the 15-inch and 20-inch guns that became known as the Rodman guns. His major technical contribution was a method for cooling cast iron gun barrels from the inside that greatly increased their strength, thereby allowing larger explosive charges that achieved greater projectile distances without bursting the gun. He also developed a progressive-burning powder that increased the muzzle velocity of the projectile.[51]

By the time of the American Civil War, the Allegheny Arsenal was the premier producer of ordnance and related gear for the Union armies, being able to draw "from among the numerous manufacturing establishments in its immediate vicinity artisans of every description and of great skill… (and) all the various materials required in the construction of arms and military equipment of all kinds." The wartime Arsenal was one of the largest factories in Pittsburgh, with about 950 employees at the time of the explosion, and shortly thereafter it attained a peak employment of 1,200. Male laborers were paid the 19th Century common-labor standard of a dollar a day; wages ranged from the master machinist's $3.75 a day to the girls as young as thirteen who packed cartridges with gun powder for 50-cents a day. On September 17, 1862, while the armies of North and South wrestled to a stalemate at Antietam in the bloodiest day in American military history, an explosion ripped through the Allegheny Arsenal killing 78 workers, mostly girls and young women, in Pittsburgh's worst industrial accident and the worst civilian accident of the Civil War. At two o'clock in the afternoon, the very moment when a bloody clash was occurring at a stone bridge crossing the little Antietam Creek in Maryland, a succession of three explosions rocked the Arsenal.[52]

The explosions occurred in or near the "laboratory," a large single-story, 68 by 30 foot wood frame shed divided into 14 rooms with an open court and a series of porches where the packing and filling of cartridges, shells, canister, grapeshot, etc., was accomplished. The entire day's production was still there waiting to be moved at the end of the shift to massive stone magazines for storage. As coldly reported by Symington the following day, production lost because of the explosion included "125,000 of .71 and .54 small arm cartridges, and 175 rounds of field ammunition assorted for 12-pounder and 10-pounder Parrott guns (cannons)." In his dutiful report on production losses for the day, he neglected to mention the age of the victims or their gender. In the building were 156 employees, mostly young women with girls as young as 14, plus 30 men and boys. Some months earlier, arsenal management discharged a large number of young boys and hired in their place numerous "young women and girls, as being more tractable and careful." Boys had careless habits like trying to smoke and were judged more rebellious.[53] Reporters who arrived at the scene were appalled by the carnage.

> The streets leading to the ground were filled with an excited crowd, including hundreds of frantic women, who rushed wildly through the multitude, shrieking and sobbing as though their hearts would break. We entered at the upper gate, and at the very threshold were met by evidence of the terrible force of the explosion. The grounds were covered with fragments of charred wood, canister shot, sheet iron, exploded cartridges, Minnie balls, etc., some of which had fallen fully 400 yards from the scene of the explosion….The horrors of the scene presented at this great destruction

of life were heightened by the agonizing screams of relatives and friends upon discovering the remains of some loved one whose humble earnings contributed to their comfort. Again, others were frantically rushing from one charred body to another looking in vain for a daughter or a sister who was employed in the ill-fated building. There was not a particle of clothing left on a majority of the victims, and mangled and disjointed as they were it was impossible to identify them. The very stockings were torn from their feet, rings from their fingers, and in some instances nothing but a headless trunk remained. Nevertheless, many were identified by their hair, by a scrap of the dress they wore, etc., but the greatest number never can be fully recognized. In the pit of the stomach of one headless trunk we saw there was embedded a dozen of Minnie balls.[54]

Colonel John Symington in his report the following day to his superiors surmised that the cause of the explosion was a leaking barrel of powder supplied by the DuPont company, but the coroner's jury investigation in Pittsburgh pointed to consistently careless housekeeping practices and large quantities of fine gunpowder dust that had been swept on the roadway. At least two witnesses testified (one at close range) to seeing sparks from a horse's hoofs ignite dust on the roadway as a teamster was making a delivery of powder barrels. Teamster J. R. Frick testified that "he saw fire from powder apparently dampened and mixed with dirt that made a 'fizzling' noise, between his wagon and the porch. There was always some powder spilled in these cylinder boxes by the chargers. They were brought out of the rooms to the porch and in leaving them the powder would fall out in quantities too small to be gathered up and was swept into the roadway." Frick said he saw the powder there three or four days prior to Wednesday and thought there was sufficient to ignite. Rachel Dunlap testified: "At the time of the explosion, I was standing at the door of room No. 12; I saw the shadow of a wagon; looked out and saw a blaze under the front wheel of the wagon near the horse's foot; threw up my hands and screamed...."[55]

A contractor testified that six months earlier he had furnished the stone for the new road that led to the laboratory. "Before he began stoning the road, it was bad and he considered it dangerous from the many ruts in it, which were likely to toss the barrels from side to side in the wagons. Mostly freestone was furnished, which, while blasting in the quarry freely ignites. The friction of horses' hoofs would readily strike fire from it. He had seen his own horses strike fire while passing over it." Another quarryman, William Baxter, testified that he had quarried stones from the same place and they were a "hard limestone, tinted with iron, and would readily strike fire." Moreover, he had worked in the Arsenal in the 1840s when the loading rooms were carpeted so dust could be completely shaken out once or twice daily and no stones were permitted around the laboratory. These workmen approached Symington when they noticed that "the workman's hammer drew sparks from the flinty stones." He was reluctant to renegotiate the contract for softer stone from a different nearby quarry. "It was then suggested to the commandant that the walk be covered with sawdust, tan bark or sand, all of which were easily accessible." This precautionary proposition was also rejected. When the walk was finally finished, it is said that McBride, supervisor of the laboratory, had it covered with cinders, without consulting the commandment. When Symington discovered this action, he reprimanded McBride for acting without authority and ordered the cinders removed at once.[56]

Symington had his day in a military court convened at his request on October 20, 1862. In a venue friendlier to the commandant, many witnesses, including some of those who had testified at the coroner's inquest, were extensively cross-examined; and the confusions and contradictions exposed in their testimonies made it relatively easy to discredit their incriminating assertions. Much effort was expended trying to attribute the explosion to worker negligence that was undoubtedly a factor because the whole production line was in a state of extreme speed-up and sloppy procedures were the consequence. On October 28, the military court of inquiry reached the following conclusion: "That the cause of the explosion could not be satisfactorily ascertained, but that possibly it may have been produced by the young man Smith (deceased) having jumped upon the powder barrel which may have had powder dust on the head. That Colonel Symington Commandant of the Arsenal took every care and precaution to guard against accidents of every kind. That Colonel Symington in his administration of his duties as Commandant has exhibited every evidence of zeal and integrity."[57] This incident, terrible in its own right, demonstrates the failure of authority to accept workers' suggestions, while subsequently blaming them for negligence when predictable tragedy strikes. The subsequent history of industrial Pittsburgh is replete with similar examples of the arrogance of the powerful, who ignored or suppressed the voices of workers concerning issues of both production and safety.

Eight months after the terrible explosion that ripped through the heart of the Pittsburgh war machine, the Confederate commander, Robert E. Lee, his initial invasion of the North blocked that bloody September 17 at Antietam, was preparing his second invasion of the north into the soft agricultural underbelly of Pennsylvania. Confederate raiders were active in West Virginia and John Morgan's raiders were eventually captured just west of Pittsburgh in East Liverpool, Ohio, in July 1863. As the daring Confederate cavalry leader, Jeb Stuart, and his horsemen spread fear across the state in advance of Lee's invasion, citizens of Pittsburgh and surrounding communities left their mines, riverboats, schools, offices and mills to carve vast earthen fortresses ringing the city – east, south and west - protecting the arsenal of the Union. The scope of the collective effort was impressive: in 15 days between June 18 and July 3, 1863, 37 fortification sites ringing Pittsburgh were hurriedly constructed by a workforce daily ranging from 4,000 to 11,000 men. The Jones and Laughlin iron mills took responsibility for fortifying the ridge above the South Side. African-Americans, still denied service as combatants, were permitted to form labor brigades and work on two of the forts.[58]

When the call to war came, many free blacks wanted to serve. Frederick Douglas, Martin Delany and others urged that the slaves be freed and recruited into the Northern armies. Pittsburgh claims the distinction of providing the first African-American company of soldiers, the Hannibal Guards. Commanded by an experienced white officer, William Sirwell, who had commanded the Washington Blues in the Mexican War, his company of blacks signed up for the initial three-month enlistment at the start of the war, but was refused the opportunity, because of the enlistee's race, to sign up for the three-year regiments. Many of this initial group eventually served in the famed Massachusetts Fifty-Fourth Colored Regiment or in regiments of the United States Colored Troops organized out of Philadelphia. After Lincoln's Emancipation Proclamation of January 1, 1863 explicitly authorized the recruitment of blacks into the armed forces, African-Americans fought in most major campaigns during the remaining two years of war. Until Martin Delany received his commission as a major directly from President Lincoln, however, there were no black officers. It is estimated that nearly a thousand blacks from southwestern Pennsylvania served. When the African-American Grand Army of the Republic, Pittsburgh Post #206, was formed, it was named for Colonel Robert G. Shaw of the 54th Massachusetts.[59]

On April 15, 1865, only a week after the surrender of General Lee and the end of the war, Pittsburgh learned of the assassination of President Abraham Lincoln the previous evening. The *Gazette* editorialized: "It is a fearful way in which to teach this nation a needed lesson…. That lesson has now been taught as by an overruling Providence, and we learn by it that Slavery is *not* dead. It was Slavery aimed that blow at the life of the President, and he is not a true man who does not vow that he will give himself no rest until Slavery and the spirit of Slavery are thoroughly rooted out of this land…. The South has provoked its doom and it cannot be averted. We must wipe out every vestige of Slavery…in whatever shape it exists. We must teach the rebellious people of the South that there is nothing for them but submission or expatriation; that there is no door open through which they can come back and be as they were before."[60]

Carnegie's Rise and Labor's Dream of Unity

The Civil War fundamentally transformed America from the primarily agrarian nation it had been since its founding. Government was immensely more powerful and increasingly sensitive, even subservient, to the interests of the wealthy. Business was firmly in control, and the nation was launched on a path of industrialization and expansion. While the slaves had been freed, there had been little or no thought given to what would happen to them. Even in Pennsylvania, they would not be accorded the right to vote until 1874, upon revision of the state constitution. The end of the war, the expansion of the railroads into the vast territories of the west, and the encouragement of immigration by business interests who needed workers and customers for the expanded productive forces that were being unleashed, created opportunity for both the accumulation of enormous wealth and vicious exploitation. While the capitalist was riding the winds of opportunity, workers were struggling to adapt to an incessantly changing world and to defend their standard of living through organization.

One of those who clearly saw the business opportunities was Andrew Carnegie. A son of an impoverished immigrant weaver who refused to abandon his hand loom, the 13 year old Andrew arrived in Allegheny City after the cotton mill riots of 1848 and took his first job for $1.20 a week at Blackstock's factory, the scene of the dramatic labor confrontation 3 years before. His big break came the following year when he escaped the textile mills and got a job as a telegraph boy, where he got to know every address in Pittsburgh. "What a change an entrance to a telegraph office was to me then. My 'Good Fairy' found me in a cellar firing a boiler and a little steam engine and carried me into the bright and sunny office surrounded with newspapers, pencils, pens and paper, and ringing in the ears, the miraculous tick, tick, tick of the tamed lightning and doing the work of a man. I was the happiest boy alive, carried from darkness to light."[61]

Carnegie's second big break came when he was hired to be the personal telegrapher of Thomas Scott, the superintendent of the Western Division of the Pennsylvania Railroad. He worked diligently, and upon Scott's moving to Philadelphia to become Vice President of the railroad under its President, Edgar Thomson, Carnegie became the superintendent of the Western Division at the age of 24. While many Pittsburgh businessmen hated the Pennsylvania Railroad, Carnegie used his close connection with Scott and the railroad as one of the foundations of the empire he would build. At the outbreak of the Civil War, when Scott was brought to Washington by Simon Cameron to be assistant Secretary of War, he brought Carnegie with him. There in the desperate early days of the war when Washington was in danger of being overwhelmed by the forces of the Confederacy, it was the efforts of Scott and Carnegie that secured train and telegraphic communication between the capitol and the North. Carnegie avoided serving in the military by hiring a substitute through a draft agent and returned to Pittsburgh to head the Western Division.[62]

By the end of the war, multiple investments in oil, railcars, telegraphy and iron had made him a rich man. It was his involvement in railroads that led to his investment in the Keystone Bridge Company, which in turn stimulated his expansion into iron fabrication and ultimately steel-making. Freed from the conflict over slavery, the west was opened to unbridled capitalist expansion. Carnegie invested heavily in sleeping cars, telegraphy and bridges. While he had mixed success in the first two areas, coming up against established rivals like Pullman and Western Union, bridge building became the activity that drove the early Carnegie interests. Keystone Bridge constructed many bridges over the Ohio, the Susquehanna, the Missouri, with the most spectacular being the great bridge over the Mississippi at St. Louis completed in 1874.

To build bridges, Carnegie needed massive amounts of structural iron members of great length, precise dimensions and strength. The key technical genius involved in solving the production challenges was Andrew Kloman, an immigrant from Prussia, who with his brother had a plant in Etna that produced gun carriages during the war, as well as railroad car axles of a very high quality. Andrew's younger brother Tom became involved on Andrew's behalf in a complex series of mergers and investments that led to the building of the Union Iron Mills in Lawrenceville, the result of a merger of Kloman's firm and Carnegie's Cyclops Iron Company. It was there that the first American universal mill was developed that permitted the rolling of plate of almost any desired length and thickness. Technical progress was spurred by labor unrest.

In the summer of 1867, the Union Iron Mills had its first serious labor difficulty, when the puddlers throughout the Pittsburgh area, organized in a craft union called the Sons of Vulcan, refused to accept a managerial order for a reduction in wages and went on strike. The several iron companies affected raised a fund to bring in European workers to replace the striking puddlers, and Kloman, representing the Union Iron Mills asked for German workers. Among those he received was a bright young metal worker named Johann Zimmer. Zimmer told Kloman about a rolling machine he had worked on in Prussia, on which it was possible to roll plates of various widths with finished rolled edges. This remarkable mill not only had the usual horizontal rolls of the plate-mills used in America; it also had two movable vertical rolls for rolling the edges of the plate, and these rolls could be widened or narrowed at the will of the operator.[63]

Organized labor in this period was struggling to find a way to deal with the great expansion of business power. While capital steadily advanced toward increased concentration and coordination and could thereby conjure up ample financial resources to corrupt legislatures and determine public policy, labor was by its very nature geographically spread, divided by craft and industry, split by race, gender and ethnicity. Because labor organizations tended to be either intensely local or defined along craft or trade lines, they could not easily muster the resources necessary to sustain organizations capable of providing communication and common strategy vis-à-vis the growing power of corporations and capital. In the eastern Pennsylvania anthracite coalfields between 1867 and 1874, John Siney led a successful effort to organize coal miners, winning the first contract in the industry. His efforts were thwarted by the repression initiated by the Reading Railroad against the alleged Irish terrorist outfit, the Molly Maguires. Siney also spearheaded the initial attempt to unite all coal miners into a strong national union, something that would be finally achieved in 1890 with the formation of the United Mine Workers of America.[64]

In the late sixties, an important pioneering attempt to provide national leadership to the entire labor movement was undertaken by William Sylvis of Armagh in Indiana County. Born the second of twelve children in 1828, William Sylvis learned the iron molding trade at various furnaces in central Pennsylvania and moved about 1854 to Philadelphia. He became active in the iron molders union and was elected its president at a convention in Pittsburgh in 1863. He built the organization, but undermined his own health by extensive organizing tours that would take him in a circuit through Pittsburgh, down the Ohio, up to Chicago, east to Buffalo, then to the major foundry centers of the Mohawk Valley in New York, into New England and finally home to Philadelphia. He traveled incessantly, and by 1865, the union was at its zenith. He fought diligently to protect skilled workers from the mass production techniques that were destroying the trade. "The want of a well-regulated apprentice system has filled the land with a vast number of inferior workmen who, not being masters of their own trade, are more or less subject to the whims and caprice of capitalists." During the bitter 1867 strike of six foundries in Pittsburgh, instead of a single apprentice being assigned to several journeymen as was the practice in a union shop, two molders worked fifty-six apprentices at one non-union establishment and seven journeymen directed eighty at another.[65]

As work slowed dramatically after the war, the owners were pushing hard for wage reductions and "resisting any and all actions of the Molders' Union, which shall in any manner interfere with our right to control our own workshops, and to manage our own business." Sylvis was able in 1866 to work one locality against another by calling selective strikes and having molders, who were working, provide strike relief to those who were locked out or on strike. Ever conscious of the need to muster public sympathy, he also tried without success to get the far-flung union to propose a uniform reduction in wages and thereby "disarm the bosses, and maintain peace on better terms than we can otherwise expect, and in the end we will not only save money by it, but what is of much more importance, we will save our organization." As economic conditions worsened, the 1867 strike in Pittsburgh led to the closing of virtually every foundry in Pittsburgh.[66]

These dark events brought Sylvis to the conclusion that workers could not stand against the power of employers through work stoppages that led to starvation and suffering for the laborer and their families. He attempted to challenge the power of wealth by promoting the cooperative ideal and by organizing a national labor union powerful enough to achieve social reform. Cooperative ventures by workers themselves, he hoped, could overcome class conflict and make workers the masters of their own souls. An initially successful cooperative foundry in the molders' stronghold of Troy, New York, prompted the Molders Union to try to open and operate a union-owned foundry in Pittsburgh. While $15,000 was raised through stock sales to union members and a building and furnace were purchased, the enterprise was starved for operating capital and failed. Hostility of local investors to the union effort and lack of investment money by the workers doomed the project. This failure convinced Sylvis that the cooperative organization of workers could only succeed with financial assistance from government. The railroads had been aided by massive investment of public funds, why should not the state intervene on the part of the worker as well as for the capitalist? Instrumental in organizing the National Labor Union, Sylvis was elected president at its second convention in Chicago in 1867.[67]

The 1867 convention drafted *The Address of the National Labor Congress to the Workingmen of America*. Thomas Armstrong, a prominent labor journalist from Pittsburgh, played a major role in the elaboration of this document. It defined the core goals of the National Labor Union to be the struggle for the eight-hour day, the opening of public lands to homesteaders, the promotion of consumer and producer cooperatives, and the organization of all workers into trade unions. It declared that "the success of our republican institutions must depend on the virtue, the intelligence and the independence of the working classes; and that any system, social or political, which tends to keep the masses in ignorance, whether by unjust or oppressive laws, or by over-manual labor, is injurious to the interests of the state and the individual."[68]

While Sylvis initially held the prevailing working-class animosity toward both Negro and female labor, he quickly grasped that labor could not become a national force for social reform without both. He welcomed women delegates to the union's conventions and supported women's trade unions and female suffrage. The 1868 convention became the first national labor body to call on employers to "do justice to women by paying them equal wages for equal work." This action impressed Karl Marx, who keenly followed American events from England. "Anybody knows, if he knows anything about history, that the great social changes are impossible without the feminine ferment. Social progress can be measured exactly by the social position of their sex." Fearing Negro loyalty to the Republican Party, Sylvis supported their inclusion in the labor movement: "If workmen of the white race do not conciliate with blacks, the blacks will vote against them" and "The Negro will take possession of the shops, if we do not take possession of the Negro."[69] In 1869, while preparing for the union's convention, he died suddenly at the age of 40. Deprived of his leadership, the organization he founded declined and disappeared three years later.

Building Business Empires

While labor was struggling to adapt to new realities, capital was pushing relentlessly to completely reorganize the existing order. The critical piece in laying the foundation of Carnegie's steel empire was the development of the Bessemer furnace. While steel had been made for thousands of years, it was an expensive, labor intensive and difficult process to obtain the correct level of carbon and eliminate silicon, phosphorous and other impurities. Its use was therefore restricted to swords, knives and razors that required a keen edge. The actual discovery of the principle involved in the new process was the work of William Kelly of Pittsburgh almost a decade before Henry Bessemer's famous discovery. In traditional iron making the blast of air was directed at the fire in order to attain the high temperatures needed for melting the iron and separating it from the slag. Kelly discovered that injecting air directly into the molten metal instead of cooling the metal, ignited it, and the resulting intense heat burned off the impurities, creating steel. In Kelly's case, however, the pig iron he was using in his furnace in Eddyville, Kentucky, was high in phosphorous that did not burn off and it rendered his steel friable and weak. Not understanding the source of the problem, Kelly abandoned the project, but patented his process. When Bessemer developed his method, by chance the ore he was using was low in phosphorous and he produced quality steel. Once the phosphorus issue was understood, the problem became for Bessemer finding the appropriate ore.[70]

Once the British obtained a source of low phosphorous ore in Spain, they were poised to provide steel rails for American railroad expansion that were qualitatively superior to the iron rails in use at the time. Two events led to Carnegie's aggressive entry into steel production. In 1866 a settlement was reached between a syndicate of Americans who had purchased Kelly's patent rights and Bessemer's agents, thus opening the American market to the Bessemer process. Even more important was the discovery in 1845 of enormous quantities of high quality iron in the upper peninsula of Michigan that was proven by chemical analysis in 1868 to be low in phosphorous. By the late 1860s a transportation network for the ore had been developed using canals, lake boats and rail that enabled the ore to be carried efficiently and cheaply to Pittsburgh. In 1872, Carnegie toured the Bessemer plants of Sheffield and Birmingham and returned with ambitious plans to launch the age of steel in America.[71]

Even before the dawn of the steel age, the enormous expansion of the furnace industries of glass and steel, plus the diversity of coal-fired steam-driven machinery was conferring on Pittsburgh the label, the "Smoky City." In 1868, James Parton, writing for the *Atlantic Monthly*, provided the description of the city that became picked up by many other writers as "hell with the lid taken off."

> Smoke, smoke, everywhere smoke! Smoke with the noise of the steam hammer and the spouting flame of tall chimneys....On the evening of this dark day we were conducted to the edge of the abyss, and looked over the iron railing upon the most striking spectacle we ever beheld. The entire space lying between the hills was filled with the blackest smoke, from out of the chimneys sent forth tongues of flame, while from the depths of the abyss came up the noise of hundreds of steam hammers...soon the wind would force the smoky curtains aside and the whole black expanse would be dimly lighted with dull wreaths of fire....If anyone would enjoy a spectacle as striking as Niagara, he may do so by simply walking up a long hill to Cliff Street in Pittsburgh and looking over into – hell with the lid taken off.[72]

Since steel-making on the scale envisioned required huge quantities of pig iron, there was also a need for the rapid expansion of iron production. In 1870, Carnegie, Kloman and Company constructed a huge furnace on the British model, over 75 feet high and 20 feet in diameter, on 51st Street in Lawrenceville. It was named Lucy after Tom Carnegie's wife. A few blocks away, a rival syndicate of iron manufactures built a furnace of the same dimensions named Isabella. By 1873, the two furnaces were breaking all English and American records and developing the "hard-driving" American method of blast furnace operation. While furnace production records had previously been at the 50-ton a day, 350 ton per week level, these two furnaces engaged in a ferocious competition that was reported in trade journals like baseball scores. In October of 1874, the Lucy furnace broke the 100-ton per-day mark, only to have the Isabella furnace surpass that on Christmas Eve with 112 tons. By 1881, Isabella was producing 215 tons a day; but two years later the Lucy furnace broke 300 tons. Ten years after their installation, they were producing in a day what the best furnaces in the world had been doing in a week.[73]

In 1873, Carnegie began the construction of the Edgar Thomson plant in Braddock on the former site of John Frazier's cabin and General Braddock's fateful fording of the Monongahela. He named the plant after Edgar Thomson, president of the Pennsylvania Railroad, whose main line ran beside the new facility. Thomson's good will was more important than ever, since Carnegie had a major falling out with his mentor, protector and key ally, Tom Scott. Carnegie refused to come to the aid of Scott, who was badly over-extended financially by a disastrous investment in the Texas and Pacific Railroad. To supervise the building of ET, as it was universally known, he chose Alexander Holley, the premier expert on the Bessemer process in America, who had constructed the Cambria steel plant in Johnstown, Pennsylvania. Holley brought William Jones with him from the Cambria works to take over as the new plant's superintendent. Captain Jones, a machinist, foundry, and furnace man, had served in the Army of the Potomac, fought at Fredericksburg and Chancellorsville, and left the service a captain. Jones was able to recruit the most talented men from the Cambria plant, bringing 200 skilled managers and workers familiar with the Bessemer process with him to run Carnegie's new mill.

As the mill was being constructed, the Panic of 1873 inaugurated one of the worst depressions in the country's history. While others panicked, Carnegie had the cash reserves and the contacts with European sources of capital to ride out the storm and turn it to his advantage. Since suppliers were desperate for his business, he was able to negotiate reduced prices for machinery and equipment. Construction workers were available in great numbers and at low wages, while the railroads were cutting rates to hold customers. It is estimated he built the great Edgar Thomson mill at three-quarters what it would have cost three years earlier. Holley's plan for ET included two Bessemer converters, a rolling mill, two Siemens' open-hearth furnaces, machine and blacksmith shops, boiler, gas and water works. The Siemens' open hearths from Germany were among the earliest constructed in the United States. They were capable of producing higher-grade steel than the Bessemers; and once the problem of removing phosphorus from low-grade ores was solved at Carnegie's Homestead Works, the open hearth surpassed the Bessemer in the mass production of steel.[74]

While Carnegie's activities in these years were to define the character of Pittsburgh as the "Steel City," other important Pittsburgh enterprises had their roots in this period as well. H. J. Heinz, Thomas Mellon and George Westinghouse all developed businesses around 1869 that would become major factors in the industrial growth of the city. Henry John Heinz was the first-born son of German immigrants living in Birmingham on the south side of the Monongahela. The family moved to the north bank of the Allegheny when he was five. The H. J. Heinz operation began as a food processing and pickling operation in Sharpsburg on the Allegheny, with the initial product being grated horseradish sold in clear glass bottles. Heinz developed 160 acres in Sharpsburg for garden crops and had substantial production in sauerkraut, pickles and vinegar. This endeavor like many others was swept away in the depression of the mid-1870s, and Heinz declared bankruptcy in 1875. Heinz was undeterred, however. He got his business going again and eventually paid off every debt, carrying a list of them around for years in a little notebook entitled "Debts of Honor."[75]

If Carnegie was the expansive, wheeling and dealing, empire builder who loved the public stage and H. J. Heinz, the focused if plodding businessman, who built his fortune by concentrating his efforts on what he knew best, then Thomas Mellon became the archetype of the relentless, meticulous financier who understood that the "money-making part of the business lay in the background." Founder of the family fortune, Thomas Mellon was born in Northern Ireland and his family settled in Westmoreland County in 1818, when he was five years old. Descendent of a soldier for Cromwell in Northern Ireland, Thomas maintained a strong disdain for "blindly ignorant and superstitious" Catholics. "Ireland…was duly, surrendered to England over seven hundred years ago…on the ground of their incapacity for self-government. And this incapacity has been abundantly manifested ever since." He believed that Cromwell, who had killed thousands of Irish, "was the only ruler who understood their nature, and governed them accordingly."[76]

As a boy of ten, Thomas Mellon walked the whole way to Pittsburgh where he saw a bigger world than the farm his father was preparing for him. He passed by the Negley mansion in what would become East Liberty, and for him it embodied a vision of wealth and success. Four years later, the reading of Ben Franklin's autobiography showed him the way. "For so poor and friendless a boy to become a merchant or professional man had before seemed an impossibility; but here was Franklin, poorer than myself, who by industry, thrift and frugality had become learned and wise, and elevated to wealth and fame." He looked askance at his Pennsylvania Dutch farmer neighbors since "the sentiments of many of them regarding sexual intercourse were rather loose." When he began stiffly courting Sarah Negley, he reported on his proposal and the passive acceptance of his kiss with the comment: "the transaction was successfully consummated." He reflected later, "If I had been rejected I would have left neither sad nor depressed, only annoyed at the waste of time."[77]

By the time they were married, Thomas was already a successful lawyer. Eight children were dutifully produced in the next seventeen years. He began to accumulate wealth from investments in commercial paper, mortgages, mechanics liens, pursuing judgments, claims, and foreclosures. After the 1845 Pittsburgh fire, he expanded into real estate in downtown and East Liberty and then moved into coal lands and companies. In 1859, the opportunity presented itself to run for Judge of the Court of Common Pleas. He was elected and served for the next ten years. When his second son, James Ross, asked his permission to join the military at the start of the Civil War, Judge Mellon was strongly opposed. He wrote his son: "In time you will come to understand and believe that a man may be patriotic without risking his own life or sacrificing his health. There are plenty of other lives less valuable or others ready to serve for the love of serving." Later, in his memoirs, he commented: "There is always a disproportionately large class of men fitted by nature for a service which requires so little brain work as that of the common soldier.... It is a mistake to suppose that it is the duty of every man to enlist when his country needs soldiers.... If a man is wise, and can perform the duties of private life with credit to himself and improve his conditions at home, he will avoid the folly of soldiering…a man whose life is of much value to himself or his family should stay at home." [78]

Estimating he was making too great a financial sacrifice by remaining a judge, Mellon decided not to run for a second ten-year term and instead organized a bank. On January 1, 1870, T. Mellon & Sons, in the five hundred block of Smithfield Street, opened its doors. Above the door stood a near life-size iron statue of Benjamin Franklin. Almost dragged under in the panic of 1873, Mellon recovered and saw the event as punishment for those who speculated and failed to exercise financial discipline and control. "The stock had to be boiled down to evaporate the water from it. Real and fictitious wealth had become so mixed up that the refining process of bankruptcy and sheriff sales became necessary to separate the dross from the true metal." Already, he was relying heavily on his sixth child, Andrew William (or A.W. – all the male Mellons, as well as H. C. Frick, went by their initials), who was only 15 when the bank opened. Together, the Mellon family increasingly evolved into finance capitalists who "invest money in a firm not for a return or a fixed percentage of interest but for a stake in the business itself." [79]

Westinghouse's Life-Saving Airbrake

Of all the industrialists and successful businessmen that came out of Pittsburgh, none is so attractive a personage as George Westinghouse. His goal was never the acquisition of fortune or fame, but the creation of useful things. In that, he was like H. J. Heinz but his achievements were much broader and more diverse. Born in 1845, he was the eighth child, a fourth generation American of German and Dutch-English stock. His father, also George, was a builder and inventor of agricultural machinery and small steam engines in Schenectady, New York. His shop there eventually sat near the entry of the mother plant of the General Electric Company of Thomas Edison, his son's greatest rival and competitor. The elder George held at least seven patents. These inventions displayed the same characteristics of the more than four hundred that would be created by his son. "Not one of the son's patents is a flash out of the blue sky or a vision on the horizon. Every one is calculated to meet a situation he has seen in his own practice. Everyone is for something to be made in his own shops and not one of them was invented to sell or as a speculation. Every one is worked out with such completeness of detail that a competent shop foreman could take the Patent Office drawing and specifications and build an operative machine. In each one we see the engineer and the trained mechanic." [80]

Three of the Westinghouse boys served in the Civil War. George's older brother, Albert, was killed leading a cavalry charge in 1864. George ran away at fourteen to enlist but was blocked by his father until he was 16. He served in the infantry and the cavalry, and ended up an engineer and officer in the Navy. His youngest brother Henry Herman Westinghouse became a life-long business and engineering partner. Twenty year-old George met his wife Marguerite Walker on a train and announced to his startled parents the same night that he had met the girl he was going to marry. They were affectionately married for 47 years, she passing 3 months after he did. He bought a large old house near the Homewood station of the Pennsylvania Railroad, added on to it and surrounded it with lawns and gardens. "It was the seat of a large and handsome hospitality. There were few houses in the land in which one would meet such a number and variety of interesting people as passed through that simple and comfortable home."[81]

George Westinghouse's first patent at the age of 20 was for a rotary steam engine, and his final one, designed while suffering his fatal illness, was for a wheel chair to be operated by a small electric motor. His rotary engine was a plaything that occupied him much of his life, "the equivalent of a rubber of bridge, or a game of golf…He used to relate that a small boy who had made a picture of a minister and found it unsatisfactory added a tail and called it a dog. Encouraged by this, Westinghouse turned his rotary engine around and made an excellent water meter out of it and established another industry." Early on he focused on problems of railroad safety. These concerns were heightened when he witnessed at close-hand, a head-on collision between two heavily loaded freight trains. "A short distance ahead the distorted hulks of two locomotives, and a stretch of track strewn with overturned or broken cars and the remains of what had been a solid cargo of merchandise…the day was clear, the roadbed at that point was level, the track was well railed and smooth and straight; it seemed as if a collision could have hardly occurred except through gross carelessness." When Westinghouse questioned the employees, however, one said: "The engineers saw each other, and both tried their best to stop, but they couldn't." "Why not? Wouldn't the brakes work?" "Oh, yes, but there wasn't time. You can't stop a train in a moment."[82]

Out of this incident grew the first two great companies that Westinghouse created: the Westinghouse Airbrake and Union Switch and Signal. The former created the mechanism to stop the trains in time; the second, the systems to keep two trains from ever moving into the same section of track at once. Before Westinghouse invented these critical safety mechanisms, railroading was a perilous adventure plagued by spectacular crashes with death and dismemberment a daily possibility for trainmen. As Westinghouse biographer, Frances E. Leupp, explained:

> Hand-braking was both difficult and dangerous. A brakeman stood between every two cars on a passenger train, and, at a point about a half a mile from the next stopping place, he would begin to turn a horizontal hand wheel on one platform so as to tighten slowly a chain that set the brakes on a single pair of wheels. When he had wound the chain taut he would step across to the opposite platform and repeat the operation on the hand wheel there. No matter how skilled all the brakemen on a train might be, their work was always uneven, for no two cars would respond to the brake with the same promptness, and the slower ones would bump into the quicker, adding to the hazards of the task. A freight train was harder to care for than a passenger train, because the brakeman had to ride on top of the cars in all weathers, with the liability of being knocked off by a low bridge, frozen in midwinter, or, on windy or slippery nights, missing his footing and falling beneath the cars.[83]

Aside from the safety concerns, primitive hand braking severely limited both the length and speed of trains. At the time of the Civil War, cars were made of wood and freight trains carried at most 20 cars at speeds of 11-20 miles per hour, with passenger trains of 5-10 cars attaining speeds of about 30 mph.[84]

Westinghouse tried a number of mechanical solutions to the braking problem without success. While pondering the problem in his office one day, a young woman came to his door selling magazines. At first, he brusquely dismissed her, "I never read magazines"; but she pleaded saying she was studying to be a teacher, so he took the issue of the *Living Age* and passing over the fiction he noticed an article "In the Mont Cenis Tunnel." He gave her two dollars for a three-month subscription, and that article provided the answer he sought. He read how a British steam drill, adapted by Italian engineers drilling inside the first tunnel through the Alps, was linked to a compressed air motor they had invented to solve the problem of drilling three miles inside a tunnel with limited air supply. "If compressed air could be conveyed through 3,000 feet of pipe and yet retain enough efficiency to drive a drill through the solid stone heart of a mountain chain, it could certainly be carried the length of a railroad train and still exert the force required to set the brakes on the hindmost car."[85]

In 1868, Westinghouse came to Pittsburgh to seek financing and manufacturing space to produce his new airbrake. In a famous demonstration of his initial or "straight" airbrake that year, a group of railroad men were taken for a test trip on the Panhandle Railroad in a short train equipped with the apparatus. As the locomotive approached a road crossing near the Panhandle Railroad bridge over the Monongahela, a teamster in his wagon crossed in front of the train. The investors and railroad managers got a dramatic demonstration (along with some bumps and bruises) of the brakes' stopping power. George telegraphed his father in Schenectady: "My airbrake had practical trial today on a passenger train on Panhandle Railroad and proved great success." In the next five years, over two thousand locomotives and seven thousand railcars, over a third of all rolling stock operating in the United States, were equipped with the brake manufactured at the new Airbrake plant at the corner of Liberty Avenue and 25th Street. By 1875, a major safety improvement was made with the development of the "automatic" airbrake which provided a fail-safe system; where, if a brake line was severed or the system was compromised, the brakes would automatically set and stop the train. Westinghouse was on his way and so was modern rail transportation. [86]

Meanwhile, the great Civil War had set Pittsburgh firmly on the path of mechanization and industrial discipline. The next generation would move the city from iron to steel and completely transform its generation of power, but its importance as a source of industrial might and war materials production was set and would endure more than a century. The city was becoming wealthy as well. A great new market was built in Allegheny City in 1869 (tragically destroyed nearly a century later to erect a poorly constructed and ill-fated urban mall), and a new Pittsburgh City Hall was dedicated in 1872. The market harkened back to an earlier age, albeit on a grander scale; but the new City Hall was the very symbol of modernity, since its turret clock was directly connected to the Allegheny Observatory where a highly accurate standard time was determined. A very large bell was rung eight times a day or every three hours, so that all that class of people affluent enough to possess a timepiece could set their mechanisms. Meanwhile "Pittsburgh time" was communicated by telegraph out to the railroads where it enabled timetables to be met and connections to be made efficiently. Increasingly, the city itself began to resemble a giant mechanism that shaped and dominated the life of its people with diminishing regard for day and night or the changing seasons. The age of the machine had arrived.[87]

Notes Chapter 5

[1]Laurence A. Glasco, ed., *The WPA History of the Negro in Pittsburgh* (Pittsburgh: University of Pittsburgh Press, 2004), 79.

[2]William J. Switala, *Underground Railroad in Pennsylvania* (Mechanicsburg: Stackpole Books, 2001), 81-5.; Catherine Hanchett, "George Boyer Vashon, 1824-1878: Black Education, Poet, Fighter for Equal Rights," *Western Pennsylvania Historical Magazine* (1985), 205-9.; Ervin Dyer, "Noted Hill Abolitionist Forgotten No Longer," *Pittsburgh Post Gazette*, 2004.

[3]Eric Ledell Smith, "The Pittsburgh Memorial: A Forgotten Document of Pittsburgh History," *Pittsburgh History* (1997), 8(3):109.

[4]Smith, *Pittsburgh History*, 108.

[5]Glasco, *The WPA History of the Negro in Pittsburgh*, 123-4.

[6]Glasco, *The WPA History of the Negro in Pittsburgh*, 127

[7]*The Mystery*, December 16, 1846.

[8]Glasco, *The WPA History of the Negro in Pittsburgh*, 84, 87.

[9]Switala, *Underground Railroad in Pennsylvania*, 81-3.

[10]R.J.M Blackett, "Freedom, or the Martyr's Grave: Black Pittsburgh's Aid to the Fugitive Slave," *African Americans in Pennsylvania* (University Park: Pennsylvania State University Press, 1997), 153.

[11]Blackett, *African Americans in Pennsylvania*, 149; Glasco, *The WPA History of the Negro in Pittsburgh*, 85.

[12]Irene E. Williams, "The Operation of the Fugitive Slave Law in Western Pennsylvania from 1850-1860," *Western Pennsylvania Historical Magazine* (July 1921), 152.

[13]Williams, "The Operation of the Fugitive Slave Law in Western Pennsylvania from 1850-1860," 152. This source makes no mention of Delany's speech reported below.

[14]Martin Delany, Martin Delany's Speeches, *West Virginia University Libraries*, 30 September 1850, [database online] [cited 18 March 2007].

[15]Martin Delany, *Blake or the Huts of America*, (Boston: Beacon Press, 1970), see the useful introduction by Floyd J. Miller, xi-xxv; W.E. Burghardt Dubois, *John Brown* (New York: International Publishers, 1969), 254-63; Glasco, *The WPA History of the Negro in Pittsburgh,* 88-9.

[16]Williams, "The Operation of the Fugitive Slave Law in Western Pennsylvania from 1850-1860," 154-5.

[17]Mary Ellen Leigh McBridge, "Jane Grey Swisshelm," in *Famous Men & Women of Pittsburgh*, ed. Leonore R. Elkus (Pittsburgh: Pittsburgh History & Landmarks Foundation, 1981), 34. I have excerpted this passage from McBridge's artfully edited version that does no disservice to the meaning of the original. Swisshelm's much longer and more rambling account is in *Half a Century* p. 128-32.

[18]Charles W. Dahlinger, "The Republic Party Originated in Pittsburgh," *Western Pennsylvania Historical Magazine*, (January 1921), 3.

[19]Michael Fitzgibbon Holt, *Forging a Majority: The Formation of the Republican Party in Pittsburgh, 1848-1860* (Pittsburgh: University of Pittsburgh Press, 1990), 133.

[20]Holt, *Forging a Majority*, 133-4.; John F. Coleman, *The Disruption of the Pennsylvania Democracy, 1848-1860* (Harrisburg: The Pennsylvania Historical and Museum Commission, 1975), 65-6.

[21]Sylvia D. Hoffert, *Jane Grey Swisshelm: An Unconventional Life*, 1815-1884, (Chapel Hill: The University of North Carolina Press, 2004), 27-28.

[22]Coleman, *The Disruption of the Pennsylvania Democracy 1848-1860*, 64-65.

[23]Dahlinger, "The Republic Party Originated in Pittsburgh," 3.

[24]Philip S. Foner, *History of the Labor Movement in the United States* (New York: International Publishers, 1962), vol. 1, 287.

[25]Mary Katherine Donaldson, *Composition in Early Landscapes of the Ohio River Valley: Background and Components* (Dissertation: University of Pittsburgh, 1971), 219-220.

[26]Fletcher Hodges, Jr., *Stephen Foster, Maker of American Songs*, Historical Pennsylvania Leaflet No. 3, ed. Leonore R. Elkus Harrisburg: Pennsylvania Historical and Museum Commission, 1977), 67-84.

[27]James Thomas Flexner, "The Dark World of David Gilmour Blyth," *American Heritage Magazine* (1962), 25, 77. Ironically, or maybe because Blythe's vision corresponded with their own view of the poor, many of his paintings adorn the walls of the Duquesne Club, the center of corporate power in Pittsburgh. There they compete with English landscapes and scenes of fox hunting.

[28]Herdis B. Teilman, "Mary Cassatt," in *Famous Men and Women of Pittsburgh*, ed. Leonore Elkus (Pittsburgh: Pittsburgh History and Landmarks Foundation, 1981).

[29]Holt, *Forging a Majority*, 229.

[30]Holt, *Forging a Majority*, 229-30.

[31]David H. Wollman and Donald R. Inman, *Portraits in Steel: An Illustrated History of Jones & Laughlin Steel Corporation* (Kent: The Kent State University Press, 1999), 10-20.; Ken Kobus, *Supporting Documentation for the Clinton Furnace Historical Marker* (Harrisburg: Pennsylvania Historical and Museum Commission, 2002).

[32] James J. Davis, *The Iron Puddler, My Life in the Rolling Mills and What Came of It* (New York: Grosset & Dunlap, 1922); Wollman and Inman, *Portraits in Steel*, 22-31.

[33] Foner, *History of the Labor Movement: From Colonial Times to the Founding of the American Federation of Labor*, 237; Meyer A. Sanders, "Labor," *Allegheny County: A Sesqui-Centennial Review, 1788…1938*, ed. George E. Kelly (Pittsburgh: Allegheny Sesqui-Centennial Committee, 1938), 130-132.

[34] Herbert Asbury, *The Golden Flood: An Informal History of America's First Oil Field* (New York: Alfred A. Knopf, 1942), 8.

[35] Asbury, *The Golden Flood*, 24-30.

[36] Asbury, *The Golden Flood*, 31-9, 57.

[37] Asbury, *The Golden Flood*, 102.

[38] Asbury, *The Golden Flood*, 105.

[39] Anonymous. "Western Pennsylvania and the Election of 1860," *Western Pennsylvania Historical Magazine* (1923), 31.

[40] *The Daily Post*, October 31, 1860.

[41] Arthur B. Fox, *Pittsburgh During the American Civil War 1860-1865*, (Chicora Pa: Mechling Bookbindery, 2002), 13. This book opens many doors for the person interested in Pittsburgh and the Civil War.

[42] A plaque commemorating this event is on the Allegheny County Courthouse, Grant Street.

[43] *Pittsburgh Post Gazette*, December 25, 1860; John Newton Boucher, ed., *A Century and a Half of Pittsburgh and Her People* (Cherry Hill: The Lewis Publishing Co., 1908), II: 151-3.

[44] Boucher, *Century and a Half of Pittsburgh and Her People*, 151-3.; Charles W. Dahlinger, "Abraham Lincoln in Pittsburgh and the Republican Party," *The Western Pennsylvania Historical Magazine* (October 1920), 145-76.; *The Pittsburgh Evening Chronicle*, February 15, 1861; J.H. Cramer, "A President-Elect in Western Pennsylvania," *Western Pennsylvania Historical Magazine* (July 1947), 71:206-217.

[45] Fox, *Pittsburgh During the American Civil War*, 16.

[46] Fox, *Pittsburgh During the American Civil War*, 39-61 for a description of the camps and their locations.

[47] Leland D. Baldwin, *Pittsburgh: The Story of a City, 1750-1865* (Pittsburgh: University of Pittsburgh Press, 1970) 323.

[48] Fox, *Pittsburgh During the American Civil War*, 74-78, 84-5.

[49] Fox, *Pittsburgh During the American Civil War*, 75-78.

[50] Samuel P. Bates, "The Fort Pitt Works," *The Martial Deeds of Pennsylvania*, (Philadelphia: T.H. Davis & Co., 1876), 1041-1048; 135; quoted in Fox, 135.

[51] Major T.J. Rodman, "Testimony," *Report of the Joint Committee on the Conduct of War, 1864* (Port Huron: Antique Ordnance Publishers, 1980); Fox, *Pittsburgh During the American Civil War*, 139-45; Details of the casting and machining of the Rodman gun are in *Casting the 15 in. Gun: Fort Pitt, 1864*, (Port Huron: Antique Ordinance Publishers, 1980); Edward G. Williams, "Pittsburgh, Birthplace of a Science," *Western Pennsylvania Historical Magazine*, September, 1962.

[52] Israel Rupp, *Early History of Western Pennsylvania*, (1846), 318-319; James Wudarczyk, "A Lost Landmark: A Study of the Fate of the Allegheny Arsenal," *The Western Pennsylvania Historical Magazine* (1987); James Wudarczyk, *Pittsburgh's Forgotten Allegheny Arsenal* (Apollo: Closson Press, 1935); James Wudarczyk, A Decision to Destroy: A Study of the Fate of the Allegheny Arsenal, *Notes and Documents Relating to Pittsburgh's Allegheny Arsenal*, (Pittsburgh: Carnegie Library, 1997) Wudarczyk advances the claim for it as the worst civilian disaster of the Civil War while the claim that it was Pittsburgh's worst industrial accident is the author's. Bound manuscripts of these works are available in the Pennsylvania Room, Carnegie Library; Fox, *Pittsburgh During the American Civil War*, 116.

[53] Fox, *Pittsburgh During the American Civil War*, 118-9.; Allan Becer, "An Appalling Disaster: The Allegheny Arsenal and the Great Explosion of 1862" paper present at The 26th Annual Duquesne University History Forum (Pittsburgh: 1993); *Pittsburgh Evening Chronicle*, September 18, 1862.

[54] *Pittsburgh Evening Chronicle*, September 18, 1862.

[55] *Daily Post*, September 20, 1862.

[56] *Daily Post*, September 20, 1862; Boucher, *A Century and a Half of Pittsburgh and Her People*.

[57] Becer, "An Appalling Disaster: The Allegheny Arsenal and the Great Explosion of 1862."

[58] Fox, *Pittsburgh During the American Civil War*, 182; Bill McCarthy, "One Month in the Summer of '63: Pittsburgh Prepares for the Civil War," *Pittsburgh History* (1998), 118-133;

[59] Ron Gancas, *Field of Freedom: United States Colored Troops for Southwestern Pennsylvania* (Pittsburgh: Soldiers & Sailors Memorial Hall and Museum Trust, Inc., 2004), 9-10, 37, 46, 97.

[60] Clarke M. Thomas, *Front Page Pittsburgh: Two Hundred Years of the Post Gazette*. (Pittsburgh: University of Pittsburgh Press, 2005) 99.

[61] Joseph Frazier Wall, *Andrew Carnegie* (Pittsburgh: University of Pittsburgh Press, 1989), 90.

[62] Wall, *Andrew Carnegie*, 145-91.

[63] Wall, *Andrew Carnegie*, 268. The story of the St. Louis Bridge is on pp. 269-78.

[64] Edward Pinkowski, John Siney: *The Miners' Martyr*, (Philadelphia: Sunshine Press, 1963), 55-217.

[65] Jonathan P. Grossman, *William Sylvis, Pioneer of American Labor: A Study of the Labor Movement During the Era of the Civil War* (Cincinnati: The Sylvis Society, 1986), 136, 141.

[66] Grossman, *William Sylvis, Pioneer of American Labor*, 136, 141 Quotes p. 167, 179.

[67] Grossman, *William Sylvis, Pioneer of American Labor*, 189-219.

[68] David Montgomery, *Beyond Equality: Labor and the Radical Republicans 1862-1872* (New York: Vintage Books, 1967), 177.

[69] Foner, *History of the Labor Movement: From Colonial Times to the Founding of the American Federation of Labor*, 231, 385.

[70] Wall, *Andrew Carnegie*, 261-263.

[71] Wall, *Andrew Carnegie*, 263-266.

[72] Angela Gugliotta, *"Hell With the Lid Taken Off:" A Cultural History of Air Pollution – Pittsburgh*, (Dissertation, Graduate Program in History, University of Notre Dame, 2004), 85. This dissertation, available on line, is a comprehensive account of the attitude of writers who were both impressed and repelled by the dark, satanic aspects of the premier American industrial city.

[73] Wall, *Andrew Carnegie*, 323-324.

[74] Wall, *Andrew Carnegie*, 311-321.

[75] Robert C. Alberts, *The Good Provider: H. J. Heinz and His 57 Varieties* (Boston: Houghton Mifflin Company, 1973); Robert C. Alberts, "H. J. Heinz" in *Famous Men and Women of Pittsburgh*, ed. Leonore R. Elkus (Pittsburgh: Pittsburgh History and Landmarks Foundation, 1981), 55-56.

[76] William S. Hoffman, *Paul Mellon: Portrait of an Oil Baron* (Chicago: Follett Publishing Company, 1974), 33-4.

[77] David E. Koskoff, *The Mellons: The Chronicle of America's Richest Family* (New York: Thomas Y. Crowell, 1978), 5-11.

[78] Koskoff, *The Mellons*, 25-9.

[79] Koskoff, *The Mellons*, 38.

[80] Henry G. Prout, *A Life of George Westinghouse* (New York: Charles Scribner's Sons, 1922), 6.

[81] Prout, *A Life of George Westinghouse*, 3-9.

[82] Prout, *A Life of George Westinghouse*, 8; Francis E. Leupp, *George Westinghouse: His Life and Achievements* (Boston: Little, Brown and Company, 1918), 48.

[83] Leupp, *George Westinghouse*, 47-8.

[84] Fox, *Pittsburgh During the American Civil War*, 89.

[85] Leupp, *George Westinghouse*, 52-5.

[86] Leupp, *George Westinghouse*, 71; Prout, A Life of George Westinghouse, 31; for a detailed description of the airbrake's development, see Prout, *A Life of George Westinghouse*, 21-76.

[87] *The City Hall, Pittsburgh* (Pittsburgh: Stevenson & Foster, 1874).

Chapter Six

Dominance and Resistance

The year 1877 marks an important transition in the history of the United States. The nation's hundredth birthday had been celebrated the previous year in Philadelphia with an extravagant display of national optimism. America, on the threshold of its second century, was undergoing fundamental transformation, and Pittsburgh was on the cutting edge. A new corporate industrial society was in the process of radically changing the agricultural, mechanical and commercial republic of the Founding Fathers. The great upheaval occasioned by the railroad strikes of 1877 constituted the "labor pains" of a new economic order. The expansionist designs of far-reaching empires of business began to drive the imperial politics of industrial nations while it transformed the urban and rural landscape and economy. Corporate power was achieving dominance, but fierce resistance emerged from within the new industrial workforce that it had called into being.

The Great Uprising

At the height of the centennial hoopla in 1876 came reports of the annihilation of George Armstrong Custer's Seventh Cavalry detachment at the hands of the Sioux, Cheyenne and Arapaho warriors at the Little Bighorn. While the country received the news with a shiver conditioned by more than two-hundred-fifty years of virtually continuous "Indian Wars" that were interwoven with every advance of the settlers, the Battle of the Little Bighorn marked the last major victory of native peoples against the invaders and the end of an era. As the "redskin" menace faded on the frontier, a new menace to American expansionism manifested itself in the form of labor agitators, radicals, revolutionaries, anarchists and communists. The reds replaced the redskins. The new barbarians were not on the frontier, but inside the gates, conjured up out of the bowels of the great leviathan of the new industrial order. The reds were not distinguished by color of their skin, but by the content of their thoughts - and the actions and organizations inspired by their beliefs. The sight of the blood red flag of the Commune flying for two months over the city of Paris in 1871 sparked anxiety in men of property who feared the contagion of this foreign virus. The events of 1877 confirmed their darkest fears about industrial labor and the intentions of those who aspired to organize it.[1]

The Panic of 1873 ushered in a serious depression that caused large-scale unemployment and wage reductions in many industries. Cities were especially hard hit as new technologies and efficiencies of operation impacted many traditional crafts and trades. Railroads, expanding at a phenomenal rate, were especially vulnerable as the speculative bubble burst. Furthermore, while Westinghouse's airbrakes represented a tremendous advance in terms of operational safety, their rapid implementation on the railroads, especially their aggressive installation on the Pennsylvania Railroad, threw many brakemen into the already swollen "grand army of starvation."[2] Improved braking capacity also allowed "double-heading" of locomotives, radically increasing the length of trains and causing job cuts among conductors and other railroad workers.

The "Compromise of 1877" marking the end of Reconstruction was the result of a deal between the dominant business wing of the Republican Party and Southern Democrats that secured the presidency for Rutherford B. Hayes and removed federal troops from the South. Congressional Southern Democrats abandoned their party's candidate, Governor Samuel Tilden of New York, winner of the popular vote and probably the presidency, in return for control of the two remaining Republican state governments in the South and a southern transcontinental railway. Hayes was awarded the disputed state of Florida, thereby being elected by one electoral vote. Federal troops were withdrawn from the South, leading gradually to the political disenfranchisement of the Negro and establishment of segregation. The key figure in securing the presidency for Hayes was the Pennsylvania Railroad's Tom Scott. [3]

The Pennsylvania Railroad was the dominant rail system in a nation that was becoming increasingly unified by strands of iron. In 1869, the continent was spanned from sea to sea. In the same year, the Pennsylvania took control of the Pittsburgh, Fort Wayne and Chicago Railroad, as well as extended their control over a number of smaller lines to connect to Cincinnati. By 1877, 79,000 miles of track formed the infrastructure of the new industrial order creating a unified national market. The Pennsylvania Railroad was the nation's single greatest enterprise with 6,600 miles of track and 200,000 employees. Railroads often owned mills and mines and controlled vast acreage of land, especially in the West. They attracted speculators and corrupted legislatures. They could create booms or strangle regional economies by the manipulation of rate structures. In Pittsburgh, the control of the Pennsylvania and its subsidiary lines over nearly every rail entry into the city, with the abuses commonly associated with monopoly, fueled the resentment of all social classes. It was cheaper for a Chicago merchant to ship his freight to Philadelphia through Pittsburgh than to ship it to Pittsburgh itself. For more than forty years, until 1872, the political muscle of the Pennsylvania Railroad repeatedly blocked the entry of the rival Baltimore and Ohio into Pittsburgh.[4]

By 1877, masses of unemployed gathered in the cities, while migrant workers characterized as tramps and hobos roamed the countryside searching for means of subsistence by hook or by crook. It was the participation of large numbers of unemployed that gave the railroad strikes an aspect of insurrection. Huge debts, declining freight and cutthroat competition were pushing railroads and other companies to the brink of bankruptcy. Unwilling to cut investor dividends, the railroads began to impose systematic wage cuts and undertook a concerted attack on the Brotherhood of Railway Engineers, a generally conservative body representing the most skilled and best organized trade on the roads. An agreement reached in May by the four largest eastern rail lines to end their rate wars included a joint decision to cut wages by 10%, the second such cut since the first of the year. These cuts were combined with new policies to increase the size of the trains.

Worker anger against the corporations, especially among the Irish who were concentrated in mining, canal and railroad construction, railroad operation and iron-making, was fueled by deep resentments stirred by the hangings of the so-called Molly Maguires in Pottsville and Mauch Chunk in the anthracite coalfields of eastern Pennsylvania. Franklin Gowan of the Reading Railroad engineered the executions of June 21, 1877, the first half of a total of twenty Irish Catholic labor activists, with the assistance of the Pinkerton detective agency. The hangings followed the crushing of the Workman's Benevolent Society, the first successful American coal miners' union led by John Siney, and the breaking of a strike by engineers on the Reading railroad. Gowan organized his Coal and Iron Police into a disciplined private military force that became a model for other industrial concerns.[5]

Resistance began to take shape in Pittsburgh. Meeting at Dietrich's Hall in Allegheny City, trainmen on the Pittsburgh, Fort Wayne and Chicago (a westward subsidiary of the Pennsylvania) met to discuss the need for a new organization uniting engineers, conductors, brakemen, and firemen on the three great trunk lines of the country into one solid body. They formed a secret organization, the Trainmen's Union. The leader of the organization was Robert Ammon, son of a Pittsburgh insurance man, who by the age of 25 had been expelled from university, served as a bugler in the U.S. Cavalry and sailed to China and South America. He returned from his adventures to Pittsburgh, where he took a job as brakeman on the PFW&C. In late June, a planned strike by the Trainmen's Union was aborted by the mass firings of union activists only days after the hanging of the Mollies. Company informers had succeeded in penetrating the union organization. The stage was now set for an explosion. Concerted activity by powerful employers against their employees triggered a generalized revolt that rode the rails across a continent and flared up in violent confrontations in a dozen states in a matter of a few weeks. Suppression of workers' organizations contributed to the fact that the movement had no nationally recognized leadership and lacked clearly defined goals or organized expression. The revolt was widespread and decentralized, local and intense.[6]

The spark was lit on the Baltimore & Ohio, already paying the lowest wages in the nation. While firemen had seen their wages drop from $55 a month in 1873 to a mere $30 in 1877, brakemen, whose hazardous work tended to fuel a radical attitude, had suffered an even more severe cut from $70 to $30 a month with wage cuts, job combinations and less employment. On July 11, the road announced another cut of 10%, dropping brakemen's wages to $1.50 a day. The cruelest blow came, however, on July 15 when the *Baltimore Sun* published the railroad's report to the board of directors citing the "entirely satisfactory" nature of the business and voted the usual 10% dividend for their stockholders. On Monday, July 16, the strike began when firemen deserted their engines at Camden Junction outside Baltimore. The strike quickly spread to Martinsburg, West Virginia, a major repair station on the line and a Trainmen's Union stronghold, where most of the town supported the desperate strikers. The governor quickly sent militia to the scene at the request of the company, despite the fact there had been little violence. Large crowds and defiance by strikers blocked the trains until the end of the week when President Hayes agreed to dispatch federal troops to protect replacement workers and move the freight. It marked the first time federal troops were employed in a labor dispute.[7]

Railroad workers all over the country responded to news of the strike on the B&O. Tension mounted in many towns and cities and spread out along the rails. In Pittsburgh, the strike began on Thursday morning, July 19, when a crew refused to take out an eastbound doubleheader freight train with thirty-six cars. A crowd of trainmen gathered and successfully blocked all freight trains leaving the yard. A "large and very enthusiastic meeting" of the Trainmen's Union was held in Pittsburgh that evening at the Phoenix Hall on Eleventh Street, where numerous speakers expressed their determination to continue the strike against the reduction in wages and the doubling of the length of trains (from 17 to 34 cars). When the undermanned Pittsburgh police force proved inadequate to disperse the swelling crowd of strikers estimated at 500 by the *New York Times*, the Pittsburgh militia was called out, but quickly demonstrated a lack of enthusiasm in confronting the strikers. Fraternization was rife. On Friday, July 20, the union shut down the Pittsburgh and Fort Wayne in Allegheny City, while in Baltimore militia troops fired into an angry crowd killing eleven.. In Pittsburgh, as crews came in to leave their trains and join the strike, the cars kept building up with from 900 to 1,500 jamming all available sidings. When Allegheny County Sheriff R. C. Fife attempted to read the riot act to the strikers at the East Liberty Station yards, he was met with cries of: "Give us a loaf of bread." A worker's committee met with Pennsylvania Railroad officials, Alexander Cassatt and James Pitcairn, demanding a rollback of the latest 10% wage cut and an end to doubleheaders. They were rebuffed, with Cassatt remarking: "They proposed taking the road out of our hands." Witnessing the disintegration of the Pittsburgh militia as an effective defender of property rights, Scott arranged the dispatch of the Philadelphia militia across the state on his railroad to break the strike. Introducing the Philadelphia militia into Pittsburgh provided the spark that ignited the conflagration.[8]

On Saturday morning, strikers controlled the yards and maintained the peace. The union allowed passenger and mail trains to pass freely and all freight destined for Pittsburgh to be unloaded and delivered. They detained, however, all through freight trains. In the early afternoon, around one thousand Philadelphia militiamen arrived on two successive passenger trains. A solid line of soldiers advanced with fixed bayonets from the Union Depot toward the huge crowd of trainmen, sympathetic workers, the unemployed, and a number of women and children, gathered at the outer freight depot approximately fifteen blocks up the tracks. To the soldiers' right stretched the steep bluffs of Herron Hill, to their left along the river lay the crowded streets of the Strip warehouse district that blended into the industrial and heavily Irish section of Lawrenceville. The Philadelphians forced the crowd back to the 28th Street Crossing where the yard abruptly narrowed. This action provoked pushing and shoving and an angry outcry.

The order was given to move forward with bayonets, and several people in the front ranks were stabbed. Some in the crowd let loose with a volley of stones. The troops were ordered to load their rifles. Shortly thereafter, firing broke out with many soldiers shooting directly into the crowd. Within a few minutes, approximately 20 were killed and 30 wounded. The dead included a woman and at least one child. The *New York Times* headlines describing events of July 21 include: A TERRIBLE DAY IN PITTSBURGH – A GREAT RIOT IN PROGRESS-ONE THOUSAND MILITIAMEN ON THE GROUND - THEY FIRE INTO A CROWD OF SPECTATORS - TWENTY OR THIRTY KILLED AND A NUMBER WOUNDED – THE MILITIA SURROUNDED BY A HOWLING MOB – THREE OF THEM KILLED BY THE RIOTERS, WHO APPEAR TO BE MASTERS OF THE SITUATION.[9]

The militia held its ground until evening when it retreated back to the roundhouse at 26th Street where the siege began. Pittsburgh's Sixth Regiment of militia, which had watched the confrontation with mounting anger and indignation from the nearby hillside, now known as Polish Hill, completely disintegrated. Soldiers were seen ripping off their uniforms and some joined the siege of the roundhouse. Gun shops were broken into, and the aroused crowd proceeded to put the railroad company's property to the torch. Women were noticeably active, urging on the crowd while providing food and drink to the besiegers, and assisting with the wholesale removal of goods that preceded the burning of cars. Catholic Bishop John Tuigg was very visible, moving among the crowd trying to stop the violence and destruction. The Philadelphia Blues endured a hellacious night as the rail yard became an inferno that destroyed a hundred twenty-five locomotives, more than a thousand freight cars, and thirty-nine railroad buildings. Energetic efforts were expended trying to burn down the roundhouse and gunfire was directed at the alien militia throughout the night. At dawn on Sunday, July 22, the Philadelphians marched out of the burning roundhouse.[10]

A lull in the action as dawn approached afforded the troops, who were in danger of being burnt alive, an opportunity to emerge from their defenses. They marched up Liberty to 33rd Street where they turned right and climbed the grade to Penn Avenue. Their objective was the United States Arsenal. The rioters discovered their retreat and armed men followed in pursuit. The Philadelphians marched in good order but were fired on from the street corners, alleyways, windows and housetops. They returned fire, once using their Gatling guns. When they reached the Arsenal, the federal commandant refused to admit them. He said he had but ten men and would be powerless to hold the place if the mob should attack it. He consented to take care of the wounded, and they were accordingly carried to the hospital. The Philadelphians counted six dead and thirty-seven wounded during Saturday's battle, plus three more lost during the retreat.[11]

The situation across the river in the City of Allegheny was dramatically different. Allegheny was the domain of "boss" Ammon, the young brakeman, leader of the Trainmen's Union. He made a pact with Allegheny Mayor Philips to protect railroad property, if, in return, no troops were summoned. Colonel Smith, an alderman of the town, described the situation to the Pennsylvania Legislative Committee that investigated the riots:

> Several days prior to the burning in Pittsburgh, the strikers took possession of the railroad tracks and the workshops of the Pennsylvania company operating the Pittsburgh, Fort Wayne and Chicago railroad. They threw up breastworks and held armed possession of the railroad property and even took possession of and regulated the running of passenger trains and the United States mail trains. At all interviews, they insisted that it was not their intention to destroy property but to protect railroad property, and they wouldn't commit any overt act in violation of law, as they understood it. Many of them believed that they were not violating any law and assumed that they had a right to accomplish the object they had in view by the method they were then pursuing. The authorities and the citizens of Allegheny City knew they were dealing with a powerful, intelligent, and well organized body of men, who were determined and resolute in their purposes. To have attempted to have forced these men from their position would have precipitated the same troubles that culminated in Pittsburgh a few days subsequently. So the citizens appealed to the better judgment of those strikers, they reasoned with them, and instead of irritating them, or attempting to force them, they permitted them to have their own way, believing the railroad officials and their employees, would in a few days, adjust all differences. This policy, under the circumstances, proved a wise one, as when danger came; and when the mob were burning and destroying in Pittsburgh, the strikers in Allegheny actually removed all the rolling stock out of the way of danger and volunteered to assist the organized citizens in protecting the depots and workshops and all other railroad

property in the city of Allegheny. Had the same policy been pursued in Pittsburgh, there would have been no destruction of property.[12]

Robert Ammon ran the passenger side of his railroad for three days while commanding his army of strikers. He personally welcomed Pennsylvania's governor to Allegheny City guaranteeing him safe passage upon his hasty return from Montana, while forcing him to address the strikers upon his arrival. When Ammon urged his followers to abandon the strike, however, they deserted him, and he withdrew from the field.[13] The stark contrast between the events in Allegheny City and Pittsburgh give credence to the judgment rendered on the strike by Mother Jones in her *Autobiography*:

> The strikers were charged with the crimes of arson and rioting, although it was common knowledge that it was not they who instigated the fire; that it was started by hoodlums backed by the business men of Pittsburgh who for a long time had felt that the Railroad Company discriminated against their city in the matter of rates. I knew the strikers personally. I knew that it was they who had tried to enforce orderly law. I knew they disciplined their members when they did violence. I knew, as everybody knew, who really perpetrated the crime of burning the railroad's property. Then and there I learned in the early part of my career that labor must bear the cross for others' sins, must be the vicarious sufferer for the wrongs that others do.[14]

On Wednesday, July 26, President Hayes, convinced by his political mentor, Tom Scott, that the strikers were waging war against the United States, decided that state and federal troops should "open the road to Pittsburgh." Accordingly, with a special train provided by the Pennsylvania Railroad as a mobile command post, a contingent of troop trains carrying six hundred US Army troops and two thousand state militiamen armed with Gatling guns arrived in Pittsburgh on Saturday, July 28. The rail companies reasserted control of their property and their employees. Allegheny County was forced to pay $1.6 million to the Pennsylvania Railroad for damages incurred in the riot. Once the corporation's control was re-established over the Pennsylvania's rails, Federal troops with the National Guard marched into the anthracite coalfields to break the persistent miners' strikes there. They occupied the anthracite region for three months.[15]

Remaking the Craftsman's City

While the railroad strike collapsed under the weight of federal suppression and inadequate labor organization, the 1870s and 80s marked a highpoint of worker power and influence in Pittsburgh. Public opinion in the city and surrounding towns overwhelmingly blamed the Pennsylvania Railroad and its political allies for the debacle, not the working classes of the city, and certainly not the railroad workers' attempt to organize for better wages and conditions. When a Committee of Safety was organized by the pro-labor Republican William McCarthy to reestablish order in the city, it included representatives of the Amalgamated Association of Iron and Steelworkers, the Knights of Labor and Thomas A. Armstrong, editor of the National Labor Tribune and an articulate exponent of labor's interests in the city. Labor Republicans like McCarthy and the former puddler and leader of the Sons of Vulcan, Miles Humphery, a three-term legislator and chief of the Pittsburgh Fire Department, demonstrated labor's power when it could achieve unity among a working-class base that was continually swelling with new blood and diverse ethnic constituencies.[16]

In 1876 in Pittsburgh, the puddlers, organized into the Sons of Vulcan, united with independent organizations of heaters, rollers, roughers and roll hands to form the Amalgamated Association of

Iron and Steel Workers. Craft traditions, very strong in the furnace industries of iron and glass-making, were destined to be undermined by rapid technological change. In both industries, the owners traditionally provided the equipment and materials to the workers and then marketed the finished product. Craftsmen supervised, hired and paid their work crews according to rules established by the union. The workers, in effect, were organized sub-contractors, selling skill, knowledge and "close and careful teamwork," while getting paid by the amount of production. They worked hard in dirty and dangerous places, but they enjoyed a high degree of autonomy and control over the pace of production and the composition of the work team. As "noble sons of labor," they fostered a spirit of mutualism and an ethic of class and craft solidarity. Their ability to control hiring, however, tended to create strong family and ethnic ties inside of various crafts which could lead to serious divisions. An ability to foster intense loyalty, as well as dominate serious skill training in specific areas, helped many craft union organizations to survive into the 21st Century.[17]

Because of its geographical position between the East and Midwest, and its strong labor traditions, Pittsburgh became the site of many important union organizational meetings over the years. In 1881, the Federation of Organized Trades and Labor Unions of the United States and Canada, an organization that took the name American Federation of Labor in 1886, held its founding convention at Turners Hall (later site of the William Penn Hotel). One hundred seven delegates representing fifty-five organizations with an estimated membership approaching a half-million were present. The convention united in an uneasy alliance craft-based trade unions and members of the Knights of Labor, especially District Assembly 3 of the Knights centered in Pittsburgh. The Knights had started in Philadelphia (District Assembly 1) in 1869, spread to Reading, and then westward to Pittsburgh. Neither exactly a trade union, nor a political party, the Knights rejected the exclusiveness of the trade unions and advocated the union of all labor, skilled and unskilled, with the goal of achieving a cooperative commonwealth through education. They supported compulsory arbitration and posed cooperation as the answer to capitalist competition, "making knowledge a standpoint for action, and industrial and moral worth, not wealth."[18]

Once the Knights of Labor overcame Catholic resistance by downplaying the early Order's secrecy and rituals, the organization made spectacular progress; in 1886, it crested as a movement reaching nearly a million members. It gradually declined in the 1890s. In 1885, the Knights of Labor Salespeoples' Assembly No. 4907 was organized and was considered the most influential "white collar" union in the country until it was destroyed in the 1907 depression. By 1890, the Machinists' Union was one of the first local labor organizations to gain the eight-hour day. In 1894, the Bakery Workers Local 12 organized and succeeded in reducing the hours of work from 14-16 hours a day to 9 hours by 1914.[19]

The Federation of Organized Trades and Labor Unions initially attempted to unite the job focus of the craft unions with the broader social vision of the Knights. At the Pittsburgh convention, it issued a militant call to action:

> Whereas, a struggle is going on in the nations of the civilized world between the oppressors and the oppressed of all countries, a struggle between capital and labor, which must grow in intensity from year to year and work disastrous results to the toiling millions of all nations if not combined for mutual protection and benefit. The history of the wage-workers of all countries is but the history of constant struggle and misery engendered by ignorance and disunion; whereas the history of the non-

producers of all ages proves that a minority, thoroughly organized, may work wonders for good or evil.[20]

Despite the ringing preamble, the organization of craft unions in the AFL evolved into the vehicle for a "pure and simple" or business unionism that eschewed a broad attack on capitalist philosophy in favor of a focused struggle to increase pay, influence working conditions, and control the hours of work. It accepted the strike as labor's central weapon and vigorously supported the broad-based struggle for the eight-hour day. Its major figure, Sam Gompers, an energetic and articulate cigar-maker, was supported by the influential New York carpenters union chief, Peter J. McGuire. McGuire, a socialist, was at the origins of both Labor Day and May Day. Calling for a national holiday honoring labor in September, he organized the first Labor Day march in 1882 in New York City. It was adopted by Congress in 1894 and signed into law by President Cleveland, at least partly to counter the growing popularity of May Day as International Workers' Day. In 1884, McGuire's carpenter delegates introduced a resolution at the Federation of Organized Trades and Labor Unions' Chicago convention, calling for the imposition of the eight-hour day through direct action by workers starting May 1, 1886.[21]

This proposal to change society from below by direct, spontaneous, decentralized action found fertile ground in Chicago where anarchist ideas had made great progress. Chicago anarchist leaders, Albert Parsons and August Spies, had participated in the founding meeting of the United States branch of International Working People's Association in Pittsburgh that issued an influential "Pittsburgh Manifesto" declaring that attempts to change the system by peaceable means were futile. The direct call to the grassroots of labor organizations to "put the eight-hour-work-day in practical operation" precipitated a chain of events centered in Chicago that led to the Haymarket Riot, the hanging of key anarchist leaders, and the adoption of May 1 as International Workers' Day by socialist, communist and anarchist movements world-wide. In Pittsburgh, the United Labor Day parade boasted 12,000 participants by 1887.[22]

Working class ferment and energy was not simply political. In the 1880s the city was a roaring, energetic, plebian place full of bars and boisterous street life. Ethnic bands, parades, picnics, numerous newspapers and broadsides, theaters that specialized in variety shows, "roaring farces," minstrels, and melodramas with "special effects, animals, and numerous female extras" provided diversion and entertainment. Local fire company parades, baseball teams, and rowing clubs were staples of working class life. In the neighborhoods, horse racing, boxing, wrestling, cockfighting and bowling were popular. Working class culture was rich, participative, public and uninhibited, unlike that of the Scots-Irish Presbyterian elite, described as "keen and steady... singularly devoid of the usual vanities and ostentations, proud to possess a solid and spacious factory, and to live in an insignificant house." Part of the reaction to the great social upheaval of 1877 was a major effort by the powerful local establishment to regain political and cultural control over the city. This upper-class determination to assert control coincided with the massive increase in their wealth resulting from industrialization. As they realized the importance of displaying wealth and power in civic life, their tastes in the private realm became more opulent and refined as well.[23]

While the uprising of railroad workers stimulated debate and organization in the ranks of labor, the great rebellion stirred the rich and powerful to action as well. The worker revolt of 1877 triggered a "great wave of armory building" in cities across the nation. A movement was started to train state militias in crowd control. Pennsylvania, whose militia had "disgraced" itself by its divided loyalties in 1877, was completely reorganized.

> The militia, or as it was now referred to, the national guard was centralized along military lines.... A tight chain of command extended from the adjutant-general down to the rank and file.... To encourage enlistment, the state reduced the term of service from five to three years and increased the stipends for active duty. To tighten discipline, it created a system of military justice, under which errant guardsmen could be court-martialed and drummed out of service. At great expense, the state set up a summer camp where guardsmen spent as many as fourteen days a year on field maneuvers and other military tasks. [24]

The 1877 upheaval marked a fundamental shift in governmental priorities. Armories were not constructed in the South to protect the fragile rights of recently emancipated slaves, but in northern cities to protect property against labor unrest. Over the following 25 years, state militias would be employed over 100 times in American industrial disputes. The disciplined troops dispatched to Homestead in 1892 little resembled the Pittsburgh militia of 1877. In addition, the recently formed Chamber of Commerce initiated a law-and-order campaign that aimed to create a larger and more professional police force. It succeeded in molding the city charter of 1887 to its specifications by imposing standards of professional efficiency and military discipline on a larger and better-financed police force.[25]

With its medieval fortress aspect, nothing more dramatically symbolized the majesty and power of the law than the Allegheny County Courthouse and Jail designed by H. H. Richardson. Richardson's impact on national architecture was great for a short while, but his solid stone and brick masonry construction faded before the advance of steel skeleton buildings fed by the rolling mills. Steel frame buildings and improved elevator construction meant that the general five-story-maximum imposed by walk-up conditions was lifted. Indicative of the transition, Westinghouse built a solid masonry building at Penn Avenue and Ninth Street in 1889 adjoining his Garrison Alley Plant; but when Carnegie built the Carnegie Building five years later, he let its steel frame skeleton stand naked for a year to demonstrate the use of steel in construction. Once the new construction principles were understood, the height of buildings began to ratchet steadily upward. These developments drove up the daytime population density downtown, given the steady increase in office workers and other commuters who lived out along the commuter rail lines, or were served by the proliferation of horse-drawn, then cable, then electric trolley lines.[26]

Reinforcement of the city's police powers paralleled the rise of the Magee-Flynn Republican political machine in the 1880s. Christopher Magee used his position as city treasurer in the 1870s to build an extensive ward-level political organization built on patronage and corruption that challenged labor's hold on the neighborhoods. The political machine, source of patronage and jobs, as well as the highly selective enforcer of laws and regulations, became the mediator between the city and the poor, polyglot, overcrowded tenement districts, and thereby began to supplant the trade union as the central vehicle for the integration of the immigrant into the American way of life. "Small businessmen such as saloonkeepers, contractors, building supply proprietors, real estate and insurance agents, many of whom could benefit directly from city contracts, made up much of the machine's membership. Few blue-collar workers or immigrants were involved."[27]

By controlling utility and transportation franchises, construction contracts and bank deposits in a rapidly growing city where new arrivals were hungry for work, Magee was able to extend the machine's influence into the union halls, ethnic organizations and veterans' groups by dangling jobs and contracts. The fire department especially became an important patronage vehicle once it was "professionalized" and under city control. Politicians themselves increasingly became professionals who served the machinery of power and were highly sensitive to money and influence. While reform Republicans, or even a Democrat, occasionally won the office of mayor, Magee's control of city council and contractor William Flinn's hold on the county row offices meant that political administration, governmental contracts and permits were firmly in the machine's hands. While old Judge Thomas Mellon took a dim view of Christopher Magee's wide-ranging interests and protectorates that included taverns and brothels, Andrew Mellon, with his close friend Henry Clay Frick, took a more pragmatic approach and quietly became benefactors and shareholders in the spreading system of machine control.[28]

Lincoln Steffens, in his muckraking book, *The Shame of the Cities*, described Pittsburgh politics as "hell with the lid on." Corruption had always existed to a degree in the town, but the local political "elder statesmen" that Steffens interviewed in 1903 told him:

> It was occasional and criminal till the first great corporation (the Pennsylvania Railroad) made it business-like and respectable.... As corporations multiplied and capital branched out, corruption increased naturally, but the notable characteristic of the "Pittsburg plan"[29] of misgovernment was that it was not a haphazard growth, but a deliberate, intelligent organization. It was conceived in one mind, built up by one will, and this master spirit ruled...the whole town − financial, commercial and political.... Boss Magee's idea was not to corrupt the city government, but to be it; not to hire votes in council, but to own councilmen; and so...he nominated cheap or dependent men for the select and common councils. Relatives and friends were the first recourse, then came bartenders, saloon-keepers, liquor dealers, and others allied to the vices, who were subject to the police regulation and dependent in a business way on the maladministration of the law.[30]

The Pennsylvania Railroad controlled the Pennsylvania legislature where its representative sat on the floor of the Senate as the "51st senator." While Chris Magee was an affable and genial man, his partner William Flinn was a bulldog-faced enforcer who engineered his own election as state senator. Their deal with Boss Matthew Quay of the Pennsylvania Senate exchanged Magee and Flinn's support to Quay in the legislature for their complete control over all legislation affecting Pittsburgh. "Magee and Flinn, owners of Pittsburg, made Pittsburg their business...and prepared to exploit it as if it were their public property."[31] Flinn hired E. M. Bigelow, a cousin of Chris Magee as impresario, his Director of Public Works, who launched an extremely ambitious public works program that specified stone and asphalt controlled by Flinn and bluestone Belgian block quarried in a Mellon-owned quarry in Ligonier. When a reform mayoral candidate, George W. Guthrie, was leading in the ballot count until one in the morning in the contentious race of 1896, the returns suddenly ceased. When the official count was rendered three days later, the machine had triumphed by a thousand votes.[32]

While the second-generation Mellon financiers were comfortable in their mutually profitable relationship with the machine, ideological middle-class Presbyterian reformers targeted the perceived degeneracy of the Catholic immigrants. Their instrument was the Law and Order League that focused on the enforcement of liquor licensing and Sabbath laws, often carried out in a hard-edged and mean-spirited fashion. The goal of these efforts was to restrict access to alcohol. In this it differed from the very strong local temperance reform movement led by Francis Murphy of the Young Men's Temperance Union and the Catholic Total Abstinence Union. For these working-class movements of the late 1870s, temperance was an issue of voluntary self-control and self-respect. Their crusades, supported by unions, idealized the sober independence and manliness of the worker needed to supply disciplined soldiers in the army of labor. The Law and Order Leaguers, conversely, were viewed by workers as agents of repression who directed their moral fury at the teeming industrial slums full of alien populations. Their activities in enforcing the Sabbath provoked outraged response. League enforcers "swooped down upon crippled cigar vendors and 70-year-old candy sellers with a cool self-righteousness working people attributed to class and ethnic bias." The League's campaign against prostitution, a business largely protected by the Republican machine, produced much heated rhetoric but little action or reform in the machine-controlled city.[33]

Another manifestation of the Catholic community's efforts toward self-improvement and community progress was the founding of what became Duquesne University. In 1878, Bishop John Tuigg of Pittsburgh granted Joseph Strub, a German member of the Holy Ghost Congregation, permission to open a college in the city to give instruction in classical, scientific, and commercial subjects, as well as provide religious training. After four years, what was first known as the Pittsburgh Catholic College moved from a site on Wylie Avenue to Boyd's Hill, a bluff overlooking the Monongahela. There, in 1855, Old Main, an imposing five-story building, was constructed that constituted the highest point in the downtown for years. The bricks were made by the Holy Ghost brothers from local clay. While the goal of the founders was to provide a classical education, the students who came were looking for a job-related education, even though most industrial management jobs in the city were not open to Catholics. Gradually the tenement houses behind the college were purchased and the school expanded to occupy almost the entire bluff. The school emphasized participation in sports and organized one of the earliest collegiate football or "American rugby" teams. In 1910, the school became the first Catholic College to receive a university charter from the Commonwealth of Pennsylvania as the Duquesne University of the Holy Ghost. Its law school opened the following year.[34]

Division and Growth in the Ranks of Labor

Worker organizations faced many challenges as sharp philosophical and tactical differences emerged between the Knights, skilled craft unions, embryonic industrial unions like the Trainmen's Union, radical groups like the anarchists (who had significant followings in the German and Italian communities), and third-party advocates in the Greenback Labor Party. While rapid technological and business organizational changes were constantly altering the terrain of struggle and modifying the terms of engagement with corporate power, ethnic and racial divisions along with rising tensions between immigrants and native born workers bedeviled union efforts to form stable organizations or develop coherent strategies. Labor Republicans, working-class Democrats and third-party efforts attempted to offer political solutions to working-class problems; but many labor activists directed more energy into their unions, churches, neighborhoods, ethnic and fraternal organizations than they allocated to a political process that was increasingly unresponsive and corrupt.

Perhaps the most intractable problem for labor organizations as they encountered a massive wave of immigrant workers, many with foreign tongues and alien heritages, was how to overcome ethnic and racial divisions. By 1900, in Allegheny County, over 190,000 foreign workers had joined the more than 270,000 second-generation workers with foreign parents in a rich and complex ethnic stew.[35] While East European laborers maintained remarkable support and engagement with the skilled, largely Irish, tonnage men at the Homestead Works in 1892, these same groups split bitterly

17 years later in the strike at McKees Rocks. Various ethnic groups were recruited to break strikes. Irish were set against Welsh and English miners in the anthracite; and in a dramatic incident in the bituminous fields, coal operators contracted with labor brokers to obtain armed Italian strikebreakers at the Buena Vista mine, southeast of Pittsburgh. The New York-based Italian Labor Company had been formed to protect Italian laborers from "unwarranted attacks of Irish workmen" in labor disputes. Two hundred Italian workers were introduced into the striking mines of the Panhandle railroad southwest of Pittsburgh where the contractor William Griffin bragged both about their desperate need of work and their armament.

> They are disposed to work…and to be peaceable; but they are not cowards and when aroused will be perfect desperadoes. Many of them were brigands in Italy. Many of them belonged to the Papal Army. Take them away from their arms and they would be of no account, but they are adept in the use of all kinds of arms, and are particularly skillful with their peculiar knives. You observe the shape of them – like a pruning hook….[36]

Charles Armstrong operated the Buena Vista and Osceola mines and employed a total of 275 men at the two locations. In October 1874, Armstrong fired the men at the Buena Vista mine for being "too bossy" and interfering with his right to weigh and measure the coal. A perennial issue for miners paid by the bushel or ton was the fair weighing of production; as the old mining song admonished, "keep your hand upon the dollar, and your eye upon the scale." Armstrong imported 173 Italian miners and armed each with "rifle, bayonet and revolver." Numerous shooting incidents occurred in Buena Vista as the whole community rallied against the importation of armed strikebreakers. On Saturday, November 29, a group of armed Italians crossed the Youghiogheny River and entered Buena Vista allegedly to seek a doctor for one of their wounded. Fighting broke out, and the Italians retreated to the mine side of the river where firing continued across the water. When evening came, a detachment of over one hundred Buena Vista residents, reinforced by local farmers, crossed the river and took up positions on a hill overlooking the mine. Caught in a crossfire, the Italians tried to surrender, but the firing was only stopped by the brave actions of two young Italian sisters who walked into the open, where "endangered and unprotected, (they) appealed by their presence to the humanity of the mob so forcefully that the firing was instantly ended, and the carnage was over." Three Italians were dead and eight were wounded. The Italians left the next day and the local jury refused to hold any of those charged with their deaths responsible.[37]

The most enduring and debilitating division, however, one that would undermine worker solidarity for more than a century, was the racial animosity fostered between blacks, hungry for decent paying jobs, and whites of various ethnic groups, trying to defend their hard-won and modest gains. While ethnic tensions among whites tended to dissipate in the second and especially the third generation as "mixed" ethnic marriages, churches and neighborhoods became more common, the racial line proved more intractable. From 1870 to 1900, Pittsburgh's black community grew from a little over 1,000 to over 20,000. In 1900, Pittsburgh, with a population of nearly 322,000, not including the nearly 130,000 inhabitants of Allegheny City, was the sixth largest American city and also had the sixth largest black community. In 1869, as a result of the Fifteenth Amendment, Pennsylvania's black males were restored the vote. In 1875, Pittsburgh Public Schools became one of the first systems to desegregate, an action that may have helped students, but eliminated black teaching opportunities altogether since black teachers were not allowed to teach in the Pittsburgh Public Schools until after World War II. Blacks owned small businesses but had very few opportunities with the town's large and powerful corporations except for low-level service jobs. In the union-dominated construction trades, blacks were generally restricted to heavy labor, hod-carrying, and teamster work. In most mines, mills and factories, blacks could only find work, usually temporary and hazardous, as strikebreakers. Since many craft unions operated as ethnic enclaves, it was difficult for any outsider, let alone blacks, to gain admission.[38]

Under slavery, blacks often did blacksmithing and other metal work. The premier Southern artillery works, the Tredegar Iron Works of Richmond, Virginia, the South's answer to the Fort Pitt Foundry during the Civil War, employed a workforce that was nearly half black slaves. After the war, there was a migration of skilled black metalworkers toward the North. While the great engineer of the early steel industry in America, Captain Bill Jones in Braddock, asserted the superiority of a multi-ethnic workforce including blacks, factory jobs for blacks were few and far between. The notable exception was during a strike. Blacks were first used as a group to break puddlers' strikes in 1875 at Pittsburgh Bolt and the Black Diamond Steel Works. At the 1881 AFL founding convention, a black delegate from Pittsburgh, Jeremiah Grandeson, had issued a prescient warning:

> We have in the city of Pittsburgh many men in our organization who have no particular trade, but should not be excluded from the Federation. Our object is, as I understand it, to federate the whole laboring element of America. I speak more particularly with a knowledge of my own people, and declare to you that it would be dangerous to skilled mechanics to exclude from this organization the common laborers, who might in an emergency, be employed in positions they could readily qualify themselves to fill.[39]

Subsequently, when blacks started a union effort at the Black Diamond mill, they were able to forge some level of unity with the Amalgamated that had asserted the eligibility of blacks for membership at their Pittsburgh convention. Blacks, however, were again employed as strikebreakers during disputes at the Solar Iron Works in 1888 and 1889. Jack Whitehead, credited with recruiting the first permanent mobile force of strikebreakers for rent, introduced 40 skilled African Americans from Birmingham, Alabama, into the Clinton Mills on Pittsburgh's South Side in 1891 and successfully broke a strike there. These early attempts at using racial division to break worker organization were greatly expanded in the early decades of the 20th Century.[40]

Despite ethnic and racial divisions, there was still a steady growth in worker organizations in the skilled trades. The rapid expansion of mills and shops, the construction of large buildings and extensive housing, the spread of traction lines and utilities conjured up enormous demand and provided ample opportunities for worker organization. The primary building material in the second half of the 19th Century in Pittsburgh was locally fabricated bricks. The Bricklayers' Union No. 2 was founded in the early 1870s and helped organize a national union affiliated with the Knights of Labor and then the American Federation of Labor. Another of the early organized trades was the Carpenters District Council of Western Pennsylvania chartered on July 12, 1877. By 1900, strong Carpenter locals were organized in Pittsburgh, Homestead, New Castle, Connellsville, Wilkinsburg and Carnegie. Dozens of new unions sprang up. Local 12 of the Sheet Metal Workers started out as the Tinners' Union of Pittsburgh Local No. 1, organized in 1880, until it affiliated with the national organization. Prominent among the newcomers was Local 3 of the Bridge, Structural and Ornamental Ironworkers or Bridgemen. The local played a major role in the organization of the Ironworkers national union, hosting its founding 1896 convention in Pittsburgh, at Moorhead Hall, Second and Grant Street. Pittsburgh was chosen because, as the "City of Bridges," "more bridge builders are employed here than in any city in the country."[41]

In the 1890s, Westinghouse's harnessing of alternating current spurred the rapid expansion of electrical usage for diverse applications. Inside wiremen, who did industrial, commercial and residential work, tended to be locally based and politically active; linemen, who strung the web of electrical lines across the country, tended to be both individualistic and politically radical. The union's goal was to assure a monopoly over skilled workers in the trade. Once the allegiance of the skilled labor market was assured, contractors were forced to come to the union to compete in the market. With a standard wage established, contractors had to compete on the basis of their relative skill to organize and bid the job, not on their ability to reduce wages. What made unionism attractive or at least palatable to contractors was the immediate availability of an adequate supply of qualified workers for exactly the amount of time it took to complete a job. This freed contractors from having personnel departments or even large numbers of permanent employees. The union's ability to supply a pool of skilled manpower on demand served well an industry whose labor demand fluctuated dramatically with the vagaries of both weather and the construction market. In June 1898, the union reached an initial agreement with the Pittsburgh Electrical Contractors Protective Association that was "a reasonable one and makes the two hearts beat as one for the success of both."[42]

Local 5 of the National Brotherhood of Electrical Workers hosted the seventh annual convention of their national organization in 1899. At that convention, held in the Knights of Labor hall on Wood Street, the union accepted its first Canadian members and changed its name to the International Brotherhood of Electrical Workers or IBEW. Over the course of the 20th Century, Local 5 grew into a major force inside the building trades and in local politics. Its aspiration was to set a standard of quality and safety in its business, to make its work "a certificate of character" as expressed in the union's 1903 by-laws:

> Our endeavors shall be…to defend our rights and advance our interests as electrical workers, thereby creating an authority whose seal shall constitute a certificate of character, intelligence and skill, and thus maintain an organization where all worthy members of our trade can freely participate in the discussion of those practical problems upon the solution of which depends their welfare and prosperity as workers. We aim to foster fellowship and brotherhood, and to shield from aggression the isolated defenseless toiler who may be destitute and unfortunate, and also to provide for the decent burial of deceased members….[43]

Political involvement produced a City Council ordinance that allowed only union men to work on city buildings. Reporting on the agreement, the local correspondent to the *Electrical Worker* wrote: "Everybody in Pittsburgh believes in unions for working people…. Without a union, the working class is like fishing without a hook. You have to wait a long time before you can get a bite."[44]

Beautiful Dreamers: Brashear, Langley and "Nellie Bly"

Many ambitious and creative people were attracted to or emerged out of the growing and vigorous metropolis at the headwaters of the Ohio. Two of the most endearing are "the man who loved the stars," John Brashear, and the archetypal investigative reporter, Elizabeth Cochrane or "Nellie Bly." John Brashear, an associate of Samuel Langley, was descended from pioneer stock. His grandfather entertained the Marquis de Lafayette at his Brownsville tavern in 1825. The eldest of seven children, Brashear's life was irrevocably set in 1849, when at the age of nine, he first gazed through a telescope at the craters of the moon and the rings of Saturn. Trained as a pattern maker and mechanic, he was hired at the Zug & Painter rolling mill, where, as a millwright, he was charged with keeping the machinery running. "I have gone into the mill on a Thursday morning and worked, with very few intervals of rest, until twelve o'clock Saturday night. When a breakdown in the machinery took place, it had to be repaired in the quickest possible time, as men were thrown out of employment, iron-melts wasted, and orders remained unfilled." He reported that the most melancholy experience in his life was on the occasion of an explosion in the mill. A worker asked him to repair a plate which he removed to his bench. An explosion then occurred that caused the collapse of a crane, crushing the man on the very spot they had been standing immediately before. Brashear reported he "frequently had to tear down and rebuild a piece of machinery where some poor fellow had lost his life." [45]

He studied star charts but was forced to search for spots high enough to see the stars above the thick smog of the mills. Leaving his job during the 1867 puddlers' strike, he soon found another rolling mill job in the South Side; and when that establishment failed in the Panic of 1873, he took a job at a local glass works. In 1870, he purchased land on the hillside above 22nd Street in South Side and built a cottage for himself and his wife. He bought a small adjoining house that he equipped as a workshop and set out to construct a telescope. After three years work, he completed his first instrument and felt emboldened to reach out to Samuel Langley, the director of the Allegheny Observatory on Pittsburgh's North Side. Langley encouraged Brashear, and Brashear soon established an international reputation for finely crafted astronomical tools including spectroscopes, prisms, object glasses, parabolic mirrors and large reflectors for many of the world's most important observatories. [46]

Samuel Langley is best known as the director of the Smithsonian Institute and for his experiments with flying machines. His fascination with flying started during his 24-year tenure as the director of the Allegheny Observatory as well as a professor of astronomy and physics at the Western University of Pennsylvania. One of his practical achievements was the use of the Observatory clock to furnish highly accurate time to the Pennsylvania and other railroads on a contract basis. Supported by philanthropist William Thaw, whose fortune came from investments in the rail and iron industries, he conducted experiments on solar radiation, making accurate measurements of temperatures in the sun's spectrum. In 1886, he and Brashear attended a meeting where a French-born, American engineer, Octave Chanute, presented a summary of attempted flights in America and Europe. Langley approached the problem theoretically, trying to determine the power necessary to overcome the earth's gravity and then how to guide a flying machine through the air. In 1891 Langley left Allegheny City to become director of the Smithsonian Institute in Washington, D.C., where he took his research proving the theoretical basis for heavier-than-air flight and applied it to model flying machines. After the failure of several manned flights and the success of the Wright brothers' machine at Kitty Hawk, Langley abandoned his efforts. He died shortly afterward in 1906. Wilbur Wright paid homage to Langley's work and his "great influence in determining my brother and myself to take up" the study of flight. [47]

Besides making equipment for major astronomical observatories, Brashear also built a business that helped amateur astronomers build their own telescopes, never forgetting the immense joy and sense of achievement he experienced as he built his own first instrument. [48] He eventually succeeded Samuel Langley as the director of the Allegheny Observatory and with the patronage of philanthropist, William Thaw, he oversaw the construction of the new Allegheny Observatory in Riverview Park. When Brashear died, his ashes were placed with his wife's in the base of the telescope at the new Observatory. Brashear was widely known and loved in Pittsburgh for his generosity of spirit. He wrote near the end of his distinguished career:

The happiest days of my life have been spent in endeavoring to lend a helping hand to the other fellow; whether he was a prince or a pauper, a savant, or a poor chap seeking for some little knowledge of things good and beautiful, a teacher of men, or a lover of kiddies; and while my love of the beauties of the skies has not abated one jot or tittle from the time I had my first view in my old home town to the day I write this paragraph, my chief joy has been to hand these beautiful things over to the other fellow, that he, too, might share in them.[49]

Another extraordinary individual who rose from the working class to achieve world fame was Elizabeth Cochrane, better known by her *nom de plume*, Nellie Bly. Born in Armstrong County and schooled in Indiana, Pennsylvania, she moved to Pittsburgh at the age of eighteen. Responding to a column in the *Pittsburgh Daily Dispatch* that decried the fad of hiring women in offices, she wrote a scathing and lengthy letter signed "Little Orphan Girl" stating that girls had a right to lead interesting, useful and profitable lives. The editor was so impressed by her earnestness and spirit that he put an announcement in the paper asking the anonymous writer to send in her name and address, so thereby "she will confer a favor and receive the information she desires." When she came to the paper, he hired her and gave her the pen name of Nellie Bly after a popular song by Stephen Foster.[50] She launched her journalistic career with a series of articles about divorce, a normally taboo topic for the pages of a daily newspaper. She became a tireless and daring investigative reporter visiting factories and slums to describe the work and the daily life of Pittsburgh's working-class women. She posed questions about, for example, the working-class widow that made the comfortable, uncomfortable.

Can they that have full and plenty of this world's goods realize what it is to be a poor working woman, abiding in one or two bare rooms, without fire enough to keep warm, while her threadbare clothes refuse to protect her from the wind and cold, and denying herself necessary food so that her little ones may not grow hungry; fearing the landlord's frown and threat to cast her out and sell what little she has, begging for employment of any kind that she may earn enough to pay for the bare rooms she calls home, no one to speak kindly to or encourage her, nothing to make life worth the living…. If sin in the form of man comes forward with a wily smile and says, 'Fear no more, your debts shall be paid' she cannot let her children freeze or starve, and so falls. Well, who shall blame her? Will it be you that have a comfortable home, a loving husband, sturdy, healthy children, fond friends – shall you cast the first stone?[51]

Too impatient to perform the usual duties assigned women on newspapers, she constantly resisted attempts to rein her in and force her to concentrate on more womanly interests such as reporting on fashion and the activities of service organizations. After nine tumultuous months as a columnist and reporter at the *Dispatch,* determined to do what "no other girl had done," Bly decided to win her spurs as a serious reporter by going to Mexico. She had been part of an entertainment committee for a visiting Mexican delegation to Pittsburgh and used the occasion to collect invitations and contacts. For six months she traveled extensively in the company of her mother and reported on the politics and the life of the Mexican people. Her reports back to Pittsburgh expressed a warm sympathy for the common people, but a low opinion of the Mexican press. "Mexican papers never publish one word against the government or officials and the people who are at their mercy dare not breathe one word against them, as those in position are more able than the most tyrannical czar to make their lives miserable."[52]

In 1888, Bly left Pittsburgh to join the staff of Joseph Pulitzer's *World* in New York City, where she wrote a pioneering report on the plight of people committed to insane asylums. Feigning mental illness, she had herself committed to the insane asylum on Blackwell's Island. Her articles describing "Ten Days in a Mad House" led to reform and increased funding for mental health treatment in the state. Her most famous adventure came when she set out to better the fictional achievement of Jules Verne's Phineas Fogg, who, in the pages of a novel, made it around the world in 80 days. Carrying only a 20 pound satchel, she beat Verne's fantasy by nearly 8 full days. Her landing in San Francisco and her entire trip across the United States by train to New York was applauded by enthusiastic crowds and serenaded by brass bands. After marrying, settling down, and then running her husband's business after his death, Nellie returned to journalism. Her final story concerned the electrocution of an inmate at Sing Sing prison that constituted a plea against capital punishment.[53]

Westinghouse, Tesla and Alternating Current

Engineering genius, an enormous capacity for work, an incessant pursuit of improvement in design and manufacturing of what were often revolutionary technical devices, drove George Westinghouse to envision and manufacture an extraordinary variety of inventions. In 15 intensely creative years (1881-1895), he garnered 150 of the 361 patents he was granted. He secured his first patent at the age of 19, and his final patent was granted in 1918, four years after his death. Besides his revolutionary airbrake, he advanced the development of railway signals with interlocking switches, and a safe mechanism for coupling railroad cars; he was a leader in railroad electrification, developing the first mainline electric locomotive and the modern trolley driven by a single reduction motor with one gear and pinion; he perfected a steam engine to propel large ships and developed a system for transmitting and using natural gas in various ways including to drive large motors. His greatest achievement was his involvement in the creation of the alternating-current system of generating, transmitting and utilizing electricity for power and light.[54]

In 1884, while Westinghouse was deeply involved with issues of railway safety control, the expansion of several separate business enterprises, and the exploration of the emerging field of alternating current, he took time at home to invent many useful devices for natural gas transmission and utilization. Mrs. Westinghouse had to surrender a portion of her flower gardens around Solitude in Hazelwood to a drilling rig as her husband went searching for natural gas. At 3 am, as his men were slowly passing 1,560 feet drilling depth, they struck a gas pocket and with an explosive roar the drilling apparatus was flung into the air while gravel, sand, and mud were thrown everywhere. The workmen had fled for their lives with the warning roar and were uninjured. The phlegmatic Westinghouse reportedly asked his wife: "All things considered, are you satisfied with the experiment?" "Oh very well," she responded cheerfully: "The house still has a roof on it, and the kitchen isn't wrecked." The force of the gas blew hundred pound rocks into the air with ease. It took a week for Westinghouse to invent an industrial scale stopcock and gradually reduce then shut off the pressure. The illuminating quality of the gas was dramatically illustrated when a draw pipe allowing some gas to escape was ignited.[55]

> The next instant, like a lightning flash connecting heaven and earth, a pillar of fire
> shot a hundred feet upward into the sky and was followed by a steady fountain of
> flame that was a marvelous study of colors. At its base was a jet of blue, brightening
> into pale yellow as it ascended, then becoming a dazzling white, and expanding like

a tubular fan, the outer edges passing through various shades of yellow and orange into a sort of Indian red. The gas lamps of the city dwindled to little points of light, and persons on the street not less than a mile away were able to read distinctly the finest newspaper print by the light of the gigantic flambeau on the heights of "Solitude."[56]

After organizing the Philadelphia Gas Company, Westinghouse turned to the problem of safe gas transmission. He developed double piping to contain leaks, systems of pipes of graded capacities that allowed greater pressure in mainline pipes with step-downs in pressure at the consumer end. He invented safety shutoffs that helped to automatically regulate the system along with meters and valves to control and measure the flow. The rapid expansion of natural gas usage gave Pittsburgh industries less than a decade of relief from the traditional coal dust and soot that so defined the city. As local supplies of natural gas declined, coal once more supplanted it for most industrial usages except glassmaking where natural gas was clearly superior.

Westinghouse's invention of the airbrake and automatic coupling systems increased the safety and efficiency of rail operations greatly, but the increased speeds and increased traffic that resulted caused serious control problems. In 1881, Westinghouse organized the Union Switch and Signal Company out of a number of existing signaling companies and, by combining their best ideas with many of his own, established the Switch as the preeminent company in the railroad controls industry, a position it held for nearly a century. The original plant was in downtown Pittsburgh on Garrison Alley off Penn Avenue between 9th and 10th Streets. There, Westinghouse and his engineers adapted principles of electro-pneumatic controls to signals, switches, and crossing-gate mechanisms to create safety controls that operated reliably in extremes of weather and usage. The first installation of automatic block signaling was made on the Pennsylvania Railroad between East Liberty and Wilkinsburg in 1884. Interlocking electrified controls made urban transit systems that subordinated the movement of trains into an integrated network possible.[57]

Over the years, the Switch created many railway safety devices including cab signaling that brought electronic speed controls into the engineer's cab, but the most significant work ever done in its engineering department were the experiments conducted between 1884-86 on various types of electrical apparatus. These experiments demonstrated to Westinghouse the limitations of the direct current machines built by Thomas Edison's General Electric plant in Schenectady New York. Edison was creating a vast array of electric generators, motors and electric lighting devices that were intrinsically limited by the fact that direct current could only be transferred short distances effectively since electrical resistance encountered increases directly with the distance traveled.

Hearing of interesting developments with alternating current in Europe, developed by Lucien Gaulard, a Frenchman, and John Gibbs, an Englishman, that allowed the transmission of electricity at high voltage to be reduced by local transformers, Westinghouse immediately purchased the U.S. patent rights to the Gaulard-Gibbs transformers. In late 1886, the Switch was moved to its new home on a 45-acre site in the suburb of Swissvale situated next to the main line of the Pennsylvania Railroad. In the fall of 1886, a dynamo at the Garrison Alley plant successfully lit 400 lamps 4 miles away in Lawrenceville. It was the first successful transmission of electricity for any considerable distance using alternating current in the U.S. Greensburg, 30 miles east of Pittsburgh, became the first town to purchase the Westinghouse alternating current system. In 1888, an electric meter was developed that could accurately measure and regulate the amount of electricity dispensed or applied.

The Garrison Alley plant served as the home base of the Westinghouse Electric until a massive new industrial complex was built in East Pittsburgh along Turtle Creek starting in 1894.[58]

The great leap forward with alternating current was made possible by the collaboration between Westinghouse and the brilliant inventor, Nikola Tesla. Born of Serbian parents in what is today Croatia, Tesla's father was an Orthodox priest and his mother a gifted inventor who developed numerous useful house and farm appliances. Nikola was an extremely talented student with extraordinary mathematical and mechanical abilities. He was subject to powerful visions accompanied by flashes of light that made it difficult for him to distinguish the real from the imaginary. At times his senses were so hypersensitive that a ticking watch or the buzzing of a fly caused him acute pain. Upon first seeing an engraving of Niagara Falls as a youth, he conceived of a huge waterwheel to harness its currents, a feat he and Westinghouse achieved some 25 years later. He encountered the direct current motor while in technical school and began his search for a an efficient device that would not need a commutator to reverse the direct current so that it could propel a rotating shaft. While working at the Central Telephone Exchange in Budapest, he was struck with a vision of how an alternating current could solve the direct-current motor problem.[59]

Walking in a city park while witnessing a sunset, he was reminded of a passage from Goethe's Faust:

> The glow retreats, done is the day of toil;
> It yonder hastes, new fields of life exploring;
> Ah, that no wing can lift me from the soil;
> Upon its track to follow, follow soaring!

> "As I uttered these inspiring words, the idea came like a flash of lightning and in an instant the truth was revealed. I drew with a stick on the sand the diagram shown six years later in my address before the American Institute of Electrical Engineers. The images were sharp and clear and had the solidity of metal."[60]

When Tesla arrived in New York in 1886, Edison's direct current system, financed by J. P. Morgan, ruled supreme. The Edison system, however, needed separate generating stations every mile or so; and the noise and pollution occasioned by decentralized power sources and the dangers of bare wire transmission systems were immediately evident. Tesla explained his alternating current system to Edison, who instead, of being grateful, saw his whole empire threatened by such ideas. With no money, Tesla, however, went to work for Edison, improving the safety of his DC system in record time; but Edison refused to pay him the $50,000 he had initially offered and instead gave him a ten dollar a week raise. At the end of 1887, Tesla filed for seven U.S. patents in the field of polyphase AC motors and power transformers. On May 16, 1888, Tesla provided a demonstration of a powerful little AC motor and the principles behind it to the prestigious American Institute of Electrical Engineers at Columbia University. Westinghouse hurried to Tesla's New York lab and paid him $60,000 for the patents, plus Westinghouse stock, and eventually hired and brought him to Pittsburgh to advise on the adaptation of his motor for mass production. Tesla defined the sixty-cycle alternating current standard that remains in use to this day.[61]

With Tesla's advances married to Westinghouse's organizational and manufacturing capacities, an all-out industrial war broke out with Thomas Edison. While seduced by the dramatic possibilities and spectacular visibility of electricity, the public, stimulated by sensationalist newspapers accounts, was also becoming increasingly alarmed by the rising death toll associated with electrical usage. During the Great Blizzard of 1888 in New York, 400 people perished, many electrocuted by collapsed electrical lines that writhed and spit sparks on Gotham's streets. Edison and his powerful financial allies secretly financed and promoted the use of alternating current in an electric chair as a "humane way" to execute criminals. A Westinghouse generator was employed in 1889 to execute a man accused of killing his wife, and great publicity was generated around the gruesome results that included the victim's spinal cord bursting into flames. The Edison interests described the process as being "Westinghoused."[62]

Edison and his allies could not overcome the inherent technical superiority of the Tesla-Westinghouse system with slander. By 1891, Tesla had become a U.S. citizen and was engaged in collaboration with Westinghouse that culminated in the triumph of successfully lighting the 1893 Chicago World's Fair, or Columbian Exposition. Westinghouse's bid was nearly half as expensive as Edison's million-dollar bid, because Edison needed two separate transmission systems to service both lights and motors, while Westinghouse's system was unitary. On May 1, 1893, the Columbian Exposition opened to 100,000 spectators who were wowed by Buffalo Bill's Wild West Show, Bell Telephone's first long-distance phone call from New York to Chicago, and the first Kinetoscope, or peep show, featuring Algerian belly-dancing girls. A director of Pittsburgh's Engineer's Club, George W. Ferris, designed, built, and operated the first Ferris Wheel as America's answer to France's Eiffel Tower. It was a massive structure capable of lifting 36 cars with 60 passengers in each car on a trip above the Chicago skyline. Nearly 1.5 million visitors took the ride. With all this, the most spectacular event was the lighting of the Fair by President Grover Cleveland as 100,000 incandescent bulbs burst into light to the accompaniment of Handel's *Hallelujah Chorus*. The sight provided author L. Frank Baum with the inspiration for the Emerald City in his book, *The Wizard of Oz*. At his personal exhibit, Nikola Tesla revealed himself as a real life wizard when he took the stage and had two million volts of electricity pass through his body creating a halo of electric flames surrounding him.[63]

After their public relations triumph in Chicago, the Westinghouse-Tesla combine undertook the spectacular engineering feat that sealed the victory for alternating current. A prestigious international committee, chaired by the renowned British physicist, Lord Kelvin, an early proponent of Edison's direct current system, was established to award a contract to harness the power of Niagara Falls. In October of 1893, the Niagara Falls Commission awarded Westinghouse a contract to build the power generation facility with ten Tesla designed generators. At midnight, November 16, 1896, the switch was thrown and a thousand horsepower of electricity surged to Buffalo. Within a few years, Niagara's power was illuminating Broadway's Great White Way.[64]

Urgently needing room to expand production for Niagara Falls and other projects, Westinghouse began the construction of the massive Westinghouse Electric and Machine Works complex in 1894 in East Pittsburgh. The Electric lay directly downstream along the Turtle Creek from the new Airbrake plant constructed in Wilmerding in 1890. From Solitude, his home in the eastern suburb of Homewood, Westinghouse could reach his three main enterprises, the Switch, the Electric, and the Brake, by short commuter trips along the Pennsylvania's mainline east out of Pittsburgh.

The Glassblowers Lament

Pittsburgh ruled as the nation's main glassmaking center throughout most of the 19th Century. A large skilled glass-making workforce evolved and grew. The union representing workers in the decorative and table glass and bottle production was the American Flint Glass Workers Union, founded in Pittsburgh on July 1, 1878, and headquartered in the city between 1886 and 1904, when it moved its offices to Toledo.[65] Many of the flint glass workers were also active in the Knights of Labor. As late as 1880, Pittsburgh's glass factories were largely concentrated in the densely populated South Side, downriver from the sprawling J&L Iron and Steel Works. Over forty percent of window and plate glass in the country was still produced within the city. The transition from coal to natural gas as the fuel of choice and the supplanting of the river boats by the railroads as the dominant transportation vehicle helped decentralize production and move it out of Pittsburgh. In 1888, H. Sellers McKee moved his glass house out of South Side to an "exclusive city of glass in Pittsburgh's suburbs," that he named Jeannette, after his wife. With the rapid growth of the natural gas industry, there was a boom in glass-making with 115 glass works in Western Pennsylvania, 29 in Allegheny County by 1900. One characteristic of the glass industry was its employment of young boys aged 10 to 16. Of 6,053 glassworkers in Allegheny County in 1885, 1,470 were children and youths under 16, while only 141 were women. Child laborers included gatherers, tending boys, and carrying boys, who did lifting, placing, and sweeping for pay that ranged from 30 cents to a dollar a day. Attempts to regulate the age, or the amount of night work a child could do, were fiercely resisted by the glass industry that often successfully obtained exemption from child labor laws.[66]

Expanded and decentralized production, plus increased specialization, spurred automation and undermined the power of skilled workers to control production. In 1830 with the flat glass process, the blower did or supervised the entire process; by 1880 he was increasingly a specialist. "No longer did he preside over the variety of tasks involving all aspects of the production process nor did he continue to make his hourly trips to the pub. Instead he blew more cylinders, supervised fewer men and boys, and constantly defended his wage rates from attack by his employer." In 1880, the separate window glass trades united into the Knights of Labor Local Assembly 300, a body that evolved into a national craft organization. A key issue was the threat posed by the importation of skilled Belgian and English glassblowers. They attempted to control the situation by allowing small numbers of immigrants into the union, seeking legislation to limit the importation of contract labor, and organizing a truly international labor union. Glass workers from five countries met in England in 1884 for that purpose. Ironically, the significant jump in Pennsylvania production fueled by natural gas discoveries undermined the large Belgian glass export industry, and drove skilled but unemployed Belgian workers to the U.S. where they curtailed the power of skilled American union workers.[67]

In 1881 a Pittsburgher, Philip Arbogast, introduced a semi-automatic bottle-blowing machine. In the 1890s, Michael Owens at Libbey Glass in Toledo developed automatic blowing machines for lamp glasses and light bulbs. These technological improvements dramatically cut labor costs and directly undermined the skilled union glass blower. For the 18 years of its existence, Local Assembly 300 buttressed the health of the industry by matching supply to demand, restricting output, and regulating the supply of labor. In 1897 Local Assembly 300 fragmented into local and regional unions as industrial expansion broke the union's control of the labor supply. While technological advances increased production, economic depression reduced demand. "By 1903, unlimited production, unrestrained apprenticeship policies, and private agreements between workers and employers had eliminated the last remnants of the order and stability LA 300 had once brought to the industry." By 1906 automation had decreased the labor costs involved in the production of a gross of beer bottles from $1.47 to $.10. Within 10 years, 100 Owens bottle machines were producing 360 million bottles a year, reducing the necessity for both skilled and child labor. Subsequently, automation and the high capital costs necessary to compete drove many smaller companies out of the market and forced consolidation.[68]

The following lament, written by a veteran glass blower, expresses the experience of many as they witnessed the breaking of skilled worker control over the production process:

A glassblower sat on a foot-bench one day,
His face sad, grim and set
And a look in his eyes that I saddened to see,
For I knew that he saw things that once used to be.
He saw L.A. 300, before the great fall,
The peer of all unions, the pride of them all;
And a look of deep loyalty shone in his face.
As he mused that no act of his brought it disgrace.

He remembered the time, all old glassworkers do,
When a man could go home, when his days' work was through
With his chin in the air and his job safe and sound,
As independent a man as could ever be found.
He worked ten months a year, and the wages were good,
He had two months vacation, as a glassblower should;
He had plenty to eat and good clothing to wear,
No fear of the future, no worry or care.

And then along came a firm with a blowing machine,
And the end of the hand-blower plainly was seen.
The highly skilled blower, with muscles like steel,
Soon the sting of vexation and hunger would feel.
As he likened the past to the present he knew
That his work-days were numbered, all ill-paid and few;
So he pensively mused, in his own sordid way,
And wondered where he would end up some fine day.[69]

Odd Couples: H.C. and A.W., Andy and Charlie

The relationship between Henry Clay Frick and Andrew Carnegie has fascinated generations of writers; many books have focused on their strained and difficult alliance and subsequent bitter split.[70] Frick, the hard-driving, fiercely competitive, focused, single-minded coke king, and Carnegie, with his contradictory persona: hypocrite or schizophrenic; the merciless competitor who destroyed his rivals or the great benefactor and humanitarian, loved and admired for his spectacular generosity. Frick's control over the fuel that powered Carnegie's mills and melted his ore drew the two men into an uneasy alliance that provides an engaging dramatic subplot to the great struggle over the nature of American labor relations. At least as important, but much less studied, is the close friendship and alliance between A.W. and H.C., Andrew W. Mellon and Henry Clay Frick that operated discretely out of the public view, but significantly impacted the history of Pittsburgh and the nation.

Born poor, Henry Clay Frick had the good fortune to have a maternal grandfather whose distillery producing *Old Overholt Rye Whiskey* made him the wealthiest man in the Mt. Pleasant area and an object of admiration to the young boy. H.C. was 19 and working as the old man's secretary when he died at the age of 86. The Overholt lands rested above the rich Connellsville coal seam, a sub-section of the great Pittsburgh seam that provided a fuel largely free of sulfur and ash, with a fibrous density that made it the finest metallurgical coal. In 1871, Frick approached Thomas Mellon, who knew his family, for a loan. Mellon was attracted to the zeal and business commitment of the 20 year-old. With the loan, Frick bought farmland, installed his first 50 ovens, and applied to Mellon for money to build 50 more. By 1873, Frick and Company owned 400 acres and 400 ovens. An investigator sent out by old Judge Mellon to evaluate H.C., reported: "Lands good, ovens well built; manager on the job all day, keeps books evenings…knows his business to the ground."[71]

In 1879, as H.C. passed his 30th birthday, he lit up a cigar to celebrate his becoming a millionaire. In 1880 he invited Thomas Mellon's son Andrew to accompany him on a trip to Europe. They became lifelong friends and allies, sharing a predilection for collecting paintings that continued on a grand scale their entire lives and led ultimately to the magnificent Frick collection in New York City and Mellon's National Gallery in Washington D.C. The following year, Frick married Adelaide Howard, who was introduced to him by A.W., and it was during their honeymoon that the newlyweds were invited to meet Andrew Carnegie in New York City. After the gathering had completed a toast to the happiness of the couple, Carnegie proposed a second toast to Henry Clay Frick and, he added without warning, to the success of the Frick-Carnegie partnership. It was a grand gesture of ensnarement, despite Carnegie's mother's arch comment ("Ah Andra, that's a verra good thing for Mr. Freek, but what do we get out of it?"). Carnegie knew very well what he got: control over coke production and over the coke king as well. Thus was launched an uneasy partnership.[72]

Within two years, Carnegie bought out Frick's partners and thereby controlled the majority of the coke king's company. By 1882, H. C. Frick and Company owned 3,000 acres of coal and 1,026 coke ovens. In addition, Frick organized the Morewood Coke Company. With 470 ovens, his Morewood works was the largest in the coke region. In the fall of 1886, Tom Carnegie, Andrew's brother and close business partner, died and Frick was chosen to become the new chairman of Carnegie Steel and a partner in the steel side of Andy's business. In 1887 a strike by coke workers provoked Frick's wrath, but as he marshaled forces to suppress the revolt, Carnegie, urged on by Phipps and others who did not want an interruption in the supply of coke, ordered Frick to meet the strikers' demands. Frick, furious at losing operational control of the coke empire he had built, resigned with an angry letter protesting "so manifest a prostitution of the Coke Company's interests in order to promote your steel interests." After, financial considerations and ego mollification, Frick returned as president six months later, and in January 1889, Frick was made the chairman of Carnegie Bros. & Company.[73]

While Frick achieved his goal of becoming a millionaire by age 30, another of Carnegie's bright, ambitious proteges made an even more dramatic climb from poverty to power. Charles Schwab was the child of German parents from the intensely Catholic town of Loretto 83 miles east of Pittsburgh which had grown up around a charismatic Russian, Prince Gallitzin, an Orthodox convert to Catholicism. Schwab was educated by the Franciscans, who introduced him to bookkeeping, surveying, mathematics, and engineering. While he was first in his class in those subjects, his teachers were totally unsuccessful in teaching him the Franciscan virtues of poverty, chastity, or obedience. He grew up in a very happy family and demonstrated a genius for interacting with people, especially young ladies. To disentangle one romance, his parents sent him at the age of 17 to work for a friend of the family in a store situated just outside the gate of the Edgar Thomson (E.T.) Steel Works that occupied the vastly altered site of General Braddock's bloody defeat more than a century earlier. Charlie Schwab's initial vehicle on his climb to the top of the world's biggest steel producer was Captain Bill Jones, who regularly came into the store to buy cigars. Jones was impressed by the young man and hired him as a surveyor in the plant's engineering department. Schwab took an interest in the chemical properties of steel and performed construction design projects for Jones. [74]

Meanwhile, Carnegie, in a series of articles for the *Forum* magazine in 1886, coinciding with the May Day strikes and Haymarket violence, asserted that "the right of the working man to combine and form trades union is no less sacred than the right of manufacturers to enter into conferences and associations with his fellows, and must be sooner or later conceded.... What we must seek is a plan by which men will receive high wages when their employers are receiving high prices for the product and hence are making large profits; and *per contra*, when employers are receiving low prices for products, and therefore small if any profits, the men will receive low wages."[75] This was Carnegie's famous sliding scale. His position was more than a little disingenuous since it was the unprecedented quantity of metal his company was dumping on the market that was forcing prices down. In a subsequent article, however, he penned words that would haunt him the rest of his life:

> To expect that one dependent upon his daily wage for the necessaries of life will stand peaceably and see a new man employed in his stead is to expect much.... The employer of labor will find it much more to his interest, wherever possible to allow his works to remain idle and await the result of a dispute than to employ a class of men that can be induced to take the place of other men who have stopped work. Neither the best men as men, nor the best men as workers, are thus to be obtained. There is an unwritten law among the best workmen: "Thou shalt not take thy neighbor's job."[76]

In fact, while Carnegie was championing the rights of workers and playing the role of industrial statesman, he was busting union organization at the Edgar Thomson works in Braddock. There, an intense struggle was going on over the issue of the twelve versus eight-hour day and the role of worker organization in the mill. Braddock was a stronghold of the Knights, who accepted both skilled and unskilled workers as members. The Amalgamated Association had several lodges there as well. On the management side, "hands-on, all-over," Captain Bill Jones, the key to Carnegie's phenomenal production records at Edgar Thomson, was a brilliant engineer and organizer of production who patented more than fifty inventions that improved and accelerated the production process. The Jones Mixer, in particular, eliminated the time-honored production of "pigs" by allowing up to 250 tons of hot iron to be collected and stored prior to going to the Bessemer furnaces to make steel. Captain Jones, a hard-driving manager, who constantly encouraged the competitive spirit of his workers to set production records, nonetheless was a proponent of three eight-hour shifts, especially in the Bessemer departments because of the intensity of the work.[77] As early as 1881, in an address to the British Iron and Steel Institute concerning advances he helped attain at both the Cambria Iron Works and E.T., he made a number of observations:

> ...The development of American practice is due to the *esprit de corps* of the workmen after they got fairly warmed to the work. As long as the record made by the works stands the first, so long they are content to labor at a moderate rate; but let it be known that some rival establishment has beaten that record, and then there is no content until the rival's record is eclipsed.... Another marked advantage which the American works have is the diversity of nationality of the workmen. We have representatives from England,, Ireland, Scotland, Wales, and all parts of Germany, Swedes, Hungarians, and a few French and Italians, with a small percentage of colored workmen. This

mixture of the races and languages seems to give the best results, and is, I think, far better than a preponderance of one nationality.... In increasing the output of these works, I soon discovered it was entirely out of the question to expect human flesh and blood to labor incessantly for twelve hours, and therefore it was decided to put on three turns, reducing the hours of labor to eight. This proved to be of immense advantage to both the company and the workmen, the latter now earning more in eight hours than they formerly did in twelve hours, while the men can work harder constantly for eight hours, having sixteen for rest. [78]

Carnegie initially accepted Jones' rationale, but in 1886, the year of his magnanimous article and at the height of labor's push for the eight-hour day, he returned E.T. to the two-shift schedule while cutting both workers and wages. Some workers who were getting $120 a month for an eight–hour day dropped to $60 for a twelve-hour one. This action provoked a strike and the firing of 700 men, followed by a temporary compromise where the three-shift system was restored for a time. At the end of 1887, however, Carnegie closed the works and discharged his workers pending an agreement on his terms. In May, Carnegie declared the mill non-union and opened the gates only to those who would sign an agreement to not join a union. Out of work for more than five months, many men returned, and formal union bargaining at E.T. was effectively ended.[79]

In 1886, on Jones' advice, Carnegie appointed Schwab superintendent of the Homestead Works where his job became the installation of the new open-hearth furnaces. He visited open hearth steel facilities in Scotland and brought back the basic open-hearth steel-making process to Homestead. In the same year; Schwab and Carnegie's cousin, George Lauder, visited armor plate works in Europe. Since armor plate required high quality open hearth steel, the Homestead Works and Schwab learned about the armaments industry and government contracting together. Schwab went on to build Bethlehem Steel into the prime producer of naval armor plate. In September 1889, in the course of breaking loose a slag jam with an iron bar, an explosion was triggered and Captain Jones was killed. Schwab was named to succeed him at Edgar Thomson, a bare ten years after he had entered the plant as a surveyor, and where reputedly Bill Jones had asked him if he could drive stakes. Schwab is supposed to have answered: "I can drive anything." Like the other highly competitive industrialists of his age, he was most adept at driving men to increase production.[80]

The rise of the great industrialists and businessmen like Carnegie, Frick, Mellon and Schwab holds enduring fascination for the American public. With the exception of Westinghouse and a lesser degree of Heinz, none of the Pittsburgh-bred corporate giants were themselves great inventors of useful products. Rather they were driven, even ruthless, men who were present at a particularly opportune time of major technological breakthroughs achieved against the backdrop of a world with abundant and easily accessible natural resources and labor power. These resources could be harnessed and controlled in new ways by the ambitious men who rose to direct giant organizations and accumulate vast wealth. The instruments of government — courts, legislatures, and law enforcement agencies — swayed by the power of their money, exercised little regulation or moderating social control. The captains of industry made over society in their image and were applauded by the press, promoted as role models for youth, and portrayed as the epitome of success.[81]

Johnstown, Mammoth and Morewood

Steel, coal, railroad and banking magnates exercised increasing power over local, state, and even national governments. Extensive and diversified holdings made them able to rise above any purely local struggle, to starve workers out while destroying their organizations. Sometimes, however, the arrogance and high-handedness of some of them aroused public opinion on the workers' side. Among the events stirring public animosity toward Henry Clay Frick at the time of the struggles at Homestead were the Johnstown Flood of 1889, the Mammoth Mine explosion and the Morewood Massacre, both in 1891. While these events hardly endeared Frick and the growing ranks of very wealthy men in Western Pennsylvania to the general public, their immense power over the region's political and economic life gave them a significant measure of insulation from the consequences of their actions.

As the men of power in Pittsburgh began to cultivate culture and leisure to compliment and embellish their pursuit of fortune, they began to acquire properties where they could escape the smoke and grit of their investments, relax and cultivate relationships that might profit their businesses. Frick and other prominent Pittsburghers, including Andrew Carnegie, Andrew Mellon, Robert Pitcairn, Henry Phipps, and Philander Knox, purchased a very large abandoned canal reservoir, three miles long, a mile wide and up to seventy feet deep, that became the South Fork Fishing and Hunting Club. Well-appointed "camps" were erected and the lake stocked with varieties of fish including a thousand black bass imported by train from Lake Erie. Extensive logging and erosion along the valley increased the flow of the runoff. The dam, a leftover from the great canal days of the 1840s, was flattened and lowered at the top to allow carriages to pass. Despite warnings about the integrity of the dam, nothing was done to strengthen it. The valley below the dam had steep sides like a sluice that provided little resistance to the velocity of the wave when the dam let loose. A violent storm the night before continued most of the day, and flooding was already serious in lower Johnstown reaching a depth of ten feet in some parts of town even before the catastrophe struck.[82]

At 4:07 pm on May 31, 1889, the dam ruptured, sending a 60 foot wall of water and debris roaring down the valley toward the 30,000 inhabitants of the pioneering steel town of Johnstown. It first devastated Carnegie's old rival, the Cambria Iron Works, and then swept into town with the debris of homes, wagons, dead bodies, trees, draft animals, railroad tracks and bridges, a freight car with 60 tons of pig iron, pianos and household goods, all interwoven with telephone and electric wire. The mass piled on top of a stone railroad bridge where a horrific fire raged after the draining of the waters. In all, more than 2,200 people were killed. Captain Jones, his roots in the Cambria Iron Works, led a contingent of 300 men from the Edgar Thomson works to the aid of the stricken town. A Pittsburgh engineer, Arthur Kirk, was called on to help clear the 800 foot long "drift" formed by debris with dynamite.[83]

Born in Allegheny City, Mary Roberts Rinehart was a prolific and successful novelist, writing over fifty books. Many of her novels were set in Pittsburgh, including her best known work *The Circular Staircase.* As a child she witnessed many spring floods along the Allegheny, but one was seared in her memory.

> Floods then were an act of the providence of God. No one referred to man's criminal folly in deforesting the hills and over grazing the plains. They came, were lived through, came again....One flood, however, was man-made....I was wakened one early morning and taken to the river bank. Something dreadful had happened; a dam had given way, and my mother's eyes were red and swollen. We stood by the river, on a bit of high land, and saw houses sweeping by and all sorts of strange things. Men were watching too

for now and then a body was salvaged. My mother continued to cry. That was the Johnstown flood, and a very dear friend of hers had been on a railroad train and was lost.[84]

Despite predictions of lawsuits against the millionaire members of the South Fork Fishing and Hunting Club, accusations by the Cambria County coroner's jury of the club's culpability and screaming denunciations of guilt from New York and Chicago newspapers, Pennsylvania newspapers were more circumspect, rarely mentioning the club and not naming its members. The club maintained a low profile, donating a thousand blankets. Club members were equally restrained in their generosity. Carnegie, who was in Europe when the dam broke, donated $10,000, Frick gave $5,000, Mellon, a mere $1,000; half of the sixty club members donated nothing. The complete membership list was kept out of the press for more than a year, and the club's lawyer, James Reed, partner with Philander Knox, the club's secretary, "understandably took the position that the Flood was an Act of God and that the organization could not be held legally responsible for the breaking of the dam." Not a nickel was ever collected from the South Fork Fishing and Hunting Club through damage suits. Mr. and Mrs. Andrew Carnegie, showing more courage and generosity than the rest of the bunch, came to town the following September and agreed to build a new library where the old one stood. In time nearly all those whose opinions mattered agreed that the flood was "a visitation of providence."[85]

Two other dramatic events in the heart of the Coke King's realm in 1891 helped shape public perceptions of Mr. Frick. The first was the Mammoth Mine Explosion that with its 109 victims equaled the Avondale mine fire of 1869 as the state's worst mine disaster to that point.[86] As in most mine disasters of the period, the true death toll was hard to ascertain because of the difficulty of reaching bodies in collapsed mine sections and, because of the practice of paying by the ton and allowing subcontracting, companies often did not even know how many men and boys were below ground.[87] The Connellsville paper first reported 134 dead, but only 84 bodies were intact enough to be identified.

> The first party went down the shaft to Flat No. 4. Three hundred feet from the shaft they found a wall of earth, coal wagons and human bodies, which blocked further progress. This was tunneled through and the party turned off at right angles along a haulage road. At the extremity of this was found a man, with his head completely severed from his body.... In the haulage road of Flat No. 4 thirty-five bodies were found, and fifteen were counted in one heap in Flat No. 2. One man had both legs blown off. The body of a boy was found with a stick driven through his arm. Fire Boss William Snaith was torn almost to pieces, and a rubber boot was found still encasing the foot and leg of a miner. The big pumps, which lift tons of water out at a time, were broken and shattered as if they had been made of straw.... Nearer the scene of the explosion, huge slabs of slate and coal are torn from the roof. Sections from the walls are blown down the roadway, stout coal cars are broken into small pieces, and the iron work tangled into fantastic shapes. The bodies found beyond Flat No. 3 showed that they were killed by concussion, being struck with or against something. Further out many of the men were burned to death, and still further from the explosion center they died from suffocation.[88]

The deaths were horrific, but the plight of the families, often large and totally dependent on the working members to survive, was equally devastating. Death or severe injury to a father was one of the prime drivers of child labor in the coalfields. The *Connellsville Courier* (Jan. 30, 1891), referring to the voracious appetite of industry, headlined its account: "The Modern Moloch: Drenches His Altar in the Blood of Many Brave Men." The paper described the burial of the 79 Catholics in two long trenches:

> During the service the vast concourse of people remained hushed and silent, but when the words ceased and the clods began to rattle on the coffins, the spell was broken, and sounds of bitter grief arose. Women rushed frantically forward sobbing and calling upon their dead ones, and no one in that vast concourse thought it unmanly to shed a tear. Then in one part of the throng was heard again in a thin treble voice the strains of the Slavic funeral dirge. It was taken up here and there until the accents of woe seem to fill the air and appeal to the very heavens. The strains died away as gradually as they arose, night draped her veil over the scene, and slowly and sadly the army of mourners filed out of the cemetery.[89]

The Mammoth disaster fueled mounting discontent in the coal and coke operations of the H. C. Frick Company. Antagonism was mounting between the "Hungarians" and the company. Long hours, low pay, plus unhealthful working and living conditions sparked work stoppages and marches by strikers (often holding aloft the American flag) on neighboring mines and oven batteries to shut them down. In January 1886, a bloody confrontation prefigured the Morewood massacre of 1891. Anti-immigrant sentiment was growing:

> These Hungarians are the most difficult class of laborers to manage when they are peaceful, or to pacify when they are enraged. Few of them speak English, they live here in the same squalid fashion as in Hungary. They know nothing of American life or manners, or of the courts, or of working-men's rights. Their only idea of carrying a point is of carrying it by physical force. Many of the men have done service as soldiers, and they know how to fight, and are not afraid to resist officers of the law. Indeed, they have no other notion of an officer than as of an enemy in war…. The disturbance has demonstrated that the employers who brought the Hungarians to take the place of native or naturalized laborers that commanded higher wages are not likely to profit by the experience.[90]

Shortly after the Mammoth explosion, on February 10, 1891, Frick's agreement on a wage scale for the coke workers expired. After some negotiation, Frick posted notices outlining the rates on the sliding scale principle that he was offering on a take-it-or-leave-it basis. Frick pinpointed the central issue: "We concluded that we would end the thing once and for all, and determine whether we had a right to employ whom we pleased and discharge whom we pleased." This action triggered a series of marches and protests by the coke drawers. On Thursday morning around 3 am, a group of several hundred strikers left a midnight rally in Mt. Pleasant and marched on Morewood. As they approached the mine, deputies opened fire killing seven men, with two others dying shortly after. Six of the dead were listed as Hungarian, or Polish/Hungarian; two were Italians. Events like Morewood cemented the Slavic workers' loyalty to the skilled men of the Amalgamated during the 1892 Battle of Homestead. The hard attitude and tough tactics of Henry Clay Frick were known to them.[91]

Shifting Battleground

The 1892 Battle of Homestead marked the violent culmination of a sustained decade-long struggle over the organization of work inside the most technologically advanced steel mill of its time. The Homestead

Works was among the pioneers of the transition from the age of iron to the age of steel. High quality structural steel rolled at Homestead dramatically changed the urban landscape. Its alloyed steel armor plate helped the United States build the world's most powerful navy. But Homestead in 1892 also marked the triumph of capital over labor at the point of production, and this watershed event inside Carnegie's steel mills profoundly impacted the labor and industrial history of the United States.

In 1881 a group of Pittsburgh investors, led by the embittered Andrew Kloman, set out to build a Bessemer mill at Homestead to rival Carnegie's Braddock mill. Led by William Clark, an aggressive and hard-driving manager, the mill was erected in record time and almost immediately encountered labor difficulties. Confronted by union activity, Clark closed the mill on New Year's Day 1882 and demanded of the 200 workers an "ironclad agreement" in the form of an individual contract that the workers would not join a union or engage in concerted activity. The issue was complete management control. Virtually the entire work force refused to "sign away our rights as freeborn citizens." They were subsequently discharged *en masse. Iron Age,* an industry publication, framed the issue inversely: "The strike resulted from a refusal (by management) to recognize the union as a party to the control of their own works." Thus, from its very origins at Homestead, the labor-management struggle was defined as property rights versus democratic rights. For Frank Gessner, leader of the Homestead Knights of Labor, it was a matter of "cruel greed" on the part of the owners: "The real question…is whether the (steelworks) is to be operated by the honest skilled labor of the Amalgamated Association, or whether it is to take its place as a 'scab' works, to be operated only by those who will severally sign away their rights, and become as much the property of the company as ever were the Negroes on the tobacco plantations of Virginia or the cotton fields of Louisiana."[92]

The strike lasted from January 5 to March 14 when the company agreed to recognize the union, giving it the power to fill openings with union men. The conflict was bitter with housing evictions of striking workers and a violent attack on scabs in the tenements where they were housed. Two policemen were badly beaten after they fired into a crowd of steelworkers. This fierce struggle had the unintended consequence of driving the floundering group of Pittsburgh owners into the arms of Andrew Carnegie, who bought the mill at a bargain price and immediately began an expansion of the works. He decided to concentrate on rail production in Braddock and focus on the rolling of structural beams at Homestead.[93]

In an astonishing sequence of events, the Homestead scenario was replayed in the town of Duquesne, a few miles upriver from Braddock and Homestead. A group of Carnegie's old rivals from the Solar Iron Company and Black Diamond Steel built a new mill to challenge Carnegie's preeminence. The experienced mill operators introduced a radical innovation in operations by running freshly poured ingots from the soaking pits directly into the rolling mills. The elimination of the reheat step made the process more continuous and significantly less costly. Carnegie understood the threat immediately. He drafted a circular to the nation's railroads charging that the process employed by the new Allegheny Bessemer (Duquesne) plant would produce defective rails. Drawn in tighter by Carnegie into the web of his interests, Frick, now chairman and a partner in Carnegie Steel, waited for his opportunity to pounce. As labor troubles broke out, including several work stoppages, and quarrels erupted among the partners as their costs mounted, Frick tendered an offer of a million dollars in bonds to be paid in five years. The rivals were forced to accept. By the time the bonds became due, the Duquesne mill paid for itself six times over without Carnegie having to pay a cent for its purchase. Once Duquesne was in his grasp, the improved process developed there was promptly introduced in both the Braddock and Homestead mills.[94]

By 1897, Carnegie's mills controlled almost half of the nation's construction steel capacity. Metal frame skeletons transformed the skyline of American cities. Spans of steel vaulted across mighty rivers and bays. From the Brooklyn Bridge and the Empire State Building to the ill-fated towers of the World Trade Center, and in thousands of other massive structures, steel from Homestead cast its physical shadow over the nation's land and waters. Mighty plates of forged and tempered alloy steel rolled at Homestead constituted the building blocks of the fleet that humbled Spain in the Spanish American War and carried the banner of "manifest destiny" to the shores of the Philippines, Puerto Rico, and Cuba. After a modicum of soul-searching, Andrew Carnegie accommodated his pacifist principles to his hunger for lucrative military contracts by consenting to make armor plate because it was "defensive" and only incidentally highly profitable. Unlike Bethlehem, Homestead never did produce heavy guns, but the superiority of its nickel alloy steel plate helped fuel "an arms race based on fear of technological innovations that might render a fleet and, therefore, an entire nation defenseless." An international arms build-up was fed from Homestead and its rival Bethlehem.[95]

Steel is iron containing enough carbon (.1-.5%) to be hardened by sudden cooling, but not enough to make it brittle like cast iron. Steel combines the ductility and malleability of wrought iron with the casting capability of pig or cast iron. Malleable or wrought iron was traditionally made in relatively small furnaces by puddling which required constant attention by a team of experienced, skilled workers. Modern steel making grew out of an increased ability to sustain high temperatures and precisely adjust the chemistry of a heat to obtain the exact characteristics of the metal desired. Increasingly large-scale steel production demanded continuity and the automation of the process. In the mid 1870s, the most advanced Bessemer technology was installed by Holley and Jones at Carnegie's Braddock mill across and up river from Homestead. While Bessemers were initially installed at Homestead, it became primarily an open-hearth shop. The Siemens-Martin open-hearth furnace developed in England and France used an acid-lining technology. Employing a process developed by Thomas and Gilchrist in 1879, the first large-scale, commercial, basic-lined open hearths in America were built at Homestead in 1888. Basic-lining materials (dolomite and limestone) produced a slag that tied up impurities such as phosphorous and sulfur, producing superior steel. [96]

Open-hearth steel's quality allowed it to challenge the Bessemer process for supremacy. The speed of the Bessemer process permitted less control over the chemistry. "The unpredictable failures associated with Bessemer steel reduced its appeal to fabricators of tanks, pressure vessels, bridges, and steel-framed buildings." Overcoming the quality control limitations of the Bessemer process, alloyed open hearth steel quickly established its dominance for specialized products such as armor plate, boiler plate, and flange steel used in construction. The more manageable nature of the open-hearth process also meant that crucial process decisions could be made by engineers or chemists in a metallurgical laboratory rather than by teams of skilled workers wresting iron from ore by fire, muscle, and experience, as had been the tradition in iron production. Precise metallurgical analysis became the hallmark of the open-hearth method. Open-hearth production was a very slow process compared to the Bessemer method, taking from 8-12 hours to produce a heat. On the other hand, open-hearth furnace size could be greatly increased (fifty ton average at Homestead in the 1880s), so separate batches could be "cooked" or adjusted to the same metallurgical consistency, and giant ingots processed from combined pours. In 1892 Homestead achieved the rolling of a 72-ton ingot.[97]

The steel magnates, of whom Frick and Carnegie were the most aggressively competitive, relentlessly increased the scope and pace of production. Carnegie rarely concerned himself with the costs of new construction; it was operational costs that mattered. His ruthless pursuit of lower costs generated his opposition to unions and tarnished his reputation as a philanthropist. In iron manufacture prior to the late 1880s, "iron-makers saw no way to increase productivity and profit other than through machinery designed to maximize the efficient employment of skill: better heating furnaces, faster and stronger rolls, etc....That is, they tried to make individual craftsmen more productive." In the steel mills, on the other hand, engineering improvements radically increased production while reducing the role of skilled labor in the production process. The men ceased being manipulators of raw materials and molten metal and became tenders of machines and thereby more easily trained and replaced.[98]

Homestead distinguished itself by the size and organization of its open-hearth pattern and the constant improvement of material-handling equipment like overhead cranes, hoists, charging machines, and buggies. It was praised as the industry model for its "economy of operation, due to the convenience of handling and the small amount of labor involved." Continuous production with sequenced material-handing mechanisms reduced the need for teams of experienced workers acting in concert at critical moments of a dynamic process. The development of three high rolls with hydraulic tables made continuous rolling possible, and by 1892 virtually all the mills at Homestead were so equipped. Open hearth technology itself, which created the possibility of enormous castings, greatly accelerated the general tendency toward ever increasing size and scale of the machinery.[99]

> It is at Homestead that wonders are performed as amazing as those of the Arabian Nights. Here machines endowed with the strength of a hundred giants move obedient to a touch, opening furnace doors and lifting out of the glowing flames enormous slabs of white-hot steel, much as a child would pick up a match-box from the table. Two of these monsters, appropriately named by the men "Leviathan and Behemoth," seem gifted with intelligence. Each is attended by a little trolley-car that runs busily to and fro... no sooner does it seem to see its giant master open a furnace door and put its great hand for a fresh lump of hot steel, than it runs back like a terrier to its owner and arrives just as soon as the huge fist is withdrawn with a glowing slab... And no human hand is seen in the operation. In another place lady-like machines seem to dance lightly in front of the furnaces, occasionally stretching out a hand, seizing a red-hot billet, and waltzing with it to the rolling mill....In yet another place a comical being runs busily about carrying hot things round corners.... And all the while he holds in one hand a long rubber tube, like a boy at a Maypole. This contains the electric wires that give him life and intelligence.[100]

These "electric wires" that gave the machine "life and intelligence" indicate another factor driving increased mechanization of the plant. The rapid development of both direct and alternating current electric power in the 1880s provided dramatic new ways to automate production and eliminate labor. Important advances in electrical generation, transmission, and motor technology were taking place in the neighboring plants of George Westinghouse. Homestead was the first big plant to install electric cranes and by 1892 the entire plant was lighted by electricity. The impact of electric crane installation on employment was immediately evident. *Iron Age* observed in 1894 that "electric cranes in the yards of the Homestead Steel Works, Homestead, Pennsylvania, are rapidly displacing many Hungarian laborers, and they are leaving that place in large numbers for other points."[101]

Technological change provided the context within which Carnegie and Frick felt they could attack the steelworkers' union in its Homestead stronghold and eliminate any interference by the union in their radical reshaping of the production process. In fact, "...one of steel's attractions for capitalists was precisely the belief that application of scientific principles to the production of steel would free them from dependence on skilled labor." On the other hand, technological changes placed workers in an extremely difficult position as they tried to defend entrenched and cherished positions on a battleground that was constantly shifting.[102]

Union of Iron in an Age of Steel

The Amalgamated Association of Iron and Steel Workers was the most powerful labor organization of its time and Pittsburgh was its home base. The steelworkers of Homestead were inheritors of a more than 3,000 year craft tradition surrounding the making and shaping of iron. In many parts of the world this craft was associated with magic and its practitioners considered a race or caste apart. The puddlers' union, the "Sons of Vulcan" founded in Pittsburgh in 1861, reflected in their name this ancient tradition of a mythical and quasi-divine origin for the craft. More prosaically, they were an organization of workers that imposed self-governing order and regulation on a dangerous workplace.

The Amalgamated Association of Iron and Steel Workers, founded in Pittsburgh in 1876, was an organization incorporating earlier organizations representing distinct skilled trades in the iron industry (puddlers, heaters, rollers, roughers, wire-drawers, etc.). The preamble to the Amalgamated's constitution posed a poignant question: "Are we to receive an equivalent for our labor sufficient to maintain us in comparative independence and respectability, to procure the means with which to educate our children and qualify them to play their part in the world drama?" In 1891 the Amalgamated reached its peak formal membership of 24,000 members and was the most powerful member organization of the American Federation of Labor. During the decade of the 1880s, practically all of the iron mills in Allegheny County were unionized. James Bridge in his *Inside History of the Carnegie Steel Corporation* estimated the union's supporters, if not members, at 70,000 and stated that: "Except in a few small works, there was not a wheel turning nor a fire burning from Maine to Texas that was not cared for by an Association man."[103]

Steel mills however were proving difficult to organize, especially when they were not extensions of pre-existing iron mills. Technology advances were a two-edged sword. Amalgamated President Weihe asserted "the genius of the country should not be retarded," realizing that improved productivity brought immediate, tangible gain to skilled workers paid by the ton. On the other hand, technological improvements and resulting job reductions helped Carnegie eviscerate union organization at his Braddock mill in 1885. Rapid organizational change in the steel industry was a serious challenge for a union whose methods were tied to a craft whose standards were fixed and uniform. The union was reluctantly forced to abandon a common tonnage scale in the steel mills since the wide variation in productivity made imposing a common standard impossible. "The Association accepted the principle that increased output through mechanical advance necessitated rate adjustments. At Homestead, for example, the men took sizable cuts in the settlement of the victorious strike in 1889. The tonnage rate was half that at the unimproved mills at Jones and Laughlin."[104]

At Homestead the union was deeply entrenched after relatively successful struggles in 1882 and in 1889. In the community and on the shop floor, steelworkers played a leading role. "The strength of the Homestead lodges lay in the superior production of its members, their ability to enlist the support of the unskilled workers, and most importantly, the almost monolithic support of the community." In 1892, the burgess (mayor) and a majority of councilmen were steelworkers. The town was prosperous and the mill was relatively clean, being new and fueled by natural gas. The town was hardly the sooty, fearful, crowded industrial slum depicted by Byington and Fitch less than twenty years later, but truly a "worker's republic" flowering at the end of an era.[105]

After the achievement of a contract in 1889, the union consolidated its power on the shop floor. Frick felt the 1889 agreement had given the union the authority "to hire and fire as well as determine the working conditions within the plant." Another business observer provided this jaundiced viewpoint: "Every department and sub-department had its workmen's 'committee', with a 'chairman' and a full corps of officers, who fearing that their authority might decay through disuse, were ever on the alert to exercise it. During the ensuing three years hardly a day passed that a 'committee' did not come forward with some demand or grievance... The method of apportioning work, of regulating the turns, of altering the machinery, in short, every detail of working the great plant, was subject to the interference of some busybody representing the Amalgamated Association."[106]

Radically increased production meant falling prices and greatly increased profits for the most technologically advanced firms like Carnegie's. While willing to adjust the wage formula via the famous "sliding scale" to reflect declining prices down to a guaranteed minimum, the Amalgamated still wanted wages in some measure to reflect the vastly increased production of metal, so as to share in the productivity gains of the industry. Carnegie, on the other hand, wanted wages to be directly linked to the falling prices increased production was creating. Both the company and the workers were prospering from Homestead. Company sources claimed the top skilled tonnage workers were making $10-$15 a day. While supervisors were reportedly outraged that some steelworkers showed up to work in carriages, the Homestead Works was virtually a money machine for Carnegie and his partners. Just prior to the 1892 strike, Carnegie would enjoy a record 4.5 million dollar profit and would exclaim: "Was there ever such a business!"[107]

The central economic issue in the strike centered on the question of whether rapid productivity advances which drove down the price of the product should depress wages in step with prices or increase them in line with productivity. As an Amalgamated man framed the issue, the union would not accept the "doctrine that because one man, with these improved plants, can do the work that four or five used to do, he must at the same time accept a lower scale than used to be allowed in the days of handwork."[108] Terrance Powderly of the Knights of Labor identified the issue at Homestead as the price of labor and the right of workers to a "voice in fixing that price."

> The Amalgamated Association, and all the other bodies of organized workmen, stands in the same relation to the men as the corporation does to the capitalist whose money is invested. One invests money, that is, his capital; the other invests his labor, which to him is not only his capital but his all. That the workman should have the same right to be heard through his legitimately appointed agent, the officer of the labor organization, that the corporation has to be heard through the superintendent or agent, is but equity. This is the bone of contention at Homestead, and in fact everywhere else where a labor organization attempts to guard the rights of its members.[109]

Working conditions were steadily improving under the union regime. Sunday work was practically abolished. The inexorable pressure in union shops was for shorter hours, more holidays and overtime pay. Wage disparities, however, caused tensions between groups of workers. Mechanics outside the Amalgamated, who erected and repaired the machinery that the tonnage men operated, earned one-half or one-third the top tonnage rates. At one point, it appeared the mechanics might not support the Amalgamated's strike. Unorganized laborers earned even less but still more than common labor outside the mill. Ultimately, however, both the craftsman mechanics and the largely immigrant labor gang supported the Amalgamated leadership. The union was looked to by virtually all workers in the mill as the source of their prosperity and protection. Few were inclined to trust their livelihood to the tender mercies of Henry Clay Frick.[110]

The Battle of Homestead

The famous 1892 confrontation at Homestead was preceded in 1889 by a dress rehearsal that created divisions within the company and led to a three-year agreement that established a formal bargaining relationship between the company and its workers. The union at Homestead was the most powerful of any within the Carnegie domain and the only one working on a straight tonnage basis on a negotiated scale, rather than on the sliding scale based on price fluctuations. The 300 skilled production workers at Homestead thus enjoyed wages significantly higher than at any other mill in the country. Before Carnegie left for Scotland on his annual vacation, he came to Braddock on March 30, 1889, to dedicate the first Carnegie library in America and delivered an "Address to Workingmen" where he affirmed the necessary partnership between employer and employed.

> Believe me fellow workmen, the interests of Capital and Labor are one. He is an enemy of Labor who seeks to array Labor against Capital. He is an enemy of Capital who seeks to array Capital against Labor.... We walk through these mills (in Braddock) knowing that instead of Labor and Capital standing face-to-face, jealous and distrustful of each other, we and our workmen are now practically partners, sharing in the present depression of prices together, but also bound to share in the advances in prices which must come sooner or later.

Carnegie then dramatically read a letter from a Homestead man who asked him to "do something for Homestead." Carnegie replied: " 'Do something for Homestead,' well we have expected for a long time, so far in vain, that Homestead should do something for us....Our men there are not partners. They are not interested in us." While he was alienated from the union stronghold at Homestead, Carnegie was interested in providing for his old neighborhood in Allegheny City. On the morning of the day in September, 1889 that Captain Jones was killed in a furnace accident in Braddock, Carnegie visited the new library that was under construction in Allegheny City. He wrote his wife about the feelings that welled up in him at the sight of the magnificent structure that was in a sense the spiritual heir of the first quasi-public library founded there by Colonel James Anderson in the 1850s that the young Andy had used extensively as a "working boy though not bound." [111]

> If ever there was a sight that makes my eyes glisten it was this gem....A kind of domestic Taj, its tower a pretty clock, so musical in tone too, for it kindly welcomed me as I stood feeling – "Yes, life is worth living when we can call forth works such as this!...The big words Carnegie Free Library just took me into the sweetest reverie and I found myself wishing you were at my side to reap with me the highest reward we can ever receive on earth, the voice of one's inner self, saying secretly, well done![112]

Confronting his first strike, William Abbott, the superintendent at Homestead, advertised for strikebreakers almost immediately after the July 1, 1889 expiration of the agreement. He hired one hundred Pinkertons as a reserve force if needed. These actions aroused the workers; and when the Allegheny County sheriff, Alexander McCandless, and 125 deputies tried to escort a small group of immigrants and Negroes into the plant, 2,000 Homestead men, women and children gathered and forced them to withdraw. As the scabs tried to disembark, the *New York Times* reported that they were "hooted and hissed, jeered and cursed, until they turned and fled the town, with stones flying all around them." Abbott then panicked and signed a contract that included the sliding scale as Carnegie wanted with, however, an elevated floor below which the scale could not slide and, most importantly, gave exclusive bargaining rights with control over hiring and firing to the Amalgamated. [113]

The negotiated sliding scale was attached to the price of the 4" billet, however; and subsequently Carnegie's political operatives achieved a tariff bill in Congress that raised duties on all plates, beams, and structural steel, except for the 4" billet whose tariff was reduced, causing its price to fall. These political shenanigans prompted John McLuckie, steelworker and Burgess of Homestead, to call the company's actions "a gigantic conspiracy assisted by vicious legislation to wrong the workman of what he is entitled to, a fair days pay for a fair day's work." Tariff protections had been very important to the growth of American manufacturing and a key issue in Pittsburgh politics for much of the preceding century, but as U.S. industry emerged as a world leader, they were increasingly less of an issue for technological innovators such as Carnegie. Support for protectionism had long provided a common political interest for workers and capitalists alike; but Carnegie's blatant manipulation of the tariff eroded worker support for the tariff's traditional champion, the Republican Party. McLuckie, in a speech to workers in the weeks leading up to the strike, said: "You men who voted the Republican ticket voted for high tariff and you get high fences, Pinkerton detectives, thugs and militia. [114]

While in New York preparing to leave for Europe on vacation, Carnegie composed a memo to the Homestead workers on April 4, 1892, proclaiming that Homestead would be run non-union upon expiration of the contract. Since the Homestead mill was to be integrated with Braddock and Duquesne into Carnegie Steel on July 1, 1892, Andy's democratic sensibilities demanded that the majority should rule. "As the vast majority of our employees are Non-Union, the Firm has decided that the minority must give way to the majority. These Works, therefore, will be necessarily non-Union after the expiration date of the present agreement." Frick, who preferred to keep the men in the dark about his intentions, ignored Carnegie and did not post the notice. His hostile intentions became increasingly clear in June, however, as he surrounded the mill with a ten foot high, sturdily built wall with gun ports, topped by electrified barbed wire and electric search lights. In negotiations, Frick insisted on lowering the guaranteed floor on the sliding scale and stood firm on the December 31 proposed expiration date of the contract, a provision he knew would be totally unacceptable to the men since a contract expiration in winter would allow the company "to starve us into submission."[115]

The Amalgamated led by the chairman of the Advisory Committee and leader of the successful 1889 strike, Hugh O'Donnell, began to organize the town on a "thoroughly military basis," establishing pickets on eight-hour shifts, river patrols, and a signaling system from the roof of the newly constructed Bost Building, where the union rented the top floor as a battle headquarters. All strangers were interrogated upon entering town. The Slavic workers were organized into a reserve brigade of 800 workers with 6 squads; each assigned a "cool-headed, conservative American" to help control their radical natures. While O'Donnell assumed military command, "Honest John" McLuckie was the spokesperson of the community. On July 3, he told a reporter: "We do not propose that Andrew Carnegie's representatives shall bulldoze us. We have our homes in this town, we have our churches here, our societies and our cemeteries. We are bound to Homestead by all the ties that men hold dearest and most sacred. The Carnegie Company has imported men of all nationalities in places that are east of us and west of us and south of us. They have never imported a man into Homestead, and by [God] they never will."[116]

While the town was celebrating a subdued July 4 where drinking was frowned on, Frick was making final arrangements with Robert Pinkerton to import his agents on barges upriver to Homestead before dawn on July 6. On July 5, acting on a request from Frick "to protect our property from violence, damage and destruction, and to protect us in its free use and enjoyment," the Allegheny County sheriff and two deputies proceeded to the Bost Building headquarters of the Amalgamated where they met with 50 unionists who were coordinating the strike. The union offered to provide deputies to the sheriff to preserve the peace and protect company property, and then escorted him around the mill to show there had been no violence or damage. The sheriff refused the union's offer of guards, said he was satisfied there had been no violence or destruction, but he would send a small force of deputies to Homestead that afternoon. A private caucus of the union followed, at the end of which the Advisory Committee asked the sheriff to enter the room, and Chairman O'Donnell announced the Advisory Committee had formally dissolved. The union was washing its hands of responsibility for any disorder or violence that might happen as a result of the company actions. Each member of the committee removed his badge of office; O'Donnell then added them to a pile of official-looking documents and set them on fire.[117]

At 2:30 a.m. on July 6, 1892, Homestead received telegraphic word the Pinkertons were coming. The result was described by a reporter for the *New York Herald* as "the uprising of a population." His report from the scene opened:

> Like the trumpet of judgment blew the steam whistle of the electric light works at twenty minutes to three o'clock this morning. It was the signal for battle, murder and sudden death, though not one of the thousands who heard and leapt from their beds to answer its signal dreamed of how much blood was to flow in response to such a call..... Not men alone, but women, too; women armed with clubs as they joined the throng which streamed up the Pennsylvania and Pittsburgh and McKeesport tracks picking its way with a fleet-footedness born of long practice over the ties....The leader of the women, a white haired old beldam who has seen forty strikes in her long life, strode to the front, and brandishing the hand billy which she always keeps around the house for just such emergencies, shrieked aloud, "the dirty 'black sheep'....Let me get at them." This was Mrs. Finch, the leader of the Amazons wherever this dark dahomey land of labor goes to war. High and shrill and strong for her years as the voice of the lustiest fisherwoman who marched on Versailles, it rose in the night air and a hundred voices answered it, "Good for you Mother Finch, Damn the black sheep. We'll send them home on stretchers."[118]

At the break of dawn, two 140-foot barges, each with 150 men on board, slowly passed the town on their approach to the mill. Crowds jeered and yelled from the bank. Some shots were fired, mostly in the air, with one hitting the pilot house of the steamboat *Little Bill*. As the boat approached the plant's landing dock and anticipated shelter within the stoutly constructed walls of Fort Frick, the wall was breached while workers also streamed into the plant through train track entries. The crowd assembled along the top lip of the sloping riverbank, perhaps twenty-five feet above the July water level, at the site where the newly constructed pump house and water storage tower overlooked the mill's landing dock. While many in the crowd were still urging restraint, a tragic-comical scene ensued between Billy Foy, a well known Salvation Army character from the town and son of a steelworker, and Pinkerton Captain Heinde. When the captain announced: "We are coming ashore...and there are 300 men behind me and you cannot stop us;" Foy responded, "If you come, you'll come over my carcass." In exasperation,

Heinde struck him with a cane to the head; two shots rang out almost simultaneously, and both Foy and Heinde were wounded.

"Then for the first time the slouched hats (Pinkertons) behind the bulwark of the barges took a hand. A row of rifles gleamed in an instant from the side of the shoreward vessel, and in an instant more a sheet of flame ran all along her clumsy hulk from stem to stern."[119] Three steel workers were killed in this initial volley, including steelworker George W. Rutter, 46 years old, who survived several bloody Civil War campaigns, only to die in battle at his worksite. Among the 300 Pinkertons, most were green recruits; less than 50 had guard or strike-breaking experience. When steelworker Martin Murray was wounded trying to get up the riverbank, the Slovak, Joseph Sotek, was shot in the head and killed trying to rescue him. A high percentage of the killed and wounded proved to be Eastern Europeans. [120]

At this point, the steamer Little Bill left for Braddock with the severely wounded captain and five other injured Pinkertons. The Pinkertons made a second attempt to exit the barges around 8 a.m. and were repulsed; but John Morris, a popular young worker with a family, was shot in the forehead as he peered out of the Pump House. The march through the streets to return his body to his wife helped fan popular fury. The deaths of the German Catholic, Henry Striegel, and Slovak, Peter Faris, who was armed only with a loaf of bread, spread the pain to all the major ethnic groups. The situation for the men in the barges became increasingly desperate as the day wore on. When the paddle boat tried to return to rescue them, it was driven off by gunfire. Attempts were made to burn the barges with oil, a burning flatcar was rolled down the rail spur at them, dynamite was thrown, an old cannon was fired from the opposite side of the river hitting one of the barges, but also overshooting and killing 23 year-old Silas Wain, an English striker who was to be married in the coming weeks.[121]

As the afternoon wore on, worker reinforcements arrived from South Side. National leadership of the Amalgamated tried to calm the crowd and stop the bloodshed. O'Donnell helped convince the crowd to allow the Pinkertons to surrender and then be brought to trial. He personally exposed himself to fire and accepted the Pinkertons' surrender around 5 p.m. As the captured men were led in a column through the mill, a 600-yard gauntlet formed. The prisoners were marched behind an armed phalanx of steelworkers carrying the American flag. At first, there were just jeers and catcalls from the crowd, then slaps and blows began to rain on them. Many were beaten severely, cursed and abused with the women in the lead and friends and families of the dead urging them on. "The women were the most virulent and savage after the surrender and it was due largely to their acts and to their goading of the men that the leaders were unable to restrain the mob." McLuckie and the union men were finally forced to intervene and threaten the crowd with their guns to stop the vengeance. While no one was killed in the gauntlet, the total number of Pinkertons listed as wounded exceeded two hundred: and one traumatized Pinkerton was said to have subsequently leapt to his death when he heard there was a worker mob prepared to meet his train in Chicago. Shortly after midnight, the Pinkertons were put on a train to Pittsburgh in the company of Christopher Magee and Sheriff McCleary. As O'Donnell promised, there would be a trial, but it would be the union leaders who would be tried as criminals, not the Pinkertons.[122]

"The coolest man in Pittsburgh appeared to be Henry Clay Frick. He sat in his magnificently appointed office and smoked cigars. While the battle raged, he displayed absolutely no emotion and refused any discussion with the Amalgamated. 'The men upon our properties now are not strikers, they are lawbreakers.... The supremacy of the law is the only question involved.'" On the day following the battle, Frick only agreed to be interviewed by a single reporter from the *Philadelphia Press* with a verbatim transcript being released to all others. He clearly defined the central issue as to whether the company would have "absolute control of our plant and business at Homestead." In testimony several months later to a U.S. Senate committee, Frick defined the union issue as "whether we had a right to employ whom we pleased and discharge whom we pleased." Not surprisingly John McLuckie saw it differently: "I do not wish this little affair at Homestead to be considered a war between labor and capital. That was a war…between laboring men, because these Pinkertons and their associates were there under a consideration; they were there under pay, and the person who employed that force was safely placed away by the money that he has wrung from the sweat of the men employed in that mill, employing in their stead workmen to go there and kill the men who made his money."[123]

Senator John Palmer of Illinois was among those that understood the central issue for workers. The company's private armed force was in contempt of the authority of the state of Pennsylvania, and the Homestead men had a right to insist on the permanency of their employment during good behavior. "Those large manufacturing establishments would have to be, hereafter, regarded as political establishments in a modified sense, and their owners would have to be regarded as holding their property, subject to the correlative rights of those without whose services their property would be utterly valueless. That only conceded to them a right to a reasonable profit on the capital invested in their enterprises." At the funeral of John Morris, Methodist pastor James McIlyar posed a question. "Of what use can the combinations of capital and trusts be without the broad shoulders and horny hands of the toilers? These are the bone and sinew of the land; these are they who make its wealth and give it its prosperity." Father Bullion, pastor at St. Mary Magdalene, asserted with Senator Palmer "that a workman has a certain right on account of the length of time he has been employed – not the deed of the property, but a certain claim – and that when he protects that property he is doing only what is right. As long as he does nothing wrong he has the right to expect permanent employment; and hence it is wrong for a mob to come here and deprive the workman of the right that is his."[124]

The four days following the strike were spent in mourning the dead and receiving expressions of solidarity from around the country, including sympathy strikes at Carnegie facilities in Lawrenceville and Beaver Falls, but not in Braddock. The joining of the massive funeral processions of John Morris and Peter Faris symbolized the close ethnic collaboration between the Amalgamated's skilled English speakers and the Slavic laborers. On July 10, Democratic Governor Robert Pattison ordered the state's entire contingent of National Guard, 8,500 men, to Homestead. The strikers, demonstrating their belief in the legitimacy of their resistance, planned to meet the troops at the Homestead station as "friends and allies with brass bands and welcoming speeches." General George Snowden soon disabused the strike leadership of the idea that they would receive any consideration from the government by disembarking the troops two stops before Homestead in Munhall and immediately surrounding the mill with soldiers.[125] When the strikers' delegation put forward one of their own, Ollie Coon, ex-captain of the militia, to speak on behalf of the locked-out men and the Amalgamated, Snowden replied:

> I neither know nor care anything about them…. I am not here to look after the strike or the Amalgamated Association or pay any attention to either. I do not accept and do not need at your hands the freedom of Homestead. I have that now in my possession, and I propose to keep the peace…and I want it distinctly understood that I am in absolute control of the situation.[126]

With the government clearly lined up in defense of property rights, the hiring of replacements went ahead at full speed. The women of Homestead reportedly turned a cold shoulder on the occupying soldier boys. Waitresses who refused to serve General Snowden and his officers were fired and replaced by Negro waiters. Arrest warrants were issued for seven strike leaders, including McLuckie, O'Donnell, Sylvester Critchlow and four others. McLuckie got roaring drunk and surrendered, was given bail after a night in jail, and upon release was driven through Homestead in triumph. The others initially hid to ascertain McLuckie's fate, then they too surrendered and were charged with second-degree murder. With between fifty and one hundred reporters on the scene, no labor conflict in American history ever received such detailed and comprehensive eyewitness coverage both nationally and even internationally, especially in England where Carnegie was a major figure and politically active.[127]

On the afternoon of July 23, an assassination attempt on the life of Henry Clay Frick in his offices in downtown Pittsburgh had a decisive impact in swinging public opinion against the strikers. Alexander Berkman, a Russian-born anarchist, who had worked briefly in Pittsburgh for John Most's German anarchist paper, *Freiheit*, returned to Pittsburgh posing as a labor agent capable of providing strikebreakers for the Homestead mill. Being told that Frick was too busy to see him, Berkman forced his way into the office, got off two poorly aimed shots that wounded Frick, then managed to superficially stab him several times before being subdued. Frick's calm determination during and after the attack won him extensive praise, even grudging admiration from workers, though initial reports of the attack elicited cheers from many. W. L. Iams, a guardsman from Waynesburg with the state's occupation forces, upon hearing the news, shouted: "Three cheers for the man who shot Frick!" Refusing to apologize, Iams was arrested, strung up by his thumbs for twenty minutes, his hair and beard completely shaved on the right side of his head, stripped of his uniform and drummed out of camp. He marched with his head thrown defiantly in the air and was received as a hero by many in Greene County.[128]

Raids followed on Pittsburgh anarchist organizations mostly centered in Allegheny City, but few had much sympathy for Berkman, including even John Most, whose *Science of Revolutionary Warfare* included bomb-making instructions. Berkman's lover and steadfast ally Emma Goldman defended him her whole life. But the bitterest rejection Berkman experienced was from a Homestead striker. During his incarceration, he encountered Jack Tinford, the steelworker accused of throwing dynamite at the Pinkerton barges. When Berkman attempted to explain that he acted for the people, indeed for Tinford himself, Tinford countered that steelworkers "don't believe in killing: they respect the law. Of course, they had a right to defend their homes and families against unlawful invaders. But they welcomed the militia to Homestead. They showed their respect for authority. To be sure, Frick deserves to die. He is a murderer. But the mill-workers will have nothing to do with Anarchists." Berkman, appalled at his rejection by a worker who had fought the Pinkertons, could not understand Tinford's failure to grasp the historic significance of Homestead. "How proud I should be in his place: to have fought on the barricades, as he did! And then to die for it, - ah, could there be a more glorious fate for man, a real man? To serve even as the least stone in the foundation of a free society, or as a plank in the bridge across which the triumphant People shall finally pass into the land of promise?"[129]

The mill gradually filled up with replacement workers. In September, the entire twenty-nine member union Advisory Committee was indicted for treason against the Commonwealth of Pennsylvania; but, in the end, no one was convicted. In November, the Democratic candidate, Grover Cleveland, won the presidency, helped by popular resentment against the Republicans over Homestead. On November 13, the strike was declared ended, and many of Homestead's steelworkers found themselves blacklisted for life. McLuckie remained politically active for a while; but when his wife died, he went to Mexico where he worked for the Sonora Railway and remarried. An acquaintance of Carnegie's tracked him down and offered him money from Carnegie. McLuckie refused, saying sarcastically, "Well that was damn white of him." The incident was reported by Carnegie in his autobiography as an exoneration.[130] Carnegie returned to Homestead for the last time in 1898 to dedicate his magnificent library. Fifteen-hundred school children with small American flags sang "Annie Laurie" in his honor; 6,000 workmen were lined up respectfully outside as 1,500 invited, important guests took their place in the library's music hall to hear Andy declare:

> By this meeting, by your welcome, by these smiling faces, all the regretful thoughts, all the unpleasant memories, are henceforth and forever in the deep bosom of the ocean buried. Henceforth, we are to think of Homestead as we see it today. This building, which I now dedicate, may it indeed be an emblem of peace, reconciliation, mental confidence, harmony and union.[131]

A Watershed in Labor History

The defeat of the Amalgamated had dire consequences. Employment at will became the foundation of American industrial relations. Workers were unprotected and wages plummeted. The 12-hour day and the 7-day week became the norm for the bottom half of the workforce; Sunday rest, holidays and the concept of overtime all but disappeared. Health and safety standards deteriorated, so much so, that by 1907, Crystal Eastman found that 195 men were killed in the iron and steel industry in a single year in Allegheny County. Business commentators wondered why the Carnegie interests were so intent on destroying a labor organization that imposed uniform wage scales on the industry, since such uniformity could only help the most technologically advanced sector that Carnegie controlled. The smashing of the Amalgamated led to the ratcheting down of the general wage level, which had the effect of slowing the pace of technological innovation. Without high labor costs, owners had less incentive to automate. Over time, degraded labor undermined investment in innovation and new technology.[132]

Furthermore, the breakdown of the direct linkage between worker process control, productivity and pay, and its replacement by hourly wages, even when accompanied by complex incentive systems imposed by management, undermined worker interest in the efficiency of the mill or success of the company. Attempts by the corporations to reestablish this link through stock sales or profit sharing were of minimal success because they removed the issue from the shop floor. There, the ancient link between more metal and more pay was direct and comprehensible. In place of negotiated tonnage rates as a vehicle for sharing in the profits generated by productivity increases, unilaterally imposed incentive systems based on tonnage became the instrument of speedup. John A. Fitch, one of the most perceptive observers of the steel industry, wrote: "On each man rests the necessity for handling the steel as fast as it comes. The procession must not be halted. Put a strong, swift man at the head of the first gang and the steel does its own driving... When the rate is judiciously cut from time to time, the tonnage system of payment becomes the most effective scheme for inducing speed that has yet been devised. Devices to develop it (speed)...become, when there is no common organization of the men to balance them and resist the encroachment, a system of exploitation."[133]

Perhaps the most devastating consequence of the union defeat, however, and one which in the long run led most directly to the industry's decline, was the exclusion of the workers from any involvement or participation in decisions regarding the organization of production. Management asserted absolute control over the production process and labor lost its ability to negotiate. Workers retained their innate intelligence and indispensability to production, but they developed a culture of resistance and silence toward authority. Their intelligence, imagination, and experience were not consulted. Their silence reinforced the stagnation of the industry and in time contributed to its decline. As Fitch remarked: "A plan which penalizes independent thinking and democratic action does not make for healthy progress," and "the inertia of corporation control...gives rigid uniformity to bad standards as well as good...."[134]

A sad denouement to the Homestead story came in 1894 as the populist leader Jacob Coxey led a march of his unemployed army under the banner of the "Commonwealth of Christ" through Pittsburgh and Homestead. He was on his way to Washington, D.C. to lobby for a federal "Good Roads" plan to solve the deepening unemployment problem. The marchers' goal was to reach Washington by May 1. His march, which set the precedent for other more famous marches on Washington in the 20th Century, left Massillon, Ohio, on Easter Sunday. On April 5, several hundred made the march from Exposition Field in Allegheny City to Homestead. That same day in Connellsville a mass rebellion in the Frick coalfields led to a shootout where twelve strikers were killed, bringing back memories of the Morewood massacre two years before. Among the press who met the marchers in Homestead was a melancholy reporter, Hugh O'Donnell. Coxey's forces and local sympathizers packed the Opera House for speeches where two years before O'Donnell had called for the workers' strike vote against Carnegie Steel. O'Donnell, estranged from his fellow workers following his attempt to reach a personally brokered settlement with Carnegie, felt himself "doomed to wander in the desert of ingratitude." He must have felt a bitter taste from the memory of the once proud, disciplined, and independent steel workers, compared to the chaos of the rag tag "army" of unemployed marching to the capital to beg politicians for relief.[135]

Notes Chapter 6

[1]Allan Pinkerton, *Strikers, Communists, Tramps, and Detectives* (New York: Arno Press & The New York Times, 1969).

[2]*1877-The Grand Army of Starvation*, VHS. Edited by Charles Musser, (New York: American Social History Productions, 1984). A brilliant labor history documentary video on the strike produced and narrated by James Earl Jones.

[3]C. Vann Woodward, *Reunion & Reaction* (Garden City: Doubleday Anchor Books, 1956), explains Scott's role in the splitting of southern from northern Democrats, securing the presidency for Hayes with a guarantee of federal support for a southern transcontinental railroad route in which he had a direct financial stake.

[4]Philip S. Foner, *The Great Labor Uprising of 1877* (New York: Monad Press, 1977), 13-15, 55; Ken Kobus and Jack Consoli, *The Pennsy in the Steel City*, (The Pennsylvania Railroad Technical and Historical Society: Kutztown Publishing, 1996) explains the consolidation and extension of the Pennsylvania Railroad's operation around Pittsburgh in detail; Joseph S. Clark, "The Railroad Struggle for Pittsburgh," *The Pennsylvania Magazine of History and Biography* (Philadelphia: Historical Society of Pennsylvania, 1924).

[5]Robert V. Bruce, *1877: Year of Violence*, (Chicago: Quadrangle Paperback, 1977) 37-9; Donald L. Miller and Richard E. Sharpless, *The Kingdom of Coal: Work, Enterprise, and Ethnic Communities in the Mine Fields* (Philadelphia, PA: University of Pennsylvania Press, 1985), 136-170; Kevin Kenny, *Making Sense of the Molly Maguires* (New York: Oxford University Press, 1998), 245-256.

[6]Foner, *The Great Labor Uprising of 1877*, 29; Bruce, *1877*, 59-63.

[7] Foner, *The Great Labor Uprising of 1877*, 34-44.

[8] Foner, *The Great Labor Uprising of 1877*, 58-60; *New York Times*, July 20, 1877; Edward Winslow Martin and James Dabney McCabe, *The History of the Great Riots and of the Molly Maguires* (New York: Augustus M. Kelley Publishers, 1971), 83-86.

[9]Foner, *The Great Labor Uprising of 1877*, 63-5; Bruce, *1877*, 142-8. The accounts of Foner and Bruce deviate rather substantially as did contemporary newspaper accounts. In particular, Bruce has the Pittsburghers firing the initial shots. Foner has three small children killed citing *The Irish World and Industrial Liberator*, probably an exaggeration, while Bruce has one four year old girl dying of an amputation after a leg wound.

[10]Foner, *The Great Labor Uprising of 1877*, 34-6.

[11]Martin and McCabe, *The History of the Great Riots and of the Molly Maguires*, 99-100. The number of Philadelphia casualties on Saturday is on p. 122 and the estimated killed in the retreat is on p.100; Foner, *The Great Labor Uprising of 1877*, 63-64.

[12]Pennsylvania Legislature, *Report of the Committee Appointed to Investigate the Railroad Riots in July 1877* (Harrisburg: Lane S. Hart, State Printer, 1878), 256-7.

[13]Foner, *The Great Labor Uprising of 1877*, 68-9.; Pinkerton, *Strikers, Communists, Tramps, and Detectives*, 231-40. Foner's book contains the most complete account of the strike as it spread out across various roads and a detailed chronology. Allan Pinkerton's *Striker's, Communists, Tramps and Detectives*, contains an illustration, showing Bob Ammon doffing his cap to the crowd from the back platform of a rail car while Pennsylvania's Governor speaks, with the inscription: "Bob Ammon compelling Governor Hartranft to address the strikers at Allegheny City."

[14]Mary Field Parton, ed., *The Autobiography of Mother Jones* (Chicago: Charles H. Kerr Publishing Company, 1977), 15-16; The insurrectionary character of the 1877 uprising is celebrated in Jeremy Brecher, *Strike!* (Cambridge: South End Press, 1997), 1-22.

[15]Foner, *The Great Labor Uprising of 1877*, 73-77; Jerry M. Cooper, "The Army of Strikebreaker-The Railroad Strikes of 1877 and 1894," *Labor History*, 1977, 184-85.

[16]Francis G. Couvares, *The Remaking of Pittsburgh: Class and Culture in an Industrializing City, 1877-1919* (Albany: State University of New York Press, 1984). 5-8.

[17]Couvares, *The Remaking of Pittsburgh*, 11-23; In Allegheny County in 2006, there are 26 crafts represented in the Pittsburgh Building Trades Council.

[18]Barbara Floyd, Richard Oram, and Nola Skousen, "The City Built of Glass," *Labor's Heritage* (October 1990), 2:75; The union had its headquarters in Pittsburgh from 1886 to 1904, when it moved to Toledo; A nearly complete account of the convention compiled from Pittsburgh newspapers can be found in a series of three articles in the Western Pennsylvania Historical Magazine, v.6, n.4 (1923), v.7, n.1 & n.2 (1924); Philip Taft, *Organized Labor in American History* (New York: Harper & Row, 1964), 87.

[19]Meyer A. Sanders, "Labor," *Allegheny County, A Sesqui-Centennial Review, 1788...1938*, ed. George E. Kelly, (Pittsburgh: Allegheny County Sesqui-Centennial Committee, 1938), 139.

[20]Philip Taft, *The A.F. of L. in the Time of Gompers* (New York: Harper & Brothers, 1957), 11-12.

[21]For the relationship between Labor Day and May Day see Philip S. Foner, *History of the Labor Movement in the United States*, Vol. II: *From the Founding of the American Federation of Labor to the Emergence of American Imperialism* (New York: International Publishers, 1955), 96-104.

[22]Foner, *History of the Labor Movement*, Vol II: *From the Founding of the American Federation of Labor to the Emergence of American Imperialism*, 105-114; James Green, *Death in the Haymarket*, (New York: Pantheon, 2006), I.

[23]Couvares, *The Remaking of Pittsburgh*, 31-50.

[24]Robert M. Fogelson, *America's Armories: Architecture, Society, and Public Order* (Cambridge: Harvard University Press, 1989); Robert Michael Smith, *From Blackjacks to Briefcases* (Athens: Ohio University Press, 2003), 4-5.

[25]Eric Foner, *Reconstruction: America's Unfinished Revolutions 1863-1877* (New York: Harper & Row Publishers, 1988), 62-63.

[26]Walter C. Kidney, *Landmark Architecture of Allegheny Country* (Pittsburgh: Pittsburgh History & Landmark Foundation, 1985), 59-63.

[27]Joel A. Tarr, "Infrastructure and City-Building in the Nineteenth and Twentieth," in *City at the Point: Essays on the Social History of Pittsburgh*, ed. Samuel P. Hays (Pittsburgh: University of Pittsburgh Press, 1990), 233.

[28]Burton Hersh, *The Mellon Family: A Fortune in History* (New York: William Morrow & Company Inc., 1978), 81-5; Couvares, *The Remaking of Pittsburgh*, 64-7.

[29]Clarke M. Thomas, *Front Page Pittsburgh: Two-Hundred Years of the Post-Gazette* (Pittsburgh: University of Pittsburgh Press, 2005), 106-7. In 1891, a decree from the U.S. Geographic Board required post offices in all municipalities ending in "burgh" to become "burg," and for every "borough" to become "boro." This order was finally rescinded in 1911, in part because of the political clout of U.S. Senator George Oliver, the publisher of the *Pittsburgh Gazette*.

[30]Lincoln Steffens, *The Shame of the Cities* (New York: Hill and Wang, 1957), 103.

[31]Steffens, *The Shame of the Cities*, 116.

[32]Steffens, *The Shame of the Cities*, 111-114. The extraordinary Quay-Flinn "Mutual Political and Business Advantage Agreement" can be found on p.111-114.

[33]Couvares, *The Remaking of Pittsburgh*. Working-class temperance movements are discussed p.51-61; Law and Order League approach, p. 75-79.

[34]Joseph F. Rishel, *The Spirit That Gives Life: The History of Duquesne University, 1876-1996*, (Pittsburgh: Duquesne University Press, 1997), 1-16.

[35]Bertram J. Black and Aubrey Mallach, *Population Trends in Pittsburgh and Allegheny County, 1840-1940*, ed. Roy Lubove (New York: New Viewpoints, 1976), 264-278.

[36]Herbert G. Gutman, "The Buena Vista Affair, 1874-1875," *The Pennsylvania Magazine of History and Biography* (1964), 257.

[37]Gutman, *The Pennsylvania Magazine of History and Biography* 264-273.

[38]Laurence Glasco, "Double Burden: The Black Experience in Pittsburgh," in *City at the Point: Essays on the Social History of Pittsburgh*, ed. Samuel P. Hays (Pittsburgh: University of Pittsburgh Press, 1990), 73-74.

[39]Alfred P. James, "The First Convention of the American Federation of Labor, Pittsburgh Pennsylvania: November 15-18, 1881," *Western Pennsylvania Historical Magazine*, 7(1):31.

[40]Dennis C. Dickerson, *Out of the Crucible: Black Steelworkers in Western Pennsylvania, 1875-1980* (Albany: State University of New York Press, 1986), 8-20; Stephen H. Norwood, *Strikebreaking & Intimidation: Mercenaries and Masculinity in Twentieth-Century America* (Chapel Hill: University of North Carolina Press, 2002), 6.

[41]University of Pittsburgh Archives, "Labor Legacy," <http://www.library.pitt.edu/labor_legacy/>.; Raymond J. Robertson, *Ironworkers 100th Anniversary, 1896-1996: A History of the Ironworkers Union* (The Ironworkers Union, 1996), 18-19.

[42]Charles McCollester, "Pittsburgh's IBEW Local 5: The Formation of a Century-Old Electrical Craft Unions," *Pittsburgh History* (1996), 86.

[43]McCollester, "Pittsburgh's IBEW Local 5," 85-86.

[44]McCollester, "Pittsburgh's IBEW Local 5," 85.

[45]John A. Brashear, *A Man Who Loved the Stars* (Pittsburgh: University of Pittsburgh Press, 1988), 40-5.

[46]Brashear, *A Man Who Loved the Stars*, 39-87.; Tim Palucka and Sherie Mershon, *The Engineers' Society of Western Pennsylvania: Celebrating 125 Year of Engineering* (Tartentum: Word Association Publishers, 2006), 29-31.

[47]William F. Trimble, *High Frontiers: A History of Aeronautics in Pennsylvania* (Pittsburgh: University of Pittsburgh Press, 1982), 30-45.

[48] In 1974 shortly after the author came to Pittsburgh, the Brashear Center in South Side was still conducting lens grinding classes for amateur star-gazers.

[49]Brashear, *A Man Who Loved the Stars*, xxiv-xxv.

[50]Foster's tune was called *Nelly Bly*. Through miscommunication, the byline first appeared as Nellie and the designation stuck.

[51]Brooke Kroeger, *Nellie Bly: Daredevil, Reporter, Feminist* (New York: Times Books, 1994).

[52]Kroeger, *Nellie Bly: Daredevil, Reporter, Feminist*.

[53]Hanice H. McElroy, ed., *Our Hidden Heritage: Pennsylvania Women in History* (Washington, D.C.: American Association of University Women, 1983), 363-365.

[54]Westinghouse Electric Corporation, *George Westinghouse 1846-1914* (Wilmerding: George Westinghouse Museum Foundation, 1946), 3-4.

[55]Francis E. Leupp, *George Westinghouse: His Life and Achievements* (Boston: Little, Brown, and Company, 1918).; Henry G. Prout, *A Life of George Westinghouse* (New York: Charles Scribner's Sons, 1922) 224-232.

[56]Leupp, *George Westinghouse*, 113.

[57]Mary Brignano and Hax McCullough, *The Search for Safety: A History of Railroad Signals and the People Who Made Them* (Pittsburgh: American Standard Inc., 1981), 102-116, 128-30, 156.

[58]Leupp, *George Westinghouse*, 132-40.

[59]Margaret Cheney and Robert Uth, *Tesla: Master of Lighting* (New York: Barnes & Noble Books, 1999), 3-11.

[60]Cheney and Uth, *Tesla*, 11.

[61]Cheney and Uth, *Tesla*, 13-27.

[62]Cheney and Uth, *Tesla*, 23-7.

[63]Cheney and Uth, *Tesla*, 27-33; Prout, *A Life of George Westinghouse*, 134-140.

[64]Prout, *A Life of George Westinghouse*, 142-58; Luepp, *George Westinghouse*, 134-40.

[65]Floyd, Oram and Skousen, "The City Built of Glass," 75.

[66]Anne Madarasz, *Shattering Notions* (Pittsburgh: Historical Society of Western Pennsylvania, 1988), 51-54.

[67]Richard J. O'Connor, *Cinderheads and Iron Lungs: Window-Glass Craftsmen and the Transformation of Workers Control, 1880-1905* (Dissertation: University of Pittsburgh, 1991), 28, 85, 106, 138-146.

[68]O'Connor, *Cinderheads and Iron Lung*, 257; Madarasz, *Shattering Notions*, 57-59.

[69]O'Connor, *Cinderheads and Iron Lungs*, 258. The poem was originally printed in the 1907 proceedings of the Third Convention of the Amalgamated Window Glass Workers of America, 1907.

[70]Les Standiford, *Meet You in Hell: Andrew Carnegie, Henry Clay Frick, and the Bitter Partnership That Transformed America* (New York: Crown Publishers, 2005).

[71]Kenneth Warren, *Triumphant Capitalism: Henry Clay Frick and the Industrial Transformation of America* (Pittsburgh: University of Pittsburgh Press, 2000), 10-13.

[72]Joseph Frazier Wall, *Andrew Carnegie* (Pittsburgh: University of Pittsburgh Press, 1989), 481-486.

[73]Wall, *Andrew Carnegie*, 483-97.

[74]Robert Hessen, *Steel Titan: The Life of Charles M. Schwab* (Pittsburgh: University of Pittsburgh Press, 1975).

[75]Wall, *Andrew Carnegie*, 524.

[76]Wall, *Andrew Carnegie*, 525.

[77]Tom Gage, "Hands-on, All-Over: Captain Bill Jones," *Pittsburgh History* (Winter 1997-98), 158-65.

[78]James H. Bridge, *The Inside History of the Carnegie Steel Company* (New York: The Aldine Book Company, 1903), 109-10.

[79]John A. Fitch, *The Steel Worker* (The Pittsburgh Survey), (Pittsburgh: University of Pittsburgh Press, 1989), 114-5.

[80]Fitch, *The Steel Workers*, 15-30; Kenneth Warren, *Industrial Genius: The Working Life of Charles Michael Schwab*, (Pittsburgh: University of Pittsburgh Press, 2007) 4-16.

[81] I am indebted for comments along these lines made by John Hoerr in a letter concerning his reading of a manuscript of this chapter.

[82] David G. McCullough, *The Johnstown Flood* (New York: Simon and Schuster, 1968), 58-59, 79-83.

[83]Standiford, *Meet You in Hell*, 23-24.

[84]Mary Roberts Rinehart, *My Story*, quoted in David Demarest, *From These Hills, From These Valleys*, (Pittsburgh: Pittsburgh University Press, 1976), 102.

[85] Ralph H. Demmler, *The First Century of an Institution: Reed Smith Shaw & McClay* (Pittsburgh, 1977) 19; McCullough, *The Johnstown Flood*, 255-264.

[86] In 1999 a granite grave marker was placed by the Pennsylvania Labor History Society on the long gentle mounds where the remains of 79 of the 109 victims of the Mammoth Mine Disaster were buried in a mass grave at St. John's cemetery in Mount Pleasant.

[87]The difficulties involved in determining the real numbers are described meticulously and explained clearly in Davitt McAteer's recent book. *Monongah: The Tragic Story of the Worst Industrial Accident in U.S. History*, (Morgentown: West Virginia Press, 2007).

[88]Connelsville Courier, January 30, 1891.

[89]Connelsville Courier, January 30, 1891.

[90]David R. Demarest, Jr., ed., *The River Ran Red: Homestead 1892* (Pittsburgh: University of Pittsburgh Press, 1992).

[91]Demarest, Jr., *The River Ran Red*, 7; US Senate Report, November 23, 1892; Emoke Pulay, "The Shorts Fired at Morewood," *The Connelsville Courier*, April 10, 1891.

[92]Paul Krause, *The Battle of Homestead 1880-1892: Politics, Culture, and Steel* (Pittsburgh: University of Pittsburgh Press, 1992), 177-181.

[93]Mark Brown, "Technology and the Homestead Works: 1879-1945," in *Canal History and Technology Proceeding*, ed. Lance E. Metz (Easton: Canal History and Technology Press, 1992), provides the most complete source for the technological advances at Homestead.

[94]Wall, *Andrew Carnegie*, 497-8.

[95]Mark Brown, "Technology and the Homestead Works: 1879-1945," 190-193; The author is also indebted to several conversations with and presentations on steel technology at Homestead by William Gaughan, a former management employee at the Homestead works; Wall, *Andrew Carnegie*, 645-6.

[96]Krause, *The Battle for Homestead 1880-1892*.; Demarest, Jr., *The River Ran Red*, 19.; Bradley Stoughton, *The Metallurgy of Iron and Steel*, 4th ed. (New York: McGraw Hill Book Company, 1934).

[97]Brown, "Technology and the Homestead Works," 187-8; *Scientific American*, August 27, 1892, 132.

[98]Wall, *Andrew Carnegie*, 26-49; Couvares, *The Remaking of Pittsburgh*, 31.

[99]*The Engineering and Mining Journal*, November 5, 1887; *Iron Age*, October 22, 1891, 682; *American Manufacturer and Iron*, May 10, 1889. *The Engineering and Mining Journal* for November 5, 1887 describes the reversing mils for rolling armor plate.

[100]Bridge, *The Inside History of the Carnegie Steel Company*, 164-6.

[101]Brown, "Technology and the Homestead Works," 205; Harry B. Latton, "Steel Wonders", *The River Ran Red*, ed. David R. Demarest, Jr. (Pittsburgh: University of Pittsburgh Press, 1992), 13-15; "Electric cranes installed in the structural mill beam yards by early 1892 displaced many laborers." *The Pittsburgh Times*, June 1, 1892. *Iron Age*, February 22, 1894, 382.

[102]Brown, "Technology and the Homestead Works," 194.

[103]Sharon Trusilo, "Amalgamated Association of Iron and Steel Workers," in *The River Ran Red: Homestead 1892*, ed. David R. Demarest, Jr. (Pittsburgh: University of Pittsburgh Press, 1992), 16-17; Fitch, *The Steel Workers*, 87; Bridge, *The Inside History of the Carnegie*

Steel Company, 154.

[104] Wall, *Andrew Carnegie*, 539; David Brody, *Steelworkers in America: The Nonunion Era* (New York: Harper & Row, 1969), 51. "Technological improvements at Edgar Thomson in 1885 had displaced 57 of the 69 men on the heating furnaces, and 51 of the 63 men on the rail-mill train, so depleting the membership of the lodges there that Carnegie Brothers succeeded in closing down the union at the plant."

[105] Brown, "Technology and the Homestead Works," 206; Paul Krause, *Labor-Republicanism and 'Za Chleborn': Anglo-American and Slavic Solidarity in Homestead* (DeKalb: Northern Illinois University Press, 1986).

[106] Wall, *Andrew Carnegie*, 539; Bridge, *The Inside History of the Carnegie Steel Company*, 201-202.; Fitch, *The Steel Workers*, 102. "A prominent official of the Carnegie Steel Company told me that before the strike of 1892, when the union was firmly entrenched at Homestead, the men ran the mill, and the foreman had little authority....changes for the improvement of the mill could not be taken without the consent of the mill committee."

[107] Bridge, *The Inside History of the Carnegie Steel Company*, 202; Wall, *Andrew Carnegie*, 536.

[108] Wall, *Andrew Carnegie*, 551.

[109] T.V. Powderly, "The Homestead Strike," *Pittsburgh*, ed. Roy Lubove (New York: New Viewpoints, 1976), 29-30.

[110] Demarest, Jr., *The River Ran Red: Homestead 1892*, 34-7.

[111] Demarest, Jr., *The River Ran Red: Homestead 1892*, 1-2; Andrew Nasaw, *Andrew Carnegie*, (New York: Penguin, 2006), 42-44.

[112] Nasaw, *Andrew Carnegie*, 373.

[113] Nasaw, *Andrew Carnegie*, 169-171; Demarest, Jr., *The River Ran Red: Homestead 1892*, 28.

[114] Wall, *Andrew Carnegie*, 529-30; Demarest, Jr., *The River Ran Red: Homestead 1892*, 28-34.

[115] Wall, *Andrew Carnegie*, 555; Demarest, Jr., *The River Ran Red: Homestead 1892*, 30-40.

[116] Demarest, Jr., *The River Ran Red: Homestead 1892*, 40-56.

[117] Demarest, Jr., *The River Ran Red: Homestead 1892*, 66-7.

[118] Demarest, Jr., *The River Ran Red: Homestead 1892*, 76; Krause, *The Battle for Homestead 1880-1892*, p. 17. Margaret Finch ran the popular Rolling Mill House Saloon. The reference to Amazons and Dahomey stems from the contemporary struggle of the Fon people of Dahomey, the heart of the Slave Coast and home of Voudou, against the French. As a French expeditionary force prepared to march out of the conquered capital, Abomey, the African women with concealed guns under their garments fired on the French from behind as their men launched a surprise attach from the front.

[119] Demarest, Jr., *The River Ran Red: Homestead 1892*, 78.

[120] Demarest, Jr., *The River Ran Red: Homestead 1892*, 78; Krause, *The Battle for Homestead 1880-1892*, 16-20.

[121] Demarest, Jr., *The River Ran Red: Homestead 1892*, 76-78.

[122] Demarest, Jr., *The River Ran Red: Homestead 1892*, 115; Krause, *The Battle for Homestead 1880-1892*, 33-34.

[123] Demarest, Jr., *The River Ran Red: Homestead 1892*, 7, 94-101; *The World*, July 7, 1892; *Pittsburgh Commercial Gazette*, July 8, 1892, McLuckie Testimony, July 13, 1892.

[124] Demarest, Jr., *The River Ran Red: Homestead 1892*, 97, 109-118.

[125] Demarest, Jr., *The River Ran Red: Homestead 1892* 107, 129-132.

[126] Demarest, Jr., *The River Ran Red: Homestead 1892*, 135.

[127] Demarest, Jr., *The River Ran Red: Homestead 1892*, 148-153, 158-159.

[128] Demarest, Jr., *The River Ran Red: Homestead 1892*, 162-175.

[129] Alexander Berkman, *Prison Memoirs of an Anarchist* (Pittsburgh: Frontier Press, 1970), 57-59.

[130] Demarest, Jr., *The River Ran Red: Homestead 1892*, 184-200.

[131] Demarest, Jr., *The River Ran Red: Homestead 1892* 206-7.

[132] Fitch, *The Steel Workers*, 64-5.; Crystal Eastman, "Work Accidents and the Law," *The Pittsburgh Survey* (New York: Russell Sage Foundation, 1910), 51.

[133] Fitch, *The Steel Workers*, 184-185, 189, 191.

[134] Fitch, *The Steel Workers*, 213, 200.

[135] John A. Grant, *Coxey's 38-Day March: Through the Alleghenies in Search of Economic Justice* (Pittsburgh: The Council of Alleghenies, 1999), 50-6.

Chapter Seven

The Triumph of Capital

1895 – 1909

In the hundred years from 1800 to 1900, Pittsburgh's relationship with its land and waters changed drastically. The great flocks of birds that once blackened the sky, the panther, the wolf, the woodland buffalo, already precarious at the century's dawn, were gone. The lush pristine landscape, the towering trees, the rivers teeming with an astonishing diversity of fish, turtles, crustaceans, and amphibians, had disappeared. The rivers were nearly lifeless by 1900, serving as drains for the untreated sewage of hundreds of thousands of people, with uncounted tons of toxins and metals discharged from mills and factories, mixed with the acidic discharge from hundreds of mines. Millions of tons of sulfuric acid leached from coal mines into the region's waters annually, annihilating the rich diversity of aboriginal stream life. Along with the environmental toll, the industrial capitalist organization of production was taking enormous profits out of very low-paid and hard-working immigrant families. With the defeat of industrial unionism, the power of the company spilled from the workplace into the community. The managers of the new industrial order demanded unfettered control over their workers, with the right to dictate the terms of employment and even regulate the life of working-class communities.

Industry, Environment and Empire

In 1897, massive fish kills were reported: "The discharges from the many coal mines lining the banks of this stream have strongly impregnated the water with sulphur, which is causing havoc among the finny tribe…. At Hazelwood, it is reported that fully 500 fish were taken out of the river by a crowd of Hungarians, who with clubs and other weapons waded into the shallow water and captured the fish as they floated about in a stupefied state."[1] The once-forested hillsides, stripped of their virgin timber, the giant oaks, beeches, maples and hickories, the spectacular sycamores, were gone. The air laden with the coal smoke from tens of thousands of industrial furnaces and boilers, home heating and cooking stoves, sat in the river valleys dulling the regenerative power of the land, and resting heavily on the hearts and lungs of the inhabitants.

The rivers themselves were dark, murky, oil and sludge-filled, garbage-littered waterways cut off by railroad tracks and riverside factories from the drab industrial towns that sprang up upon what

153

once were rich agricultural bottomlands. The dark and turgid waters became crowded highways where huge tows of barges laden with iron ore, coal, limestone, gravel, and sand asserted the right of way. Individual watercraft virtually disappeared amid the tows and barges. Where the sharp cry of the hawk and the trill of the songbird once filled the orchards and fields of the industrious farmer, the air now reverberated with the clash of metal, the blast of great, angry furnaces, the incessant rumble of machinery, the screech of steel wheels on steel rails. In 1800, barely 1,500 people lived in the little town at the forks of the Ohio, while ten times that number was spread across the county. A century later, 775,000 souls populated the county and over forty percent of them lived inside the city limits. If the City of Allegheny (annexed by Pittsburgh in 1907) is added, the combined urban population exceeded 450,000 or 58% of the county's population, even without the inclusion of the mill towns stretched out along the three rivers.

The urban population was not restricted to Pittsburgh and Allegheny City. From 1870 on, the Monongahela Valley, which had until then remained mostly farm or woodland with few industries other than boat building and coal mining, began a fifty year period of explosive growth along the lower forty miles of the river valley. McKeesport from 1870 to 1890 claimed to be the fastest growing community in the nation with its population swelling from 2,500 to 20,751. Braddock, in the forty years between 1870 and 1910, saw its population increase from 1,290 to 19,357. While enormous resources and talent were focused on the rational integration of the gigantic machines of production, the physical and spiritual needs of the communities that provided the workers who sweated and toiled in the cavernous structures of iron and masonry amidst unforgiving machinery and relentless fires received substantially less attention. While managers and skilled workers, often descendents of the earlier agricultural landowners, moved up the steep slopes to the ridges to escape the constant noise and smoke, immigrants and blacks were tightly packed into the dismal row houses and dreadful tenements, themselves crammed onto the narrow strips of bottom land that bordered the mills and shops. As late as 1930, Homestead had 116 persons per acre, while Braddock had more than 131.[2]

In 1894, writer Theodore Dreiser came to Pittsburgh where he lived for six months. He rode the trolley out to Homestead where he found "so depressing" the "sense of defeat and sullen despair." He vividly described the opposing worlds of the rich and poor which were coming to characterize the region as much as fire and smoke.

> Along the river sprawled for a quarter mile or more the huge low length of the furnaces, great black bottle-like affairs with rows of stacks and long low sheds or buildings paralleling them, sheds from which came a continuous hammering and sputtering and the glow of red fire. The whole was shrouded by a pall of grey smoke, even in the bright sunshine. Above the plant on a slope which rose behind it were a few moderately attractive buildings grouped around two small parks, the trees of which were languishing for want of air. Besides and to the sides of these were the spires of several churches, those soporifics against failure and despair. Turning up side streets one found, invariably, uniform frame houses, closely built and dulled by smoke and grime, and below, on the flats behind the mill, were cluttered alleys so unsightly and unsanitary as to shock me.... The streets were mud tracks. Where there were trees (and there were a few) they were dwarfed and their foliage withered by a metallic fume which was over all. Though the sun was bright at the top of the hill, down here it was gray, almost cloudy, at best a filtered dull gold haze....

On another day I explored the east end of Pittsburgh, which was the exclusive residence section of the city and a contrast to such hovels and deprivation as I had witnessed at Homestead and among the shacks across the Monongahela and below Mt. Washington. Never in my life, neither before nor since, in New York, Chicago, or elsewhere, was the vast gap which divides the rich from the poor in America so vividly and forcefully brought home to me. I had seen on my map a park called Schenley, and thinking that it might be interesting I made my way out the main thoroughfare called (quite appropriately, I think) Fifth Avenue lined with some of the finest residences of the city. Never did the mere possession of wealth impress me so keenly. Here were homes of the most imposing character, huge, verandaed, tree-shaded, with immense lawns, great stone or iron or hedge fences and formal gardens and walks of a most ornate character. It was a region of well-curbed, well-drained and well-paved thoroughfares. Even the street lamps were of a better design than elsewhere, so eager was a young and democratic municipality to see that superior living conditions were provided for the rich. There were avenues lined with wee-cropped trees, and at every turn one encountered expensive carriages, their horses jingling silver or gold-gilt harness, their front seats occupied by one or two footmen in livery, while reclining was Madam or Sir, or both, gazing condescendingly upon the all too comfortable world about them....[3]

Pittsburgh was beginning to adorn itself, however, with cultural and recreational facilities that countered to some degree its grimy and sordid industrial slums. The city had refused Andrew Carnegie's offer of a public library in 1881; and he had gone on to build spectacular edifices in Braddock, Allegheny City, Homestead and Duquesne. Pittsburgh finally decided to support the operation of a library system with tax funds, a requirement of the donor. On November 1, 1895, Carnegie's magnificent library in Oakland was dedicated, marking the beginning of a public library system that opened branches in Lawrenceville, West End, the Hill District, Mt. Washington, and Hazelwood by the turn of the century. At the dedication speech, Carnegie revealed his plans to adorn his new museum in Oakland with a grand hall of architecture where, through life-size architectural casts, museum-goers could compare and contrast masterpieces throughout the history of art. Carnegie outlined his vision for the hall that was completed in 1907: "Already many casts of many of the world's masterpieces of sculpture are within its walls. Ultimately, there will be gathered from all parts of the world casts of those objects which take the highest rank. The museum will thus be a means of bringing to the knowledge of the masses of the people who cannot travel many of the most interesting and instructive objects to be seen in the world." Carnegie, however, stipulated that fig leaves (available from a supplier for 75 cents) or draping be employed on classical statuary, so that "nothing in the gallery or hall will ever give offense to the simplest man or woman."[4]

In 1900, the trustees of the Carnegie Institute honored Andrew Carnegie with a banquet where he announced his intention to found a technical school. He initially provided a million dollars and over the years he contributed $36 million dollars to what became known as Carnegie Technical Institute and later Carnegie Mellon University. Citing the benefits of manual labor and holding up the examples of George Westinghouse and John Brashear, Carnegie said that if Pittsburgh would provide the land, he would provide the money. He concluded his speech with the phrase: "My heart is in the work," which became a part of the Tech's official seal. The first director, Arthur Hammerslag, was an electrical and mechanical engineer who had helped to establish trade schools in New York

City. Initially, the school focused on practical, vocational training leading to diplomas or certificates, not bachelor's degrees.[5]

The recreational needs of the upper and professional classes were also receiving some attention. In 1899, the city's first golf course was established in Homewood and the first auto race took place in Schenley Park. Victor Herbert, whose operettas were hits on Broadway, became the director of the Pittsburgh Orchestra. In 1903, Henry C. Fownes, a Welshman who forged his family fortune in steel, coal and banking, began building a world-class golf course out along the Allegheny in Oakmont. On June 19, 1905, the "Nickelodeon," the first all-motion picture house in the United States, was opened by Harry Davis and John P. Harris at 433-435 Smithfield Street. The first two short films, *Poor but Honest* and *The Baffled Burgler,* were a great success with crowds marveling at the moving images.[6]

What the city squandered in natural beauty and wealth, it seemed to make up in muscle and power. New bridges spanned the rivers. The beautiful Smithfield Bridge finished in 1883, designed by Gustav Lindenthal, from Brno, Moravia (now part of the Czech Republic), replaced John Augustus Roebling's suspension bridge. The Lindenthal bridge has two lenticular spans of 360 feet each, and the flexibility of the structure derives from the pin-connected eye bars of the catenaries. From the side, the structural outline resembles two lenses. Unfortunately, the final Roebling bridge in Pittsburgh, the elegant Sixth Street Bridge, was torn down in 1892, because of the increased weight demands of trolleys. The Brady Street Bridge connected South Side and Oakland in 1896. Two bridges met at the Point: the Union Bridge over the Allegheny was a privately owned wooden toll bridge built in 1874 that came down in 1907; the Point Bridge, across the mouth of the Monongahela, was a steel suspension bridge, built in 1876 and replaced in 1927.[7]

Steel bridges crossed valleys and ravines carrying pedestrian, wagon and trolley traffic along with the occasional automobile by the new century; railroad bridges and "hot metal" industrial spans connected the steel rails that lined virtually every river bank. New trolley lines carried office workers and mill men to work, prompting complaints from middle-class patrons about "grimy workmen," immigrant Slavic and Italian industrial workers covered with "oil, sweat and dust."[8] Steel rail inclines climbed Mt. Washington initially in the 1850s to transport coal from the mines. In 1870, the Monongahela Incline opened for passengers with an adjoining freight incline later added beside it for wagons. Three years later in 1873, the Duquesne Incline, with its two distinctive red coaches and interior wood paneling, opened for passengers further west along the ridge in Duquesne Heights. Eventually 15 passenger inclines linked the river plains to the ridges above, but only the original two passenger ones survived into the 21st Century. Pittsburgh had become the city of steel and steelworkers, and as such cast its shadow across much of the 20th Century. While steel was transforming Pittsburgh, it was also changing America's position and role in the world.

In 1898, a young woman reporter for the *Pittsburgh Leader,* Willa Cather, wrote an article about the patriotic procession and burial in Allegheny City for Lieutenant Friend W. Jenkins, killed by an explosion on the Battleship Maine, the incident used to justify the Spanish American War. The outbreak of war proved less than lamentable for other local observers, however, chief among them, the President of Carnegie Steel, Charles Schwab. Questions about the quality of Homestead's armor plate following the 1892 strike fueled Naval and Congressional investigations in the mid 1890s with Schwab the target. Homestead's armor plate was dramatically vindicated at Manila Bay. Big Steel, especially the armor mills at Bethlehem and Homestead, had proved its usefulness toward the implementation of American imperial designs. The shells that wrecked such damage on the Spanish fleet were made at the Firth Sterling Steel plant in McKeesport. Cornering the outgunned and decrepit Spanish forces, the flagship Olympia, easily absorbed most of the enemy fire and then devastated the Spanish fleet without losing a sailor. Tours were given after the battle to demonstrate how little effect the Spanish artillery had on the ship's alloyed steel armor. Ground troops in the Philippines like the Tenth Regiment Pennsylvania Volunteer Infantry from southwestern Pennsylvania experienced a much more arduous and hazardous mission, however, especially as the indigenous insurgents against Spain began to understand that the Americans, who had once heralded the rebels as freedom fighters, were not leaving anytime soon and in fact, had their own designs on the place. The arrogant rhetoric common in American accounts of that time finds painful echo in more recent imperial adventures.[9]

> A new era has opened up in the history of that wonderful land with its liberation from the Spanish yoke. The dense ignorance and semi-savage barbarities which exist there must not be expected to yield too rapidly to the touch of human kindness and brotherly love with which the Christian world will now visit those semi-civilized and untamed children of nature. Nevertheless, western civilization and western progress will undoubtedly work mighty changes in the lives of these people, in the development of that country, during the first quarter of the 20th Century, which ushers in the dawn of its freedom.[10]

Willa Cather had arrived at the Baltimore and Ohio Station in Pittsburgh on July 3, 1896, at the age of 22, the year following her graduation from the University of Nebraska. She became one of America's noted writers, whose best known works such as *Oh Pioneers!* reflect her youth in Nebraska. She came to Pittsburgh at the invitation of an investor, James Axtell, who hired her to edit and, as it turned out, mostly write, a *Home Monthly* magazine that he envisioned as a rival to the *Ladies Home Journal*. Cather quickly moved on to become a writer for the *Pittsburgh Leader* and numerous other outlets. She was prolific, providing a stream of stories and book reviews for a wide range of national and regional magazines. From 1901 to 1906, she took a position as a Latin and later English teacher, first at Pittsburgh Central and then Allegheny High School. She became highly active in the city's social and cultural spheres, where the children of the wealthy and the children of the middle-class were coming in increasing contact and mix.[11] In 1899, she met the relatively wealthy Isabelle McClung, daughter of the judge who presided at the trial of Alexander Berkman for the attempted assassination of Henry Clay Frick. They toured Europe together, and in 1901, she moved into the McClung household and lived there for over five years. The relationship was the great romance of Cather's life; and when Isabella died in 1938, Cather said that Isabella had been "the one for whom all her books had been written."[12]

Cather wrote a lot of articles about life in Pittsburgh for a newspaper in Lincoln, Nebraska. While she mostly covered the cultural scene, her extensive wanderings around the city led her to describe places like Pottersville, a collection of shacks built as housing for scab workers during the 1892 strike. "One six room boarding house reported seventy inmates, some of the rooms accommodating twenty lodgers. This of course was only made possible by the twelve-hour shift system. Every bed does double duty, and every floor is a bed. As soon as one set of men get up and go to work, another set, tired and dirty, creep into the same sheets and go to sleep." In her most famous story set in Pittsburgh, *Paul's Case,* she documents the longing of a middle-class Pittsburgh student to escape his "highly respectable street, where all the houses were exactly alike, and where business men of moderate means begot and raised large families of children, all of whom went to Sabbath School and learned the shorter catechism, and were interested in arithmetic; all of whom were as exactly alike as their homes, and of a piece with the monotony in which they lived." To escape to New York and briefly achieve a facsimile version of his glamorous dreams, Paul steals from his employer and ultimately commits suicide. Cather did leave Pittsburgh for New York, when offered the prestigious job as an editor of *McClure's Magazine*. What Pittsburgh provided Cather was the opportunity to exercise her writing skills and to teach English, something she really enjoyed, especially her final year at Allegheny in 1906. She was a rarity in that institution, a young teacher. Her teaching was forceful and forthright; some thought her manly. Her energy and her youth made her a force in the classroom and the school. Though Cather worked for many years in New York, she maintained two places of retreat, Red Cloud, Nebraska and Pittsburgh. She often visited Pittsburgh to see Isabella and write.[13]

Seeds in the Mellon Patch

The sons of Thomas Mellon developed the Midas touch through shrewd investments in a rapidly expanding production economy. While the family produced numerous talented businessmen, the unquestioned leader among Judge Mellon's sons and grandsons was Andrew. William Larimer Mellon wrote of A.W.: "When it came to investments that jaw of his did not relax any more than the doors of a locked iron safe until his mind had explored every possibility of losing some of his money." From the time of Judge Mellon, the family steadily extended their real estate holdings. Through political contacts on the local and state level, requisite licenses and permits were awarded that extended Mellon control over gas and electrical distribution and into the traction or trolley systems that were opening up suburban communities to the growing ranks of professionals, clericals, and skilled workers. Control over trolley lines led to expanded real estate investment beyond the Golden Triangle, and the development of new amusement parks such as those at Kennywood and Idlewild provided profitable anchors for suburban car lines with their growing middle class patronage. In 1898 the Mellon-owned Monongahela Street Railway Company leased Kennywood, a rustic picnic grove popular since the 1860s. The Monongahela Railways chief engineer, George Davidson, designed the park's layout around a man-made lagoon. A bandstand was built in 1900 and the first roller coaster in 1902. "Since the Monongahela Street Railway Company paid a single charge for all the electricity their system used, they covered Kennywood with thousands of incandescent light bulbs…. At night Kennywood seemed to be a magic fantasy-land of lights and reflections." [14]

Andrew Mellon extended his father's coal investments through the Monongahela River Consolidation Coal and Coke, or "River Coal." It exercised control over 96 of 102 working mines along the river and 44 boat companies that serviced them with a fleet of tugboats and 3,000 barges. Mellon with his ally H. C. Frick also held extensive holdings in Pittsburgh Coal that controlled extensive rail-accessed coal properties.[15] Andrew Mellon retained a close alliance with Frick until the latter's death in 1919. They were partners in innumerable enterprises. Frick's great fortune was housed in Mellon's banks, and H.C. was a central figure in both the key Union Trust and Mellon National Bank operations. Mellon helped Frick disengage Andrew Carnegie from his steel company and make an enormous fortune in the process. Subsequently, the two of them threatened a confrontation with the newly birthed U.S. Steel by uniting Sharon Steel, controlled by ally Christopher Magee, and Mellon-controlled Union Steel's state-of-the-art wire and nail mill in Donora. Using techniques developed in the struggle with Standard Oil, the Mellon-Frick consortium threatened aggressive competition, showed that they meant business by serious investment, and then sold out at an inflated profit. "Once again the Mellons had increased their fortunes essentially by making their enterprises nuisances to their competitors."[16]

In 1889, A.W. began financing a revolutionary process to produce aluminum developed by the Pittsburgh Reduction Company headed by Alfred Hunt. This company used an electrolytic method, invented by Charles Hall of Ohio in a backyard garage, to precipitate alumina from clay. By 1891, the company had expanded out of its original factory on Smallman Street in the Strip District to a large plant in New Kensington, east of Pittsburgh, which became the mother plant of the aluminum industry. Since the new process required large amounts of electricity, aluminum and electricity grew together. In 1894 the company built a large plant at Niagara Falls to benefit from its cheap and abundant electricity generation. While Hall was the inventor and technological leader, the operations end of the aluminum business was assumed by close Mellon ally, Arthur Vining Davis, who was hired by the Pittsburgh Reduction Company as a 21-year-old graduate of Amherst College. Upon Captain Hunt's death upon his return from service in the Spanish American War, Andrew's younger brother, Richard Beatty Mellon or R.B., became president of Alcoa's Board, a post he ceded to Davis in 1910. In 1893 federal judge William Howard Taft ruled in favor of the Pittsburgh Reduction Company's control of Hall's process over rival claims by Hall's previous employer. This ruling put the company that became Alcoa in a monopoly position that it retained by various means for more than a half-century. Mellon Bank remained the main investor in what, in 1907, became the Aluminum Company of America and, by the mid-1920s, Mellon owned over a third of Alcoa's stock directly. Up until 1909, Alcoa's legal monopoly to produce Aluminum in the United States was based on Charles Hall's original patent. To ensure its position after the expiration of the patent, the company entered into agreements with European producers, in effect dividing world production between them. In 1911, the Department of Justice filed suit against Alcoa for participation in foreign cartels and other unfair competitive practices. This was only the first of a long series of governmental investigations of Alcoa's business practices.[17]

Another of the Mellon "crown jewels," Carborundum, also depended on large amounts of electricity. Using clay, powdered coke, and powerful charges of electricity, Edward Acheson produced an extremely hard abrasive that could scratch glass like a diamond. President of a small electrical utility company in the Monongahela Valley, Acheson had worked for both Edison and Westinghouse. He called his new material "carborundum" and incorporated a company of the same name to produce the material for industrial grinding, cutting, and polishing. Like many other young inventors of the period, he made the pilgrimage to the office of A. W. Mellon for a loan. Once the corporation constructed its large facility at Niagara Falls, its success required expansion and new loans. By the late 1890s, the Mellons were moving their men into operational control; and Acheson himself was ousted and replaced with a Mellon man in 1900. The Mellons, A.W. and R.B., attacked Acheson for lax management and failure to show a profit, although Acheson had invented the product and led the company through the difficult development stage. Acheson, who in his memoirs referred to the powerful Mellon brothers only as bankers "A" and "B," wrote about the takeover: "The business of the Company was then on a fine basis, being ready to enter upon a period of great prosperity, but no profits had yet been made. I had created an entirely new industry, worked out and patented the many details of manufacture, created a stock to supply demands from the trade, proved the value of carborundum as an abrasive and established a demand for same, and all this while the country was passing through a great financial depression." By the end of the decade, the company was profitably producing ten million pounds of caborundum abrasive per year. William Larimar Mellon wrote about the takeover: "the Carborundum Company began to grow in strength and its usefulness expanded wonderfully. That usefulness to America and civilization can scarcely be exaggerated."[18]

The Mellons had extensive interests in oil in Western Pennsylvania primarily through investment in the J. M. Guffey Petroleum Company. While Pittsburgh was the center of the nascent oil industry in the 1860s and 70s, an aggressive Cleveland refiner named John D. Rockefeller learned the secret of vast wealth and power in the petroleum business was not the production but the transportation of oil. The Mellons dominated oil production in proximity to Pittsburgh; but since Rockefeller controlled the network of pipelines serving a growing national market, they needed to create their own pipeline outlet to the east to compete. After a complex series of maneuvers and political manipulation of the Pennsylvania legislature, Rockefeller was able to block their pipeline attempt, forcing the Mellons to sell their Crescent Pipeline Co. to him, albeit at a price that almost doubled the Mellons' total investment.[19]

Andrew's cousin, "W.L." William Larimer Mellon, operated as a wildcatter in Western Pennsylvania. As oil and gas exploration moved south from its origins in northwest Pennsylvania, the Mellons became major players in the Coraopolis fields west of Pittsburgh in the 1890s. Their financial involvement with mineral and oil prospector James M. Guffey paid huge dividends: first, in a lucrative silver mining operation in Nevada through the Trade Dollar Consolidated Mining Company, but especially later, when Guffey discovered an enormous gusher in 1901. Called "Spindletop," it tapped into the great coastal oil fields near Beaumont, Texas, and eventually fed the giant oil refinery at Port Arthur. In only three years, Spindletop's production equaled the entire output of Pennsylvania's wells. Its largesse broke the Rockefeller hegemony over the oil industry and made Texas a major player in world oil markets. While Rockefeller eschewed production and concentrated on delivery, W.L. was determined to create an integrated company that combined production and distribution. Andrew Mellon invested substantially and became the treasurer of the J.M. Guffey Petroleum Company. Problems developed almost immediately between the free-wheeling Guffey and the Mellons, especially since the refining of the heavy, asphalt-based, sulfur-laden, "sour," Texas crude posed multiple obstacles compared with the pure, "sweet," Pennsylvania oil, whose production was already in decline. Also, the massive output of the new Texas and Oklahoma fields drove down the price of oil to five cents a barrel. The resulting financial problems squeezed Guffey and allowed the Mellons to increase their stake and gain a majority share. In 1907 they deposed Guffey, renamed the operation Gulf Oil, initially with Andrew Mellon, and then with William Larimer Mellon as president.[20]

In 1900, McClintic-Marshall, one of America's great construction firms, was formed by two Lehigh University graduates who worked for Pittsburgh's Shiffler Bridge Works. Specializing in structural steel, with large facilities in Pottstown, Rankin and Carnegie, the firm became a major force in construction with projects that included Grand Central Terminal, the George Washington and Golden Gate Bridges, the Waldorf-Astoria Hotel and Chicago Merchandise Mart, as well as the Cathedral of Learning for the University of Pittsburgh. Its most famous project was the construction of locks for the Panama Canal, where it underbid all other contractors by a million dollars and ended up losing two million. A.W. and R.B Mellon financed the company for a sixty percent interest. Another steel fabrication business the Mellons came to control was the Standard Steel Car Company, which operated a major manufacturing facility in Butler, north of Pittsburgh. The Schoen family initially built Pressed Steel Car Company in McKees Rocks into the dominant rail car manufacturer; but they lost control of it to Pittsburgh banker Henry Hoffstot, who in turn expanded the factory in McKees Rocks into a major production center. Standard's main plant in

Lyndora, outside Butler, became Pressed Steel Car's bitter rival. The Mellons came to control eighty percent of Standard Steel Car before they divested.[21]

As the Mellon interests swelled to dominate Pittsburgh and regions well beyond, there was only one major Pittsburgh industry that escaped their control. George Westinghouse's giant electrical and rail controls empire had resolutely resisted takeover. In 1890, a financial panic had shaken Westinghouse, who was constantly investing his profits into new plants and production facilities. He went to the Mellons for assistance but refused to accept their money when they demanded the power to name his general manager. Westinghouse was able to find alternative financing in New York. In the financial panic of 1908, Westinghouse was overextended and cash-strapped. A coalition of financiers including New York bankers and the Mellons moved in and stripped Westinghouse of control over his greatest achievement, the Westinghouse Electric Corporation. While he retained control of the Switch and the Airbrake, the loss of the Electric broke his heart.[22]

While the Mellon family steadily expanded its reach and became one of the richest families in America, money did not always ensure happiness and domestic tranquility. Andrew Mellon abhorred the media spotlight that followed men like Andrew Carnegie, Charles Schwab and John D. Rockefeller. Personally shy and diffident, he preferred to exercise power quietly and indirectly whenever possible. In 1900, at the age of 45, A.W. accompanied his close friend, Henry Clay Frick, on a trip to England. On the voyage Frick introduced Mellon to Nora McMullen, the 19-year-old daughter of Alexander McMullen, whose family fortune came from the brewing of Guinness Stout. After a brief courtship, the couple was married in September of 1900. In 1901, a daughter, Ailsa, was born, and six years later, a son Paul. The marriage was decidedly not a happy one, however. Nora was vivacious, gay, educated and beautiful. Coming from a bright and jovial English manor, she entered into a home and an extended family that was devoted to business and the acquisition of fortune.[23] In an eloquent statement composed as their marriage was disintegrating, Nora revealed the extent of their incompatibility:

> I saw myself in the role of the mistress of the manor who lightens the burden of the peasant... I would go into my husband's American towns and plan and plant and win the love and affection of his people and give them an heir that I would bring up good and kind and generous, a master of his fortune, not its slave....Then my boy was born, as fine a baby as any mother ever was blessed with. But my joy was saddened by the dread of the thought that this baby was to grow up to stand alone as the master, not of a loyal set of workmen, devoted tenants and affectionate servants, with an intelligent appreciation of the master's trials, but as the master of an unreasoning hoard of wage slaves, with an instinctive hatred for the man in the manor that knows them less than they know him....I wanted him away from gray-smoke and dust-filled air of my husband's gold and grim estate. I wanted him to grow big and strong, prizing health more than wealth, in himself and in others. I wanted him to grow up as master not as slave of his fortune: to use it not as a club to dominate with, but as a magic wand to spread health, happiness and prosperity.... I wanted my baby boy to inherit not a town of stony walls, but a town of human hearts.... Nights that I spent in my baby boy's bedroom, nursing these thoughts for his future, my husband, locked in his study, nursed his dollars, millions of dollars, maddening dollars, nursed larger and bigger at the cost of priceless sleep, irretrievable health and happiness. Always new plans, always bigger plans for new dollars, bigger dollars, robbed him and his

family of time he could have devoted far more profitably to a mere "Thank God we are living."[24]

In early 1909, Nora began to have a rather open affair with a man 15 years younger than her husband. Initially, Andrew and Nora agreed to a divorce and a sharing of the children; but, at the last minute, as the children were about to leave on a ship for England with their mother for six months, A.W. decided to keep the children and returned by train to Pittsburgh. Nora followed closely in the following train, returning to their house where a terrible and bitter conflict erupted over custody of the children. Nora defiantly took up residency to assert her right to a share of the children. Her husband marshaled the best lawyers in Pittsburgh and spread the house with 13 listening devices to hear his wife's conversations. On September 14, 1910, A.W. sued for divorce on grounds of adultery, naming Nora's lover, Alfred Curphey. The Pittsburgh papers remained silent for fear of Mellon power. Mellon allies demonstrated their muscle in the Pennsylvania legislature by pushing an amendment to the state's divorce law, eliminating the right to a trial by a jury in a divorce case and allowing hearings of evidence in private. The bill passed 168 to 0, without debate.[25]

It was a Philadelphia paper, the *North American,* that broke the story, and as the eastern press weighed in on the side of the beautiful and sympathetic Nora, Mellon lost control of the story and the case. Pittsburgh papers, bound by a network of debts to the Mellon interests, still did not cover the juicy story about its richest citizen that was unraveling in the east. One of the most revered of news reporters, George Seldes, got his start with the *Pittsburgh Leader* where he was assigned to cover the Mellon divorce trial. To his amazement, he was the only reporter there, since the local papers knew they were not going to print anything.

> Although the Mellon divorce case was headlined in New York and other cities, only the *North American* had the enterprise to ship in bundles of hundreds of copies for sale in our fair city – but the moment the Mellon forces heard about it, they created another sensational news item; they sent the Pittsburgh police into the streets by the dozens, the papers were grabbed, the newsboys clubbed, their property destroyed. The next day's bundles were bought up at the railroad station. All copies that escaped confiscation changed hands easily at one dollar each.[26]

To add insult to injury, Nora's lover, Curphey, who claimed, probably fraudulently, to be a former captain in Britain's Boer War, showed up in Pittsburgh and presented himself at Mellon Bank, with a reporter from the Philadelphia *North American* in tow. He came "to teach Mr. Mellon, that, no matter who he is, he owes some respect to an English woman even though she is his wife…. If I did not have such a decided advantage over him I could find it in my heart to thrash him." Mellon got a court order to remove the children from his own house to a court appointed matron. His daughter, Ailsa, broke down sobbing several times in her mother's arms, begging not to be separated. "Momma, please momma, save me! Don't let them take me away! Don't! Don't! I don't want to go to papa; he doesn't like us, momma." The children gone, Nora and her entourage were forcibly removed from A.W.'s house as neighbors watched. Nora eventually agreed to a private hearing, and the children were assigned six months to each parent. The whole wrenching affair had a profound effect on the children, Ailsa and Paul, who remained distrustful of both father and mother and reportedly of all close relationships for the rest of their lives.[27]

Charles Schwab's Dinner Speech

On the night of December 12, 1900, at a dinner in his honor held by eighty New York bankers and corporate leaders, Charles Schwab, now president of Carnegie Steel, outlined a vision of an integrated, centrally managed steel industry to an enthralled audience that included banker, J.P. Morgan. Schwab was not simply speculating about some ideal theoretical model where greater efficiency, best practices, and superior management would lower costs and increase profits for all. His vision provided a compromise solution that could guarantee stability and profits, head-off a brutal industrial war that was brewing between the Carnegie and the Morgan steel interests, as well as solve the bitter legal and personal feud between Andrew Carnegie and Henry Clay Frick.

Carnegie held his partners and management in a legal "Iron Clad Agreement" that provided him with virtual total control over his minority partners including Phipps, Frick, and Schwab. While the iron-clad agreement for workers was essentially the yellow dog contract, an agreement not to act concertedly, strike, or join a union; for managers and partners, it was the power of the corporation, essentially the power of Andrew Carnegie, to pay off shares at book value for the dissolution of partnership upon action of three-quarters of the voting shares in a company where Carnegie personally controlled over fifty-five percent. All senior management except one received relatively modest salaries and were paid as shareholders whose worth increased with time, but who could lose most of their accrued value if they lost their job. The only upper-level manager paid a full salary, at his insistence, had been the indispensable organizer of the modern steel mill, Captain Bill Jones. He received a salary equal to the president of the United States ($25,000) and, therefore, was the only subordinate willing to push the implementation of an eight-hour day for workers even if it might diminish profits.[28]

The war between the two great egos of Frick and Carnegie was rooted in the structural dependency of Frick on Carnegie and the deep resentment he bore over that fact. Frick's loss of control over the coke company that bore his name and his belief that Carnegie diverted profits from the coke operation, where Frick had a larger share to the steel side where he was a more junior partner, spurred the animosity. Unlike the other Carnegie partners who rose up with or under Andy, Frick saw their relationship as between two sovereigns, not one of subordination. Resentment was fanned by Carnegie's hypocrisy over the Homestead battle where he initially supported Frick fulsomely in public, but insinuated to many, how things might have been different if he had been there. Carnegie resented Frick's heavy handedness, fearing it might tarnish his carefully constructed image of benevolent paternalism. Tension erupted in 1894 when Frick wrote to Carnegie: "…I have become tired of your business methods, your absurd newspaper interviews and personal remarks and unwarranted interference in matters you know nothing about." Carnegie replied: "No one values you more highly as *a partner*, but as for you being Czar and expecting a man shall not differ from you and criticize you, No. Find a slave elsewhere, I can only be a man and a friend." Frick bristled with contempt at Carnegie's holier-than-thou attitude in his 1898 Homestead library dedication speech, where he again expressed doubt in that highly charged public forum whether the 1892 tragedy at Homestead would have occurred if he could have talked to the men.[29]

The breaking point was reached over a verbal agreement between the two men concerning the price of coke and the sale of some coal properties that Frick and his silent partner Andrew Mellon wanted to sell to the coke company at a million dollar profit. In response, Carnegie moved to abolish the post of Chairman, implement the "Iron Clad Agreement," and buy Frick out at book value.

Carnegie dispatched Schwab to get the necessary votes. Carnegie's oldest partner and financial officer, Henry Phipps, Jr., his next-door neighbor in Allegheny City as a boy, who stood to lose the most if Carnegie could so easily discharge a senior partner, dissented unsuccessfully. Frick, in his office at the Carnegie building, was confronted by Andrew Carnegie and informed that he was invoking the "Iron Clad." Frick started for Andy with raised fists, shouting: "For years I have been convinced that there is not an honest bone in your body. Now I know that you are a goddamned thief. We will have a judge and jury of Allegheny County decide what you are to pay me."[30]

In court filings, Frick made public the extent of the wealth and power of the Carnegie interests, embarrassing a Republican Party still committed to high tariffs for the protection of a supposedly vulnerable domestic steel industry. Carnegie still controlled his company, but it had become too large for him to run it in the way he was accustomed. His infatuation with dinosaurs seemed an apt symbol for the greater vulnerability of the corporate behemoth he had created. In fact, Carnegie was increasingly removed from his own creation. He had spent 18 months in 1897-98 between Scotland and the French Riviera without once stepping foot in the smoky city that was the source of his wealth. Under pressure by his partners and the need to reach a settlement with Frick, Phipps arranged the merger of Carnegie Steel and Frick Coke on April 1, 1900, and re-capitalized the new entity, The Carnegie Company, at $320 million. Under the new valuation, Frick's share rose from $4.9 million to more than $31 million. Carnegie's share was nearly $175 million.[31]

The lawsuit was dropped, but Frick and Carnegie never spoke again and Frick's enmity remained unrelenting. In Pittsburgh, Frick built his Frick Building alongside and looking down upon the Carnegie office building. In New York, Frick built a magnificent mansion at Seventieth and Fifth Avenue that outshone Carnegie's residence and housed in it one of the greatest private art collections in the world. The blood, sweat and tears of tens of thousands of workers blasting, shoveling and pushing coal, tending banks of hot, smoky coke ovens, or laboring in the dark satanic mills were morphed into brass, marble, and fine hardwoods to display masterpieces by Velasquez, El Greco, Turner, Degas, Vermeer, Frans Hals, Rembrandt, Van Dyke, Goya, and others. One of Frick's favorite paintings, the *Expulsion from the Temple* by El Greco, showing an angry Christ expelling the money-changers from the holy of holies, was seen by Frick as himself driving the union from the Homestead mill. His daughter, Helen, preserved his beautiful, but relatively modest Pittsburgh mansion, Clayton, as a shrine to his memory. In 1919, Carnegie's attempt at a reconciliation meeting prompted Frick's famous response: "Tell Mr. Carnegie, I'll meet him in Hell."[32]

While this bitter internal conflict was being worked out, Carnegie's empire was under attack from without. While Carnegie's company dominated the production of primary steel products like plate, structural shapes and rails, and his 3 million tons of steel production almost equaled the combined production of his five major competitors, he was increasingly vulnerable as investors like J.P. Morgan and Andrew Mellon began combining various companies that produced finished products like tube, wire, nails, sheet, tinplate and other goods. They were organizing combinations of steel fabricators and threatening to expand primary production at Federal Steel controlled by Morgan, and Sharon Steel controlled by the Mellons, thereby cutting Carnegie out as a supplier. Carnegie, his fighting instincts aroused and seeing the looming battle as "a question of the survival of the fittest," was inclined to go to war by expanding into fabrication. Schwab argued forcefully for expansion of the Duquesne mill into the wire and nail business. Part of the Carnegie war plan included building a tube mill at Conneaut on Lake Erie straddling the Pennsylvania-Ohio line. On another front, Carnegie was preparing to take up the old railroad fight against the Pennsylvania Railroad and its new president Alexander Cassatt. He encouraged Jay Gould in his efforts to expand his Wabash railroad and reach Pittsburgh from the west. A mighty conflict seemed in the offing.[33]

Carnegie's other option was to cash in his chips and sell out. It was in this context that the dinner speech of Charles Schwab to New York investors pointed the way to increased profits and the avoidance of industrial warfare. Carnegie's partners were increasingly resistant to pouring all their ballooning profits into aggressive expansion, when a buyout could bring them immediate and enormous gain. Schwab's speech presented Morgan with a vision of the kind of orderly, controlled, risk-avoiding, and predictably-profitable universe he desired. Carnegie was disruptive and dangerous. "Carnegie was to Morgan what the Anabaptists had been to Calvin, the fanatical enthusiast who in excess of fervor would destroy God and Calvin's orderly plans for the universe."[34] Schwab played the role of trusted intermediary, even enlisting Carnegie's wife in the plan to ease Andy out of the business. Schwab made the pitch to his boss and asked Carnegie for his price. When Schwab carried Carnegie's figures totaling 480 million dollars to Morgan, he accepted. On March 2, 1901, the birth of United States Steel Corporation was announced to the world. Capitalized at 1.1 billion dollars, it was the world's first billion-dollar corporation, and Charles Schwab, aged thirty-nine, midwife at the corporation's birth, was named its first president.[35]

In the Monongahela Valley, the new corporation included the three main Carnegie mills in Braddock, Homestead, and Duquesne; plus the National Tube Works in McKeesport, the largest producer of steel pipe in the country; the Donora Works, specializing in wire, rods and nails; and the Christy Park Works in McKeesport that made specialty tube products, especially artillery shells. In 1904, the corporation purchased the Clairton Coke Works, which by 1918 included more than six hundred by-product coke ovens, making it the largest facility of its kind in the world. In the summer of 1901, shortly after the birth of the corporation, the Amalgamated Association declared a strike that engaged over sixty thousand of the steel corporation's workers, mostly in Illinois. Since the union had been broken in the Carnegie mills, and the largest independent steel producer in the Pittsburgh area, Jones and Laughlin, had expelled the union from its mills in 1897, the strike had relatively little impact on the Pittsburgh region. Termed "one of the most humiliating defeats ever imposed on an American trade union," the strike weakened the Amalgamated to the point that it was virtually irrelevant as a vehicle for worker resistance. A subsequent organizing effort in 1909 by the Amalgamated was easily defeated.[36]

Crimes of Passion

The most famous jailbreak in Pittsburgh was the escape of John and Ed Biddle with Mrs. Katherine Soffel, the wife of the warden, from Richardson's stone-walled, fortress-like prison on January 30, 1902. Memorialized in countless news reports and articles, a play and a movie, and around many a Pittsburgh kitchen and dining room table of rich and poor alike, the tale of the "Biddle Boys" and Mrs. Soffel concerned love and betrayal, an upstairs-downstairs story of class and ethnicity. In the words of Pittsburgh poet Haniel Long, the story told by his grandmother:

... [left] us with the memory of a heroine
who saw love and death as one, and a hero
who could make of love more than a means of escape.
Criminals all, true; yet criminals
are human beings too – how does it matter?

And there are criminals, and criminals –
but love bears witness to its mystery
wherever one can find it.[37]

The Biddle brothers were from Canada and had allegedly committed a run of crimes in Chicago and Cincinnati before perpetrating a string of twenty or thirty robberies in Pittsburgh. Newspapers turned that alleged feat into "99 robberies in 99 days." The Biddles were dashingly good-looking and were robbing local stores using two female accomplices, Jessie Bodine and Jennie Zeppers, as decoys. In the incident that led to their capture, they were robbing a grocery store in Mt. Washington, owned by George Kahny, along with a fifth accomplice, Walter Dorman, an ex-lover of Bodine's who later fingered the Biddle brothers. When Kahny left the store to check on his house, he was murdered, perhaps by Dorman or one of the women. The following day, however, the boarding house where the five robbers were staying was raided by police, and, in a shootout, city detective James Fitzpatrick was killed by a bullet, probably fired by Ed Biddle. The Biddles were captured and put in the county jail. Their trial attracted great attention, especially among a legion of female admirers. Dorman turned state's evidence and directed responsibility for both killings toward the Biddles, who subsequently were sentenced to be hanged.[38]

While occupying cells one and two on death row, the Biddles attracted the attention of Katherine Soffel, the 35 year-old wife of the warden and mother of four children, who regularly visited prisoners and read them the Bible for their consolation and edification. She took an especially keen interest in the soul of Ed Biddle. She brought the brothers saws that they used to cut through the bars under the cover of her skirts while she was reading to them. On the night of the escape, she provided the guns they used to overpower the guards. It was believed she drugged her husband and sent messages to the Biddles from the warden's quarters, visible from their cell, by pointing to various parts of her anatomy. She used her keys to open the prison exit and fled with the brothers. They crossed to Allegheny City and took the Perrysville trolley to the end of the line and began to walk. It was a bitter winter day with deep snow. Mrs. Soffel was slowing the escape, so the brothers stole a horse and sleigh and headed north on the road to Butler where they were overtaken by former "Rough Rider" Charles C. "Buck" McGovern and a posse on horseback. A gun battle ensued. Accounts varied widely as some claimed the Biddles shot themselves, and other versions had the two riddled with bullets. Both died of wounds the day after the gunfight.[39]

Mrs. Soffel was shot once in the breast, in some accounts by herself and in others by Ed Biddle, allegedly at her request. She survived, and after serving just 20 months in jail, she left prison in "a pretty black quarter cut suit and wore a handsome sable around her neck." Her "good behavior and submissive nature" made her a "model prisoner in every respect." In fact the *Pittsburgh Press* gushed: "The awful pangs of remorse which accompanied the retribution of her rash act will be stored away in the archives of memory, remote and safe from all gaze of the public, and with a spirit purified by meditation in solitude, she steps on the threshold of the world to begin a new life."[40] Buck McGovern, who had served with Teddy Roosevelt's "Rough Riders" in Puerto Rico during the Spanish American War, later became Allegheny County Commissioner.

Another dramatic crime of the period had a Pittsburgh connection. Harry K. Thaw, from Allegheny City, was one of the ten children of William Thaw, the millionaire philanthropist, who was a generous patron to John Brashear among others. A wealthy playboy of mercurial and unstable temperament, Harry married one of the most sought after women of his time, Evelyn Nesbit, at the Third Presbyterian Church of Pittsburgh. Nesbit, known after her pinup as "the girl on the red velvet swing," was a chorus girl and model, who had been the lover of actor John Barrymore and the famous New York architect Sanford White. On June 25, 1906, Harry and Evelyn were at dinner prior to a play in the Madison Square Garden Theater that White had designed. Seeing White, Thaw approached his table, believing him guilty of unspeakable acts toward Evelyn as well as actually preying that night on other young girls.

> There I saw him 30 feet in front of me; and as he watched the stage, he saw me. I walked towards him and about fifteen feet away I took out my revolver. He knew me and he was rising and held his right hand towards, I think, his gun, and I wanted to let him try, but who was next? A man, a dozen men might have maimed me, cut off the light, allowed him to escape and rape more American girls as he had; too many, too many as he ruined Evelyn. Half-rising he gazed at me malignantly. I shot him twelve feet away. I felt sure he was dead. But I wanted to take no chances. I walked toward him, and fired two more shots. He dropped…. I walked…straight to Evelyn. She uttered a cry: "My God, Harry, what have you done?" I held her close and told her: "It is all right, dearie, I have probably saved your life." Then I kissed her.[41]

The trial was the sensation of the decade as the bizarre sexual behavior of the very rich was paraded before the public eye. Thaw's mother hired the best lawyers money could buy and mounted a defense based on Thaw's insanity. Allegedly, when he saw White that night, he had a "brain storm" or mental explosion that rendered him incapable of responsible judgment. The jury could not reach a verdict. Thaw spent some time in a mental institution before winning acquittal in a retrial. Insanity as a legal defense and the word "brainstorm" entered into American life and language.[42]

The Pirating of Allegheny

Baseball gradually attained its stature as the "national pastime" following its introduction among troops in the Civil War. Amateur sports of all types, but especially rowing, baseball, and boxing, proliferated among the working and middle classes. The rise of professional sports teams as an expression of Pittsburgh identity originated with baseball. The city was a place where people admired physical strength and prowess, personal effort, and sports competition among schools, neighborhoods, towns, and villages. A rich and extensive network of amateur leagues built around neighborhoods and occupational groups extended through the middle class neighborhoods and industrial towns out into the surrounding countryside's teams of farmers and miners. Professional teams came to embody local values. While teams like the Yankees adopted pinstripes and exuded the power of money, the teams of Pittsburgh from their earliest days emphasized blue-collar grit and toughness.

In 1869, a Pittsburgh amateur team, the Olympics, steamed down the Ohio to challenge baseball's leading professional club, the Cincinnati Red Stockings. The Reds humiliated the Olympics 54-2. In 1876, when the National League awarded eight franchises without one for Pittsburgh, the town's first professional baseball team, the Alleghenys, was formed and joined the International League. After two seasons, the team disbanded. Amateur teams still ruled in Pittsburgh, and one of the best was the all-black Keystones. Racial exclusion toward black ball players was already hardening into place. In 1882, a reconstituted Alleghenys joined the American Association. Finally in 1887, the team was awarded a National League franchise. The following year, the team obtained a good-field, no-hit centerfielder named Billy Sunday. Perhaps his name predestined him, but he would go on to become a fiery evangelist (though famously failing to reform Chicago, "the town that Billy Sunday could not shut down"). On his revivalist tours, he often illustrated his bible-thumping sermons with a demonstration of "sliding into God's home plate and being called safe."[43]

In a dramatic manifestation of mounting union sentiment nationwide, a players' union, simply called the "Brotherhood," was formed in 1890 to negotiate a profit-sharing arrangement with the owners to supplement their rather modest player salaries. Upon the refusal of the owners to negotiate, the players, including most of the stars, pulled out of the National League to form a rival league. Nearly the entire roster of the Alleghenys left for the Brotherhood's Players League team, the Burghers. The union team captured use of Exposition Park and drew the bulk of the fans, while the Alleghenys limped through a 23-113 season. Billy Sunday was almost the only regular player to stay with the Alleghenys. The Players League lasted only one season because of a lack of financial backing and business experience. In the aftermath of the player revolt, a dispute over a player signed by the Pittsburgh team in the reconstituted National League earned the team the nickname "Pirates." Probably to shake the Allegheny name after the previous humiliating season, what was an accusation was adopted as the official team name. Management also imposed a $2,400 a year salary cap. That same year a skinny catcher named Cornelius McGillicuddy, but called by every one "Connie Mack," joined the team. After being injured in a spiking incident, Mack went on to coach the Pirates for two years and the rival Philadelphia Phillies for decades.[44]

In 1900, the National League decided to reduce the number of teams from 12 to 8. The Louisville club, owned by businessman Barney Dreyfus, was cut from the roster. Dreyfus was enticed to bring an impressive collection of players to Pittsburgh, where he was named the president of the team. Fred Clarke, a future baseball hall-of-famer, was his player-manager. Dreyfus remained president of the Pittsburgh ball club for 32 years. Among the players he brought to Pittsburgh was the man, Honus Wagner, who firmly established professional baseball in the minds and hearts of the city. Wagner, known as "The Flying Dutchman," or to friends simply as "Dutch," was born in Mansfield, now known as Carnegie, an industrial suburb southwest of Pittsburgh along Chartiers Creek. He attended a German Lutheran school, then he followed his father into the coal mines. Following the normal path for a miner boy, he started at the breaker, sorting coal from slate, and then moved into the mine as a loader. Wagner recalled: "I seldom saw daylight except on Sundays and holidays.... I'd start for work very early in the morning when it was still dark and return home in the dusk and darkness of the evening. I worked on what was known as a 'boy car.' I loaded a ton of coal a day in one of those cars for 70 cents a ton. That's why it was called a 'boy car,' because it was all a boy of nine could handle. My pay averaged about $3.50 per week."[45]

Wagner, who loved hunting, fishing, and beer drinking almost as much as he loved baseball, was an intimidating physical presence on the field. "Wagner was a bulging, squat giant, with a wide, thick chest and legs so bowed one could have rolled a barrel through them. Weighing around 190 pounds, he had big awkward-looking feet and great gangling gorilla-like arms. The arms hung loosely hinged from his wide shoulders and from the ends dangled great hams of hands."[46] He also played professional basketball for 20 years with a Carnegie-based team during the off-season. In 1900, his first year as a Pirate, Wagner led the team to a second place finish and, with a batting average of .381, became the National League's batting champion, a feat he would achieve eight times. In 1901, playing shortstop for the first time, he led the Pirates to their first pennant, beating the Phillies by seven-and-a-half games. In 1902, perhaps the greatest Pirate team of all time had a phenomenal 103-36 record and finished 27½ games ahead of Brooklyn – the widest margin in major league history. The following year, the National League recognized and made an accommodation with the rival American

League that included a "World Series" championship. Pittsburgh repeated as National League champion with Honus Wagner and Fred Clarke leading the league in hitting; but in the first World Series, they fell in eight games to the Boston Pilgrims, whose players included among other standouts, a young pitcher named Cy Young.[47]

While Honus Wagner kept up his dominating batting, the Pirates slipped to second in 1905, third in 1906, second in 1907, and second again in 1908. Prior to the 1908 season, Wagner demanded a $10,000 a year salary and threatened to go home and open a garage in Carnegie if he did not get it. "Barney had to convince me that $10,000 a year in baseball was better than the garage business." He got his price. In that same year, he famously refused to allow a cigarette company to use his picture on a baseball card, not because he was against tobacco since he both smoked and chewed, but because he did not want to be a negative influence on young people. The company printed seven cards as a demo, and the single one that has survived is the most valuable baseball card in history.[48]

Similar to the Pittsburgh baseball club's "pirating" of the Alleghenys, the City of Pittsburgh pirated the City of Allegheny itself (today's North Side) in 1907 through a combined referendum where Allegheny City was annexed against its will. After several attempts at annexation failed beginning in 1867, an annexation bill was introduced into the legislature in 1903, and in 1905, enabling legislation was passed. In June 1906, the annexation vote acquired a simple majority of the combined vote. State law provided for "the union of cities which are contiguous or in close proximity, by the annexation of the lesser to the larger." Pittsburgh pursued its takeover through the legislature and then defended the election procedures in state court, ending with a favorable decision by the U.S. Supreme Court on November 18, 1907. Pittsburgh with a population of approximately 350,000 and 62,000 voters absorbed Allegheny City with 150,000 people and 24,000 voters. Pittsburgh cast 31,117 votes for the merger and 5,323 against, while Allegheny City voted 12,307 against the measure and 6,747 in favor.[49]

The lawsuit filed by citizens of Allegheny City pointed to the financial health of their city compared to the deep indebtedness of the city of Pittsburgh, as a result of Bigelow's extensive park building, the excavation and removal of the 'hump" on Grant Street, the construction of a water filtration plant, and an electrical generation facility. They argued that Pittsburgh's action, given the additional taxes and burdens imposed on the smaller city, constituted a "taking" or a depreciation in the value of their property. The Supreme Court ruled unequivocally that municipalities are subject to "the absolute discretion of the state." "Municipal corporations are political subdivisions of the state, created as convenient agencies for exercising such of the governmental powers of the state as may be intrusted to them.... The state, therefore, at its pleasure, may modify or withdraw all such powers, may take without compensation such property...with or without the consent of the citizens or even against their protest."[50]

In 1909, insult was added to injury when the Pirates moved from their old Allegheny City home in Exposition Park, where rising water from the river occasionally inundated the field, to the new Forbes Field, constructed in Oakland adjacent to the University of Pittsburgh. The stadium, like the avenue on which it was located, was named for the British General who founded Pittsburgh. The stadium, the nation's first steel and concrete structure of its type, was opened in 1908 during Pittsburgh's sesquicentennial, the 150th anniversary of Forbes' entry into the smoldering ruins of Fort Duquesne. Fittingly, the stadium entry was located at Forbes Avenue and Bouquet Street, named for the tough Swiss mercenary Colonel Bouquet, who had been instrumental to the success of Forbes' mission. Built along the edge of Panther Hollow, the stadium encased a wonderfully eccentric field with a very short right field (300 feet), a long left field (365), and a very deep center field that reached 462 feet in left center. In 51 years, no pitcher ever posted a no-hit game on that field. On June 30, 1909, Mayor Christopher Magee threw out the first ball from his box seat, before more than 30,000 fans. Pittsburgh now had a real major league stadium, and the city, extended to enclose the Forks of the Ohio, boasted of a population over 600,000, seventh largest in the nation.[51]

That year, 1909, Pittsburgh won the pennant by six-and-a-half games over Chicago and faced the Detroit Tigers, led by the redoubtable Ty Cobb. The series matched two industrial cities and featured a legendary match-up between Wagner and Cobb, two of the greatest hitters and base runners in baseball history. Cobb was famous for aggressive base running and effective use of razor-sharp spikes. The Pirates won the series in seven games with Wagner batting .333 and Cobb only .231, avenging their embarrassing loss to the upstart American leaguers in 1903. The hero of the series for the Pirates was Babe Adams, who pitched and won three games. The three games held in Pittsburgh drew almost 83,000 fans. The series was the occasion of a legendary encounter whose very existence has been questioned in recent accounts. It was a story recounted by Honus Wagner many times over the years and entered baseball lore as a permanent fixture. "Once after Cobb reached first base, he yelled to Wagner: 'I'm coming down on the next pitch, you big krauthead.' 'I'll be waitin' for you,' called Honus. As he took Gibson's throw, Wagner tagged Cobb so vigorously in the mouth that he loosened several of Ty's teeth." Honus Wagner won his eighth and final batting title in 1911, but the Pirates would not win another pennant until 1927. Wagner retired as a player in 1917, returning to his home in Carnegie. He had hit better than .300 in 15 consecutive seasons, played in 2,800 games, and stolen 722 bases.[52]

Death on the Job

As Pittsburgh, the great pioneering center of the new industrial order, entered the 20th Century, the toll in human life exacted by its industry, construction, and abysmal public health infrastructure was steadily mounting. Deadly construction accidents included the collapse of the Wabash Bridge over the Monongahela in 1903. The bridge marked an attempt by the ill-fated Wabash Railroad to break into the important freight and passenger hub of Pittsburgh, long dominated by the Pennsylvania Railroad. The bridge had to be constructed at a significant height above the surface of the Monongahela to pass over tracks and roads to enter a long tunnel through Mt. Washington. On October 19 at 8:30 am, as the central span was being extended out over the river, it collapsed onto passing coal barges. Ten ironworkers were killed, and three were injured. A passerby described the scene: "They fell through the air like flies…. The men were shrieking and yelling as they fell. Some were clinging to the pieces of iron and beams. Others had become separated from the falling mass and dropped through the air. The entire mass fell with a sickening thud on the barges beneath. One of the barges was sunk immediately. It seemed that few of the men on the barges saw the mass falling on them. If they did it was too late. Several of the men at work on the barges jumped into the river just before the wreckage from above struck the barges." Hearing of the accident, 400 structural ironworkers from all over the city, including Local 3 president, C. P. Fitzgerald, made their way to the scene and began removing steel to assist the search for survivors. [53]

The mounting death toll in the burgeoning bridge and structural iron-working trades was a subject of growing concern and organizational focus for the newly formed International Association of Bridge and Structural Iron Workers at their convention in Toronto in 1904. Seven years earlier in

1896, only five blocks from the site of the Wabash bridge collapse, Pittsburgh Ironworkers Local 3 had hosted the founding convention of the Bridge and Structural Iron Workers International Union at Morewood Hall.[54]

The strength of the Ironworkers Union demonstrated that while unionism was dealt an almost mortal blow in the industrial sector after the Homestead strike of 1892, labor organization was thriving in virtually every craft and skilled trade sector in the city. On February 10, 1908, the Pittsburgh Building Trades Council was organized with many organizations that have remained a part of the life of the city for more than a century including: Asbestos Workers (Insulators) Local 2, Bricklayers Local 2, Bridge and Structural Ironworkers Local 3, Electrical Workers Local 5, Engineers Local 95, Building Laborers Local 11, Common Laborers 1040, Roofers Local 3, Steamfitters Local 449, the Cement Finishers, Sheet Metal Workers Local 12, and the Carpenters District Council. The carpenters were probably the oldest construction union with the Carpenters District Council of Western Pennsylvania chartered in 1877, followed by the Plumbers, organized in 1879. The Sheet Metal Workers Local 12 was founded in 1880 as Tinners and Cornice Workers of Allegheny County Local 1, and several Pittsburgh local leaders served as officers of the national organization in its early years. Most of the building trades organizations dated from the 1880s. The Bricklayers were the highest paid construction workers and were the first to achieve the eight-hour day in 1896. By 1900, most of the other building trades had secured the eight-hour day as well. In 1908, after twenty years of rivalry between the American Federation of Labor and the powerful Knights of Labor District Assembly No. 3, that had more or less functioned as the city's central labor organization, the Iron City Trades Council was formed and established itself as the city's dominant labor federation. In 1925, it changed its name to the Pittsburgh Central Labor Union.[55]

The International Union of Steam and Operating Engineers Local 66 was chartered in 1901. An organization of steam engineers involved in hoisting and excavation, the organization held its Sixth Annual Convention in 1902 in Pittsburgh. The union was continually involved in jurisdictional disputes with miners, ironworkers, electricians and stationary engineers over attempts by steam engineers to leave those unions and join the operators. Local 85 of the Amalgamated Transit Union was chartered on May 21, 1897 and in 1903 hosted the Eighth International Convention of the trolley operators' union. The Pittsburgh convention was the largest gathering yet for the union as representatives of 84 locals gathered from the United States and Canada. Notable for the attendance of the first female delegate, elected to represent employees of the Chicago Elevated Service, the convention established its first Defense Fund to support members on strike and pay costs associated with the arbitration of disputes.[56]

The low numbers designating many of Pittsburgh's local unions often indicate that these organizations were among the founding entities of their respective national unions. This is strikingly true of the Pittsburgh Firefighters Local 1 which was organized on May 5, 1903. The first union president, Frank Jones, represented the union at the 1904 AFL convention in San Francisco. He called on the labor federation to unionize the fire service across the nation. Jones was fired by the Department for his efforts and the local union members banded together to pay his salary until his reinstatement two years later. As early as 1899, Pittsburgh Police threatened to strike over long hours, poor pay, no vacations, and forced assessments for "campaign funds." Police were not compensated for working parades or attending court hearings. Pittsburgh's Fraternal Order of Police also carries the designation of "Local 1."[57]

By the first decade of the 20th Century, Pittsburgh's building trades unions had daily wage rates higher than those of any other group of workers in the Pittsburgh district. With 15,000 members, they controlled about 75 percent of all men working in the trades. Some trades like plumbers, bricklayers, elevator constructors and steamfitters were over 90 percent union. In an article, "The Wage Earners of Pittsburgh," co-authored by the legendary labor historian and economist John R. Commons, the reasons for this relative strength were outlined. They also help explain why the construction trades have been able to survive organizationally into the 21st Century.

> Turning to the building trades we find a set of workmen who have forced their daily rates of wages higher than those of any other men in the district. At least four things have helped them do this: First, the skill required in the trades; second, the closely allied unions; third, the seasonal character of the work; and fourth, the fact that the work has to be performed at a particular place, at a particular and usually limited time, under constant pressure from the purchaser.[58]

While concern over wages and hours were common to all unions, health and safety issues were paramount for many occupations. In no industry was the death and injury toll on workers worse than in the coal industry. In Pennsylvania alone, the death toll in the coal mines exceeded one thousand men per year for twenty-six of the thirty years between 1890 and 1920. The state's worst year was 1907 when 1,514 miners died on the job, with 806 killed in the bituminous fields and 708 in the anthracite.[59] On January 25, 1904, at 8:15 am, an explosion ripped through the Harwick Mine whose extensive workings ran approximately 550 feet below the towns of Cheswick and Springdale, Pennsylvania, on the Allegheny River, 15 miles northeast of Pittsburgh. Methane gas or "fire damp" accumulated in the tunnels because ice as thick as three feet formed around airshaft intakes in the bitterly cold weather, choking the ventilation system and restricting the flow of life-giving oxygen. Varying accounts told of from 177 to 186 men killed, including either 2 or 8 rescuers. Most of the dead were miners in the deep mine; but several workers were killed at the tipple by the force of the explosion; and four Italians who were reportedly working in the main entry shaft fell into the pit and were covered by falling elevator weights. The dead included Polish, English, Russian, Irish, and an exceptionally large contingent designated "Hungarian" that included Slovaks and Croatians but also a substantial group of 58 members of the first Hungarian Reformed Church of Homestead.[60]

The mine inspector said "none of the bodies showed any sign of suffering before the victims met death, which was caused by the ignition of fire-damp and dust in No. 1 monkey butt, on the south side of the mine by a blown-out shot. The shot was placed 18 inches over on the solid coal and lighted by gas, which, by the fine particles of coal dust suspended in the air, traveled into every place in the mine like a streak of lightening, carrying destruction in its path until it finally expended its force up the air and hoisting shafts." [61] A mule was blown into the air and fell dead several feet from the mine entrance. The only survivor was a young 16-year-old German immigrant named Adolph Gunia, who would normally have been with his father and brother deep in the mine and like them killed; however, since someone failed to come to work, he filled in as a trapper, putting coal cars onto the elevator at the shaft's base. Badly burned and bleeding beneath a pile of debris with water rising around him, he was extracted and carried all the way to Pittsburgh's St. Francis Hospital in an ambulance pulled by a team of mules. Two rescuers were killed by "afterdamp," the build-up of poisonous gases especially carbon monoxide after the blast. Selwyn Taylor was a mining engineer who was with the first rescue team that entered the mine and rescued Adolph Gunia. Daniel Lyle, a coal miner with a wife and five children from Castle Shannon, died in a subsequent rescue attempt when overcome by gas. Andrew Carnegie donated $40,000 toward the relief fund for wives and orphans of the deceased. Three months later, he established a $5 million trust to endow the Carnegie

Hero Fund, so that "heroes and those dependent on them should be freed from pecuniary cares resulting from their heroism." In the century following the Harwick disaster, more than eight thousand awards were made.[62]

Most of the bodies, burned beyond identification, were buried close by the present Cheswick Power Plant in land donated by St. Mark's Lutheran Church. It is believed that up to 165 remains of bodies lie there. In a stunning decision, the Allegheny County Jury Inquest recommended censuring the Allegheny Coal Company for breaking the law, charging negligence by the mine foreman and the fire boss (both killed), and recommending murder charges for the mine inspector and mine superintendent.[63]

This terrible tragedy was not, however, the worst in Pennsylvania mining history. On Dec. 19, 1907, an explosion killed 239 men and boys, many Hungarian immigrants, at the Darr coal mine near Jacob's Creek and Van Meter along the Monongahela River in Westmoreland County. Some of the dead were from the closed Naomi mine, near Fayette City, which exploded on Dec. 1, killing 34. In Olive Branch Cemetery, 71 Darr miners, 49 unknown, are buried in a common grave. Over 3,000 coal miners died in the month of December, 1907, the worst single month for fatalities in U.S. coal mining history. This month included the deadliest event in the bloody history of American coal mining, the Monongah, West Virginia, explosion that took the lives of 362 miners. While the Monongah Disaster happened on the Roman Catholic feast of St. Nicholas, the Darr Mine explosion happened the day after the mine reopened following celebrations for the Eastern Orthodox and Byzantine Catholic (Carpatho-Rusyn) feast of St. Nicholas. Since hundreds of men at both locations were spared because of religious duties or hangovers, this strange coincidence became known as the "Miracle of St. Nicholas." At Darr, up to two hundred Eastern Europeans were spared because they were sleeping off the effects of the celebratory feast. This caused the majority of the deaths to be among the American-born miners.[64]

Mrs. John Campbell was the wife of a sixty-year-old miner who had quit one mine because of dangerous conditions there and had told her about the gaseous atmosphere at Darr. Waiting for her husband come out of the mine for his noon meal, she felt the house shake and heard a great rumbling sound. "She went to the door and saw great columns of smoke belch from the mine…She had been a miner's wife too long not to realize the importance of that rumbling. She threw up her hands and gave one despairing scream and ran with a few of her neighbors to the mouth of the mine. There in agony she watched and waited, wringing her hands and praying, hoping against hope until someone gently led her aside and told her that her husband's body was the first one found." He had nearly been clear of the mine but was overcome by gas. As the coroner worked to identify the men, they were kept in the mine and not released to be buried. The stench of death emanated from the mine entry and could be smelled a mile distant. Horses and mules needed to remove the bodies refused to enter the mine even when whipped. The owner of the mine, the Pittsburgh Coal Company, claimed they paid the burial expenses, but then it was discovered that every miner had been forced to buy an insurance policy as a condition of employment. The mine had a reputation for poor management and adamant refusal to deal in any way with the miner's union. Relief was slow in coming to the 542 widows, children and other dependents, since the Monongah disaster in West Virginia was getting most of the national press coverage.[65]

The reckless all-out expansion of mining to feed explosive growth in steel production and power generation absorbed a seemingly relentless flow of immigration into a world with few safety controls and no amenities. From 1870 to 1900, the number of miners increased fivefold, from one hundred thousand to over one half-million. While thousands of miners were dying from explosions, rock falls, electrocution, suffocation, equipment failures and other causes, uncounted thousands of others were dying young, or suffering for prolonged periods, from the debilitating effects of what became known as "black lung." Doctors in the 19th Century had documented numerous cases of the "black spit" of miners who expectorated "a fluid closely resembling black paint." In 1869 a doctor from Pottsville in the anthracite region noted the great excess of old women in mining towns and the fact that few miners lived past 55 years of age. He provided a clinical picture of a typical veteran miner: "A peculiar asthmatic character of cough is generally noticed; emphysema is detected on physical exploration, and the sputa are black, often streaked with blood. Miner's asthma is chronic bronchitis, with thickening of the air passages, emphysema and nervous distress in breathing….The black expectoration is observed for years after ceasing work in the mines." In 1881 a professor of medicine wrote part of his report on the ailment with the fluid from a miner's lung.[66]

Unfortunately, there was no known remedy for the disease. The only solution to the problem was prevention: adequate ventilation at the mine face, adequate protective equipment, good training and excellent mine organization, all areas of serious expense and relative rarity. It was far more cost effective to use corporate power to block or redirect the attention of the small and poorly funded public health community in other directions. Public health officials' attention was diverted toward the unhygienic personal habits of mine employees, especially among the multilingual immigrant hordes and the obvious deficiencies in the sewage arrangements of the mining towns. Public health officials concentrated on contagious disease like typhoid fever, not on the widespread incidence of miners with severely damaged lungs. Inside the mines, Pennsylvania inspectors directed their attention toward methane detection and the explosiveness of coal dust rather than on any chronic effect the dust might have on the men who worked in the pits.[67]

After the 1902 anthracite strike, revered mine leader John Mitchell raised the issue in a national forum: "When we look upon the enormous fortunes that our labor has made possible, with the innumerable comforts and luxuries that it brings to the people at large, and then examine the paltry pittance we undergo [sic], the dampness we must endure, the foul air we must breathe, and the peculiar rheumatic and lung troubles super-induced by these conditions, which we must bear, we naturally feel that we are being unjustly dealt with." Following the strike, a regular drumbeat was initiated to counteract claims of coal dust inhalation's dangers. Samuel Haythorn at the University of Pittsburgh in 1911, after a ten-day test on a guinea pig and an eighty-seven day test on a single rabbit, concluded the blackened tissue of the lung only marked a harmless discoloration. Researchers began to contend that coal dust guarded miners from tuberculosis, unlike silicosis dusts that fostered tubercular infection. Others argued the sulfur or other chemicals in coal acted as an antiseptic that guarded against bacteria. By 1915, the industry journal *Coal Age* felt able to announce that "the atmosphere of the mine is now vindicated." Furthermore, in an article on a miner who lived to be 98, they asserted: "There are no healthier men anywhere than in the mining industry." By 1920 the introduction of mechanized mining cutters and power drills produced qualitatively higher levels of dust, while powered belts and equipment meant the constant circulation of microscopic mineral dust throughout the mine.[68]

Crystal Eastman came to Pittsburgh at the age of 26 in 1907. Graduate of Vassar with a Masters from Columbia University, she placed second in her Law School class at New York University. Initially hired for two months by Paul Kellogg of the *Pittsburgh Survey*, she stayed more than a year investigating the industrial accidents that occurred in Allegheny County during 1906-07. Her study of the 526 workplace deaths in a twelve-month span analyzed the hazards of various occupations and detailed the profound impact the deaths had on workers' families. She also highlighted the inadequacy of the law in regard to worker protection and exposed the pitiful levels of compensation paid for worker death and injury. Her classic *Work Accidents and the Law* is one of the most important contributions to the cause of worker health and safety produced in the United States. "This one bolt of statistical lightening started the safety ball rolling."[69] Following her stay in Pittsburgh, she was commissioned by the governor of New York in 1909 to investigate work accidents and recommend legislation, which led to that state's workers' compensation law. The courts struck down New York's law shortly before the Triangle Shirtwaist fire that killed 146 women. The resulting outrage helped to propel workers compensation laws through many state legislatures including Pennsylvania's. She campaigned against World War I and, with social worker Jane Addams, founded the Woman's Peace Party. She was also a founding board member of the American Civil Liberties Union. With three other women she wrote the Equal Rights Amendment in 1923.

What distinguishes Crystal Eastman as a safety researcher is the rigorous and detailed collection of data combined with a deep compassion for the plight of the worker and the family who faced the consequences of industrial death and injury. As she investigated 526 industrial deaths and 509 hospitalizations of workers in Allegheny County, and followed 132 families of married men for up to eighteen months after the accident, she interviewed witnesses and family members and composed a view of industrial safety that was worker-centered. Her findings completely contradicted the truism, invariably repeated to her by managers she interviewed, that "95 percent of our accidents are due to the carelessness of the man who gets hurt." This attitude reflected the state of law in Pennsylvania that in 1901 was the most one-sided in favor of the employer of any state in the nation. The rule in Pennsylvania was that if "the negligence of the party contributed in *any* degree to the injury he cannot recover damages or compensation." Upon detailed analysis of accidents, she determined that in only 32 percent of fatalities was personal responsibility a factor, and, of these, most were due to inattentiveness caused by long hard hours of heat, noise, and speed or to a recklessness on the part of the worker that, like with brakemen, was part of the trade. Most safety investigators examined the circumstances of an accident, assigned blame, and perhaps made specific and narrow remediation proposals. Eastman investigated the social and familial impact of the industrial carnage along with straightforward recommendations for both policy and practice.[70]

> If we were to regard the year's industrial fatalities in Allegheny County as one overwhelming disaster in which the dead numbered 526, its most appalling feature would be that it fell exclusively upon workers, breadwinners. Among those killed there were no aged helpless persons, no idle merry-makers, no irresponsible children. The people who perished were of those upon whom the world leans. [71]

A crippling injury to a breadwinner could be more devastating than death.

> When a man dies as a result of an injury there is at least one less consumer in the family. When a man is disabled by injury, the number in the family remains the same, and their situation is further complicated by the presence of a sick man to be fed and cared for - an invalid whose recovery is delayed by the very conditions of increasing poverty and anxiety which his injury caused and which his recovery alone can terminate.[72]

The enormous number of lost limbs stimulated a thriving prosthesis industry in Pittsburgh that advertised in labor and ethnic journals offering a mechanical fix to the carnage caused by an indifferent industrial order. The efforts of reformers like Eastman and the *Survey* had an impact on publicity-conscious companies, especially U.S. Steel, which was facing federal anti-trust pressures.

At the same time as Eastman's work, inside U.S. Steel, William Dickson, assistant to Charles Schwab, began a campaign for both improved safety and compensation for injury and death. He produced a study for Judge Gary that reported a total of 405 fatalities in all divisions of U.S. Steel in 1906. In 1908, a safety committee was established, initially as "a species of self-defense" in regards to the negative publicity that was being generated over the corporation's abysmal safety record. By 1914, when its "Safety First" campaign was inaugurated, it did succeed in significantly cutting the death toll. Dickson, citing growing litigation involving jury trials that were beginning to award significant damages to injured workers, urged the corporation to adopt policies such as those in many European countries where "the cost of industrial accidents…be made a part of the cost of production and that men injured and the families of men killed should be given compensation or relief irrespective of employer negligence." Dickson's reforming zeal, which also included urging the discontinuation of the twelve-hour day and Sunday labor, caused him to be passed over in 1911 as successor to William Corey as U.S. Steel president. However, a gradual corporate recognition of the devastating personal, social, and political cost of wholesale industrial death and dismemberment, plus concern over the increasingly successful use of lawsuits by injured employees, helped open the way for the passage of state workers' compensation laws in subsequent years.[73]

The Pittsburgh Survey and the New Corporate Order

Pittsburgh in the first decade of the 20th Century underwent one of the most comprehensive and meticulous examinations of life, work, community, and public policy ever done on any American city. Commissioned by the Russell Sage Foundation, the *Pittsburgh Survey* was published in six volumes (four major books and two collections of articles) between 1909 and 1914. With a combination of scholarship, investigative reporting, and personal engagement by the authors, the *Survey* revealed in excruciating detail the high costs, terribly uneven development, and social depravation that accompanied the shower of local millionaires, with their mansions along Fifth Avenue, who appeared in the aftermath of the creation of U.S. Steel or rode on the crest of the ever expanding Mellon empire.

Of the four single-author works, three were by women who combined rigorous methodology with a human eye for the family and community consequences of workers' low wages, long hours, and abysmal working conditions. Illustrated by the brilliant photographic work of Lewis Hine, the volumes put a face and a social context on the plight of workers described by the *Survey's* researchers. Hine's photography was complemented by the sensitive portrait drawings of Joseph Stella. Stella came to Pittsburgh immediately after the Monongah mine disaster where he was commissioned to illustrate an account of the disaster for *Charities and Commons,* a publication that became *The Survey* magazine. He produced 100 drawings, a third of which were published with the *Survey's* books and articles about Pittsburgh. While the study fueled public debate, it made little immediate change in the way things were done in Pittsburgh. U.S. Steel tore down some awful and highly visible tenement buildings called Painter's Row that stood on the south side of the Monongahela opposite the Point; they had been highlighted in the *Survey* as one of Pittsburgh's worst. While Crystal Eastman's study helped achieve workers' compensation legislation in many states, reform efforts in Pittsburgh were largely driven by the concerns of the elite or the middle-class and lacked the muscle of labor involvement until the 1930s.[74]

Like Crystal Eastman, Elizabeth Beardsley Butler was a young college-educated woman who was a dedicated social investigator. Before coming to Pittsburgh, she worked for the Consumer's

League in New Jersey that encouraged women to buy only clothes produced under decent working conditions. She visited over four hundred shops and factories in the course of research for her volume, *Women and the Trades: Pittsburgh 1907-8*, perhaps contracting tuberculosis from the numerous visits and interviews she conducted in dank tenements and unventilated workplaces. She died the year after the publication of her book in 1911 at the age of 26. She worked hard to provide a comprehensive overview of the working conditions of 22,000 female wageworkers, primarily in manufacturing. She wrote:

> Look down from Mt. Washington at the merging of two dull brown rivers, at the irregular succession of bridges, at scows and small river craft slowly finding way from wharf to wharf; and on either shore, at the black enclosures, gleaming now with leaping flames, now with the steady white-hot glow of Bessemer converters, but everywhere swarthy from the rising columns of black smoke. The cry of…the first metal smiths rings again in the blows of the miner's tools and in the shouts of gangs of furnace men and engine crews in the recesses of the mills.
>
> Nevertheless, in this city whose prosperity is founded in steel, iron and coal, there has come into being beside the men a group of co-laborers. If we listen close enough, we hear the cry…not only from the gangs of furnacemen, but from the girl thread makers at the screw and bolt works, and from the strong-armed women who fashion sand cores in foundries…. We shall hear answering voices in many other workrooms, in the hum of machines in a garment factory, in the steady turn of metal rolls in a laundry, and even the clip of a stogy roller' knife in a tenement loft. For Pittsburgh is not only a great workshop, it is many workshops; and in these workshops women stand beside the men. Forced by individual and group necessities, they have found a place in industry in the steel district of the Alleghenies.[75]

With the consolidation of corporate political power, the collapse of the Knights of Labor and other labor reform efforts like the Greenback Labor Party, organized labor was forced into a defensive mode where it remained dominated by the mostly male, skilled craft workers of the AFL. The adherence of skilled workers in specific and vital trades to union organization gave them bargaining power and the ability to achieve contracts. Meanwhile, employers exercised broad dominion over unskilled and semi-skilled workers, especially in the growing industrial sector. This situation prompted reformers to concentrate their efforts on protective legislation for women and children. While the concept of special protective legislation for women workers remained controversial until the 1960s when they were largely abandoned under the banner of equality, such reform efforts kept alive the notion that governmental action was needed to establish fair labor standards until the enactment of such legislation in the 1930s.[76]

In his introduction to the third of the *Survey* books written by a woman, Margaret Byington's *Homestead: The Households of a Mill Town*, Paul Kellogg posed two questions of national significance raised by the book: first, how does local government deal with a powerful national industry, the second concerns the family: "Here is a town dependent on one of the great industries of America, which has profited by brilliant invention, by organizing genius, by a national policy of tariff protection. It was studied at the close of one of the longest periods of prosperity known by our generation. What has that prosperity brought to the rank and file of the people whose waking hours are put into the industry?"[77]

The inequalities that loomed so large in the greater social context could get especially nasty on the local borough level. Around the turn of the century, creative political gerrymandering carved wealthy supervisory and professional enclaves that garnered the taxes paid by industrial properties, leaving the more densely populated working-class districts with school and borough taxes that were substantially higher than in the adjoining enclaves. The Borough of Edgewood, for example, was created to include all but the front gate of the Union Switch & Signal under its taxing authority, while Swissvale's government, where most of its blue collar employees lived, got very little tax benefit from the facility. A similar situation existed between Homestead and Munhall. "Although Homestead had the largest population and concentration of low-paid workers, most of the mill property was placed in Munhall, whose borough and school taxes were little more than half the rate of Homestead. Since assessors tended to value smaller properties at the highest rates, the large industries contributed a disproportionately small share of taxes. In contrast to the industrial sector, the civic sector was hopelessly atomized." The burden on the working poor was accentuated by the fact, common to all the industrial towns, that while mill property was assessed at thirty percent of its value, residential property was assessed at eighty percent of market value.[78]

Low corporate taxes and poor residents combined to create schools in Homestead that were visibly inferior and manifestly more dangerous than those in Munhall. Byington described the Second Ward school: "The first grade room had 34 double seats, or 68 students for one teacher – an excessive number. Drinking water was brought in buckets from a well in the yard; the toilets were cemented privy vaults flushed only by waste water from the yard and by rain water from the roof, except in dry season when the flushing was done by a hose. Heat was provided by sheet-metal incased coal stoves situated in the rooms, and there was no system of ventilation." Byington was constantly frustrated by the climate of fear among residents that stifled free conversation. "Many of them expressed the belief that my own investigation was being made by the corporation to find out whether wages would stand another reduction." Byington decried the overwork and mental fatigue that undermined family life, and the stultifying loss of initiative that had settled on the town. Where once individual skill provided a measure of control and pride over one's work, mechanization and the growing rigidity of the corporate work organization meant that, fifteen years after the great labor battle, the workers of Homestead "feel that their conditions of life are determined by forces too large for them to do battle with."[79]

It was this dispiritedness in the face of overwhelming corporate control over industrial organization under the non-union regime that formed the central subject of John Fitch's *The Steel Workers*. "Following Carnegie and Frick's victory at Homestead, steel manufacturers carried to new lengths their internal policy of reducing cost by increasing output and lessening dependence upon human labor." The goal was to make the entire process as mechanical as possible and then let the machines drive the men at a faster and faster pace, while the slightest resistance was instantly repressed. Work organization was pyramided with lines of promotion, and the workforce "held together by the ambition of the men lower down." At the apex were the five percent of highly skilled rollers and heaters who directed gangs of men and were essentially foremen. At the base of the pyramid were the ethnic laborers, mostly Slavs, unskilled men that constituted sixty percent of the workforce, who were paid at day-rates and were generally interchangeable and dispensable. In between were what Fitch considered "the real steelworkers," men of moderate earnings, essential to the industry, but also tied to it because they possess skills only useful in steel-making, while the common laborers could dig ditches or heave coal anywhere as well as work in the mill. It was the "real" steelworkers who saw their pay, tied to the tonnage rates, decline from five to thirty percent following the 1892 battle while their hours increased.[80]

Indeed, a major consequence of the union's defeat was the extension of working hours. The union had virtually eliminated Sunday work at Homestead prior to 1892. After the union defeat, sections of the mill with eight-or-ten-hour work saw the imposition of the twelve-hour standard and Sunday work became mandatory. Less than one percent of the 17,000 steel corporation employees had the eight-hour day in 1907, while seventy-nine percent worked twelve. Overtime pay was eliminated around 1900, and holidays were reduced to two: July 4 and Christmas. Under the union, all legal holidays and the Amalgamated's annual Labor Day picnic were honored.[81] Worst of all, the institution of the swing shift, where the seven-day men had to change each week from day-turn to night-turn and then back again, created the "long-turn" or 24-hour workday twice monthly. This swing system had no rational justification, but effectively excluded a large group of the workforce, especially blacks and immigrants, from any participation in the political and civic life of the mill towns. It was impossible to run for office or effectively participate in local politics with the man-killing swing shift. Fitch highlighted a fundamental conflict between private interest and the public good in the American economic system that endures until this day.

> A proper economic policy from the standpoint of the individual may be absolutely uneconomic from the standpoint of society. Such men as have plundered our forests and wasted our coal deposits have followed an economic policy individually sound, but the policy is today denounced as at enmity with the public good. If the man who wastes and destroys *natural* resources is a public enemy, what of the corporations that exploit *human* resources?[82]

The *Survey* drew conclusions about Pittsburgh that drew attention to the terrible disparity between the economic efficiency of its business enterprises and the political paralysis of its social institutions. It saw a city submitting to "an altogether incredible amount of overwork by everybody." Behind enormous tonnages from the mines and mills and the huge accumulation of capital in bankers' vaults lay a terrible impoverishment of community. "Certainly no community before in America or Europe has ever had such a surplus, and never has a great community applied what it had so meagerly to the rational purposes of human life. Not by gifts of libraries, galleries, technical schools, and parks, but by the cessation of toil one day in seven and sixteen hours in the twenty-four, by the increase of wages, by the sparing of lives, by the prevention of accidents, and by raising the standards of domestic life, should the surplus come back to the community that created it."[83]

The civic failure was nowhere more starkly expressed than in the number one and two rankings in typhoid deaths in the country by Pittsburgh and Allegheny City. Over a nine-year period from 1898 to 1907, the typhoid death-rate in Pittsburgh was 130 per 100,000 population; Allegheny City was 104. In comparison, Chicago was 24; New York, 18; Paris 17; Vienna, 5; Berlin, 4.[84] How such a dismal state of public health could exist was explained by an examination of thirty-five years of typhoid in Pittsburgh by the *Survey*. Public water supplies were pumped directly from sick rivers.

> The rivers commonly carry in solution the soluble chemical products of the mills along their shores - organic and inorganic; acid and alkali; oils, fats, and other carbon compounds; and in addition, investigators of the river contents have gathered up dead animals, flesh-disintegrated and putrescent, as well as the off-scourings of iron and steel mills, tanneries, slaughter-houses, and similar industries. Nor is this all. Seventy-five up-river towns, with an estimated population of 350,000 inhabitants,

in the Allegheny or its tributary valleys, and in the Monongahela Valley a long string of towns - Swissvale, Homestead, Braddock, Rankin, and McKeesport – all furnish their supply of common sewage as a further contamination.[85]

With working-class organizations weakened and under attack, reform efforts in Pittsburgh were driven by elites rather than the result of mass movements. Reformers used the rhetoric of democracy and the public interest, but their goal was to improve the efficiency of government by cementing business control. In 1911, reformers broke the old ward election of councilmen and school boards, undeniably and often outrageously corrupt, but which did provide lower and middle class groups some power. Reform placed the city council and school board directly into the hands of the upper class. Reform was seen as contingent on the suppression of local autonomy and self-determination, and its replacement by centralized professional administration. Professionalism and centralized control was augmented by technology. In response to the trolley strike of 1909, the Pittsburgh Bureau of Police established its first police motorcycle unit with five motorcycles from Harley-Davidson. Elite political efforts directed toward the smooth management of corporate control have endured to the present.[86]

While Andrew Carnegie had grossly undervalued Carnegie Steel in order to keep share values low and plow capital constantly back into expansion and technological advance, the creation of U.S. Steel created vast numbers of rich shareholders by watering the stock. The more than one billion dollars of nominal capital involved at the moment of its birth was backed less than fifty-percent by tangible assets. As one of the principal organizers of the corporation admitted, the creation of the corporation had been "to convert a lot of doubtful assets into cash." As the character of steel-making shifted from aggressive expansion to effective utilization of assets, the old Carnegie boys like Charles Schwab were marginalized, and the corporation increasingly was dominated and then completely controlled by Judge Elbert H. Gary, chairman of the corporation's executive committee. Ironically, the creation of the stable and highly managed steel industry envisioned by Schwab in his dinner speech pushed him, with his more aggressive and freewheeling style, to leave the corporation in the summer of 1903 and put his competitive talents to work for Bethlehem Steel. For 25 years, Judge Gary dominated U.S. Steel and was the recognized leader of the steel industry. His leadership was not especially favorable to the position of Pittsburgh.[87]

After the formation of U.S. Steel, the corporation purchased both Union Steel and Sharon Steel in an effort to bring Henry Clay Frick and his Mellon allies firmly into the fold and forestall any rivalry from that direction. Gary's prime concern was to establish firm prices and predictable operations. One of the mechanisms to establish price stability was the "Pittsburgh Plus" price system that priced steel at the mill price in Pittsburgh plus the cost of transport to the supplier. The same price was charged whether they actually got the steel from the Pittsburgh mills or from mills that were much closer. This policy, stabilized demand for Pittsburgh steel, but also, advantaged independent steel firms and U.S. Steel plants far from Pittsburgh, but near their customers, especially the new mega-mill in Gary, Indiana, opened in 1908-1909. Pittsburgh's aging mills were able to compete, but they were starved for capital to modernize. Furthermore, Pittsburgh's dominance was undercut by the advancement of by-product coke furnaces that reduced the dependency of the industry on high quality Connellsville coal, the proximity of which provided one of Pittsburgh's key advantages. Expanded use of lower quality coal permitted lakefront mills like those in northwest Indiana, closer to expanding western markets for rails, bridge, and structural steel, to exceed the production of the western Pennsylvania mills by the late 1920s. Also, while the corporation's steel production increased from 8.9 to 13.4 million tons from 1901 to 1913, its percentage of the total steel market fell from 65.7 percent to 53.2.[88]

Pittsburgh's industrial locations were cramped and confined to river bottoms that made expansion and innovation difficult. On the other hand, the corporation's Gary works sprawled several miles deep along ten miles of lakefront, and the greater space allowed for efficient materials flow and production organization. Chicago was also the rail hub of the nation, and the large and diversified metalworking industry that developed there provided a wide range of consumer manufacturing that in turn drove demand for basic steel. "Chicago metalworking far exceeded its metal-making industry; around Pittsburgh the reverse was true." Furthermore, once Pittsburgh's traditional industrial base of steel, glass, electrical, aluminum, chemicals, and food processing was established, these large industries resisted the entry of other manufacturing into the region because of the competition for both space and labor. While Pittsburgh was a revolutionary innovator during the last quarter of the 19th Century, in terms of industrial development, during the course of the first quarter of the 20th Century, the area became increasingly conservative.[89]

The McKees Rocks Strike of 1909

The search for labor, tractable enough to work long hours for low wages in dismal working conditions, was reaching its limits. Slavic workers, in particular, drew the line at McKees Rocks down the Ohio River just below Pittsburgh in the summer of 1909. Unlike Homestead where the leaders of the union struggle were fluent both in English and local politics, the new immigrants were divided by language and culture among themselves and from the surrounding town. The eastern and southern European origins of the workers shaped the character of the rebellion and help explain its obscurity. In the McKees Rocks strike, the fighting spirit and organizational ability of these new immigrants sowed the seeds of future industrial unionism.

The Pressed Steel Car Company was situated in the Schoenville section of McKees Rocks downriver from O'Donovan's Bridge, constructed near the placement of the later, much grander, McKees Rocks Bridge, completed in 1931 across the Ohio River. The population of McKees Rocks was divided into three parts. The old settlers, mainly Scots, English, and German, owned much of the business and real estate, and many lived on the higher ground above the industrial and commercial "Bottoms"; the next, second and third generation workers, mainly Irish and German, performed most of the skilled craft and maintenance work in the factory. Many of these lived outside the town or across the O'Donovan Bridge in Woods Run, an area that had once had a thriving iron industry. Among the 6,000 workers at the Pressed Steel and affiliated plants, there were 16 distinct nationality groups. The Slavs, referred to as "Hunkies" because of their origins in the multi-ethnic Austro-Hungarian Empire, were regarded with contempt by the corporation and by many native born workers as "the least intelligent, the least independent…the most content to be driven like slaves."[90]

Pressed Steel Car fabricated railway cars on an assembly line basis. The company purposely split the workforce into nationality and language groups in order to communicate with them, but also to keep the groups divided. The plant had the reputation of being a "slaughterhouse" with serious accidents an almost daily occurrence. Lurid accounts in the press called the plant "the last chance": "When some poor 'Hunky,' as they even familiarly call themselves now, is maimed and mangled in his work, some foreman or other petty "boss" pushes the bleeding body aside with his foot to make room for another living man, that no time be lost in the turning out of pressed steel cars. The new man often works for some minutes over the dead body until a labor gang takes it away." A former county coroner, Joseph G. Armstrong, testified about the appalling death toll. "It seemed to me that the deaths averaged about one a day. Many of the deaths resulted from men being struck by heavy moving cranes and the dogs suspended from the cranes. Investigation made it look to me as though a lot of young fellows who were operating the cranes did not care much whether or not a "hunky" laborer was hit every now and then."[91]

The work organization was both relentless and subject to constant speedup. The rail cars moved on a belt-driven track through the plant. The men worked in pools or teams and were only paid for the completed car. Since the rates were not published, no one knew what was owed them at week's end. Workers complained of a plant-wide system of extortion. Workers had to pay to get a job and then to keep it. A system of company stores and housing regulated life beyond the gates of the factory and enforced a system of industrial servitude. Father A.F. Toner, the Catholic pastor of St. Mary's Church, wrote: "Men are persecuted, robbed, and slaughtered, and their wives are abused in a manner worse than death – all to obtain or retain positions that barely keep starvation from the door. It is a pit of infamy where men are driven lower than the degradation of slaves and compelled to sacrifice their wives and daughters to the villainous foreman…to be allowed to work. It is a disgrace to a civilized country. A man is given less consideration than a dog, and dead bodies are simply kicked aside while men are literally driven to their death."[92]

On Saturday, July 10, 1909, the men were paid, and many were shorter in their pay than usual. A demand was raised to know the pay rate. Upon management's refusal to talk, shop after shop walked out until virtually the entire plant was struck. The company immediately contacted Pearl Berghoff, "king of the strikebreakers," who was in between efforts to break two bitter trolley strikes in Philadelphia using Negro replacements against union drivers. He had developed a quasi military organization with "nobles," often college blue bloods seeking adventure; "guards," who were little more than thugs; and "finks," who were men with some industrial skill, but who acted as professional strikebreakers without expectation of remaining at work after the conflict. Under this umbrella were recruited masses of fresh immigrants, blacks and other workers hired under false pretenses.[93] The experience of a young German Fred Reiger was not atypical.

> I was walking in New York near the Bowery and a man came up and said, "Would you like to work for the Erie Railroad for $2 a day?" We agreed. After visiting the agency we were taken to the Erie station. Ninety men were there. At midnight we were placed in a coach and traveled all night and all the next day, all the time without any food…. Sometime during the night after we had been traveling rapidly, the car was stopped, the door opened – which had formerly been locked – and we found ourselves in the yard of the Pressed Steel Car Company plant at McKees Rocks. We were strikebreakers.[94]

Berghoff received five dollars a day for each body delivered to the plant. He quickly mobilized some 500 strikebreakers, who began arriving on the morning of July 14. Most entered the plant by rail, but deputies initially escorted contingents on foot to the plant gate.

> When they reached the gate they were greeted by a storm of bricks, stones and clubs… Terrified, the strike-breakers broke ranks and ran for their lives, leaving the policemen to look out for themselves. The latter drew their revolvers and this act seemed to further enrage the already maddened crowd. With the men shouting oaths and the hundreds of women in the crowd screaming with rage, the strikers closed in and began a hand-to-hand battle. A policeman fired into the crowd, his shot striking a man in the stomach,

inflicting a wound that will probably prove fatal. An instant later, he was seized by a giant "Slav," who disarmed him and turned the revolver on the policeman…. Policemen were seized by groups of four and five strikers, who disarmed them and beat them with their own clubs. Stones flew so thick and so wildly that strikers were knocked down and their heads split open by their own friends. Several women were knocked down and trampled on by the crowd. After a few minutes fighting, the policemen were scattered throughout the mob of men and women, temporarily converted into bloodthirsty savages fighting desperately.[95]

In the evening, a company-hired boat, the *Steel Queen,* attempted to land with 300 scabs. Gunfire erupted and the boat retreated. On July 15, 300 deputy sheriffs and 200 state constables, including 62 mounted state police referred to by strikers as the "Black Cossacks," surrounded Preston and began evicting the strikers from company-owned houses. Mounted police charged the strikers and their families, and they responded with rocks. The troopers fired into the crowd. Over one hundred were injured in the subsequent melee including Stowe Township Police Chief John Farrell, who was shot in the arm and stabbed a dozen times.[96]

Meeting on the Indian Mound, the strikers elected a committee of ten who went to Pittsburgh to present their grievances. Frank N. Hoffstot, president of the Pressed Steel Car Company, declared his determination to fire the strikers and never negotiate with them. "They are dead to us. There are more than enough idle men in Pittsburgh to fill any vacancy." The native born, English-speaking workers, who performed the more skilled tasks for higher pay, didn't work in the gangs nor did they live in the company housing. Some of the skilled among them had successfully negotiated short-term contracts. While most of them supported the strike at the beginning and had no love for Hoffstot, they began to seek ways to make their own deal. Among the immigrants, however, were workers who had experience in labor and revolutionary struggles in Europe. There were Hungarians who had participated in a great railway strike, Russians who had witnessed "Bloody Sunday" in 1905, and Germans with experience in the metalworkers union. While the official strike leadership, called the "Big Six," was dominated by skilled native-born leadership, the foreign leadership formed the "Unknown Committee" which remained behind the scenes but commanded the loyalty of the immigrants. After American workers led by the "Big Six" made a deal with management on July 31 that the immigrant workers rejected, the immigrant's leadership recruited the support of the Industrial Workers of the World (IWW). The IWW helped bring attention to the struggle in labor circles. William Trautman, IWW general organizer, arrived in McKees Rocks; and, following his arrest, Joe Ettor took his place. IWW leader Big Bill Haywood also came to rally the workers.[97]

Workers and their families organized a 24-hour watch system. Pickets checked every trolley and ferry to intercept anyone who didn't have legitimate business in town. They selected 16 separate rally speakers to cover all the principal languages of the strikers. At mass meetings from the "Indian Mound," they stood along the ridge of rocks, looking down on the Bottoms that once sheltered Queen Aliquippa's village and cornfields. The line of speakers positioned along the ridge could be heard translating and making speeches urging worker solidarity and resistance to oppression before great crowds assembled in multiple language groups on the flats below. Newspaper reporters coming to town expecting a confused foreign rabble were impressed with the discipline and organization of the strikers. The District Council of Carpenters announced its support. "We sympathize with these poor men and their wives and children, whose condition is worse than the African slave." The *Pittsburgh Leader* raised funds to feed the strikers and 20 wagonloads of food were sent by Pittsburgh unionists and sympathetic merchants, prior to the July 31 agreement and the entry of the Wobblies onto the scene. The craft unions that dominated Pittsburgh organized labor, especially its politically active and voting contingent, were mainly sympathetic to the "American" workers. Since the foreign born population of the county now exceeded fifty percent of the total population, concerns about the immigrants, their living conditions, and their political intentions were widespread among the native born.[98]

Violence escalated in August as matters came to a head. On August 11, a Croatian striker, trying to prevent the entry of strikebreakers, was killed by a Negro deputy. Five thousand workers formed a funeral cortege, with American and nationality flags flying, and marched from McKees Rocks across the length of the North Side to St. Nicholas Croatian Church overlooking the Allegheny River (not to be confused with St. Nicholas Croatian Church in Millvale, only a few miles farther upriver). On August 15, a second gun battle prevented another steamer from landing replacement workers. On the 17th, 8,000 strikers and their supporters rallied at Indian Mound. The IWW took public control of the strike and recruited 3,000 members into the Car Builders Industrial Union. The tension continued to build until August 22, which became known as "Bloody Sunday." Strikers boarding a trolley searching for scabs were confronted by an armed deputy who opened fire. In the ensuing fight, the deputy, Harry Exler, was killed. A company of state troopers was called in to restore order; and in the bloody confrontations that followed, ten more men including eight strikers were killed. The next day, the troopers stormed through "Hunkeyville" attacking men and women indiscriminately.[99]

The conflict began to attract national and even international attention. On August 25, ignoring threats on his life, the Socialist leader and oft-times candidate for President, Eugene V. Debs, then at the height of his powers and popularity, addressed a crowd of 10,000 from the Indian Mound. He called the strike the "greatest labor fight in all my history in the labor movement"; one that signaled "a new spirit among the unorganized, foreign-born workers in the mass production industries who can see here in McKees Rocks the road on which they must travel - the road to industrial unionism."[100]

Most of the strikebreakers who numbered approximately one thousand inside the plant by early August were recently arrived immigrants recruited under false pretenses. Their condition became increasingly desperate. Strikebreakers who complained or whispered a wish to go home were beaten. The Austro-Hungarian consul formally protested their condition as peonage. In late August, 60 of the strikers secretly hired on as scabs and, penetrating the plant, convinced 300 of the remaining 400 workers to leave the stockade. Strikebreakers told numerous stories of false recruitment, brutality and ill-treatment in the plant. One of the strikebreakers told a reporter: "They treated us like dogs. Of all the promises made when we were hired, not one was kept. We were practically starved, and what little food we did get was moldy. Everyone who ate it got sick. When we dared complain we were beaten and kicked. Everyone swore at us and called us vile names. We were made to work whether we were sick or not, and when we said that we wanted to quit, the bosses threatened to blow our heads off with big revolvers…."[101]

On September 8, a settlement offer was proclaimed by C. A. Wise, the leader of the moderate Big Six, which seemed to concede ground on some of the most egregious worker issues that triggered the strike: a pay increase, posting of wage rates, modifications of pooling, ending the abuse of families in housing and eliminating the graft in job assignments. Workers and their families were hungry, so they proclaimed victory and marched into the plant. Once there, however, the company began to backtrack from the agreement. This triggered a walkout by 4,000, primarily immigrant workers, on September 15. The following day, 2,000, mostly native born workers, marched behind a huge American flag toward the immigrant worker picket line. The immigrants opened their ranks and allowed the marchers to enter the gate unscathed, and most of the immigrants followed the Americans inside shortly after. The skilled men exercised their shared management control by slowly squeezing out the IWW supporters and other resisters. From a claimed membership of 6,000 inside and outside the plant in the immediate aftermath of the strike, by 1912 the IWW chapter had dwindled to only 20 members.[102]

The Battle of Homestead lasted from dawn to dusk. McKees Rocks saw two months of sustained collective resistance in the form of mass meetings, social organization, street fighting and even gun battles. At Homestead, most of the union leaders were first or second generation Irish fluent in English and included very well known local political figures such as Homestead Burgess John McLuckie. At McKees Rocks, the leaders of the immigrant forces remained hidden; and the pivotal forum was the almost daily mass meeting on the "Indian Mound," not the institutions of local government.[103] At Homestead, the immigrant, foreign-tongued workforce constituted something over ten percent of the employees; at McKees Rocks, the ratio was reversed with immigrant workers constituting over seventy-five percent of the workers. At Homestead, the union workforce grew up with the town and dominated local government. At McKees Rocks, the strikers were relative newcomers, not property owners or officials. Prior to the organization of the union, the language groups found organizational expression and protection through churches and ethnic organizations. At both Homestead and McKees Rocks, the women of the community were deeply and dramatically involved.

The strike was ultimately broken by a deepening split between the 3,500 immigrant workers and the 1,500 or so "American" (second generation, English speaking) workers, many of whom were Irish skilled and semi-skilled workers. The complex ethnic character of the strikers was poorly understood by the press.[104] This confusion was understandable since the political boundaries of central and eastern Europe, constituted at the time by the Austro-Hungarian, Russian and Prussian empires, did not reflect the ethnic or linguistic character of the populations. Thus, the main groupings of the strikers were often characterized as "Russians, Hungarians, Slavs, and Italians." In fact, the largest ethnic groups were probably the Croatians, Poles and Ukranian/Carpatho-Rusyns. Croatia was a part of the Austro-Hungarian Empire, and Poland, which disappeared as a nation in 1796, was divided into Russian, Austro-Hungarian, and German zones of administration. Poles could be characterized as Russian or Hungarian by immigration officials or police, yet be clearly identified as Polish by family, friends, and neighbors. On the ground, the newspapers' term "Russian" might include Russians, Ukrainians, Carpatho-Rusyns, Serbs, and even Bulgarians, since these groups were often described as Russians because of their Eastern Catholic or Orthodox religion.

Clearly the rich ethnic stew and the secrecy that worker organizations adopted because of fear of arrest or deportation rendered press interpretation and public understanding difficult. Among the workers at McKees Rocks were workers who had extensive experience in the strikes and rebellions of central and eastern Europe. Their insurrectionary proclivities and industrial rather than craft organization made them open to assistance from the radical organizers of the Industrial Workers of the World. Unlike the Homestead workers, they did not express their rebellion in the rhetoric of American rights and living standards that might have bridged somewhat the gap between them and the skilled American-born worker. The employer's refusal to bargain with the employees no matter their strength of organization, the justice of their grievances, or the degree of their support, remained intact. The rights of property trumped the democratic rights of association, recognition, and collective bargaining. While workers gained improved conditions from the struggle and won a measure of respect, the violence of their struggle stimulated public fear of the immigrant worker and increased attempts to "Americanize" them. This Americanization did not speak to rights or standards, but emphasized loyalty and duty. The 1909 McKees Rocks strike stands as a milestone in American immigration and labor history.

The Construction of an Immigrant Society

The McKees Rocks strike signaled the definitive end of an image of the immigrants as passive drones unwilling to struggle for their rights. The central, eastern and southern European immigrants that now made up a majority of the region's population were also creating vibrant and successful communities centered around churches, fraternal organizations, ethnic clubs, and neighborhoods. The Catholic Church, especially, became an institution that linked older immigrant groups like the Irish and the German Catholics to the Italians, Poles, Slovaks, and Croatian newcomers. The burgeoning Catholic school system helped create a certain level of solidarity among groups that stood outside the traditional Presbyterian, Episcopalian, Methodist power structure; and as the second generation emerged out of the great immigrant wave with voting rights and a greater political consciousness, the base was being laid for the political sea change that characterized the 1930s. The church provided a vehicle, simultaneously, for the expression and retention of old world identities, as well as the opportunity for gradual assimilation to American culture. Through "mixed" ethnic marriages among Catholics of various national origins, the old ethnic divisions were diluted.

Perhaps the most dramatic expression of the internal strength and cohesion of immigrant culture was the extraordinary flowering of religious architecture in Pittsburgh during the early decades of the 20th Century. Considering the low wages and miserable working conditions present in Pittsburgh's dark satanic mills, it almost defies comprehension that such magnificent houses of worship could blossom in the midst of such hard scrabble towns and neighborhoods. In the McKees Rocks Bottoms, scene of such bitter fighting, the spires and domes of St. Mark's Slovak Catholic, St. Mary's Ukrainian Orthodox, Holy Ghost Byzantine Catholic, and St. Nicholas Russian Orthodox churches rose up between 1914 and 1922, bearing witness to the fierce communal spirit of the place. The entry to the South Side was framed by the onion-shaped domes of St. John the Baptist Ukranian Church (1895), while the iron bells of St. Paul's Monastery rang out over a neighborhood crowded with a dozen notable congregations. On the North Side, there was the huge German church of St. Boniface, and on Troy Hill the Shrine of St. Anthony's, built in 1880 by Father Suibertus Mollinger to house his collection of 5,000 holy relics, said to be the largest in the Western Hemisphere. In the Strip District out along the Allegheny stood St. Stanislaus Kostka Polish Church, followed by great bulk of St. Augustine's German Church and up on the side of Polish Hill, the great baroque domed Church of the Immaculate Heart of Mary.[105]

Both the Catholic and the Jewish communities gave expression to their increased presence and power by building great houses of worship in Oakland at nearly the same time. St. Paul's Cathedral was dedicated in 1906, and the massive Rodef Shalom synagogue designed by Henry Hornbostel opened the following year. The ubiquitous Henry Hornbostel also designed the Allegheny County Soldiers and Sailors Memorial in Oakland and the City-County Building on Grant Street. Rodef Shalom, with a large, influential and mostly German Jewish membership that included Henry Kaufmann, philanthropist and founder of Pittsburgh's premier department store, had played an important role in the elaboration of Reform Judaism in the United States. In 1885, the congregation hosted a conference of 19 American

Reformed rabbis who drafted the famous *Pittsburgh Platform*. This document rejected Christian ideas of heaven and hell, asserted that the Bible was an ethical guide and not the infallible word of God, and declared that Judaism was a religion but not a nation, and that it was designated by God to bring "truth, justice and peace among all men." An indication of the importance that this German Jewish community had achieved was the visit by President William Howard Taft to Rodef Shalom in 1909. It marked the first time that an American president made an official visit to a Jewish synagogue. Taft's speech was a plea for tolerance of various religious beliefs and his visit signified a legitimization of the Jewish community. The composition of the community was itself undergoing a major shift as a second wave of poor, largely Orthodox, Jewish immigrants from Eastern Europe was settling in the Hill District.[106]

The mainline Protestant churches rebuilt their downtown sanctuaries, the Episcopal Trinity Cathedral and the First Presbyterian Church, in early and late English Gothic styles flanking the old burial ground on Sixth Avenue, situated directly across the street from the bastion of upper-class influence and power, the Duquesne Club. First Presbyterian adorned a particularly impressive interior with extraordinary woodwork and spectacular Tiffany glass windows. Given the enormous disparities in wealth during this period between the worshippers at these two downtown edifices and those that crowded the immigrant churches to experience a bit of heavenly beauty and communal affirmation, it is all the more impressive to visit immigrant churches like those in Homestead: St. Michael the Archangel (Slovak) with its wonderful variegated tile interior and the statue of St. Joseph the Worker on its tower; St. Mary Magdalene (Irish), with its interesting brick façade, vaulted wood ceilings and beautiful stained glass; and St. John the Baptist Byzantine Catholic Cathedral with its two striking towers. By various means, houses of worship express in a concrete way the attitude and aspirations of their congregations. Churches like First Presbyterian exuded power and wealth. Places of worship like the Slovak St. Michael the Archangel, the Polish Immaculate Heart of Mary, and the Jewish Rodef Shalom expressed the aspirations, pride and solidarity of communities determined to survive and thrive in their adopted land.[107]

Notes Chapter 7

[1] Nicholas Casner, *Devastation and Renewal: An Environmental History of Pittsburgh and Its Regions*, ed. Joel A. Tarr (Pittsburgh: University of Pittsburgh Press, 2003).; *The Pittsburgh Leader* (October 14, 1897), 89-109.

[2] John Hoerr, *And the Wolf Finally Came: The Decline of the American Steel Industry* (Pittsburgh: University of Pittsburgh Press, 1988), 91, 165-166.

[3] Theodore Dreiser, *A Book About Myself* (New York: Boni & Liveright, 1922), 390-392, quoted in E.R. Schmidt, ed., *Pittsburgh Regional Ecology* (California PA, Vulcan Press, 1971), 70-71.

[4] Mattie Schloetzer, "Andrew Carnegie's Original Reproductions: The Hall of Architecture at 100," *Western Pennsylvania History,* Fall 2007, 39, 43.

[5] Edwin Fenton, *Carnegie Mellon, 1900-2000: A Centennial History,* (Pittsburgh: Carnegie Mellon University Press, 2000), 1-28.

[6] Robert I. Vexler, *Pittsburgh: A Chronological & Documentary History, 1682-1976* (New York: Oceana Publications, 1977), 48-9.; Samuel A. Schreiner, Jr., *Henry Clay Frick: The Gospel of Greed* (New York: St: Martin's Press, 1995), 150.; Stefan Lorant, *Pittsburgh: The Story of an American City* (Garden City: DoubleDay & Company, Inc., 1964), 611; Robert Dvorchak, "Golf the way it's meant to be," *Pittsburgh Post-Gazette,* June 10, 2007.

[7] Walter C. Kidney, *Pittsburgh's Bridges: Architecture and Engineering* (Pittsburgh: Pittsburgh History and Landmark Foundation, 1999), 56, 7, 103, 109-110, 125.

[8] *Pittsburgh Press*, October 18, 1899.

[9] Kathleen Byrne and Richard Snyder, *Chrysalis: Willa Cather in Pittsburgh* (Pittsburgh: Pittsburgh Historical Society of Western Pennsylvania, 1980), 14.; Robert Hessen, *Steel Titan: The Life of Charles M. Schwab* (Pittsburgh: University of Pittsburgh Press, 1975), 90-102.; Alden March, *A New History of the Spanish-American War* (Philadelphia: American Book & Bible House, 1899), 46-54.

[10] March, *A New History of the Spanish-American War,* 43.

[11] Ethel Spencer, *The Spencers of Amberson Avenue: A Turn-of-the-Century Memoir*, ed. Michael P. Weber and Peter N. Stearns (Pittsburgh: University of Pittsburgh Press, 1984).

[12] Byrne and Snyder, *Chrysalis*, 1-53; Denise Riffle, *Willa Cather: The Pittsburgh Years, 1896-1906,* (Pittsburgh: University of Pittsburgh Press, 1993). I am indebted to an excellent student paper submitted in 1993 by Denise Riffle in my IUP Pittsburgh Class.

[13] Byrne and Snyder, *Chrysalis*, 78-96.

[14] William Larimer Mellon, *Judge Mellon's Son* (Pittsburgh: Private Printing, 1948); David E. Koskoff, *The Mellons: The Chronicle of America's Richest Family* (New York: Thomas Y. Crowell, 1978), 112; "Kennywood's Beginning Year," *Amusement Park Annual* (March 1980).

[15] Harvey O'Connor, *Mellon's Millions: The Biography of a Fortune; The Life and Times of Andrew W. Mellon* (New York: John Day Company, 1933), 64-67.

[16] Koskoff, *The Mellons*, 114-116. Union Steel's base, the town of Donora, was named for its operational head, William Donner, and A.W.'s wife Nora.

[17] Charles C. Carr, *ALCOA: An American Enterprise* (New York: Rinehard & Company, Inc., 1952), 43-4; David Cannadine, *Mellon, An American Life,* (New York, Vintage Books, 2008), 221-223; Koskoff, *The Mellons,* 79-82.

[18] Koskoff, *The Mellons*, 85-88; Edward Acheson, "A Pathfinder: Discovery, Invention, and Industry," *Educational Biographical Sketches of Eminent Investors* (New York: The Press Scrap Book, 1910), 114.

[19] Koskoff, *The Mellons*, 91-97.

[20] O'Connor, *Mellon's Millions*, 1-3-110; Cannadine, *Mellon: An American Life*, 121-122, 177-180; Craig Thompson, *Since Spindletop: A Human Story of Gulf's First Half-Century* (Pittsburgh: Gulf Oil Corporation, 1951), 9-24.

[21] Mellon, *Judge Mellon's Sons*, 305-309; Koskoff, *The Mellons*.

[22] O'Connor, *Mellon's Millions*, 54-55.

[23] Cannadine, *Mellon: An American Life*, 142-152.

[24] Koskoff, *The Mellons*, 128-9.

[25] Koskoff, *The Mellons*, 131-135. The bitterness and humiliation suffered by Andrew Mellon can be gauged by the report of George Seldes, who worked at the *Pittsburgh Leader* for a time. "The most intimate affairs of a man and a woman were [disclosed] by the Mellon lawyers, providing at times nuances of vulgarity." Seldes in an oral interview told Koskoff that the Mellon lawyers claimed that the couple was "unfitted sexually – unfitted in the actual sense of the word. Their sexual organs were unfitting: his too large or hers too small…sexual intercourse was a horrible experience to both of them." This is a mighty claim for an older man with a woman who bore two children! p. 131-132.

[26] George Seldes, *Witness to a Century* (New York: Ballantine Books, 1987), 19.

[27] Koskoff, *The Mellons*, 137-141; A very complete recent account of the marital breakdown is in Cannadine, *Mellon: An American Life,* 186-214.

[28] Kenneth Warren, *Triumphant Capitalism* (Pittsburgh: University of Pittsburgh Press, 1996), 217.

[29]Joseph Frazier Wall, *Andrew Carnegie* (Pittsburgh: University of Pittsburgh Press, 1989), 166, 716-717.

[30]Schreiner, *Henry Clay Frick*, 162.

[31]Wall, *Andrew Carnegie*, 714-793.

[32]Description of the Frick Collection in the Michelin Guide *New York City*: "one of the highlights of a visit to New York", 6th edition, pp. 71-72, 212; Martha Frick Symington Sanger, *Henry Clay Frick* (New York: Abbeville Press, 1998), 212; Schreiner, *Henry Clay Frick*.; Wall, *Andrew Carnegie*, 764; James H. Bridge, *The Inside History of the Carnegie Steel Company* (New York: The Aldine Book Company, 1903).

[33]Wall, *Andrew Carnegie*, 765-782.

[34]Wall, *Andrew Carnegie*, 784.

[35]Kenneth Warren, *Charles Schwab: Industrial Genius* (Pittsburgh: University of Pittsburgh Press, 2007), 68-92.

[36]Hoerr, *And the Wolf Finally Came*, 89; Robert R. Brooks, *As Steel Goes,…: Unionism in a Basic Industry* (New Haven: Yale University Press, 1940), 28-30.

[37]Haniel Long, *Pittsburgh Memoranda* (Pittsburgh: Brenton Books, 1990), 41.

[38] Many students over the years of my teaching a senior synthesis course on Pittsburgh did research papers on Mrs. Soffel and the Biddle Boys. I am particularly indebted to two of the best efforts by Gretchen Fulmer and Natalie Benton.

[39]"Warden McNeil's Story of the Biddle Boys Escape," *Pittsburgh Sun-Telegraph*, 1938.; Charles Owen Rice, "Biddley Byes," in *Fighter with a Heart*, ed. Charles McCollester (Pittsburgh, University of Pittsburgh Press, 1996); A Hollywood film, *Mrs. Soffel*, starring Diane Keaton and Mel Gibson was shot on location at the Allegheny Courthouse and Jail where the real events took place.

[40]*Pittsburgh Press*, October 10, 1903.

[41]Harry K. Thaw, *The Traitor* (Philadelphia: Dorrance and Company, 1926).

[42] E.L. Doctorow, *Ragtime* (New York: Random House, 1975).

[43]John McCollister, *The Bucs!: The Story of the Pittsburgh Pirates* (Lenexa: Addax Publishing Group, 1998), 21-28.

[44]McCollister, *The Bucs!*, 17-18.

[45]William Hageman, *Honus: The Life and Times of a Baseball Hero* (Chicago: Sagamore Publishing, 1996), 2.

[46] Frederick G. Leib, *The Pittsburgh Pirates* (Carbondale: Southern Illinois University Press, 2003) 54.

[47]McCollister, *The Bucs!*, 38-55; Roger I. Abrams, *The First World Series and the Baseball Fanatics of 1903*, (Boston: Northeastern University Press, 2003); Dan Bonk and Len Martin, "The First World Series & Its Pittsburgh Connections," in *Western Pennsylvania History*, (Fall 2003), 11-23.

[48]McCollister, *The Bucs!*, 58-60.

[49]Charles W. Dahlinger, "Old Allegheny," *Western Pennsylvania Historical Magazine*" (1918), 221-223.

[50]Roy Lubove, *Twentieth-Century Pittsburgh: Government, Business, and Environmental Change* (Pittsburgh University of Pittsburgh Press, 1995), 1; U.S. Supreme Court, "Hunter v. City of Pittsburgh," ed. 207 U.S. 161 (1907), 27.

[51]McCollister, *The Bucs!*, 64.

[52]McCollister, *The Bucs!*, 98-99; Hageman, *Honus.*; Leib, *The Pittsburgh Pirates*, 151.

[53]*Pittsburgh Press*, October 19, 1902.

[54]Raymond J. Robertson. *Ironworkers 100th Anniversary, 1896-1996: A History of the Iron Workers Union*, (The Iron workers Union, 1996), 33-34.

[55]Meyer A. Sanders, "Labor," *Allegheny County, A Sesqui-Centennial Review, 1788…1938*, ed. George E. Kelly, (Pittsburgh: Allegheny County Sesqui-Centennial Committee, 1938), 136-139.

[56]Marlin S. Thomas, *A Chapter in the Development of Local #66 I.U.O.E.*, (Pittsburgh: I.U.O.E., 1981); F.A. Fitzgerald, editor, *The International Engineer: Fifty Years of Progress: 1896-1946*, (December, 1946), 11; Amalgamated Transit Union Staff, *ATU 100 Years: A History of the Amalgamated Transit Union*, (Amalgamated Transit Union, 1992), 14-19.

[57]*Pittsburgh Professional Fire Fighters: 100th Anniversary*, (Pittsburgh Fire fighters, 1974), 26; "Demands of Policemen," *The Pittsburgh Leader*, October 19, 1899.

[58]John R. Commons & William M. Leiserson, "Wage-Earners of Pittsburgh," *Wage-Earning Pittsburgh* (The Pittsburgh Survey), (New York: Survey Associates, 1914), 144-147.

[59] Department of Environmental Resources, *Annual Report on Mining Activities, 1991* (Harrisburg: Commonwealth of Pennsylvania, 1991), 14-15, 92-93.

[60]Department of Environmental Resources, *Annual Report on Mining Activities, 1991*, 14-15, 92-93; John Asmonga and Linda Asmonga, *Comparison of the Harwick Miners Surnames*, (Unpublished, 1906); *Pittsburgh Press*, January 28, 1906 and February 1, 1906.

[61]Department of Mines of Pennsylvania, *Report: Part II Bituminous 1904* (Harrisburg: Harrisburg Publishing Co., 1905).

[62]*Pittsburgh Press*, January 26, 2004; The most complete collection of information on the Harwick Mine disaster was assembled by Linda and John Asmonga and printed in the newsletter of the *Homestead & West Mifflin Historical Society* in February 2004.

[63]*Homestead & West Mifflin Historical Society*, 2004.

[64]Mine Safety and Health Administration, U.S. Department of Labor, "Mine Disasters," (2000).

[65]Carlton Jackson, *The Dreadful Month*, (Bowling Green, Ohio: Bowling Green State University Popular Press, 1982), 91-106.

[66]Alan Derickson, *Black Lung: Anatomy of a Public Health Disaster*, (Ithaca: Cornell University Press, 1998), 1-7. This book is a powerful, documented study of how corporate interests overrode public health interests and fiercely resisted the development of occupational medicine.

[67]Derickson, *Black Lung*, 17-21.

[68]Derickson, *Black Lung*, 43-59.

[69]C. William Verity, "The Pioneers," *National Safety Congress* 1 (1972), 33.

[70]Crystal Eastman, *Work Accidents and the Law* (The Pittsburgh Survey), (New York: Russell Sage Foundation, 1910), 11-15; Albert S. Bolles, *The Legal Relations Between the Employed and Their Employers in Pennsylvania Compared with the Relations Existing Between them in Other States*, ed. Bureau of Industrial Statistics (Harrisburg: W.M. Stanley Ray, 1901), 178.

[71]Eastman, *Work Accidents and the Law*, 119.

[72]Eastman, *Work Accidents and the Law*, 144.

[73]Gerald G. Eggert, *Steelmasters and Labor Reform, 1886-1923* (Pittsburgh: University of Pittsburgh Press, 1981), 43-58; Steward Slavishak, "Artificial Limbs and Industrial Works' Bodies in Turn-of-the-Century Pittsburgh," *Journal of Social History* (2003).

[74]Elizabeth Beardsley Butler, *Women and the Trades: Pittsburgh, 1907-1908*, Pittsburgh Series in Labor History (Pittsburgh: University of Pittsburgh Press, 1984), x-xiii; Maureen Weiner Greenwald, "Women at Work through the Eyes of Elizabeth Beardsley Butler and Lewis Wickes Hines," Introduction to Elizabeth Beardsley Butler, *Women and the Trades* (Pittsburgh: University of Pittsburgh Press, 1984); Stephen May, *Carnegie Magazine*, (July-August 1991).

[75]Butler, *Women and the Trades*, 17.

[76]Greenwald, "Women at Work through the Eyes of Elizabeth Beardsley Butler and Lewis Wickes Hines," 20-21.; Margaret Byington, *Homestead: The Household of a Mill Town* (Pittsburgh Survey) (Pittsburgh: University of Pittsburgh Press, 1974).

[77] Paul U. Kellogg, "Editor's Foreword," in Margaret Byington, *Homestead: The Households of a Mill Town* (Pittsburgh: University of Pittsburgh Press, 1974), vi-vii.

[78]Lubove, *Twentieth-Century Pittsburgh, Government, Business, and Environmental Change*, 15. Information on the Swissvale-Edgewood situation was provided to the author by former Swissvale Major Charles Martoni.

[79]Byington, *Homestead*, 119, 173-176.

[80]John A. Fitch, *The Steel Workers* (Pittsburgh: University of Pittsburgh Press, 1989), 139-157.

[81]Fitch, *The Steel Workers*, 168-177.

[82]Fitch, *The Steel Workers*, 206.

[83]Edward Devine, "Pittsburgh the Year of the Survey," *The Pittsburgh District: Civic Frontage* (Pittsburgh Survey) (New York: Arno Press, 1974), 3-4.

[84]Frank E. Wing, "Thirty-Five Years of Typhoid," in *The Pittsburgh District: Civic Frontage* (New York: Arno Press, 1974), 66.

[85] Wing, "Thirty-Five Years of Typhoid," 65.

[86]Lubove, *Twentieth-Century Pittsburgh, Government, Business, and Environmental Change*, 20-27; Joseph Tersak and James Craig, "Pittsburgh, PA Police: 98 Years of Police Motorcycles," *The Mounted Officer*, 2007, 10.

[87]Warren, *Triumphant Capitalism*, 22-27.

[88]Warren, *Triumphant Capitalism*, 32-50; While Warren traces the complexities and varying impact at different times on the Pittsburgh mills, Harvey O'Connor's concise description of the system demonstrates how it operated as a two-edged sword, both extending the life and reinforcing the technological stagnation of the Pittsburgh mills in *Steel Dictator* (New York: The John Day Company, 1935), 170.

[89]Warren, *Triumphant Capitalism*, 59, 61.

[90]Philip S. Foner, *History of the Labor Movement in the United States*, Vol. 4: *The Industrial Workers of the World, 1905-1917* (New York: International Publishers, 1965), 282.

[91]*Pittsburgh Leader*, July 15, 16, 1909.

[92]*Pittsburgh Leader*, July 20, 1909.

[93]Edward Levinson, *I Break Strikes!: The Technique of Pearl L. Bergoff* (New York: Robert M. McBride and Company, 1935), 52-69. Although Berghoff's "nobles" tended to be experienced gangsters, an interesting book by Stephen H. Norwood, *Strikebreaking & Intimidation: Mercenaries and Masculinity in Twentieth-Century America* (Chapel Hill: University of North Carolina Press, 2002), discusses the recruitment as strikebreakers of both college youth and African Americans as an expression of masculinity.

[94]Levinson, *I Break Strikes!*, 79; Norwood, *Strikebreaking & Intimidation*.

[95]*Pittsburgh Leader*, July 14, 1909.

[96]*Pittsburgh Leader*, July 15, 1909.

[97]*Pittsburgh Leader*, July 17, 1909; Bill Haywood, *The Autobiography of Big Bill Haywood* (New York: International Publishers, 1974), 241.; Foner, *History of the Labor Movement*, Vol.4: *The Industrial Workers of the World, 1905-1917*, 287-90.

[98] Foner, *History of the Labor Movement*, Vol.4: *The Industrial Workers of the World, 1905-1917*, 288.

[99] Foner, *History of the Labor Movement*, Vol.4: *The Industrial Workers of the World, 1905-1917*, 290.

[100] Foner, *History of the Labor Movement*, Vol.4: *The Industrial Workers of the World, 1905-1917*, 291.

[101] Levinson, *I Break Strikes!*, 79; *Pittsburgh Leader*, August 27, 1909.

[102] Melvyn Dubofsky, *We Shall Be All: A History of the Industrial Workers of the World* (New York: New York Times Books, 1969), 200-209.

[103] While the location of workers' rallies and meetings was uniformly described as being held on the "Indian Mound," the actual location was the long narrow ridge that separated the "Bottoms" from the Ohio River. On the eastern extremity of this long ridge, a burial mound rested for approximately 1,900 years until its excavation by the Carnegie Institute in 1896. The ridge itself is often mistakenly referred to as the "Indian Mound" to this day.

[104] It is to be hoped that the upcoming centennial of the McKees Rocks Strike will inspire an extensive investigation of the various local and national, foreign language, journals and papers that might enrich our understanding of the 1909-1919 era especially from the point of view of the immigrant Ukrainian, Rusyn, Croatian, Polish, Slovak, Serbian, Italian, etc. communities that formed there.

[105] For a description of churches and buildings discussed see Walter Kidney, *Landmark Architecture of Allegheny Country*, (Pittsburgh: Pittsburgh History & Landmarks Foundation, 1985).

[106] Jacob Feldman, *The Jewish Experience in Western Pennsylvania: A History, 1755-1945* (Pittsburgh: Historical Society of Western Pennsylvania, 1986), 52-53; Barbara Burstin, *A Jewish Legacy: Pittsburgh*, Documentary video, Carnegie library of Pittsburgh.

[107] Kidney, *Landmark Architecture of Allegheny Country*.

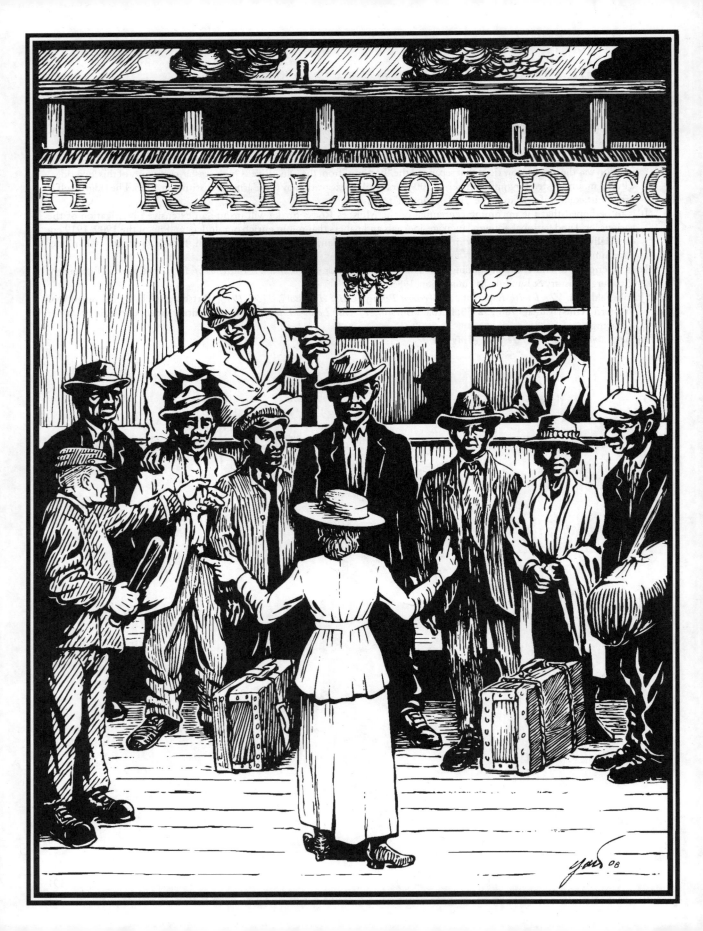

Chapter Eight

The Americanization of Labor

1910 - 1919

The questions "who is an American?" and "what is an American?" were central political issues in the first half of the 20ᵗʰ Century. They have reemerged early in the twenty-first. Who is an American? The "100% American" questions the loyalty of the immigrant and the civic aptitude of the descendents of slaves, or natives, or orientals, or "hunkies," or Catholics, etc. However, unlike nations where one's ancestors lived in the same location for many hundreds of years, a degree of insecurity accompanied the demand for a pedigree in the United States given our anti-royalist, democratic, revolutionary roots. Only Native Americans had any degree of antiquity to their claim on this land. "What is an American?" on the other hand, goes to the question of meaning. Is an American someone who has loyalty to a set of ideals including freedom of speech, assembly, and religion, who pledges allegiance to a government that provides for the common defense and promotes the general welfare? Or, does being an American come wrapped in an Imperial flag, demanding unregulated private control of the nation's wealth and lifeblood, and use of its military to pursue ambitions of expansion and domination at home and abroad?

American Rights and Wrongs

White Protestant elites, at the pinnacle of their power, felt threatened in the sea of strangers they had conjured up out of the depths of Europe and the afflictions of Africa. Questions of identity and loyalty were deeply contested in Pittsburgh before, during, and after World War I. America, the polyglot, the great mixing pot, melts only slowly over time. People share an always changing landscape, the uneven mixing of hundreds of distinct groups, a land of widely varying ties and shifting loyalties. On the Republican establishment side, there was a split developing between the city's small businessmen, skilled artisans, and municipal workers, whose particular interests benefited from the decentralized ward system, and the bankers, corporate leaders and professionals, who were interested in the rationalization and systemization of government in the hands of the new social elite - people with citywide and cosmopolitan viewpoints. In 1911, these elite-based reformers achieved the citywide election of the City Council and a centralized School Board.[1]

On the labor side, there were intense splits in philosophy over the degrees of appropriate resistance to a war rooted in the conflicting imperial ambitions of the European powers. These divisions were compounded by acrimonious debates over whether the American system could be reformed through the ballot and workplace organization, or needed to be swept away by an international proletarian revolution with completely new governmental or organizational forms. There were socialist, anarchist and communist variants on the revolutionary vision, once "the greedy parasites" of big business were overthrown. Ironically, most of the left was internationalist in viewpoint, but deeply fragmented by nationality. Radical political seeds found fertile ground in the industrial and coal towns of Western Pennsylvania, where dozens of nationalities had a significant, and often sharply distinct, presence; yet the work life was so brutal and the political life so controlled, workers naturally banded together as a class. Once news of the Russian Revolution was received in late 1917, many activists felt that all workers should unite to defend the first workers' state. As the decade ended, the defeat of union organizing efforts in steel, plus the fear spread by federal governmental raids targeting immigrant radicals, forced unions into a dozen-year fight for survival. Most radicals initially looked with hope to Russia as a guide and model. For a significant part of the left, once the Russian revolution occurred, organizational issues and policy positions inside the United States became linked to the fate and direction of the Soviet system.[2]

The dozen years from the start of the McKees Rocks strike in 1909 through the bitter aftermath of the 1919 steel strike gave newly arrived immigrants and the children of immigrants a stern lesson in the practical limitations of American democracy. Consistently, the central issue for workers through the entire period was the "denial of the right of any employee to any voice regarding the conditions of his employment." The determination of corporations "to rule at any cost" and impose "silence and acquiescence as the price of a job" was becoming the unifying rationale of big business' labor relations. As in steel, coal companies were willing to go to extraordinary lengths to keep unions out of their mines and "retain absolute authority over the coal pits." In Westmoreland County, just to the east of Pittsburgh, immigrant miners rose up in what some called a "miners' insurrection" and others a "civil war." The strike affected 17,000 miners at its peak, and when it was ended after sixteen bitter months, the devastation wrought upon coal patch communities was severe.[3]

> Of the existence of civil strife, the observer needs no signs or tokens. It is here in its grim realities elbowing the customary routine of the farms and villages of this old Pennsylvania countryside. Tented hill-sides shelter evicted families, processions of rough clad miners led by fife and drum, flying Old Glory, tread the township roads, mounted troopers rattle six-shooters at their hips, rations by the wagon load are daily distributed by the union commissary, people have been arrested, half a dozen men have been shot dead, and non-participants, Pittsburgh business men and others who made overtures toward peace, have been labeled "presumptuous and officious."[4]

The Westmoreland coalfields lay between the Pittsburgh region where the UMWA held sway, and the Connellsville coke region where Frick's determined resistance kept unionization at bay. The mostly Slavic strikers demanded the eight-hour work day standard of the union mines, rather than their ten-hour stint. They also wanted to be adequately compensated for "dead work," such as separating clay or slate from coal and pumping water out of the mine. Finally, they wanted a check-weighman independent of the company to assure fair pay for the full tonnage of coal extracted by hard labor. The young Phil Murray got forced out of one mine and blacklisted in others for raising "a little cane with the weigh-boss, because there was no union check-weighman at the mine." During the same period, he was a leader in the fight to obtain a workers' compensation law in Pennsylvania. Before his marriage, he roomed for three months with Pat Fagan's family, and as a result they became lifetime friends and allies. During the strike, Fagan recalled hiding three fellow mineworker organizers from the state police and mine deputies in St. Bartholomew's Church in Crabtree where he had been baptized. One of the organizers, Van Bittner, was a 32nd degree Mason and the other a Greek. "I was the only Roman among them." Another organizer friend of Fagan's during that strike was George Chip who later became middleweight boxing champion. The Westmoreland mines did not pay by the ton, but rather by the wagonload, an imprecise measure that invited abuse. The central issue for workers was, of course, unionism itself or, from the owners' point of view, any "interference with the employers' absolute determination of the labor contract."[5]

The strike was defeated by a downturn in the coal market and the fact that the extensive relief efforts, costing the UMWA in excess of a million dollars, could not be sustained. Technological change and steady immigration flow undermined union efforts. The strikers were mostly immigrants without deep roots in the mining towns. "They could pull up stakes and look for work in adjoining districts, thus relieving the strike commissary. At the same time, not only funds but leadership had to be drawn largely from the outside, for this was not the settling down of a resident work-people to a long-continued struggle in the towns they had grown up in." Coal companies could just keep recycling immigrants who seemed available in an inexhaustible supply. The strategy was increasingly feasible since the traditional hand miner was being replaced by mechanization, requiring more unskilled and semi-skilled workers and less of the quasi-independent, pick, shovel, and dynamite-wielding, all-round miner. [6]

The widespread use of dynamite during this period in mining and construction impacted the bitter struggle happening at the same time between U.S. Steel and the Ironworkers or Bridgemen's Union, nationally, and intensely in the Pittsburgh area. With unionism crushed in the steel production end, the corporation targeted its extensive fabrication business in bridges, industrial and commercial buildings to be open shop, refusing recognition to any labor organization. Previously, most of the erection had been done union. A bitter struggle raged from 1908 to 1911, and sporadically thereafter, as the National Erectors Association hired professional strikebreakers and what the union called "a network of spies, detectives, thugs, provocateurs" to break the union organization. Writer Harvey O'Connor commented on the struggle:

> The bridgemen were foes worthy of Steel's metal. Men who walked nonchalantly along girders and beams hundreds of feet above ground, who faced constant peril of death, who migrated across the continent, following the ever-shifting demands of bridge and building erection, cared little for the Corporation's threats. Fear would have been a grave handicap in a calling whose death rate was three times that of anthracite mining, six times that of ordinary construction, fifteen times more hazardous than work in the iron and steel mills.[7]

Ironworkers responded with more than one hundred bombings directed against worksite property nationwide. "At some 70 sites where explosions took place companies quickly gave the Ironworkers Union recognition. No one was ever killed in any of these explosions and the average loss of property was about one thousand dollars." A good number of these worksite explosions occurred in the Monongahela Valley, and the union gradually regained contractors, especially with the wartime boom and skilled labor shortage. The national union, however, came under concerted attack following an explosion at the *Los Angeles Times* printing plant that killed twenty people. The charismatic national

Secretary-Treasurer of the Ironworkers, John McNamara, was arrested, charged with planning the attack and defended in court by Clarence Darrow.[8]

In 1912, Democrat Woodrow Wilson, in a four-way race, won the presidential election. Socialist Eugene V. Debs received 900,000 votes for president, nearly six percent of the total, winning industrial towns like Turtle Creek, Wilmerding, and Whitaker, placing second to Teddy Roosevelt in Swissvale, and to Woodrow Wilson in East Pittsburgh. Nationally, socialists were elected mayors in 56 large and small cities. Additionally, the Industrial Workers of the World (IWW) were a growing, internationalist, "One Big Union," that vigorously opposed the AFL in the name of industrial union organization. While the IWW espoused industrial insurrection and the general strike, the organization also popularized non-violent, free speech fights as a tactic to challenge corporate control of communities. While working-class militancy was on the rise, strong, broad-based, middle class reform movements were also advancing a wide range of causes including municipal reform, women's suffrage, child labor protections, public education, workplace safety, and workers' compensation for death and injury on the job. The mounting political ferment for progressive reform was increasingly resisted, both locally and nationally, in the name of national preparedness, security, and loyalty, especially as the nation became increasingly drawn into an intensifying European war.

The women's suffrage movement was gaining significant support in the nation, and Pittsburgh was taking the lead in Pennsylvania. The right of women to vote had been championed by Jane Grey Swisshelm in the 1840s, and Susan B. Anthony spoke in support of female suffrage in Pittsburgh in 1880. The first recorded local suffrage group began in Wilkinsburg in 1889, and a columnist, Elizabeth Angus Wade, wrote numerous columns on the subject for three local papers under the pseudonym of "Betsy Bramble." Her columns relied, however, on racist and anti-immigrant arguments. "Consider yourselves, men, and see yourselves as we see you. Ignorance is the basis of despotism, and yet here you are thrusting the ballot into the hands of ignorant slaves….Here you are draining countries of their most degraded and dangerous classes and thrusting the ballot into their hands…while you deny it to your own best and moral citizens."[9]

In June 1904, a group of young Pittsburgh women led by Mary Flinn and Jennie Bradley Roessing organized the Allegheny County Equal Rights Association. Mary Flinn was the daughter of political boss William Flinn. She married John Lawrence and founded the Home for Crippled Children. In 1969, she sold the couple's beautiful estate, Hartwood Acres, to Allegheny County for the purpose of a county park. In 1907, the founding convention of the Pennsylvania Women's Rights Association was convened in Pittsburgh, and Roessing was elected president. The group sponsored numerous parades and marches; the first in Pittsburgh included two hundred women and eight men. The group visited all sixty-seven counties in the state in a truck with a Liberty Bell replica mounted on it and a sign that read: "The Liberty Bell will not ring until women win the right to vote." Their efforts were supported by the *Pittsburgh Leader,* whose publisher, Alex Moore, was the husband of Lillian Russell, an outspoken activist for women's rights. In 1913, the women's rights convention endorsed child labor legislation, called for reduced hours and increased pay for women and children, and mandated that the Union Label should appear on all its literature in the future in recognition of the Pennsylvania Federation of Labor's support for women's rights.[10]

Opposition to the vote for women was spearheaded by an association headquartered in Philadelphia that issued a pamphlet, "What is Feminism: Containing Doctrines on Divorce, Attacks on The Home, The Family, The Church and Christian Marriage." The liquor lobby opposed the women's vote out of justifiable fears that it would strengthen the Prohibition movement. The suffrage movement, on the other hand, was extending its reach to African-American women. On May 2, 1914, a large pro-suffrage parade with fifteen hundred women and a hundred automobiles made a circuit through Pittsburgh. Two black women's organizations, the Lucy Stone Suffrage Club, whose secretary was Daisy Lampkin, and the Anna H. Shaw Suffrage Club were given a place of honor marching in front of the Equal Rights Federation of Pittsburgh. Following the war, Pennsylvania became the seventeenth state to ratify the Nineteenth Amendment, and on August 26, 1920, Pittsburgh Mayor, E. V. Babcock issued a proclamation celebrating the ratification of the amendment, whereby "American womanhood has finally achieved its emancipation and enjoys for the first time full citizenship in the republic." The organization that led the struggle evolved into the League of Women Voters.[11]

Democracy in the Workplace

Turtle Creek flows into the Monongahela River at the location of the Edgar Thomson plant in Braddock, eight miles above Pittsburgh's "golden triangle." The area became known as the "Electric Valley" because, along its length, George Westinghouse constructed a complex of factories that pioneered many developments in electrical equipment manufacturing. In Wilmerding, where Westinghouse established personal headquarters in the massive stone general office building, referred to by the locals as the "Castle," he created not only a production apparatus but also a paternalistic company town and model factory. Great pride was taken in the town's sewer system and the modern toilet facilities installed in the workers' housing, built and financed by the company. While the defeat of unionism in the steel industry in 1892 brought the twelve-hour day and the seven-day week to the iron and steel mills, work in a Westinghouse plant was generally cleaner and the hours shorter. The basic work week was six ten-hour days until Westinghouse initiated a Saturday half-holiday, thus establishing a fifty-five hour work week. A hard worker and a skilled mechanic himself, Westinghouse enjoyed the respect and affection of many of his workers. The panic of 1907, however, caused him to lose control of the Westinghouse Electric Company to a group of bankers in league with the Mellons. He maintained operational control, however, over the Airbrake and the Switch until his death in 1913.[12]

Aggressive introduction of incentive pay, time studies, and piecework systems, according to the scientific management theories of Frederick Taylor, into the Westinghouse Electric, Machine, and Meter plants led to a rapid deterioration in labor relations in the Turtle Creek Valley. While George Westinghouse was a workhorse who successfully opposed craft union organizing attempts in 1903 and 1907, he respected skilled workers and surrounded himself with bright young engineers who helped him build complex production and distribution systems. Westinghouse Electric workers fiercely resisted the Taylor system as an assault on craft skills and workers' autonomy whose aim was complete managerial control. "Scientific management was by its very nature discontented management. Its efficiency experts and time-study men moved about tirelessly from one department to the next, and then back to those they had already reorganized once or twice before." Taylorism advocated "the gathering up of all this scattered craft knowledge, systematizing it and concentrating it in the hands of the employer and then doling it out again only in the form of minute instructions, giving to each worker only the knowledge needed for the performance of a particular relatively minute task.... When it is completed, the worker is no longer a craftsman in any sense, but is an animated tool of the management."[13]

Taylor began his work on scientific management in the 1880s. By World War I his ideas and many variations on them were influential all over the industrial world. The rise of industrial unionism was at least partially a response to this systematic attack by corporate management on the power and solidarity of established skilled craftsmen, such as machinists, molders, and foundry men. In addition, there were strong organizational stirrings among workers in brand new industries, such as the manufacture of complex electrical generation, motor and transmission systems, and the production and utilization of aluminum, where there were no traditional crafts or jurisdictions. The Taylor system especially affected the approximately 1,500 women workers at the Electric, concentrated in areas where work was tedious and often unhealthy. In 1909, during the course of her study for the *Survey*, Elizabeth Beardsley Butler described women's work in the foundry core room, the mica-splitting room, and the coil winding department. One of her concerns at the time, poor ventilation, provoked the walkout that triggered the 1914 strike. "Mica filling the air and the dust from the mica scattered about….diseases of throat and lungs, sometimes tuberculosis, among old employees…..Some 650 women also staffed the coil winding department, each working fast at winding coils by hand or machine, or at pasting mica at the long tables…in the midst of the ceaseless whirr of a thousand wheels."[14]

Westinghouse workers described the Taylor system as "the last word in man killing." "The piece work system… is applied to small work. The hardship exists from the fact that the rate is so small that a man has to work himself to the point of exhaustion to make anything. This system is in vogue, in the punch shop, better known as the slaughter house, so called because of the great number of fingers that have either been torn off or haggled so badly that they had to be amputated. Nearly all employees of the punch shop have mutilated fingers."[15] Butler pinpointed the alienation engendered by the Taylor production system, especially as it affected women workers: "In going through the plant, my guide asked a winder if the coils on which she was working were not for a motor of a certain sort, and she replied, 'I don't know: We're just told to do them this way.' The women do not consciously coordinate their work with that of the other departments of the factory or see in it significance beyond the mechanical execution of the tasks allotted. They are operators solely, cheaper than men, who are speeded to the limit of their strength, then dropped for a force of new and as yet untried recruits."[16]

The Socialist Party out-polled the two major parties in elections in the Turtle Creek Valley in 1910 and 1912, but there was also a strong contingent of advocates for revolutionary direct action among the Industrial Workers of the World (IWW) and other radical groups. Fred Merrick, editor of the radical paper *Justice*, a strong supporter of the IWW's 1913 stogie maker's strike in Pittsburgh, advocated direct action. The "Stogie Strike" in Pittsburgh's Hill District successfully united a majority of the 2,000 Russian, Romanian, and Austrian Jewish women who rolled the short cheap worker's cigars in a four-month strike that achieved a measure of union recognition in many of the small shops. During Eugene Deb's 1912 presidential run, a free speech campaign was mounted at the gates of Westinghouse, where many activists were arrested for their agitation against worsening working conditions inside Westinghouse.[17]

The free speech struggle was rooted in the radical culture shared by Jewish, Croatian and Italian workers at the Westinghouse plant who lived in Homewood, an East End neighborhood of Pittsburgh that had become an important residential district for Westinghouse workers. The movement started in August when Fred Merrick and another man were arrested for speaking to a group at the corner of Homewood Avenue and Kelly Street, a location where community gatherings had occurred for years without incident. On August 3, 1912, a mass meeting of up to ten thousand gathered to protest the arrests; "to protest against industrial slavery; to protest against capitalism; to protest against tyranny." Twenty, including nine women, were arrested at the largely peaceful demonstration. To protest these arrests, a third and larger meeting of fifteen thousand gathered for a night rally. Forty-five were arrested and crowded into six small cells where thirty-six prisoners were already housed. Subsequently, a grand protest meeting at Kennywood Park heard IWW leader Big Bill Haywood speak to fifteen thousand on behalf of the IWW's Joe Ettor and Arturo Giovanitti, arrested for murder during the Lawrence textile strike.[18]

In January 1914, discontent erupted at the Westinghouse Electric when the company instituted layoffs and imposed a reduction in hours. A large street meeting chose officers and a ten-man executive committee; then at a large indoor meeting a "speaker from each prominent nationality spoke and women first were recognized among the leadership...At this meeting, the enthusiasm of the girls became especially manifest and they were recognized by having a girl put on the speaker's list." A resolution "Announcing Plan of Organization to Take In All Workers From Every Department Without Regard to Craft, Nationality, Sex, or Age" was adopted. The new union, called the Allegheny Congenial Industrial Union (ACIU), envisioned an organization unifying all industrial workers. Asserting that Pittsburgh had become "a synonym of slavery" among the workers of America and "of all the working hells in this district Westinghouse is recognized as the chief penitentiary," the resolution called on all workers of the Pittsburgh district to raise the flag of industrial revolt. [19]

Unseasonably hot and humid weather, breaking existing records, probably helped spark the initial incident on June 3, when 23 men walked out of the Westinghouse machine plant protesting poor ventilation and were joined by women in the Micarta section. "These men and others stated that the lack of oxygen in the air in the plant caused them to be sick more than half the time." At a mass meeting at the Turtle Creek playgrounds later that evening, a committee of nine volunteered to present a list of grievances to the company. The union demanded recognition and the establishment of a grievance procedure, the reinstatement of all laid-off workers before new people were hired, and suggested work -sharing by means of an alternating or rotating layoff policy during slow times. The final demand was for the elimination of all bonus, premium, and piecework systems associated with Frederick Taylor's scientific management approach.[20]

After management refused to meet with the union committee, a strike was called. Crude banners were hastily lettered, and the first disorganized pickets were at the gate as the main body of workmen left the plant that evening. The early morning picket line effectively shut down the plant. The *Pittsburgh Leader* reported that by Friday afternoon 7,250 workers were on strike at the Electric, Machine, and Meter plants in East Pittsburgh. Local newspapers began to note a novel aspect of the work stoppage. Women workers, who constituted about twenty percent of the workforce, were actively leading the picket lines. Some 400 female pickets were at the front gate of the plant that first morning. Led by Bridget Kenny, an intense young Irish woman who the *Pittsburgh Leader* dubbed the "Joan of Arc of the Strikers," women became the shock troops of the union in a deliberate tactic to avoid violence. The paper commented: "a feature of the strike is the placing of 3,000 girls and women as pickets at the various entrances. This has been done on the presumption that no men workers will have the temerity to pass these guardians." An early morning mass meeting was held at the Turtle Creek ball fields, where "the idle men were instructed by four leaders, two men and two women, to remain away from the plants and to conduct themselves in an orderly manner." The meeting "was most enthusiastic, and later, headed by approximately 1,000 girl workers, the men strikers against tyrannical oppression and injustice, marched around the immense plants. During this parade many of the workmen in the plants stopped their machines, grabbed their coats and dinner pails and joined the parade." The women continued through the streets of East Pittsburgh and Turtle Creek blowing horns, and from a high bridge outside the plant, they called out to acquaintances inside to join them on strike. Twelve thousand people were reported to be marching about the town on the first day.[21]

The same afternoon, 4,000 strikers met and divided into 60 departmental groups, each electing 2 delegates to the strike committee. A committee of 12 was selected to negotiate with the company. Strikers met with railroad union representatives, requesting them to refuse to handle freight in the struck plants. The union issued an appeal to the stockholders and directors of Westinghouse, attacking Taylorism's attempt to usurp the skill and knowledge of the workman on behalf of management control. "In regard to the Taylor-made bonus system, we say that with all its possibilities for good in increasing production there is no other system we know of that can produce more hardship and unjustice [sic]." The letter goes on to say: "A system that ignores the soul of man won't work with man very long." Numerous accounts of the strike noted the high degree of organization and low level of violence during these exciting and tumultuous events. During the first days, some jostling of non-strikers was reported, and a guard drew a revolver brandishing it in strikers' faces; but generally the activities were marked by discipline and restraint. The strike appeared to an observer from the *Survey* as an exercise in "pure democracy" where decisions were made and discussed in large open-air meetings. Bridget Kenny, secretary of the ACIU, addressed an appeal to local saloonkeepers to close their establishments for the duration of the stoppage. The union required pickets to sign a pledge to do all in their power "to keep any person from doing another bodily harm, whether it be strike breaker or not."[22]

The company's first attempt to build a "sneak bridge" across Turtle Creek so that strikebreakers could get from railcars into the plant without passing through the picketed gates failed. "Sixty carpenters got off a train at the station in East Pittsburgh yesterday and were immediately surrounded by pickets....The carpenters had been engaged by a Braddock contractor to build a covered bridge from the railroad station to the works. When informed that a strike was on and this bridge would be used to take men, cots and other camp paraphernalia into the plant, the carpenters who were all union men refused to work." In another incident, drivers with two large truckloads of groceries for management and office workers in the plant turned back to Pittsburgh upon learning of the strike. The *New York Times* reported the Machinists union of Pittsburgh had resolved not to handle any work contracted out from the struck plants.[23]

At a Sunday mass rally, union leaders and sympathetic local clergy appealed for non-violence. While the company had allegedly brought former Pittsburgh Pirate pitcher and nationally known revivalist preacher, Billy Sunday, to town in March to counter mounting union sentiment, the Catholic pastor, Reverend William Cunningham at St. Colman's in Turtle Creek, and many of the local Protestant clergy, supported the workers' efforts. Ironically, the large wood and canvas "tabernacle" that had been constructed at the Turtle Creek playground for Billy Sunday was leased by the strikers, christened the "Labor Tabernacle," and re-commissioned for an "industrial revival." "At times as many as ten nationalities would be represented in different parts of the immense hall, with interpreters translating to their fellow countrymen the words of the speaker." In the months preceding the strike, the Reverend Edward Golden, an Episcopalian priest, was transferred out of St. Margaret's parish in Wilmerding, and then threatened with excommunication for preaching "Christian Socialism." In response to his bishop's actions, the clergyman stated the point clearly: "The issue is a better manhood for all or money for the few. Whether the present degrading capitalism shall continue or whether humanity shall realize a decent type of human society."[24]

By Monday, June 8, the entire Westinghouse Electric complex of plants, including the Machine and Meter plants, was effectively shut down. The company received cables and telegraphs from Westinghouse road workers from as far away as South America who immediately laid down their tools upon confirmation of the strike. Strikers wrote: "The silence from inside the works had a stimulating influence for it proved, more conclusively than anything could, that the monster, that the obstinacy of the bosses and their inhuman treatment of employees, were being given a just rebuke."[25] On Tuesday, the strikers adopted a new tactic. ACIU officials and Bridget Kenny, who emerged as the most public and assertive leader of the strikers with her brigade of 1,000 working girls, led a mass march to Wilmerding and the Airbrake plant two and one-half miles away. "Surprise was manifest on the faces of all the borough officials and business men as the column of silent, grave-visaged men and women stepped past to the beat of the drums, always forward without a marcher leaving the ranks, and then turned and marched back to the strikers' headquarters in East Pittsburgh… This quiet and orderly display of power had a great effect on the employees in the Wilmerding factory." Following it, a large number of men joined the union and later were willing if necessary, to go on a sympathy strike.[26]

On Thursday, June 11, a meeting of Local 2 of the ACIU at the Union Switch and Signal plant in Swissvale voted to go on strike in response to the reported importation of gunmen into East Pittsburgh and Turtle Creek. A planned march from East Pittsburgh to the Trafford foundry was immediately rerouted. George Hartshorn, ACIU organizer and the first Switch employee to be fired for union activity, led the parade. Heading the 5,000 marchers was a band on a large truck and a caravan of automobiles, decked with bunting and American flags, carrying women strikers. "Following the automobiles, with the fair enthusiasts saluting everyone on the way, was an army of men with eyes turned toward the front and with the stamp of a purpose on their faces….When the column passed through the towns of East Pittsburgh and Swissvale, the businessmen and citizens showed them sympathy for the cause by serving the workers coffee, lemonade, ice cold buttermilk and other summer beverages and sandwiches." The East Pittsburghers' parade, arriving at noon on a fair-weather Friday, emptied the Switch of most of its workers. Newspapers variously estimated that from eleven-hundred to fourteen-hundred of the seventeen-hundred shop men at the Switch went out that first day. Management warned workers, if they failed to return to work on the following Monday, they would lose their jobs.[27]

One night, the company made a second attempt to build a bridge across Turtle Creek to provide direct access from commuter trains to the plant. Within a few minutes, pickets roused a large body of strikers who surrounded the company men. "With these men Miss Kenny and her army of strikers engaged in friendly conversation, reminding one of the days of the Civil War when the soldiers of the North and South chatted and swapped tobacco across the battle line during a lull in the fighting. Then the strikers built a bonfire on the banks of the creek about which strikers and company men mingled in the most friendly fashion. Songs were sung, although it was the small hours of the morning. Finally all efforts at completing the bridge were given up and the strikers and company men dispersed, leaving the strikers' pickets on duty as before. Before dawn, however, 300 strikers constructed their own bridge out of railroad ties down at water level to facilitate their passage across the creek, and they christened it "Picket's Bridge."[28]

On Monday, June 15, the Westinghouse Company, in an open letter to employees in several Pittsburgh papers, announced it would remain an open shop and reserved the right to determine the compensation of employees based on the service they performed. The strikers in turn asserted their right to organize based on "rights guaranteed in the constitution and institutions of this country" and noted that: "They have enlisted the support of all those who have realized that the great progress of our age is steered by the formations and concentration of organizations on the part of the employers, which if not restricted by corresponding organizations of the employees, would eventually abridge and abolish the rights of the millions who due to their station in life have to be an employee in these highly organized and perfected industrial enterprises."[29]

The Switch's threat to fire strikers if they failed to report to work on Monday was unsuccessful. While the company claimed that 400 shopmen and 300 office workers reported to work, the union responded that only "about 100 men, the majority of whom are aged or employed in special tasks" actually entered the plant. Newspaper accounts estimated that over 1,500 of the 2,000 total shop and office employees remained out. E. M. Herr, president of the Electric, and George Prout, president of the Switch, seemed to take different stands. In a meeting with the striking committee on June 24, Herr reiterated that the plant would remain an "open shop." Prout, on the other hand, while asserting the need for the strikers to return to work, answered the strikers' grievances specifically: discharged union men's cases would be taken up with the relevant foreman; all departments would be allowed to elect a committee for adjustment of all matters; the eight-hour day demand would be taken under consideration; overtime would be paid at time and a half during the week and double time on Sundays and holidays; time and a half for piece workers would be considered. By the following Saturday, June 27, Switch workers voted to return to work. Prout, attempting to counter union claims of victory, asserted in a telegraph to the *New York Times*: "This walkout was an IWW effort, thinly disguised, and the men went out without presenting any grievances, demands or requests. No concessions whatever have been made by the company." A statement by the strike committee asserted: "We feel that by returning victorious we will be better able to help our fellow workers at East Pittsburgh, both financially and morally, than by the continuance of our strike." It is noteworthy that the Electric was under the harder-edged management of the bankers; while at the Switch and Brake, the old Westinghouse regimes were in place. [30]

The Switch workers' optimism, however, was ill-founded. At the Electric plant, Herr remained unmoved and prepared for confrontation by publishing notices in Pittsburgh newspapers on June 27 that all employees not reporting to work by Tuesday, June 30, would be considered as having left the company's employment. On Sunday, June 28, a mass meeting of 6,000-7,000 workers in East Pittsburgh voted unanimously not to return to work. Outside intervention, however, helped tip the scales against the strikers. Monday morning began with angry pushing and shoving at plant gates. Twenty Westinghouse gunmen, who had until now been kept out of sight, appeared armed with rifles on the main bridge and hurled insults at the pickets. The crowd roughly handled two company men on motorcycles, striking one in the head with a brick, and they roughed up the East Pittsburgh chief of police. These events provided Allegheny County Sheriff Richards with a justification to summon the state constabulary. [31]

Late that afternoon, a picket on motorcycle scout duty reported the approach of thirty mounted troopers from Greensburg. A large body of strikers met the "Cossacks" a mile east of Turtle Creek and escorted them into East Pittsburgh. "As the troopers, covered with dust, rode two abreast along Braddock Avenue, one of the girl strikers sprang out in front of the horses with tears flowing down her cheeks and waving an American flag. At a sharp command the horses were reined in and the girl cried out, "Oh, have you come here to shoot us down?" Captain L. G. Adams, in command, raised his hat and with his other hand saluted the flag, as did each of his troopers, as he said: "We, young lady, we came here to keep peace and order." Captain Adams said afterward the incident had impressed him more than anything that had occurred in his life as a "Cossack." Headlines in the *Pittsburgh Press* screamed "Troops Enter East Pittsburgh," while the day's second story reported on the assassination of Archduke Ferdinand of Austria in the distant Balkan city of Sarajevo, the incident that triggered World War I. [32]

The strikers maintained an orderly discipline toward the troopers that drew praise from the officers. On their part, the state troopers were generally well behaved, declaring to strike leaders their job was to be "like umpires at a baseball game." Despite this professed neutrality, the Westinghouse Company quartered and fed the horses and men, and the troopers took the first man they arrested to the company office rather than to the borough jail "a few rods distant." On July 1, the strikers again voted unanimously to refuse to go back to work. While the company extended the deadline for returning to work to July 2 and continued the pledge to meet and adjust grievances after the strikers returned, some officials at both the Machine and the Meter companies told newspapers that they would "stand by the strikebreakers." On July 2, moreover, the company greatly increased new hiring, prompting a July 3 secret ballot vote on the company's vague and now outdated commitments. The strikers voted 3,063 to 1,983 in favor of staying out, publicly demonstrating significant slippage in the strikers' resolve. Herr then announced he would no longer talk to the strikers; and on Monday, July 6, the companies opened employment offices seeking skilled workmen in Philadelphia, Cleveland and Detroit. "In view of the fact that a large number of employees have already returned and that applications are constantly being received from others, it is impossible to grant any further extension but that the companies' doors are open, and any of the employees coming back would receive full consideration from the companies."[33]

On Thursday, July 9, the last great meeting of the strikers drew 5,000 to the Tabernacle. Rejecting a proposal to return the next day, they decided unanimously to march back to work on Monday morning "impressed with the belief that by returning as a body they might gain more advantage than by returning individually." The workers were urged to look after their less fortunate fellows and maintain the solidarity that had made the strike such a success. The strikers claimed victory in that the company had agreed to meet with committees of the workers to solve grievances. Despite the vote, many of the remaining strikers bolted and retuned to work on Friday. On the final Monday morning, the remnant of the strike army marched to the plant. They found themselves forced to pass like cattle between rails to the company gates where the company officials told some of them to go work for the union. Sources variously estimated between 1,000 to 3,000 workers remained unemployed.[34]

Black Migration

As war production increased and the labor supply tightened, African-Americans were widely recruited in the South, then systematically used to undermine labor's efforts to organize. Driven north by low wages, tightening Jim Crow segregation and lynching, cotton crop failures caused by the advance of the boll weevil infestation of cotton, and the serious drought of 1916, Southern black labor saw in northern factories the hope of steady employment and the possibility for social advancement. While earlier recruitment of blacks after the Civil War had focused on skilled iron workers for employment as strikebreakers, the great wave of black migration between 1910 and 1920 was stimulated by railroad companies, steel mills, and munitions plants to replace the reduced flow of unskilled immigrant labor. Employment as unskilled labor was not always reliable, however, as production demands fluctuated, and material handling was increasingly automated. While the flow of foreign immigration to the United States constricted by nearly two-thirds, from more than a million to 350,000 a year, the number of foreign-born working in Pittsburgh's industries declined by more than 10,000. Concurrently, the number of black industrial workers swelled from 2,550 in 1910 to 14,610 in 1919 while the local black population climbed from 25,623 in 1910 to 37,725 in 1920.[35]

While the African-American industrial workforce grew significantly, the percentage of blacks in skilled industrial jobs dropped from over a third to less than ten percent. In addition, unskilled blacks were increasingly channeled into the "Negro jobs" that employers defined as hard labor in high temperatures, such as tearing down and rebuilding furnaces, cleaning up spilled metal and slag, clearing hot metal from shearing operations, stoking furnaces and charging coke ovens. Outside the mill as well, blacks were being hired on asphalt crews, stoking coal in boilers and working over hot stoves in restaurants. Blacks in industry tended to be injured in industrial accidents at a rate somewhat worse than immigrants and at double the rate of native white workers. Like the immigrants, blacks suffered from access only to substandard housing. Many of the strikebreakers of 1919 were housed in bunkhouses or in dilapidated boarding houses adjoining the mill properties for many years. In addition, blacks suffered exclusion from many public facilities. Most downtown Pittsburgh restaurants would not serve blacks, and they were only allowed in the balconies of most movie theaters, even in the mill towns.[36]

Like the immigrant societies, black society grew up around the churches. The church "performed the most vital social functions for a people restricted in expression in most spheres....With freedom and growth of the community, the aspirations of the Negro grew. And the church largely made possible their satisfaction. Not only did it develop religious doctrine and give moral guidance, it also established all means of social communication and expression, choral music, literary societies, dramatic clubs, bands and orchestras. Through the doors of the church for many years the Negro found his chief entry into the world he wanted to inhabit." Supplementing the churches was the growth of black fraternal and social organizations such as the Elks and black veterans' groups that established their own legion halls. Extremely important over the years was the development of a strong independent newspaper, the *Pittsburgh Courier*, taken over by Robert L. Vann in 1910, shortly after its founding by Edwin Harleston.[37]

Robert Vann arrived in Pittsburgh in 1903 at the age of 24, a recipient of an Avery Scholarship to the Western University of Pennsylvania. His light color, slim nose and straight hair led the registrar to suggest that he register as someone from India to make things easier on himself. Vann refused and affirmed his blackness with pride his entire life. He was welcomed into the local black elite and became a member of the prestigious Loendi Club. He graduated from the university in 1906 and was admitted into the law school as the only black in his class. To support his studies, he worked nights and early mornings as a dining car porter on the P&LE Railroad between Connellsville and Pittsburgh. Upon graduation from the University of Pittsburgh Law School in 1910, he became one of only five black attorneys practicing in Pittsburgh. Asked to help incorporate a fledgling African American newspaper, Vann would dedicate most of his life to making it a significant and influential force in and on behalf of the black community.[38]

Vann found ample causes to champion. The healthcare available to the black community was abysmal. Black schoolchildren never saw a black teacher. Many downtown restaurants refused to serve blacks, department store clerks ignored them, theaters segregated them in the balconies, while the Nickelodeons charged blacks double the price for inferior seats. When Daisy Lampkin, Vice President of the *Pittsburgh Courier* and one of Pittsburgh's most prominent black women, went to visit a friend at the Penn Hotel, she was forced to use the freight elevator. Inadequate housing and lack of opportunity bred crime. While Vann sympathized with unions, he was acutely aware of the job hunger of the black community. When Kaufmann's department store fired its union drivers during an organizing campaign, Vann helped recruit 76 black replacement drivers who after the strike was settled were "found wanting" and dismissed. By the 1930s the *Pittsburgh Courier* had a national reach with 70,000 subscribers and Southern and Eastern editions, in addition to its City edition.[39]

The industrial corporations were interested in promoting stability and discipline within their black workforce. Where corporate efforts directed at immigrants stressed "Americanization" and loyalty, corporate policies toward blacks tended to focus on the migrant's leisure and the dangers of "fast living." The city with its pool halls, taverns, brothels, and gambling offered many distractions and temptations for rural migrants that the corporations saw as distractions from work. The Pittsburgh Urban League, founded in 1915, encouraged and cooperated with the welfare efforts of the local corporations. In 1918, the Homestead Steel Works became the first to establish a community center for black workers and their families that provided educational and recreational opportunities. Black welfare officers were appointed by local corporations and directed by their personnel departments to assist the recruitment and retention of black labor.[40]

Pittsburgh blacks also developed their own community institutions and political entities. The Pittsburgh Branch of the NAACP was founded in 1915 and soon had branches in many mill communities. Initially more popular, a black nationalist organization, the Universal Negro Improvement Association, founded by Marcus Garvey in Harlem in 1914, spread rapidly, with its highpoint coming in the early 1920s. Emphasizing black racial pride and self-help enterprises, the movement had chapters in many area mill towns and attracted some support from local clergy. Black sports were not dependent solely on corporate largesse. Cumberland Posey, son of a steamboat and coal company owner, who played basketball at both Duquesne University and Penn State, became involved in 1911 with the team that gained national fame in the 1930s as the Homestead Grays. His Homestead Grays Athletic Club included a basketball team and a stable of boxers.[41]

With the great migration, the African-American community reasserted itself as a significant presence in Pittsburgh. It was, however, fragmented internally as well as geographically. The "Old Pittsburghers" formed a distinct social set from the new migrants. While the recent arrivals spread out, working in the mills and living in the industrial towns and neighborhoods along the rivers, the Pittsburgh-born blacks tended to live higher up in older African-American neighborhoods. A few worked as skilled workers and professionals, but most took domestic, clerical, and service positions. Furthermore, while the Hill District was the center of African-American cultural life in Pittsburgh, the black community was dispersed into enclaves in city neighborhoods in the North Side, Beltzhoover in the south, and Homewood in the east, or in distinct sections of the surrounding mill towns; thus, their political clout tended to be diluted.[42]

May Day in Braddock

The dissolution of the 1914 Westinghouse strike left grievances over Taylorism and the speed-up unresolved and thwarted the demand for workplace organizational rights. As the terrible trench warfare in Europe displayed the horrors that modern industrial advances brought to war, division over U.S. involvement in the European war deepened. War orders, especially munitions, increased rapidly in 1915. Discontent and agitation increased as employment began to swell and workers felt their leverage. Between August and October 1915, a young ambitious mineworker working as an organizer for the American Federation of Labor, John L. Lewis, spent six weeks in the Turtle Creek Valley organizing among the electrical workers, but, despite large mass meetings that Lewis addressed, an attempt to organize a strike at the Westinghouse Electric was defeated by a three-to-one vote of the workers.[43] It was at this time that Lewis met Pat Fagan and Phil Murray for the first time. Lewis had been attacked and beaten by several men in Turtle Creek. Murray traveled into Pittsburgh to meet Lewis, who apparently was planning some personal revenge on those he thought responsible for the attack. Fagan tells the story:

> Well, the first time that Murray ever met Jack Lewis was in the old Labor Temple on Webster Avenue in Pittsburgh. Murray went up to meet him, and there he was in a fight with two boilermakers. One was lying in the corner, and Lewis was after the other one. Murray asked, "Is there a fellow by the name of John Lewis here? "Yes." Lewis said, "But I'm busy now, see you in a few minutes." So Lewis and Murray got acquainted in the old Labor Temple.[44]

Between 1915 and 1916, there were 4,924 strikes nationally involving 2,000,000 workers. On April 21, 1916 (Good Friday), less than two years after the first Westinghouse strike, a second walkout of 14,000 workers at the Electric occurred. Whereas the 1914 strike had been well organized, peaceful, and disciplined, the 1916 walkout was chaotic and marked by violent incidents. With war orders feeding demand for labor, and immigration from eastern and southern Europe disrupted by war, labor scarcity fueled a spirit of rebellion among the workforce. On March 16, a walkout over pay rates occurred, and Westinghouse Electric responded with a raise. The International Association of Machinists (IAM) attempted to organize skilled men in the company's huge machine shops; but a resurgence of the industrial union organization, called this time the Allegheny Industrial Union, led by Charles Hall, proved more popular. The "Congenial" part of the union's title was dropped, appropriately enough, since the mood of the workers was decidedly angrier and less congenial. On April 20, Hall was fired for union activity; and, the following day, 14,000 Westinghouse workers walked off the job.[45]

Fred Merrick, revolutionary socialist and editor of the paper *Justice*, worked at a luncheonette with Bridget Kenny, heroine of the 1914 strike. At strike meetings, Merrick gave inflammatory speeches to workers. He professed skepticism about any organization because they all bred "autocracy." He urged the workers to be like "Indians of olden times" and fight for their rights. At one meeting, he brandished a shotgun and revolver and urged the stockpiling of weapons. A young, energetic and charismatic 20 year old woman, Anna K. Bell, became the new "Joan of Arc of the Westinghouse strike." On Sunday, April 30, strikers were told to report for duty the following morning at 5:00 a.m. for a mass march on the Edgar Thomson Works, only two miles downstream from the East Pittsburgh plant. On May 1, a huge parade of approximately 4,000 East Pittsburgh marchers with red flags flying and led by a Lithuanian band broke through the gates of the Edgar Thomson Steel Works and called on immigrant steelworkers to strike. The crowd then broke into groups and invaded a series of plants, American Steel and Wire in Braddock, Standard Chain Works and McClintic Marshall Construction in Rankin, all of which were forced to shut down. As many as 36,000 workers were out.[46]

Despite the erosion of its workforce, the mighty Edgar Thomson plant refused to close; thus, a second electrical worker march was set for May 2. After making a circuit of previously shut down facilities in Braddock and Rankin and setting pickets, the main body of marchers returned to the gates of Edgar Thomson. There, Coal and Iron Police, detectives and company guards, estimated by the press to be 1,700 in number, were barricaded in the plant. After taunts and rocks were directed at the police, shots were fired, provoking a charge upon the gates of the mill. Several attacks were repelled and, by late afternoon, three people were dead and thirty wounded. Governor Martin Brumbaugh dispatched more than a thousand infantry and cavalry of the National Guard. Strike leaders including Merrick, Bell, Hall and twenty-seven others were arrested. The strike began to unravel as 1,500 toolmakers marched back into the plant on May 8. The IAM tried to provide leadership after the collapse of the AIU, but on May 17 the strike was ended. In subsequent trials, Merrick declared he had lost all faith in unions and supported direct action by workers. Merrick and a dozen others served time in jail, Bell and Kenny were acquitted, and charges against Hall were dropped.[47]

War, Revolution, Disease

From 1914 on, the European combatants' insatiable appetite for war materials, especially munitions, sparked a tremendous surge in Pittsburgh manufacturing that created gigantic profits for the powerful corporations that dominated civic and economic life. A French military leader observed that, "Pittsburgh steel was everywhere along the battle front." Westinghouse Electric alone produced over five million shells and five hundred million half-inch bullets for the British Army and garnered war contracts of $1,475,000,000. Massive outputs of shells and grenades, shafts and propellers, armor plate for ships and tanks, rail cars and braking units, gas masks and optical equipment, earned Pittsburgh the title of the "arsenal of the world." "By the time the United States entered the war in April 1917, the Pittsburgh district had 250 great war plants, employing 500,000 men and women, day and night, seven days a week." U.S. Steel was particularly well prepared for a surge in international demand, since it had created an international marketing infrastructure with sixty agencies scattered around the world, with warehouses in China, South Africa, South America and Australia. "…It was natural that when the warring nations of Europe looked outside for help in steel and iron, they thought first of the Steel Corporation." Help, indeed, it did; and in 1916 the "corporation with a soul" registered earnings of $333,500,000, double that of any previous year.[48]

The last of the great Mellon "crown jewels," as the core family businesses were termed, was the Koppers Company. Its importance and expansion was directly linked to the world war. Dr. Heinrich Koppers, a German inventor, developed a process to distill and capture the by-products of coal combustion. The Koppers process salvaged gas that was used for industrial and home heating, tars used in roads and a variety of other applications, and chemical by-products such as toluol, the base ingredient for TNT. Dr. Koppers developed his new process in Germany, and he was brought to the United States in 1908 by U.S. Steel to build by-product coke ovens for its use. As war clouds gathered, Dr. Koppers became anxious about mounting anti-German sentiment, the possibility of war, and the seizure of his patents and operations. Following the German attack on Belgium, the demand for the by-products of Dr. Kopper's ovens skyrocketed. "With the advent of war came the realization that the striking power of a nation in modern warfare is largely determined by its supply of coke….Altogether the company played a most important part in the successful prosecution of the world conflict." In 1915, the Mellons moved in, reorganized, and effectively secured control of the company, leaving the inventor with a 20 percent share. When the United States declared war on Germany, the Koppers Company, undoubtedly motivated by the deepest patriotic sentiment, notified Attorney General Palmer of the German inventor's stake-holding, whereby his share was confiscated and sold at auction to the sole bidder - the Mellon interests.[49]

The war was good for Alcoa, too. Aircraft parts, fuses, bullet heads, helmets, radiators, three million meat cans and bacon containers, and especially the ubiquitous aluminum mess kits, required for doughboys through Mellon influence, increased both the company's volume of production, as well as a price to the government for the metal that was 50 percent higher during wartime. Ninety percent of Alcoa production in the U.S. and Canada was dedicated to the war effort. The Mellon Institute for Industrial Research provided British troops with the first gas masks on the Western Front, not long after the Germans launched the initial gas attack on Canadian soldiers at Ypres in 1915. Mellon Institute was also instrumental in developing a reliable aviation fuel.[50]

The negative side of the region's war ledger of course factored in the loss of Pittsburgh soldiers. Close to 60,000 residents of Allegheny County joined the armed services, and 1,527 were killed in the conflict. A Pittsburgh soldier from Bloomfield, Thomas Enright, who already had extensive military experience in America's growing imperial involvement around the globe, was among the first three Americans killed in World War I. He had been in China, fought against the Moros rebellion in the Philippines, and was part of General John Pershing's expedition in pursuit of Pancho Villa in Mexico. He became part of the 16th Infantry Division that marched in Paris on July 4th 1917. Pershing wrote in his memoirs: "The first appearance of American combat troops in Paris brought forth joyful acclaim from the people." The division's chief of operations was George C. Marshall of Uniontown. On November 3, 1917, Enright was one of three American soldiers killed in a German attack, his head nearly severed by a trench knife. After the war, Enright's body was returned to Pittsburgh where it lay in state at Soldiers and Sailors Memorial Hall, taken in solemn procession to St. Paul's Cathedral for a funeral mass said by Bishop Hugh C. Boyle, and then buried in St. Mary's Cemetery in Lawrenceville.[51]

Many Western Pennsylvanians who served in World War I were assigned to the Eightieth Division, a direct descendant of the "Old Eighteenth," itself descended from the Duquesne Greys, organized in the city in 1831. The Eightieth took part in the Meuse-Argonne offensive and suffered in excess of 6,000 casualties. Many Pittsburghers were also part of the "Iron Division" of the Pennsylvania National Guard that served in France with distinction. Pittsburgh sent 500 airmen into the service, second only to New York City. William Thaw of Pittsburgh became a famous ace pilot first with the legendary Lafayette Escadrille and then with the American Air Service in France. He was decorated numerous times for flying missions behind enemy lines or downing German air machines.[52]

One of the most challenging war contracts fell to the Union Switch and Signal, contracted to produce 2,500 80-horsepower Le Rhone airplane engines in September of 1917. After many engineering problems caused by inadequate working drawings, production began slowly in the summer of 1918; but by September, production reached 345 engines with an increase each month until 546 were produced in January 1919, when the contract was cancelled because of the end of hostilities. Union Switch and Signal, despite numerous engineering and production problems, was able to meet the challenge. Once the war ended, however, contracts were cancelled, and production ceased. The intense effort did nothing to erect a foundation upon which an aviation industry could grow and develop in Pittsburgh.[53]

As the European war expanded, it cut the former flood of immigrant Eastern and Southern Europeans to a relative trickle. Labor shortages stimulated labor militancy. Between 1915 and 1916, there were 4,924 strikes in the United States involving 2,000,000 workers. Rapidly rising prices, caused by near full employment and the shift away from consumer to war production, put a severe strain on workers' budgets. Furthermore, the pace of labor conflict did not decline upon the declaration of war by the United States; it accelerated. In the first six months of American involvement, there were nearly 3,000 strikes. As direct action and unsanctioned wildcat strikes spread, American Federation of Labor President Samuel Gompers moved the organization decisively, first toward "preparedness," and then into outright support for the war. He wrote in his autobiography: "I was convinced that…the time has come when the world could not exist part democratic and part autocratic. It was an issue on which there could be no real neutrality, and therefore propaganda for neutrality was propaganda to maintain autocracy. Those not actively for democracy were in effect against it."[54]

The American Socialist Party, on the other hand, unlike many of its European sister parties that abandoned oft-repeated pledges of opposition to capitalist war in the patriotic fervor stirred by nationalist war fever, affirmed "its allegiance to the principle of internationalism and working class solidarity the world over." It proclaimed its "unalterable opposition to the war just declared by the government of the United States." Leading Socialist, Eugene V. Debs, winner of six percent of the nation's vote for president in 1912, and imprisoned for opposition to the war, told the court that sentenced him: "The five percent of our people who own and control all of the sources of wealth, all of the nation's industries, all of the means of our common life – it is they who declare war; it is they who make peace; it is they who control our industry. And so long as this is true, we can make no just claim to being a democratic government – a self-governing people."[55]

After Wilson was reelected in 1916 with the boast that "he kept us out of war," German battlefield success, followed by the military collapse of Russia, raised the possibility that Germany might win the war. Labor discipline became more urgent for war industries with large investments in France and England. Gompers supported governmental action against the Socialists and the IWW. "We all had to shift from freedom of action, thought, and speech that belongs only to peace over to circumspection and control made imperative by war dangers….Things that can be done safely in times of peace arouse suspicion and condemnation in time of war." In November of 1917, Wilson became the first American president to address an American Federation of Labor convention and paid tribute to Gompers and his "patriotic courage." Wilson indicated: "I like to lay my mind alongside of a mind that knows how to pull in harness. The horses that kick over the traces will have to be put in corral." Intolerance toward opposition to the war extended to educational establishments as well. Three University of Pittsburgh students were arrested for attempting to hold an anti-war meeting on campus, where a minister, who was a veteran, was scheduled to speak. At their trial, the Allegheny County Court dismissed the charges with the judge stating: "College students are not intended to be empty tanks into which wisdom is to be poured."[56]

Labor shortages and a relatively friendly federal government gave renewed impetus to labor organizing. The failure of the AFL to develop appropriate industrial union structures hampered its efforts; still in 1917, the old Amalgamated Association of Iron and Steel Workers successfully organized the Pittsburgh plant of Jones and Laughlin, but after a month-long strike the effort collapsed. The mineworkers' union was growing vigorously, adding 50,000 members in the summer of 1918 alone. Companies with the power to grant military exemptions to critical workers could revoke them to eliminate agitators. "Thus a workman exempted at the manufacturer's request becomes his slave," charged a complaint to the War Labor Board about U.S. Steel. The patriotism of Samuel Gompers was buttressed, moreover, by the solid union gains made during the period. An AFL Declaration on March 12, 1917 pledged labor's support for the war: as long as capital did not benefit from the war; that work and wages conform to "principles of human welfare and justice"; and that organized labor be represented on the boards of all war agencies. President Wilson, anxious to blunt radical labor opposition to the war responded: "I am for the laboring man. Justice must be done him or there can be no justice in this country." Wilson's policies were administered by his Secretary of

Labor, William B. Wilson of Pennsylvania, former UMWA District 2 and Knights of Labor local president. Early in 1918, a War Labor Conference Board was created to establish "principles and policies that will enable the prosecution of production without stoppages of work." Among the principles so established was labor's right to organize into trade unions without interference.[57]

The Socialist Party declined rather dramatically after 1914. Internal divisions over varieties of opposition to U.S. involvement in the war, debates about the meaning of the Russian revolution, the combined force of both moderate reform and the repressive policies of Woodrow Wilson, all diluted the Party's appeal. The Socialists made only modest headway among immigrant steelworkers. The Bolshevik phase of the Russian Revolution in November of 1917, coming not long after U.S. entry into the war in April, had a momentous impact on the public perception of labor conflict. First, the triumph of the anti-war Bolsheviks meant the collapse of the Eastern front, triggering the dispatch of an American expeditionary force into Russia to fight against the Red government. Second, the surprising seizure of power in Russia by its small communist party inspired a sweeping "red scare" in the U.S., orchestrated by a combination of business, government, and press, that focused upon the presumed danger posed by a Slavic immigrant workforce concentrated in heavy industries essential for war production. In reality, however, the two rival Communist parties formed during the 1919 strike, were more concerned with factional strife between themselves, and with heated polemics against the Socialists and the IWW, than they were in taking advantage of the industrial upheaval that was occurring. One of the main Communist leaders admitted later that, among all the delegates of the two tiny parties, "it would have been difficult to gather together a half-dozen delegates who knew anything about the trade union movement."[58]

Anxiety levels in Pittsburgh, indeed worldwide, were increased by the devastating Flu Epidemic of 1918. The worst pandemic in modern human history, the influenza started among American military in Kansas in March 1918 and, in less than a year, it killed an estimated twenty-one million people worldwide – more than twice the number slaughtered in the 1914-1918 "Great War" itself. Influenza followed the American forces to Europe and then swept through the French and German armies, reaching China and Japan by summer. Pittsburgh remained unscathed, however, until the fall of 1918. While Philadelphia raged with the fever, Pittsburgh received an order from the State Health Commissioner on October 4 closing all places of amusement in the state, including saloons, college football games, movie houses, and public funerals. The order provoked near universal protests by politicians, newspapers and the general public. From October 4 to 7, there were 284 reported cases in the city; on the fifth day, October 8, 453; and on the sixth day, 784. Hospitals were overwhelmed, and any patient capable of being sent home was cleared out. The mayor cancelled all church activities and closed the playgrounds. Churches, clubs, and settlement houses became sick wards. A tent hospital of 300 beds was set up in Washington Park. The deaths began piling up: on October 15, 39 died; October 16, 61; October 17, 75; October 22, 121; October 23, 133. The city was soon struck with a shortage of gravediggers and coffins as well as hospital beds.[59]

Many surrounding towns were worse off than Pittsburgh. Elizabeth had 900 cases. Coal patch and mill towns with their close and cramped quarters were hit especially hard. In Rossiter, Indiana County, one out of five residents had the flu. Carnegie Steel had 2,600 workers off sick. Bishop Canevin of the Catholic Diocese ordered relief stations to be set up in all 27 city wards; sisters served as nurses, and church buildings became infirmaries. On October 29, the death toll crested at 176, and within days, movie houses, saloons and some politicians began pushing hard for an end to the restrictions on gatherings. On November 6, the death toll dropped below 100; two days later, new cases declined to 189 from 585 a week earlier. There was a spike in infections following the November 11 Armistice signing that ended the war and triggered mass celebrations. When it was over, Pittsburgh counted 4,500 dead with 700 children orphaned. Altogether, in Pennsylvania, 40,000 died.[60]

The end of the war in November of 1918 with its slowing of production increased worker anxieties in an era without unemployment compensation or government welfare programs. In February, a shipyard strike in Seattle erupted into a two-day general strike, where virtually all activities in the city including shops, theaters and schools were shut down and up to 100,000 workers idled. Social tension built in the steel towns of Western Pennsylvania during the "red summer" of 1919. A terrible race riot erupted in Chicago, and racial animosities were on the rise in the mill towns and coal fields, as blacks, recruited by companies to replace immigrant labor, provided leverage against union organization. During U.S. involvement in the First World War, April 6, 1917, to November 11, 1918, labor negotiations and a measure of union recognition came with federal government policies intended to sustain national production by arbitrating labor disputes. Many unions enjoyed de facto recognition. Once the armistice was declared ending World War I, however, the partial labor truce began to unravel. The government began to dismantle wartime regulations. As the volume of work declined, worker demands for shorter work hours, especially the end of the twelve-hour swing shift system in steel, became more urgent to share the available work and avert mass layoffs. Mineworkers had agreed not to strike during the war, and price increases had outstripped wage gains. Because the national bituminous coal agreement, supposed to expire April 1, 1920, was repudiated by most operators in early 1919, local wildcat strikes began to break out providing a context of mounting labor unrest leading to the upheaval in steel. In the 1919 mineworker convention, the union officially endorsed the nationalization of the mines and a thirty-hour workweek. Railroad unions had previously endorsed the Plumb Plan calling for the nationalization of the railroads. To many the specter of Bolshevism haunted the land, and the breakdown of order was epitomized when the Boston Police went on strike in September 1919.[61]

War-induced labor shortages forced companies to raise wages to retain workers who discovered they could move with relative ease to another job. The cost of living, however, rapidly outstripped wage increases as consumer goods production stagnated in favor of war production. The cost of living showed a steady increase: from August 1915 to June 1917 (29%), to June 1918, (58%); to December 1918, (74%); and by December 1919, the cost of living had increased nearly 100 percent. Workers increasingly demanded higher wages, shorter hours, overtime pay, and above all union recognition, so that their numerous grievances could be addressed in an ongoing manner. The number of strikes increased steadily during the war as workers tried to improve their position. Unrest peaked in 1919 as four million workers, 20 percent of the total American workforce, participated in 3,374 work stoppages. Union membership steadily increased from two million members in 1916 to over four million in 1920.[62]

Public sector workers, including Fire Fighters, were suffering the effect of wartime wage freezes combined with steadily mounting inflation. In February, 1918, an aggressive leader, John "Knockers" Conley was elected president of Fire Fighters Local 1. The *International Fire Fighter,* noted that he had "a wonderful pair of lungs." Assisted by Attorney William Brennan, the union vigorously protested the city's granting of a much higher wage increase to police than to the firemen. Firefighters worked a much longer work week and the wages paid to the two groups had always been equal. At a meeting at Pittsburgh's Labor Temple, the Fire Fighters Local 1 voted to strike at noon on Saturday. Only 15 out of 918 members ignored the union and continued to work. While their meeting was still in progress, news was received of a blaze out of control on Penn Avenue. The entire assemblage dashed to the fire, extinguished it as "volunteers," and then returned to the Labor Temple. After seven-and a half hours, the strike was settled. Fire Fighter Harry Weinand recalled: "I think the unselfish response of the striking Firemen to the fire at Penn Avenue was the most memorable event. In spite of the fact I was married and had two children, I went on strike with the Fire Fighters. After the strike I was elected steward, and for 40 years thereafter served as union steward on the job,"[63]

For steelworkers and miners, the key issues were union recognition and a shorter work week without a reduction in pay, since they could barely survive on what they were making as it was. U.S. Steel, however, led employer opposition to unions. Judge Gary wrote to the union organizing committee: "Our corporation and subsidiaries, although they do not combat labor unions as such, declines to discuss business with them. The Corporation and subsidiaries are opposed to the 'closed shop.' They stand for the 'open shop,' which permits one to engage in any line of employment whether one does or does not belong to a labor union. This best promotes the welfare of both employees and employers." [64]

Free Speech Struggles and the Murder of Fannie Sellins

The underlying causes of worker unrest in steel were the brutally long hours and low pay, combined with dangerous and unhealthy conditions. With 12-hour workdays and swing shifts, workers had little energy for family, recreation, education, or even religion. The strength of the steel companies' resistance to unionism rested on their immense economic resources combined with their near total control over the towns where their facilities were located. For unions to have a chance, they had to crack the corporate political control of the mill towns. In this effort, they were provided with a powerful argument by the drumbeat of war propaganda asserting that the terrible battlefield sacrifices of the World War were necessary to "make the world safe for democracy." The assertion of democratic and human rights by union activists countered to some degree the corporation's efforts to blame all unrest on revolutionary foreign ideologies. Fr. Adalbert Kazinci, who provided sanctuary to strikers in his Braddock church, St. Michael's, testified before a U.S. Senate Committee: "Most of them work on Sunday; and they do not see the inside of a church more than once in six months, because they are forced to work.... Some get a Sunday off, perhaps once in six months; but it is not taking care of their souls." A colorful and flamboyant figure, Kazinci became an outspoken and articulate defender of the workers' cause. Strike leader William Z. Foster, referring to the Slovak Catholic pastor, said: "Through the dark night of oppression, a bright beacon of liberty gleamed from Braddock."[65]

With the end of the war and the reduction of governmental efforts to impose a labor-management truce, class conflict and revolution were in the air both at home and abroad. German workers occupied the Ruhr steel and coal regions, while the Bolshevik revolution in Russia both alarmed capitalists and encouraged increasingly radical workers. After his stunning success organizing packinghouse workers in Chicago's stockyards, William Z. Foster, former anarcho-syndicalist who later became one of the central figures in the American Communist Party, convinced the conservative AFL to provide authorization for an organizing drive in steel. In the summer of 1918, the convention of the American Federation of Labor headed by Samuel Gompers voted to attempt "to establish democracy in the iron and steel industry." While the AFL's sanction was useful, it was a commitment backed by few resources and an unwieldy organizational structure based on an unstable coalition of craft unions. Foster's organizing drive made surprisingly rapid gains among the steel workers of the Midwest in late 1918, but he quickly realized it would be the former Carnegie mills in the

Monongahela Valley where the battle would be the most intense and resistance to unionization the fiercest.[66]

Realizing that a frontal attack on Pittsburgh was beyond his means, Foster devised a flank attack. The outlying steel districts that dot the counties and states around Pittsburgh, like minor forts about a great stronghold, were first to be won. Then the unions, with the added strength of numbers, were to make the drive on the citadel. Critical to success of the union organizing drive was mounting a challenge to the system of joint corporation-government control that subjected the mill towns to a virtual dictatorship. Foster and his organizers developed an organizing strategy based on concentrating forces, holding winnable free speech fights, and establishing union outposts. "This resolved itself into a plan literally to surround the immediate Pittsburgh district with organized posts before attacking it. Before unions could be organized, first free speech and free assembly had to be established."[67]

Organizing began on the upper Monongahela River 40 miles above Pittsburgh and worked down – establishing momentum in Donora, then Monessen and Clairton, before attacking the Steel Corporation's bastions: McKeesport, Duquesne, Braddock and Homestead. With very limited resources and only a dozen or so organizers, the AFL's Foster began the great drive on Pittsburgh, "the despair of unionism for a generation," ever since the defeat at Homestead in 1892. The free speech campaign was launched on April 1, 1919, "Mitchell Day," traditionally a day of mineworker celebration held in honor of the revered United Mine Workers of America (UMWA) president John Mitchell, leader of the great 1902 Anthracite Strike. J. L. Beaghen, AFL organizer and president of Pittsburgh's Bricklayers' Union, was in charge of the "Flying Squadron" of union organizers. UMWA organizer William Feeney, defying a prohibition on union meetings by the mayor of Monessen, led a march of 10,000 union miners into the town. Feeney, Foster, Mother Jones, UMWA District 5 President Phil Murray, and James Maurer, president of the Pennsylvania Federation of Labor, spoke at rallies and the union entered the mills of Monessen. The next target was Donora where Feeney organized a worker boycott of town merchants to break free speech prohibitions and successfully unionized the American Steel and Wire plant there. Victory at Clairton followed.[68]

The really tough fights lay ahead as the population density of union miners decreased, while the numbers of company managers, professionals and their small business allies increased. Union forces moved next on McKeesport, "the heart of the conspiracy against free speech and free assembly," where Mayor George Lysle took a strong stand against any union meetings. When initially challenged by mass street meetings, Lysle retreated and granted a permit to hold "a mass meeting in Slavish Hall on White Street," but he required that no foreign language be used and a list of speakers be submitted for approval. The union, however, began holding meetings without restricting the languages spoken or submitting speakers' lists. The manager of the National Tube Company, U.S. Steel's pipe-making subsidiary, then organized "at least five hundred of their bosses, detectives, office help, and 'loyal' workers to intimidate the men who were entering. About three hundred more would be sent into the hall to disrupt the meetings. And woe to the man they recognized, for he was discharged the next morning. The organizers, running the gauntlet of these Steel Trust gunmen, carried their very lives in their hands."[69]

Across the Monongahela, James Crawford, Duquesne Mayor and part owner of a large tin mill in McKeesport, arrested Foster, Beaghen and Mother Jones for trying to hold a meeting on several lots the union leased in an "obscure part of town." Crawford famously proclaimed: "Jesus Christ himself could not hold a meeting in Duquesne." Mother Jones replied: "I have no doubt of that, not while you are mayor. You may remember, however, that He drove such men as you out of the temple." In Braddock, the colorful and flamboyant Slovak priest, Fr. Adelbert Kazinci, provided the only reliable meeting space for the union and the strikers, and Braddock became the heart of the strike in the U.S. Steel plants in the Mon Valley. Braddock was also the location where the African American labor was strongest; at the peak of the strike, blacks briefly became a majority of the unskilled labor force.[70]

While the union organizing drive was moving down the Monongahela River toward Pittsburgh, the city's attention was riveted on a labor conflict that immediately impacted business operations and the daily routine of its citizens. At midnight on August 14, 1919, 3,000 union trolley operators of Division 85 of the Amalgamated Association of Street Carmen struck, despite the lack of sanction for the stoppage by their international union. They angrily rejected a modest raise proposed by a mediator and demanded a 12 cent hourly raise. The strike prompted the cancellation of a Pirate game while ads offered "Car Strike Specials" on automobiles and jewelry. On August 25, the strike culminated in street actions that "led to riots and subsequent destruction of company property" by large crowds storming the trolleys and blocking the operation of the cars by 300 scab operators recruited in New York City.[71]

Homestead, called by Foster "that sacred shrine of Labor," was both the largest mill and key symbolic target. Ironically, the mayor, P. H. McGuire, was a striker in 1892, but someone who Foster described as "fully recovered from his unionism." On Wednesday, August 20, when Mother Jones came to Homestead, it marked the culmination of several attempted mass street meetings in the town that led to the arrests of Beighan and Foster. Repeated efforts to acquire a meeting hall that would permit union gatherings or foreign languages to be spoken were blocked.

> Applications for a "permit" brought forth an instant refusal on the alleged grounds that some Slavish interpreters had been used at a previous meeting....This effectively closed the hall, but Mother Jones, with characteristic contempt for the edicts of Kaisers of high and low degree, declared she would speak on the streets if a hall could not be secured. So, at the appointed hour, the hall still being closed, in an automobile across the street, Mother Jones, accompanied by several organizers, appeared. Her presence immediately fired the great crowd with the wildest enthusiasm. Organizer J. L. Beaghen arose in the machine and began to explain why a hall could not be secured and the necessity which determined Mother Jones to speak on the street.
> Beaghen was at once arrested, but Mother Jones, veteran of a thousand battles, commenced to hurl her defiance at the crowd of police scattered among the thousands of spectators. Her venerable white hair, her body, bent and twisted from hardships and exposures of her forty-year fight, lent an almost tragic aspect to the situation. She simply electrified the crowd; even the police were awestruck for the moment. When they recovered sufficiently, they ordered Organizer J. G. Brown, who was in the machine, to drive on, hoping thus to stop the meeting. Upon his refusal to do so he was also arrested. The police then commandeered the services of a colored auto mechanic and forced him to drive the machine with Mother Jones in it to the police station.[72]

The large crowd, estimated variously from 1,000 to 8,000, followed Mother Jones to the jail and tension mounted. Mother Jones was urged to disperse the men, which she did, saying: "Boys we live in America! Let us give three cheers for Uncle Sam and go home and let the companies go to hell!" The Homestead *Messenger* had a more jaundiced report. Under the headline "Labor Agitators Try to Hold a Meeting Without a Permit," the paper downplayed the numbers, saying when 'Mother

Jones and the other speakers appeared at the corner of Eighth Avenue and McClure Street, the shouting of the followers brought the usually large crowd that is attracted when anything unusual occurs on the street....The crowd following the speakers and at the municipal building were almost all foreigners." When they tried to reconvene the hearing the next day, a thousand or more men again appeared at the Homestead Borough Building. It was announced that the Burgess was out of town, and the trial was postponed to August 25 and moved to Pittsburgh. [73]

Mother Jones and the three labor leaders were fined for "violating a borough ordinance, which prohibits street speaking without a permit." In one of the most famous incidents of her colorful career, Mother Jones described the exchange: "A cranky old judge asked me if I had a permit to speak on the streets. 'Yes, sir,' said I. 'I had a permit.' 'Who issued it?' he growled. 'Patrick Henry; Thomas Jefferson; John Adams! Said I." Jones left Pittsburgh immediately after the hearing, reportedly to seek a meeting about the suppression of labor's civil liberties in the mill towns with Attorney General Palmer. Late in the afternoon following Mother Jones' departure, August 26, 1919, the *Times-Gazette* headlined "WOMAN LABOR LEADER SLAIN IN MINE RIOT: 2 KILLED, MANY HURT AS STRIKERS ATTACK BRACKENRIDGE GUARDS - Battle Starts When Employees, Accompanied by Mrs. Fannie Sellins, a Labor Organizer, Open Fire from Hillside With Revolvers – Men Enraged by Killing, Charge in Force, But Are Put to Flight. Two persons, one of whom Mrs. Fannie Sellins, organizer for the United Mine Workers of America, Secretary of the Allegheny Valley Trades Council and a woman labor worker of national repute were shot to death and five others wounded in a strike riot at the entrance of the Allegheny Coal and Coke Company near Brackenridge late yesterday."[74] The following day, the same paper reported:

> "Mrs. Sellins was known throughout the country as a skillful organizer and assisted the mine workers' unions in many campaigns for new members. She formerly resided in St. Louis, having come from there to New Kensington about two years ago. She was called a very attractive woman, personally, and her efforts had attracted wide attention among miners.... Mrs. Sellins has been with the striking miners at the Brackenridge mine for five weeks, perfecting their organization and acting as a picket. She leaves one son and three daughters. Her body was removed to the undertaking establishment of H. W. Flick, Fourth Avenue, Tarentum, where several hundred persons gathered last night to view her body."[75]

Born Fannie Mooney, Fannie Sellins was a garment worker, and like her better known predecessor Mary Harris Jones, was a seamstress and a widowed mother of four children. As a union leader and negotiator for 400 women locked out of a garment factory in St. Louis in a struggle that lasted more than two years, Sellins achieved national recognition as a fiery orator at support meetings across the country, collecting money for the strikers and organizing a boycott of the company. In 1913, she came to Pittsburgh to work for the United Garment Workers of America, but then joined a United Mine Worker drive to organize miners in West Virginia. She described her work as the distribution of "clothing and food to starving women and babies, to assist poverty stricken mothers and bring children into the world, and to minister to the sick and close the eyes of the dying."[76]

Despite an injunction by a coal-operator friendly judge who prohibited all UMWA organizing in Colliers, West Virginia, on the basis of personal employment or "yellow dog" contracts that forbade membership in a union as a condition of employment, Fannie spoke out against this effort to stifle free speech and association at a miners' rally:

> I am free and I have a right to walk or talk any place in this country as long as I obey the law. I have done nothing wrong. The only wrong they can say I've done is to take

215

shoes to the little children in Colliers who needed shoes. And when I think of their bare little feet, blue with the cruel blasts of winter, it makes me determined that if it be wrong to put shoes upon those little feet, then I will continue to do wrong as long as I have hands and feet to crawl to Colliers.[77]

Sellins was jailed for contempt of court, but after a series of legal battles and a petition campaign led by the mineworkers' union, she was pardoned by President Woodrow Wilson in December 1916. She returned to Pittsburgh and was hired by Phil Murray onto the staff of District 5. There, she confronted one of the central dilemmas facing the union organizer in this period – the importation of scab labor – especially the cynical use of African-Americans as strikebreakers. The boll weevil cotton infestation devastated black sharecroppers and triggered a mass African-American exodus toward the war-swollen industries of the North. On February 24, 1917, at the train station in Tarentum, she and union organizers met a group of a hundred black workers, some with their families, recruited by the Allegheny Coal and Coke Co. to break strikes in Vandergrift and Leechburg. Sellins' eloquence helped inspire many of the intended strikebreakers to leave the train and accompany her to New Kensington.[78]

In the summer of 1919, Fannie Sellins was assigned to the Allegheny Valley to direct picketing for striking miners at Allegheny Coal and Coke, a subsidiary of Allegheny Steel. Less than a week before her death, she participated in a rally in Natrona aimed at recruiting steelworkers into the union. On the day of her murder, she was meeting with the wives of mine and mill workers in an immigrant community referred to as "Ducktown," because of the large flocks of fowl kept by the largely Polish and Slovak residents. Indicative of Sellins' ability to gain black miners' support for the union, several were with her on the picket line that day. Reportedly some Greeks and some "free born Americans" were acting as strikebreakers. In late afternoon, as they were leaving the mine, a scuffle broke out between picketers and guards. Sellins and a group including women and children were approaching the picket line when the deputies moved in, beating and then shooting Joseph Starzelski. Sellins remonstrated with the guards who then turned on her. Trying first to shelter the children, she was apparently struck in the face with a blackjack or the butt of a shotgun, whereupon she attempted to flee through a miner's yard. Photos of the crime scene show five bullet holes in the gate where she attempted to escape. The large rock beside the gate where Sellins was shot the final time at close range can be seen to this day. The autopsy describes two bullets to the head, one apparently from behind and the other from the front as well as a depressed fracture running from her left eye to above her right ear.[79]

Despite the lurid press accounts of an armed attack on the deputies by the strikers, all those wounded by gunfire were strikers: one in the arm, another in the foot, one in the mouth, and one in the back. The lone deputy injured had cuts and bruises on his face, perhaps caused by a rock or brick. Allegheny County Sheriff W. S. Haddock arrested eight men as leaders of the "premeditated" attack on the mine guards including three who had been hospitalized and Michael Szanfracki, a former coal miner and war veteran who was allegedly Sellins' bodyguard. It is possible the company's naming of Joseph Starzelski as a strikebreaker was a way to claim a serious casualty on the Coal and Iron Police side in keeping with the characterization of the incident as an armed attack by union forces. The fact the UMWA honored both Starzeleski and Sellins at the monument erected over their graves makes it highly unlikely, however, that he was a scab.[80]

The labor press, however, had a very different view of the bloodshed. *The Amalgamated Journal* under the title "Another Labor Martyr" wrote: "Mrs. Fannie Sellins, one of the best known organizers in the labor movement in America, was deliberately assassinated near the mouth of the Allegheny

Coal and Coke Company's mine at Brackenridge, Pa., about 5 o'clock, Tuesday, August 26, 1919. It is reported on the most reliable authority that she was talking to four little girls when the assassin fired three bullets into her head." Many versions of the story speak of her efforts to protect the children who were with her. Mother Jones later referred to her as the "young girl whom the constabulary had shot as she bent protectively over some children." Several accounts claimed that the guards shouted "Kill the …!" The newspaper of the Chicago Federation of Labor wrote: "Mrs. Sellins was dragged by the heels to the back of the truck and a deputy took a cudgel and crushed her skull before the eyes of a throng of men, women, and children, who stood powerless before the armed men."[81].

Fannie Sellins' funeral was held in St. Peter's Church, New Kensington, on August 29, 1919. Thousands of people attended. Phil Murray wrote a strong letter of protest to President Wilson and the governor calling for an investigation. The funeral cortege that accompanied the bodies of Sellins and Starzelski was said to be the largest in the town's history. Succeeding generations of the family who owned the yard where she was killed tended flowers around the boulder for decades. [82]

The original coroner's jury, convened on the night of Sellins' death in Tarentum, listing her occupation as "labor organizer," ruled her death a "prob(able) murder" stating she "came to her death from gunshot wounds in the hands of unknown person."[83] A month later, however, when the Allegheny County Coroner's Jury seated in downtown Pittsburgh met, the perpetrator remained unknown despite numerous eyewitnesses. The county coroner's jury judgment reflected the anti-foreign hysteria that gripped the "better class" of people as the great steel strike entered its fourth day. The death was "due to gun shot wound in left temple from gun in the hands of person or persons unknown to the Jury during an attack on Sheriffs Deputies on Aug. 26, 1919." The jury ruled that:

> Death…was justifiable and in self-defense and also recommend that Sheriff Haddock be commended in his prompt and successful action in protecting property and persons in that vicinity and the judgment exercised by his deputies. We also Criticize and deplore the action of Alien or Agitators who instill Anarchy and Bolshevism Doctrines in the minds of UnAmericans and uneducated Aliens (sic).[84]

Mother Jones clearly saw herself in the younger Fannie Sellins. The photo of her battered face was hung in every steel organizer's office. Labor reporter, Mary Heaton Vorse, wrote about seeing Fannie's photo in William Z. Foster's office and wrote of its impact. "From its inconspicuous place it dominated the office. Whoever came in turned to look at it." One day in that Pittsburgh office of the strike organizer, Vorse encountered Mother Jones standing in front of the picture:

> When the strike was still young I came in one day. A little old woman stood before it. Her hair had the pure white of extreme age. She wore a basque with lace on it, and a bonnet that had a touch of purple. A very neat old woman who looked like everybody's grandmother. She was standing before the picture and talking as though to herself. "I often wonder it wasn't me they got. Whenever I look at the picture of her I wonder it's not me lying on the ground. They shot her from behind when she bent over children to protect them. They knew what they were doing. They went out to get Fannie Sellins. Bending over them children with her back turned, they shot her."[85]

On September 8, two weeks following Fannie's murder, Mother Jones addressed the United Mine Workers' convention in Cleveland:

> A woman was murdered in Pennsylvania the other day (Mrs. Fannie Sellins). You fellows didn't amount to a row of pins! You ought to have lined up fifty thousand

men and women and gone there and cleaned up that gang that murdered that woman in cold blood. You haven't any manhood in you! You want Congress to investigate. How very thoughtful you are! They got Congress to investigate for you. Not on your life! Why didn't you do as we did in West Virginia? We do business down there.[86]

The day Fannie Sellins' body was laid out in her brother's New Kensington home, the Pittsburgh street car strike entered its 13th day and seemed headed for renewed confrontation. U.S. Attorney General Palmer authorized the appointment of additional federal deputies to protect rail company property. At a meeting of 500 members of the Chamber of Commerce, Mayor Babcock was met with "hisses and hoots" over his "apparent helplessness to quell the disturbances that have swept the city during the last several days." With 3,000 strikebreakers in town and the international union pressing for a settlement, the local union leadership was under great pressure. The Pittsburgh Central Labor Union, however, endorsed the strike at their executive board meeting. After receiving assurances that the replacement or "emergency workers" would give way to returning strikers, the leadership of the local strongly urged acceptance of the six cent raise awarded by the War Labor Board, instead of the twelve cent union demand. While the membership had twice rejected this settlement in spite of the international union's endorsement, mounting public pressure and the threat of replacements turned the tide. With local leadership now strongly in favor of it, the agreement was approved 2,082 to 408.[87]

The 1919 Steel Strike

As the steel strike approached in late September, the Mon Valley took on the aspect of an armed camp. "Pennsylvania at the present time presents all the aspects of war, with the exception that only one side is equipped with the implements of war."[88] The fifteen miles of the Mon Valley from Pittsburgh to Clairton, with a half-dozen major mills that defined the heart of the U.S. Steel empire, witnessed the greatest display of private force masquerading as public order in American history.

> All are surrounded by newly uniformed and recently deputized gunmen, carrying heavy rifles, wide cartridge belts, pockets bulging with blackjacks, and the butt of a heavy revolver protruding significantly from its leather holster fastened to each well-groomed body. At the several entrances of each steel mill are mounted one to a half-dozen machine guns, and around these stand from a dozen to a hundred bosses, some with a police cap on their heads, others with a blue coat, still others without any sign of authority in their apparel. But all have a deputy sheriff's star – there are more than 10,000 in the section referred to. Many new men have also been appointed to the police forces of each of the boroughs and cities along the river. In addition to all this there is a large force of the unspeakable state Constabulary in the district, clothed with blanket police authority, who ride horseback without a particle of warning down the sidewalks of the small steel communities, swinging their vicious clubs and shooting right and left.[89]

Following a meeting of the National Organizing Committee in Pittsburgh on September 17, the strike was scheduled for September 22. By September 30, Foster claimed 365,000 strikers, making the strike the largest in American history to that date. Ultimately, however, the strike broke upon the rock of repression and corporate organization in the Steel Valley of Pittsburgh. The strike was between 30 to 50 percent effective in the Mon Valley, though exaggerated claims on both sides made it difficult to ascertain the truth. Nearly total in Monessen, Donora and Clairton, it was weak and ineffective in Duquesne and McKeesport. In Braddock and Homestead, it was supported almost exclusively by Slavic unskilled workers, so the mills were able to claim only a 25 percent drop in production while using the skilled and semi-skilled English-speaking workforce, black workers and strikebreakers. Meanwhile in Chicago, Gary, Youngstown, Lackawanna, Buffalo, Johnstown, Sharon, and nearby Brackenridge, the strike was nearly 100 percent effective for several weeks and in some cases for two months and more.[90]

On the second day of the strike, newspapers extensively excerpted a revolutionary pamphlet called *Syndicalism* that William Z. Foster had written in 1912. "Leader of Local Steel Strike Wrote Book in Which He Declares Himself a 'Syndicalist' and Preached Most Revolutionary Doctrines," headlined *The Pittsburgh Leader*. The mass of immigrant steel workers were transformed overnight into dedicated revolutionaries seeking the overthrow of capitalism and civilization. While Foster was the organizer for the conservative American Federation of Labor and kept his radical opinions on industrial unionism more or less to himself, the discovery of his little red book gave the press the "Bolshevik" connection they sought. The Interchurch World Movement report on press conduct during the strike noted: "No copy of the original book, out of print for several years, was found in the possession of any striker or strike leader. A reprint, which was a facsimile in everything except the price mark and the union label, was widely circulated from the middle of September on by officials of the steel companies.... In McKeesport, for example, it was mailed to all the pastors in the city....The book's relation to the strike, therefore was in no sense causative; it was injected as a means of breaking the strike."[91]

Workers in Braddock and the other U.S. Steel dominated towns of the lower Mon Valley inherited the burden of the Homestead workers defeat in 1892, while facing even more daunting odds. William Z. Foster wrote: "At Homestead Carnegie and Frick stuck a knife deep into the vitals of the young democracy of the steelworkers." By 1919, the organizations of resistance had been weakened, while the instrumentalities of corporate power were at their most domineering. The corporation virtually owned the towns where its mills operated. Long hours and swing shifts, the foreign origins and diverse languages of the immigrants, many of whom were not citizens, effectively excluded unskilled workers from civic life and political participation. Corporate dominance extended to the press. Local newspapers and all the Pittsburgh dailies spoke with virtually one voice. From mid-September through October 1919, a series of 30 full-page ads in the Pittsburgh papers trumpeted in huge type: "Be a 100% American. GO BACK TO WORK, GO BACK TO WORK." The central message carried by these imposing ads, printed ten months after the German surrender, without any indication they were paid for by the Steel Corporation, was that it was un-American for steelworkers to be on strike.[92] One ad text, repeated in seven foreign languages, Russian, Italian, Polish, Lithuanian, Croatian, Slovak, and Magyar, said in part:

> Now that the fighting with arms has ceased, are you going to be less loyal to America? Are you going to give Germany a chance to win the vital battle of industry? Why are you stopping work? What are the motives of the men who ask you to quit? Do they love you? Do they love America and the American ideals of government? Or do they seek power for themselves and trouble for America....Go back to work - Stick to the job and thank God that America is still the land of the free and the home of the brave.[93]

As the Interchurch report noted: "the point of view taken in these advertisements was exactly the point of view which dominated the news and editorial columns of the Pittsburgh papers from the beginning to the end of the strike and...no Pittsburgh papers pretended to offer at any time a consistent and thorough examination of the causes of the strike from any other view." The press's unified antagonism to the worker's cause or plight was reflected, according to the report, by a number of indicators: their acceptance of lucrative company advertisements; their dissemination of the company line that the men on strike were chiefly radicals or revolutionaries; their silence as to actual industrial grievances; their silence on the issue of free speech and assembly; their accounts of violence and disorder from the employers' and officials' point of view without investigation of such incidents; their publishing of inaccurate statements concerning the number of men on strike and the number of men returning to work; and finally their effectual suppression of news that might have inspired a fair-minded examination of repressive conditions in the Pittsburgh district.[94]

Homestead in 1892 played out in the public consciousness as a well-articulated struggle between two clearly defined antagonists. By contrast, events during the Great Steel Strike of 1919 smoldered under the heavy cover of a concerted and well-organized effort to suppress public discussion of the issues involved in the conflict. The unskilled and semi-skilled workers, largely of central and eastern European ancestry, remained faceless and voiceless, portrayed in the press as ignorant, disloyal, and alien.[95] In Braddock, the Slovak priest, Fr. Kazinci, provided protection for strike meetings in the sanctuary of St. Michael's church. When the company threatened to foreclose on the mortgage of his church, he said he would place a sign on his steeple: "This church destroyed by the Steel Trust." His church became a target and parishioners were twice attacked.[96]

> On Monday last at 10 a.m. my congregation leaving church, was suddenly, without any cause whatever, attacked on the very steps of the Temple of God, by the Constables, and dispersed by the iron-hoofed Huns…. It was the most magnificent display of self-control manifested by the attacked ever shown anywhere. They moved on, with heads lowered and jaws firmly set, to submit. Oh, it was great; it was magnificent. They, these husky, muscle-bound Titans of raw force walked home…only thinking, thinking hard.[97]

Slovak workers from surrounding mill towns flocked to hear Fr. Kazinci. Reporter Mary Heaton Vorse witnessed the crowds of workers crossing from Homestead to Braddock to hear the priest. After his sermon in Slovak to the packed congregation, Vorse asked the priest what he had preached. "He said, 'I preach to them about their own weapons. Against them are violence, lies, repression. They have only their patience, their faith, their endurance - and then I told them the story of the Pharoah. He would not let the Children of Israel out of bondage." Not all the religious voices were supportive, however. Just a short distance down the street at the Irish parish in Braddock, whose church building had been donated by Charles Schwab, the pastor, Fr. Molyneux, wrote in a widely distributed pamphlet: "The strike is not being brought about by intelligent or English-speaking workmen but by men who have no interest in the community, are not an element of our community…. But you can't reason with these people. Don't reason with them…knock them down."[98] Fr. Kazinci addressed the issue of his parishioners' patriotism when he testified before a U.S. Senate Committee investigating the strike:

> We have an Americanization course taking place, and they have been instructed to go and attend those night schools, but they are not a very great success, for the simple reason that the men are overworked, working 10 to 13 hours a day; and they do not feel like going to the schools and depriving their families of their own company and society even after those long hours…. The conditions under which they live are bad for America. The housing conditions are terrible. The work conditions, the hours of work, are absolutely impossible, and I think that it tends to make the men disgusted with the country….[99]

Despite such bitter judgments, a certain America, one representing the ideals of political freedom and national independence, remained deeply attractive to many immigrants. At the end of the first week of the strike, 50,000 Poles from throughout the region marched through Pittsburgh's South Side with 3,000 veterans in the lead to "pay homage to America for liberating Poland." In fact, Pittsburgh played an important role in support of President Wilson's championing of the self-determination of nations such as Poland and Czechoslovakia. On April 3, 1917, Ignace J. Paderewski gave a speech to delegates of the Polish Falcons at a convention in Pittsburgh's South Side that initiated a movement to recruit a Polish army in the U.S. to fight on the side of the Allies and create an independent state. Paderewski, a renowned pianist, later served as prime minister of an independent Poland. On January 8, 1918, President Wilson in his "Fourteen Points" spoke of a "united, independent and autonomous Poland with free, unrestricted access to the sea."[100]

On May 31, 1918, a meeting in Pittsburgh declared the intent of Czechs and Slovaks to form a new democratic nation. Later that year, Thomas Masaryk, author of the declaration, became President of Czechoslovakia. The "Hunky Strike" of 1919 marked an important stage in the Americanization of the Slavic immigrants as they struggled to come to terms with the meaning of their adopted land. Some immigrants left for the old country during the strike; some were permanently replaced by the steel companies. The foreign-born percentage of the steel workforce dropped from 68 percent to 47 percent from 1910 to 1920. Immigration, slowed by the war, was sharply curtailed by Congress, first in 1921 with the Emergency Quota Act and even further in 1924, with the National Origins Act. In the same period, the percentage of African-Americans working in steel rose from 3 percent to 13 percent.[101]

The reason for the weakness of the strike in the Pittsburgh region was the broad array of forces marshaled against union activity. Every town government was firmly controlled by American-born mill managers and professionals. Virtually every mayor deputized "loyal employees" while the Allegheny County Sheriff alone deputized 5,000 men. The Mayor of McKeesport swore in 3,000. Foster estimated the corporation could count on as many as 25,000 men under arms in the Monongahela Valley from Pittsburgh to Donora. In addition, the Interchurch World Movement report documented the multiple layers of private detective companies that "spied, secretly denounced, engineered raids and arrests, and incited to riot." The state contributed the hated "Cossacks," the small, but splendidly mounted and well-equipped state police force, used to push strikers off the streets and ride down gatherings. Finally, there were the activities of the Bureau of Investigation and various agencies of military intelligence that provided a federal police dimension to the layers of repression in the mill towns. It targeted the "reds" of the IWW and anti-war Socialists. The Military Intelligence Division operated primarily through the Plant Protection Services (PPS), whose "agents used the cover of fire and safety inspections to set up and oversee volunteer internal 'secret service' operations in mills and plants with war contracts." Papers were filled with accounts of "foreigners" or "aliens" arrested for failure to "move on" or for being "suspicious persons." The strike committee estimated 20 were killed nationwide (18 of them strikers) from strike-related violence.[102]

The steel strike began to fade in the Pittsburgh district in November. It officially ended shortly after the dawn of the New Year. At the moment when the steel strike was fading in Pittsburgh, the mineworkers, under the untried leadership of John L. Lewis, who achieved power through a series of resignations without ever having been elected to any position within the union, launched a national strike of 400,000 coal miners. The miners were striking for the six-hour day to spread the work and for a significant pay raise to recover from the price increases brought by wartime inflation. Miners at their national convention authorizing the strike in September had called for the nationalization of the mines and a labor party. Sweeping injunctions, the threat of arrest against the leadership, and the hostility of the Wilson administration which considered the nation still formally at war, caused Lewis to try unsuccessfully to cancel the strike. Lewis declared: "I will not fight my government, the greatest government on earth," but it took nearly two months to get the miners back to work with a 14 percent pay raise, but no shortening of hours. Lewis betrayed his inexperience by failing to link the miner's struggle to the organizing effort in steel, and his political weakness by failing to extend the strike into the anthracite.[103]

Despite the defeat of the organizing drive in steel, the struggle was a major factor in the abandonment by U.S. Steel of the 12-hour day in 1923. Reformers such as John Fitch, writing for the *Survey,* and the investigators of the Protestant social gospel-inspired Interchurch World Movement, writing about the 1919 strike, highlighted the brutality of the 12-hour workday. U.S. Steel sponsored several rebuttals to church criticism, including a tome by Arundel Cotter entitled *United States Steel: A Corporation with a Soul*, but public opinion was overwhelmingly critical. Mounting political pressure caused President Harding to appeal personally to Gary. Finally, Gary acceded, allowing the President to make the momentous announcement: "I have received a joint communication from the large majority of steel manufacturers of America in which they have undertaken to abolish the twelve-hour day in the American Steel industry at the earliest moment that the additional labor required shall be available." The bitterness of the 1919 strike nurtured a spirit of resistance that resurfaced in the 1930s, returning unionism to the steel industry forty-five years after the Homestead battle. Unfortunately, however, the strike also revealed the dark side of an America: where patriotism was used to suppress and harass the foreign born, where racism was cynically exploited to divide workers, and where elementary civil liberties were flagrantly denied.[104]

In the lower Mon Valley, especially, the strike was truly a "Hunky Strike" of foreign-speaking workers, primarily Slavs. American unionists, contemptuous of the organizational ability of the Slavic workers, were proven wrong in their evaluation of these workers as "submissive, unorganizable slaves." Recognizing the relative weakness of American born workers in the strike, Foster paid high tribute to the foreign immigrants. "Throughout the whole affair they showed an understanding, discipline, courage and tenacity of purpose that compared favorably with that shown in any organized effort ever put forth by workingmen on this continent....Their solidarity was unbreakable; their fighting spirit invincible. They nobly struggled onward in the face of difficulties that would try the stoutest hearts. They proved themselves altogether worthy of the best American labor traditions."[105]

The great social tragedy of the strike involved the importation of black strikebreakers into the industrial towns before and during the strike. Blacks, who felt the sting of craft union discrimination and exclusion from the ranks of much of organized labor, were the most resistant of workers in the mills to the strike call and prime recruits to replace striking workers from the outside. In Homestead and Rankin where the 1,737 blacks composed nearly 15 percent of the non-management workforce, only eight joined the union and only one went on strike; only six of three hundred joined at Clairton, and none at the Duquesne mill. Foster estimated that, nationwide, blacks constituted a body of 30-40,000 strike breakers. The historic exclusion of black workers from most craft unions, dominated as they were by American-born workers, prepared the way for their employment as strike breakers against the Slavs. In 1925, after the failure of the industrial drive, only 518 Pittsburgh blacks were union members. In Braddock, black workers were the key to continued operation of the mill where they worked, ate, and slept inside the plant for the initial three weeks of the strike. At Duquesne and Monessen, blacks were sworn in as deputies to keep the mills operating.[106]

William Attaway in his novel, *Blood on the Forge*, about the 1919 strike from an African-American perspective, described the attitude of black leadership "The union organizers made a desperate effort to induce the black men to join the movement toward the strike. But the steel interests had bought the black leaders....A victory for the mill owners [they said] would be a victory for the Negro worker. The black worker had never advanced through unions. He had advanced fighting alongside the owners." Attaway described the new-found feeling of power that came with being deputized. "Always within him was that instinctive knowledge that he was being turned to white men's uses. So always with him was a basic distrust of the white. But now he was the boss. He was the law. After all, what did right or wrong matter in the case? Those thrilling new words were too much to resist. He was a boss, a boss over whites." The achievement of power and authority was a powerful incentive to become a strikebreaker. Strikebreaking "allowed African-American men to challenge openly white society's image of them as obsequious, cowardly and lacking the ability to perform well under pressure. It enabled them to violate the prevailing norms of conduct for black men in the South, which required that they act deferentially in the presence of whites, avoid eye contact, and step aside on the sidewalk."[107]

Foster placed primary blame for black strikebreaking on the racist practices of many unions. "Many of them sharply draw the color line, thus feeding the flames of race hatred. This discriminatory practice is in direct conflict with the fundamental demand that all the workers be organized, without regard to sex, race, creed, politics or nationality. It injures Labor's cause greatly." However, Foster also recognized that most of the black leadership, ministers, politicians, and professionals were strongly opposed to the efforts of even those unions who were trying to recruit blacks. "They look upon strike breaking as a legitimate and effective means of Negro advancement. Time and again, they have seen their people, by use of it, readily work their way into trades and industries previously firmly sealed against them by the white workers' and white employers' prejudices. Nor can they see any wrong in this taking advantage of the white man, who has so brutally oppressed them for centuries. On the contrary, they consider it a justified retaliation. They are in a race war." The mill owners played the card of racial division vigorously, to the point of deputizing and arming black workers as a fighting force alongside management. The African-American imports had the added attraction of being loyal, at least initially, to the Republican party of Abraham Lincoln because of the party's anti-slavery origins.[108]

John Fitch, author of the *Pittsburgh Survey*'s study of labor conditions in the steel industry, called the 1919 strike a "strike for freedom."

> Kings and autocrats have fallen since the last wholesale discharge of Steel Corporation employees who tried to organize. Labor organizations as much as any other group made it possible to win the war. The government itself had laid down the dictum that men should be free to organize and to bargain collectively.... With the right of collective bargaining now accepted as a fundamental right, are steel workers to continue any longer to be subject to a regime of absolute dictatorship, with no opportunity to express themselves as to the conditions under which they are to work, with discharge the penalty if they join a union?[109]

After the strike, the World Church Commission summarized the goals of various groups of strikers as follows: "Besides the skilled workers who struck principally against arbitrary (or autocratic) control and besides the mass which struck mainly against the twelve-hour day, a large portion of the skilled and unskilled struck also against wages which statistics indicate, were actually inadequate to maintain an American standard of living." While dangerous working conditions and brutally long hours were the prime factors driving the rebellion of the Slavs, virtually the entire press in the Pittsburgh region depicted the struggle as a battle of American industry against subversion. To the press, the strike was a continuation of the war. Fighting the Hun became fighting the "hunky"; being 100% American meant supporting the company. According to the Interchurch Report, the "solidarity of opinion, arising naturally from national efforts to 'mobilize public sentiment' and to overwhelm obstructionists to the country's war policy, notoriously continued beyond the war and on behalf of others than the government."[110]

This interpretation was given governmental affirmation when the breaking of the great steel strike was followed by government deportation raids against left wing immigrant activists. While the threat of Bolshevism was trumpeted by press and government, in fact, the organized left was weakened by internal divisions as well as by a program of governmental repression during the war that was aimed primarily at anti-war Socialists and direct-action Wobblies. After the war, in May 1919, the minority pro-Bolshevik left wing of the Socialist Party of America was expelled, taking most of the foreign language federations with them into the Communist Party of America, which became dominated by the former Socialist Party foreign language federations. A rival Communist Labor Party also competed for adherents. Tensions with the government increased exponentially in June when eight nearly simultaneous bomb blasts went off nationwide, one at Attorney General A. Mitchell Palmer's house in Washington D.C. and two in Pittsburgh. The bombings resulted in a single death in New York City, and both bombs in Pittsburgh were probably placed at mistaken locations. Anarchists appeared to be responsible. Months later, Pittsburgh's Communist Party was first convened on November 2, 1919 at the International Socialist Lyceum with representatives of twenty-two former Socialist foreign-language federations. Two months later, both Communist organizations, and the Union of Russian Workers, became the prime target of deportation raids led by Attorney General Palmer.[111]

On January 2, 1920, raids on people identified as "Reds" were carried out simultaneously across the country, and the press heralded the apprehension of 2,500 Communists. These numbers were probably exaggerated by the publicity-hungry Attorney General and J. Edgar Hoover, the young and ambitious director of the Bureau of Intelligence. The official number arrested in Pittsburgh was 233, but a recent examination of the local record claims only 39 detentions with 17 of those released after a few days. Many arrested as dangerous aliens were in fact citizens and some of those native born. The raids were highly successful, however, in creating a climate of fear in many immigrant communities, and they also solidified the clandestine organizational tendencies of the American Communists who were guided as well by the prestige of the Soviet experience.[112] A young Croatian girl from Troy Hill, eight years old, recalled the sense of fear that gripped the immigrant communities upon word of the Palmer raids and orders from the Communist Party to "go underground."

> Strikers seeking to defend their living standard were called "reds" and "Bolshevik agents." The "Red Menace" replaced the wartime hatred of the "Hun." The effort to crush the labor movement, drive down wages, and restore open shops in industry made life very dangerous for foreign-born activists….Mama became more and more worried as increasing numbers of people we knew were picked up. My parents felt that they, too, might be hunted down just for being foreign-born and communist. Some of Palmer's men were ignoring citizenship papers which my parents had long held. The word came to lie low and avoid all meetings, halls, and offices.[113]

In Russia, the seizure of state power by a small (little more than 10,000 members) but highly disciplined minority armed with revolutionary theory fed both the paranoia of government and the conviction of dedicated revolutionaries. Revolutionary organizations, though small, might provide the leadership for a working class movement that could overthrow capitalism and fundamentally reshape the economic order. So while the two American communist parties represented somewhere between 25,000 and 40,000 members, versus the reformist AFL's membership of 3,260,068, their small numbers could apparently be overcome by doctrine and discipline. The Russian experience offered the lesson to a divided and demoralized American left that "revolutionaries had to hold themselves in readiness for the right moment. Then, despite all setbacks and lack of mass following, superior revolutionary principles and determination would carry them through to victory." The Communist Party's quasi secret character and obsession with theory stood in sharp contrast both to the more open and formally democratic organization of the Socialist Party, and the flamboyant free speech traditions of the IWW's anarcho-syndicalist approach.[114]

To many strikers and their supporters, the struggle was about a fundamentally different America - the democracy for which they had sweated and bled to defend. If America could not guarantee freedom of speech and the right of assembly inside its own borders, what significance did its high sounding ideals have in the assembly of nations? As Mother Jones said:

> During the war the working people were made to believe that they amounted to something.... Up and down the land the workers heard the word, "democracy." They were asked to work for it. To give their wages to it. To give their lives for it. They were told that their labor, their money, their flesh were the bulwarks against tyranny and autocracy. So believing, the steel workers, 300,000 of them, rose en masse against Kaiser Gary, the President of the American Steel Corporation. The slaves asked the czar for the abolition of the twelve-hour day, for a crumb from the huge loaf of profits made in the great war, and for the right to organize. Czar Gary met his workers as is the customary way with tyrants. He could not shoot them down as did the Czar Nicholas when petitioned by his peasants. But he ordered forth his two faithful generals: fear and starvation, one to clutch at the worker's throat and the other at his stomach and the stomachs of his children.[115]

In the end, Mother Jones expressed both the bitterness of defeat and the fierce hope that inspired the struggle. The fire of resistance was smothered, but the embers of 1919 would spark a fire that would sweep the industrial valleys in the 1930s.

> The strike was broken. Broken by the scabs brought in under the protection of the troops. Broken by breaking men's belief in the outcome of their struggle. Broken by breaking men's hearts. Broken by the press, by the government. In a little over a hundred days, the strike shivered to pieces.
> The slaves went back to the furnaces, to the mills, to the heat and the roar, to the long hours - to slavery. At headquarters men wept, I wept with them. A young man put his hands on my shoulders.
> "Mother," he sobbed. "It's over."
> A red glare from the mills lighted the sky. It made me think of Hell.
> "Lad," I said, "It's not over. There's a fiercer light than those hell fires over yonder! It is the white light of freedom.[116]

Notes Chapter 8

[1]Paul Kleppner, "Government, Parties, and Voters in Pittsburgh," in *City at the Point: Essays on the Social History of Pittsburgh,* ed. Samuel P. Hays (Pittsburgh: University of Pittsburgh Press, 1989), 169-170.

[2]Philip Foner, *History of the Labor Movement of the United States*, Vol. 8: *Postwar Struggles:1918-1920* (New York: International Publishers, 1988). See Chapter 3, "The U.S. Labor Movement and the Bolshevik Revolution," 42-62.

[3]John Fitch, "The Labor Policies of Unrestricted Capital," *The Survey* (April 6, 1912), 27; Paul U. Kellogg, "Westmoreland Strike Called Off," *The Survey* (July 29, 1911).

[4]Shelby M. Harrison and Paul U. Kellogg, "The Westmoreland Strike," *The Survey* (December 3, 1910), 345.

[5]Harrison and Kellogg, "Westmoreland Strike Called Off," 360-362; Pat Fagan, *Interview* by Alice Hoffman, September 24, 1968.

[6]Harrison and Kellogg, "Westmoreland Strike Called Off," 360-362.

[7]Harvey O'Connor, *Steel Dictator* (New York: The John Day Company, 1935), 180.

[8] Raymond J. Robertson, *Ironworkers 100th Anniversary, 1896-1996: A History of the Ironworkers Union* (The Ironworkers Union, 1996)

[9]Jennie Benford, "Sisters Anxious for the Ballot: Pittsburgh Suffragists"; Elizabeth Voltz, "Local Women Make Long Fight to Secure Privilege of Ballot and Share in Credit for Victory," both articles in *Pittsburgh Women's Suffrage Folder,* Carnegie Library, Western Pennsylvania Room; *Legendary Ladies: A Guide to Where Women Made History in Pennsylvania: Greater Pittsburgh,* Pennsylvania Commission for Women. See <www.WomenMadeHistoryInPa.com>.

[10]George Swetnam, "Pittsburgh's Determined Suffragettes," *Pittsburgh Press,* Nov. 4, 1956; *Pittsburgh Post,* October 31, 1913; *Pittsburgh Post,* May 3, 1914.

[11]"Mayor Proclaims Saturday Noon for Noisy Celebration on Ratification," *Pittsburgh Post,* August 27, 1920.

[12]Francis E. Leupp, *George Westinghouse: His Life and Achievements* (Boston: Little, Brown, and Company, 1918), 18.; Charles McCollester, "Turtle Creek Fights Taylorism: The Westinghouse Strike of 1914,"*"Labor's Heritage"* (Summer 1992).; Harvey O'Connor, *Mellon's Millions: The Life and Times of Andrew W. Mellon* (New York: John Day Company, 1933), 54-55; "Smulls Legislative Handbook and Manual of the State of Pennsylvania," 1913, 600-613.

[13]William Foley and Thomas Pierce, *History of the Great Westinghouse Strike* (Unpublished Manuscript). This is an eighty-two-page typed manuscript discovered by David Demarest of Carnegie Mellon University and now in the possession of the author. It appears to be a carbon of an original manuscript intended for publication. Descriptions in the narrative are confirmed in detail by photos and newspaper accounts of the 1914 strike. William Foley and Thomas Pierce were among a delegation from the strike executive committee who visited with Senator Boise Penrose toward the end of the strike; *Pittsburgh Post Gazette,* July 3, 1914; David Montgomery, *The Fall of the House of Labor: The Workplace, the State, and American Labor Activism, 1865-1925* (Cambridge: Cambridge University Press, 1987), 323; Harry Braverman, *Labor and Monopoly Capital* (New York: Monthly Review Press, 1984), 20-28.

[14]Elizabeth Beardsley Butler, *Women and the Trades: Pittsburgh, 1907-1908* (Pittsburgh Survey), (Pittsburgh: University of Pittsburgh Press, 1984), 215-16.

[15]*Pittsburgh Leader,* June 21, 1914.

[16]Butler, *Women and the Trades,* 219.

[17]Montgomery, *The Fall of the House of Labor,* 317-318.; "Stogy Makers and the IWW in Pittsburgh," *The Survey,* November 29, 1913.

[18]Jacob Margolis, "The Streets of Pittsburgh," *International Socialist Review* 13:4 (1912), 313-320.

[19]*Justice,* January 31, 1914; Foley and Pierce, *History of the Great Westinghouse Strike.*

[20]*Daily News,* June 5, 1914; *Pittsburgh Press,* June 6, 1914; *Pittsburgh Leader,* June 7, 1914; *Pittsburgh Post,* June 7, 1914. Strike issues were extensively reported.

[21]*Pittsburgh Chronicle Telegraph,* June 6, 1914; *Pittsburgh Leader,* June 5, 1914.; *Pittsburgh Leader,* June 6, 1914; *Pittsburgh Leader,* June 9, 1914; *Pittsburgh Chronicle Telegraph,* June 5, 1914.

[22]*Pittsburgh Dispatch,* June 7, 1914; *Pittsburgh Press,* June 7, 1914; *Pittsburgh Leader,* June 7, 1914 The original "unjustice" is retained; George Michales, "The Westinghouse Strike," *The Survey,* August 1914.

[23]*Pittsburgh Leader* June 8, 1914; Foley and Pierce *History of the Great Westinghouse Strike,* 10, 16; *New York Times* June 8, 1914.

[24]Golden's problems in Wilmerding are recounted in *Pittsburgh Leader,* Jan. 30, 1914.

[25]Foley and Pierce, *History of the Great Westinghouse Strike,* 19; *Pittsburgh Press,* June 8, 1914; *Pittsburgh Leader,* June 8, 1914.

[26]Foley and Pierce, *History of the Great Westinghouse Strike,* 21-22.

[27]Foley and Pierce, *History of the Great Westinghouse Strike,* 27-28; *Pittsburgh Gazette-Times,* June 13, 1914; *Pittsburgh Sun,* June 12, 1914; *Pittsburgh Chronicle Telegraph,* June 12, 1914.

[28]*Pittsburgh Leader,* June 13, 1914; *Pittsburgh Press,* June 13, 1914.

[29]*Pittsburgh Dispatch,* June 15, 1914; Foley and Pierce, *History of the Great Westinghouse Strike,* 36-37.

[30]*Pittsburgh Gazette-Times,* June 24, 1914; *Pittsburgh Press,* June 24, 1914; *Pittsburgh Gazette-Times,* June 30, 1914; *New York Times,* June 30, 1914; *Pittsburgh Leader,* June 28, 1914.

[31]Foley and Pierce, *History of the Great Westinghouse Strike,* 60; *Pittsburgh Leader,* June 29, 1914; *Pittsburgh Leader,* June 30, 1914.

[32]Foley and Pierce, *History of the Great Westinghouse Strike,* 57-59.

[33]Foley and Pierce, *History of the Great Westinghouse Strike,* 58-59; *Pittsburgh Leader,* June 30, 1914; *Pittsburgh Leader*, July 2, 1914; *Pittsburgh Chronicle Telegraph*, July 3, 1914; *Pittsburgh Chronicle Telegraph*, July 6, 1914; *Pittsburgh Chronicle Telegraph*, July 7, 1914; *Pittsburgh Press*, July 5, 1914.

[34]*Pittsburgh Leader,* July 10, 1914; *Pittsburgh Press,* July 10, 1914; Foley and Pierce, *History of the Great Westinghouse Strike,* 69; *New York Times,* July 10, 1914. The New York Times estimated 1,000. The *Chronicle Dispatch* figured 1,800, and strikers Foley and Pierce counted 3,000.

[35]Dennis C. Dickerson, *Out of the Crucible: Black Steelworkers in Western Pennsylvania, 1875-1980* (Albany: State University of New York, 1986) 27-36; Peter Gottlieb, *Making Their Own Way, 1916-1930* (Urbana: University of Illinois Press, 1987), 94-95, 121.; William O. Scoggs, "Interstate Migration of Negro Population" *Trade Unionism and Labor Problems,* ed. John R. Commons (New York: A.M. Kelley, 1920), 121-2.

[36]Gottlieb, *Making Their Own Way,* 99, 124; Dickerson, *Out of the Crucible,* 61-62.

[37]Laurence A. Glasco, ed., *The WPA History of the Negro in Pittsburgh* (Pittsburgh: University of Pittsburgh Press, 2004), 231, 248.

[38]Andrew Buni, *Robert L. Vann of the Pittsburgh Courier: Politics and Black Journalism* (Pittsburgh, University of Pittsburgh Press, 1974), 3-54.

[39]Buni, *Robert L. Vann of the Pittsburgh Courier,* 55-83.

[40]Gottlieb, *Making Their Own Way,* 129-130.

[41]Dickerson, *Out of the Crucible,* 75.

[42]Rob Ruck, *Sandlot Seasons: Sport in Black Pittsburgh* (Urbana: University of Illinois Press, 1993), 11.

[43]Melvyn Dubofsky and Warren Van Tine, *John L. Lewis, A Biography* (New York: Quadrangle Books, 1977), 28-29.

[44]Pat Fagan, *Interview,* Alice Hoffman, September 24, 1968.

[45]Carl I. Meyerhuber, Jr., *Less Than Forever: The Rise and Decline of Union Solidarity in Western Pennsylvania, 1914-1948,* (London: Associated University Presses, 1987), 32-37.

[46]Meyerhuber, *Less Than Forever,* 37-41; Montgomery, *The Fall of the House of Labor,* 321-326.

[47]Meyerhuber, *Less Than Forever,* 37-41.

[48]Frank R. Murdock, "Some Aspects of Pittsburgh's Industrial Contribution to the World War," *Western Pennsylvania Historical Magazine* (October 1921), 215-222; Frank C. Harper, *Pittsburgh of Today: Its Resources and People* (New York: Pennsylvania Historical Society, 1931), 1:395-397; Ida M. Tarbell, *The Life of Elbert H. Gary: The Story of Steel* (New York: D. Appleton and Company, 1925), 253-263.

[49]David E. Koskoff, *The Mellons: The Chronicle of America's Richest Family* (New York: Tomas Y. Crowell, 1978), 120-122; Frank C. Harper, *Pittsburgh of Today: Its Resources and People* (New York: The American Historical Society, 1931), 2:654.

[50] Koskoff, *The Mellons,* 82-83; O'Connor, *Mellon's Millions,* 90-92.

[51]Michael Connors, "Finding Private Enright," *Pittsburgh Post-Gazette,* November 11, 2007.

[52]Harper, *Pittsburgh of Today,* 1:402-404; William F. Trimble, *High Frontiers: A History of Aeronautics in Pennsylvania* (Pittsburgh: University of Pittsburgh Press, 1982), 82.

[53]Trimble, *High Frontiers,* 94-102.

[54]Samuel Gompers, *Seventy Years of Life in Labor* (New York: Cornell University, 1984), 190.

[55]James Weinstein, *The Decline of Socialism in America, 1912-1925* (New York: Vintage, 1969), 93-118; John Steuben, *Labor in Wartime* (New York: International Publishers, 1940), 53, 104-106.

[56]Gompers, *Seventy Years of Life in Labor,* 192; Steuben, *Labor in Wartime,* 62; George E. Kelly, ed., *Allegheny County, A Sesqui-Centennial Review, 1788...1938.* (Pittsburgh: Allegheny County Sesqui-Centennial Committee, 1938), 95.

[57]David Brody, *Steelworkers in America: the Nonunion Era,* (New York: Harper Torchbooks, 1960), 200-208.

[58]Foner, *History of the Labor Movement in the United States,* 8:20-62; Theodore Draper, *The Roots of American Communism* (New York: Viking Compass, 1963). American Communist leader Charles Ruthenberg quote, 198.

[59]Kenneth A. White, "Pittsburgh in the Great Epidemic of 1918," *The Western Pennsylvania Historical Magazine* (1985), 221-235.

[60]White, "Pittsburgh in the Great Epidemic of 1918," 232-242.

[61]Meyerhuber, *Less Than Forever,* 45-65; Foner, *History of the Labor Movement in the United States,* 8:63-101; 141-169.

[62]David Brody, *Workers in Industrial American: Essays on the Twentieth Century Struggle* (New York: Oxford University Press, 1980), 45; Philip Taft, *Organized Labor in American History* (New York: Harper Row, 1964), 362.

[63]*Pittsburgh Professional Fire Fighters: 100th Anniversary,* (Pittsburgh Fire fighters, 1974), 27-29.

[64]O'Connor, *Steel Dictator,* 101.

[65]The Interchurch World Movement, *The Steel Strike of 1919* (New York: Harcourt, Brace and Company, 1921), 71; William Z. Foster, *The Great Steel Strike and Its Lessons* (New York: B.W. Huebsch, Inc., 1920), 117.

[66]David Brody, *Labor in Crisis: The Steel Strike of 1919* (Urbana: University of Illinois Press, 1987), 63-69; Foster, *The Great Steel Strike and its Lessons,* 34.

[67]Foster, *The Great Steel Strike and Its Lessons,* 50.

[68]Foster, *The Great Steel Strike and Its Lessons,* 52-54.

[69]Foster, *The Great Steel Strike and Its Lessons,* 54-7; Brody, *Labor in Crisis,* 91-95.

[70]Mary Harris Jones, *The Autobiography of Mother Jones* (Chicago: Charles H. Kerr, 1977), 218. Foster has the quote as: "Jesus Christ himself could not speak in Duquesne for the A.F. of L."; Dickerson, *Out of the Crucible,* 89; Fr. Adalbert Kazinci's last name is sometimes rendered Kazincy.

[71] *Pittsburgh Press*, August 25, 1919; *Pittsburgh Press*, August 26, 1919; *The Gazette Times*, August 26, 1919.

[72] *The Bridgemen's Magazine*, October 1919, 511-12.

[73] *Homestead Daily Messenger*, August 21, 1919.

[74] *The Gazette Times*, August 27, 1919.

[75] *The Gazette Times*, August 27, 1919.

[76] James Cassedy, "A Bond of Sympathy: The Life and Tragic Death of Fannie Sellins," *Labor Heritage* (Winter 1992), 8(4).; *St. Louis Labor*, August 30, 1919.

[77] Cassedy, "A Bond of Sympathy," 40.

[78] Cassedy, "A Bond of Sympathy," 43. I am indebted to Rich Gazarick for access to the manuscript of his book on Fannie Sellins, *Black Valley*.

[79] Cassedy, "A Bond of Sympathy," 44-5.

[80] A beautiful UMWA memorial statue stands over the graves of Sellins and Starzelski in the Union Cemetery in Arnold PA. A state historical marker marks the cemetery.

[81] *The Amalgamated Journal*, August 28, 1919; Meyerhuber, *Less Than Forever*, 54-55; Philip S. Foner, ed., *Mother Jones Speaks: Collected Writings and Speeches* (New York: Monad Press, 1983), 315.

[82] Cassedy, "A Bond of Sympathy," 45-6.; J.R. Borland, "Coroner's Press Report, August 26, 1919" (Tarentum: University of Pittsburgh Archives, 1919); The author had the opportunity to locate the site of Sellins's murder thanks to Tony Slomkoski, who got a marker placed at a war memorial in Natrona Heights. After the ceremony, a neighbor came and took us to the boulder where Fannie was killed and told of the flower that had been tended there in her honor. Tony has kept alive the memory of Sellins with an annual Labor Day commemoration in her honor.

[83] Borland, "Coroner's Press Report, August 26, 1919."

[84] "Coroner's Jury Verdict (Fannie Sellins)," Coroner's Office (State of Pennsylvania, County of Allegheny, 1919).

[85] Mary Heaton Vorse, *Men and Steel* (New York: Boni and Liverirght Publishers, 1920), 69.

[86] Foner, *Mother Jones Speaks*, 309-10.

[87] *The Pittsburgh Press*, August 26, 1919, *Pittsburgh Press*, August 27,1919.; *Pittsburgh Press*, August 28, 1919.; *Pittsburgh Press*, August 29, 1919.

[88] Anonymous, "National Committee of Organizing Iron and Steel Workers," *The Bridgemen's Magazine* (October 1919), 509.

[89] Anonymous, "National Committee of Organizing Iron and Steel Workers," 509. This unsigned article from the Bridge and Structural Ironworkers International publication is the single best account of the arrest of Mother Jones by an eyewitness.

[90] Accurate figures are difficult to determine. *The Pittsburgh Leader* which advertised itself as "Pittsburgh's One Clean Newspaper" cited claims on the first day of the strike by the company of 15-20,000 out of 100,000 steelworkers in Allegheny County, while the union claimed 85,000, and "neutral observers" estimated 25%. It was probably between 30-40% successful overall in Allegheny County, though percentages varied greatly from mill to mill. A week into the strike the superintendent of the Homestead Works admitted that production had dropped by a third while claiming that only 2,500 out of 10,000 were on strike *(The Pittsburgh Leader*, Sept. 28, 1919). Foster's claims for Homestead (9,000) and Braddock (10,000) are exaggerated or reflect the highest level of participation: *The Great Steel Strike*, p.100.

[91] *Pittsburgh Leader,* September 23, 1919. Among other things, the pamphlet stated: "When the psychological moment arrives, the working class, hungering for emancipation will adopt the only method at its disposal and put an end to capitalism with the general strike"; The Interchurch World Movement,*The Steel Strike of 1919*, 34-35.

[92] Foster, *The Great Steel Strike and Its Lessons.*; The Interchurch World Movement, The Commission of Inquiry, *Public Opinion and the Steel Strike: Supplementary Reports of the Investigators to the Commission of Inquiry, the Interchurch World Movement* (New York: Harcourt, Brace, and Company, 1921), 90-5, Reprinted in facsimile edition, (New York: Arno Press, 1969).

[93] *Pittsburgh Post*, October 2, 1919.

[94] The Interchurch World Movement, *Public Opinion and the Steel Strike*, 96-7, 147-8. Newspapers would print that the mills had returned to normal while accepting ads that demanded that strikers return to work. Many jokes circulated among strike organizers that while the newspapers were reporting only tens of thousands on strike, they were faithfully recording company reports of hundreds of thousands returning to work.

[95] Russell W. Gibbons, "Dateline Homestead," in *The River Ran Red: Homestead 1892*, ed. David R. Demarest, Jr. (Pittsburgh: University of Pittsburgh Press, 1992), 158-159.

[96] Gibbons, "Dateline Homestead," 158-159; Foster, *The Great Steel Strike and Its Lessons*, 117.

[97] Foster, *The Great Steel Strike and Its Lessons*, Fr. Adalbert Kazincy, Letter to William Z. Foster p.121-2.

[98] Vorse, *Men and Steel,* 75-6; The Interchurch World Movement, *Public Opinion and the Steel Strike*, 278-9.

[99] The Interchurch World Movement, *Public Opinion and the Steel Strike*, 276-7.

[100] "Poles Hold Monster Demonstration," *Pittsburgh Leader*, September 26, 28, 1919; Norman Davies, *God's Playground: A History of Poland*, II (New York: Columbia University Press, 1982). A state historical marker on 18th Street at Carey Way near Carson Street marks the site of the Paderewski's Polish National Army speech, p. 387.

[101] Dickerson, *Out of the Crucible*, 98. Foster estimated the number of strikers at 365,000, but he almost certainly overestimated the Mon Valley Carnegie mill totals. 250-300,000 participants is probably realistic. v. *Pittsburgh Leader,* September 26, "Many foreigners with big bank accounts have made arrangements to return to their former homes as soon as passports can be secured." The Pittsburgh Declaration on Czechoslovakia is commemorated by a state historical marker on Penn Avenue at Ninth Street.

[102]Foster, *The Great Steel Strike and Its Lessons*, 97, 223; The Interchurch World Movement, *Public Opinion and the Steel Strike of 1919*, 3; Allegheny County Sheriff Haddock stated to Senate investigators that "no public meetings were to be permitted or conducted in any foreign tongue." *Pittsburgh Sun*, Oct. 25. The *Sun* reported on October 16 that meetings in Pittsburgh itself were restricted to the Labor Temple and the Croatian Hall on the North Side. They were specifically banned in the steel-making district of South Side.; Charles H. McCormick, *Seeing Reds: Federal Surveillance of Radicals in the Pittsburgh Mill District, 1917-1921* (Pittsburgh: University of Pittsburgh Press, 1997), 12.

[103]Philip Foner, *History of the Labor Movement of the United States*, 8:141-148.

[104]Charles Hill, "Fighting the Twelve-Hour Day in the American Steel Industry," *Labor History* (Winter 1974), 15:34; Brody, *Labor in Crisis*, 177-188.

[105]Foster, *The Great Steel Strike and Its Lessons*, 200-1.

[106]Dickerson, *Out of the Crucible*, 86-90.; Brody, *Labor in Crisis*, 162; William J. Tuttle, *Race Riot: Chicago in the Red Summer of 1919* (New York: Athenium, 1970), 108-56; "Steel Workers Sleep in Own Homes," *Chronicle Telegraph*, October 21, 1919. Skilled workers in Braddock remained inside the mill for nearly a month.

[107] William Attaway, *Blood on the Forge* (New York: Monthly Review Press, 1987), 226-7, 246; Stephen H. Norwood, *Mercenaries and Masculinity in Twentieth-Century America*, (Chapel Hill: University of North Carolina Press, 2002), 80; That such incidents were not the invention of a writer of fiction v. "Steel Strikers and Negroes Engage in Furious Gun Battle," *Pittsburgh Press*, Oct. 9, 1919, describing a clash in Donora.

[108]Foster, *The Great Steel Strike and Its Lessons*, 209-10.

[109]John A. Fitch, "A Strike for Freedom," *The Survey* (September 27, 1919), 891.

[110]The Interchurch World Movement Report, *The Steel Strike of 1919*, 87.; The Interchurch World Movement Report, *Public Opinion and the Steel Strike*, 155.

[111]McCormick, *Seeing Reds*, 102, 168-9.

[112]McCormick, *Seeing Reds*, 170.

[113]Freida Truhar Brewster, "A Personal View of the Early Left in Pittsburgh," *The Western Pennsylvania Historical Magazine*, v. 69, n.4, (October, 1966), 361-362.

[114] Draper, *The Roots of American Communism*, 103.

[115]Jones, *The Autobiography of Mother Jones*, 209-10.

[116]Jones, *The Autobiography of Mother Jones*, 224-225.

Chapter Nine

Mellons' Rule and Capital's Crash

On November 2, 1920, from the roof of the tallest building at the Westinghouse Electric plant in East Pittsburgh, the first commercial radio station, KDKA, broadcast the results of the presidential election. The saintly socialist, Eugene V. Debs, imprisoned in the Atlanta federal penitentiary for his opposition to World War I, received more than one million votes as Socialist Party candidate for president of the United States. Reflecting voter desire for a "return to normalcy" after foreign war and domestic upheaval, Republican Warren G. Harding easily defeated Democrat James M. Cox. This election not only inaugurated a radio industry that changed mass communication and politics, but it unexpectedly propelled Pittsburgh's Andrew W. Mellon into national political power, characterized by many as "the Secretary of the Treasury under whom three presidents served."

Hard Money

The naming of Andrew W. Mellon as Treasury Secretary came as a surprise, since though A.W. was fabulously wealthy, he had long avoided both the public limelight and the conspicuous consumption of many of the wealthy, preferring to exercise control over his Pittsburgh-based empire from behind the scenes. Mellon's closest ally, H. C. Frick, had been deeply involved in Republican Party politics and represented Mellon interests on the state and national levels. A.W. had gotten involved in public policy issues slowly, financing anti-League of Nations efforts, and supporting the Association of Foreign Language Newspapers that acquired foreign-language papers with the purpose of promoting pro-business "Americanism" to immigrants. With Frick's death in 1919, he began to play a larger role in state and national Republican affairs, and, in 1920, he was named a delegate to the Republican National Convention. His nomination as Secretary of the Treasury was engineered by his close political allies, Pennsylvania senators, Philander C. Knox and Boise Penrose. Successor to Matthew Quay as Pennsylvania's political "boss," Boise Penrose, described as "possibly the most dissolute person ever to rise to major national importance in an American political party," was one of the most powerful men in the U.S. Senate. His most notable achievement was the creation of the infamous "oil depletion allowance" that allowed oil company reserves to be counted as a liability against taxes on production. Weighing in at 350 pounds and "habitué of whorehouses across the Commonwealth," he was "paymaster for the oligarchy" and reliable blocker of reform legislation. One of his final gifts to the nation was Andrew Mellon in charge of the Treasury of the United States.[1]

Andrew Mellon's banker philosophy became the nation's economic policy during the 1920s and into the beginning of the Great Depression. Harding had proclaimed: "We want less government in business and more business in government." With Mellon as Secretary of the Treasury, America got both. His key goals were cutting the size of government, reducing governmental debt assumed during the world war, and reducing taxes, especially on the upper brackets. Mellon pushed successfully for a reduction of taxes on the wealthy, while resisting inheritance and gift taxes. Mellon was also a staunch defender of the tariffs that protected his family's steel investments and their control of aluminum production. The fact that these economic policies were advanced by the nation's third largest taxpayer was seen by many as a conflict of interest. While Mellon benefited personally and enormously from the governmental policies he pursued, he could be a guardian of fiscal responsibility when the question was tax money directed toward the lower orders. He opposed any governmental purchase of the agricultural surplus of American farmers in order to relieve starvation in Europe after the war, and to support declining domestic crop prices. Despite the dire situation faced by many of the two million troops demobilized into a contracting economy, he opposed any early payment of the Bonus Bill for veterans of the World War as a subsidy to a special interest group, incompatible with his plan for lower taxes on the wealthy while reducing governmental debt. Mellon, however, as a former stockholder in Frick's Overholt distillery, and consumer of fine wines, was decidedly lukewarm about enforcing prohibition, a function of his office.[2]

Like his close ally H.C. Frick, Mellon was coldly and fiercely anti-union and anti-labor, as were most of those who served with him in the three successive Republican administrations. He heartily disapproved of the young Henry C. Wallace, secretary of agriculture, who championed the interests of farmers over that of business and industry. All the relative civility of wartime industrial labor relations was buried, as the courts and the administration let the anti-monopoly regulations of the so-called reform Clayton Anti-Trust Act go unenforced, while, simultaneously, conservative courts were ruling that the Clayton Act could be used against unions as combinations in restraint of trade. In 1921-22, national strikes of coal miners and railroad workers were crushed by a combination of federal troops and court injunctions. The large corporations were reasserting political control.[3]

Shortly after A.W.'s confirmation to the Treasury, both Boies Penrose and Philander Knox died, forcing Mellon to take a direct hand for a while in the state Republican Party, a job he poorly understood. Eventually, however, Joseph Grundy, president of the Pennsylvania Manufacturers Association, became the leader of the state Republicans and the prime instrument for Mellon control over the Commonwealth's policies. Their mutual enemy was Gifford Pinchot, an independent, good-government politician who served two separate terms as Pennsylvania governor. Since the Pennsylvania governor at that time was not allowed successive terms, Mellon's arch-conservative ally, John S. Fisher of Indiana County, was elected and served from 1927 to 1931, sandwiched in between two Pinchot terms as governor. Pinchot's view of the Mellon machine, especially its leaders Andrew and William Larimer Mellon, state Republican Party chair once Grundy was moved to the Senate, can be gathered from his farewell address to the legislature in 1927:

> The special interests who buy votes with excessive expenditures for campaign funds, and politicians who steal votes in elections, have combined to bring upon Pennsylvania dishonor which it will take years to live down.... For many years politics in this state has been run as a part of the business of certain moneyed interests. These inter-

ests invest in politics as they do in mills or mines or banks, and for the same purpose-
to make money. But instead of property, they buy men and votes, favors and legislation. What these interests buy is non-interference, tax exemption, extortionate rates
allowed public utilities and other special privileges for themselves at the expense of
the people. Any such machine must include a body of the lowest politicians...men
who depend for their living and their power on liquor, crime and vice... (and) such of
the ostensibly respectable elements of the community as are willing to shut their eyes
to make common cause with gangsters, vote thieves, dive keepers, criminals and har-
lots, because of the social and financial eminence of the Mellon name.[4]

Another key ally in state politics was David Reed, chief counsel for U.S. Steel, who succeeded
Philander Knox in the Senate. When Harding died in office, he was succeeded by his vice President,
Calvin Coolidge, who then easily won his own term in 1924. In Pittsburgh, the Democrats almost
disappeared when their presidential candidate John W. Davis received only eight percent of the vote,
while Robert LaFollette, running on a local Socialist-Labor Party ticket, gained 36 percent of the
vote, a full twenty points above his national average. When he called "Andrew Mellon the real President of the United States" in a speech in Pittsburgh, "Fighting Bob" La Follette demonstrated why
his anti-corporate campaign inspired such enthusiasm among the working class of Pittsburgh. "It is
unnecessary to demonstrate to a Pittsburgh audience that private monopoly does in fact control
government and industry."[5]

Like Andrew Mellon, who was shy and taciturn in public, "Silent Cal" Coolidge was someone
with congenial views on public policy and the role of government. Coolidge gained the vice-presidential nomination with Harding on the strength of his public opposition to the Boston Police strike
of 1919, as governor of Massachusetts. His philosophy was simple: "The business of America is
business." In the 1920s, wealth was venerated, and financial success was confounded with moral
worth. A contemporary critic, Harvey O'Connor, wrote of Mellon: "Probably at no other time in
American history could a man so aloof from the mass of his fellow-men, so lacking in the common,
homely touch or the dramatic appeal, have achieved such prestige. It was a tribute to the single-
minded concentration of the articulate classes in the country on one aim - the acquisition of wealth.
All other issues faded into insignificance." In this climate, Andy Mellon's backers began to hail him
as "the greatest Secretary of the Treasury since Alexander Hamilton." When Coolidge declared that
he would not be a candidate again in 1928, William L. Mellon orchestrated a "Mellon for President"
campaign that generated little enthusiasm for the aged multi-millionaire.[6]

Mellon's relationship with Herbert Hoover, the Republican candidate in 1928, was strained.
Hoover was the most progressive cabinet member in the Harding and Coolidge administrations.
Hoover won the election against the Catholic Democrat Al Smith, but, harbinger of elections to
come, Smith received 48 percent of the vote in the City of Pittsburgh. With waves of new ethnic
voters emerging out of the mill towns, the Republicans barely carried Allegheny County. The Catholic vote, stimulated by Al Smith's candidacy, was swelling Democratic numbers, as immigrants attained citizenship and their children reached voting age in increasing numbers. The 79 year-old
A.W. did not offer to retire, and Hoover, in order to reassure big business, kept him on board. Mellon
would prove to be an albatross around Hoover's neck as the Great Depression unfolded.[7]

The American Plan

In the 1920s, unions in virtually all fields, even the construction craft unions, came under sustained attack. In the summer of 1920, the electrician's Local 5 correspondent was reporting that work was slack and prospects were not bright. "The Carpenters and the Bricklayers have been on strike for four months so you can figure for yourself that we cannot have very much in sight. We have at present about one hundred unemployed." Furthermore, the new power plants being constructed at Cheswick and Springdale were being done non-union.[8] Hard times and an increasingly hostile attitude on the part of contractors who were determined to impose the anti-union "American Plan" formed the backdrop for conflict. A fourteen-month strike/lockout, which for IBEW Local 5 stretched from May 1921 to August 1922, marked a turning point in Pittsburgh construction unions' history. The local's longest work stoppage, it was followed by the adoption of dispute resolution mechanisms which solidified a significant measure of collaboration between the building trades locals and the local unionized construction firms. Andy Johnson, who played an important leadership role in the electricians union for many decades, recalled the bitter struggle that erupted a few months after he was accepted as an apprentice.

> Prior to May, 1921, our contractors insisted that we take a 20 percent reduction in wages and operate under the open shop. The members could not see either the reduction or the open shop, and instructed the business agent to see that our conditions and our wages were not relegated to the waste basket on May 1, 1921. As a result of those instructions it was necessary for him to take our members away from four shops that insisted in putting into effect the reduction and the open shop. This lasted until May 15, 1921, when the balance of the contractors who were in the Association voted to lock out the balance of our members, and did it by putting notices in their envelopes that on and after May 15, 1921, the wages would be $8 per day and open shop.[9]

On July 15, the Building Trades unions joined together to present a united front, since "the fight now being waged by the organized employers is not for the purpose of bringing about a fair and equitable wage readjustment, but has for its ultimate object the putting into effect the open shop plan in the building industry." Vowing joint action on "any job where non-union workmen of any craft are employed," they promised to resist the lowering of their standard of living to a "level unbearable". Four days later, IBEW Local 5's board gave Business Agent Mike Gordan the authority to carry out coordinated action with the other unions.[10] Harry Kluppell the Local's correspondent to the *Electrical Worker Journal* reported on conditions and spirits among the men seven months into the strike.

> We have been locked out since the 16th day of May and are still on the street. We have not yet asked for a penny from the outside. Those who have been fortunate enough to keep going have come to the assistance of the needy. We have lost a few by desertion; not over eight or ten....The membership of Local #5 can hold up their heads and be proud of the fact that they have stuck together and battled for the things to which every American is entitled: The right to organize and collectively bargain for the wages they are to receive and the conditions under which they shall work.[11]

Andy Johnson remembered that "we had a strike fund to try to help those that were out, and we went out to the country and we bought so many chickens and so many turkeys and so many hundreds of pounds of potatoes and we delivered them to the men that were on strike, helping out as best we could during that time." As the strike entered its second year, the IBEW received important assistance from their fellow construction unions, many of which had settled earlier with their contractors. "The Pittsburgh Building Trades Council have done all in their power morally to try to get the Electrical Workers and their contractors together to adjust their grievances, but so far have been unsuccessful. From now on the Pittsburgh Building Trades are going to use the only weapon that is left to them, that is, they are striking the jobs where those contractors who are unfair to the Electrical Workers are employed on, and we feel that it will only be a short while that the general contractors will stand for a condition of that kind." With the weight of all the construction unions now thrown into the fray, a settlement was finally reached on August 5, 1922. "We are now working under strictly union shop conditions and the wages are ten dollars a day....Right now the by-word is 'Harmony', and every brother wears that big happy smile, and the local is healthier in every way for it. I mean, morally, numerically and financially, with a closed shop agreement and most of the brothers working."[12]

The bitter experience of the 1921-22 strike/lockout led to the establishment of the Council on Industrial Relations that strengthened cooperative relationships with the unionized contractors. "With the settlement of the strike, we went into what is now known as the Council on Industrial Relations. If we reach an impasse with our employers today, the question is submitted to the Council on Industrial Relations that's made up of five men from the union and five men from the contractors, and their decisions are final and binding on the parties. Therefore, we are known today as a "strikeless" industry."[13] Unlike industrial unions that expressed the class-based antagonism between industrial workers and bosses, skill-based craft unions had to deal differently with a spectrum of contractors that ranged from cooperative to hostile.

The case of Sargent Electric provides a striking example of the mutual loyalty that could exist between a contractor and a local union.

> During the lockout...when all the contractors with the exception of one major contractor, went non-union, the only one that stayed with the union was Sargent Electric Company. Sargent would bid on a job and then try to get it financed. The banks were in league with the non-union contractors, and wouldn't lend them any money. Sargent was able to get the Liberty Tunnel lighting and power project and money was short. Those who worked on the tunnel didn't get an hourly rate, but whatever they could scrape together at the end of the week, they gave them to take care of their lunch money and their car fare with what few pennies was left. But we weathered the storm and came through it with flying colors.[14]

Ed Sargent Sr. also remembered the lockout and the determination of his father who had once been bounced out of his job for associating with union men.

> We stayed union and almost went bankrupt in 1922 because we were employing most of the local union. They were working for us. We were paying them union scale and the other fellows were paying non-union scale.... It is the best thing we ever did because everywhere we went we could talk about the fact that we were the only electrical contractor that stayed union in Pittsburgh in 1921. That built a lot of loyalty and the IBEW has always been good to us everyplace we went. We always got good men and we could cooperate with them. We got our jobs done on time and we got them done right.[15]

While efforts to break skilled craft unions of largely American-born workers were being wrapped in the flag of Americanism, even more virulent anti-union, anti-Catholic and anti-immigrant sentiments were being stirred up by radical organizations like the Ku Klux Klan. The spectacular rise of the Klan in states like Pennsylvania and Indiana in 1923 and 1924 was the culmination of wartime 100% Americanism drives and a reaction to the large Slav and Italian populations in the mill and mining towns. The restrictive Immigration Act of 1924 marked a significant victory for nativists like James J. Davis, later elected Pennsylvania senator, who worried that "the United States was in danger of sliding into the hands of descendants of such poor human stock…that the ideals of our founders will not have the ghost of a chance to remain dominant in the Republic." While the Klan was concerned about the growing black population which more than doubled in the state from 1910 to 1930, Catholics were especially targeted for their supposed divided loyalties between America and Rome, their rituals and iconography that smacked of paganism, their sectarian schools, and their non-recognition of Protestant marriage. For the Klan in Pennsylvania was above all a militant Protestant movement, strongly supportive of Prohibition and in many cases closely linked to the Masonic orders. Its strongholds were in the coal and steel regions of the state where the old nativist, agricultural and commercial order felt most threatened. Allegheny County alone claimed thirty of the Commonwealth's sixty-seven Klaverns. Wilkinsburg, on the Pittsburgh's eastern border, was a stronghold, and old-timers in Mt. Washington told of at least one cross-burning overlooking the city where Catholics from St. Mary's reputedly put the Klansmen to flight. Internal splits and scandals led to the movement's rapid decline in the late 1920s with smaller groups remaining active during the 1930s mainly in the rural coal fields where they focused on anti-union activity.[16]

A Revolution in Communication and Transportation

World War I stimulated intensive research into wireless telegraphy and telephony. By war's end there were three major corporations with a keen interest in the potential of radio: Westinghouse, AT&T, and General Electric. None of the three, at that point, realized its potential as an entertainment medium; all were looking at wireless as a replacement for telegraph and telephone, enabling them to sell voice messages between individuals and businesses. Dr. Frank Conrad, an engineer at Westinghouse, had done extensive work on wireless telephony. Two stations were established to develop a wireless telephone transmitter: one at the Westinghouse Electric plant and the other in the second floor of Conrad's garage on Penn Avenue about five miles distant. His station was licensed as 8XK in April 1920. As more and more amateur ham radio operators began picking up his broadcasts, he began playing records to supplement talk, and as the volume of requests increased, he started regular two-hour broadcasts two nights a week.[17]

Conrad's boss in the engineering department at Westinghouse, Henry Phillips Davis, seeing an advertisement by Horne's department store for receivers capable of receiving Conrad's musical broadcasts, understood "that a station sending out entertainments, concerts, records of current events on regular schedules, was the key to the future. He believed that once such entertainment was broadcast, persons would demand 'ears' with which to hear it." Subsequently Davis described his excitement in a speech at Harvard University: "We became convinced that we had in our hands in this idea the instrument that would prove to be the greatest and most direct means of mass communication and mass education that had ever appeared. The natural fascination of its mystery, coupled with its ability to annihilate distance, would attract, interest, and open many avenues to bring happiness into human lives. It was obviously a form of service of universal application that could be rendered without favor and without price to millions eager for its benefits." [18]

On October 27, the new station was licensed by the Department of Commerce and assigned the call letters KDKA. Election dispatches from all over the nation were received via telegraph by the *Pittsburgh Post* and then telephoned to the "rough box affair on the roof" where they were broadcast to between five hundred and a thousand local listeners who heard the news "from the evening sky." The election returns were read all through the night and into the following morning by Leo Rosenberg, who became thereby the nation's first radio announcer. KDKA was the location of many broadcasting firsts. In 1921, it broadcast the first church service at Calvary Episcopal Church in Shadyside; the first live band concert conducted in a tent on the roof of Westinghouse; the first boxing match featuring Johnny Ray and Johnny Dundee at Motor Square Garden; the first play-by play of a National League baseball game; the first football broadcast, the University of Pittsburgh vs. West Virginia University; the first coverage of a presidential inauguration; the first time signal; and the first barn dance. Frank Conrad went on to discover the advantages of broadcasting on shorter wave lengths of 100 meters, rather than the 360 meter length then used. These improvements greatly facilitated daytime reception and increased the reach of KDKA radio. [19]

As revolutionary as the radio was in the creation of a mass consciousness, new methods of travel were not limited to sound waves. The 1920s saw the emergence of two competing transportation systems, the trolley and the automobile. For forty years, from 1920 to 1960, a healthy balance was maintained in the Pittsburgh region between the communal public trolley and the individualistic private automobile to the benefit of all. The 1920s saw the great flowering of the electric trolley system in, around, and out of the city. Indeed, in 2008, eighty years after they were spoken, the words of Edwin M. Herr, veteran of the 1914 strike and still president of Westinghouse Electric in 1928, resonate with sad irony, as the nation struggles with the wars and environmental degradation incumbent on petroleum dependency, and the region's public transportation system at the dawn of the 21st Century teeters on the brink of collapse.

> Let us imagine, if we can, Pittsburgh without electric traction. We can scarcely conceive what it would mean to eliminate the wonderful system of street and interurban railways which carry people to and from their daily tasks and furnish a means of rapid communication between the central hive of industry and the many thriving outlying communities which surround it. Without electric traction Pittsburgh's progress would have been spelled in very small letters – her present development would have been absolutely impossible. [20]

The last horse-drawn trolley made its run on the South Side in 1922. The powerful Westinghouse single reduction motors that drove the electric trolleys were ideally suited to Pittsburgh's rugged terrain. Trolleys connected the mills and the workshops to towns and suburbs. Housing and businesses spread out along the suburban lines and clustered around stops. The trolley opened up Oakland as it emerged after the turn of the century as the city's university and research center, as well as the location of its major sports venues and arenas: Forbes Field, Pitt Stadium, and the Duquesne Gardens. The Amalgamated Association of Street and Electric Railway Employees, Division 85, completely organized the trolley system and eventually many of the bus lines in the city. In 1924 trolley operators went on strike to restore wages cut in 1921. Mayor William Magee asked the city council to authorize the purchase of tear gas and riot guns to protect citizens and property. After three days, the strike ended without a wage increase but with the concession by the companies that they would pay half of the operator's uniform costs.[21]

The changing transportation system affected many unions, especially the Teamsters. The Teamsters locally were organized in 1890 and, by 1904, had established rates of $9 a week for single-horse wagons and $10 for two-horse vehicles. As trucks took the place of wagons, intense competition and chaotic conditions prevailed in a decentralized new industry. In 1928, General Teamsters Local 249 was established and became the driving force inside the Teamsters Joint Council No. 40 that during the 1930s organized virtually "everything on wheels." Various Teamster locals organized bakery, milk, refuse, newspaper, produce handlers, construction, and taxicab drivers. The Teamsters became a powerful force for the advancement of unionism, since their mobility and refusal to cross picket lines assisted many building trades unions to organize contractors and industrial unions to organize plants. Reflecting the movement from steam power to gasoline and diesel engines, the operating engineers dropped "steam" from their title and became the International Union of Operating Engineers (IUOE) in 1928.[22]

Wealthy Pittsburghers, however, preferred the luxury and privacy of the automobile. They also liked the public to pay for road construction and maintenance through taxes, while public money for mass transit or rail was provided begrudgingly and seen as socialistic. Furthermore highway contracts provided fertile opportunities for graft and kickbacks, while construction jobs provided a base for the patronage that reinforced the Republican machine's political control. While the Mellons owned important trolley lines, they were not anxious for governmental subsidies that might lead to public regulation, but they were anxious that the huge oil production capacity they controlled had a market. The first gas station downtown was opened by Gulf Oil at Liberty and Water Street in 1919. In 1922, the city was shocked by a record five auto fatalities in a single day. In 1923, the Boulevard of the Allies was completed and fitted with the first unified traffic light system. At $1.6 million per mile it was said to be the most expensive road construction job in the world at the time. In 1924, the fifth transit strike in fifteen years led to a traffic jam in the new Liberty Tunnels that caused people to become ill from the air. Better ventilation had to be installed. In 1929, Saw Mill Run Boulevard was opened to traffic, and the Roadway, later named for City Councilman P. J. McArdle, was opened to Mt. Washington. Airmail service started to Cleveland in 1927 with air passenger service following in 1928. In 1929, the "Canalization of the Ohio" celebration drew 100,000 citizens as the Ohio's system of locks and dams now created a year-round Pittsburgh pool of stable, navigable depth. Until then, it remained possible to wade across the Monongahela during a summer dry spell.[23]

While foreign immigration slowed as a result of federal legislation restricting it in 1921, Pittsburgh's population showed steady growth from 588,343 in 1920 to 669,817 in 1930, primarily reflecting elevated first and second generation immigrant birth rates. Population growth leveled off with the Depression, however. The total remained above 600,000 for more than three decades from 1930 to 1960, reaching its peak of 676,806 in 1950, followed by its, at first gradual, then precipitous decline to its population of 340,000 in 2000. In 1926, R. B. Mellon, president of Mellon Bank, was elected chair of the Allegheny County Planning Commission. While Andrew ran the financial business of the nation, R.B. oversaw Pittsburgh and played an important role in state politics. An attempt to create a "greater Pittsburgh" including surrounding boroughs and townships was defeated in the legislature, but, in 1928, a constitutional amendment passed to allow Pittsburgh and Allegheny County to consolidate into a metropolitan district. Pittsburgh voters supported the proposal 8 to 1, but the requirement for a two-thirds vote margin in a majority (62 out of 123) of municipalities killed the plan, as only 47 municipalities approved the merger by the required margin.[24]

Public morality became a contentious issue since Sunday entertainments and all Sunday games, except the gentlemanly, upper-class pursuits of golf and tennis, were banned. Prohibition and the Blue Laws provided abundant opportunities for the corruption of police and politicians. Selective enforcement or non-enforcement of the laws provided a handy way to keep political operatives in line. In 1926, police were turned out to break up illegal games, and when the Pittsburgh Symphony defied the Sunday ban in 1927, nine members of the Symphony's Executive Board were arrested and given nominal fines. Charged with violating the Act of April 22, 1794, prohibiting "worldly employment" on the Sabbath, and therefore concerts charging admission, the convictions were overturned by the Allegheny County Court with the judge stating: "What lover of nature has not been thrilled with the singing of birds on Sunday morning...? They at once unconsciously lift the mind to the praise and adoration of the Creator, and if nature sings on Sunday, why not men?" Frick Park, Helen Frick's monument to her father, opened that summer, and in 1928, the Stanley Theater featured a movie picture accompanied with sound track as the "talkie" *Tenderloin* opened to mixed reviews. Even more portentous in its consequences than bestowing voice on movie actors, Frank Conrad at Westinghouse in 1928 demonstrated the feasibility of broadcasting talking motion pictures by radio, thereby planting the revolutionary seed of television.[25]

Truth and Money in Academia

Oakland in the 1920s was becoming a great center of research, education and entertainment. During the late 19th Century, Western University languished as an appendage to the Allegheny Observatory on Observatory Hill in Allegheny City, failing to excite either Andrew Carnegie or the Mellons to contribute significantly to the school. In 1901, John Brashear, named acting chancellor, built the new observatory in Riverview Park. When its new chancellor, Samuel Black McCormick, moved the university officially to Oakland in 1909 and changed the school's name to the University of Pittsburgh, "the university was small in enrollment, small in faculty, small in dollars, small in traditions, and very much smaller in fame" than the prestigious eastern universities or the great state universities to the west. The timing was right, however, because Carnegie Tech and Mellon Institute were proving the importance of intellectual capital in the growth of both industry and commerce, and the Mellons were beginning to look for ways to unload some of their vast holdings of capital for both political and tax purposes. [26]

Key to the success of the university was its emergence as a collegiate football power under the coaching of Glenn Scobey "Pop" Warner, who came to Pitt with experience coaching at Cornell, Georgia, and at the Indian School in Carlisle, where he had assisted in the development of the great Native American athlete Jim Thorpe. He produced four straight undefeated teams (1915-1918) that outscored opponents 863 to 17. He began a Pitt football tradition that resulted in 27 winning seasons in a row. The extraordinary collegiate football success of Pop Warner was continued by Coach Jock Sutherland. In 1925, the new 60,000 seat Pitt stadium constructed by the alumni-based Athletic Council opened with a 28-0 Pitt victory over Washington and Lee. To maximize the use of its new investment, Pitt scheduled 36 straight home games. In 1927, a Pitt-Penn State match drew 45,000 fans, and Pitt represented the east in the Rose Bowl against a Stanford team coached by their former coach Warner, only to lose the game on a disputed play. In 1930, a record 60,000 fans witnessed Pitt play Notre Dame and in 1932, 65,000 witnessed Pitt's first defeat of the Fighting Irish by a score of 12-0.[27]

In 1927, Chancellor John Bowman announced plans for an ambitious 42-story Gothic "Cathedral of Learning" as the centerpiece for the university on a fourteen acre plot donated by the Mellons. Bowman had been summoned to Washington shortly after A. W. Mellon's accession to the Treasury to advise on medical services mandated for soldiers disabled by tuberculosis and mental illness. The chancellor seized the opportunity to press the secretary for increased Mellon family donations to the university. A.W. at first resisted, but Bowman's persistence was repaid when Mellon retired the university's substantial debts, and donated the large plot of prime real estate where Bowman constructed his grandiose Cathedral of Learning. The University also expanded and strengthened its medical school, which had been basically a group of teaching laboratories without a directly affiliated hospital. This problem was solved by both expanding existing institutions and creating new ones. Thus Magee Hospital for Women, Children's Hospital, Presbyterian Hospital, Eye and Ear, and Falk Clinic were united into the University of Pittsburgh Medical Center with affiliated schools of Dentistry and Pharmacy.[28]

While Chancellor Bowman was a visionary in bricks and mortar, he also had an autocratic style that suppressed dissent and provoked unrest within the university. Bowman was concerned about a dozen or more talented faculty who were becoming deeply involved in civil liberties issues around the 1927-28 coal strike, and who constituted the core of a revived Pittsburgh ACLU chapter. The Pittsburgh ACLU had been founded on April 11, 1920, at the Jewish Labor Lyceum in reaction to the Palmer raids. Shortly afterward, members of the local group were arrested in Duquesne along with William Z. Foster in an attempt to hold a meeting, but the chapter was moribund until a professor's group at Pitt began doing research for school teachers seeking a raise. When the UMWA struck the coal companies on April 1, 1927, Colston Warne, who had done his doctoral work on the cooperative movement, and William Nunn, another economist, joined with District 2 mineworker leader, John Brophy, to found the Pittsburgh Labor College. When Warne began to speak out publicly on "The Human Effects of the Coal Strike," he was summoned by Chancellor Bowman and ordered to be silent. In response, he became the ACLU coordinator for the coal regions. Then, in December 1928, Nunn and Frederick Woltman, a graduate student in psychology and secretary of the Pittsburgh ACLU, wrote an article for H. L. Mencken's *American Mercury*, entitled "Cossacks." It assailed the conduct of state police in recent coal strikes. In response to increasing pressure from the Chancellor, Nunn and Woltman wrote publicly to Pennsylvania's Governor Fisher, former officer in the Clearfield Coal Company, outlining cases of police abuse. In early 1929, a dramatic example of the abuse of private police powers erupted on the front pages of the newly minted *Pittsburgh Post-Gazette*.[29]

Pittsburgh's newspapers were consolidated and reorganized during the 1920s. In 1923, the *Daily Dispatch* and *The Leader* were shut down, and the *Pittsburgh Press* was sold to the national Scripps-Howard syndicate. Paul Block was a publisher who owned papers in Newark, New Jersey, Lancaster, Pennsylvania, and especially the *Blade* in Toledo, where the enterprise maintained its headquarters. He and William Randolph Hearst both had entertained a relationship with an actress and Ziegfeld Girl, Marion Davies. Instead of the arrangement promoting rivalry, the two men managed to collaborate on a complex purchase and ownership swap of two of Pittsburgh's morning and two of its evening papers. When the smoke cleared, Block owned and merged both morning papers, the Republican *Gazette-Times*, linear descendent of the town's first newspaper, and the historically Democratic *Post* into the *Post-Gazette.* For his part, Hearst combined two of the three remaining evening papers into the *Sun-Telegraph* to compete with the *Press.*[30]

Shortly after the reconfiguration, Paul Block launched an editorial attack on one of Pennsylvania's most hated institutions, the Coal and Iron Police. On February 10, a group of private company police had gone to the home of a part time miner, John Barcoski, to buy moonshine from his mother. The policemen were drinking, and one got into an argument with Barcoski. The policeman arrested the miner and then on the way to the police barracks beat him to death with his revolver. The incident prompted State Representative Michael Musmanno of Stowe Township near McKees Rocks to draft a bill repealing the 1865 law that permitted railroad, and later coal and industrial, companies, to employ police forces. Musmanno launched a personal, public campaign against the corporate police and produced a book and a movie, both called *Black Fury,* built around the incident. When the coal owners' ally, Governor Fisher, vetoed the repeal bill, the *Post-Gazette* printed a Cy Hungerford cartoon that portrayed Fisher as Lady Macbeth, with blood dripping from his hands and the Musmanno bill anchored to the floor with a dagger. It was only in 1935 that Democratic Governor George Earle abolished the hated private police forces completely and for good.[31]

Following the Barcoski affair, on April 22, 1929, a meeting was called at the University of Pittsburgh by William Albertson, student chair of Pitt's small Liberal Club, to demand the release of Tom Mooney and Warren Billings, who it was widely believed were falsely accused of throwing a bomb into a patriotic parade in Montana and sentenced to life imprisonment. Pitt authorities reacted swiftly, suppressing the meeting and disbanding the club. Woltman and Albertson were "severely rebuked" by the Pitt dean L. P. Sieg. Meanwhile, members of the Liberal Club defiantly attempted to hold several meetings on campus, leading to the expulsion of Woltman, Albertson and a third student, Albert McDowell. Bowman stated that "the issue was that the club, with its president known as a Communist and aided by organizations or individuals outside and in Pittsburgh was using the name of the University to advance its propaganda and publicity." At about the same time, Frederick Woltman was dismissed from his instructor's position on the grounds that he had made public confidential conversations with the administration. The dismissal of Woltman, who had been serving as the secretary of the ACLU branch, elicited a formal protest from the ACLU, which also offered legal representation to the expelled students. An American Association of University Professors campus visit and investigation was also critical of the administration. Albertson, after working for labor and radical causes for many years in New York City, returned to Pittsburgh where he became the organizational secretary of the Communist Party in Western Pennsylvania.[32]

Without tenure, twelve out of the eighteen Pitt members of the civil liberties group left the university, some because contracts had not been renewed, others because they objected to a climate of fear and did not want to stay. In his letter of resignation from the university, April 28, 1930, Colston Warne wrote that he was leaving because of differences with the Chancellor over "my ideals of academic freedom, scholarly research, and educational policy." Chancellor Bowman apparently advised Warne during one of their interviews: "A person in academic circles has no place in heated controversies. Nothing is gained and the institution is imperiled." Warne believed otherwise.[33]

> I have seen liberal students unjustly expelled and faculty members censured, demoted, or dismissed, when they voiced minority opinions on pressing social issues. Possibly some day – I hope not too late – the trustees and administrators of the University will come to appreciate that education is not built of forty-story cathedrals or stadia which seat seventy-thousand people. Education is the product of scholars dedicated to the

search of truth wherever it may lead. Pittsburgh does not deserve a great university until it can learn the difficult lesson of the value of ideas, unpopular though they may, on occasion, be to large industrialists.

Five years have shown me the potentialities of this city. If only its vision of bigness in material things could be translated into an ardent quest of the truth, it could become the center of a new world of thought. Chancellor Bowman, however, has wished conformity....[34]

Boxing and Baseball

Conflicts between academic freedom and the power of money impinged very little on the public consciousness. Sports, on the other hand, loomed large in the public eye. Oakland was becoming the center of sports activity with highly successful football programs at Pitt and Carnegie Tech, and boxing at Duquesne Gardens. Meanwhile, the Pirates were beginning to make some noise at Forbes Field. The broadcasting of Pirate home games by KDKA was at first resisted by team management out of fears that access to games on the radio might cut attendance. In fact, the radio helped extend the game's reach directly into homes across the region, stimulating attendance especially by women and youngsters. Pirate fans were a feisty bunch and after several physical confrontations between fans and police over possession of foul balls, the ball club announced: "Fans who attend games at the National League baseball park here may keep balls knocked into the stands without fear of being molested by a policeman." In 1925, the Pirates won the National League pennant by 8 ½ games over the rival Giants of John McGraw. They were led by swift outfielder, Kiki Culyer, and stellar fielding and hard hitting third baseman, Pie Traynor. Culyer hit .357 with 26 triples and 17 homeruns, including eight inside-the-park homeruns, a record that still stands. This feat was undoubtedly helped by the spacious confines of Forbes Field. Nearly the entire lineup hit over .300. In the World Series, the Pirates were stymied by the Senators' great pitcher, Walter Johnson, in the first and fourth games, and with the Series tied at three apiece, they faced him again. The Pirates staked the tired Johnson to a 4-0 lead, but they fought back to go ahead 9-7 and win the game. Mass pandemonium broke out on the streets of Oakland as the nearly 43,000 fans left the stadium, but, this time, all over town and out into the region, celebrations erupted. Radio was extending and magnifying the rich Pittsburgh-centered sports market.[35]

After a disappointing third-place finish in 1926, the Pirates came back late in the following season to edge the Cardinals for the pennant. The team was again led by the spectacular fielding and steady hitting of their star shortstop Pie Traynor. The team's muscle came in disarmingly small packages; namely in the form of Paul and Lloyd Waner, nicknamed "Big Poison" and "Little Poison." Both were small, especially Lloyd, who was well under 150 pounds. Paul won the batting title in 1926 with a .380 average and 237 hits, while Lloyd hit .355. Lloyd's 223 hits that year remain the most ever achieved by a rookie; 198 of them were singles. The brothers were very fast and notoriously difficult to pitch to. In the 1927 World Series, however, the Pirates faced the "Murderers' Row" Yankee lineup, led by Babe Ruth and Lou Gehrig. Some argued that the Series was won during batting practice for Game One at Forbes Field, though this account is fiercely contested by many Pittsburghers. In 18 seasons of play, it was claimed, no one had ever hit a ball into the second tier of seats in right field. The Babe took four swings in batting practice. He drove the first pitch into the second tier; the second, into the first tier; the third, high up in the second tier. On the fourth pitch, he drove the ball

242

high against the façade of the second tier roof, only eighteen inches from clearing the stadium. Despite "Little Poison" batting .400 and his older brother .333 in the Series, the Yanks dominated and won four straight. While the Waner brothers and Pie Traynor continued their batting heroics into the 1930s, the Pirates would not participate in a World Series again for 33 years.[36]

Alongside the more genteel baseball, boxing was the sport that defined Pittsburgh in the first half of the 20th Century. Life in Western Pennsylvania for the working class was a constant struggle that bred toughness and fostered competition. For many men, fighting in bars under the influence of alcohol was a release from the pressured machine and metal work that they performed. The purpose of bar fighting was to demonstrate dominance or impose respect, not commit murder or cause serious injury – at least, not usually. Not uncommonly, men might fight and then go back and have a few drinks together. Fighting proved manliness and self-worth. Boxing for money required no sophisticated equipment or specialized venue, yet contests drew rabid crowds and generated large gates. Ethnic tensions were acted out, and manliness expressed. It was a heavily working-class sport, but attracted wagers from the wealthy. Criminal and political organizations hovered around the fight game. Fighters fought continuously, often monthly and sometimes more often, to earn money, afford training, stay in the game, climb up the rankings and negotiate a shot at the title.

The only fight Gene Tunney ever lost was to one of the toughest fighters in boxing history, Pittsburgh's Harry Greb. Their fight in Madison Square Garden on May 23, 1922 was for the Light Heavyweight Championship of America. Greb, naturally a middleweight, fought successfully against boxers from Light to Heavyweight classifications. Called the "Pittsburgh Windmill" for his aggressive, relentless, swarming style, Greb fought in 299 professional fights, winning 261. Greb rarely trained, because he fought so often. In one year, 1917, he fought 37 officially recorded bouts, and in 1919, he fought forty-four fights, only five less than Rocky Marciano fought in an entire career! In 1920, Greb was invited to spar Jack Dempsey for three rounds. Greb, thirty-five pounds lighter and five inches shorter, completely dominated the famed "Manassa Mauler." Dempsey was so embarrassed by the display that he demanded a rematch the following day, but Greb, much quicker and faster, at one point delivered fifteen unanswered punches. Dempsey warned Gene Tunney about Greb: "Funniest hitter in the world. He makes you think you are in a glove factory and shelves of them are tumbling down on you. He can slap you to death." When Greb fought Tunney, five hundred Pittsburghers came by train in a group to witness the bout. Famous sports writer, Grantland Rice, called the Tunney-Greb match "perhaps the bloodiest fight I ever covered." A great fighter – and bar room brawler – Greb handled Tunney, "the Greenwich Village Irishman with the crew cut." "like a butcher hammering a Swiss steak."[37] Tunney, in an excerpt from his autobiography, described the first fight:

> In the first exchange of the fight, I sustained a double fracture of the nose which bled continually until the finish. Toward the end of the first round, my left eyebrow was laid open four inches…. In the third round another cut over the right eye left me looking through a red film. For the better part of twelve rounds, I saw this red phantom-like form dancing before me. I had provided myself with a fifty-per-cent mixture of brandy and orange juice to take between rounds in the event I became weak from loss of blood. I had never taken anything during a fight up to that time. Nor did I ever again.
>
> It is impossible to describe the bloodiness of this fight. My seconds were unable to stop either the bleeding from the cut over my left eye, which involved a severed ar-

tery, or the bleeding consequent to the nose fractures....At the end of the twelfth round, I believed it was a good time to take a swallow of the brandy and orange juice. It had hardly got to my stomach when the ring started whirling around. The bell rang for the thirteenth round; the seconds pushed me from my chair. I actually saw two red opponents. How I survived the thirteenth, fourteenth and fifteenth rounds is still a mystery to me. At any rate, the only consciousness I had was to keep trying. I knew if I ever relaxed, I should either collapse or the referee would stop the brutality. [38]

At the end it was estimated that Tunney lost two quarts of blood, while Greb was unmarked and his plastered down hair was still in place. What was not known then was that Greb also was carrying many wounds as a result of his brutal profession, and had only been fighting with one functioning eye since a fight the previous year against Kid Norfolk, the "Black Thunderbolt," where he was gouged in the right eye, suffering a detached retina. Harry Greb fought the best fighters of his day in four weight classes. He bet heavily on himself. To increase the odds against him and thereby improve his winnings, he put on calculated displays, like staggering into a New York City hangout bar for sportswriters at lunchtime on the day of a fight, with a woman on each arm, stinking of alcohol. Greb, however, did not drink. He held the World Middleweight championship for three years. In the Greb-Tunney rematch, Tunney won a close decision and then beat Greb two more times convincingly. Tunney was on his way up; Greb on his way down. Harry Greb's gutsy work ethic and his tragic young death in a hospital made him a hero to many Pittsburghers, including Gene Kelly and Billy Conn. [39]

The fight game struck a deep chord with Pittsburgh's working-class. Life for most workers was a constant struggle. The manly art of self-defense was mirrored and then magnified in the many struggles around the common defense that characterized the 1920s and 1930s. Workers adopted a combative attitude rooted in the harshness of their daily experience.

Coal Wars

The defining labor struggles of the 1920s occurred in the coal fields surrounding Pittsburgh. In fact the decade from 1923 to 1932 marked the darkest period in the United Mine Workers history, as governmental and corporate attacks nearly destroyed labor's strongest organization. Declining demand for coal, consistent overproduction, increased mechanization, and cut-throat competition between operators, who were themselves controlled by large financial interests, combined with an autocratic union leadership that exacerbated internal divisions within the organization, led to the near total collapse of the coal miners' union. John L. Lewis, who succeeded to the presidency in 1919 because of the illness of the union's president, Frank Hayes, was elected president in 1920 by 62 percent of the vote. His vice-presidential candidate, Phil Murray, director of District Five, was narrowly elected over a leader of the union's radical wing, Alexander Howat. With the union's Secretary-Treasurer, William Green, the mineworkers' leadership thus included three men who played central roles in American labor history over the next three decades, and more. Lewis and Murray successively headed the Congress of Industrial Organizations (CIO), with Murray assuming the first presidency of the United Steelworkers of America (USWA). William Green subsequently presided over the American Federation of Labor (AFL) during the split that created the CIO and into the 1950s. [40]

A bitter crisis was looming in coal. All out warfare erupted in West Virginia in May 1920. As Baldwin-Felts private detectives were evicting striking miners in Matewan in Mingo County, a gun battle broke out between them and town officials seeking to stop the evictions, led by Mayor Cabbell Testerman and Sid Hatfield, chief of police. Eleven Baldwin-Felts guards and three townspeople, including the mayor, were killed. More than a year later, an unarmed Sid Hatfield and Ed Chambers were gunned down by Baldwin-Felts men on the steps of the courthouse. This provoked a march of ten thousand armed miners on Logan County, where they were met by state National Guard and a squadron of airplanes under the command of General Billy Mitchell. At one point, the miners were bombed in the first recorded incident of aerial warfare in an industrial dispute. With the arrival of federal troops, the miners surrendered their weapons, and many local unions were crushed.[41]

With these desperate struggles as background, the bituminous coal agreement expired in 1922. Unionized operators went on the offensive, demanding wage reductions in excess of 30 percent, while the union essentially attempted to defend previous gains. The battle cry became "No backward steps!" The central battleground in the strike was Western Pennsylvania and Eastern Ohio. The union's strike was deeply complicated by the virtually spontaneous eruption of the non-union mines in central Pennsylvania, especially in the perennial battleground areas of Somerset, Fayette and Cambria counties. There, tens of thousands of non-union miners massively joined the union strike, seeking protection under the UMWA contract. This expansion of the strike into the non-union fields was advocated and strongly supported by UMWA District 2 president John Brophy. Brophy, a socialist by politics and Catholic by religion, was becoming an articulate and widely respected opponent of Lewis's dictatorial ways, while at the same time opposing growing Communist Party organization in the union. He led a movement inside the miners' union, with a social-democratic view influenced by the British trade union example, which called for the creation of a Labor Party and the nationalization of the coal industry. Miners also supported the Plumb Plan supported by the rail unions calling for the nationalization of the railroads. As president of District 2, he formulated what he called "The Miners' Program," because he believed that the stubborn intransigence of the coal operators had destroyed collective bargaining. "The true interest of the public would be served by our proposals to end the waste, unreasonable profits, exorbitant prices, unemployment, outrageously high accident rate, planlessness and indifference to public needs characteristic of the industry."[42]

> The private ownership of the great natural resource of coal is morally indefensible and economically unsound. It means that coal is mined for the profit of a comparatively few "owners," instead of for the use and service of the public. It results in chronic mismanagement of the mines. It results in exploitation of the miner, through overwork, underpay, inadequate safeguards, bad housing, accidents, and, then, long and unnecessary periods of enforced idleness. It results in unemployment when millions of consumers need coal. It results in high prices for coal when democratic methods of production would reduce the cost, increase the production and give a good American life to the miners.[43]

Brophy was not naive about the difficulties involved in the organization of the non-union mines. In 1919 during the previous contract struggle, Brophy had experienced first hand the difficulties in organizing the unorganized mines when employers were free to organize "small armies of guards and spies on their payrolls and controlled absolutely the local and county officials."

> Organizers and strikers had no rights; officers charged with keeping 'law and order' drove union men out of town, arrested them on trumped-up charges, and maintained a reign of terror against anyone who dared call his soul his own. Courts eagerly provided the most extreme injunctions against any person or activity the operators ob-

jected to. Men who went on strike were brutally evicted from their homes; no mercy was granted to young or old. Even pregnant women were turned out to bear their children in tent colonies or in chicken coops and other temporary shelters.[44]

With coal stockpiles high, and the non-union mines under the control of the Mellon, Rockefeller and Morgan interests free to operate and increase production, Brophy believed that striking union miners were doomed unless they spread the strike to the non-union mines. With approval from the union's national policy committee, Brophy printed and distributed 20,000 strike cards with the following message:

> STRIKE CALL TO NON-UNION MEN
> Miners of Non-Union Fields of Pennsylvania
> Fellow Workers RISE! STRIKE!
> This is your fight...
> QUIT WORK APRIL 1ST!
> Join our fight. Make it your fight
> You will get
> > A checkweighman
> > Correct weight
> > Decent wages
> > Your independence as free men and miners
> DROP YOUR TOOLS
> LEAVE THE MINE![45]

Over the weeks following the April 1st "Mitchell Day" strike call, the hard-scrabble patch towns serving the unorganized and captive mines across the state rose in rebellion, as an estimated 100,000 non-union miners in Pennsylvania and West Virginia joined the 600,000 striking union miners. In Pennsylvania, the shutdown spread from the western bituminous fields into the anthracite fields, effectively shutting coal production in the entire state in both union and non-union mines. While unilaterally imposed wage and tonnage rate cuts in the non-union mines helped fuel the walkout, very quickly it became clear that the fundamental issue was the very right to have a union. "The strike for union," as it became known, was a cry for freedom from arbitrary company dictation over wages, hours, and working conditions. Workers wanted fairness and the protection of a contract. A miner from Windber, just south of Johnstown, where the conflict was especially bitter, was quoted: "We are no longer slaves and we are done loading three ton for two. We will never return under a scab system. We want union to protect our rights." Brophy, in his testimony before the Coal Commission, stressed that the reason that the non-union miners struck and held on with such tenacity was "to secure their rights as free Americans against the state of fear, suspicion and espionage prevailing in non-union towns....To put an end to the absolute and feudal control of these coal operators."[46]

When the former union operators agreed to settle with Lewis and the UMWA on August 15 after four-and-a-half months because of declining coal stocks, the approach of cold weather, and mounting political pressure on the national level, Brophy tried to keep some union mines in District 2 out on strike in solidarity with the non-union miners by refusing to sign a contract with any company unless all their mines, union or non-union, were included in any agreement. The UMWA International cut strike support, but District 2 voted in favor of a $1 assessment from every miner's pay to provide assistance to the non-union miners on strike. District 2 miners contributed more than a million dollars to the non-union strikers.[47]

Berwind-White responded by evicting strikers en masse from its mine patch housing surrounding Windber. The union moved strikers to union mines and towns, where possible, and upon the onset of winter they adapted barns, chicken coops and built barracks. In December 1922, while relief efforts were under way to provide shoes and blankets for the strikers and keep them from starvation, the tax report on the estate of Mrs. E. J. Berwind revealed that she had left her husband a half a million dollars in jewels, including a diamond-studded dog collar worth more than $22,000. An innovative corporate campaign was launched against Berwind-White in New York City, since the Berwind-White company supplied fuel for the city's subways. Picketing and protests led New York City's Mayor Hylan to appoint five officials to an investigative committee that visited Windber. The New Yorkers were appalled by conditions in the coal towns around Windber and stated in their report that the living conditions of the miners employed in the Berwind-White mines "were worse than the conditions of slaves prior to the Civil War" and quoted a miner who explained that their condition was worse than slave because "the slave owners housed, fed and clothed their slaves, while at Windber, if the miner does not do as he is bid by the Coal Company, he and his family are kicked out of their home and are left to starve and freeze to death like dogs."[48]

In January 1923, with an estimated 40,000 still on strike in Pennsylvania, Lewis called off the strike in the Connellsville coke region and cut relief to the remaining strikers in District 2. At the same time, Brophy and the nationalization committee of the union issued their answer to the coal crisis in a pamphlet entitled *How to Run Coal* that urged nationalization of coal, a policy that the business-union, Republican, John L. Lewis, did not support. Many strikers and their families were forced to leave the coal fields, and the number of striking miners fell to 6,000. Finally, in August 1923, nearly a full year after the ending of the national strike, the new locals constituted at the non-union mines voted to end the strike. In that same summer, the Ku Klux Klan made a spectacular surge in Western Pennsylvania targeting immigrants and Catholics with an emphasis on 100% Americanism. An armed clash between Catholics and the Klan in Carnegie, where a Klansman was killed, spurred recruitment. Klan membership in Pennsylvania peaked that year at 125,000 members. In the following year, the Indiana, Pennsylvania branch of the Klan hosted 35,000 at its first annual picnic at its new "Klan farm." UMWA District 2 was its primary organizational antagonist in Central Pennsylvania.[49]

After the 1922-1923 strike, the UMWA's share of the nation's coal production slid from 60 percent, where it had been in 1919, to 28 percent in 1925. Brophy helped buttress the union's hold in central Pennsylvania with an ambitious District 2 labor education program headed by Paul Fuller. Classes were run on labor history, public speaking, parliamentary procedure, and the economics of the coal industry. With his close ally, the Pennsylvania AFL president, James Maurer, Brophy supported local and national labor education efforts, including the Workers' Education Bureau of the AFL and the Brookwood Labor College. During three summers from 1924 to 1926, Brophy and Fuller organized eleven "Labor Chautauquas." An example was the gathering in 1925 in the union stronghold of Nanty Glo, where the program included seven evenings of state and national speakers, combined with vocal and instrumental music provided by local talent. National mineworker leaders such as Murray and Green, socialist leaders like Maurer and the fiery orator, Kate Richards O'Hare, as well as labor educators like Clint Golden, provided lectures and participated in workshops with lively discussion. Entertainment at a 1926 Chautauqua "included the Radcliffe Family which consisted of Mother Radcliffe, pianist, Father Radcliffe, violinist, and the 'Misses Mary and Virginia, singers, whistlers and dancers,' as well as 'the six-year-old Kovolchek twins of Sagamore in a boxing bout' and 'little 3-year-old Wolevine Elkins of Sagamore, soloist and Charleston dancer.'"[50]

The precipitous decline of the UMWA after the 1923 strike fueled internal opposition to the autocratic rule of John L. Lewis. Powers Hapgood, a young Harvard-educated radical, who Brophy described as "sincere, friendly, and courageous to the point of foolhardiness" had joined with Brophy in 1921 to help expose conditions in the non-union mines. They remained close allies throughout the strike, and later in 1926 when Brophy decided to challenge Lewis for the UMWA presidency. Brophy rejected Lewis's defensive strategy and autocratic practices. He saw himself as "the only person prominent in the Miners' Union who was both more interested in policy than personal conflicts, and uncommitted to one of the radical parties." He was confronted with the fact that the best organized anti-Lewis faction inside the union was the Communists. "The Communists worked hard, but for their own purposes, and could not be trusted from one day to the next. Besides, I had no use for their program, any more than they had for mine. They would "support" me to injure Lewis, and to get a chance to talk to miners who would otherwise ignore them, but they would cut my throat on a moment's notice if the "line" called for it." Brophy launched his campaign under the "Save the Union" banner, and Lewis responded with a brutally negative red-baiting campaign accusing Brophy of being "part of a Bolshevik plot to take over America." Despite an official count showing Lewis the winner by 170,000 to 60,000, Brophy very possibly was the winner in an honest count. Lewis won crushing pluralities in paper locals that had no working miners, and Brophy was able to document instances where the local tallies that heavily favored him were reversed for Lewis in the official tally. Brophy, who had to step down as district director to run for the presidency, found himself unemployed, with a wife and two small children, and his only work experience being as a miner or a union official, "neither experience…marketable."[51]

Phil Murray remained faithful or at least subservient to Lewis, and when dispatched to refute Brophy's charges of election fraud, spoke "more in sorrow than in anger to his 'old friend John Brophy.'" After Brophy's defeat, the Communists abandoned their strategy of boring from within the miners' union and convened a convention to form a separate organization, the National Miners Union. Brophy felt that "dual unionism played into the hands of the operators" and refused to endorse the effort, despite having been "expelled from the union by the international executive board, without notice and without trial." He respected the "incredibly hard working" Communists in the miners' union, but felt they were motivated less by devotion to the cause of labor than they were to the advancement of their party. "I had very little experience with Communists at that time…. I knew that my friend Maurer detested them, but not much else. I had had dealings with Socialists, but Socialists did not conceal their identity or their purposes. And, more important, men like Jim Maurer were immovable in their devotion to democracy, while the Communists would accept anything they could use for their purposes."[52]

The struggle for democracy both inside unions and at the workplace was confronted squarely by mineworker John Brophy. His appreciation for the need for labor education, so that workers could effectively organize vibrant and healthy organizations, was ahead of its time. His recognition of both the strengths and limitations of Communist organization among workers pinpointed an issue that would profoundly affect and ultimately divide the American labor movement over the next 25 years. Principled opposition to Communist Party organization, combined with a deep commitment to union democracy, labor education, and organizing the unorganized, made Brophy a lonely figure. His life personified the difficulties inherent in simultaneously opposing powerful capitalist economic organization and union bureaucracy, while also rejecting the Communist doctrine and party discipline that increasing numbers of labor activists were accepting as the only practical alternative to the power and destructiveness of capitalism.

The culmination of the mine wars of the 1920s in Western Pennsylvania was the 1927 strike of the 200,000 union miners of the Central Competitive Field that included the bituminous regions of Pennsylvania and Ohio. Begun on April 1, the strike attempted to defend the $7.50 a day standard set by the 1924 Jacksonville Agreement. Operators, under pressure from increased production in the non-union southern mines, demanded a 20 percent wage reduction. At the low end of the scale, Alabama miners only made $4.50 a day. While in 1920, Pennsylvania and Ohio had produced 60 percent of the nation's coal, by 1927, their share had dropped below 40 percent. A central battlefield in the strike was the Rossiter mine in Indiana County, northeast of Pittsburgh, near Punxatawny. The town was named for E. W. Rossiter, the treasurer of the New York Central Railroad, which owned the coal company. The conservative governor of Pennsylvania, John Fisher, had been a director and attorney for the coal company. He was a close personal friend of Judge Jonathan Langham, who issued several of the most sweeping anti-union injunctions in the history of the United States. Langham's injunction "forbade picketing, marching or gatherings for meetings or rallies. It prohibited the disbursement of union funds for use by striking miners. The order also forbade newspaper advertisements and other means of communication seeking to aid the cause of the strikers or urging miners to leave their jobs. Judge Langham's prohibition against singing hymns and holding church services on lots owned by the Magyar Presbyterian Church situated directly opposite the mouth of the mine was especially infuriating to the miners."[53]

In the midst of the strike in April 1927, Sacco and Vanzetti, accused of robbing a bank and killing a policeman in Massachusetts, were executed. A mass protest in the Allegheny Valley at the Acmetonia Grove turned violent. John Begovich remembered: "A couple of Italian guys came to get support for Sacco and Vanzetti. That was a famous trial. These Italian fellows were giving a speech and holding a big American flag. The police broke the flag. The supporters took the broken staff and fought back. I was scared. The State police came on mounted horseback and broke up the demonstration by shooting and using tear gas." According to newspaper accounts, as the 30 troopers moved on the crowd of 1,500 protestors, a woman pushed her way to the platform and cried: "We pay taxes, we can meet if we want to." Troopers rode their horses into the crowd scattering people in every direction. When two troopers moved on a small group of men: "A man reached into his pocket. A revolver flashed in the bright sunlight and three shots rang out. (Trooper) Downey gasped and crumpled to the ground." The state trooper died of his wounds, and despite an extensive search the shooter escaped.[54]

In October 1927, with winter approaching, the company began evicting miners and their families from their housing. The union responded by building barracks that were subdivided into twenty rooms, each measuring 10 feet by 20 feet. Eleven Protestant denominations joined Roman Catholic and Greek Orthodox parishes and the Jewish community in relief efforts. The Reverend James Cox of old Saint Patrick's Church in Pittsburgh's Strip District collected food and clothing for the miners, as did a Businessmen's Relief Committee from Pittsburgh. Unions organized support efforts. The Operating Engineers collected funds for the coal miners, calling the vicious wage cuts and the disregard for life in the coal fields "the toughest, grimmest fight for human rights since the World War period." In February 1928, the Interstate Commerce Committee of the United States Senate came to Indiana County to investigate conditions in the coalfields. Among the senators was Robert

Wagner of New York, who was appalled at the sweeping nature of the injunction, especially the prohibitions against assembly and free speech. "Had I not seen it myself...I would not have believed that in the United States there were large areas where civil government was supplanted by a system that can only be compared with ancient feudalism." Wagner would go on to co-sponsor the Norris-La Guardia Act of 1932 limiting the use of labor injunctions and introduced the National Labor Relations Act or "Wagner Act" in 1935, that established the recognized parameters of American labor relations for the next fifty years. [55]

By July 1928, the strike had been crushed, and the United Mine Workers membership had dropped to one quarter of its numbers in 1919. One consequence of the 1927-1928 strike was the large scale importation of black strikebreakers into the mining regions of Western Pennsylvania, especially in the coke regions controlled by the H. C. Frick company. Racial violence erupted in the "Black Valley" of the Kiskimenitas prompting Robert Vann of the *Pittsburgh Courier* to print warnings to Southern blacks to expect exploitation in non-union "death-traps." While the white miners were hardly immune from racist sentiments, the fact that the UMWA prohibited membership in the Ku Klux Klan (as well as the Communist Party), gave hope to black miners that some protection could be afforded them in union mines. Pittsburgh Coal, controlled by the Mellons, took the lead in union busting. It hired two hundred industrial police and mounted searchlights on gun towers at its mines. Radical miners responded with violence, and the Bethlehem mines reported 500 incidents involving guns or dynamite at its mines. While the miners' union had suffered a serious defeat, the UMWA leaders, Lewis, Phil Murray and Pat Fagan, had not capitulated, and their resistance paved the way for the union's resurgence in 1933-34. [56]

Out of the Depths

The coal miners of Western Pennsylvania, wages slashed, contracts negated, their union organization decimated by operator attacks and bitter internal divisions, also faced a steady decline in employment because of increased mechanization. While Pennsylvania bituminous coal production reached its historic peak production of 177 million tons in 1918, in the decade between 1919 when the state produced 147 million tons and 1929 when production nearly reached 142 million tons, employment in soft coal was reduced by more than 45,000 miners. The anti-union drive in coal was supplemented by the application of the principles of scientific management to the mines. The goal, as a mine superintendent remarked in 1923, was "to standardize every operation down to the minutest detail so that no responsibility will fall to the worker." As in steel and glass two generations earlier, expanded managerial control marched in tandem with technological advances. Electric drills, improved blasting powder, better ventilation and major advances in mine haulage were undermining the job control of the traditional miner. At the same time, an angry revolt was spreading inside the shrinking miners' union. The Communist-led National Miners Union became a significant force in Western Pennsylvania for several years prior to the election of Franklin D. Roosevelt and the resurgence of the UMWA. [57]

The nature of traditional mining practices meant that skilled miners worked in their own "rooms" without supervision, almost as an independent contractor. With control over the pace of production and largely beyond the reach of management, the miner enjoyed "the miner's freedom," a significant degree of autonomy. So while the companies might control the miner's above ground community through armed guards, spies, company housing and stores, management still relied on the skill and initiative of the miner to produce coal. Indeed, since economic control over the miner's housing and purchases provided a significant amount of the operator's revenue, the need to keep a large number of families in economic dependency militated against the implementation of new technology that reduced the number of miners and depressed the demand for housing and retail purchases. Conversely, the resistance of miners to managerial control of their lives both below and above ground, plus the significant gains in wages that accompanied the extension of unionization during and immediately after World War I, pushed employers toward mechanization.[58]

The key technological advance in coal mining was the loading machine. Many varieties and models were tried. The Mellons' Pittsburgh Coal Company, the nation's largest, set aside its Somers #2 mine as a testing site for various innovative mining machines. All the loaders had some sort of mechanism at the front to gather the coal, with a conveyor connected to a hopper car that could itself be unloaded onto a continuous belt conveyor system to move the coal out of the mine. It was at the Mellon's test mine that a consulting mining engineer, Joseph Joy, developed what became known as the Joy Loader, which established itself as the industry standard. With his headquarters in Franklin, Pennsylvania, north of Pittsburgh, Joy "was more responsible for the complete mechanization of coal mines than any other engineer in the United States." While many miners felt directly threatened by mechanization, the miners' union historically embraced technological improvements while striving for a voice in their implementation. While bituminous fatalities reached their second worst level at 3.8 deaths per 1,000 miners in 1929 (the record of 4.4 per thousand was set in 1907, the worst year for mining fatalities in U.S. history), the death rate subsequently dropped dramatically from a combination of unionization and mechanization, reaching a ratio of 1.03 per 1,000 in 1938.[59]

Depression and the abrupt slowing of economic activity caused a steep drop in Pennsylvania coal production from 1929's 142 million tons to 74 million tons in 1932. Adding to the general misery caused by unemployment was the bitter and brutal struggle that erupted inside the ranks of the union miners themselves. Following the defeat of John Brophy and his Save the Union movement, radical miners based in the Communist Party founded a rival organization to the UMWA, the National Miners Union (NMU). The NMU was the first dual union set up by the communists, a step strongly opposed by William Z. Foster, the party's best known leader, who believed in working within the existing unions of the American Federation of Labor. Due to politics internal to Russia and between Russia and other communist parties, Stalin, who was consolidating his own dictatorial power, embraced the left-separatist option, which subsequently gained ascendancy inside the American party. The NMU had little organizational presence in the non-union fields, but proved to be a bitterly divisive force in the remaining union strongholds.[60]

The National Miners Union was literally born in blood on the streets of Pittsburgh. Its founding convention was scheduled to open September 9, 1928, at the Labor Lyceum on Miller Street in the Hill District. The Labor Lyceum, built in 1916 by the Hill District branch of the Allegheny County Socialist Party, carried a seal carved in its stone façade "Workers of the World Unite!" Predominately a center for Jewish trade unionists, it was the site for the first meeting of the Pittsburgh American Civil Liberties Union in early 1920, not long after the Palmer Raids. The NMU claimed that more than six hundred delegates were to gather at 9 a.m. on a Sunday morning, but they were met by an estimated 1,000 UMWA loyalists. Fighting began around 8 a.m. with some delegates barricaded in the Labor Lyceum hall. The Pittsburgh Police arrived late and allegedly directly aided the UMWA supporters. While the ACLU supported the dissident miners' right to assemble, the defense of arrested individuals was undertaken by the Communist Party's International Labor Defense organization and local activist attorney Henry Ellenbogen. A delegation of local liberal clergy, lawyers, doctors and professors organized by Professor William Nunn of the University of Pittsburgh demanded that the convention be allowed to meet and have police protection. Police raids were conducted however on various locations where dissident miners were staying, and over one hundred of them were detained for varying lengths of time. The convention was reconvened the following day in the friendlier confines of East Pittsburgh, and the organization was officially launched.[61]

In 1931, the Pittsburgh region became a major battlefield between the rival miner organizations. In June, the NMU called a strike that quickly turned violent. On June 8, serious rioting near Pittsburgh resulted in the death of two miners and a state trooper. At Ellsworth, down the Ohio, a marching column of strikers battled Coal and Iron Police who met them behind barricades. On June 13, the Pittsburgh Terminal Company, the state's second largest coal company, signed an agreement with the UMWA to forestall the advance of the radical NMU. By the end of the month, Pittsburgh Terminal Coal reported 90 percent of the miners had returned to work under the UMWA terms. On June 16, a sweeping injunction was issued forbidding the NMU to picket or gather at the Consolidated Coal Company mine at Wildwood in Washington County. Seven thousand miners protested the injunction in front of the county courthouse; then, on June 21, an armed battle erupted in Wildwood where deputies killed one and injured twelve. Radical miners had gathered from as far away as Harmarville in the Allegheny Valley. Theresa Orzechowski Molchan remembered: "I know how mean companies were. I lived through it. Lots of people were hurt. Trucks came to support the strike, they picked up miners to go to Wildwood on a picket line. The state police and local police laid-in-waiting – they had machine guns, too. They wounded many." On June 27, 2,000 striking NMU miners and families gathered in Arnold for the funeral of Mike Phiapovich, "who was killed by deputy sheriffs and coal and iron policemen in an outbreak of shooting following the throwing of a rotten egg by a small boy at a strikebreaker." On June 29 a riot broke out between the two union factions in Canonsburg where more than one hundred people were injured at a meeting where Murray and Fagan spoke and were pelted with rocks. Late that evening, two men accosted UMWA leader Pat Fagan, who was sitting smoking his pipe on his porch in Brookline. One of the men pulled a gun. Fagan wrestled him to the ground and in the struggle shot and killed the man with his own weapon before the other man fled. Fagan was charged, but acquitted. [62]

On June 30, a massive police presence was mustered to meet a Hunger March of miners that the NMU predicted would assemble 50,000 protesters. Newspapers estimated that about 8,000 miners, families and sympathizers marched from West Park on the North Side over the Manchester Bridge, along the fringe of the Golden Triangle to the Sixth Street Bridge and then back to the start. While contingents of radical miners walked all the way from McKeesport and New Kensington to take part in the march, Ironworkers Local 3 settled a four-week strike that secured them a five-day week at $1.25 an hour at such construction sites as Mellon Institute, the Gulf Building and the Arsenal trade school. While Pennsylvania Senator David Reed, speaking that day to a gathering of Republican women in Beaver County, compared the travails of President Hoover to those of Abraham Lincoln, the *Post-Gazette* described the miners' march in temperatures that reached into the nineties. "Under a pitiless sun which streaked the faces and bodies of all with perspiration, past solid phalanxes of police at street intersections, the marchers cheered, sang and shouted their grievances at the thousands of curious bystanders who gathered to see what striking miners looked like."[63]

On its editorial page, the generally pro-business *Post-Gazette* commented on:
"…the tragedy in the outbreak of industrial warfare in the bituminous coal industry.

On the one hand are the sorely tried miners, willing to work but unable to make a decent living for their families, driven almost to desperation by the ills of a sick industry....On the other hand are harassed and discouraged operators, losing money and markets through cut-throat competition, just about ready to close up the mines and quit the struggle, but reluctant to face the facts of the situation and stumbling along without effective leadership. The one hope of finding a way out of the existing morass of bankruptcy, hunger and ruin is cooperation and recognition of mutual interests."[64]

By the winter of 1932-33, the coal industry was in a state of complete demoralization. Some insight into the terrible poverty and bitter strife that characterized the early years of the Great Depression can be gleaned from an extraordinary account written by Lauren Gilfillan who graduated from Smith College in 1931. Unable to find a job, she went into a mining town southwest of Pittsburgh to write a book about her experiences. The town she chose was probably Avella, called Avalonia in her book, *I Went to Pit College*. She hired a driver who dropped her at night with bag and typewriter in hand on the edge of town where she appealed to a local family for lodging. She had accidentally stumbled on a stronghold of the National Miners Union, and she was soon walking picket lines, attending strike meetings, and accompanying a group of Young Communist League activists and ragged children to beg on the streets of Pittsburgh for money to support the miners' struggle. At first she was welcomed and befriended by a series of absolutely destitute families, but she drew the suspicion of the Communist leadership, who denounced her as a capitalist spy and agitated the rank-and-file against her. A young Slovak miner with literary ambitions became deeply attracted to her. His refusal to denounce her got him expelled from his position as a leader in the Young Communist League.[65]

The book describes scenes of the most abject poverty verging on starvation. At one house where she stayed a night, she discovers that a young girl who had been with her on the begging excursion to Pittsburgh had just died from illness brought on by privation. The husband of the eldest daughter had been arrested for strike activity, and his wife had composed a letter to him in jail, but could not afford a stamp. They offered Gilfillan their only bed. "We put the children to bed early. If they sleep a lot they don't go hungry." They had traded their stove for a baby cradle, so their breakfast consisted of cold black coffee and a few cold cooked potatoes. Ever the reporter, she managed to convince a young miner to smuggle her into the mine. When she learned that his brother was crushed by a mine car, she asked him about accidents.

Once I was working at the entry six feet in the entry six feet away from this fella and he got hit by a rock all of a sudden. Great big rock fell on him, bendin' his head beneath his knees, slow-like. Smashed him to death. He laid there unconscious for a while and the blood spurted out of his ears. Jesus! I'll never forget it."...You can git killed in many ways. Choke dust gits in with the air when you are firing a shot, and there is a mine explosion. The roof can cave in. You can get electrocuted. Maybe there is a premature shot. When there is a big fall, the air will go up the entry sixty miles an hour knockin' down everything. Maybe you're walking up the main entry and you get knocked down by a motor and killed. If the motor and cars jump the track you ain't got a chance....Minin' wasn't such a bad job - afore the strike. It gets you. A young fella starts workin' when he is fifteen, 'n' most likely he's a miner all his life and likes it, and his kids is miners most likely. You don't often quit minin' fer good... It gets you where you live, the smell of coal or something….It's the hardest work there is, but it gets in your blood 'n' you ain't satisfied with nothin' else. You ain't satisfied with minin' either, and there you are.[66]

As her day underground wore on, eight hours passed, and her companion still had four cars to load. The pay for a ton of coal was seventy-seven cents "in good times," but after the strike of 1922, it was cut to forty cents, and her companion says: "now it's twenty-six, 'n' what can you do?" Her head splitting from the acrid smoke of dynamite, fearing the murky figures in narrow black tunnels, breathing the air "chill, damp and stuffy – the stiffness of palpable darkness," she decided to walk out alone.

My knees trembling with trepidation, I edged forward, very slowly at first, pushing at the darkness with my hands, avoiding inky pools into which my pit lamp cast a dull unpleasant glow at my feet, keeping between the two railroad tracks running in front of my trudging boots, shuddering away from the deadly wires threading the coaly wall above my head, listening fearfully for the buzz of rails, peering constantly behind me for an oncoming light. I was sick of this world, unknown, bewildering, foreign. The smell of coal and sulphur had numbed my weary wits….Now I stood upright at the junction of the left entry and the main entry. A red light shone there, and under it a man – Negro or white I could not tell in the obscurity – holding a bucket between his knees and devouring a sandwich held in pitchy hands. He looked at me, his eyes like twin white moths in his black face, but he said nothing and continued to eat….Now I was facing down the main entry, the main thoroughfare of the mine. An interminable black corridor stopped with darkness. The long line of tracks narrowing ever so gradually to a needle-like V. Beyond the V, nothing….On and on over the tracks, one foot scrapping after the other. I seemed to get nowhere. Timelessness. Walking aimlessly in an endless nightmare. Buzz! Zing! I looked frantically behind me. A light was floating back there in the black. The sound grew rapidly louder. I leaped to the outside of the track, my head missing the singing wire. I began to run, desperately, scraping my fingers against the rough unyielding wall of coal. My arm dropped through the solid surface into a black pocket. A manhole! I fell into it panting. My haven of safety….The motor flashed by; the cars slid past. The wire above shot blue sparks. When it was gone, I stepped again between the tracks. There before my eyes, far away as at the little end of a telescope, I saw a tiny square of light.[67]

As Gilfillan reached the mouth of the drift mine, she began to run toward the daylight. She felt the sunlight as a tangible substance, "a holy oil anointing me, a yellow water flowing over my body."

I stood alone on the tracks in front of the pit mouth, breathing in the air in gulps, looking at the green trees and the grass, and the gloriously wide blue sky. I dodged away from the black tipple, a huge black skeleton on which crawled black figures and coal cars ascending and descending. I ran away from the uproar of grinding machinery and falling coal. As I turned toward the woods, I met several men. None of them gave me a second glance….I climbed the hillside into the woods. I lay down in a sunny spot in the tall grass about me. I buried my nose in the warm fragrant earth. I fell asleep. [68]

Crash and Depression

Following Hoover's reelection in 1928, the stock market soared. While Secretary of the Treasury Mellon was mildly concerned about a possible market correction and attempted to slow the speculative frenzy, he was reluctant to support a rise in the low interest rates that were feeding the gambling instincts of an increasingly broader segment of the population. In September, the market began to fluctuate wildly and then in late October was struck by a wave of liquidation. On October 29, sixteen million shares were sold, a record that stood for 39 years. Approximately a third of the value of the nation's stocks held on Labor Day evaporated by Thanksgiving. The speculators and small investors who had jumped on for the ascent were wiped out in the subsequent crash. The Mellon family itself, however, was secure behind the bank's huge cash reserves and privately held crown jewels like Gulf, Alcoa, Koppers, and Carborundum that were not publicly traded. The great tidal wave of failures passed over their enterprises, but left them intact. The only company they unloaded during the depression was Standard Steel Car, their Butler based rival to McKees Rocks' Pressed Steel Car, which they sold to Pullman Standard. [69]

Initially the crash only seemed to affect the 3 percent of Americans who owned stock; however, conditions steadily worsened on European markets. Treasury Secretary Mellon remained upbeat, seeing the crash as a purification, similar to the view his father Judge Mellon had of the depression of the 1870s, a purgative needed to cleanse the economy of its excesses. He also finally achieved his goal of getting Treasury out of Prohibition and moving that headache to the Justice Department. With pressure for federal employment measures increasing, Mellon oversaw the construction of the Federal Triangle, "the greatest piece of neoclassical construction the world had ever seen," that included the Departments of Justice, Labor, Post Office, National Archives, and the Interstate Commerce Commission. Their cold massive facades evoked a power-of-the-state message not unlike edifices constructed by Mussolini, Stalin and Hitler in the same era. 1930 brought a steep decline in production, especially in steel and auto. Four million workers were unemployed by the November elections, when the Republicans lost control of both houses of Congress. [70]

By 1931, Andrew W. Mellon was increasingly under attack for incompetence and hard-heartedness. His coldness and political insensitivity was evident in his stubborn opposition to the early release of promised bonuses to the veterans of World War I. As late as May 1931, he remained unmoved by the worsening situation. "Conditions today are neither so critical nor so unprecedented as to justify a lack of faith in our capacity to deal with them in our accustomed way." This was "no time to undertake drastic experiments which may conceivably result in the breaking down the standard of living to which we have become accustomed." He seemed oblivious that his own standard of living was qualitatively different and much more secure than that of the majority of his fellow citizens. In 1930, Andrew Mellon's wealth had reached its zenith. In a career noted for acquisitions and investment, not spending or giving, he began to do both. He built buildings with government money in Washington and in Pittsburgh, where a grandiose federal building was constructed on Grant Street. He also accelerated his purchases of portrait art, acquiring masterpieces by Rembrandt, Franz Hals and Raphael. His brother and operations manager R.B. constructed the monumental East Liberty Presbyterian Church, with no assistance from Andrew, of whom it was said that the only time he entered the sanctuary was at the time of his funeral. [71]

Mounting anti-Mellon sentiment probably was also a factor in his stepped-up donations to the University of Pittsburgh and especially Mellon Institute. He began distributing large chunks of his fortune to his children, Ailsa and Paul, as well as to his former wife Nora, with whom he reconciled. Perhaps sensing the growing fragility of his earthly empire, he wrote her: "The old love was in my heart even while I was obtuse and blind, and it makes me heartsick to think of you all this time suffering so sadly alone." Disappointingly for him, his son Paul showed little interest in the management of the great Mellon Bank and its extensive tentacles, preferring his studies at Cambridge and fox-hunting with the British gentry. One mechanism that Andrew used to reduce potentially staggering tax liabilities as a Democratic majority swept into office with Franklin Roosevelt in 1932 was the donation of his extensive art collection to the National Gallery. The depression and accompanying social crisis in Europe was putting great numbers of famous paintings on the market at vastly reduced prices. A.W.'s biggest haul of old masters came from the Hermitage Museum in Leningrad, where Stalin willingly unloaded Czarist treasures for hard cash to support industrialization and war preparation efforts. It was in the management of the National Gallery that son Paul would find his niche in the Mellon world order.[72]

The winter of 1930-31 was harsh and economic conditions worsened. By early 1931, 28 percent of Allegheny County workers were unemployed. The Mellons began to lose their grip on state politics. Their bitter enemy, Gifford Pinchot, returned to the governorship. They were unsuccessful in their attempt to oust the unpopular Republican Charles Kline from the mayor's office. While Pennsylvania's Republicans still outnumbered Democrats 4 to 1 in 1930, the political tide was shifting dramatically. Faced with mounting poverty and anger in the city that they once dominated, Andrew ignored local appeals and donated the bulk of his fabulous collection of paintings to Washington D.C, not to Pittsburgh, where most of the wealth represented in those paintings had been wrung out of generations of the region's miners and mill workers. A mounting political liability for President Hoover, Andrew left the Treasury for a gilded exile as U.S. Ambassador to the Court of St. James in England. While there, he would make his final significant contribution to the family wealth by obtaining highly lucrative oil concessions for Gulf Oil in a little known Arab sheikdom at the end of the Persian Gulf named Kuwait.[73]

Kuwait became a British Protectorate after the collapse of Ottoman rule during World War I. British Petroleum already had extensive holdings in Iraq, Iran and Saudi Arabia, and it was becoming increasingly clear that the Middle East would become the center of global oil production. In November 1931, while A.W. was still the Treasury Secretary, he arranged for a meeting between the Secretary of State and representatives of Gulf Oil, who lobbied for vigorous governmental pressure on the British to open opportunities for American oil interests in the Arab states. The British, French and other European nations were highly susceptible to American pressure since deepening economic depression made it increasingly difficult for them to meet their massive World War I debt payments to the U.S. Treasury that Secretary Mellon had steadfastly resisted forgiving. Mellon pressed hard and without embarrassment, urging "fairness" to American oil interests, in this case those of his own company. A State Department memo of December 27, 1932, noted that: "the ambassador is not at all bashful pressing this matter himself." Gulf and British Petroleum produced a deal, and the concessions obtained by Gulf in Kuwait became the company's principal source of crude oil.[74]

Mellon remained ambassador to England until the March 1933 inauguration of Franklin D. Roosevelt. On his seventy-eighth birthday, his ship docked in New York City, where he boarded a train for Pittsburgh. There was a stirring in American political life caused by capital's calamitous crash, such that even someone as exquisitely shielded from the realities of working-class life and the worldwide economic trauma as Andrew Mellon could sense the radical nature of the impending storm. Speaking to an audience of Americans before he left England, he said: "…we who are left over from the last century continue to look on the last decade as merely a prolongation of all that has gone before. We insist upon trying to make life flow in the same channels as before the war, whereas the years since the war ended are in reality the beginning of a new era, not the end of an old."[75]

Voices from the Street

As the Depression deepened, causing a sharp drop in both production and consumption, assurances from national figures like Secretary Mellon and President Hoover that the economy was "fundamentally sound" and would soon rebound sounded increasingly hollow to the swelling ranks of the unemployed, and the increasing numbers of skilled and white collar workers reduced to two or three-day work weeks. By November of 1932, the price of U.S. Steel and General Motors stocks, the two leading industrial indicators of the day, declined to a mere eight percent of their record highs in 1929. "Hoovervilles" of the homeless grew up along railroad tracks and under bridges. Homeless women slept in city parks while able-bodied men sold apples and pencils, or shined shoes along downtown streets. An extensive shanty town sprouted around St. Patrick's Church in the produce district of the "Strip" that closely bordered the business district stretching out between the Pennsylvania Railroad yards and the Allegheny River. Many hundreds of men formed up daily for a chance at a hard day's work loading and unloading wagons, trucks and railcars. Work for the professional middle class was contracting, and recent college graduates were unsuccessfully searching for work. At Duquesne University, where the young Charles Owen Rice was beginning what would become a seventy-year journalistic career writing for the student newspaper, many of his fellow students struggled mightily to stay in school since there were few other alternatives.

> In Duquesne University, Pittsburgh, one student is an undertaker's helper, one a railroad fireman, one a laborer in a steel mill, one cuts granite tombstones and another sells newspapers. A student who has become an expert on glass works a regular eight-hour shift in a glass factory 40 miles from Pittsburgh and "commutes" to take a full-time course at Duquesne….An enterprising student buys old text-books from sophomores and sells them to freshmen. An athletic young man is serving as first aid instructor for a coal company. One Duquesne student is reputed to hold 27 odd jobs on the campus and in the city. Among other things, he is editor-in-chief of the school newspaper and official announcer at the major league baseball games at Forbes Field.[76]

One of the characteristics of the labor and political scene in Pittsburgh was the extent to which Catholic activists working on behalf of workers and the unemployed tended to blunt the appeal of Communism for the growing underclass. The depression struck just as the church was becoming a major political and social force in Western Pennsylvania. By 1940, the Catholic Diocese of Pittsburgh was the seventh largest in America, and its 322 parishes served the needs of 622,000 Catholics. Furthermore while older Catholic communities like the Germans and especially the Irish remained powerful in the hierarchy, the Catholic working class of the mines and mills was heavily Slovak, Croatian, Polish and Italian. With the influx of large numbers of Greeks, Serbians and Ukrainians, Pittsburgh, also, became the American center of the Orthodox Church. Carpatho-Rusyns constituted several large Byzantine or Greek Catholic congregations. Pittsburgh's corporate leadership, on the other hand, was overwhelmingly Protestant. Key business and social organizations like the powerful Duquesne Club and the Masonic orders excluded Catholics, Orthodox, Jews, blacks and women alike. At many area companies, a Masonic ring was required to rise above the level of a foreman prior to World War II.[77] While the Jewish population maintained a slow but steady migration out of the Hill District into the middle-class enclave of Squirrel Hill, a network of Jewish merchants spread throughout the mining and mill towns providing a welcome alternative to the company stores. The American electorate expanded by forty percent from 1920 to 1936, with second generation immigrants providing the bulk of the growth. In Allegheny County, with its ballooning population of second generation ethnic voters, the growth of the electorate was even more spectacular; it increased 120 percent between 1924 and 1936. As an example, in 1930 in Pittsburgh's Polish Hill, 30 percent of the ward voted Democrat, with 11 percent voting Republican, but nearly 60 percent did not or could not vote. By 1940, over 60 percent of those eligible voted Democratic, while only 27.5 percent did not vote.[78]

As economic conditions worsened, Catholic, Protestant and Jewish religious organizations increasingly became centers of relief and assistance to the unemployed. Father James Cox, born in predominately Irish Lawrenceville in 1886, became a renowned champion of the downtrodden and Pittsburgh's first famous "labor priest." Cox worked his way as a steelworker and taxi cab agent through Duquesne University, then on to St. Vincent's Seminary in Latrobe, and was ordained a priest in 1911. He was assigned as a chaplain to a hospital on the Western Front during World War I, and upon his return, he obtained a masters' degree in economics at the University of Pittsburgh. He was assigned to Old St. Patrick's Church, a small, poor parish that had a certain stature as the oldest in the city. He liked to recall that when he was assigned to St Patrick's, he was the youngest pastor of the oldest parish in the diocese. He began to broadcast a mass every day at noon over radio station WJAS in 1925, a practice that continued until his death in 1951. He established the gardens surrounding the church as an "oasis of beauty" in the hard-working Strip with the stations of the cross and a replica of the grotto at Lourdes. Deeply devoted to Mary, the mother of Jesus, he led many pilgrimages to Lourdes in France. His fine-voiced homilies also included passionate demands for social justice that made him a political force in Pittsburgh. He was an advocate for the taxi cab drivers during several violent strikes in the twenties and early thirties. He became the protector and provider of food, fuel and clothing for an expansive shanty town where he served an estimated two million meals from 1930-1934.[79]

While Cox served as a vice-chair of Pittsburgh's ACLU chapter and protested Pitt Chancellor Bowman's suppression of leftwing activists, he became increasingly concerned about the Communist Party's organization of Unemployed Councils, which were very active in Chicago and Pittsburgh. While he supported the Communists' civil liberties, he deeply opposed their atheism and link to Soviet Russia. Communist front organizations were not interested in providing direct assistance to the unemployed as was Cox. They focused on staging confrontations over housing evictions and organizing angry mass demonstrations against the failures of local and national government. They were most interested in attracting converts to their revolutionary aims. On March 6, 1930, on a day when Cox's taxi men were striking the Yellow, Green and Checker cab companies, and federal agents were being stoned by neighbors as they seized $7,000 worth of wine from the Italian Club in the shadow of the Bloomfield Bridge, the Communists staged their largest unemployed demonstration in Pittsburgh. Starting in front of the Pennsylvania Railroad station, more than 5,000 men, carrying banners that said "Fools Starve, Men Fight," marched onto Grant Street toward the City-County Building, which "presented the appearance of a besieged fortress with firemen on guard before the locked doors of the Grant Street side and police and mounted policemen standing by with tear gas, maces and riot sticks." Aggressive police action broke up the march on Grant Street.[80]

In December of 1931, the Communists staged a much ballyhooed march on Washington that failed to generate the mass participation expected. A bit more than fifteen hundred marchers rode into Washington on trucks singing the *Internationale* and were greeted by a nearly equal number of District police, who under the restrained command of General Pelham Glassford, kept the protestor's actions contained without arrests or violence. In response, Cox decided to organize his own march on Washington, calling his movement "The Commonweal of Christ." He found an ally in Henry Ellenbogen, Jewish graduate of Duquesne University and close political associate of David Lawrence, the Democratic Party chair of Allegheny County. Surprising nearly everyone, on January 5, Cox assembled an estimated 45,000 men from the adjoining slums and stricken mill towns to join his crusade or to see it off. Six hundred trucks and cars were there to carry the marchers – many of whom were unable to find space for the trip. By the time the caravan reached Johnstown, an observer counted nine hundred seventy-eight trucks and cars. Weapons, women and alcohol were not allowed on the trip.[81] One witness, Elmer Cope, a Protestant ironworker who became a Socialist Party unemployed organizer, came to believe that Cox was sincere and "has the workers truly at heart."

> I went down to see the gang off thinking that only a small crowd would be there. I was completely stunned when I saw that milling mob, lining Penn Avenue for twelve solid squares, and clamoring for a way to get to Washington. When I left home I had no intention of doing more than seeing the gang off, but the turn-out was so intriguing that I went to Wilkinsburg, then to Johnstown, and later Harrisburg and Washington....All along the road were thousands of jobless workers walking toward Washington hoping that trucks and cars would pick them up. One group of men arrived at Blairsville, about twenty-five miles from Pittsburgh, on foot and, giving up all hope of getting rides on trucks, boarded freight trains. When this gang reached Washington two days later they had increased in number to 600 strong.[82]

Six thousand men left Pittsburgh; twenty thousand marched through Johnstown, Governor Pinchot greeted Cox effusively. "Command me! Whatever you want me to do I will do; you are the master of ceremonies." As Cox passed through the Gettysburg battlefield that evening, he reflected on the "monument –dotted farm lands...peopled by the specters of an army that fought to free civilization from the curse of poverty and unemployment; a battle that will end in final victory when every man has a job that will permit him not only to exist, but enjoy a real American standard of living." On January 7, 1932, the 12,000 man "army" swept into Washington carrying American flags and were given a respectful hearing by official Washington. Cox presented petitions personally to President Hoover and to Congress calling for public works, a federal relief program for the needy, and a soak-the-rich tax plan. According to *Time* magazine, Andrew Mellon paid the expenses for 276 stragglers to return to Pittsburgh. On January 16, following his triumphal return to Pittsburgh, Cox held a massive rally of nearly 60,000 supporters in Pitt Stadium voicing the same demands.[83]

For the Communists, Cox was a fascist in the mold of a Mussolini. Cox gave a certain credence to such characterizations with his organization of the Blue Shirts, a uniformed organization that for a while claimed several hundred thousand adherents. In June of 1932, Cox, as a former army chaplain, joined the World War I Bonus Army marchers in Washington, where he presented their petition to Vice-President Charles Curtis. The jobless veterans of World War I flocked from all over the country to demand that the bonus that they were promised in 1919 be redeemed before the twenty-year maturation date, since their need was urgent and immediate. They carried signs that read: "Cheered in '17, Jeered in '32." Over twenty thousand veterans set themselves up in encampments around the city and were determined to stay until the bonus was paid. While the House passed the requested funds, the Senate defeated the measure. Tension began to build in the city, and conditions in the camps deteriorated. On July 28, as police tried to clear veterans who were occupying an abandoned armory, fights broke out and Hoover ordered the army to clear the city. In a display of force out of all proportion to the threat, cavalry, infantry, a mounted machine gun squadron and six tanks, commanded by General Douglas MacArthur, with Dwight Eisenhower and George Patton in supporting roles, moved on the veterans' encampments. The operation was delayed an hour so that MacArthur could don a "tunic, service stripes, sharpshooter medal and English whipcord breeches." Thousands of veterans with their wives and children fled the city virtually without resistance. Two veterans were killed; a couple of dozen people were injured, including an eleven-week baby who died from injuries; an eight year-old boy was partially blinded; and more than a thousand veterans were gassed.[84]

This ignoble event proved to be the most unpopular single action of Hoover's presidency. Father Cox wired Hoover: "Told you last January there would be riots and probably revolution because of your attitude toward the unemployed...you are treading on dangerous grounds." In August 1932, Cox announced his candidacy for President on the Jobless Party ticket. In October, however, after Roosevelt attacked laissez-faire capitalism and quoted Pius XI's encyclical, *Reconstructing the Social Order,* Cox endorsed Democrat Franklin D. Roosevelt declaring: "This is not only an economic crisis, it is a human crisis. The old system is broken down. A new order must come."[85]

The Rise of Davey and the Democrats

David L. Lawrence was the most successful politician in the history of Pittsburgh. He ended more than seventy years of Republican domination of the city by building a powerful and inclusive political machine while making a rare transition from an effective urban boss to a sophisticated modern political leader. On June 18, 1889, Davey Lawrence, the fourth and youngest child of Irish parents, with roots in Galway and Belfast, was born in the Point District community that had become a stronghold of Irish laborers in the years following the Irish potato famine of 1845-1850. The Point had deteriorated into a jumble of old houses, tenements, warehouses, retail and machine shops, alongside the Exposition, Mechanics and Symphony Halls. The ill-fated Wabash Railroad built a constricted terminal on the Monongahela side of the district just after the turn of the century. The Lawrence family lived above their shoe repair shop, two blocks from the Blockhouse, the only remaining relic of Fort Pitt and the French and Indian War. David's devoutly Catholic mother, Catherine, ran the household with an iron hand and inculcated in her son a lifelong habit of daily Mass, a spirit of compromise and a sense of obligation toward helping those less fortunate. "She emphasized employment for her children over education and expected them to lead hard-working, moral, blue-collar lives."[86]

Dave Lawrence was an apprentice politician from the age of nine, when he got a part time job as helper for the First Ward alderman, running errands, passing leaflets and readying halls for political functions. The Lawrence family were active Democrats in terms of state and national elections, but operated in the city essentially as a sub-branch of the powerful Flinn-Magee Republican machine. His political mentor was William J. Brennan, a former machinist at J&L who worked his way through school to become a lawyer. Brennan, who defended steelworkers arrested during the 1892

Homestead steel strike, became the chairman of the Allegheny County Democratic Party in 1901. Lawrence went to work for him in 1903 at the age of fourteen. They remained lifetime associates who shared religion, ethnic and class origins, as well as education by the formidable Sisters of Mercy. Brennan's ability to deal successfully with wealthy Republicans, while acting as a spokesman for organized labor, was a skill that Lawrence came to share. Lawrence's ties to labor came from his father and especially his two brothers who were officers in the carpenters and plumbers union locals. Like Brennan, Lawrence, who always wore a suit and tie, developed a very formal political style that was practical rather than ideological. His experience running a small insurance business made him a fiscal conservative. His fundamental loyalties were personal, and he expected personal loyalty in return. Early friends who remained influential in his political career included Art Rooney, with whom he shared a love of horse racing, boxing, baseball, and of course football, and Jimmy Kirk, an Irish Catholic youngster from the Point who Lawrence hired as his stenographer and who became his closest personal friend and confidante. Critical to his career was his close relation to Brennan's successor as Allegheny County Democratic chairman, Joe Guffey, who picked Lawrence to succeed him when he advanced to the National Democratic Committee. Another more problematic ally was Jimmy Coyne, the Republican boss of Allegheny County in the 1920s, who began as a superintendent for the Booth-Flinn Construction Company and became the owner of a popular Oakland bar. They remained friends despite Coyne's manifest corruption and the shifting sands of political fortune.[87]

In 1924, Lawrence, supporting the presidential candidacy of Al Smith, attended his first national political convention, a chaotic affair that lasted 17 days and required 103 ballots to select John W. Davis, a New York lawyer, as the Democratic nominee. The election was a disaster for the Democrats and strengthened Lawrence's commitment to Al Smith in 1928. While Hoover defeated Smith in that election, Smith's local vote was the best showing for a Democrat in many years, as he won a third of the county's boroughs and townships, and fourteen of the city's wards, only losing the city by 8,000 votes. Still, many thought Lawrence's first decade as Democratic chairman a dismal failure, and there were calls from within the party for his resignation. Lawrence, however, was beginning to build a grassroots organization by integrating the blue-collar, ethnic and Catholic voters at the committee level. Smith won decisively in the Irish and German North Side, the Eastern European South Side, Polish Hill, Lawrenceville, and the Point. The national results, however, convinced Lawrence that a Catholic candidate could not win at the national level, a conviction that he would maintain all the way up to the nomination of John F. Kennedy in 1960. In 1931, this conviction led Lawrence and Guffey to move away from Smith, who they both greatly admired, toward the candidacy of Franklin D. Roosevelt.[88]

While the Republican Party was imploding and the base of the Democratic Party growing stronger, Lawrence personally suffered his most humiliating political defeat in 1931. Preferring to remain behind the scenes, he reluctantly agreed to become Democratic candidate for County Commissioner. The Republicans were deeply split between the corrupt old guard of James Coyne and Mayor Charles Kline, and Republican reformers led by Charles "Buck" McGovern, tracker of the infamous Biddle boys. Lawrence's longtime business partnership and political understanding with Coyne led reform Democrats to abandon and newspapers to ignore him. Traditional machine voter fraud was rife. The *Pittsburgh Press* printed photos of abandoned lots and billboard locations where registered voters allegedly lived. On August 30, the *Press* charged that registrants in the upcoming primary outnumbered the adult population of the city by 11,000 votes. Mayor Kline meanwhile was indicted on forty-six charges of malfeasance in office and was widely ridiculed for an expensive Persian rug that he purchased for the Mayor's office, at a time when a third of the city's workers were without employment. While William Mansfield, the Republican machine candidate, got the most votes, independents McGovern and Joe Barr took the other two commissioner's seats, breaking the machine's control of patronage. Lawrence, tarred by charges that Coyne and Kline were secretly backing him to block the reformers, came in fourth place. After the election Mayor Kline was convicted and received a prison term, though he died of a stroke before serving any time in jail.[89]

At the 1932 Democratic National Convention, Lawrence and Guffey helped Franklin Roosevelt to victory with 55 delegate votes through four ballots, more than any other state. In the campaign, Lawrence focused his efforts on strengthening the Democratic organization in the blue-collar wards and mill towns, but he also made an extremely important overture to Robert Vann, the influential editor of the nationally distributed *Pittsburgh Courier*. Vann had faithfully supported three Republican presidents, but had little to show for his efforts in terms of concrete gains for blacks. In March of 1932, at the urging of Guffey and Lawrence, Roosevelt invited Vann to Hyde Park to discuss a role for Vann in a future Roosevelt administration. Vann responded by forming a Black Democratic Club in Allegheny County and turned his newspaper into a powerful organ of support for the Democratic presidential candidate. In a speech that was widely circulated in the press and as a pamphlet, Vann charged that "the Republican Party under Harding absolutely deserted us. The Republican Party under Coolidge was a lifeless, voiceless thing. The Republican Party under Mr. Hoover has been the saddest failure known to political history....It is a mistaken idea that the Negro must wait until the party selects him. The only true political philosophy dictates that the Negro must select his party and not wait to be selected....I see millions of Negroes turning the picture of Lincoln to the wall. This year I see Negroes voting a Democratic ticket....I for one shall join the ranks of this new army of fearless, courageous, patriotic Negroes."[90]

Lawrence's outreach to the black community reflected his vision of a multi-ethnic alliance where each constituent group received a share in the organizational power and, if successful, a share in the political spoils. He also made inroads into the Pittsburgh business establishment that provided badly needed funding to the party. Michael Benedum, who made his fortune in oil and was a longtime ally of William L. Mellon, switched allegiance to the Democrats. As the 1932 election approached, Guffey and Lawrence convinced Roosevelt to give a major campaign address at Forbes Field. On October 19, 50,000 enthusiastic Democrats, regaled by black and ethnic bands, heard Father James Cox and Robert Vann announce their support for Roosevelt. Michael Benedum introduced Roosevelt as the Greentree Fife and Drum Corps in brilliant green uniforms led a single open automobile with a single passenger through the center field gate to the delirious ovation of the crowd. The Democrats were on the march.[91]

[1]David E. Koskoff, *The Mellons: The Chronicle of America's Richest Family* (New York: Thomas Y. Crowell, 1978), 159-162; Burton Hersch, *The Mellon Family: A Fortune in History* (New York: William Morrow and Company, 1978), 197-199.

[2]David Cannadine, *Mellon: An American Life,* (New York: Vintage Book, 2006), 278.

[3]Cannadine, *Mellon,* 277- 280.

[4]Harvey O'Connor, *Steel Dictator* (New York: The John Day Company, 1935), 265.

[5]Bruce M. Stave, *The New Deal and the Last Hurrah, Pittsburgh Machine Politics* (Pittsburgh: University of Pittsburgh Press, 1970), 36.

[6]O'Connor, *Steel Dictator,* 228-255.

[7]Stave, *The New Deal and the Law Hurrah,* 35.

[8]H.L. Kluppell, *Electrical Workers Journal,* 1920.

[9]*The Electrical Worker,* August 1923.

[10]Letter from the Building Trades Council read at Advisory Board Meeting of July 19, 1921.

[11]*The Electrical Worker,* July 1922.

[12]Andy Johnson, *Interview,* November 27, 1990; *The Electrical Worker,* July, 1922; M.L.Brush, *The Electrical Worker,* Jan. 1924.

[13]Andy Johnson, *Interview,* November 27, 1990.

[14]Andy Johnson, *Interview,* November 27, 1990.

[15]Edward J. Sargent, *Interview,* Aug. 21, 1991.

[16]Philip Jenkins, *Hoods and Shirts: The Extreme Right in Pennsylvania, 1925-1950.* (Chapel Hill: University of North Carolina Press, 1997), 62-75; I first heard about the cross burning(s) on Mt. Washington from old-timers at a bar in Duquesne Heights in the mid-1970s. In discussions with Msgr. Charles Owen Rice, whose family lived on Bailey Avenue across from Grandview Park in the 1920s, he corroborated the story saying that he believed that his Uncle Joe had played a role in organizing Catholic neighbors against Klan cross-burning intrusions. Rice was fourteen in the summer of 1923. For background, see: Charles McCollester, ed., *Fighter With a Heart: Charles Owen Rice, Pittsburgh Labor Priest* (Pittsburgh: University of Pittsburgh, 1996), 14-17.

[17]*Encyclopedia of Radio and TV Broadcasting,* p. 36; Gleason Leonard Archer, *The History of Radio* (New York: Arno Press, 1971), 199-201.

[18]"Pittsburgh's Broadcasting Pioneers," *The Literary Digest* (September 2, 1992), 30.; Archer, *The History of Radio,* 201, 307.

[19]*Encyclopedia of Radio and TV Broadcasting,* pp. 39-43: Archer, *The History of Radio,* 203-213.

[20]E.M. Herr, "Pittsburgh and the Electrical Industry," *Pittsburgh and the Pittsburgh Spirit,* (Addresses at the Pittsburgh Chamber of Commerce, 1927-1928), 223.

[21]Amalgamated Transit Union Staff, *ATU 100 Years: A History of the Amalgamated Transit Union,* (Amalgamated Transit Union, 1992), 43.

[22]Meyer A. Sanders, "Labor," *Allegheny County, A Sesqui-Centennial Review, 1788…1938,* ed. George E. Kelly, (Pittsburgh: Allegheny County Sesqui-Centennial Committee, 1938), 135; F.A. Fitzgerald, editor, *The International Engineer: Fifty Years of Progress: 1896-1946,* (December, 1946), 29.

[23]Mel Seidenberg, Lois Mulkearn, and James W. Hess, "Two Hundred Years of Pittsburgh History; A Chronology of Events Complied," in Stefan Lorant's *Pittsburgh: The Story of an American City* (Garden City: Doubleday & Company, Inc., 1964), 616-620. This chronology and that already cited by Vexler are an ongoing point of reference for summarizing contextual elements that surround the main story.

[24]Seidenberg et al., "Two Hundred Years of Pittsburgh History: A Chronology of Events Complied," 616-620.

[25]Seidenberg et al., "Two Hundred Years of Pittsburgh History: A Chronology of Events Complied," 616-620; George E. Kelly, ed., *Allegheny County, A Sesqui-Centennial Review, 1788…1938* (Pittsburgh: Allegheny County Sesqui-Centennial Committee, 1938), 94-95.

[26]Robert C. Alberts, *Pitt, the Story of the University of Pittsburgh, 1787-1987* (Pittsburgh: University of Pittsburgh Press, 1986), 46-67.

[27]Alberts, *Pitt, the Story of the University of Pittsburgh,* 115-117.

[28]Alberts, *Pitt, the Story of the University of Pittsburgh,* 89-117.

[29] David L. Rosenberg, "The Re-formation of the Pittsburgh Chapter of the American Civil Liberties Union 1928-1930," Unpublished paper delivered at the *Pennsylvania Labor History Society* meeting, October 4, 2003. A copy of this paper is on file at the Archives Service Center, University of Pittsburgh.

[30]Clarke M. Thomas, *Front-Page Pittsburgh: Two Hundred Years of the Post-Gazette* (Pittsburgh: University of Pittsburgh Press, 2005), 153-155.

[31]Thomas, *Front-Page Pittsburgh,* 160-162.

[32]Alberts, *Pitt, the Story of the University of Pittsburgh,* 144-147; Steve Nelson, James R. Barrett, & Rob Ruck, *American Radical* (Pittsburgh: University of Pittsburgh Press, 1981), 373-374.

[33]David Rosenberg, "The Re-formation of the Pittsburgh Chapter of the American Civil Liberties Union 1928-1930," Unpublished paper delivered at the *Pennsylvania Labor Histor Society* meeting in 2003. I am grateful for permission to refer to David Rosenberg's paper on the "purge of professors that followed the purge of the students."

[34]*Letter,* April 28, 1930, Colston E. Warne to Dr. S.B. Linhart, Secretary, University of Pittsburgh, reproduced in Rosenberg's paper can be accessed in the John G. Bowman papers, Liberal Club file, Archives Service Center, University of Pittsburgh.

[35]John McCollister, *The Bucs!: The Story of the Pittsburgh Pirates* (Lenexa: Addax Publishing Group, 1998), 83-85.

[36]McCollister, *The Bucs!,* 86-92; a more skeptical view of the incident is offered by Frederick G. Lieb, *The Pittsburgh Pirates,* p. 231, who observes that the Pirates went on to outhit New York in that first game, 9-6, while losing 5 to 4.

[37]Grantland Rice, *The Tumult and the Shouting* (New York: A.S. Barnes & Co., 1954), 140; Jack Cavanaugh, *Tunney: Boxing's Brainiest Champ and His Upset of the Great Jack Dempsey,* (New York: Random House, 2006), 123-136.

[38]Gene Tunney, *A Man Must Fight* (New York: Houghton Mifflin Company, 1932), 140-141.

[39]Cavanaugh, *Tunney: Boxing's Brainiest Champ and His Upset of the Great Jack Dempsey,* 130-140.

[40]Maier B. Fox, *United We Stand: The United Mine Workers of America, 1800-1990* (Washington D.C.: United Mine Workers of America, 1990), 185-186, 228-229.

[41]Fox, *United We Stand,* 250-251.

[42]John Brophy, *A Miner's Life* (Madison: University of Wisconsin Press, 1964), 155.

[43]Fox, *United We Stand,* 226.

[44]Brophy, *A Miner's Life,* 177.

[45]Brophy, *A Miner's Life,* 181-182.

[46]Mildred Allen Beik, *The Miners of Windber: The Struggles of New Immigrants for Unionization, 1890s-1930s* (University Park: The Pennsylvania State University Press, 1996), 276.

[47]Beik, *The Miners of Windber,* 290

[48]Beik, *The Miners of Windber,* 290-299; Mildred Allen Beik, *Remembering the Strike for Union in 1922-23* (University Park: The Pennsylvania State University Press, 1997), 16.

[49]Beik, *The Miners of Windber: The Struggles of New Immigrants for Unionization,* 302-314.

[50]Beik, *The Miners of Windber,* 318; Brophy, *A Miner's Life,* 212; Elizabeth C. Ricketts, *Our Battle for Industrial Freedom: Radical Politics in the Coal Fields of Pennsylvania, 1916-1926* (UMI Dissertation Information Service, 1996), 518-534.

[51]Brophy, *A Miner's Life,* 210-219; In an interview in James Dougherty's video documentary about the central Pennsylvania coalfields, "Struggle for an American Way of Life," Richard Trumka, then president of the UMWA, called Brophy "the only man who beat John L. Lewis in a union election."

[52]Brophy, *A Miner's Life,* 228-230.

[53]Irwin Marcus, James Dougherty, and Eileen M. Cooper, "Confrontation at Rossiter: The Coal Strike of 1927-28 and its Aftermath," *Pennsylvania History* (October 1992), 59(4):310-314.; Carl I. Meyerhuber, Jr., *Less Than Forever: The Rise and Decline of Union Solidarity in Western Pennsylvania, 1914-1948,* (London: Associated University Presses, 1987), 66.

[54]Jeanne Svitesic Cecil, *Our Coal-Mining Community Heritage: Harmarville, PA,*(Homestead: Steel Valley Printers, 2002), 36; *The Valley Daily News,* August 22-23, 1927.

[55]Meyerhuber, *Less Than Forever,* 82; Marcus et al., "Confrontation at Rossiter: The Coal Strike of 1927-28 and its Aftermath," 321; With the encouragement by the Reagan administration of the use of permanent replacement workers to break strikes, it is the author's view that the Wagner Act ceased to provide the "recognized parameters" of American labor relations.

[56]Meyerhuber, *Less Than Forever,* 75-90; F.A. Fitzgerald, ed., *The International Engineer: Fifty Years of Progress: 1896-1946* (December, 1946), 29.

[57]Keith Dix, *What's a Coal Miner to Do?: The Mechanization of Coal Mining* (Pittsburgh: University of Pittsburgh Press, 1988), 80.; Department of Evironmental Resources, *Annual Report on Mining Activities, 1991* (Harrisburg: Commonwealth of Pennsylvania, 1991), 92-93.

[58]Dix, *What's a Coal Miner to Do?,* 12-16; 26-27.

[59]Dix, *What's a Coal Miner to Do?,* 61-76; Department of Environmental Resources, *Annual Report of Mining Activities, 1991* (Harrisburg: Commonwealth of Pennsylvania, 1991), 92-93.

[60]Theodore Draper, *American Communism and Soviet Russia* (New York: Viking Press, 1960), 380-388; W.Z. Foster barely mentions the NMU in his *History of the Communist Party of the United States* (New York: International Publishers, 1968), 257, 286.

[61]Martin Abern, "Attack on the National Miners' Union Convention," *James P. Cannon and the Early Years of American Communism, Selected Writings and Speeches* (New York: Spartacist Publishing, 1992); David Rosenberg, "Labor Lyceums a Forgotten, Rich Labor Heritage," Pennsylvania Labor History Journal, v. 27 (December, 2005), 7.

[62]Irving Bernstein, *The Lean Years: A History of the American Worker, 1920-1933* (Baltimore: Penguin Books, 1970), 287-288; Jeanne Svitesic Cecil, *Our Coal-Mining Community Heritage: Harmarville, PA,* (Homestead: Steel Valley Printers, 2002), 86-87;Pat Fagan (son of the UMWA leader), *Interview,* Charles McCollester, December, 2007.

[63]*Pittsburgh Post-Gazette,* July 1, 1931.

[64]*Pittsburgh Post-Gazette,* June 9, 1931.

[65]Lauren Gilfillan, *I Went to Pit College* (New York: The Literary Guild, 1934).

[66]Gilfillan, *I Went to Pit College,* 99.

[67]Gilfillan, *I Went to Pit College,* 102-104.

[68]Gilfillan, *I Went to Pit College,* 104-105.

[69]Cannadine, *Andrew Mellon,* 387-394.

[70]Cannadine, *Andrew Mellon,* 395-400.

[71]Cannadine, *Andrew Mellon,* 402.

[72]Alberts, *Pitt, the Story of the University of Pittsburgh,* 90; Carradine, *Andrew Mellon* 402-414.

[73]Carradine, *Andrew Mellon* 429-463.

[74]Koskoff, *The Mellons,* 297-298; Leonard Mosley, *Power Play: Oil in the Middle East* (New York: Penguin, 1974), 77-84 for an account of how Gulf Oil lost Bahrain, but got a share of Kuwait.

[75]O'Connor, *Steel-Dictator,* 333.

[76]Gilbert Love, "College Students Are Beating the Depression" *School and Society,* June 10, 1933 reprinted in David A. Shannon, *The Great Depression,* (Saddle River, NJ: Pearson/Prentice Hall, 1961), 105.

[77]Several oldtimers assured me that this was the case at the Union Switch & Signal until the late 1940s.

[78]Kenneth J. Heineman, *A Catholic New Deal: Religion and Reform in Depression Pittsburgh* (University Park: Penn State Press, 1999), 3-9; Eric Leif Davin, "Blue Collar Democracy: Class War and Political Revolution in Western Pennsylvania, 1932-1937," *Pennsylvania History,* (Spring 2000), 249.

[79]Heineman, *A Catholic New Deal,* 15-16; Sally Witt, "Father Cox and Pittsburgh in the 1940s," *Pittsburgh History,* (Summer, 1997), 53-55.

[80]*Pittsburgh Post-Gazette,* March 7, 1930.

[81]Thomas H. Coode and John D. Petrarulo, "The Odyssey of Pittsburgh's Father Cox," *Western Pennsylvania Historical Magazine,* (July 1972), 217-221.

[82]Heineman, *A Catholic New Deal,* 22.

[83]Heineman, *A Catholic New Deal,* 23-24; Bernstein, *The Lean Years,* 432.

[84]Bernstein, *The Lean Years,* 450-454; Witt, "Father Cox and Pittsburgh in the 1940s," 225-227.

[85]Heineman, *A Catholic New Deal,* 28-30.

[86]Michael P. Weber, *Don't Call Me Boss: David L. Lawrence* (Pittsburgh: University of Pittsburgh Press, 1988), 5-8.

[87]Weber, *Don't Call Me Boss,* 7-27.

[88]Weber, *Don't Call Me Boss,* 29-36; Clarke Thomas, *Fortunes and Misfortunes: Pittsburgh and Allegheny County Politics, 1930-1995* (Pittsburgh: Institute of Politics, 1998), 30.

[89]Weber, *Don't Call Me Boss,* 37-46.

[90]Weber, *Don't Call Me Boss,* 47-50.

[91]Weber, *Don't Call Me Boss,* 51-54.

Chapter Ten

Labor's Rise

1933-1940

Three plus years of deep economic depression had undermined whatever weak labor standards existed and wiped out most of the meager gains that workers had achieved. With many unions destroyed or marginalized, the sweatshop returned; labor was increasingly transient and migratory, and the mounting misery of the bottom half of society raised the specter of mass revolt and even revolution. U.S. Senator Robert Wagner said: "We are not in a mere business recession. We are in a life and death struggle with the forces of social and economic dissolution."

A New Deal for Labor

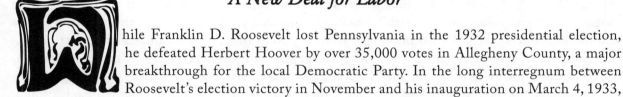 hile Franklin D. Roosevelt lost Pennsylvania in the 1932 presidential election, he defeated Herbert Hoover by over 35,000 votes in Allegheny County, a major breakthrough for the local Democratic Party. In the long interregnum between Roosevelt's election victory in November and his inauguration on March 4, 1933, a rising chorus of voices demanded action along the lines that Pittsburgh's Father Cox had indicated to President Hoover. A massive public works effort financed by increased income and inheritance taxes on the rich was needed to lift the income of the masses and stimulate production. Government unemployed relief and pension support was needed to mitigate the economic cycles of capitalism by providing basic support for the vulnerable aged and unemployed members of society. Mineworker leader Phil Murray called for a floor under wages and a ceiling over hours. Limitations on the hours of work and on child labor were needed to spread available work, improve the life and health of legions of wage workers, and stimulate technological progress.[1]

As president-elect Roosevelt completed his term as Governor of New York on January 2, 1933, an international banking crisis threatened as the French and British governments were increasingly unable to make payments on their war debts to the United States. Even more ominously, the domestic banking crisis was intensifying as Michigan banks were forced to close for a week and many other banks around the country declared a "holiday" and denied withdrawals. Mellon Bank remained as solid as a rock. In such a climate, Roosevelt had little time to formulate a comprehensive labor policy. He made, however, a bold and unconventional choice in his selection of a Secretary of Labor. Ignoring strong union support for Dan Tobin, the president of the Teamsters, Roosevelt selected Frances Perkins, who was eminently qualified and a loyal and trusted friend. He also wanted to be the first president to select a female cabinet officer. Perkins argued against his choice, urging the selection of a labor leader; but failing to shake Roosevelt's resolve, she outlined the program she wanted to pursue if she accepted, including unemployment insurance, public works, minimum wage and maximum hours, old age pensions and the abolition of child labor.[2]

In that initial meeting, neither Perkins nor Roosevelt brought up the issue of labor's right to organize or bargain collectively. This oversight was perhaps a reflection of her not being a leader from the organized, largely craft union, sector of the labor force. William Green, president of the AFL, wrote Tobin that the president should have placed a trade unionist in charge of the Labor Department, not "some college professor who learned about labor from a textbook." Perkins, however, was never a professor and knew a great deal about the plight of labor. Fifty years old at the time of her appointment, like Alice Hamilton, the great pioneer of industrial health and occupational medicine, she had lived at Jane Addam's Hull House in Chicago where she gained first-hand experience in its slums. Like Crystal Eastman and Elizabeth Beardsley Butler, she was a well-educated woman (Holyoke College and Columbia University) of the upper-middle class who devoted her life to labor reform and other progressive causes. Most of her career had been spent in New York City, where she fought against sweatshops and child labor and for restrictions on the hours of work. She was deeply affected by the horrible deaths of 146 girls in the 1911 Triangle Shirtwaist factory fire. Under Governor Roosevelt, she served as New York's Industrial Commissioner. Despite her old American stock and Protestant religion, she had fervently supported Al Smith's presidential aspirations.[3]

In July 1933, after Roosevelt's inauguration and the passing of the National Industrial Recovery Act (NIRA), Perkins made a tour of the steel communities to gain support for the legislation that included provisions for the establishment of industrial codes regulating minimum wage rates and the hours of work, and most important from the point of view of organized labor, section 7(a) that asserted: "Employees shall have the right to organize and bargain collectively through representatives of their own choosing and shall be free from the interference, restraint or coercion of employers of labor, or their agents, in the designation of such representatives or in self-organization or in other concerted activities for the purpose of collective bargaining or other mutual aid or protection." When she arrived in Homestead, she was allowed by the burgess, John Cavanaugh, coroner by trade, former policeman and county detective, to address a relatively small group in the town's council chambers in the very building where Mother Jones had been taken under arrest fourteen years earlier for speaking on the streets of Homestead with no permit save the Constitution. A larger crowd gathered outside wanted to hear and speak to the new labor secretary, but Cavanaugh, anxious to assert control over his fiefdom, refused permission for her to speak to people he considered "undesirable Reds" either on the sidewalk or up the street in Frick Park. Perkins, seeing the flag flying across the street over the federal post office, said: "We will go to the post office. There is the American flag." Inside, "Madame Secretary" got up on a chair, made a short speech, and listened as several dozen citizens asked for relief from the domination of the corporation. A new dynamic was being unveiled in the steel towns.[4]

Indeed, among the crowd demanding to speak to Secretary Perkins were a fair number of those Reds that the mayor recognized and had excluded from his Council Chamber meeting. Given the conservative timidity of the Amalgamated Association, the separatist Communist-led Steel and Metal

Workers' Industrial Union (SMWIU) had developed a nucleus of support in nearly all the large mills. Ironically, while most of corporate America viewed Roosevelt as a very dangerous man and a threat to their interests, the Communist Party was also extremely hostile to the NIRA and considered Perkins "a tried and true friend of the bosses." At her meeting in the Post Office, Pat Cush, a resident of Homestead who had participated in the 1892 strike and president of the SMWIU, pushed Perkins to read their proposed changes to the steel industry code being debated in Washington. The radicals' program included a $20 a week minimum wage for a six-hour, five-day week, no discrimination against Negroes in hiring, job placement or pay, plus a guaranteed forty hours of work supplemented by unemployment insurance at full wage rate. Perkins diplomatically termed the proposal "reasonable and debatable."[5]

Communists aside, mainstream labor leaders were overjoyed with the NIRA. Bill Green compared it to the Magna Carta and John L. Lewis to the Emancipation Proclamation. Lewis claimed that section 7(a) had been inserted at his insistence. "I fought for it and got it." He then tried unsuccessfully to convince Bill Green that the AFL should broadly interpret Section 7(a) and hail it as "a franchise to nationwide organizing" and as "the weapon for a great organizational attack." He was appalled at the "criminal appeasement" of labor leaders who remained inactive in the face of such an opportunity.

> Most exasperating were the limited mentalities of so many of our so-called leaders of labor, who could not begin to grasp the scope of the nationwide organization drive nor understand its implications. They could not recognize the simple premise that the very welfare of their own unions was completely dependent upon and contingent upon the welfare of other workers in this country. Over all this lay the shadow of the curse of the labor movement, cowardice, avarice, and those private petty fears and insecurities of individual trade union leaders who were zealously guarding and jealously fearful of their own little stakes in the empire of labor. They wanted then, as now, to repose in comfort and peace. Unfortunately, too, many leaders of many union groups are more interested in their own personal wages and peace, comfort, and order than in the constant struggle to increase the living standards of their own people.[6]

Miners at the grassroots level had already grasped the opportunity that Lewis perceived, and even more forcefully. Beaten down for a decade, they rose up and between February 1933 and July 1934 the demoralized and battered UMWA's membership swelled from less than 100,000 to more than 500,000 paid-up members. The rejuvenated mineworkers union provided the organizational and financial foundation for the mass industrial organizing drives that followed. Within weeks of Section 7(a) becoming law, the UMWA committed its treasury and 100 organizers to an organizing drive. Significant contributions to the effort were also made by the International Ladies Garment Workers Union and the Amalgamated Clothing and Textile Workers Union. In fact, the impetus for organizing came from below. The union was running to catch up and reassert its leadership. The word went out: "The president wants you to join the union." Miners believed, or wanted to believe, that the president referred to was Roosevelt. They sensed an opportunity to assert their right to organize as a legal and human right. The drive took on the character of an uprising as it spread like a wildfire. Union sentiment swept across southern Ohio, deep into West Virginia, across Pennsylvania and even into the southern, historically non-union, fields of Tennessee and Alabama.

Riding the wave of grassroots organizing, Lewis drove hard for a national agreement. In September, a comprehensive bituminous agreement for commercial mines in Pennsylvania, Ohio, West

Virginia, Kentucky and Tennessee established the 8-hour day and forty-hour week, mandated union check-weighmen, severed the miner's obligation to shop in the company stores, and banned child labor under age seventeen. Between February 1933 and July 1934, the explosive organization from below added 400,000 determined miners to the dispirited remnant of 100,000 that existed in 1933. Funds raised by this infusion of dues money provided resources for the successful organizing drives in auto and steel. The only mines standing outside the agreement were the "captive mines" that fed the steel mills.[7]

The miners at the H. C. Frick captive mines went on strike for recognition in July 1933, and by September, 70,000 miners were on strike including many from commercial mines who had a UMWA contract, but were striking in solidarity with the captive miners. An estimated 100,000 miners were affected in an area of over 1,000 square miles of rugged terrain. Led by a 44-year old Irish immigrant, Martin Ryan, president of a Frick Coal Company local union in Grindstone, Fayette County, the miners attempted to spread the strike into steel by marching into Clairton where their coal was processed into coke for the Monongahela mills. Perhaps half of Clairton's steelworkers joined the miners' picket. Shutting down Clairton threatened to shut all the Carnegie mills once supplies of coke were exhausted. When U.S. Steel appealed to Pennsylvania Governor Pinchot, he replied: "If the Carnegie Steel Company is threatened by striking miners, it has nothing but the blind and brutal conduct of affiliated officials to thank for it. The moment their officials cease to let their willful and antiquated prejudices against organized labor stand in the way of national recovery and sign the Coal Code, the trouble will be over."

While Pinchot asserted the miners' right to peaceful picketing, the miners' use of mass picketing challenged the traditional property rights of corporations to an unobstructed flow of labor. For the miner, the issue was not individual freedom versus union power, the conflict was between conflicting centers of collective power, between the employer and the union. While the Roosevelt code also sanctioned company unions, like those hurriedly organized by U.S. Steel's H. C. Frick Coke Company, the miner elevated Section 7(a) into a workers' declaration of independence affirming the right to organize independent self-governing unions of their choice. As James Gray Pope has indicated: "In 1933, the miners of western Pennsylvania brought their common law of solidarity into the realm of public struggle; building a 'jurisgenerative' movement complete with principles of solidarity, democratic forms for translating those principles into enforceable policies, and inspirational stories about section 7(a)." "Jurisgenerative" refers to the common law principle that laws derive from the practice and adhesion of the community.[8]

Under intense corporate pressure, President Roosevelt pushed Lewis to get the men to return to work on the promise of free elections, and Lewis dispatched Murray to end the strike. Summoning the strike leaders to Pittsburgh, Murray warned:

> Today you are fighting the coal companies; but tonight, if you remain on strike, you will be fighting the Government of the United States. Today you are conducting a strike; tonight you will be conducting a rebellion. Today we may say we are going to defy the greatest friend we've ever had in the history of this nation. But I tell you friends, he can turn against you strong as he's been for you.

When Murray was done, the miners' leader Martin Ryan responded: "Why do you ask 75,000 men to go back to work instead of telling one man (the president of H. C. Frick Company) to sign the contract?" While the Communists were denouncing the National Recovery Act as a capitalist plot and Lewis was most anxious about asserting organizational control of the upsurge, the miners through their pit committees were imposing union rule on the workplace from below while hailing Section 7(a) as the legal assertion of their right to organize.[9]

False Starts in Steel

Despite a more complex situation in steel than in coal, a similar feeling of optimism swept the mill towns with Roosevelt's election and the unionization of the surrounding coal mines during the summer of 1933. As labor reporter and union sympathizer, Harvey O'Connor, then living in Pittsburgh, recalled:

> Along came the New Deal, and then came the NRA, and the effect was electric all up and down those valleys. The mills began reopening somewhat, and the steelworkers read in the newspapers about this NRA Section 7(a) that guaranteed your right to organize. All over the steel country union locals sprang up spontaneously. Not by virtue of the Amalgamated Association; they couldn't care less. But these locals sprang up at Duquesne, Homestead, Braddock. You name the mill town and there was a local there, carrying a name like the "Blue Eagle" or the "New Deal" local. These people had never had any experience in unionism. All they knew was that, by golly, the time had come when they could organize and the government guaranteed them the right to organize![10]

Despite high hopes that the union organizing effort in steel would mirror the upsurge in coal, a combination of factors forestalled such an outcome. First of all, corporate resistance was much stronger in steel than in the decentralized coal industry. Furthermore, realizing the need to respond to a changed political landscape, the steel companies established company-dominated Employee Representation Plans, a form pioneered by Charles Schwab at Bethlehem Steel, to forestall worker self-organization under Section 7(a). Unlike in mining where an industrial union model had long been accepted, the AFL was still deeply divided on the issue of industrial unionism and what form it should take in steel. Steel unionism was saddled with Michael Tighe's timid, conservative direction of the Amalgamated Association that stifled rather than encouraged organizing. John L. Lewis, though conservative and autocratic in many ways, was prepared to boldly jump out in front of the rank-and-file revolt and use his powerful public persona and magnificent voice to channel and coordinate the grassroots upsurge to the benefit of his organization. Finally, given the paralysis of both the AFL and the Amalgamated, there existed no framework to support the spontaneous awakening in the mill towns.

The Communist Party, which had watched its National Miners' Union (NMU) be virtually absorbed from below into the UMWA during the uprising in coal, was in a period of strategic transition. The Communist independent Steel and Metal Workers International Union (SMWIU), though still small with perhaps 15,000 members, was probably the only organization with enough geographic reach and organizational coherence to be capable of coordinating the various strands of the rank-and-file mill workers' revolt. Due to a radical shift in international Communist Party policy, however, the radical SMWIU was disbanded in 1934 and its militants dispatched into the Amalgamated where a great deal of energy was expended in trying to resuscitate a lifeless shell. Before the SMWIU was disbanded, it conducted a number of strikes in the Ohio Valley where the NMU had also been strong. Concentrated among workers of South Slav extraction, the union conducted a short and partially successful strike at the Pressed Steel Car Company in McKees Rocks. The bloodiest event, an attack by club and rifle toting deputies and thugs from Aliquippa on an SMWIU picket line at the Spang-Chalfont plant in Ambridge, was filmed and photographed extensively, being featured in several documentary films on the era. One man was shot and killed, and nearly 100 wounded in what was manifestly an unprovoked attack. Thousands attended the funeral of the victim, Adam Petrasuski. Communist leaders Pat Cush and Mother Bloor spoke at the graveside. The radical union also planted a seed in the Turtle Creek Valley. A mass rally for Westinghouse workers in East Pittsburgh drew 600 attendees and "about 150 members" were claimed for the new local there. [11]

In response to the seizure of power by the Nazis in Germany, the Communist International moved away from attacks on socialists and other moderate leftwing forces as social fascists and abruptly promoted broad democratic alliances to forestall right-wing takeovers of governments such as France. In the United States, as elsewhere, the party was required to move from a separatist union strategy toward a "united front" policy. It should be noted here that the American Communist Party was very much a two-tiered operation. On the higher level of the party, where policy was formed, events in the Soviet Union were closely followed for signs of shifts in political direction. The party was heavily concentrated in a handful of cities with New York having one-third of the membership and Chicago, one quarter. If the membership in Detroit, Cleveland and San Francisco is added in, three-quarters of the party was concentrated in five cities. Pittsburgh was anomalous in that it had a long and sustained tradition of class struggle and unionism in coal, steel, electrical, construction, and other industries, and for this reason was a priority target for Communist Party activity, but its union culture proved generally resistant to the party-line politics of the Communists. Party policy, especially its international outlook, was shaped by a New York perspective. Its understanding of the miners and mill workers of western Pennsylvania was limited by both culture and work experience.[12]

As an international revolutionary movement with the goal of supplanting capitalism worldwide, the Communist movement was at a minimum deferential to the Russian party and its views. The movement's efforts to impose a unified strategy was a source of attraction to many around the world suffering the ravages of a profound global economic depression, but shifts in party line, theory and tactics imposed from above proved to be a source of confusion and disillusionment as well. The Communists were often effective and dedicated organizers with a level of commitment rooted in an almost messianic hope in the possibility of a new and better society achievable by the application of "scientific socialism" and revolutionary theory. Their dependence, however, on disciplined adherence to a strategy imposed by a Russian dictator who was eliminating all opposition to his rule ultimately proved to be an enormous liability. On the grassroots level, however, many militants were respected unionists who toiled tirelessly to organize workers in defense of their rights and their livelihoods and thereby earned the respect of many who did not necessarily share their broader ideological convictions. Stories of the crimes of Stalin were discounted as the propaganda of the capitalist press.[13]

When the NRA came into effect, the once proud Amalgamated Association of Iron, Steel and Tin Workers had less than 5,000 members. O'Connor wrote: "The union had been hammered on the anvil of Steel's 'open shop' labor policy until it had lost all spirit and hope. Its president breathed the philosophy of defeatism." The National Labor Board was proving itself to be a completely ineffective instrument to force corporate recognition of unions. A petition in early 1934 to President Roosevelt by 4,600 Weirton employees requesting an election languished in the courts for sixteen months until a Delaware Court struck down Section 7(a) as unconstitutional, holding that the production of steel was an intrastate matter outside the jurisdiction of the federal courts. Despite its lack of interest in organizing, the Amalgamated held the jurisdictional rights under the AFL for iron and steel production. By the time of the Amalgamated's annual convention in 1934, its membership had swollen to a number variously estimated at from 50,000 to 200,000. The union reported 129 new lodges organized with no help and mostly obstruction emanating from its leadership. Increased worker militancy was reflected in strike activity that increased from virtually zero in 1932 to 34,000 workers in 1933. Many of these early strikes were led by the radical SMWIU, but large numbers of steelworkers streamed into the Amalgamated where they quickly discovered its rigid resistance to change.[14]

The 59th annual convention of the Amalgamated Association was convened in Pittsburgh on April 16, 1934 to consider a rising chorus of calls from the rank and file for "concerted action," preferably a national strike to be coordinated with miners and railroad workers. Despite Tighe's obstructiveness, the majority of delegates voted for a strike if the steel companies did not recognize the union. Most of the emerging rank and file leaders were inexperienced and plans were poorly coordinated, so that a call for a strike in June generated a great deal of negative publicity while the corporations stockpiled both weapons and steel. Federal laboratories in Pittsburgh, specializing in "protection engineering," sold over $100,000 in riot guns, revolvers and gas grenades. President Roosevelt's promises of elections were widely seen as futile, since there was no enforcement mechanism to ensure union recognition or collective bargaining. An Amalgamated conference called in Pittsburgh on June 14th to set the date for the work stoppage actually managed to get the rank and filers to abandon the strike. The president of the AFL, William Green, addressed the convention and delivered the coup de grace to the strike effort on behalf of the Roosevelt administration.

> I come as a miner speaking to steel workers....Listen to me only as a coal miner. I
> learned my lesson in the mines. I graduated from that hard school. I know what it is
> to go through strikes of eighteen months duration with the family larder empty....We
> cannot afford to play into the hands of these autocratic barons. We must use strategy.
> In my judgment, it is my firm opinion, based on my own interest in the workers and
> my own experience, that the time will come when your wrongs will be righted, but I
> do not believe the time is here at this moment.[15]

The abandonment of the strike had a powerfully negative effect on rank-and-file steelworkers. In Braddock, workers who heard the news on the radio reportedly tore up their union cards. The last gasp of an independent radical grassroots movement in steel was expended in early 1935 when 400 steelworkers representing dissident Amalgamated lodges, 100 mineworkers, and some aluminum workers met in Pittsburgh to devise a common strike strategy. In response, the Amalgamated expelled the lodges that participated, and Pat Fagan denounced the meeting as "absolutely Red," asserting: "Those fellows don't believe in authority, law and order or anything else. They're an asinine crowd of parlor Bolshevists." In fact, many members of the Communist Party, by this time committed to working within the existing union structures, *had* joined rank-and-file militants who were pushing the Amalgamated toward organizing steel. Their participation helped provide an excuse for Tighe to expel the militant lodges. Committed to boring from within, the Communists abandoned the independent rank and file movement.[16]

As the early hopes for an industrial union in steel collapsed in disarray, there developed a separate dynamic in the steel mills inside the company-promoted Employee Representation Plans (ERPs) that had been established to ward off union organizing efforts. An embryonic radicalism began to incubate inside the Clairton and Duquesne mills especially. The Duquesne mill of U.S. Steel with 6,000 employees had been the most tightly controlled and least active of the Mon Valley mills during the 1919 Steel Strike. Mayor James Crawford ruled with an iron fist, arresting both Mother Jones and William Z. Foster when they attempted to convene a meeting in his town. From the election of Roosevelt, who carried the town two-to-one in 1932, a struggle for unionism developed on two fronts with a significant segment of the workforce pushing for reform inside the Amalgamated and another group making creative use of the company-initiated ERP as a vehicle to advance worker interests. Activism at Duquesne was rooted in the same objective conditions that prevailed elsewhere in steel. Workers were subject to unsafe working conditions and the unrestricted rule of foremen was marked by inconsistency, favoritism and discrimination. Son of a Lithuanian steelworker, author Phillip Bonosky noted: "Our town was full of men with fingerless hands, footless legs, eyes squashed back into their heads." Ethnic groups were pitted against each other. While blacks were assigned the hottest and dirtiest jobs in the mill, in the community they were denied the use of the gym, pool and club rooms at the massive Carnegie Library.[17]

Myron C. Taylor, who in 1927 succeeded Judge Gary as chairman of U.S. Steel, attempted to rationalize corporate personnel policies that varied significantly from plant to plant of the corporation. As the Depression deepened, he instituted a work-sharing system designed to keep the workforce intact in anticipation of the expected revival of economic activity. In 1934, he declared to the corporation's stockholders: "I do not believe there is a brighter page in industrial history than your corporation wrote through this Depression in its treatment of its servants." A cruel aspect of the company's policy toward its unskilled workers during the Depression, however, was its requirement for them to report every day for work even when everyone knew none was available. Workers were thus held in thrall, unable to go out and take day or part-time work. Company mortgage and rent credits as well as food distributions were counted as loans and deducted directly from paychecks once work was available. Before the New Deal programs, a worker could only receive county relief after quitting the mill, thereby losing his contributory pension if he had one and risking the loss of re-employment. With food and mortgage relief set by income level becoming available from Democratic state and federal programs, independent worker activity began to intensify.[18]

Union organizing began slowly in Duquesne where the communist SMWIU was small. By March of 1934, however, approximately 1,500 of the mill's workers had become members of the Fort Dukane Lodge of the Amalgamated. Meetings were conducted in Croatian, Italian, Russian, Hungarian and Lithuanian. Significantly 300 black steelworkers joined in the union activity. That the self-sacrificing dedication of the Communist organizer could attract people who were deeply rooted in ethnic community religious values and practices is illustrated in one of the finest working-class novels set in Pittsburgh, *Burning Valley* by Philip Bonosky. The novel, set in the early 1930s, depicts the parallel struggles of the African-American and the Lithuanian communities in Duquesne. It involves three conflicts: the primary one of workers against the corporation's control of town and mill; the second between the Catholic priests and the Communist organizer for the spiritual allegiance of the young narrator; and the struggle within the church over its allegiance to either the workers or the mill management. The book ends with the young altar server's rejection of the new, corporate-friendly, outsider priest and his carrying oranges to the Communist organizer, whose courage he admires, imprisoned in the town's jail.[19]

Initially, the mass of unskilled workers spurned any involvement in the ERP and concentrated on building the rebel movement within the Amalgamated and calling for a nationwide steel strike in

June of 1934. William Spang from the Fort Dukane Lodge became a leader in that drive. When that effort collapsed due to opposition from the Amalgamated and AFL leadership, themselves under pressure from the Roosevelt administration, membership in the Fort Dukane Lodge dropped precipitously. Spang then ran for Duquesne Council in the fall of 1934 and nearly upset an incumbent councilman who was the general labor superintendent of the Duquesne Works. While Duquesne was voting Democratic in presidential and Congressional elections, party registration and local offices remained overwhelmingly Republican, since workers feared company retaliation if they registered or ran as Democrats. Given long-standing Republican control of the county, registration information was used to maintain political control and was shared with employers.[20]

As the Fort Dukane Lodge declined in the face of the Amalgamated's intransigence, the internal plant ERP began to develop an increasingly independent attitude toward management. Representing many skilled workers, the ERP was only empowered to submit requests that management could reject without any obligation to submit disputes to arbitration. Initially at least, the company union's version of bargaining was described as being like "writing a letter to Santa Claus." So while the ERP's formal powers were nearly non-existent, the fact that for the first time in its history U.S. Steel had established a grievance procedure and a democratic process for electing worker representatives opened up a new vehicle for worker organization. The ERP gradually developed a more confrontational style beginning with safety and health issues. Its representatives, especially Elmer Maloy and John Kane, were instrumental in the gradual transformation of the ERP into a vehicle for worker expression and negotiation. It began to demand an equal sharing of the hours of work and for seniority protections that helped many unskilled workers and reduced the arbitrary powers of the foremen. With the signing of the Wagner Act July 5, 1935, with its prohibitions against company domination of worker organizations, the ERPs increasingly demonstrated independence.[21]

As U.S. Steel under Myron Taylor tried to rationalize its labor policies to make them consistent from plant to plant, the ERPs under the leadership of John Mullen from Clairton, Maloy and Kane from Duquesne and George Patterson from Chicago's South Works began to form a Central Committee with two representatives from each of the ERPs in the corporation's mills to coordinate demands for things like a five-day week, vacations with pay after ten years, and increased pensions. So while the original corporate plan had envisioned plant-based labor-management committees with equal representation, the ERPs were increasingly excluding management and joining in broader organizational alliances. In response, U.S. Steel began to try to infiltrate the ERPs with spies while stalling and delaying response to a growing list of demands submitted by them. Step-by-step, the company's own creations were moving toward genuine independent organization.[22]

Pittsburgh's New Deal

While Roosevelt's presidential victory in 1932 breached the mighty Republican fortress, it took four years of steady organizational advance for the Democratic Party to achieve solid political dominance. Roosevelt failed to carry Pennsylvania, but he carried Pittsburgh by 27,000 votes and Allegheny County by 37,000, the first Democratic candidate to do so since before the Civil War. With Dave Lawrence's long-time ally Joe Guffey in command of all federal jobs in the state, and with desperate economic conditions making jobs precious and recipients extremely grateful and loyal, patronage became the key to constructing a political machine. By September 1934, Guffey had placed 500 Pennsylvanians in Washington jobs of varying importance, and 5,000 party loyalists in federal positions within the state. Lawrence managed patronage appointments in Western Pennsylvania. In addition, he already controlled much of the local patronage and by 1935 controlled most of the state's as well. Most important, for the extension of party loyalty down into the grassroots, hundreds of thousands of blue collar jobs were created; first through the state and after 1935 through the Works Progress Administration (WPA). In Western Pennsylvania that meant 57,000 jobs. For Pittsburgh, the WPA in two years built 530 miles of water and sewage projects, new parks, pools, and playgrounds, as well as six miles of extraordinary concrete stairways connecting the city's hillside neighborhoods.[23]

Lawrence, of course, did not distribute this largesse personally, but rather through the system of ward chairmen and committeemen. While lower level jobs were generally distributed without regard for political affiliation, the channel for their distribution was primarily the ward chairman, so the Democratic Committee sank deep roots into the neighborhoods. Over time, the number of committeemen and women who were themselves on the public payroll increased. By 1960, with Lawrence in his second term as governor, three-quarters of committeemen and a third of committeewomen were on the public payroll, firefighters being especially heavily represented. On election day, the committee members were "on the job" literally, getting voters to the polls. In 1934, Lawrence reorganized and expanded the Democratic Committee structure, as 1,600 men and women were put in place to serve as the eyes and ears of the organization. He kept close tabs on its operation and personally attended ward meetings until 1959 when he left to go to Harrisburg as governor. Ward chairmen were rewarded patronage on the basis of their performance in delivering votes. Lawrence's political skill was demonstrated in his careful balancing of ethnic and interest groups that were the building blocks of the party. Termed the "Balkan succession" by commentators, the City Council seats were variously tagged the Italian, the Slav, the Irish, Jewish, black, labor, Protestant and female seats. Structural representation for key voting blocks helps explain the power, political credibility and longevity of Lawrence's system.[24]

While Lawrence was methodically extending his control over patronage and political power, he was confronted with an embarrassing struggle in the heart of his own bailiwick with his handpicked candidate for mayor of Pittsburgh, William McNair. Lawrence had nearly been persuaded to run for mayor himself in 1933, but he was more interested in building an empire, and both the state and county governments remained under Republican control. He also was not yet certain that Pittsburgh was ready for a Catholic mayor. McNair had been numerous times a Democratic candidate for district attorney, judge, mayor in 1921, and polled over a million votes running against David A. Reed for the U.S. Senate in 1928, in the years when there was little possibility of victory. He had served as Lawrence's campaign manager in his run for county commissioner in 1931. While the political sands were shifting, Lawrence preferred playing the odds and felt little need for personal aggrandizement. McNair, though a lifelong Democrat, was a Protestant blue-blood, and appeared to present no threat to the middle and upper class voters who Lawrence wanted to avoid rousing.[25]

With Republican Mayor Kline's indictment on 46 charges of malfeasance in office and subsequent resignation, the disorganized Republicans, despite a still heavy 120,000 advantage in voter registration (numbers that were heavily padded by dead and phantom voters), were crushed in the city elections of 1933. McNair and five Democratic candidates for City Council won convincingly. In local-option referendums, Pittsburghers voted six-to-one for legalizing Sunday baseball and football and seven-to-one for repealing prohibition. It proved to be a decisive defeat for the formerly formidable Republican machine, one from which they would not really recover. For the Democrats who put FDR's face on virtually every poster and ran under the banner of the NRA, happy days were here again indeed.[26]

While the 1933 election marked the crucial turning point in Lawrence's personal domination of Pittsburgh's politics, William McNair demonstrated almost immediately he was going to blaze an independent path. He told a reporter shortly after the Democratic primary: "You know, I made an agreement with Davey that I'd let the Democratic Party handle all the patronage if I was elected. But if I'm elected, who'll be the Democratic Party? As mayor of Pittsburgh I'll be the most important Democratic officeholder in Pennsylvania and I'll be the Democratic Party. How'll Davey like that?" McNair began immediately to make appointments without consulting and often in defiance of the party. His behavior became increasingly volatile, arbitrary and unpredictable. His individualistic grand-standing made great newspaper copy but was completely ineffective. He set up a desk in the lobby of the City-County Building where he met with enormous lines of the unemployed who came looking for jobs that he was unable to provide. To demonstrate to the unemployed what could be done with $500, he erected a small frame cottage on the sidewalk adjacent to the county jail, and to house the unemployed he erected a 400 foot long tent on the grounds of Mayview Hospital. These and other bizarre initiatives subjected him to public derision.[27]

> During his aborted term in office, McNair's crusades against high transit fares, the utilities, and the numbers racket came to little; his prolific use of the veto and his non-cooperation with local and federal relief authorities delayed Pittsburgh's join-ing the national recovery program; his week-long hosting of a local vaudeville show, along with appearances on radio as guest of Rudy Vallee and Major Bowe's amateur show increased his reputation as a buffoon as well as a ham. His close association with Father Peter V. Tkach, a Russian Orthodox priest, who he appointed traffic commissioner, a post many claimed did not exist; with A. Solly Mazur, facetiously labeled by the press as a "boardwalk inspector" for the municipal government; with Hunky Joe Lewandowski, a former numbers racketeer; and with Bozo Lavery, noto-rious for his criminal record yet appointed a detective by McNair, all enhanced the mayor's image as a colorful and rather curious character. In addition, McNair was twice arrested and once jailed while in office.[28]

Meanwhile, Dave Lawrence was preoccupied with gearing up the state Democratic Party to win the gubernatorial contest in 1934. In what had become a pattern, he chose George Earle, a multi-millionaire Main Line Philadelphian, who had only become a Democrat in 1931, but strongly supported Roosevelt and was serving as ambassador to Austria. Significantly, however, he also se-lected, Thomas Kennedy, Secretary-Treasurer of the United Mine Workers of America for Lieuten-ant-Governor, a move that greatly pleased organized labor. Meanwhile, he supported his mentor Joe Guffey for the U.S. Senate and thereby positioned himself to become the state Democratic chair-man. In the 1934 election, Lawrence emerged triumphant as Guffey defeated the arch-conservative Reed and Earle won the Governor's race. While Republicans held on to a narrow majority in Phila-delphia, the increasingly well-oiled Western Pennsylvania Democratic machine racked up decisive margins to carry the state. The victory of 22 of 32 Democratic candidates for the House of Repre-sentatives gave the party its first house majority in the 20th Century. Earle became the first Demo-cratic governor since 1894. From his Pittsburgh headquarters Lawrence declared: "The victory is a sweeping endorsement of the policies and administration of Franklin D. Roosevelt and the New

Deal. For the people of Pennsylvania it is a red letter day marking the emancipation of millions from the yoke of the Mellon-Grundy industrial and financial aristocracy."[29]

Following his triumph, Lawrence accepted appointment as the secretary of the Commonwealth where he managed the affairs of the state while Earle acted as the public spokesman. Ten of eighteen cabinet positions went to Western Pennsylvania allies. He effectively directed state government from 1935 to 1939. While he returned to Pittsburgh by train each weekend, his all-consuming political life left little time for family. His main recreation was found in the rich sports life of the city and card playing with his old political cronies. A pragmatist not an ideologue, he was an astute politician, adept at balancing conflicting interests and mediating compromises. Though he paid homage to organized labor, he maintained a certain distance from union leaders and at times showed a disconcerting willingness to work in partnership with the powerful and wealthy.[30]

During 1935, Republican control of the Senate stymied a push for a Pennsylvania "Little New Deal." An attempt to initiate tax reform targeting utilities, corporate income, capital gains exemptions, and a luxury tax were fiercely resisted in the Senate. A labor reform bill forbidding child labor under sixteen and establishing a minimum wage for women and children was blocked. While the Coal and Iron Police were finally completely abolished, the effects were limited because companies were still allowed to pay the salaries of local law enforcement officers, a practice that could not help but taint their neutrality. Finally after Mayor McNair fired a whole raft of public officials in January 1935, Lawrence began to push for the passage of a "ripper" bill that would abolish the post of mayor and appoint a city commissioner. McNair had deeply antagonized the party by running for governor against Earle in the Democratic primary and then endorsing the Republican candidate after he lost. In two years in office, the mayor vetoed 83 bills, 69 of these vetoes being overridden. Twenty-four out of twenty-five state representatives from the west lined up in support of the ripper, but the Republican Senate kept the bill tied up in committee. Lawrence focused his energies toward the conquest of the Pennsylvania Senate in 1936.[31]

As Lawrence geared up for the 1936 election, new Democratic registrations swelled by nearly 375,000 while Republicans added only 30,000. Republican obstructionism of the Little New Deal social agenda was deeply unpopular and 22 of 25 contested state senate seats were in Republican hands. The 1936 Democratic Convention was held in Philadelphia giving the national spotlight to the three leading Pennsylvania Democrats: Guffey, Earle and Lawrence. Roosevelt caravans crisscrossed the state with Roosevelt joining some of them in October moving through towns and neighborhoods, speaking at plant gates and town squares. The President repeated his triumphal visit to Forbes Field where he addressed a standing room crowd. He felt obliged to respond to accusations he had increased the national debt despite promises four years earlier at the same stadium that he would balance the budget. He argued his deficit spending was a necessary priming of the pump that included the payment of the World War I veterans' bonus and massive federal investment in conservation projects and infrastructure. Roosevelt opened his speech by saying that a ball park was a good place to talk about box scores.

> Compare the scoreboard which you have in Pittsburgh now with the score board
> which you had when I stood here at second base four years ago. At that time as I
> drove through these great valleys, I could see mile after mile of this greatest mill and
> factory area of the world, a dead panorama of silent black structures and smokeless
> stacks. I saw idleness and hunger instead of the whirl of machinery. Today as I came
> north from West Virginia, I saw mines operating; I found bustle and life, the hiss of

steam, the ring of steel on steel – the roaring song of industry.

And now a word as to the foolish fear of a crushing load the debt will impose on your children and mine. This debt is not going to be paid by oppressive taxation on future generations. It is not going to be paid by taking away the hard-won savings of the present generation. It is going to be paid out of an increased national income and increased individual income produced by increasing national prosperity.[32]

The Roosevelt visit also provided another huge benefit for Dave Lawrence. In a huff over being excluded from any role in the Roosevelt appearance at Forbes Field, Mayor McNair fired the only remaining organization Democrat in the city administration, Lawrence's close friend and city treasurer, Jimmy Kirk. City Council then refused to approve McNair's appointed successor and without a treasurer to sign checks, the city government ground to a halt. McNair submitted a one-page letter of resignation that Council quickly accepted, thereby sparing Lawrence the necessity of moving against the mayor in the new Democratic legislature. Organization Democrat and president of City Council, Cornelius Scully, was sworn in as mayor.[33]

Roosevelt swept the state by an astonishing 600,000 votes, the first Democratic presidential candidate to win the state since James Buchanan in 1856. Eighteen of the contested Senate seats went to the Democrats creating a two-to-one majority in their favor. Senator Coyne and the remaining remnants of Republican dominance were swept away and the new Democratic majority in the Pennsylvania House was 154 to 54. Roosevelt took every ward in Pittsburgh and, even more impressive, broke Republican power in Philadelphia by winning over all the black and Italian wards. The result was a flood of progressive legislation including the breakup of the company town and company store, substantial increase in relief funds, slum clearance and public housing, and enactment of a graduated state income tax. Only 6 of 371 bills supported by the administration failed to reach the governor's desk. The legislature often worked 12 and 14 hour sessions. Organized labor got a "Little Wagner Act" protecting workers' right to organize without coercion or interference from employers along with a Pennsylvania Labor Relations Board to enforce its provisions. Regulations were placed on public utilities, public assistance was centralized, fair trade practices upheld, a milk control board established, loan sharking practices curtailed, the first regulations aimed at controlling stream pollution instituted, a state tuberculosis hospital established, and the workers' compensation system expanded to include occupationally acquired diseases. Other legislation imposed safety regulations, prohibited employers from recruiting replacement workers during a strike and limited court injunctions in labor disputes. Perhaps the most ambitious project was the establishment of a state turnpike, initially over the two hundred mile distance from Pittsburgh to Harrisburg, the first such limited access four-lane system in the United States. Dave Lawrence oversaw the whole operation and was widely seen as a gubernatorial candidate in 1940, if Earle ran as expected for president.[34]

Floods of Change

1936 and 1937 proved to be momentous years for the Pittsburgh region. The creaking infrastructure of the region's river towns and cities was devastated by the worst flood in its history. Physical flood was followed by political landslide followed by a sea change in the nature of class relationships. It was not simply the change of one party to another. It was a fundamental shift that opened up power to many union politicians and working-class activists in the towns where they lived. The "Labor Democrats" sweep in the mill town municipal elections year extended the conquest of governmental power by the resurgent Democrats in the wake of Roosevelt's landslide victory. In the 1937 municipal elections, the corporate stranglehold over community life and politics was broken. Largely grassroots candidates running as Labor Democrats or CIO Democrats were able to sustain the Roosevelt momentum and break the local control of the Republican machines. The struggle for the organization of workers and the increased grassroots political involvement overlapped and reinforced. The labor movement had finally achieved an organizational form adapted to industrial reality that provided a vehicle for the rise of union power in steel, aluminum, glass, electrical, food processing, and especially automobile. A legal framework for industrial disputes evolved. These transforming local events took place unfortunately against the backdrop of a world sliding toward a war to be fought on a scale and intensity unequaled in human history.

On February 26, 1936, an ice jam formed on the Allegheny River and began to move slowly toward Pittsburgh flooding upstream communities along the way. On St. Patrick's Day, March 17, heavy rains and rapid snow melt combined to send water levels to nine feet above flood stage at the Point, inundating downtown streets and interrupting rail and trolley service. The water continued to rise, however, and crested around noon on March 28, at more than twenty feet above flood level, exceeding the previous flood record by five feet. The official death toll was 46 known dead. The worst affected community was the McKees Rocks "Bottoms" district, once site of Queen Aliquippa's cornfields, where thousands fled and many hundreds were trapped and needed rescue.

> More than 800 families were awaiting rescuers in the McKee's Rocks "Bottoms," the riverside district below the borough proper. More than a dozen fire companies from neighboring communities were working to bring them to safety; but while they worked, the roaring waters were smashing the flimsy houses to pieces. Exhausted and frantic, clinging to house tops and chimneys, some lost their strength when rescue seemed near and were swept into the swollen waters....Firemen were lowering ladders and ropes down from the McKees Rocks-North Side bridge, late last night for those in the "Bottoms" area who could row.[35]

The flood-caused devastation provided a sharp rise in demand for the skilled construction unions; this was especially true for the IBEW, which was called upon to rewire many of the homes and businesses of the city. This surge in employment came at the very moment when the AFL was facing an internal revolt over its conservatism and inability to effectively organize. That internal revolt led by John L. Lewis of the Mineworkers unleashed a mass organizing effort that simultaneously abetted and harnessed rank-and-file aspirations and involvement.

Despite John L. Lewis's anti-democratic and authoritarian leadership style, he clearly understood the need for a dynamic and forceful leadership to aggressively push and support mass industrial organizing. He chafed under the timid and self-serving leadership of the AFL. He understood "the foul taste of treason which the AFL left among steelworkers in 1933," the demoralizing effect of the Amalgamated's dithering over the protection of its craft jurisdictions in the face of the deep longing for effective union organization among the rank-and-file steelworkers. Lewis was a forceful personality, whose sense of the dramatic and understanding of political infighting was legendary. Like Franklin D. Roosevelt, who he came to detest, he exuded an incredible self-assurance, decisiveness and confidence. Radio served the talents of both men. For Lewis the medium magnified his dramatic presentation of labor's aspirations and made him one of the most powerful men in America. When Lewis decided to make his move, he reached out to former non-Communist rivals like John Brophy and Powers Hapgood and recruited them to his cause. With his immediate staff secure, he opened organizing positions to the Communists. Lewis had long experience and a grudging respect for the discipline and dedication of the Communists. Despite old wounds and bitter memories on their side, the Communists rallied to the CIO as the natural vehicle for their united front strategy.[36]

The Rubicon of industrial organization was crossed at the October 1935 AFL convention. At the beginning of the gathering, Lewis made the case for industrial unionism: "The labor movement is organized on the principle that the strong shall help the weak....Isn't it right that we should contribute something of our own strength, our own virtues, our own knowledge, our own influence toward those less fortunately situated, in the knowledge that if we help them and they grow strong, in turn that we will be the beneficiary of their changed status and their strength?" In conclusion he thundered: "Heed this cry from Macedonia that comes from the hearts of men. Organize the unorganized." With the industrial union resolution defeated by the conservative old guard majority, Lewis confronted the leader of the carpenters' union, Bill Hutcheson, on the final day of the convention, over his repeated *point of order* interruptions during pleas by young rubber workers for an industrial union. The miners and the carpenters, as the two largest unions in the federation were seated across the aisle from one another at the front of the hall. Lewis rose to challenge Hutcheson calling his repeated interruptions "rather small potatoes." In response, Hutcheson raised his three hundred pound frame to full extension. "I was raised on small potatoes. That is why I am so small." Lewis walked across the aisle to confront Hutcheson, whispered something to him, upon which the carpenter allegedly called him "a coal-crackin' son of a bitch." Lewis responded with a punch to the face and the two men fought, ending up wrestling on the floor. CIO publicist Len De Caux called Lewis "the John L. Sullivan of industrial organization." Lewis later recounted: "All I will say is that I never walked across an aisle so slowly and grimly as I did that day in the 1935 convention. An act of some kind, an act dramatic to a degree that it would inspire and enthuse the workers of this country was necessary. Did I say was necessary? It was essential."[37]

On the very next morning, Lewis convened a breakfast meeting of nearly 50 supporters of industrial unionism and shortly afterward formed a special self-appointed Committee for Industrial Organization within the AFL. Initially the three largest unions involved were the UMWA, Sidney Hillman's Amalgamated Clothing Workers and David Dubinsky's International Ladies Garment Workers. While many of those gathered espoused moderate socialist ideas, they all supported collective bargaining, centralized union leadership, and basic American institutions including private enterprise. Most all were enthusiastic supporters of President Roosevelt. While they were willing to utilize the strength and discipline of Communist Party members as organizers, they all had varying levels of negative experience with Communists during the party's dual-union phase. While in some ways, the party's greatest strength was the credibility it garnered as a realistic alternative to capitalism because of its global strategy and organization, the subservience of national parties to a common position on international politics and internal strategies adopted by the Communist International became a fatal flaw. As Joseph Stalin solidified his hold on both the Russian Communist Party and the Communist International, he increasingly tightened his control over the strategic decisions of the entire movement. Subsequent shifts in party line proved difficult for locally based union leaders to embrace or even understand and gave manifest credence to hostile accusations of foreign control.

By the end of 1935, the UMWA had gained important footholds in the captive mines owned by the steel companies; but steel itself had to be captured to secure the victory in coal and open the door to a union movement powerful enough nationally to balance the power of capital. The showdown came on April 28, 1936, when the old Amalgamated Association met in Canonsburg, south of Pittsburgh, while the Pennsylvania State Federation of Labor convened in nearby Uniontown. Several days before the convention John L. Lewis offered the Amalgamated a half-million dollars to launch a steel organizing drive. Delegates streamed to the convention where the old guard stalled for several days. Finally, a delegation headed by John Brophy and Pat Fagan was sent to the Amalgamated's convention where they were met by a standing ovation and an overwhelming vote to accept Lewis's offer and join the Committee for Industrial Organization.

Lewis threw down the gauntlet to the AFL on June 13, 1936, when he announced the formation of the Steel Workers Organizing Committee (SWOC) and effectively absorbed the moribund Amalgamated Association. The organizational meeting of SWOC was held in Pat Fagan's UMWA District 5 board room in Pittsburgh's Commonwealth Building on June 17, 1936. The eight-member Executive Board of the new organization included four mineworkers with Phil Murray as chairman and David J. McDonald, secretary-treasurer. Pat Fagan was on the board in his key positions as president of UMWA District 5 which included the large captive mines of U.S. Steel, Jones and Laughlin, Wheeling, Inland, Republic and Crucible steel companies around Pittsburgh, as well as in his role as president of the Pittsburgh Central Labor Council. At the meeting, Murray appointed Clint Golden, director of the Pittsburgh Region and Van Bittner, director of the Midwest Region. Golden had to step down as the Pittsburgh Regional Director of the National Labor Relations Board to take the job. Lee Pressman was appointed general counsel and Vince Sweeney, publicity director. The UMWA pledged thirty-five to forty organizers to the SWOC effort. In a policy statement, Murray emphasized "the spirit of responsibility to the whole labor movement and to the nation in which it is undertaking the gigantic task of organizing the steel industry," and stated that "the objective of the Committee is to establish a permanent organization for collective bargaining in the steel industry."[38]

A short time later, George Powers from McKeesport, who introduced the resolution to send the AFL-CIO delegation to the Amalgamated convention in Canonsburg, was summoned by Clint Golden to the SWOC headquarters on the top floor of the 32 story Grant Building and charged with opening an organizing office in McKeesport. He was thrilled by the seriousness of the operation.[39]

> …I took the elevator to the top floor. In my mind I could recall the shabby offices of the old AA located over on the west end. What a dramatic contrast! Here in the Grant Building was a modern steel workers union open for union business. People were coming and going; secretaries were busy taking notes and answering phones.[40]

Even though the CIO represented a direct organizational challenge to the AFL, ideologically it remained similar in philosophy. It espoused a "centralized and responsible" organizing strategy with hierarchical governance and a goal of collective bargaining. All decisions were made by Murray, who hired the organizers, and all money collected from members was sent to Pittsburgh to be dispersed by SWOC. Working for SWOC became a high priority for Communists in the steel-making areas. William Z. Foster claimed that 60 of SWOC's 200 organizers in 1937 were party members. Given SWOC's top-down structure and the CP's deference to Lewis, party members in steel generally remained loyal foot soldiers with little inclination to rock the boat. The party virtually abandoned its independent work in coal where it once had been strongest in order to signal its subservience to Lewis and the CIO.[41]

While Lewis and his closest lieutenants were trusted anti-communists, there were two important Communists among the central staff of the CIO: one, a feisty journalist, the Australian Len

DeCaux, was hired as publicity director of the CIO and editor of the *CIO News* on the recommendation of Brophy; and the other, more important, was Lee Pressman, general counsel of both SWOC and the CIO, who played the role of intermediary between Party leadership and the CIO's non-Communist leaders. A brilliant lawyer, considered by some the *eminence grise* of the CIO, Pressman helped facilitate the Party's role as junior partner, smoothing relations and resolving conflicts. He faithfully served Lewis and Murray through numerous twists and turns of union and party policy. When ordered, he even wrote anti-Communist resolutions for his bosses. Another group of intellectuals, more social democratic than Communist, that played an important role in advising rank-and-file militants in their relations with SWOC and the CIO included labor mediator Clint Golden, muck-raking journalist Harvey O'Connor, and economist Harold Ruttenberg. It was an indicator of Lewis's personal self-confidence and understanding of the historic opportunity that he was able to assemble such a talented and broad-based team, many of whom had been his sworn and bitter enemies.[42]

On June 21, 1936, the first mass meeting organized by SWOC was held on the Youghiogheny River bank in McKeesport, since no other location could be obtained in town. A contingent of 350 miners marched into town from Versailles joining steelworkers to hear Phil Murray call on workers "to defend your rights as Americans." On July 5, 1936, SWOC organized a rally at the Seventh Street Playground in Homestead in honor of the steelworkers of 1892. Between 2,000 to 4,000 steelworkers gathered to hear speeches by Judge Michael Musmanno and Lieutenant Governor Thomas Kennedy. The mill was operating that day, its first Sunday of work in seven years, one reason certainly for the lower than expected attendance. Indeed, one factor for the seeming lack of passion in steel was the relative success of the New Deal in getting industrial production up, while providing work and relief to the unemployed through governmental programs.[43]

On the front page of the first issue of *Steel Labor: The Voice of the Steel Workers Organizing Committee* – price one cent – there was printed the "Declaration of Independence" adopted at that Homestead rally. An accompanying illustration depicted two fists, the Steel Worker's and the Steel Owner's, rising up out of the smokestacks. Under the caption "What is," it states: "As long as there is oppression of one by the other there will always be bitter strife and test of force." Under the caption "What will be," it states: "An intelligent order will ensue when contractual relations will be established, when under union organization and union agreements, steel worker and steel owner can adjust their problems in fairness, reason and human decency." The declaration decried the "Despotism of the Lords of Steel."[44]

> ….Through their control over the hours we work, the wages we receive, and the conditions of our labor, and through their denial of our right to organize freely and bargain collectively, the Lords of Steel try to rule us as did the royalists against whom our forefathers rebelled….So we steel workers do solemnly publish and declare our independence. We say to the world: "We are Americans." We shall exercise our inalienable right to organize into a great industrial union….Through this union, we shall win higher wages, shorter hours, and a better standard of living. We shall win leisure for ourselves and opportunity for our children.[45]

After the program, the crowd proceeded up the hill to the graves of the 1892 Homestead Strikers, only one of which was graced with a headstone. The location of the unmarked graves was indicated by "a sturdily built elderly Irishman, the Communist leader, Pat Cush, whose father had served on the union advisory committee during the Homestead strike." Those gathered heard UMWA leader Pat Fagan say: "Let the blood of those labor pioneers who were massacred here be the seed of this new organization in 1936." Fagan also spoke at the massive 1936 Labor Day rally in South Park where an estimated 250,000 gathered.[46]

In later years, Pat Fagan remembered the many volunteer union organizers, including his brother who organized in Pittsburgh.

> My brother Gerald (God be good to him), he's dead now, was the youngest in the family and he helped to organize the J&L workers in the South Side and Second Avenue. He did a lot of organizing in the taverns. After the boys had a few drinks, he'd get them to sign a card. We had many meetings on the South Side in the Lithuanian Hall. At first we had a tough time getting a place to meet, but the Lithuanians would leave you meet there as often as you wanted to and they wouldn't charge you anything. They played a prominent role in organizing the men in South Side and on Second Avenue.

Roosevelt's smashing victory in November 1936, driven by a massive labor vote, set off a wave of worker activity. SWOC supporters inside the U.S. Steel ERPs became emboldened, and key company union leaders like Elmer Maloy and George Patterson made a well-publicized trip to Washington to confer with John L. Lewis and Frances Perkins. Murray convened a meeting where 250 ERP representatives from 46 plants assembled in Pittsburgh and signed SWOC membership cards and named itself the "CIO Representative Council." Sit-down strikes starting the day after Christmas at a General Motors plant in Flint, Michigan electrified the nation by introducing the plant occupation tactic into the heart of what had become the country's largest corporation. Lewis went to Flint with what he thought was President Roosevelt's backing to settle the strike through the achievement of union recognition. Roosevelt, however, resented the way that Lewis maneuvered the press into thinking he had some sort of presidential mandate. Tension and mistrust grew and deepened between the two men. Lewis gained enormous stature from his leadership under pressure. He later described the key confrontation with the newly elected and basically supportive Democratic Governor Murphy, as 2,500 National Guard troops and state police units encircled the defiant plant, who had just informed Lewis that as Governor he had to "uphold the law," and enforce a court injunction vacating the building from its six-week occupation at the point of bayonet. According to Lewis, he replied:

> Uphold the law? You are doing this to uphold the law? You, Frank Murphy, are ordering the National Guard to evict by point of bayonet, the sit-down strikers? You, Frank Murphy, by doing this are giving complete victory to General Motors and defeating all of the hopes and dreams of these men. And you are doing all of this because you say, *"to uphold the law!"* Governor Murphy, when you gave ardent support to the Irish revolutionary movement against the British Empire, you were not doing that because of your high regard for law and order....And when the British government took your grandfather as an Irish revolutionary and hanged him by the neck, you did not get down on your knees and burst forth for the sanctity and glory and purity of the law....
>
> Tomorrow morning I shall personally enter General Motors plant Chevrolet No. 4. I shall order the men to disregard your order, to stand fast. I shall then walk up to the largest window in the plant, open it, divest myself of my outer raiment, remove my shirt, and bare my bosom. Then when you order your troops to fire, mine will be the

first breast that those bullets will strike….And as my body falls from that window to the ground, you listen to the voice of your grandfather as he whispers in your ear, "Frank, are you sure you are doing the right thing?"

The governor did not serve the order and General Motors capitulated the following day. With the defeat of General Motors, the labor war looked like it might turn into a rout. A wave of plants self-organized themselves into the CIO across the country, however, many subsequent sit-downs strikes were suppressed and the Supreme Court declared them illegal. In Pennsylvania, a dramatic sit-down strike at the Hershey Chocolate plant ended when local farmers whose milk had to be dumped for lack of storage entered the plant with management encouragement and forcibly evicted the striking production workers.[47]

Meanwhile, Lewis encountered Myron Taylor while having lunch with Senator Joseph F. Guffey of Pennsylvania on January 9, 1937, at the Mayflower Hotel in Washington, D.C. With the Flint plant occupation as back drop, they began meeting privately the next two days, as well as negotiating through an intermediary. After several meetings in mid-February, Taylor presented Lewis with a formula for the recognition of SWOC. Phil Murray, who had not initially been informed of Lewis's bold venture, was assigned to work out the details with Ben Fairless from U.S. Steel. The two signed the formal accord in Pittsburgh on March 2, 1937. Reportedly, a portrait of Henry Clay Frick was removed from the room before the signing. The capitulation of U.S. Steel without a fight secured for the stockholders of the corporation the promise of continued production without labor unrest just as huge British government armor plate orders were being placed. But the bottom line was clear. The labor movement had refashioned American economic and political reality. While thousands of the steel corporation's workers streamed into SWOC, the agreement did not give SWOC exclusive bargaining rights since a contract had been hastily approved by most of the ERPs in December. In March 1937, a "flying squadron" was dispatched to Homestead by Murray where it maintained a round-the-clock picket for a week to sign up the majority of the mill's workers. The same month, a short sit-down strike, the first in steel, achieved a contract at Firth Sterling Steel in McKeesport. The victory without a battle for recognition at U.S. Steel proved to be a two-edged sword. The agreement blunted shop floor militancy and reinforced top-down organizational tendencies inside SWOC, but it also had a strongly inspirational impact on other CIO efforts, especially on the rising militancy of workers in what became known as Little Steel. There, fierce corporate resistance tested shop floor resolve. [48]

An example of how the CIO upsurge assisted other industrial union organizing efforts is illustrated by the struggle of aluminum workers at Alcoa's plants in and around New Kensington. Allegheny Valley aluminum workers had spontaneously organized an Aluminum Workers union local in 1933 in response to Roosevelt's victory and the passage of the NIRA. Stonewalled by the AFL and feeling betrayed by NIRA industrial codes that actually cut wages, a five-week strike in August 1935 ended without gains. The emergence of the CIO rekindled hope among the Alcoa workers and by January 1937, the CIO organizers inside the AFL union had gained majority support. On April 12, 1937, the constitutional convention of the Aluminum Workers of America convened and elected longtime activist, an anti-Communist Socialist, Nick Zonarich as president. Mary Peli, fired for union activity, emerged as a spokesperson for both the women and the Italian workers who composed the majority of the workforce. Successive work stoppages in 1937, 1938 and 1939 culminated in a comprehensive union contract signed by Alcoa on November 11, 1939.[49]

The restraint the Communist Party's United Front policy exercised on its most successful organizers in the great auto struggle was revealed in the party's lack of support for popular and capable Communist organizers like Wyndham Mortimer, and close rank-and-file allies like the extremely popular Georges Addes. These men were capable of attaining autoworker union leadership on the merits, but they were barred from union leadership by Party directives that reflected pressure from Murray and Lewis. The United Front strategy revealed a persistent tension between the public leadership of the above ground party organization and the often silent membership of important union leaders. Anonymous semi-secret membership engendered a "was (she) he" or "wasn't (she) he" dilemma in the assessment of the real level of Communist Party involvement, both in assigning credit for effective organizing or blame for disastrous policies.[50]

The Flint Strike went to the heart of the matter. It was essentially and starkly a struggle of property rights versus democratic organizational rights. It was an assertion of the worker's property right to a job and human right to concerted activity. While workers asserted their human right to association, representation and participation on the job, they also asserted, as had the workers at Homestead in 1892, a certain property right to the worker's most valuable asset – a job. Strikers put their lives on the line in a bitter cold winter and sustained a largely non-violent struggle. In January and February 1937, John L. Lewis became the center of whirlwind negotiations between General Motors, the Governor of Michigan and the President of the United States with the revolutionary backdrop of occupied auto plants. The sit-down strikers posed a direct challenge to private property rights that teetered on the brink of serious violence and resulted in a settlement for union recognition. Lewis, in an extraordinary negotiating tour de force, squeezed out a settlement with General Motors, while simultaneously negotiating with Myron Taylor of U.S. Steel a deal to unionize from above the vast domain of Carnegie, Frick, and Gary.[51]

The agreement between SWOC and U.S. Steel had a dramatic impact on all the players in the steel industry. Before March 2, only a handful of small companies had signed with the union. Afterwards, dozens of small companies and U.S. Steel subsidiaries ran to sign up. By May 15, SWOC had signed 110 contracts with companies employing 300,000 workers. Conversely, the major independent steel companies were appalled at Myron Taylor's betrayal and vowed to fight to the finish. Bethlehem, J&L, Republic, Youngstown Sheet and Tube, Inland, National (Weirton) and American Rolling Mills (ARMCO) took their stand as "Little Steel."

Aliquippa and Little Steel

The first battle in Little Steel took on historic dimensions. The Jones & Laughlin Steel Company was the second largest steel company in western Pennsylvania and third in the country after Charlie Schwab's Bethlehem operations outgrew it just before the First World War. It remained basically family owned with the Jones, King and Laughlin families maintaining various leadership positions. An ambitious Lehigh University graduate, Tom Girdler came to J&L in 1914, helped build the firm's war production capacity, becoming superintendent of the Aliquippa Works in 1920. Girdler was instrumental in developing the very harsh labor regime and system of community control that won Aliquippa the title "Little Siberia." Girdler, on the other hand, believed that his tightly controlled domain was "the best possible place for steelworkers to work and raise their families." Characterized as a "benevolent dictatorship," the company tightly controlled its "company town" through the Republican political machine, an efficient and at times brutal police force, and direct control over the town's housing that was broken into "plans" where thirteen separate ethnic groups were kept separate and divided. In a notorious case, a union organizer, George Issoski, crippled from a mill accident, was committed to the state hospital at Torrence by a lunacy commission for carrying 200 union leaflets into Aliquippa. Governor Pinchot had to commission an investigating committee to obtain his release. Pinchot's wife Cordelia spoke at the first public labor meeting the town had ever seen attended by over 4,000 people and participated in a parade for steelworkers during the abortive union upsurge of 1934. Corporate control was never so total at the older J&L complex that sprawled along both shores of the Monongahela in the City of Pittsburgh.[52]

Aliquippa was a tough town for unionists and it produced a tough bunch of activists. The area had been a stronghold of the National Miners Union and a small but effective branch of the Steel and Metal Workers Industrial Union was active there. Like other steel companies, J&L had initiated Employee Representation Plans after the passage of the NIRA in 1933. At the 1935 AFL Convention Phil Murray had cited Aliquippa as an example of the failure of craft-based organizing. When 6,500 of 8,000 workers organized industrially in 1933-34, the AFL came in and split the workforce into separate crafts and the entire effort collapsed. In 1935, the Supreme Court struck down the NIRA and Congress responded by passing the Wagner Act. J&L systematically fired union activists and these were the subject of unfair labor practice charges filed with the National Labor Relations Board against J&L's denial of labor rights that would go all the way to the Supreme Court. A center of union and political organizing was the Democratic Social Club, many of whose members were radical Italian political refugees from Mussolini's Italy. In 1935, the club ran a full slate of Democratic candidates, a first in the town's history. Unfair labor practice charges were filed over the dismissal of a carefully constructed list of ten workers representing all the major ethnic groups at the mill out of the hundreds who had been fired for union activity at Aliquippa. The Labor Board agreed with the unfair labor practice charge and ordered the men reinstated. J&L immediately challenged the constitutionality of the Wagner Act and the case worked its way to the U.S. Supreme Court.[53]

In June 1936, Phil Murray sent in one of his best organizers, Joe Timko, a tough former boiler-maker and coal miner who had been an elected UMWA district president in Indiana and then served as an international representative in bloody Harlan County, Kentucky, to deal with the Aliquippa situation. Timko began holding organizational meetings at the center of resistance to corporate rule, Aliquippa's Democratic Social Club, housed in the former Romanian Hall on a hillside overlooking the mill not far from the main gate. Mike Kellar, an immigrant from Yugoslavia, whose father was killed at Crucible Steel in Midland, was elected president of the Democrat Club at the beginning of 1936. As the most public face of opposition to corporate rule, Mike, who was a small man, was set upon several times and viciously beaten. On Labor Day 1936, the company and the union held rival parades in town. After the morning's official parade with town officials and company union members, the union parade including thousands of union coal miners and AFL craftsmen marched behind the fired workers carrying American flags. In November, Franklin Roosevelt carried Aliquippa, signaling the dawn of a new era. Critical to the victory was the shift of black workers out of the Republican Party into the Democratic Party and the CIO. Critical meetings held to recruit company union leaders were held in Pittsburgh's Hill District at a bar run by Cumberland Posey, owner of the Homestead Grays baseball team. Timko subsequently recruited five leaders of the company union, most notably, Paul Normile, a popular leader who publicly resigned from the ERP in January 1937 and joined SWOC. He was subsequently elected president of SWOC Local 1211.[54]

On April 12, 1937, the U.S. Supreme Court issued its eagerly anticipated decision in NLRB vs. J&L Steel. The case had become a test of wills between the extremely popular president and the aging conservative court. Frustrated by the court's repeated striking down of the key legislative achievements of the New Deal, Roosevelt threatened to "pack the court," adding six new justices out of an expressed solicitude for the age and workload of the court. With labor in turmoil and a constitutional crisis looming, the court upheld the constitutionality of the Wagner Act in a 5-4 decision, the famous "switch in time that saved nine." Since there are no explicit protections in the Constitution for the right of association, let alone labor representation or collective bargaining, the Wagner Act, like many other efforts to regulate big business, rested precariously on the Commerce Clause of the Constitution that gave Congress the power to regulate interstate commerce. The first issue the court needed to decide was whether these large manufacturing entities constitute interstate commerce because of their size and impact on the economy? While there was no question that the products of the steel mills were transported and used nationally and even internationally, the courts had long held that mines and mills, being fixed and stationary, could only be regulated in matters such as health and safety or labor relations generally by the states. The second fundamental issue that had to be dealt with was "freedom of contract," an essential aspect of American law that allowed employers, as well as employees, to sever the employment relation at will. Chief Justice Charles Evans Hughes, writing for the majority, addressed these fundamental issues, starting with labor rights as human rights:

> Long ago, we stated the reason for labor organizations. We said they were organized out of the necessities of the situation: that a single employee was helpless in dealing with an employer; that he depended ordinarily on his daily wage for the maintenance of himself and his family; that if the employer refused to pay him the wages he thought fair, he was nevertheless unable to leave the employ and resist arbitrary and unfair treatment; that union was essential to give laborers opportunity to deal on an equality with their employer....

Next, the Court addressed the issue of the application of the Commerce Clause:

> Although activities may be intrastate in character when separately considered, if they have such a close and substantial relation to interstate commerce that their control is essential or appropriate to protect that commerce from burdens and obstructions, Congress cannot be denied the power to exercise that control.... When industries organize themselves on a national scale, making their relation to interstate commerce the dominant factor in their activities, how can it be maintained that their industrial relations constitute a forbidden field into which Congress may not enter when it is necessary to protect interstate commerce from the paralyzing consequences of industrial war?

Finally, the Court addressed the central issue of employment at will or freedom of contract:

> The Act does not interfere with the normal exercise of the right of the employer to select its employees or to discharge them. The employer may not, under cover of that right, intimidate or coerce its employees with respect to their self-organization and representation, and, on the other hand, the Board is not entitled to make its authority a pretext for interference with the right of discharge when that right is exercised for other reasons than such intimidation and coercion.[55]

This monumental Supreme Court ruling addressed labor issues that went back to the early days of Pittsburgh and the conspiracy charge for organizing to raise wages leveled at the Pittsburgh cordwainers during their 1814 trial. Then, conspiracy (breathing together), conversation, and concerted activity were involved in the crime of restraining trade. One could quit work as an individual, but the crime was in the togetherness, the impact of concerted activity on commerce. In 1937, the violation by large corporations of workers' rights to free association and organization was being recognized as the source of the work stoppages and plant occupations that were causing massive disruptions of commerce. Thus, concerted activity, rather than being punished for the interruption of commerce, was *by means of the interruption of commerce* putting the systematic violation of workers' human rights by corporations under the purview of Congress and the courts.

> When news of the court's decision hit town, a parade of cars was immediately assembled. The parade moved along Franklin Avenue, Aliquippa's main business street, then climbed steep Fifth Ave. to Plan 11, a staunchly pro-union neighborhood. The "Aliquippa Ten" who were named in the NLRB complaint rode in two lead cars. One carried a sign: "We are the Ten Men Fired for Union Activity by J&L. We are ordered back to work by the Supreme Court;" the other bore a sign that stated simply, "The Workers of America are now Free Men." Pete Cekoric, a little firebrand at 5'2", told Rose Stein for the *Nation* magazine. "When I hear Wagner Bill went constitutional, I happy like anything. I say, good, now Aliquippa become part of the United States."[56]

Despite the Supreme Court ruling, J&L continued to stall and set conditions, so on May 12, SWOC called a strike. Many of the Aliquippa workers wanted an inside-the-plant sit-down, but SWOC insisted on a picket line and strike to force a recognition vote. Conditions at the front entry tunnel were tense. A supposed postal truck was stopped by women picketers at the entry tunnel and when the driver refused to let the union open the doors to check the contents, the truck was overturned to reveal food and drink for those still inside the plant. An eyewitness reported: "Aliquippa rose up against a tyranny that had held it for years. For all practical purposes, the workers took over the reins of government. They were in complete control….The strike is doing wonders for the men. Remember that Jefferson once said something about a revolution every twenty years being a blessing? The same is true of a strike. There is real solidarity now. And certainly no fear. In fact workers go out of their way to thumb their noses at company police by whom they have been cowed for years." In a dramatic gesture, George Earle, the Governor of Pennsylvania, appeared at the plant entry on the morning of the 14th. When he drove through the tunnel into the mill with SWOC organizer Timko at his side, he was confronted with gun-toting deputies. He ordered the guns removed and by noon an agreement was reached that was better than that with U.S. Steel, since it offered exclusive bargaining rights to SWOC if it won the representation election. Another parade through the whole town ensued and parties lasted through the night. The election held on May 20 in Aliquippa and Pittsburgh resulted in an overwhelming victory for SWOC, 17,028 to 7,207. One of the strike leaders in the Tin Mill, Mary Cozzucoli, recalled: "We were really happy, really happy! We had a parade….I'll tell you that street was loaded with people…celebrating, hollering, screaming. That was the best day of our lives."[57]

Aliquippa represented the highpoint of the drive for industrial organizing in 1937. While union organizing around the nation had ridden the wave of Roosevelt's landslide, the subsequent dramatic rank-and-file victory at Flint and the collapse of U.S. Steel's resistance, fed the expectation that the victory at Aliquippa was the opening salvo in a triumphal march through the recalcitrant Little Steel companies. This hope was brutally aborted at the Memorial Day massacre outside the gates of Republic's South Chicago mill. There, the longstanding animosity of the Chicago police against those considered radicals or agitators was brutally displayed when a picket line established after a march was attacked; ten marchers were fatally shot and thirty others wounded by gunshot, including a woman and three minors. Tom Girdler, elected President of the Iron and Steel Institute by his peers after the betrayal of Myron Taylor, had been preparing for war all during the previous year. Union strength in Little Steel varied greatly from company to company. Strongest in Youngstown, South Chicago and Northwest Indiana, the union was weak in Bethlehem Steel, and weaker still at National Steel in Weirton and Steubenville, and ARMCO, in Middletown, Ohio. Murray, whose fledgling organization had just swallowed a whale, needed time to regroup and consolidate. Rank-and-file pressures for a strike, however, were strong in Youngstown and in the Chicago area. Girdler began to purchase ammunition and gas grenades, establish police and community support networks and develop a public relations campaign that included distribution of tens of thousands of copies of a pamphlet entitled "Join the CIO and Help Build a Soviet America." Little Steel adopted the U.S. Steel wage and hours proposal; so that economic issues were off the table and the sole issue was recognition. [58]

As violent incidents proliferated, public opinion began to swing against the unions. In the midst of the renewed corporate offensive, and confronted by Tom Girdler's refusal to accept any mediation, Roosevelt made the fateful remark: "The majority of people are saying just one thing, a plague on both your houses." Lewis was meeting with the press when he read Roosevelt's comment. A reporter noted: "He said nothing, but his heels drummed against the desk's lower panels with a violence that just missed reducing them to splinters." Martial law declarations in Pennsylvania and Ohio prevented strikers from blocking the return to work by non-strikers and replacements. By the end of the summer, the Little Steel strike had been broken, and so was the relationship between Lewis and Roosevelt. In his Labor Day radio address, Lewis struck back vigorously at the President. "It ill behooves one who has supped at labor's table and who has been sheltered in labor's house to curse with equal fervor and fine impartiality both labor and its adversaries when they become locked in deadly embrace."[59]

Priests, Prayers and Consolidation

On June 3, 1937, a few days after the Memorial Day massacre in South Chicago, Father Charles Owen Rice, a brash, energetic young Roman Catholic priest accompanied by two older priest mentors and a group of laity, including "some nice-looking young women," joined the picket line set up by strikers for the American Federation of Labor at the H. J. Heinz Company in Pittsburgh. In this action, he was harshly criticized by Father James Cox, who had received considerable food assistance from Heinz to feed the denizens of his shantytown. While individual Catholic priests had often been supportive of union activities and the Church's official pronouncements endorsed workers' rights to join unions, many priests, especially members of the hierarchy, were conservative and wary both of the largely Protestant corporate powers on their right and the Communist and socialist organizations on their left that contested for the allegiances and souls of their parishioners. The appearance of Father Charles Owen Rice with Father Carl Hensler and Monsignor Barry O'Toole wearing their clerical collars while picketing at the gates of an iconic Pittsburgh business at such a highly charged moment made news, even a mention in *Time* magazine. The two older men soon moved on to other vineyards, but Rice was just embarking on what would become a sixty-year career as Pittsburgh's best known, most influential, controversial and at times notorious labor priest.[60]

Charles Owen Rice was born in 1908 in New York City. At the age of four his mother died, so his father conveyed Charles and his older brother Patrick to his family home in Ireland to be cared for by his own mother and an assortment of aunts and uncles. Rice was seven at the time of the Easter Rebellion for Irish independence and remembered seeing the damage done in Dublin by British artillery during its suppression. In 1920, the two boys rejoined their father in the Mt. Washington neighborhood of Pittsburgh. Rice graduated from Duquesne University in 1930, where he edited the student newspaper and was senior class president. He went on to seminary at St. Vincent's in Latrobe, was ordained a priest of the Diocese of Pittsburgh in 1934, and assigned to St. Agnes Church in Oakland. Inspired by the work of Dorothy Day and the Catholic Worker movement, he founded St. Joseph's House of Hospitality in the Hill District that evolved into a major operation, housing hundreds and feeding thousands at its peak of operation. With a small group of social activists, he formed the Catholic Radical Alliance, dedicated to the social teachings of the church and their application to the economic and social crisis at hand. Rice embraced the need for radical change. "I believe that the present social and economic system is a mess and should be changed from top to bottom." In practice, this meant an allegiance to the unionism of the CIO. "Christ's concern for the poor and the exploited is clear command to all His followers to be concerned for them. Unionism is a Christian thing." This commitment took on a double aspect: on the one hand, it was necessary for the Church to stand on the side of the poor and the worker against the power and greed of the corporations; on the other hand, it was necessary to contest the ideology and organization of the Communists for the allegiance of the workers. Between right and left, Rice perceived the radical center ground lay at the heart of the CIO where Phil Murray, a devout Catholic, stood.[61]

After his appearance at the Heinz plant, Rice was asked by SWOC to come to Youngstown where tension and violence were on the rise as the strike polarized the town. At a night time plant gate rally in the rain, Rice urged non-violence and forgiveness. "The laboring man does not demand a Godless soviet system, the SWOC does not demand it; but they do demand and we all demand that the Godless features of our own system cease and give place to an order that recognizes God and human rights and duties and justice for all." Later that summer in Canton at another strike meeting he stated: "Our profit-mad, business worshipping civilization has forgotten certain things. It has forgotten that human rights are above property rights; that there is a certain fundamental dignity in labor that must be respected; that money and profit are not the ends of industry." Rice began to accept invitations to debate prominent Communists about the church accepting a working alliance with the Communists. Debating both Party chair, Earl Browder, and *Daily Worker* editor, Clarence Hathaway, on the issue, "Can the Catholic Accept the Outstretched Hand of the Communist?" Rice answered firmly in the negative.[62]

On August 26, 1937, Andrew Mellon died and his body was brought back to Pittsburgh for burial. Three months before, he had appeared frail and rattled when he delivered the presentation address for Mellon Institute, his $10 million research facility on Fifth Avenue. He had largely succeeded in divesting himself of his assets to his family and to his charities, thereby largely dodging the New Deal taxman. His younger brother and partner, R. B., who died in late 1933, had been somewhat less successful in shielding his assets. When R.B.'s funeral cortege left his magnificent mansion with 65 rooms and 11 baths on Fifth Avenue and made its way to the massive East Liberty

Presbyterian Church, where his remains would ultimately lie, silent crowds lined the streets in a cold rain "glowering" at the limousines and luxury automobiles in a way that some of the funeral participants found frightening. The crowd's sullen response was a result both of the desperateness of the times as well as the publication the previous summer of Harvey O'Connor's *Mellon's Millions* that documented the history of the family fortune and crystallized the hostility felt by many in Pittsburgh toward their wealthiest and most prominent family. A 2007 ranking of the thirty wealthiest Americans of all time put the combined Mellon Fortune of A.W. and R.B. at $96 billion dollars and in fourth place behind John D. Rockefeller, Cornelius Vanderbilt and John Jacob Astor and just ahead of Bill Gates and Andrew Carnegie. Henry Clay Frick ranked number 26.[63]

In the fall of 1937, the final wave of the New Deal electoral surge passed over the mill towns surrounding Pittsburgh. Municipal elections were being conducted in a political universe that had changed radically since the previous round in 1933. In town after town, what became known as the "labor Democrats" were swept to power shattering the Republican machines that had for so long dominated working class life in the industrial mill towns. For the entire civic lives of most workers, local governance was an extension of corporate control. Suddenly the world was turned upside down, or right side up depending on the point of view. Workers from coke ovens, rolling mills or maintenance departments became mayors and council members of towns where they had once been targets of company and police persecution. John Mullen worked at the coke works for 11 years before becoming mayor of Clairton. Prior to his victory, dues pickets set up by SWOC to check membership in the union were broken up by police. In Duquesne, Elmer Maloy, with a strong following in the mill's open hearth division, decided to run against Jim Crawford, the town's banker, who had ruled the town with an iron fist for decades. When Maloy won the Democratic primary, Crawford decided to step down. In a rally where 1,500 crammed into the high school auditorium, Maloy was introduced by Congressman Henry Ellenbogen as: "A man risen from the ranks of labor who knows its problems." In Aliquippa, a labor-democratic slate organized by Paul Normile swept the election, with its first task being to clean out the notorious city police force. Up and down the industrial valleys, the grassroots labor Democratic activists operating locally swept every town except McKeesport, where Mayor Lysle managed to hold on until 1941.[64]

As the labor organizing wave crested, there remained consolidation of the gains. SWOC was an organizing committee and not a union. It had grown with lightning speed and had spread beyond basic steel production to a wide range of fabricating, rail and engine equipment, and machining industries. In some signed shops, the SWOC presence was weak, in others there were feisty rank-and-file groups that aggressively challenged time-honored relationships and ways of doing business. In Little Steel where SWOC was defeated, there was often vigorous shop floor organizing accompanied by wildcat strikes and continuous bargaining without a contract. In addition most of the contracts, based on the U.S. Steel deal, were set to expire after one year on February 1, 1938. Murray had assembled an experienced group in Pittsburgh with Clint Golden, as chief of staff, Harold Ruttenberg, as research director, Vin Sweeney, from the *Pittsburgh Press* as publicity director, and Lee Pressman, as General Counsel. Golden had been a railroader, a machinist, an organizer in textiles, a labor mediator for Governor Pinchot assigned to investigate the suppression of civil liberties in Aliquippa, and finally the regional director of the National Labor Relations Board in Pittsburgh before agreeing to work for Murray.[65]

To prepare for bargaining the multitude of contracts, Murray called a Wage and Policy Convention in Pittsburgh on December 14, 1937. Nine hundred and twenty-four delegates assembled from across the U.S. and Canada and submitted over eight hundred resolutions for consideration. Golden and his staff gathered all the proposals into a report that loosely defined bargaining goals but left all the power to make an agreement with Murray and the leadership. The essential business was the passage of a resolution endorsing SWOC as their bargaining agent "with full power to secure the best joint wage agreement possible." As was observed at the time, "The Steel Workers' Organizing Committee is a democracy…of steel workers and for steel workers but not by steel workers."[66]

The CIO faced a similar organizational challenge, since it was still acting as an ad hoc committee originally set up inside an unsupportive AFL. It finally convened its Constitutional Convention in Pittsburgh on November 17, 1938 with more than four million workers under contract, an impressive record of organizing accomplishment since its rupture with the AFL. Pat Fagan, as president of the Steel City Industrial Council of CIO unions, welcomed the delegates. Father Rice gave a notable benediction immediately preceding the opening address by John L. Lewis. "O Lord and Savior, Jesus Christ, You who were a worker Yourself….We pray for the victory of the worker in this country, O Almighty God, because his victory is Your victory, his cause is Your cause. A victory for labor in its struggles for decent conditions is a victory for Americanism and Christianity."[67]

Lewis in his address called attention to the fact that this constitutional convention was being held in the same city and on almost the same date as the founding convention of the American Federation of Labor 57 years earlier. While the old federation had successfully organized the crafts, it had failed again and again to bring the blessings of collective bargaining to industry. "During all those years, Pittsburgh was the citadel of non-unionism in America, the citadel of labor exploitation, and the recognized fortress of those financial interests and industrial interests in America who preferred to exploit and debase and degrade labor rather than recognize its existence or concede its right to fair treatment." What the AFL had failed to do in 54 years, the CIO had accomplished in three. Praising Phil Murray "for the super-human task that you have accomplished in the area where you live, where the headquarters of the organization you head exists." Lewis spoke of the Pittsburgh of 1938:

> The Pittsburgh area today is the most completely organized of any city or area in industrial America. Whether you come into Pittsburgh through the Ohio Valley, the Monongahela Valley, or the gateway of the Allegheny, you pass one of those great industrial plants in coming through any of those gateways, you pass a plant where the CIO has established collective bargaining, and where the employees are members of the CIO…and in every one of those plants, in every one of those corporations without exception, since the negotiation of those agreements, peaceful relations have obtained and mutual satisfaction prevails between management and labor – something of a record for an industry that for a lifetime, through oppressive measures, prevented the organization of its employees and denied to them the right to join the union of their choice.[68]

Lewis went on however to paint a dark picture of a time where "great and sinister forces are moving throughout the world."

> We stand appalled at what we witness in Europe. Whose heart can fail to become anguished as he reads in the daily press of the terrible abuses and atrocities and indignities and brutalities that are being inflicted by the German government and some of the German people on the Jews of that nation?…In Germany the labor move-

ment was first wiped out and its leaders were harried and sent to concentration camps, and now in progressive fury and increasing brutality the German government is found inflicting these pogroms on the Jewish race....When this mad, blood-thirsty wolf of the German government inflicts its will upon the defenseless people of Germany, Austria, and of Czechoslovakia, then it is possible that we will have to meet the German dictator as he tries to extend his domain into the realm of the Western Hemisphere. If that day comes, who is going to sustain the United States of America? Who is going to man its industries? Who is going to send its young men to military ranks to engage in war? Labor – Labor!...Who is going to do the suffering and dying in the future but the sons and daughters of this country? The workers of this country never make anything out of war, they merely work and sweat and fight and die. Someone else takes the profits....Not labor. And if war comes, the United States needs the cooperation of the millions and millions of workers that are members of the CIO.[69]

While John L. Lewis deserved to feel a sense of achievement for labor's significant gains under his leadership, the loss of organizing momentum, the threat of foreign war, and his deteriorating relationship with Franklin D. Roosevelt darkened his perspective as he contemplated the future.

Immigrant Dreams and Foreign Nightmares

The 1930s witnessed the coming of age of the immigrant communities in Pittsburgh. Members of the second and even the third generation of Slavic, Italian, Greek, and other immigrants were now deeply rooted citizens intensely interested in the stirrings of the body politic. Growing political power through the resurgence of the Democratic Party; better wages and working conditions through union organization; improved education in rapidly expanding public and Catholic school systems; ethnic, religious and civic organizations strengthened by tempering in a time of privation; all these factors combined to integrate and assimilate immigrants and their children, products of the vast wave of immigration that flooded into Pittsburgh from 1880 to 1920. The rise of the "ethnics," out of the furnace, out of the teeming slums, into industrial and political citizenship found expression in two important artistic and cultural works of the period: Thomas Bell's powerful novel of Slovak and Carpatho-Rusyn mill worker life, *Out of This Furnace,* and Maxo Vanka's vivid murals at St. Nicholas' Croatian Church in Millvale. Many individuals from strong ethnic backgrounds struggled with privation and hard times to achieve great things.

Pittsburgh's greatest novel, Thomas Bell's *Out of This Furnace* movingly chronicles the history and aspirations of three generations of immigrants working at the Edgar Thomson Works. Born in Braddock on March 7, 1903, Thomas Bell was christened Adalbert Thomas Belejcak. His father Michael Belejcak migrated in 1890 from the Rusyn village of Nizny Tvarozec in Austro-Hungary. His mother was Slovak Catholic. Of Bell's three younger brothers, one was murdered after a workplace quarrel and another asphyxiated by furnace gas in the mill. His father, like his mother, died of tuberculosis. In his saga of mill town life, Bell combines a meticulous description of the town and mill with a story that draws deeply on but reconfigures the story of his own family. Most importantly, the novel is written from the ethnic point of view. It combines a rich sense of particularity embedded in a distinct cultural experience that provides a counterpoint to the deep yearning for the human universals of justice, freedom and even a brand of patriotism rooted in ideals and principles.[70] In a 1946 interview, Bell stated about the novel:

My conscience dictated me to write. I saw a people brought here by steel magnates from the old country and then exploited, ridiculed and oppressed....As a small boy I could not understand why I should be ashamed of the fact that I was Slovak....I made up my mind to write a history of the Braddock Slovaks in order to tell the world that the Slovaks with their blood and lives helped to build America, that the steel they produced changed the United States into the most industrialized nation in the world....It was also my aim to strengthen in the Slovaks their pride in their origin. Finally I wanted to make sure that the hardships my grandfather, my father, my mother, and my brother, sisters, and other relatives lived through would never be forgotten.[71]

The central theme of the novel expresses the growing realization by the members of an immigrant culture of their collective and individual value that leads them to challenge power and assert their dignity as human beings and their worth as Americans. Appropriately for a novel so deeply rooted in a culture, women play an extremely important role as mothers and sisters, domestic workers and guarantors of family survival in a violent and uncertain world where many male breadwinners are killed or maimed with little compensation or regard for the impact on their large families. With many mouths to feed and clothe, husbands absent at work for eighty or more hours a week, no workers' compensation, unemployment or Social Security, women still succeeded in creating homes and a sense of community in an extremely harsh environment. The novel is also very much about class, about "bossism...the intolerable state of affairs under which some men had virtual power of life and death over others." Bell, who worked in mills and factories before becoming a writer and author of six novels, described the alienation that workers felt in a workplace where they had no power.[72]

When the General Superintendent entered the cast-house, well-dressed, papers in hand, coldly inscrutable of countenance, it was like god appearing on earth and produced a comparable chaos. Lesser bosses went into a hysteria of activity over a barrowful of cinders or a splash of metal on the tracks, hovered around him in taut, eager servility. For this was not a man like other men; this was the General Superintendent, the godlike dispenser of jobs and layoffs, life and death....Mike could guess how it must feel to be a boss, looking busy and worried, ordering men around, enjoying their fear; but the General Superintendent wasn't an ordinary man set a little above others much like himself. He was of a different species altogether, partaking of the company's inhuman incomprehensibility and like the company going his way, doing this, doing that hiring, firing, shutting down, cutting wages, raising them, and giving no reasons, maintaining throughout a cold impassability before which a man felt himself divested of humanity, to which it was impossible to appeal or reason with, one's love and hate alike unnoticed, unfelt, unwanted.

More subtly, his presence disturbed the rhythm, the relationship, between worker and job. With his appearance the furnace and the men became separate. It was now his furnace and they its servants, and his: for its well-being they were responsible now not to the furnace and to themselves, their pride in knowing how to handle her, but to him. He took it away from them. They ceased to be men of skill and knowledge, ironworkers, and were degraded to the status of employees who did what they were told for a wage, whose feelings didn't matter, not even their feelings for the tools, the machines they worked with, or the work they did.[73]

Ultimately, *Out of This Furnace*, is not only a finely constructed tale of work, family and community, it is a reflection, a meditation on what it means to be an American. The death of the first generation character, Kracha, toward the end of the novel, is used to bring the immigrant tale to a close. The fourth and final section of the book expresses the exuberant hope that seized Carnegie's old mill town in the wake of U.S. Steel's capitulation to SWOC. Steel unionism may have finally achieved recognition through a dinner discussion at the Mayflower Hotel, but the political landscape was dramatically altered in the process. "Men would soon be striding past the cops at the mill gates with union buttons on their caps, and no knightly plume had ever been worn more proudly or celebrated a greater victory." The union's victory raised a stream of questions in the mind of Dobie, the third generation protagonist who is most like Bell himself. How would the more powerful union deal with the many problems that plagued society: the economic crisis, political leadership, bossism, biased press, new technology that was eliminating many desperately needed jobs, and the environmental destruction wrecked by industry on the land?

> No nation could permit such waste of its human material any more than it could permit the waste of its substance in the eroded hills and poisoned rivers and blasted earth of the steel country....All over America men had been permitted, as a matter of business, as a matter of dollars and cents, to destroy what neither money nor men could ever restore or replace. With this result: that America was no longer, except to a few of its people, a beautiful land. Where it wasn't blighted with slums its deforested hills were being washed into the sea, or the soil of its plains was being blown in clouds across the sky.[74]

But with all of these questions now emerging with the dawn of a degree of political power, there is one thing that is certain, one solid achievement after three generations of struggle: Dobie has become an American.

> Maybe not the kind of American that came over on the Mayflower...or the kind that's always shooting off their mouths about Americanism or patriotism, including some of the god-damnedest heels you'd ever want to see, but the kind that's got Made in the U.S.A. stamped all over them, from the kind of grub they like to the things they wouldn't do for all the money in the world....If I'm anything at all I'm an American, only I'm not the kind you read about in the history books or that they make speeches about on the Fourth of July; anyway, not yet.
>
> Made in the U.S.A., he thought, made in the First Ward. But it wasn't where you were born or how you spelled your name or where your father had come from. It was the way you thought and felt about certain things. About freedom of speech and the equality of men and the importance of having one law – the same law – for rich and poor, for the people you liked and the people you didn't like. About the right of every man to live his life as he thought best, his right to defend it if anyone tried to change it and his right to change it himself if he liked some other way of living better....
>
> I want certain things bad enough to fight for them. Patrick Henry, Junior – that's me. Give me liberty or give me death. But he meant every word of it and by God I think I do too.[75]

Maxo Vanka was an extraordinary painter who led an amazing life. His two sojourns in 1937 and 1941 in Millvale, an Allegheny Valley industrial town bordering Pittsburgh, produced one of the most expressive works of immigrant art in America. The murals that fill the entire Croatian church of St. Nicholas manage to encompass in one magnificent ensemble both mystical religious aspirations and horrifying depictions of war and injustice. Full of rich symbolism and powerful imagery, the murals simultaneously provide a powerful expression of religious spirituality as well as a profound social commentary for a community on the brink of world war. The Croatian community grew rapidly in western Pennsylvania after 1890 with the first Croatian parish, St. Nicholas, established in 1895 at the upstream end of Allegheny City. The parish expanded and then divided, forming a second St. Nicholas Church in Millvale, a short distance farther up the Allegheny River. In 1921, the original Millvale church burned down and was replaced. When Father Albert Zagar became pastor in 1931, he began to look for a muralist to decorate the structure's stark white walls. Meanwhile, the young Croatian artist who would accomplish the task was slowly being drawn to Millvale, the site of what would be his greatest work.[76]

Maxo Vanka was born in 1889, the illegitimate issue of a relationship between the son and daughter of high Austro-Hungarian imperial nobility. For his first eight years, he was raised by a peasant woman, Dora Yug, "a large, buxom woman of extremely rich, open, generous nature." At this point, his maternal grandfather took him away to a family castle, where he received an education from tutors and was given the name Vanka. His well-funded education continued at an art school in Zagreb and then in 1914 at the Royal Academy of Beaux Arts in Brussels, Belgium, where he witnessed the horrors of the war at close hand during the German invasion. Meanwhile, back in Croatia in 1931, where he lived modestly on an art professor's salary with his paintings exhibited locally and abroad, he met Margaret Stetten, an American woman of culture and independent financial means. She determined to marry Maxo, a small, slim, extremely intense artist, "a species of mystic who swung gracefully between intellectual agnosticism and a profound, peasant-like faith in God, the Virgin, and all the saints and angels in heaven." Jesus-like in appearance, he was blessed with a "gift of sympathy" that attracted wild birds and woodland creatures to him and led him to the company of the lowly, the dirty and the neglected.[77]

Strong-willed Margaret prevailed and brought Maxo to New York in 1934. In December that year, they drove together to Pittsburgh where his paintings were shown at an exhibit sponsored by the Croatian counsel and seen by Father Zagar. In March 1937, through the auspices of Louis Adamic, a Croatian socialist writer who a year earlier had published a fictionalized account of Maxo's birth and youth titled *Cradle of Life,* Vanka came to Millvale to meet Father Zagar and was commissioned to paint the church. After a month working on sketches back in New York while scaffolding was constructed, Vanka returned and in eight weeks of intense work completed eleven murals covering half the church. At the dedication ceremony in June, Father Zagar thanked Vanka for his work in a passionate address that brought tears to the eyes of the congregation, as well as the artist. At a picnic feast of celebration, metalworkers and their families crowded around him exclaiming in Croatian: "You are our sun, you are our star!"[78]

The 1937 session at the church produced the dominating figure over the altar, Mary Queen of Croatia, a forceful strong-shouldered peasant queen with worker's hands holding her son who carries grapes and wheat. To her left on the wall is a scene of peasant life in Croatia, with farmers stopping to pray in the fields; on the right, the mills of the Allegheny Valley are backdrop for a procession of workers led by Father Zagar carrying St. Nicholas Church in their hands. This initial session produced the two great scenes that act as secular counterpoints to the classical, albeit expressionistic and highly symbolic representations of the Crucifixion and the Pieta painted during that same session. On a back wall, opposite Christ on the cross attended by women, there is a mural of a gangrenous dead soldier in a casket surrounded by mourning women and rows of crosses covering the hills beyond entitled: *The Croatian Mother Raises Her Children for War.* Opposite the Pieta, Mary holding her dead son brought down from the cross, is the painting: *The Immigrant Mother Raises Her Son for Industry.* Deservedly, the most famous of all the murals, it depicts Croatian women in flowing black mourning dress weeping over the body of a dead miner, while behind his weeping mother, his three brothers descend toward the mine. Vanka explained that the image came "from a disaster near Johnstown where 72 men were trapped in an explosion. The body of this son was the first brought to the surface. The mother is sorrowing over him while at the same time sending his three brothers into the mine with a rescue expedition. It actually happened that she lost all four sons."[79]

Vanka was a man of extraordinary perception and intensity, who, during the sixteen to eighteen hours that he labored six days a week, ate very sparingly. Adamic, who had almost become Vanka's publicist, published an article on the artist's murals in *Harper's Magazine* in 1938 that recounted in gripping detail, the ghostly apparition that haunted Vanka's labors, appearing often around midnight after the artist had worked fifteen hours. Strange noises and clicks, a profound chill and then a strange ominous figure appeared who walked around the church waving his arms or sat in a pew. One night, "I saw him very clearly; a man in black, an old man with a strange angular face, wrinkled and dark with a bluish tinge. He leaned on the front part of the pew, looking up, not so much at me as at everything in general: a sad, miserable gaze. I saw him for just a moment, then – nothing. He vanished. But I felt cold all over, at the same time that sweat broke out of every pore of my body….The sensation I had was more than fear; something indescribable…." Adamic's ghost story threatened to overshadow Vanka's masterpiece as the Millvale ghost initially garnered more attention than the Millvale murals themselves.[80]

In 1941, Vanka, who had moved with his wife to eastern Pennsylvania, was brought back to Millvale where he completed eleven more murals "since every inch of the church must be completed." With the horrors of World War II enveloping all of Europe, including Croatia, the 1941 murals are pointedly didactic, heavy with a hatred of war and the greed that feeds it. The Old Testament mural depicts Moses breaking the tablets of the law with "Thou Shalt Not Kill" inscribed in Croatian while a thunderbolt destroys the Golden Calf. While *Justice* holds balanced scales, in the mural *Injustice*, a nightmarish figure, wearing a gas mask and wielding a bloody sword, holds scales where bread is outweighed by gold. In the back of the church, contrasting murals depict the simple meal of the Croatian family, with the ghostly figure of Christ blessing their bread and soup, with the feast spread out before the Capitalist, an amalgam of Frick and Mellon with monocle and top-hat waited on by a Negro servant, while a poor man begs for crumbs at the foot of his table.

The most disturbing mural covers the low ceiling beneath the choir loft and pictures Christ on the cross being bayoneted by crucifix-wearing soldiers, while Mary forcefully pushes away another soldier's bayonet. Generations of Catholic schoolchildren passed under these stark and terrifying images to reach the sublimity of the sanctuary whose dome is covered by the heavenly mural *Transcendent Vision* showing Christ accompanied by angels descending into hell and ascending into heaven in a vision worthy of William Blake. The final sequence of murals were completed a month before Pearl Harbor. Father Zagar, whose congregation included both socialist and fascist sympathizers, defended the powerful anti-war message of the paintings. "It's religion, expressed in our social life. At the same time, it's completely Catholic." Vanka, who had just become an American citizen, said: "These murals are my contribution to America – not only mine, but my immigrant peoples, who also are grateful like me, that they are not in the slaughter in Europe."[81]

While Maxo Vanka and Thomas Bell provided two of the greatest artistic creations to originate in Pittsburgh out of the immigrant experience, a mythical story of questionable origins has become an acceptable vehicle for recognizing the contributions of the Slavs without any hint of politics or alienation. "The Saga of Joe Magarac: Steelman," written by Owen Francis in 1931 for *Scribner's Magazine* resulted, according to the author, from "working for a considerable number of years with a Hunkie on my either side, by sitting many evenings in their homes." It tells of the competition among the strongest of the Slavic steelworkers from the Mon Valley and Johnstown for the hand of the stunningly beautiful Mary Mestrovich, who it should be noted is looking for the "best man that ever poke 'em tap hole." The winner of this competition, who twists eight hundred pounds of steel in his bare hands, is literally a "man of steel." The aptly name Joe Magarac (or jackass in Croatian), then turns down the beautiful Mary with the immortal words: "What you tink. I catch time for sit around house with woman's? No, by Gods, not me. I joost catch time for workit dats all." Joe, a manager's dream, works 24 hours a day, and is so productive that he shuts down the Braddock mill for lack of orders. This unintended consequence of his work-loving nature causes him to commit suicide, melting himself down to provide "the best steel what we can makit for buildit new mill." Joe immerses himself in the ladle to "build finest mills that ever was." It is not surprising that many establishment depictions of the ethnic steel worker have adopted the iconography of Joe Magarac.[82]

In the 1930s, many people in Pittsburgh and elsewhere were increasingly preoccupied by the political crisis in Europe and the seemingly inexorable march toward war. Anxiety about the European crisis was felt with especial acuity by the Italian, German and Jewish communities but was shared by virtually the entire immigrant population and their descendents. Ideological divisions between left and right as well as the shifting political landscape of alliances and assaults between and within nations made for a complex political stew in Pittsburgh when it came to possible involvement (and on what terms) in the European conflict. While events in Europe impacted many ethnic groups, with several groups like the Croatians being deeply divided along left-right lines, the slide of Europe toward war had a particular impact on the city's Italian, German, and Jewish communities.

The Italian community in the Pittsburgh region with its deep ideological divisions and strong regional identities is not easy to characterize. While the rise of Benito Mussolini and his fascist movement in the early 1920s was hailed by many Italians, strong anarchist, socialist, and communist movements combined with the strong institutional presence of the Catholic Church made an exact determination of political loyalties within the community difficult to discern. The Sacco and Vanzetti executions in 1927 had stirred deep feelings in the Italian community and a state trooper had been shot and killed as troopers tried to break up a protest meeting at the Acmetonia Grove at Cheswick in the Allegheny Valley. The rather astonishing political and judicial career of Michael Musmanno is illustrative of the difficulty in branding Italian activists. Musmanno admired the anti-communism of the fascists as a law student in Rome in the 1920s, served with Felix Frankfurter and other legal luminaries on the Sacco and Vanzetti defense committee in the days before their execution, fought the Coal and Iron Police as a legislator, was a novelist and movie advisor for *Black Fury* (starring Paul Muni), was a judge at Nuremburg in the trials of the Nazis, and then ended up as a ferocious anti-communist in the 1950s. Many Catholics who were hostile to Hitler looked on Mussolini with sympathy for his accord with the Vatican. Strong regional ties also complicated matters since many Pittsburgh Italians came from the poor and politically marginal regions of Abruzzi and Calabria.

The Mafia, while never as strong in Pittsburgh as in New York, Chicago and some other towns, played an important local role in gambling and prostitution.[83]

By the 1930s, the German community in Pittsburgh was largely third and even fourth generation Americans, though Pittsburgh still had 19,000 foreign-born German speakers concentrated on the North Side. While most Germans, remembering the hostility their community had experienced in World War I, kept a low profile politically, there were a number of German organizations with sympathy for Hitler's rise in the wake of the German collapse during and after the Great War. The German American Bund strongly supported Hitler's vision of a greater Germany and organized to counteract communism and oppose Jewish-led boycotts of German goods. It agitated for the New Germany among older and often resistant German cultural associations. Much weaker than pro-Nazi groups in Philadelphia, the Bund was thrown into disarray by the Nazi-Soviet pact. The promotion of anti-Semitism based on the claim that communism was a Jewish conspiracy gained less traction in Pittsburgh than in Philadelphia or New York, since the Communist Party in Western Pennsylvania was much more Slavic in membership than Jewish.[84]

The Bund allied itself with right-wing Catholic groups like the Christian Front, but robust liberal, labor Catholicism represented by Charles Owen Rice and Philip Murray that vigorously supported both industrial unionism and the Democratic Party of Lawrence and Roosevelt left little room for political extremism among the faithful. Rice, in particular, forcefully and unambiguously confronted in his weekly columns and radio broadcasts anti-Negro sentiment among Catholics, as well as the anti-Semitism of Father Charles Coughlin of Royal Oak, Michigan. About the Jews, Rice said in a broadcast in 1939: "It is poppy-cock to prate of the Jews killing Christ. We killed Christ; our sins did it. The Jew has no monopoly on sin and no monopoly on the guilt for Christ's death. Of all the sins that tortured Christ on the cross be it noted, among the most excruciating were the sins of hatred and intolerance perpetrated upon his people in his name." As far as race hatred, Rice in 1938 singled out his Irish conferees for forgetting their own persecution and their adoption of the "race prejudice of the Anglo-Saxon." "Before any Catholic says 'The Negro must keep his place,' let him find out what right he or any other lump of the slime of the earth has to assign any race to an inferior place....In God's providence, we shall see black faces shining high above us in Heaven, if we haters of men manage to get there."[85]

An Irish success story of the period was that of the great dancer Gene Kelly. Gene Kelly was born the third of five children in 1912 in East Liberty. His father was a traveling salesman for the Columbia Phonograph Company whose earnings were squeezed by the Depression. Encouraged by his father's love for sports, Gene, the middle child, was an adept skater, baseball and hockey player, as well as skilled with his fists. His mother, Harriet, was determined that her children would succeed in the theater and formed "The Five Kellys" performing group with her children. Gene's hero was Harry Greb who gave him a few boxing lessons. This training proved useful, since Gene was often taunted by his peers for dancing, which some considered an indication of homosexuality. At Peabody High School, Gene was outstanding in hockey, gymnastics and football, as well as starring in school plays and writing poetry for the school paper. Harriet convinced a local dance school to let her open a branch for them in Johnstown, and Gene became the head teacher while still in his teens. With the Depression deepening, Harriet took over the Pittsburgh studio and the Gene Kelly School of Dance was born. When Gene was admitted to Penn State, he ran the Johnstown operation on the weekends.[86]

All his life, Gene Kelly detested racism and prejudice. With some other activists he protested the exclusionary policies against Jews by the fraternities at Penn State. "I'd come from a family where prejudice was never mentioned." He danced and learned from black dancers and once got a standing ovation from Cab Calloway's band after an audition. A heterosexual, he was often mocked by drunks in small venues as gay. He transferred to the University of Pittsburgh to save money and, in 1933, entered its Law School, where he was recruited to stage Pitt's annual Cap and Gown Varsity Show complete with burly athletes in drag. He built up the Pittsburgh dance school and developed a first rate staff of dance teachers. One of his many students was a young Jewish boy, Myron Kopelman, who years later as Myron Cope became the much loved and highly distinctive voice of the Pittsburgh Steelers' football broadcasts. Preferring baseball, Myron suffered through a year at the dance school. "And later, along with millions of others, I loved hearing Gene Kelly sing and dance his way through *Singin' in the Rain.* 'I studied dancing under Gene Kelly,' I occasionally mentioned to make an impression on a girl." Theater and dance was a way out of hard times and the Depression pushed talent his way. The 1936 Johnstown Flood wiped out the Kelly operation in that town. After various attempts to break into the big time in Chicago and New York, his mother gave him a one way trip to New York City, where one of the greatest careers of American theater and cinema was launched.[87]

Recently, Gene's wife Patricia Ward Kelly, recalled just who Gene Kelly was:

> Graduated with a degree in economics from Pitt, Gene was not only a gifted dancer, director and choreographer; he was also a most civilized man. He spoke multiple languages, wrote poetry, studied history; he actually read the treatises of Marx and Engels and understood the projections of Adam Smith and John Maynard Keynes. He did the Sunday *New York Times* crossword in ink. Much of this intellectual curiosity was fostered right there in Steeltown during the depression - at the university, where Gene memorized the "new" poems of Robert Frost and read the works of Lincoln Steffens and Upton Sinclair, and in after-hours discussions at Kahn's, when he met other young men to ponder what was wrong with the country. Exceedingly articulate, Gene often conveyed more through movement than others manage with words.[88]

The Jewish community in Pittsburgh was deeply affected by Hitler's rise. On June 23, 1918, near the close of World War I, a major Zionist convention had been held in Pittsburgh to support the Balfour Declaration of the British Government that envisioned a Jewish "national home" in Palestine. A march of 10,000 demonstrated on behalf of the proposal and the convention heard newly appointed Supreme Court Justice Louis Brandeis endorse the Zionist project. In 1932, Henry Ellenbogen, labor supporter and avid Zionist, successfully ran for Congress, becoming the first Democrat to represent Pittsburgh in the Congress in the 20th Century. Confidante of Dave Lawrence and President Franklin D. Roosevelt, he served three terms and was appointed a judge of the Court of Common Pleas in 1938. As the European situation worsened, the Jewish community organized boycotts of German imports and focused their efforts toward relaxing the severe immigration quotas established in 1927. By 1938, the 19,736 Jews who successfully entered the United States comprised 29% of total immigration. After the Nazi *Krystallnacht* attacks against Jewish synagogues and shops in Germany and Austria, the U.S. government turned over the entire German immigration quota to the Jewish refugees whose numbers peaked at 43,450 in 1939, more than half of the immigration total for that year. By 1943, when the Nazi exterminations were at their peak, only 4,705 Jews managed to gain American shores.[89]

There was another side of the Jewish experience in Pittsburgh. Between 1936 and 1938, Frank Lloyd Wright designed one of the greatest works of American architecture for Edgar J. Kaufmann, Pittsburgh's "merchant prince." Edgar Kaufmann was the son of one of four brothers who migrated to Western Pennsylvania from Germany's Rhineland between the late 1860s and early 1870s. Like many itinerant Jewish merchants of the period, they sold clothes and other dry goods to farmers and especially miners, grateful for merchandise sold outside of the overpriced company stores. In 1871, the two eldest brothers, Jacob and Henry, opened a tailor shop on East Carson Street in Pittsburgh's South Side. In 1877, joined by their two younger brothers, Morris and Issac, J. Kaufmann & Brothers moved to Smithfield Street in the Golden Triangle. In 1885, Kaufmann Brothers opened a new wing at the prize intersection of Smithfield and Fifth Avenue. Edgar was born to Morris and Betty Kaufmann in 1885, the same year that a miniature statue of the Statue of Liberty was erected on the corner holding a natural gas torch. Later, a gilded clock replaced the statue and "meeting under the Kaufmann's clock" became the most popular meeting place in Pittsburgh. The store kept expanding and upgrading until by 1910 it had a million square feet of space and three thousand employees. It claimed to be the first store in the nation to purchase full-page newspaper advertising.[90]

The Kaufmann brothers were patrons of architecture and prolific builders of both commercial and public buildings. They were the prime donors toward the erection of Rodef Shalom Temple designed by Henry Hornbostel, the French-trained protégé of architect Stanford White, who famously had been shot and killed by Pittsburgh's own Harry K. Thaw over the heart-throb Evelyn Nesbitt. Henry built the Irene Kaufmann Settlement House in the Hill District to provide immigrants with classrooms, a library, baths, a laundry, and an auditorium. Morris oversaw the building of the Concordia Club in Oakland which, unlike the Duquesne Club downtown, was open to Jews. In 1909, Edgar triumphed over a large and fractious group of family claimants to the great department store by marrying his first cousin, Lillian, the vivacious daughter of his uncle Issac, thereby consolidating control over the department store into his own hands. In the 1920s, Edgar directed the building of the Young Men's Hebrew Association in Oakland. Much later in the 1950s, he would be the inspiration behind the Civic Arena as the founder and president of the Pittsburgh Civic Light Opera. Finally, he tore down Carnegie's Pittsburgh headquarters and expanded the great store that bore the family's name up against the Frick Building. Kaufmann's Department Store became the nerve center of the city.[91]

As Pittsburgh's foremost merchant, Edgar was a tireless promoter of the city. He was also a brilliant designer and publicist who gained recognition as the most creative retailer in America. After Lindbergh's solo flight across the Atlantic, he assembled a complete airplane on his ground floor. He lived the life of a renaissance merchant prince with magnificent homes, horse-riding and dog-breeding interests. Despite Edgar's business success and devotion to Pittsburgh, the Kaufmanns were loaned money by the Mellons, but excluded from the inner circles of Pittsburgh upper-class social life. The rigid class restrictions of up-scale Pittsburgh society forced women to enter the Duquesne Club by a side door and excluded Jews, Catholics and blacks from membership until well after the Second World War. Edgar's lack of religious practice and numerous mistresses, who enjoyed free Kaufmann's credit cards, kept him at some distance from the mainline Jewish community as well.[92]

Perhaps it was Kaufmann's existence as an outsider that inspired him to hire Frank Lloyd Wright to build his extraordinary home, Fallingwater, southeast of Pittsburgh. Certainly, such a creative collaboration with the maverick, Wright, would have been unthinkable for the Mellons who were steadfastly reactionary in their building tastes, normally erecting ponderous classical or medieval structures. Kaufmann had wide-ranging and eclectic tastes, becoming infatuated with Mexican muralists Juan O'Gorman and Diego Rivera, and especially the Mexican artist Frieda Kahlo in the 1930s. He was conversant with Modernist architecture in Germany and Austria. In the mid-1930s, he was introduced to Frank Lloyd Wright, America's most original architect, and together they began to plan a monumental house to straddle a waterfall on Bear Run, a small tributary of the Youghiogheny River, not far from where Washington had been defeated by the French and Indians at Fort Necessity. Considered by many the greatest work of architecture in the United States, it is one of the most visited sites in Western Pennsylvania. The juxtaposition of cubist structural shapes, surface elements from New Mexican pueblos, a massive cantilever thrusting out over the water, with the whole ensemble straddling the massive boulders of the creek, all these unique elements somehow fit organically into the primeval forest setting.[93] Wright wrote about the building:

> Fallingwater is a great blessing – one of the great blessings to be experienced here on earth. I think nothing yet ever equaled the coordination, sympathetic expression of the great principle of repose where forest and stream and rock and all the elements of structure are combined so quietly that really you listen not to any noise whatsoever although the music of the stream is there. But you listen to Fallingwater the way you listen to the quiet of the country.[94]

While Kaufmann was Pittsburgh's best known Jewish businessman, another offshoot from the extensive Jewish presence in retail dry goods and grocery businesses in Western Pennsylvania grew into Giant Eagle, the region's dominant grocery chain. In the 1930s, Joseph Goldstein combined his Eagle Grocery in the Hill District with four other family stores to form Giant Eagle. His daughter Frieda Shapira became the matriarch of one of Pittsburgh's most prominent families. Rooted in her experience as a child welfare worker, Shapira, a lifelong liberal Democrat, remained committed to social reform throughout a long life of civic engagement.[95]

All in all, the hard times of the 1930s, combined with the strong organizational upsurge from below that involved tens of thousands of citizens from all ethnic groups, increased acceptance of second and third generation immigrants in recognition of their varied contributions to the Pittsburgh scene. This process of assimilation was symbolized in the magnificent collection of nationality rooms that started to be built at the end of Chancellor Bowman's reign at the University of Pittsburgh. Chancellor Bowman's final years saw the completion of the Cathedral tower, the construction of the beautiful Heinz Memorial Chapel and the Stephen Foster Memorial. The Mellons joined with the pharmaceutical manufacturer, Joseph Lilly, who had amassed a major collection of manuscripts, sheet music, rare books, letters, and personal possessions of Pittsburgh's great composer of popular songs. Among the documents was the piece of paper found on Foster upon his death in New York City at the age of 37 with the haunting title of a song that he never wrote: "Dear Friends and Gentle Hearts." The Heinz Chapel, constructed by the Heinz Family as a memorial to Henry J. Heinz, is a jewel of a building recalling the Gothic masterpiece of Sainte-Chappelle in Paris. The non-sectarian edifice, with its magnificent stained glass windows designed and assembled by Charles Connick of Pittsburgh, became an immediate magnet for weddings and baptisms. The first four nationality rooms, Scottish, Swedish, German and Russian were completed under Bowman's regime. The next round of rooms completed in 1938-1943 took on an especially poignant significance, since many of the nations represented had been invaded, occupied, or partitioned. Following the German Room's dedication in 1938, there came the Chinese (1939), Czechoslovak (1939), Hungarian (1939),

Yugoslav (1939), Lithuanian (1940), Polish (1940) and French (1943) rooms. These classrooms came to be a great source of pride for the diverse ethnic groups that called Pittsburgh home, since nearly half of the region's population was foreign-born or the children of two foreign-born parents in 1940. Some of the rooms were financed by a small group of wealthy donors, but most were constructed through the efforts of committees that raised funds through bake sales, church benefits, donations from ethnic clubs and organizations.[96]

Though significant tensions and differences remained among ethnic groups as another world conflict approached, the process of assimilation rooted in the cooperation and solidarity necessary to build homes, religious institutions, schools, and communities, while organizing vast segments of the labor force to achieve fairness on the job, would culminate on the field of battle as the working class marched off to defend a democracy they themselves were just beginning to experience first hand.

Recognition in the "Man-Breaking City"

As rough as the economic situation in Pittsburgh was during the Depression, it proved to be a glorious time for mass participation in sports. Men had much time without work so semi-pro, industrial and sandlot leagues proliferated in many sports especially baseball, fast-pitch softball, basketball and football. This activity was overwhelmingly a male phenomenon, since aside from an occasional trip to the cinema or excursion downtown with the kids to look at the windows in the shops especially at Christmas, most married working-class women, whose traditional house work and child care duties continued unabated during the economic crisis, found little time for recreation. A notable exception to the male dominance of local sports was the phenomenal record of the Homestead Library Athletic Club women's swimming teams. Under coach Jack Scarry, the Homestead swim team sent representatives to the Olympic Games in Amsterdam (1928), Los Angeles (1932), Berlin (1936). Susan Laird was a member of the 1928 Olympic squad as was Josephine McKim who won a bronze medal. In 1932, Lenore Knight took the silver medal in the 400 meter free-style in Los Angeles, while Knight and Anna Mae Gorman won gold medals as members of the 4 x 100 meter free-style relay team. Lenore Knight went on to win a bronze medal at the Berlin Olympics in 1936.[97] While several local university's sports programs gained national recognition and a professional football team was organized in Pittsburgh that in time became the iconic symbol of the city itself, the two most important sports phenomena of the 1930s were the rise of Pittsburgh as the heart of black baseball and the city's capture of the world boxing stage on the eve of World War II. Much of the city's great success in both arenas was driven by hunger and privation as well as by pride and grit.

After 1927, the Pirates had to wait 33 years to appear in another World Series. They were, however, a highly competitive team through most of the 1930s, finishing second four times. The Waner brothers were two of the best fielding outfielders in the game and their offensive production over a combined 38 seasons was phenomenal. Combined they garnered 5,611 hits with only 449 strikeouts. Paul compiled the highest lifetime batting average for a Pirate at .340. Another extraordinary hitter from the 30s was "Arky" Vaughan who hit over .300 for ten straight years and won the National League batting title in 1935 with a .385 average. Perhaps the most storied event of the decade at Forbes Field occurred that same year when the great Babe Ruth played his final game in magnificent fashion. On May 25, 1935, the 41 year-old slugger, traded by the Yankees back to the Boston Braves where he began his career two decades before, performed his swan song before the fans of Pittsburgh. In each of his first three appearances at the plate, he hit towering home runs, the last of which was the first ever to clear the right field roof and land in Joncaire Street. In his fourth and final at-bat, he lined a single to right and left baseball as a player to the applause of the fans of Pittsburgh.[98]

A sports event that made only a modest ripple in Pittsburgh's sports consciousness at the time, but loomed very large 40 years later was the purchase by Art Rooney of a franchise in the National Football League. The team which he called the Pirates built on Rooney's organization on the North Side of a semi-pro football team that went through several name changes, including the Hope Harveys, the Majestic Radios and the J. P. Rooneys (named for Art's younger brother who served a term as a state legislator as part of the Republican James Coyne machine). The opening for professional football came with the Democratic electoral victory of 1932 and the subsequent ending of the Blue Laws prohibiting Sunday play. Saturdays belonged to college football since Pittsburgh boasted three nationally ranked college programs with the University of Pittsburgh, Carnegie Tech and Duquesne, but the enormous growth and success of the college game also produced a growing number of outstanding college stars who desired to continue to play football. The college game itself was fed by the burgeoning growth of high school football, especially in the coal and steel towns of Western Pennsylvania. Consistent losers through the 1930s, Rooney's team achieved their first winning season in 1942, the year that they changed their name to the Steelers. It was not that Art Rooney didn't try to build a winner. In 1938, he signed Byron "Whizzer" White, the star runner, receiver and kicker for the University of Colorado, for nearly $16,000 a year, three times the going rate for star players in the period. White, however, only stayed a year, then went to Oxford on a Rhodes scholarship. Eventually, he became a Supreme Court justice, named to the nation's highest court by President Kennedy.[99]

Art Rooney achieved a larger-than-life stature and by the end of his storied career was judged the most popular figure in 20th Century Pittsburgh. With family roots in coal and steel, he was born on January 27, 1901 and grew up in and around Rooney's Cafe and Bar, the North Side tavern owned by his father, a hotbed of political and sports activity. Art was a fine boxer who made the U.S. Olympic team, but decided not to go to the Games in Antwerp, Belgium, where his replacement won the gold medal. He played semi-pro and minor league baseball with his brother Dan. Talented as well in football, he declined Knute Rockne's invitation to play at Notre Dame, but did play college ball at Indiana Normal (now Indiana University of Pennsylvania), Georgetown and Duquesne. Art Rooney never held a regular job, having lasted only a couple of hours working in a steel mill. He was, however, a brilliant sports promoter and very shrewd judge of horseflesh. His successful gambling on horse racing was legendary. His football team was only one of a number of investments. With his partner Barney McGinley, he became a very successful boxing promoter, and their bank-rolling of the Pittsburgh fight scene was a major factor in Pittsburgh's rise as a major force in the boxing world.

Rooney was a pro-union Republican who despite a close friendship with Dave Lawrence remained a Republican and served the party in his youth as a ward chairman. "One thing you never do is change parties, religions or wives," he remarked. Lawrence paid tribute to Rooney as "a true-blue guy who will be with you when you die." His generosity was legendary. He could be counted on for money, food, or coal to heat the house. Legions of North Side kids were helped by the "Chief" to pursue schooling, get a job, or launch a political career. He was a friend and ally of the great black sports entrepreneurs, Cumberland Posey and Gus Greenlee; he promoted black athletes, and welcomed blacks as friends and employees. As his son Dan later related, a lot of Art Rooney's character was shaped by the working-class culture of the North Side. "We didn't think about your skin color, or your accent, or what church you went to. What mattered was that you lived up to your word, pulled your own weight, and looked out for your friends."[100]

In the 1930s, Pittsburgh suffered profound economic trauma, but, perhaps for that reason, it became a dynamic cauldron of athletic achievement. The city was the center of black professional baseball in its heyday from the late 1920s until its demise in the late 1940s following the absorption of black talent into baseball's major and minor league systems. Black owned, black-operated, the Homestead Grays and the Pittsburgh Crawfords, a team deeply rooted in Pittsburgh's Hill District, were the epicenter of black professional baseball. The two decades prior to the sport's integration constitute a period that has become a mythical, almost mystical, expression of the Pittsburgh black community's aspirations and determination before and after World War II. The swelling war economy, the triumph of unionism, the advent of government programs brought increased disposable income to both black and white workers. Black sport, music and the bar scene attracted money and stimulated economic activity in the Hill.

Pittsburgh's pivotal situation midway between New York and Chicago meant that black ball teams could compete either on the east coast or west toward Chicago and the heartland. Likewise, the best jazz players, following the east-west migratory route served by the Pennsylvania Railroad's *Broadway Limited,* passed through the Hill's clubs and helped cross-pollinate an already rich local musical scene. With the end of Prohibition, nightlife flourished and, while one political machine replaced another, public corruption and organized crime adapted. While the speakeasy retreated as the most ubiquitous underground institution, illegal gambling, especially in the form of the number's racket, became an efficient method for extracting capital out of black and working-class neighborhoods. Pittsburgh's black community, however, was blessed by the numbers game being controlled locally by Cumberland Posey and Gus Greenlee, both of whom reinvested much of their winnings back into revenue-generating, community-based operations, the two most renowned being the Homestead Grays and the Pittsburgh Crawfords.[101]

As part of corporate efforts after World War I to integrate ethnic immigrants and black migrants into urban life and the demands of industrial discipline, companies sponsored a plethora of sports teams and the city built 78 recreation centers, eight of which were in the Hill. The city's network of parks, playgrounds, bath houses, pools and athletic fields was upgraded and extended through the 1930s by the WPA and other government works programs. The Crawford Bath House with an all-black staff catered mainly to blacks. Boys and girls basketball teams operated out of it and its boxing ring served as a training center for some of Pittsburgh's finest fighters including contenders Jackie Wilson and Charlie Burley. Its sandlot ball team was an incubator for some of the greatest black stars of the Negro Leagues.

Six miles away in the neighboring industrial town of Homestead, the Homestead Grays emerged from the rough and tumble world of sandlot baseball to become the first dominant black professional team. Their rise was tied to the work of Cumberland Posey, who became team captain in 1916 and manager a couple of years later. His father "Cap" Posey spent his life around the river. By studying ship engines he became a licensed engineer and shipbuilder, supervising a local yard that built coal barges. He invested in various coal companies and formed the Diamond Coke and Coal Company, the largest black-owned business in Pittsburgh. As president of the Loendi Club, he was at the top of the social pyramid in black Pittsburgh. His son Cumberland spent time at both Penn State and Duquesne, but his passion was the sporting life. He organized the first local black basketball team, the "Montecellos," upsetting Howard University in 1911. Posey, himself, was touted as the greatest Negro basketball player in his time and his Loendi Club team beat the best black and many white teams and engaged in a storied rivalry with a local Jewish club labeled the "Second Story Morries."[102]

Cum Posey, a shrewd businessman as well as accomplished baseball coach, recruited widely through the 1920s to field the best possible team. In 1925, he signed the 49 year old Smokey Joe Williams, who some considered the greatest black pitcher ever. His team posted a record of 130 wins and 23 losses playing the best teams in black baseball and a steady stream of white sandlot and semi-pro teams. At one point in 1926, his team posted 43 straight wins. In 1928 he signed Oscar Charleston, who played for and managed the Crawfords in their heyday and became one of the first Negro Leagues' veterans to enter baseball's Hall of Fame. In 1929 Posey signed the great Cuban player Martin Dihigo and added Cool Papa Bell and Judy Johnson, among the best ball players in the world, to his roster. In 1929, the Grays joined the American Negro League and their 1930 and 1931 teams ranked among the greatest black baseball teams ever assembled. As the Grays attained national stature, the upstart Crawfords from the Hill began a sustained effort to challenge their dominance. A highly successful sandlot team, the Crawfords evolved into a powerful professional club that played with an intensity and camaraderie rooted in their origins on the streets of a dynamic neighborhood. One of their early stars Harold Tinker recalled: "I didn't play baseball because it was a pastime. I played it because I loved it. I played it with what they call reckless abandon. I ran over hills, I ran into fences, I dove into pigpens. I'll never forget that...I was baseball nuts." [103]

Gus Greenlee, one of the most powerful and successful black businessmen in Pittsburgh, owned several nightclubs including the world renowned Crawford Grill that established itself as the heart and soul of Pittsburgh's rich jazz culture, the place to be for visiting ball players and musicians. Greenlee ran speakeasies, sold bootleg liquor before the repeal of prohibition, and organized one of the most successful numbers operations anywhere. While the Hill was becoming increasingly black, strong Jewish, Italian, Syrian communities remained. White sports figures like Art Rooney, a friend of Greenlee, came to the Hill for the nightlife. The numbers racket, a grassroots gambling phenomenon, grew to become a staple of working-class life before the advent of state-run lotteries. Gus Greenlee and his partner Woogie Harris, brother of the Hill's storied photographer Teenie Harris, built up the networks run out of the Hill until the daily take reached nearly $25,000 a day. When Harold Tinker went to pick up his first pay for playing for the Crawfords, "somebody told me to go upstairs over the Crawford Grill....I walked into that room and all I could see was from here to the back of this church, were tables with adding machines and those people were sitting there counting up their money in the numbers and I stood there and was amazed." Unlike most other cities, this indigenous capital accumulation remained in the hands of local black entrepreneurs despite an invasion of out-of-town racketeers who unsuccessfully challenged local elements for control of vice and gambling.[104]

The collapse in 1932 of the rotting Republican machine led by Senator James Coyne, plus the failed attempt of the disgraced Republican mayor, Charles Kline, to take control of the numbers racket, substantially weakened the politicians' hold on illegal activities. The operation of the numbers reverted to its decentralized, neighborhood origins. Greenlee proved capable of parlaying his illegal earnings into a position of honor and affection in the neighborhood. In this, he resembled his friend and fellow Coyne supporter, Art Rooney, who controlled the numbers and the bookmaking business on the North Side. Like Rooney, Greenlee was recognized as generous, "a beautiful man," "never slow when a man needed a favor" whether it be for rent, a load of coal for a family in the winter, or help with a doctor's bill or lawyer's fee. He ran a soup kitchen across from the Crawford Grill during the Depression, gave away hundreds of turkeys at Thanksgiving and Christmas, and provided capital for college loans and small business startups. Greenlee supported the efforts of black educator Mary Bethune and bank-rolled early black politicians like attorney Homer Brown when he ran for the legislature.[105]

In 1930 the Crawfords began to challenge the Grays and on the third try defeated the mighty Homestead crew, thanks to a lanky young fastball pitcher with phenomenal speed and uncanny control, Leroy "Satchel" Paige, who won the contest in relief. Between 1932 and 1937, the two great Pittsburgh teams vied for control in the city and in the nation. The 1936 Crawfords, champions of the Negro National League, had five men, Oscar Charleston, Judy Johnson, Cool Papa Bell, Satchel Paige and Josh Gibson, in their lineup who subsequently were honored with entry into Cooperstown, baseball's Hall of Fame. Greenlee built his team the finest black-owned stadium in the nation, Greenlee Field, in the Hill. On opening day, *Pittsburgh Courier* editor Robert Vann threw the first pitch. Harold Tinker described what these extraordinary teams did for the morale of people in the hard times of the Depression. "When the Crawfords were coming along – that was a sad time for this country. Not only for blacks but for the majority of poor people – It was sad. And they would come to a ball game and forget all about their woes....We really were the Kings on the Hill...the way we come up from nothing, to be somebody."[106]

While black baseball was king, blacks were increasingly making their mark in track and boxing. In the early 1930s, John Woodruff, a black athlete from Connellsville, southeast of Pittsburgh, was setting high school records in the half-mile run. Woodruff attended the University of Pittsburgh and in the summer of 1936, he beat America's best half-miler and won a place on the U.S. Olympic track team. At the Berlin Olympics, that Hitler envisioned as a showcase for Aryan superiority, Woodruff won the 800 meter race with a torrid final kick after being forced to stop completely to escape from being boxed in. He joined Jesse Owens and three other black athletes to bring home eight gold medals for the American team. In 1940, he set an American record in the 800 meter race that stood for a dozen years. Subsequently, he served in the military through World War II and Korea and retired a lieutenant colonel. After 1937, as the fortunes of the Crawfords declined, Gus Greenlee trained and sponsored the light heavyweight, John Henry Lewis, in a title fight in St. Louis that Lewis won, becoming the first American born black to win that category. After Lewis successfully defended his title a number of times, Greenlee helped arrange a bout with reigning heavyweight champ Joe Louis. Louis had little difficulty in dispatching Lewis in not much over two minutes in the first round. There was, however, a white Pittsburgher from Lawrenceville who gave Joe Louis the fight of his life, and boxing one of the great bouts of all time, Billy Conn.[107]

Pittsburgh claims the honor of being the home of nine champion boxers over the years. Its status as a boxing town reached its peak at the hinge of history in 1940-41. In 1941, Sammy Angott of Washington, Pennsylvania won the lightweight title from Lou Jenkins. A year earlier, Fritzie Zivic, "the Battling Croatian," one of four boxing brothers from Lawrenceville, defeated the highly regarded Henry Armstrong in Madison Square Garden to become the Welterweight Champion. Zivic was a fierce competitor who fought best against the toughest opponents and gained notoriety as a dirty fighter who did whatever it took to win. He often fought twenty or more opponents a year, and his fights with East Liberty's Billy Conn were the stuff of legend and controversy. Their first contest in 1936 "was to be a nice pleasant boxing bout between pals, but as it worked out, the boys used everything but knives, with the result that the town was treated to as swell a boxing feud as you would care to gaze at." Conn said about Zivic: "It was like going to college for five years, just boxing him ten rounds....He put an awful face on me, busted me all up with everything. He did everything but kick you." Fritzie described his style as follows: "I'd give 'em the head, choke 'em, hit 'em in the balls, but never in my life used the thumb, because I wanted no one to use it on me....You're fighting, you're not playing the piano, you know." Zivic lost two out of three fights with a tough, black fighter with a devastating punch, Charley Burley, who many aficionados of boxing claim was one of the greatest boxers of the era, despite never having the opportunity for a title fight. Thwarted in his quest for a championship, Burley went to work for the city of Pittsburgh as a garbage collector in the late 1940s.[108]

Conn's father worked 40 years at Westinghouse Electric as a steamfitter, but Billy was convinced that fighting with his fists beat working in a factory. Conn was trained and managed by a tough Pittsburgh featherweight, Harry Pitler, known by his fight name of Johnny Ray, who had been a close friend of Harry Greb. Conn, 17 years old in 1935, got to see the man who would make him famous at close range when he served as an assistant for the "Brown Bomber," Joe Louis, the night Louis defeated the German Hans Birkie at the Duquesne Gardens in Oakland. Louis knocked out the German in the eighth round and tipped Billy twenty bucks. A memorable local adversary for Billy Conn was Teddy Yarosz, a middleweight champion from Monaca, who had worked at the Aliquippa steel mill. He ran six miles every day and walked the thirty miles from Monaca to Pittsburgh twice a month. When Conn won a split decision before a huge crowd at Forbes Field, a near riot erupted between partisans of the two fighters. A second split decision for Conn set up a third match which turned into a dirty, vicious brawl that Yarosz won.[109]

In 1939, Billy Conn defeated a popular Italian fighter, Freddie Apostoli, in a 15 round bloodbath before a packed house of 19,000 at Madison Square Garden and thereby won the opportunity to fight Melio Bettina for the light heavyweight championship of the world. Conn defeated the champion twice to secure the crown, and he began to seriously dream of moving up to heavyweight to challenge Joe Louis. Conn, not yet 21 and extremely handsome, was the hottest thing in Pittsburgh. In between the two Bettina fights, a former major league baseball player for the Pirates and an East Liberty bar owner with fierce fighting instincts of his own, "Greenfield Jimmy" Smith invited Conn down to his summer place on the Jersey Shore where, as fate would have it, he met Smith's pretty, blonde, fifteen year-old daughter, Mary Louise. The unsuspecting father let the boxer take his daughter to dinner, where Billy announced to the girl his intention to marry her. Once Conn began making the big money, he moved his mother, Maggie, to a new house on Fifth Avenue in Shadyside. [110]

Meanwhile on October 4, 1940, Fritzie Zivic defeated Henry Armstrong in Madison Square Garden, one of the greatest boxers of all time, earning the welterweight championship of the world. Zivic had intended to fight clean so he would not alienate the pro-Armstrong crowd and referee. Reportedly, however, Armstrong started the dirty stuff. He had chosen the wrong person. Fritzie recalled:

> I busted him up, cut him here, cut him there. I'd get him in the clinch. He'd have his head down trying to give you that head, I'd come up on the side. When the eye was cut, I'd rub it with laces to open it up a bit more. Then he's watching this cut and I'd cut this [other] eye. His mouth was cut real bad. He was too proud to spit the blood out. He swallowed it. Swallowing the blood made him sick.

By the final round, Armstrong was covered with blood and his eyes were nearly swollen shut. Moments before the bell in the final round, Zivic floored the champ and secured the title.[111]

The summer of 1941 marked the hiatus between two eras as the country was just climbing out of its worst economic crisis and still blissfully ignorant of how profoundly everything would change six months later once the Empire of Japan launched its attack on the American fleet at Pearl Harbor. Joe DiMaggio was tearing up baseball on his way to a consecutive game hitting record. As Conn's fight with Joe Louis approached, his beloved mother, Maggie, was on her deathbed and Mary Louise reached her eighteenth birthday. Billy Conn was absolutely determined to wed Mary Louise despite her father's fierce opposition. Before the fight, Conn told his mother that the next time she saw him; he would be the heavyweight champion of the world. She replied: "No son, the next time I will see you will be in paradise." At the weigh-in, Louis outweighed Conn by more than thirty pounds, 199 ½ to 169. The night of the bout, the Pirates had a home game, but in order to get some people in the stands, they announced that play would be suspended during the fight to allow the blow-by-blow account to be broadcast to the crowd.

All over Pittsburgh, radios were on in every bar and house, the sound of the fight wafting through every open window into the streets. Every Negro heart on the Hill beat for the great Joe Louis; every Irish ear in Lawrenceville, East Liberty and Greenfield listened intently to discern the fight's ebb and flow. Louis was defending his title for the nineteenth time, his seventh in seven months. The bout garnered the greatest hype of any fight since Louis had squared off against Max Schmeling, the darling of Hitler's Third Reich. Louis won the first two rounds, but Conn came back strong in the next two and even went toe-to-toe with the champ, slugging it out with the slugger. In the fifth round Louis cut Conn deeply over the right eye, but the eighth and ninth rounds were won handily by Conn. Conn sensing victory came on strong in the 11th and 12th and rocked Louis at the round's end with a crushing left. The *Pittsburgh Press* described the mood shift as the rounds progressed among the listeners at Forbes Field from "feigned amusement, then deep interest…profound amazement and finally sheer delirium." As Frank Deford wrote in his famous article on the fight: "This was the best it had ever been and ever would be, the 12th and 13th rounds of Louis and Conn on a warm night just before the world went to hell."[112]

All Conn had to do to win on rounds was to hold on. Instead he itched to knock out the champ. Louis, however, connected with a vicious right and followed with a flurry of punches on the stunned Conn that brought him down for the count with only two seconds left in the 13th. Conn's classic response was "What's the use of being Irish, if you can't be dumb?" His beloved mother, Maggie, died shortly after the fight and Billy married Mary Louise in Philadelphia, the day after the funeral, with a church cleaning lady as the maid of honor. Their marriage endured a lifetime. Initially, however, there was not much opportunity for connubial bliss, since after Pearl Harbor, Billy entered the service. When he returned home on leave for the christening of his first-born, Art Rooney was the godfather. At a family gathering organized to make family peace, Greenfield Jimmy started badgering his son-in-law and a fight broke out with the result that Conn broke his hand on his father-in-law's skull and so ended his chance for a serious rematch with Joe Louis. Conn and Louis, however, became lifelong friends and would sometimes get together in Pittsburgh or New York for dinner on the anniversary of the fight.[113]

Pittsburgh's robust fight scene reflected the essence of a working-class culture pushed to the edge of survival. "Depression fighters" they were called. Men came out of the fire and soot, the darkness and the danger of the mills and the mines, and headed for the bars and the streets where they exercised their individual fighting spirits. Fisticuffs were ubiquitous and seldom led to serious injury. Once a man said enough or went down, the former adversaries might well repair back to the bar for further libations. If they were serious about the art, they entered the ring and showed their grit and determination before the howling crowd. On the ball field, court or gridiron, players exulted in the camaraderie and solidarity of the team, a neighborhood, a crowd. In the ring it was man to man, tribe to tribe. Big fights were arranged at the Duquesne Gardens, a converted trolley barn across from St. Paul's Cathedral in Oakland. There, Irish were pitted against Italians, Poles against Jews, blacks against whites. The complex variables of race, nationality, religion and ethnicity expressed themselves not only in language, music and art, but especially in Pittsburgh, through the intense physicality of working-class contests. Soon a distant and terrible conflict would soak up all the energy, the violence and anger in men's hearts, and the fight game would never be quite the same.

Denouement

As the terrible decade of the 1930s came to a close, it seemed that the world was coming apart. The global economy remained weak and brutal imperialist invasions on three continents by Germany, Italy and Japan provoked deep concerns. Civil conflicts were brewing in many parts of the globe. While the depression-driven upsurge of unions in America had instituted legal reforms that somewhat moderated the power of money and shifted the balance of political power, labor's gains, though significant, were fragile. In 1938 an economic downturn helped Republicans make large gains in Congress. Political attention was shifting from the New Deal social agenda toward the deepening European crisis and the possibility of American involvement in war. David Lawrence, who to all appearances had concluded a 20 year march to unparalleled Democratic organizational power that rivaled Boise Penrose and Matt Quay, the great Republican bosses of the past, was in legal difficulty. In addition, the Republican resurgence in the elections of 1938 and 1940, following their crushing defeat of 1936, slowed the momentum of the Little New Deal and opened cracks in the Democratic Party. But no division so shook the core of the left-labor-liberal coalition as deeply as did the bitter conflict between John L. Lewis and Franklin D. Roosevelt that led to the rise to power of Pittsburgh's Phil Murray. Murray emerged as the most important American labor leader of the 1940s, whose actions shaped the American labor movement and impacted Pittsburgh in profound and lasting ways.

While Pittsburgh on the eve of the Second World War had ceased being a primary driver of industrial innovation, it still remained a mighty producer and employer as European and then American orders for armor plate and the other myriad accoutrements of war began to arrive. Its mills, though often aging, were still capable of enormous production. Nearly anything mechanical and electrical could be made in the complex network of small specialized machine and fabrication shops that surrounded and complimented its metals, glass, railroad and electrical industries. Its workforce was second to none. It gained a reputation as a tough labor town because workers throughout Pittsburgh's history struggled to set rules and then mold attitudes and behaviors as to what constituted a fair day's work, as well as a fair day's pay. The rights of workers' organizations to assert a claim to a type of work or the jurisdiction over a particular field was challenged in 1937 when the National Society of Professional Engineers sought to restrict the term "engineer" to someone with a degree or diploma. The Operating and Stationary Engineers Union successfully fought to defend the identity of the practical engineer whose technical knowledge was gained through experience and whose training was provided by the union. The practical knowledge of equipment was indispensable, especially in the early days, given that most power equipment was custom-made for a particular job. The Operating Engineers also won an important ruling from the AFL when the federation ruled against claims by the Teamsters Union and awarded jurisdiction to them for all power-driven equipment used on all types of building and other construction.[114]

The rising tide of industrial unionism also floated the boats of the craft unions of the AFL. By 1937 the AFL which had resisted industrial unionism suddenly "got religion" and launched aggressive organizing drives that swelled its numbers at the same time as the CIO surge. Carpenters organized lumber and sawmill workers; machinists went after aircraft and other metal workers; the IBEW evolved from being strictly a craft union into seeing the need to organize the suppliers of the wire, cable, boxes, relays, switchboards, which were the stock in their trade. IBEW organizer, Andy Johnson, remembered: "Prior to the Wagner Act, the IBEW consisted purely of journeymen electricians. Then the Wagner act came in, we could see that it was necessary to protect our work....Otherwise, if some organization got in and happened to have a strike and we couldn't get the materials, we would be out in the street. So, to protect ourselves, we went into the industrial end of the industry." The ironworkers, makers of bridges and skyscrapers, were also forced to organize "upstream" to protect their flanks by securing both fabricators and the suppliers of hardware. By August 1937, the AFL had swollen to three and a half million members, larger than it was before the split. By 1938, the construction industry in Pittsburgh was 98% unionized.[115]

In Pittsburgh, the resurgence of the AFL was assisted by the 1936 flood that required an enormous clean-up and reconstruction effort. The Pennsylvania Turnpike's construction also played an important role in rebuilding and reorganizing the building trades unions while extending the reach of many Pittsburgh-based locals. A dramatic example was IBEW Local 5. Many IBEW locals had become inactive during the Depression. Mike Gordan, Local 5's business agent, used the building of the Turnpike east of Pittsburgh from 1938 to 1940 as a vehicle for union growth.

> We had to establish a wage rate from one end of the Turnpike to the other....It was Mike's idea to pick up these defunct local unions all through the territory which the Turnpike went through....We held meetings in Johnstown, Altoona, Indiana, Washington, Punxsutawney, DuBois, and State College, and all the territory that Local 5 now covers. And people who belonged to these defunct local unions made application, and if we knew what their history was and what their abilities were, they were made members of Local 5.[116]

The organization of the Pennsylvania Turnpike by the construction unions was the product of a bitter and sustained struggle that produced some violent confrontations. Contractor Bob Fay remembers the Turnpike's construction as one of the bloodiest battlegrounds of the era.

> There were equipment burnings and fights on both sides. Management had their goon squads and labor had their goon squads and it was a war....It was one of the biggest jobs in the country at the time. It was a new concept to have a turnpike. There were contractors from all over the country working on the original 160 mile section and things were quite violent for the length of that job....But after the war, people that were going to be organized were generally organized. They were learning to live in the union system and many of those violent problems finally ended, thank God.[117]

By 1938, organized labor was at the peak of its power in Pittsburgh, Allegheny County, and all of Southwest Pennsylvania. Pittsburgh City Council included Charles Anderson of the Plumbers, Peter J. McArdle of the Iron Workers, and Thomas Gallagher of the Glass Workers. In Allegheny County, the two majority Commissioners were John J. Kane of the Printing Pressmen and John S. Herron of the Bricklayers, while John Heinz of the Firefighters was Allegheny County Sheriff. The CIO's Phil Murray was a member of the Pittsburgh Board of Public Education and the UMWA's Pat Fagan was a member of the Pennsylvania Labor Relations Board. Public employees were organizing. Postal employees organized into separate Letter Carrier and Postal Clerks Unions. State, County and Municipal Employees, Liquor Control Board, and County Maintenance Workers formed local unions marking a breakthrough in public sector union organizing. Musicians, motion picture operators, sign painters, bartenders, barbers, laundry workers, retail clerks, stage employees and actors all formed or expanded local organizations. The Hotel and Restaurant Alliance grew to 6,000 members by the late 1930s. The Amalgamated Transit Union won the right to represent drivers at the Greyhound Bus Company.[118]

Teachers (mostly female) began to organize despite a long history of being kept subservient to school administration (nearly all male). Anne Leifer, one of the organizers of the Pittsburgh Federation of Teachers, judged teachers "a justifiably fearful lot." The first uprising of the teachers came over the issue of a teacher's right to marry. In 1935, 200 female teachers petitioned the Board of Education for permission to marry. In one instance, a principal tried to force teachers in his school to sign a letter denouncing as immoral a teacher who had secretly married and became pregnant. All the teachers refused to sign. With support from the Philadelphia Federation of Teachers, a bill was passed through the "Little New Deal" legislature on April 27, 1937 giving Pittsburgh's female teachers the right to marry. Anne and Herb Leifer got married on April 30, 1937 followed by about 200 more couples in that spring. "Some of the best and strongest teachers in the city joined the union during 1937-38," Anne recalled.[119]

At the very moment of labor's political triumph, the deepening division between the AFL craft unions and the CIO's industrial unions was sealed by a formal break. The CIO claimed four million members nationally and over 87,000 members in Allegheny County, but many of those members were barely integrated into the workings of their locals. While unionism was spreading into almost every aspect of working-class life, the two labor federations were poised to go to war. John Frey of the AFL Metal Trades Council led the attack, calling the CIO a front for the Communist Party (CP) with 145 known members of the CP on its payroll. Several attempts at a negotiated reunion were thwarted despite heavy pressure from President Roosevelt and Labor Secretary Perkins. Finally, in meetings held in February and May 1938, the AFL Executive Council revoked the charters of ten of the CIO unions, including that of the UMWA and the Amalgamated Association of Iron and Steel Workers. In Pittsburgh, the Pittsburgh Central Labor Council expelled all delegates from locals affiliated with the CIO, which then formed the Steel City Industrial Union with Pat Fagan as its president. No longer able to function as a committee of the AFL, Lewis convened the CIO's Constitutional Convention in Pittsburgh at the end of 1938.[120]

It was no secret that Lewis demanded loyalty and no one had been more loyal to him than Phil Murray. In 1938, when Lewis unveiled his selection of CIO officers at the founding convention as the Committee of Industrial Organizations became the Congress of Industrial Organizations at a fraternal hall on the North Side in Pittsburgh, there was one surprise. While Murray and Sidney Hillman of the Amalgamated Clothing Workers were carried over to the formally new organization in their vice-presidential positions, John Brophy, the Secretary of the Committee on Industrial Organization that issued the call for the convention, was not anointed an officer in the new organization despite being very popular and endorsed by nearly every delegation. Brophy wrote:

> The evidence accumulated before him (Lewis) of support for me probably was the worst thing that could have happened. He wanted no equal, especially not a man he had had on his payroll, one notoriously subject to the vice of thinking for himself. It was not so much that I would be a rival to Lewis, but that I would become independent of him and with the prestige of election on my own merits, would be listened to when I disagreed with him.[121]

Lewis, in fact, wanted to install his daughter Kathryn as Secretary, a course resisted by Hillman and even Murray. Lewis claimed to oppose Brophy because with him there would be three miners in the four CIO officer positions. When Murray offered to withdraw in Brophy's favor, Lewis glowered and selected James Carey, the president and only anti-Communist officer of the United Electrical, Radio and Machine Workers Union (UE). By making the young Carey a CIO officer, Lewis probably helped the Communists solidify their hold on the UE by pulling Carey's attention away from the internal struggles around the union's direction. [122]

After achieving an almost unimaginable gain in political power in only five years, the Democrats seemed adrift. An economic downturn in 1937-38 cooled voter enthusiasm for the New Deal and in 1938, Republicans made significant gains in Congress. Lewis harbored presidential ambitions, and relations with Roosevelt were openly hostile. Lewis increased his criticism of Roosevelt's economic policies urging more public works, more subsidized housing and more generous Social Security payments. He was also taking an increasingly aggressive anti-war stance against involvement in the looming European conflict. He stood for continuing domestic reform, not foreign wars, and threatened to lead a left-wing, farmer-labor coalition to either take over or secede from the Democratic Party.[123] In his traditional Labor Day network radio address to the nation, Lewis thundered:

> War has always been the device of the politically despairing and intellectually sterile statesman....It provides employment in the gun factories and begets enormous profits for those already rich. It kills off the vigorous males who, if permitted to live, might question the financial and political exploitation of the race....Labor in America wants no war, nor any part of war. Labor wants the right to work and live – not the privilege of dying by gunshot or poison gas to sustain the mental errors of current statesmen.[124]

Lewis's mounting hostility to Roosevelt was a source of deep discomfort for other CIO leaders, especially Sydney Hillman and Phil Murray. Unease in the labor movement only increased as news of the Hitler-Stalin non-aggression pact, signed on August 19, 1939, burst upon the political landscape. This agreement was disorienting for the American Communist Party initially and devastating in the long run. The action was especially harmful to Communist support within the Jewish community. The change in party line dictated by the dominance of Stalin and the Soviet party within the Communist movement undercut an American party that had gained a good deal of respect and acceptance in liberal circles for its resolute resistance against fascism and Nazism. That resistance had provided the rationale for the whole United Front strategy. [125]

Unlike the Soviet imposition of the dual-union strategy in 1929 that only affected a small and relatively isolated party, this accord shook an organization that had gained a significant measure of influence in the labor movement and among a wide array of progressive political forces in the nation. Initially, the rumors of a German-Russian accord were met with derision by American Communist leaders, including Earl Browder who proclaimed that "there is as much chance of Russo-German agreement as of Earl Browder being elected President of the Chamber of Commerce." Caught completely off-guard by events, the party continued to urge support for Poland and Roosevelt's policies. The Soviet invasion of Eastern Poland in mid-September revealed the true nature of the accord and Communist parties worldwide were forced to shift course and denounce the looming European war as one between two imperialisms and therefore something that the Communists could not support. When word came from Russia that the party was to abandon its support for President Roosevelt, Lewis and the Communist Party found themselves on the same page.[126]

Meanwhile, General George C. Marshall, named Chief of Staff of the United States Army on the very day that Hitler started the Second World War with his attack on Poland, a nation that Britain and France were pledged to defend, returned to Uniontown, Pennsylvania, south of Pittsburgh to make a speech. Born in Uniontown in 1880, Marshall had a distinguished military and civilian career culminating with his service as Secretary of State and Secretary of Defense. Once he left home at the age of seventeen for the Virginia Military Institute, he returned home only sporadically over a long career that took him to the Philippines to fight the insurrection there, then to France as Chief of Operations for the First Infantry Division in France during World War I. From 1924 to 1927, he served in China. During the depression of the 1930s, he was assigned to work with the National Guard and the Civilian Conservation Corps, where he developed a deep respect for the American civilian soldier.[127] A week after being named Chief of Staff, Marshall made a trip home to revisit the scenes of his youth. In a speech before four hundred guests at the White Swan Hotel, he recalled hunting pheasant along Braddock's trail and picnicking by his grave. He recalled the momentous events at the nearby glen where George Washington had attacked Coulon de Jumonville's small force and thereby precipitated a worldwide conflict that ultimately cost France its North American empire and led to a revolution against England by her colonists. He told the assembled:

> I will not trouble you with the perplexities, the problems and requirements for the defense of the country, except to say that the matter is so great and the cost, unfortunately, is bound to be so high, that all we should do should be planned and executed in a businesslike manner, without emotional hysteria, demagogic speeches, or other unfortunate methods which will befog the issue and might mislead our efforts. Finally, it comes to me that we should daily thank the good Lord that we live where we do, think as we do, and enjoy the blessings that are becoming rare privileges on this earth.[128]

The 1940 election marked a watershed in American political and labor history as John L. Lewis attempted and failed to sway the presidential election. For as long as Roosevelt was expected to step down in 1940, Lewis may well have harbored his own presidential ambitions. Once it became clear that Roosevelt was going to run again as war enveloped Europe, Lewis allegedly proposed himself to Roosevelt as his vice-presidential candidate. According to Lee Pressman, the CIO's legal counsel's version of the story, when Lewis argued that Roosevelt might be defeated without a labor man on the ticket, Roosevelt responded: "That's very interesting, John, but which place on the ticket are you reserving for me?" When Roosevelt declined and in a surprise move picked Henry Wallace as his running mate, Lewis reverted to his Republican roots and supported the candidacy of Wendell Wilkie while adopting a militantly isolationist position on the war.[129]

Lewis's stand put enormous pressure on pro-Roosevelt CIO leaders like Brophy, Hillman, Carey, and especially Phil Murray, and effectively aligned Lewis with the Communist minority inside the CIO. The Republicans were equally in disarray as Roosevelt named prominent Republicans as Secretaries of War (Henry Stimson) and of the Navy (Frank Knox). Both parties' political conventions were confronted with Hitler's conquest of Poland, Denmark, Norway, Holland, Belgium and France. While the Republicans were isolationist and anti-New Deal, they nominated Wilkie, an interventionist supporter of most of the New Deal's programs. Roosevelt, himself, torn between a desire to retire, yet harboring a deep concern over who might succeed him as president, waited until the convention. When a statement was read stating his wish not to run, a massive "We want Roosevelt" demonstration erupted that secured him the nomination.[130]

In October, Wilkie's campaign began to make progress since most Americans in fact did not want to go to war. In agreement with Lewis, he made a speech in Pittsburgh where he quoted Abraham Lincoln saying that "Labor ...is the superior of capital," and pledged to support collective bargaining, social security, minimum wage and maximum hour legislation. On the evening of October 25, 25 to 30 million Americans tuned in their radios to listen to the speech of John L. Lewis. Before the address Lewis called Pat Fagan, UMWA District 5 Director and close ally of Phil Murray, and said: "I'm going to make a speech tonight, and I want you to listen to it." Fagan, who was in fact on his way to make a speech that night for Roosevelt in Uniontown, replied: "I will." Lewis in his radio address attacked the president heartily for war preparation and for not leaving the presidency after two terms. "The President has said that he hates war and will work for peace, but his acts do not match his words....Personal craving for power, the overweening abnormal and selfish craving for increased power, is a thing to alarm and dismay....America wants no royal family." Roosevelt could only win with labor's support and Lewis passionately urged his listeners to deny it to him. After endorsing Wilkie ("He was born of the briar and not to the purple. He has worked with his hands and knows the pangs of hunger"), Lewis threw down the gauntlet. If labor voted for Roosevelt, he would resign as CIO president. Ending with an emotional appeal to mothers, Lewis implored them "with the sacred ballot, (to) lead the revolt against the candidate who plays at a game that may make cannon fodder of your sons." Fagan heard Lewis's speech in the car on the way back to Pittsburgh and immediately sent a telegram: "Listened to your speech. Still for Roosevelt."[131]

Lewis's endorsement of the Republican candidate caused consternation among the liberal left and inside the CIO. Murray maintained a stony silence. Hillman openly attacked Lewis's action. The Communists followed Lewis reluctantly. While they applauded his rejection of Roosevelt and foreign war, they had a difficult time embracing Wilkie, the Wall Street lawyer. For most of 1940, Lewis positioned himself as the angry voice of the political left, attracting Communists, pacifists, isolationists, radicals of many stripes with a populist message of jobs and peace. In a striking demonstration of miners' feelings, Murray received more than double the number of locals' nominations for President at the UMWA convention that year than did Lewis. Van Bittner, a tough miner organizer from West Virginia and longtime Lewis supporter, summed up the feelings of most inside the CIO: "I am 100% for John L. Lewis as head of the CIO and also 100% for the reelection of Roosevelt." The election results revealed Lewis's political miscalculation. Roosevelt won by five million votes (down from eleven million in 1936) and his support was strongest among industrial workers including coal miners.[132]

The consequences of Lewis's political gamble were substantial. The New Deal coalition was deeply wounded and eventually the labor movement was split into three as Lewis took the powerful miners' union out of the CIO. The Roosevelt wing of the labor movement, led by Murray and Hillman, was now deeply embedded in government operation, industrial policy, and party politics. Mainstream labor sentiment was moving centrist labor leaders toward the view that involvement in the war was inevitable and the key issues were: How soon would it start? How prepared would the nation be? An important expression of this political tendency was the campaign by Father Rice in his *Pittsburgh Catholic* columns to overcome the Irish antipathy to England and support Roosevelt's aid to an England besieged by the Nazis. They trusted Roosevelt personally to lead in the crisis. For the Communists, the Hitler-Stalin pact cut them off from the liberal left, and their new-found fervor for isolationism uncomfortably allied them with some of the most reactionary right-wing forces in the country.

The 1940 CIO Convention brought the organization to the very hall in Atlantic City where, in October 1935, Lewis punched Hutcheson and provoked the industrial union secession movement. Great anticipation and anxiety gripped the 2,600 delegates, hardened local union politicians representing the majority of the factories, mines and mills in the nation. As Lewis made his way to the podium, the delegates stood, applauded and demonstrated enthusiastically in a demonstration led by miners, Communists and other delegates that lasted 43 minutes. Lewis could probably have swept the convention up into an election by acclamation, but instead he launched into what was described alternately as a valedictory or a eulogy. He made clear his determination to leave the presidency by the end of the convention and so largely removed himself from overt criticism except by Hillman. Murray and his supporters, in an indirect attack on Lewis's policies, attacked an easier target – the Communists – for their subservience to foreign dictation.

Murray was deeply conflicted about taking over the leadership of the organization. His only paid position was as vice-president of the UMWA, so Lewis signed his paycheck. He knew that Lewis expected him to continue as his agent, something that given his interventionist leanings and close relationship with Roosevelt would be impossible. He had served Lewis for more than twenty years as his chief administrator, negotiator and trouble-shooter. Relations between the men had not always been smooth as Murray, as head of SWOC, resented being kept uninformed about the steel negotiations with Myron Taylor. Murray in turn had not consulted Lewis before launching the Little Steel strike in the euphoria following the victory at Aliquippa.[133]

Murray was the only candidate acceptable to Lewis and the mineworkers as well as Hillman and the Roosevelt loyalists. Faced with a situation where it was either him or likely chaos, Murray, nominated by Lewis, was unanimously elected the second president of the Congress of Industrial Organizations. His deeply conflicted loyalties and painful acceptance of his duty was openly displayed in the grim picture of the convention gavel being passed; Lewis glowering, Murray bowing like a knight accepting a commission from his lord. Echoing the most poignant moment at the end of Lewis's opening speech, where Lewis, with tears streaking down his face, said: "We can't stop to weep and wear sackcloth because something that happened yesterday did not meet with our approval or that we did not have a dream come true....You know when you first hired me I was something of a man, and when I leave you in a day or two I will still in my own mind be something of a man." Murray in his acceptance speech alluded to those sentiments in words that have often been interpreted as self-questioning, rather than as assertions or even a muted warning to his long-time leader. "I think I am a man. I think I have convictions, I think I have a soul and a heart and a mind....With the exception, of course, of my soul, they all belong to me, every one of them."[134]

The Lewis-Murray relationship had endured more than two decades of close collaboration between two men who were profoundly different in temperament and lifestyle. Lewis acted and lived like a monarch. He rarely socialized with workers and preferred the company of the powerful whether in the political, business or social world. He had no firm religious beliefs and eschewed alcohol. Murray on the other hand was humble and unpretentious, uncomfortable in the limelight or in high society. He enjoyed a few beers with his friends and socialized regularly with miners and mill workers. Murray was also a devout Catholic who was deeply influenced by the Church's social teaching. While Lewis lived in a wealthy D.C. suburb and took his vacations on the Florida coast or in Jackson Hole, Wyoming among the rich and powerful, Murray stayed close to home and family. He deeply enjoyed sitting on a family member's porch in the coal patches swapping tales with mineworkers. Lewis felt no inferiority in high social and political circles, wheeling and dealing there with confidence. Murray, on the other hand, had been the guy who for decades had been called upon to explain union policy to the rank-and-file, as well as doing the detail work on negotiations and organization. He avoided the limelight and felt uncomfortable at the social gatherings of the rich and powerful. Labor historian Melvyn Dubofsky memorably tagged them as "labor's odd couple." Their differences dovetailed perfectly for more than two decades, however, and made them an effective team. In 1941 Murray's political, union and personal conscience began to increasingly conflict with his loyalty to Lewis. At that point, he stepped out on his own.[135]

Notes Chapter 10

[1] Irving Bernstein, *Turbulent Years: A History of the American Worker, 1933-1941* (Boston: Houghton Mifflin, 1971), 14-25.

[2] Bernstein, *Turbulent Years*, 10-11.

[3] Bernstein, *Turbulent Years*, 11-13.

[4] William Serrin, *Homestead: The Glory and the Tragedy of an American Steel Town* (New York: Random House, 1992), 174-176.

[5] *Steel and Metal Worker*, v.1 n.1, (August-September, 1933).

[6] Saul Alinsky, *John L. Lewis, An Unauthorized Biography* (New York: G.P. Putnam's Sons, 1949), 67-69.

[7] Bernstein, *Turbulent Years*, 34-45; James Gray Pope, "The Western Pennsylvania Coal Strike of 1933, Part I: Lawmaking from Below and the Revival of the United Mine Workers," *Labor History*, 44:1, (2003), 15-18.

[8] James Gray Pope, "The Western Pennsylvania Coal Strike of 1933, Part I," 15-29, quote 18. *juris-generative refers to the common law notion that the laws derive from the practice and adhesion of the community.

[9] Harvey O'Connor, *Steel Dictator* (New York: The John Day Company, 1935), 154-157; Staughton Lynd, "The Possibility of Radicalism in the Early 1930s: The Case of Steel," *Radical America*, 6:6, (November-December 1972), 41-42; Pope, "The Western Pennsylvania Coal Strike of 1933, Part I: Lawmaking from Below and the Revival of the United Mine Workers," 42-48.

[10] Harvey O'Connor, *Personal Histories of the Early CIO*, quoted in Staughton Lynd, "The Possibility of Radicalism in the Early 1930s: The Case of Steel," *Radical America*, v.6 n.6 (November-December, 1972), 39. Lynd's influential article was an important reinterpretation of the 1930s at the time when many activists of the 1960s decided to enter the mines and mills to organize for a more democratic America. The present author includes himself among those activists, as he worked with Staughton and Alice Lynd in East Chicago, Indiana, in the movement against the Vietnam War and organizing with Staughton a forum called "Rank-and-File," where labor activists from the 1930s to the 1960s spoke about labor organizing history. Subsequently, in 1973, I arrived in Pittsburgh committed to finding a place in the area's mills.

[11] Lynd, "The Possibility of Radicalism in the Early 1930s: The Case of Steel," 46-54; The Spang-Chalfant footage figures prominently in the half-hour segment on Aliquippa in the PBS series on *The Great Depression*; *Steel and Metal Worker* (October, November, 1933).

[12] Harvey Klehr, *The Heyday of American Communism: The Depression Decade* (New York: Basic Books, 1984), 161-165.

[13] Harvey A. Levenstein, *Communism, Anticommunism and the CIO* (Westport: Greenwood Press, 1981), 20-26.

[14] O'Connor, *Steel Dictator*, 185-195.

[15] O'Connor, *Steel Dictator*, 217.

[16] Lynd, "The Possibility of Radicalism in the Early 1930s: The Case of Steel," 51-52; Robert R. R. Brooks, *As Steel Goes: Unionism in a Basic Industry* (New Haven: Yale University Press, 1940), 68-69.

[17] James D. Rose, *Duquesne and the Rise of Steel Unionism* (Urbana and Chicago: University of Illinois Press, 2001), 44-47.

[18] Rose, *Duquesne and the Rise of Steel Unionism*, 51-62.

[19] Philip Bonosky, *Burning Valley* (Urbana and Chicago: University of Illinois Press, 1998).

[20] Rose, *Duquesne and the Rise of Steel Unionism*, 72-75, 99. I am grateful to John Hoerr for pointing out the use by local political bosses of county registration information.

[21] Rose, *Duquesne and the Rise of Steel Unionism*, 103, 117.; Brooks, *As Steel Goes*, 105.

[22] Rose, *Duquesne and the Rise of Steel Unionism*, 128.

[23] Michael P. Weber, *Don't Call Me Boss: David L. Lawrence, Pittsburgh's Renaissance Mayor* (Pittsburgh: University of Pittsburgh Press, 1988), 67-68.

[24] Weber, *Don't Call Me Boss*, 67-76; Clarke M. Thomas, *Fortunes and Misfortunes, Pittsburgh and Allegheny County Politics, 1930-95* (Pittsburgh: Institute of Politics, 1998), 31-33.

[25] Weber, *Don't Call Me Boss*, 56-7; Bruce M. Stave, *The New Deal and the Last Hurrah: Pittsburgh Machine Politics* (Pittsburgh: University of Pittsburgh Press, 1970), 56-57.

[26] Weber, *Don't Call Me Boss*, 55-61; Stave, *The New Deal and the Last Hurrah*, 65-66.

[27] Weber, *Don't Call Me Boss*, 86-88

[28] Stave, *The New Deal and the Last Hurrah*, 85-86.

[29] Weber, *Don't Call Me Boss*, 91-93, 101.

[30] Weber, *Don't Call Me Boss*, 106-115.

[31] Weber, *Don't Call Me Boss*, 115-119; Stave, *The New Deal and the Last Hurrah*, 88-108.

[32] *Pittsburgh Post-Gazette*, October 2, 1936.

[33] Weber, *Don't Call Me Boss*, 124-127.

[34] Weber, *Don't Call Me Boss*, 120-124; Kenneth C. Wolensky, "An Activist Government in Harrisburg: Governor George H. Earle III and Pennsylvania's "Little New Deal," *Pennsylvania Heritage*, v. XXXIV, n.1, (Winter 2008), 18, 20.

[35] *Pittsburgh Post-Gazette*, March 19, 1937.

[36] Alinsky, *John L. Lewis*, 64-78; *Minutes of the Organizational Meeting of the Steel Workers Organizing Committee of the Committee for the Industrial Organizations*, June 17, 1936. Copy in possession of the author courtesy of Russ Gibbons.

[37] Alinsky, *John L. Lewis*, 76-78; Robert H. Zeiger, *The CIO: 1935-1955* (Chapel Hill: University of North Carolina Press, 1995), 23.

[38] Pat Fagan, *Interview* by Alice Hoffman, September 24, 1968, Penn State Archives, 32.

[39]George Powers, *Cradle of Steel Unionism, Monongahela Valley, PA,* (East Chicago, Indiana: Figueroa Printers,1972), 69-84.

[40]Powers, *Cradle of Steel Unionism,* 85.

[41]Robert H. Zeiger, *The CIO: 1935-1955,* 38; Harvey A. Levenstein, *Communism, Anti-communism and the CIO,* 49-50.

[42]Levenstein, *Communism, Anticommunism and the CIO,* 46-49.

[43]John Hoerr, *And the Wolf Finally Came,*(Pittsburgh: University of Pittsburgh Press, 1988), 262-263; *Pittsburgh Press,* July 6, 1936; *Pittsburgh Post-Gazette,* July 6, 1936.

[44]*Steel Labor,* August 1, 1936; George Powers, *Cradle of Steel Unionism,* 93-94.

[45]*Steel Labor,* August 1, 1936.

[46]*Steel Labor,* August 1, 1936;

[47]Jim Young, "Bitter Pill in Chocolate Town: The Sit-down Strike of 1937," *Pennsylvania Labor History Journal* (December 2005), 12-13.

[48]Brooks, *As Steel Goes,* 98-109; Powers, *Cradle of Steel Unionism,* 98-107; Melvyn Dubofsky and Warren Van Tine, *John L. Lewis: A Biography,* 273-275.

[49]Carl I. Meyerhuber, Jr., *Less Than Forever: The Rise and Decline of Union Solidarity in Western Pennsylvania, 1914-1948,* (Selinsgrove: Susquehanna University Press, 1987), 179-192.

[50]Harvey A. Levenstein, *Communism, Anticommunism and the CIO,* 42-46.

[51]Jim Pope, "Worker Lawmaking, Sit-Down Strikes, and the Shaping of American Industrial Relations, 1935-1958," *Law and History Review,* Vol.24, Issue 1, (Spring 2006).

[52]David H. Wollman & Donald R. Inman, *Portraits in Steel: An Illustrated History of the Jones & Laughlin Steel Corporation* (Kent, Ohio: Kent State University Press, 1999), 84-98; Brooks, *As Steel Goes,..,* 112-114; James Green, "Democracy Comes to "Little Siberia,"*Labor's Heritage,* v.5, n.2, Summer, 1993, 6-11.

[53]Congress of Industrial Organizations, *CIO 1935-1955: Industrial Democracy in Action* (Washington: Industrial Union Department, AFL-CIO, 1955), 7.

[54]Brooks, *As Steel Goes,..,* 110-119; James Green, "Democracy Comes to "Little Siberia," 16-18.

[55]Richard C. Cortner, *The Jones and Laughlin Case* (New York: Alfred A. Knopf, 1970), 163-165.

[56]Steve Kocherzat and Charles McCollester, "NLRB v. Jones & Laughlin Supreme Court Ruling," *Aliquippa's Struggle and Labor Law Reform* (Homestead: Steel Valley Printers, 2000), 5.

[57]Brooks, *As Steel Goes,...* 121-127; Wollman & Inman, *Portraits in Steel,* 108-112; James Green, "Democracy Comes to "Little Siberia," James Green, "Democracy Comes to "Little Siberia,"20-22.

[58]Bernstein, *Turbulent Years,* 478-497; The events at Aliquippa and the Memorial Day massacre at Republic Steel were the subject of an episode in the PBS television documentary *The Great Depression* entitled "Mean Things Happening." James Green's article in *Labor's Heritage,* "Democracy Comes to Little Siberia" derived from his research done to produce that segment..

[59]Bernstein, *Turbulent Years,* 496; Alinsky, *John L. Lewis,* 168

[60]Charles Owen Rice, "America's Darkest Decade," in *Fighter With a Heart: Charles Owen Rice, Pittsburgh Labor Priest,* edited by Charles McCollester, (Pittsburgh, University of Pittsburgh Press, 1996), 23-29.

[61]Rice, *Fighter with a Heart,* 23-33; Neil Betten, *Catholic Activism and the Industrial Worker* (Gainesville: University Presses of Florida, 1976), 77-84.

[62]Rice, *Fighter With a Heart,* 35-48.

[63]David E. Koskoff, *The Mellons: The Chronicle of America's Richest Family* (New York: Thomas Y. Crowell, 1978), 305-306, 339-340; Louis Uchitelle, "The Richest of the Rich, Proud of a New Gilded Age," *New York Times* (July 15, 2007). The separated Mellon fortunes ranked the brothers 14th and 15th.

[64]Eric Leif Davin, "Blue Collar Democracy: Class War and Political Revolution in Western Pennsylvania, 1932-1937," *Pennsylvania History,* v.67, n.2, (Spring 2000), 240-297.

[65]Thomas R. Brooks, *Clint: A Biography of a Labor Intellectual, Clinton S. Golden* (New York: Atheneum, 1978), 180-185; Vincent D. Sweeney, *The United Steelworkers of America* (Pittsburgh: USWA circa 1956), 40-46.

[66]Brooks, *Clint.*

[67]*Proceedings of the First Constitutional Convention of the Congress of Industrial Organizations,* (Pittsburgh: November 14 to 18, 1938), 8.

[68]*Proceedings of the First Constitutional Convention of the Congress of Industrial Organizations,* 9-10.

[69]*Proceedings of the First Constitutional Convention of the Congress of Industrial Organizations,* 10-11.

[70]Considered one of the classic expressions of the immigrant experience, *Out of This Furnace* has been the University of Pittsburgh Press's best seller with over 200,000 copies sold.

[71]Quote in Dave Demarest, *Afterword,* to Thomas Bell's, *Out of This Furnace: A Novel of Immigrant Labor in America* (Pittsburgh: University of Pittsburgh Press, 1976), 418; I am grateful for the information provided on the contentious issue of Thomas Bell's origins by Peter Oresick. Bell identified himself as Slovak, but the place of his birth and the fact that he identifies the religion of the fictional Dobrejcak family (based on Bell's family the Belejcaks) as Greek Catholic indicates a Carpatho-Rusyn ethnicity. The Carpatho-Rusyns or Ruthenians were one of the three original ethnicities of Czechoslovakia and inhabited the Carpathian mountains and were divided among Poland, Ukraine and Czechoslovakia jurisdictions. Bell who was quite secular in his viewpoint accepted the Slovak designation.

[72]Bell, *Out of This Furnace,* 409.

[73]Bell, *Out of This Furnace,* 165-166.

[74]Bell, *Out of This Furnace*, 408.

[75]Bell, *Out of This Furnace*, 410-412.

[76]David Demarest, *Maxo Vanka's Millvale Murals* (Millvale, Pa: St. Nicholas Croatian Catholic Church, 1995); David Leopold, *The Gift of Sympathy: The Art of Maxo Vanka* (Bucks County, PA: The James A. Michener Museum, 2001), 11-23.

[77]Louis Adamic, "My Friend Maxo Vanka," *My America: 1928-38* (New York, Harpers, 1938), 156-166; Leopold, *The Gift of Sympathy*, 19-23.

[78]Louis Adamic, "My Friend Maxo Vanka," 170-171; Leopold, *The Gift of Sympathy*, 19-23.

[79]Leopold, *The Gift of Sympathy*, 30.

[80]Adamic, "My Friend Maxo Vanka," 176-179.

[81]Leopold, *The Gift of Sympathy*, 33-35.

[82]Owen Francis, "The Saga of Joe Magarac: Steelman, A steelworker takes his place beside Paul Bunyan," Scribner's Magazine, November 1931, reprinted in the Standard Dictionary of Folklore, Mythology and Legend, v. 2, Edited by Maria Leach and Jerome Fried, (New York, 1970), 505-511; Clifford J. Reutter, "The Puzzle of a Pittsburgh Steeler, Joe Magarac's Ethnic Identity," *Western Pennsylvania Historical Magazine*, v.63, n.1, (January 1980) 31-36. I am indebted to John and Linda Asmonga for these articles and to Ed Salaj, Homestead steel worker for first pointing out to me that Joe was a jackass.

[83]*The Valley Daily News*, August 23-24, 1927; Louis Joughin and Edmund M. Morgan, *The Legacy of Sacco and Vanzetti*, (Princeton, NJ: Princeton University Press, 1948), 52-353.

[84]Phillip Jenkins, *Hoods and Shirts: The Extreme Right in Pennsylvania, 1925-1950*, (Chapel Hill: University of North Carolina Press, 1997), 136-165.

[85]Rice, *Fighter With a Heart*, 52-55.

[86]Alvin Yudkoff, *Gene Kelly: A Life of Dance and* Dreams, (New York: Back Stage Books, 1999), 4-20.

[87]Alvin Yudkoff, *Gene Kelly: A Life of Dance and* Dreams, 20-45; Myron Cope, *Double Yoi!: A Revealing Memoir by the Broadcasting/ Writer*, (Sports publishing, L.L.C., 2002), 8.

[88]Patricia Ward Kelly, "George Bush is No Gene Kelly," *Pittsburgh Post Gazette*, March 24, 2008. This letter to the editor was provoked by a comparison of George Bush to Gene Kelly after the president did a clumsy soft-shoe while waiting for John McCain. She forcefully rejected the comparison saying it represented not only a transformation but a considerable slight. If Gene were in a grave, he would have turned over in it. When Gene was compared to the grace and agility of Jack Dempsey, Wayne Gretzky and even Pittsburgh's own Roberto Clemente, he was delighted, but to be linked with a clunker - particularly one he would consider inept and demoralizing - would have sent him reeling.

[89]Jacob Feldman, *The Jewish Experience in Western Pennsylvania: A History 1755-1945*, (Pittsburgh: The Historical Society of Western Pennsylvania, 1986), 224-285.

[90]Franklin Toker, *Fallingwater Rising: Frank Lloyd Wright, E. J. Kaufmann and America's Most Extraordinary House*, (New York: Alfred A. Knopf, 2003), 34-39.

[91]Franklin Toker, *Fallingwater Rising*, 41-48.

[92]Franklin Toker, *Fallingwater Rising*, 49-60.

[93]Franklin Toker, *Fallingwater Rising*, 70-75; 134-192.

[94]Franklin Toker, *Fallingwater Rising*, 133.

[95]Barbara Burstein, *A Jewish Legacy: Pittsburgh*, Video documentary, Carnegie Public Library; Sally Kalson, Frieda Shapira: Committed to Social Reform, *Pittsburgh Post-Gazette*, July 8, 2003.

[96]Robert C. Alberts, *Pitt, the Story of the University of Pittsburgh, 1787-1987* (Pittsburgh: University of Pittsburgh Press, 1986), 132-142.

[97]Mary L. Solomon, *Legacy to a Mill Town: Carnegie Library of Homestead*, (West Homestead, 1998), 70.

[98]Thomas E. Schott, "Pittsburgh Poison: The Waner Boys," in *Pittsburgh Sports: Stories from the Steel City*, ed. Randy Roberts (Pittsburgh, University of Pittsburgh Press, 2000*)*, 78-91; John McCollister, *The Bucs: The Story of the Pittsburgh Pirates*, 107.

[99]Rob Ruck, "Art Rooney and the Pittsburgh Steelers," in *Pittsburgh Sports: Stories from the Steel City*, ed. Randy Roberts (Pittsburgh: University of Pittsburgh, 2000), 251-254.

[100]Ruck, "Art Rooney and the Pittsburgh Steelers," 258-262; Dan Rooney, *Dan Rooney: My 75 Years with the Pittsburgh Steelers*, (New York, Da Capo Press: 2007), 21, 27.

[101]Rob Ruck, *Sandlot Seasons: Sport in Black Pittsburgh* (Urbana: University of Illinois Press, 1987).

[102]Ruck, *Sandlot Seasons*, 124-128.

[103]Ruck, *Sandlot Seasons*, 124-136; Rob Ruck, "I Lived Baseball: Harold Tinker and the Pittsburgh Crawfords," in *Pittsburgh Sports: Stories from the Steel City*, ed. Randy Roberts (University of Pittsburgh Press, 2000), 97.

[104]Ruck, *Sandlot Seasons*, 137-147; Ruck, "I Lived Baseball," 105.

[105]Ruck, *Sandlot Seasons*, 147-151.

[106]Ruck, *Sandlot Seasons*, 155-158; Ruck, "I Lived Baseball," 109.

[107] Frank Litsky, "John Woodruff, an Olympian, Dies at 92," *New York Times*, November 1, 2007; Ruck, *Sandlot Seasons*, 165-169.

[108]Harvey Boyle, *Pittsburgh Post-Gazette* quoted in Randy Roberts, "Between the Whale and Death," *Pittsburgh Sports: Stories from the Steel City*, ed. Randy Roberts (University of Pittsburgh Press, 2000); Andrew O'Toole, *Sweet William: The Life of Billy Conn*.(Urbana and Chicago: University of Illinois Press, 2008), 33; Harry Otty, *Black Dynamite: harles Duane Burley*, http://cyberboxingzone.com/boxing/burley.htm>.

[109]Andrew O'Toole, *Sweet William: The Life of Billy Conn*.(Urbana and Chicago: University of Illinois Press, 2008), 5-25.

[110]Andrew O'Toole, *Sweet William: The Life of Billy Conn*, 45-49, 75-78, 90-136.

[111]Randy Roberts, "Between the Whale and Death," *Pittsburgh Sports: Stories from the Steel City*, 23-24.

[112]Frank Deford, "The Boxer and the Blonde", *Sports Illustrated*, June 17, 1985; These paragraphs owe much to a conversation with sports writer Roy McHugh.

[113]The author waited on Conn and Louis when they had dinner at Christopher's Restaurant in Mt. Washington in 1975.

[114]F.A. Fitzgerald, Editor, *The International Engineer: Fifty years of Progress: 1896-1946*, (December, 1946), 37-48.

[115]Andy Johnson, *Interview* by Charles McCollester, (November 27, 1990); Bernstein, *Turbulent Years*, 685-687.

[116]Bill Branthoover, *Interview* by Charles McCollester, (May 5, 1991).

[117]Bob Fay, *Interview* by Charles McCollester, (undated 1987).

[118]Meyer A. Sanders, "Labor," *Allegheny County: A Sesqui-Ccentennial Review, 1788…1938*, Ed. George E. Kelly, (Pittsburgh: Allegheny Sesqui-Centennial Committee, 1938), 138-139; Amalgamated Transit Union Staff, *ATU 100 Years: A History of the Amalgamated Transit Union*, (Amalgamated Transit Union, 1992), 66-67.

[119]Kathy Gensure, "The PFT's Inception and Early Days – Reminiscences on a Time Gone By." Interview with Anne Leifer, Albert Fondy, and Joseph Zunic, *Pittsburgh Federation of Teachers' 50ᵗʰ Anniversary Book*, 1985.

[120]Meyer A. Sanders, "Labor," *Allegheny County: A Sesqui-Ccentennial Review*, 143-144.

[121]Bernstein, *Turbulent Years*, 699.

[122]Robert H. Zeiger, *The CIO, 1935-1955*, 93.

[123]Melvyn Dubofsky and Warren Van Tine, *John L. Lewis: A Biography* (New York: Quadrangle/The New York Times, 1977), 330-332.

[124]Dubofsky and Van Tine, *John L. Lewis*, 332.

[125]Levenstein, *Communism, Anticommunism and the CIO*, 84-85.

[126]Klehr, *The Heyday of American Communism*, 386-396.

[127]John A. Garrity, Ed., *Dictionary of American Bbiography*, Supplement Six, 1956-1960, (New York: Charles Scribner's Sons, 1980), 428-433.

[128]Forrest C. Pogue, *George C. Marshall: Education of a General (1880-1939)*, (New York: Viking Press, 1963) 348-349.

[129]Dubofsky and Van Tine, *John L. Lewis*, 340-341. Dubofsky and Van Tine raise doubts about the accuracy of Lewis's approach to Roosevelt despite its recounting by both Pressman and Frances Perkins.

[130]Bernstein, *Turbulent Years*, 714-715.

[131]Bernstein, *Turbulent Years*, 719: Dubofsky and Van Tine, *John L. Lewis*, 357-358. Pat Fagan, *Interview* by Alice Hoffman, Penn State Archives, (September 24, 1968).

[132]Dubofsky and Van Tine, *John L. Lewis*, 360-361.

[133]Melvyn Dubofsky, "Labor's Odd Couple: Philip Murray and John L. Lewis," in *Forging a Union of Steel: Philip Murray, SWOC and the United Steelworkers*, eds. Paul F. Clark, Peter Gottlieb, and Donald Kennedy (Cornell: ILR Press, 1987), 40.

[134]Dubofsky, *John L. Lewis*, 365-370.

[135]Dubofsky, "Labor's Odd Couple," 30-44.

Chapter Eleven

Victory and Division

The enormous volume and diversity of the Pittsburgh region's production, result of the genius and effort of its peoples, played a major role in the victory of the allied armies in World War II. The working-class of southwestern Pennsylvania donned uniforms in massive numbers. Hardened by depression and struggle, older workers, females, and minorities toiled long hours in factories and mines to send forth a seemingly endless supply of the implements of war. The region's women contributed heroically, maintaining families and gardens, entering the mills and workshops in record numbers as welders, machinists, and other trades formerly closed to them, replacing men fighting on Pacific beaches and in the ruined cities of Europe. Organized industrial labor under the leadership of Pittsburgh's Phil Murray consolidated its institutional power and extended its presence in American life. Inside the house of labor, however, serious divisions arose. John L. Lewis led his coal miners from their position as labor's shock troops, the spearhead of its resurgence, to the margins of the broader labor movement. Of even greater consequence, the issue of Communism and its place in American unionism came to a head in post-war Pittsburgh. A political civil war between right and left factions inside the region's third largest industrial union shaped the character of the labor movement for decades, providing unions a measure of acceptance, while narrowing labor's aspirations and constricting its place in society.

Mobilization or Neutrality

he Electric Valley stretched along the Turtle Creek from Trafford, through Wilmerding, Turtle Creek and East Pittsburgh to its juncture with the Monongahela Valley at the upriver edge of Braddock's Edgar Thomson plant. Centered in East Pittsburgh on the lower reaches of the creek, nearly contiguous with the Braddock steel mill, the massive Westinghouse Electric complex at its peak in the 1940s employed more than 30,000 workers. Immediately upstream from the electrical assembly and machine shops of the Electric was the Westinghouse Airbrake, a separate corporate entity from the Electric, which together with its sister Union Switch and Signal operation employed approximately 10,000 at wartime production levels.

While the founders of the United Electrical Workers (UE) were radicals and activists of various political tendencies, the Communist Party faction came to dominate the national union and was powerful in UE 601 at the Electric, especially among those older skilled workers who emerged out of the intense union struggles of 1914 and 1916 to become the leaders and organizers of the local in the 1930s. The union pioneers of the Turtle Creek Valley in the 1930s tended to be activists in the highly skilled non-production areas like the main tool room and the generator division. Key union leaders like Logan Burkhart, who had spent time in jail for resistance to World War I and openly professed Communist beliefs, Porter Mechling and Mike Fitzpatrick were shaped by those pre-World War I struggles and the repression that followed. The tradition of radical women unionists, embodied by Bridget Kenny in 1914 and Anna Bell in 1916, was carried on in the 1930s by union activists Rose Meer, Rose Shylock, and Margaret Darin. Margaret "Peg" Darin and later her younger sister Evelyn became important UE leaders. In 1934, Peg attended the famous Bryn Mawr Summer School for Women Workers where she experienced a world of culture and intellectual curiosity that propelled her into a leading role in the organization of the Westinghouse plants.[1]

An important factor in the divisions that ultimately split the electrical workers into warring camps was the contrasting attitudes of various activists toward religion, especially Catholicism. Many of the most effective left-wing leaders of the UE were former Catholics who for various personal and/or ideological reasons harbored bitter feelings toward the church. On the national level, this was true of the brilliant young secretary-treasurer of the union, Julius Emspak, who at the age of nine witnessed his fiercely anti-clerical mother demand that a cross be removed from his father's casket before being lowered into the ground. Emspak began to work at GE's main plant in Schenectady, New York at fourteen, but returned to school after finishing a tool and die apprenticeship. Using a GE loan, he graduated from Union College and did a year's graduate work at Brown. He returned, however, into the plant as a worker and was quickly chosen as an officer in the fledgling union. He was only 33 years old when elected secretary-treasurer of UE at its founding convention.[2]

On the other hand, half or more of the Westinghouse workers were practicing Catholics. On the national level, this was true of its president, James Carey, who himself was only 26 when elected president of the UE at that same founding convention. Fourth of eleven children, he was brought up in a Catholic home and looked for inspiration to the labor encyclicals of Popes Leo XIII and Pius XI that stressed the importance of Catholic-led unions and the cooperation of labor and management for the common good. Typical of the Catholic union leadership in the Turtle Creek Valley was Phil Conahan, his father, like Phil Murray, a devout Catholic and union coal miner. He became a leader of the anti-Communist faction whose political base was the younger, less-skilled, production machinists and assemblers in the plant. A religious man, he was active in the Ancient Order of Hibernians whose members contributed many anti-Communist activists to the struggle. In 1940, Catholic social unionism and Communist social revolutionary ideals began a nearly two decade long political struggle that bitterly divided the Turtle Creek Valley's families and communities as well as the electrical workers union.[3]

On March 21 and 22, 1936, with the full support of Lewis's CIO, an electrical worker organizing convention was held during a blizzard in Buffalo, New York. Fifty delegates representing two distinct groups – locals in the radio and appliance industries on one hand and the large electrical manufacturing industrial plants on the other – convened and founded a united organization. Representing each of the two wings, Carey and Emspak set up the headquarters of the new union in New York City. They claimed 15,000 members in an industry of 300,000. On October 11, 1936, UE Local 601 was formed and adopted its constitution. In the summer of 1937, however, James

Matles led fourteen machine locals with 15,000 members into the organization. A disciplined and effective organizer, James Matles was a leader of the Communist-controlled Steel and Metal Workers Industrial Union. When the Communists abandoned their dual union strategy, he took his following into the International Association of Machinists for a short time; then, as the CIO emerged, he led them out of the Machinists into the UE. Of Jewish parentage, Matles emigrated from Romania and became a skilled machinist, tough negotiator, and union militant in the New York area who came to the attention of William Z. Foster, the leader of the industrial wing of the Communist Party. At the September 1937 convention of the fledgling organization, Matles joined Carey and Emspak at the head of the UE as director of organization.[4]

Tension within the UE began to manifest itself almost immediately in response to the international political situation. Carey initially was drawn into supporting various Communist front organizations, but in 1938 his position was complicated by his surprise selection by John L. Lewis as the secretary-treasurer of the CIO. During 1938 and most of 1939, the UE followed the strongly anti-fascist line of the Communist Party, but as the UE gathered in September 1939 for its convention, confusion reigned over the meaning of the Hitler-Stalin pact signed a couple weeks earlier. Shortly after the convention, however, the new political direction was indicated when the *UE News* came out strongly for neutrality. Taking this position, they found themselves allied with Lewis and Green but moving away from Murray and Carey who both supported the war preparedness policies of FDR. Carey publicly voiced his objections to UE foreign policy and Communist influence in the union for the first time in Pittsburgh in early 1941. In February, the right-wing UE Local 615 at the Allis Chalmers plant in Pittsburgh tried to pass an amendment barring Communists, Nazis, and Fascists from leadership positions in the union. In opposition to the majority of the union's executive board, Carey supported their right to pass such restrictions.[5]

Meanwhile Westinghouse Electric organized company-controlled workers' councils and steadily raised wages in the late 1930s to attract workers and forestall union organization. While the corporation refused to sign a contract, it did negotiate grievances with the UE on the shop floor level, and by 1939 the union could claim the support of a clear majority of workers inside the Electric plant. Westinghouse resisted formally recognizing the union, however, until 1940 when in the *Heinz* case the U.S. Supreme Court ruled that the NLRA required companies to sign written contracts and not simply consult with unions in their plants. Heinz and many other local companies signed their first union contracts at this time. The Electric, Airbrake, and Switch signed first contracts with the UE. The membership of the UE grew more than any other union in this period, adding 116,123 new members between August 1940 and August 1941.[6]

While the UE's position on foreign policy was heavily influenced and at times determined by the Communist Party, there was little proselytizing on the shop floor, and the union's shop floor behavior was generally democratic and effective. Furthermore, a high level of local and district autonomy derived from the fact that the union was organized out of distinct industrial building blocks and held annual local, district, and national elections. Interest in building a strong rank-and-file oriented, class-conscious, militant organization to defend workers' interests was shared by most union members. Intense political debate, fierce election struggles and effective shop floor organization, especially through an extensive and vigorous steward system, made the union powerful. These characteristics distinguished the UE sharply from the USWA, whose organizational form came from the highly centralized mineworkers and whose largest employer was organized from above. Until SWOC became the USWA in 1942, Phil Murray appointed all regional and district directors, and staff men were paid and dependent on the international union. Inside UE, as the anti-Communist struggle deepened over national and international politics, the commitment of both right and left factions to active shop floor struggle against the company remained a legacy of the union's founding rank-and-file organizational principals.[7]

Meanwhile, in early 1941, the energetic anti-Communist labor priest, Charles Owen Rice, entered the fray in East Pittsburgh supporting an anti-Communist insurgent group against the local's leadership. He was the organizer and chaplain of the Association of Catholic Trade Unionists (ACTU) chapter in Pittsburgh. His Catholic Radical Alliance had dissolved into the national group, so Rice dominated the local chapter and was a force on the national Catholic labor scene. He gained stature from Pittsburgh's importance for labor, as well as a close relationship with Phil Murray whom he deeply admired. Days after the Nazi attack on Soviet forces, he wrote in the *Pittsburgh Catholic*:

> Members of the Communist Party in America for the past two years have been violently anti-war. In the American trade union movement they have hampered the defense effort and have been a big factor in the wildcat defense strikes that have slowed down our re-armament effort. They have shown themselves to be utterly disloyal to the United States and loyal only to Communism and Soviet Russia.
>
> Germany is now fighting Russia. We may expect the Communists to execute another brazen about-face. They will be super-patriots. They will become avid partisans of the aid-Britain and speed re-armament movement. They will set out to fool the loyal workers of the nation into thinking that they have democracy's best interests at heart.[8]

Rice's attack picked up momentum as the Nazi's surprise invasion of the Soviet Union on June 21, 1941 had thrown the Communist members of the union's leadership into the uncomfortable position of moving from denouncing Roosevelt as a war mongerer to calling for the opening of a western front to assist the Soviets in their resistance to the Nazi onslaught. Carey denounced his opponents in the UE in his president's column in the union's newspaper, noting that "the 'imperialist blood bath' becomes 'a peoples war for freedom'" and asserting that "political acrobats in pink tights posing as labor leaders are a disgrace to the union and insult the intelligence of the membership." The prime target of Rice's attack in East Pittsburgh was Charles Newell, the business agent of UE Local 601, who had been assigned to the local by the international union. In elections held shortly after the Japanese attack on Pearl Harbor, the right-wing slate took control of the local and expelled Newell as business agent. On the national level, on the other hand, James Carey was narrowly defeated as president of the UE by Albert Fitzgerald, the candidate of the left-wing forces. Matles and Emspak remained the real powers and continued to run the union. Carey retained his position, however, as secretary-treasurer of the CIO.[9]

The other major opponent of war mobilization, of course, was John L. Lewis. The German attack on Russia made little impact on his anti-war stand, however. Instead, it pushed him into a bizarre alliance with right-wing Republican isolationists and separated him from a labor movement and a society that was moving toward accepting the inevitability of war. Lewis genuinely abhorred war and abhorred Roosevelt even more. He believed that the United States should complete the CIO revolution and organize the American economy on a new basis where a powerful labor movement would renew and strengthen the nation from below. In 1937 he had asserted: "If we can free them (the workers) from industrial servitude, we can, in the fullest sense, free them from the political shackles which in the past have restrained and limited their strength. There is no reactionary force which can stand against the untrammeled and crystallized voice of two-thirds of our population represented by labor..." In a 1940 attack on the president, he stated: "War kills off the vigorous males who, if permitted to live, might question the financial exploitation of the race."[10]

From the time of his resignation as CIO president until the Nazi attack on the Soviet Union, Lewis tried to stay out of CIO affairs and let Murray run the organization. This was difficult because Murray's Washington office was still in the Washington D.C. headquarters of the UMWA where he remained a vice-president of the mineworkers. Union leaders after meeting with Murray would inevitably go to Lewis's office to consult with the man most of them still perceived as the personification of the CIO, as well as the man who signed Murray's paycheck. Left wing labor leaders, in particular, supporting Lewis's anti-war stance, remained firmly in his camp and lauded his resistance to Roosevelt's war mobilization efforts. All this changed abruptly when the Communists switched their political line and their allegiances when Hitler launched his attack on Russia. The left wing which had previously lionized the great John L. now launched a vicious attack on his anti-war position, calling him an opportunist and even a fascist sympathizer. In a climactic meeting with Murray on October 18, 1941, Lewis determined that Murray was turning his back on him as well. Murray was very weak, just recovering from a heart attack. Lewis, who had also suffered a serious heart attack six months prior, was loath to push Murray too hard, but determined that Murray was either "a fool or a liar or both." He told Murray: "Well from now on, Philip, you go your way and I'll go mine."[11]

Pittsburgh at War

Scattered all around the neighborhoods of Pittsburgh and the surrounding mill towns and coal patch communities are hundreds of World War II memorials to those who served and to those who died in the war. Official figures show some of the highest military service rates in the nation, despite the exemption of some skilled occupations as critical for the war effort. One out of every seven persons in Allegheny County (including men, women, and children) served in the military during the war – 197,411 from the county with 95,694 from the city itself. The two top draft boards in terms of numbers of recruits in the state were Carnegie and Brentwood and the highest ratio of servicemen to citizens came out of the North Side and the South Side. The North Side sent an incredible rate of one service man or woman for every 5.5 persons. Extraordinary citizen mobilization complemented the military one. Price controls, rent controls, and credit controls were imposed. Gasoline and rubber use was curtailed, prompting a swelling of trolley utilization. Cars were encouraged to pick up hitchhikers. In 1943 one thousand Allegheny County high school students signed up for farm work during the summer to assist the war effort.[12]

It is impossible to do justice to the military experience of the hundreds of thousands of southwestern Pennsylvania soldiers, so a few stories will have to represent them. James W. Knox of Emsworth, subsequently Allegheny County controller and Democratic county commissioner, was sitting in Dr. Benjamin Williams' political science class at the University of Pittsburgh on the morning after Pearl Harbor. As can be imagined, deep anxiety and intense feeling gripped the young students facing a future that had suddenly changed irrevocably. Professor Williams told them: "Well, the cards are on the table. The winner takes all, leaving the vanquished with nothing but his eyes to weep with. But we will win because we will out-produce them." Knox, who grew up just downriver from the massive Dravo shipyard on Neville Island, whose production of LSTs (Landing Ship-Tanks) and other war vessels fulfilled the prophecy of his Pitt professor, went on to serve on and command LSTs in the Mediterranean, Atlantic, and Pacific. Knox commanded LST 491 at Utah and Omaha beaches during the Normandy landing. On the way in, they carried tanks, trucks and troops; then, on return trips to England, they transformed the ship into a field hospital with seven operating rooms, six doctors and forty-five nurses. Fourteen thousand wounded were transported in this way from the bloody beaches at Normandy to the hospitals of England. Knox later remembered: "We were too busy to be scared."[13]

The first soldier from Allegheny County to win the Congressional Medal of Honor was Mitchell Paige from West Mifflin. He single-handedly held off a Japanese attack at Guadalcanal on October 26, 1942. A platoon sergeant in command of a machine gun section, after all his men were killed or wounded, he continued firing from three machine gun emplacements and then took the last 150 pound machine gun and two ammunition belts and charged the remaining Japanese. "Every time I fired, the kickback knocked me down." His main trophy was a Japanese colonel's sword scarred by his machine gun bullets. After 26 months in the service, more than a thousand citizens assembled to cheer him on his arrival in McKeesport by train. Making a beeline for his wife, Stella, he said: "All I want to do at home is relax." A posthumous Congressional Medal winner was Arthur Mathies of Finleyville, who refused to bail out of a badly damaged Flying Fortress that he was attempting to land in England after a bombing mission and thereby abandon his badly wounded pilot and co-pilot. In total, ten men from Southwest Pennsylvania won the Congressional Medal of Honor in the war.[14]

The most famous Pittsburgh World War II warrior was Charles E. "Commando" Kelly, the first Congressional Medal of Honor winner in the Italian campaign, and, with Audey Murphy, the most decorated American soldier in the war. During the Depression, at age 16, Kelly quit Latimer school on the North Side to work in a bottling plant to help his widowed mother support the family. During the Anzio campaign, he was credited with killing 40 German soldiers and holding the town of Altavilla single-handedly. He went on to be awarded two Silver Stars and two Bronze Stars. Never impressed with his medals, he remarked: "These medals will just be a lot of brass after the war and I'll just be another ex-soldier." His life was dogged by tragedy and he died poor and in obscurity on the North Side. A legendary family from Pittsburgh was the "Fighting Grossmans," which included eight brothers from the Hill District, six in the army and two in the navy, who came to symbolize sacrifice and patriotism during World War II. After the eighth brother enlisted, draft board workers wrote President Roosevelt: "We can say that no more loyal or enthusiastic American youngsters can be found anywhere." The President responded by sending a letter of appreciation to Samuel and Della Grossman, parents of the boys. [15]

One of the most extraordinary Pittsburgh war stories was lived by the black reporter for the *Pittsburgh Courier,* Frank Bolden. Bolden graduated from Pitt in 1934; but, when he tried to get into medical school, he was told "we'd like to admit you if you were white." He tried to get a job teaching in the Pittsburgh schools, but there were no black teachers. He then went to work for the *Pittsburgh Courier,* which was at the peak of its power with 14 editions weekly (including ones for the Caribbean, England, and Africa), a circulation of 400,000 and 350 employees. His first stories were about Wylie Avenue, which "begins at a church and ends in a jail." He wrote about the lively cultural and sports life of the Hill and was encouraged by editor Robert Vann to write and agitate about social issues confronting the black community: fair housing, employment discrimination, the anti-lynching struggle, and the integration of the armed forces. He was famous for such pronouncements as: "No man can make you feel inferior without your consent;" and "Make the stumbling blocks into stepping stones and keep moving."[16]

One of the first two African-Americans accredited as a journalist by the Armed Forces, Bolden was assigned to the 93rd Infantry and accompanied the initial all-engineer convoy, whose truck drivers were black Americans, over the tortuous Burma Road to establish a supply line to assist the Chinese in their resistance to the Japanese invasion of their country. He interviewed Winston Churchill and Joseph Stalin, Chiang Kai-shek, Mahatma Gandhi and many other world leaders of the period. He penned an eloquent tribute to his fellow soldier: "This is G.I. Joe, the rugged dough-boy, your son, your husband, your sweetheart, my buddy – the greatest piece of fighting machinery the world has ever known. Through the torrid heat of summer and zero cold of winter, I have seen him fight the hardships of malaria and dysentery, of painful heat rash and frostbite, and the eternal monotony of loneliness and the longing for home – all for fifty dollars a month, and room and board, so we might remain free."[17]

The policy of restricting black soldiers to segregated units was a bitter pill for African-Americans who wanted to serve their country, but it also provided a showcase for units that won glory and recognition for the skill and devotion of their service. None were more famous in this regard than the famous Tuskegee Airmen, whose ranks included 56 men from the Pittsburgh region (including 8 from the small black community in Sewickley), 25 of whom were graduates of the University of Pittsburgh. Colonel Lee Archer, with 160 career missions and 5 confirmed "kills," was an ace of the Tuskegee fighter units, called the "red tails," because of the unit's distinctive tail decoration, that accompanied Allied bombing raids over North Africa, Italy, Germany, and Romania. In the landings at Anzio in Italy, the red tails flying close cover for Allied bombing missions shot down 17 German fighters. Three black Pittsburgh airmen were killed in combat: Elmer Taylor of the Hill, James Wright of Beltzhoover, and Carl Woods from Lawrenceville. In a principled challenge to segregationist practices in the military, a large contingent of the Tuskegee airmen were arrested for defying orders and insisting on their right to enter an officers' club on an airbase in Indiana. Following the war, many of the Tuskegee pilots tried to get jobs in commercial aviation, but none were successful.[18]

Jean Monnet, the architect of modern post-World War II Europe, labeled the United States the "Arsenal of Democracy" and Pittsburgh was the heart of the matter. Hitler's Germany built its armies on an industrial culture that perfected the machinery and mechanics of war. The Empire of Japan also built a formidable war machine whose air and navy struck a deadly blow against America's Pacific fleet. The great industrial region that stretched from Youngstown to Johnstown provided a key component in the enormous human effort that was expended to defeat the armies, navies and air forces of the Axis powers. The Pittsburgh region's achievement was all the more astounding given the level of military service among the blue collar production-based communities. Pittsburgh served as the forge of American industry. Steel in all types and shapes – castings, forgings, alloyed armor plate, structural beams, shell casings – poured out of its shops and mills. Machines, engines, drive shafts, generators, gears and motors in thousands of variations and in untold numbers were carried on freight cars and steel rails, themselves fashioned in its workshops, to the shipyards and ports that carried warfare to Europe, North Africa and East Asia, as well on to the waters of the Atlantic, Pacific and Mediterranean. Landing craft and PT boats were mass produced in her barge construction yards to transport the Allied armies to the beaches of Normandy, Sicily, Tarawa and

Iwo Jima. Pittsburgh's rail tonnage was measured in hundreds of millions of tons exceeding New York's and Chicago's; river tonnage exceeded that of the Suez and the Panama Canals.[19]

The steel industry was, of course, at the heart of America's war production. The volume of Pittsburgh's steel production more than doubled from 1939 to 1942. The United States in its peak war year produced more than Germany could in three and Japan in nine years. Coal production increased by 168%. Government investment poured into the coffers of local corporations to rapidly expand war production. U.S. Steel inaugurated a $700,000,000 expansion program, nearly two-thirds of which was underwritten by the taxpayer. Alcoa and Westinghouse also saw their private corporate investments buttressed by public money at a nearly two-to-one ratio. Conversion of industries to war production had to be achieved while new facilities were being simultaneously added. The expansion and conversion of plants required large numbers of construction as well as production workers. The AFL construction unions had to expand training and membership to respond to the demand for skilled manpower. The enormous wartime increases of production in steel were added to a level of rolled steel production that by 1940, stimulated by European war orders, already exceeded that of the 1929 pre-Depression levels.[20]

U.S. Steel initially resisted the construction of vast additional facilities, especially if built by the government. They feared President Roosevelt's inclination toward government regulation and planning for large-scale industry, a direction that was strongly supported by the steelworkers' Phil Murray as a way to permanently and structurally insert labor at the table inside the American industrial system. As Irving S. Olds, successor to Myron Taylor as chairman of U.S. Steel, expressed it in 1940: "In this country, we cannot disassociate our system of free enterprise from democracy, because it is the very heart and soul thereof." Ultimately, government largesse proved too difficult to resist, however; and the corporation embarked on major expansion, especially in the Pittsburgh region. Government investment, however, proved to be a two-edged sword. Most of U.S. Steel's increased war production came from Pittsburgh which moved back ahead of the Chicago region during World War II and again became the world's largest steel center. The Pittsburgh region produced 23% of the nation's steel and Chicago, just under 20%. However, U.S. Steel's percentage of total U.S. production slid from nearly 46% in World War I to under 32% at the end of the Second World War. While the war brought huge government investments into the industry and ended the Depression, the emphasis on heavy, alloyed, plate products reinforced product lines that would make Pittsburgh poorly placed to adapt to post-war consumer-driven economic expansion that vastly increased the consumption of flat-rolled sheet for automobiles and appliances, as well as bar and beam materials for road and building construction. The wartime destruction of much of European and Japanese steel capacity allowed the corporation to put off for a full generation a rethinking and reorganization of its product line and production facilities.[21]

The largest wartime steel plant expansion in the nation was made at Homestead. There, 11 open-hearth furnaces, a slab mill, 160-inch plate mill, a forge, and machine shops were added. Employment swelled from 12,000 to 15,000 and workers' hours increased. To accommodate the enormous increase in the mill's size, 120 acres of land were cleared along the river using governmental eminent domain powers, completely obliterating the town's teeming ethnic wards downstream from the mill. More than eight thousand inhabitants of the lower wards, forty percent of the town's population, were displaced. In a short time, 1,225 homes, 12 churches, 5 schools, 2 convents, 28 saloons and numerous shops and clubs (the Lithuanian Club, Turner Hall, Sokol Hall, Rusyn Hall and others) were torn down. The wards below the tracks were largely Catholic with substantial numbers of blacks. Many were forced to move to public housing projects that initially excluded blacks. Most of Homestead's whorehouses were forced to close or move. Evelyn Marshall, Homestead's most famous madam, quickly relocated and upgraded her facilities in anticipation of the war boom. The "Hill" part of town above the tracks initially housed the skilled workers and management who were largely Protestant, but the displaced "Ward" people gradually moved up the hill into the upper town.[22]

As a youngster, Ed Sninsky watched President Roosevelt, who was to his Lower Homestead neighborhood "a combination of Caesar Augustus and a Greek god," pass through Homestead during his 1940 presidential campaign. "The crowd was immense and filled with exultant joy." Sninsky, whose family was one of the last to move out of the lower ward in January 1942, watched the demolition of the old neighborhood from the High-Level Bridge with his pre-teen friends. He described the ritual in Homestead which occurred in so many American towns when the draftees were ordered to present themselves for service:

> The draftee with his family would walk to the railroad station on Amity Street followed by many friends, neighbors and all of us kids. I was standing up front when the draftee and family approached somebody at the train station holding a clipboard and a pencil and, as he checked the name of the draftee, there occurred probably the most dramatic single moment which defines, other than the death telegram, the sorrowful poignancy of war. The draft supervisor with clipboard in his left hand, would gently nudge the draftee to one side and simultaneously with the pencil, in his right hand, nudge the parents off to the opposite side thus creating a separation, which for the earliest draftees would last five years, and, unfortunately for some, forever.[23]

New blast furnaces were built at Edgar Thomson in Braddock to provide iron for the Homestead open hearths. Electric furnaces and a heat-treatment plant were constructed at the Duquesne mill. A naval ordnance subsidiary plant directly under Homestead management was opened in Charleston, West Virginia. By mid-1942, the corporation's plate production reached 3.6 million tons. The brand new Irvin Works hot strip plant built in 1939 to produce light-gauge flat-rolled metal for cars and appliances was converted to produce plate up to an inch thick and 72 inches wide. The Pittsburgh District served as the nation's major producer of bombs, high-caliber shells and heavy ordnance, with the district producing 1.7 million bombs and 9.7 million shells ranging from 20 millimeters to 8 inches. At U.S. Steel's Christy Plant in McKeesport where tube steel from the National Tube Works was shaped into shells and packed with explosives, over 1,000 women were employed operating machines, driving trucks and tractors, inspecting and packing bombs and shells:[24]

> The young women work seriously, eagerly, along with the men, in all parts of the bomb and shell plants.... "I have never seen a girl shrink at any job," commented Mrs. Kennedy (assistant manager of Industrial Relations). "They plunge into grease up to their elbows, slap it on by the handfuls, get themselves splashed with oil, and then talk excitedly about how much they like their work."[25]

At the war's peak, employment at U.S. Steel nationwide attained 340,000 workers. At the same time, J&L's total employment, concentrated in Western Pennsylvania, reached nearly 40,000. J&L produced enormous quantities of shell forgings, bomb casings, fragmentation components, oil and chemical drums, wire rope, as well as ship parts, especially its line of Junior beams and channels. Its fabrication facilities made LST sections that were assembled in coastal shipyards. Its most distinctive contribution was the 5x7x5 foot "steel box," that could be connected and used to build movable piers, causeways, and "rhino ferries" – where 30 were linked together and driven onto beaches by outboard motors. While J&L's harsh labor relations improved with its acceptance of the union, the company also dropped its paternalistic attitude toward a community it no longer controlled. J&L's wartime president and chairman, H. Edgar Lewis, cautioned the community in 1940: "The days when J&L would build swimming pools, homes and public buildings and present them – complete and wrapped in an attractive package – to the people of Aliquippa are over."[26]

Numerous other local steel and fabrication companies made specific contributions. Allegheny Ludlum's alloyed steel was widely employed in diverse and critical applications. Crucible Steel's specialty alloys went into cutting tools, aircraft parts, machine-gun and small arms parts. Pittsburgh-Des Moines supplied oil, water and gas tanks, pontoon units and many other products. Pittsburgh Steel produced large quantities of explosives. In Butler, north of Pittsburgh, the American Bantam Car Company had been founded by the English Austin Car Company to build the small fuel efficient car that was their specialty. The Depression disrupted production, but in 1938 production was resumed under the name of the American Bantam Car Company. In 1940, the U.S. Army sent out bid designs for a go-anywhere reconnaissance vehicle to 135 companies. Bantam was the smallest of the three companies that submitted designs, but its design became the prototype for the Jeep, later mass-produced by Willys and Ford.[27]

U.S. Steel converted a part of its large Ambridge bridge construction facility to the production of LSTs that complemented the large Neville Island facility of the Dravo Corporation. Dravo constructed football field sized, 328 foot long - 50 foot wide LSTs as well as destroyer escorts, minesweepers and sub-chasers in an assembly line operation. Dravo had previously developed welded barge construction, replacing the earlier method of hot riveting plates together. By 1935 a method of building ship preassembly segments inside large shops and then welding them together in a final assembly building before moving to a launching berth guaranteed a 24-hour operation, rain or shine, under controlled conditions to ensure high quality standards. The first LST, with its revolutionary design and front bay opening, the largest combat ship ever constructed on the inland waters of the United States, was launched on September 7, 1942. During the war, Dravo launched an LST every 6.1 days; and in the two-month push prior to D-Day, the yards produced a ship every 3.5 days. The Neville Island yards expanded from peacetime employment of less than 1,500 to a peak of 16,000 workers (16% female) in 1944. The sign at the entry to the Neville Island yards proclaimed "We Can. We Will. We Must."[28]

Given the importance of aluminum in the construction of airplanes and the prodigious expansion of American air power during the war, the demands on aluminum production were enormous. From an average production level of 185,000,000 pounds in the previous decade, wartime expansion increased production tenfold by 1944 to 2.1 billion pounds annually. In 1943 Alcoa reported that it employed a large number of women, including 23 grandmothers, at its New Kensington plant. This expansion was largely financed through the government and helped Pittsburgh's Alcoa expand its facilities and extend its reach to control both sources of bauxite ore and purchase the enormous quantity of electricity needed to create aluminum. Another core Pittsburgh company, H. J. Heinz, made contributions to war production with enormous amounts of processed food rations for soldiers and civilians in the U.S., Britain and Russia, but most famously included the construction of plywood glider planes by female workers in its Pittsburgh plant. These gliders, able to elude enemy radar, were used to send spies and reconnaissance probes deep into enemy-occupied territory.

Reconnaissance missions employing gliders proved important as part of the Normandy invasion of France. Another established Pittsburgh firm, Blaw-Knox, designed mills and produced a bewildering variety of parts and products and became known as the "department store of fabricated steel products." Its most significant contribution, however, came in its design work for plants producing synthetic rubber. The Japanese conquest of Southeast Asia cut off the supply of natural rubber and a substitute had to be developed quickly.[29]

The 40,000 employees of the Westinghouse Electric Corporation in 1941, about a third of whom were located in the East Pittsburgh plant, by the end of the war had increased to 115,000 employees including many employed in dozens of large new facilities. The mother plant in the Turtle Creek valley employed nearly thirty thousand workers at its peak wartime production. Westinghouse's electrical expertise was critical to developing and manufacturing complex electrical systems for warships and airplanes. Westinghouse also built steam propulsion equipment for hundreds of fighting and merchant ships. Motors and generators from the East Pittsburgh plant were a major component in supplying the power that drove the manufacturing production of America and its allies. The company helped develop and improve radar that could detect enemy planes over one hundred miles distant, developed the "walkie-talkie," a two-way portable radio system for ground combat communication, made gyroscope gun-mounts for tanks, precipitators used in the production of optical gun sights, as well as systems controls for oil and gas delivery systems. The Nuttall plant in Trafford built precision gears and during the war built over one thousand milling machines designed for war production.[30]

The shortage of factory workers promoted a "white collar rush to the factories," where the *Sun-Telegraph* reported on lawyers, preachers, barbers, and funeral directors working in the mills.[31] The problem that wartime mobilization caused those trying to organize war production is illustrated by an account contained in a multi-volume post-war report by Westinghouse to the government:

> Manpower shortage made it necessary that we take vocational school trainees and specialize them in gear hobbing. About 34 people (in September 1941)…received nearly eleven months training on the intricate job of cutting gears….Our plan was to use these men as key operators to help and assist in the training of the future personnel….We had just about reached our peak of production when the War Labor Board ruled that this highly essential class of work would be non-essential. We lost all of our boys who were draft age within the first year. Thirty-two of the thirty-four trainees went to the armed forces at a time when they were most needed.[32]

The movement of troops, supplies, and materials was an enormous logistical task that devolved primarily on the nation's rail system. It took 75 trains to move an army division – soldiers, support personnel, anti-aircraft guns, tanks, jeeps, trucks – and they moved as units from bases to ports. The rail infrastructure that moved 90% of the country's war traffic was stretched to the maximum. In 1939 railroads carried 26 billion ton-miles of traffic, and by 1942 the rails were carrying 64 billion ton-miles of traffic. No area in the country bore more of the load than Pittsburgh. The Pennsylvania Railroads Steel Freight Car Repair Shop in Pitcairn adjacent to the Westinghouse Airbrake plant ran night and day. The Airbrake and its sister plant in Swissvale, the Union Switch and Signal, the largest manufacturer of railroad controls in the world, expanded production to keep the railroad lines and rolling stock supplied. In addition, the Airbrake produced a great variety of shells, bomb parts, and munitions. The Switch manufactured a wide range of war materials, including automatic handguns, airplane propellers, and pioneering flight simulators to train pilots.[33]

The astonishing mobilization of an entire society including hundreds of smaller firms and shops in the Pittsburgh area was only possible through the entry of the female population into the workforce at record levels. The Pennsylvania Railroad added 4,500 female employees. The war opened 80 trolley operator jobs to women. During World War I, women had been permitted to work as operators but were refused membership in the union. In 1942 the union ruled that women employed as operators must be allowed to become members with the same rights as men. Hired during the war, Florence "Hattie" Bartosik was an operator for more than 45 years, leaving the South Hills Junction every morning at 4:01 a.m. Sixteen percent of Dravo's shipyard workers were women, and one of the iconic "Rosie the Riveter" war production images took a Westinghouse Electric worker as its model. Female workers at Westinghouse before the war were concentrated in lower paying assembly and coil winding jobs that required speed, attention to detail, concentration, and dexterity, all characteristics that female workers reputedly epitomized. During the war, women were moved into the heavier machinist jobs, running lathes, mills, drill presses, gear-cutters, grinders, punch-presses, and cranes. They remained largely excluded from skilled maintenance and tool room jobs, however. When the war ended, employment levels dropped dramatically and newly hired women were laid-off. In addition, many of the recently won union contracts secured seniority time for men who left the plants for military service, so returning service men bumped the women off their jobs.[34]

Acute demand for industrial workers triggered a wave of black migration from the south. Black workers, whose importance to both the union movement and the triumph of the Democratic Party in the industrial valleys of Western Pennsylvania had gained them a measure of respect, experienced a less hostile attitude from white workers than did the black migrants during World War I. The newcomers suffered with sub-par housing however; and like the women workers, many found themselves on the street after the war. Concentrated in the dirtiest and hottest jobs, the percentage of blacks reached 63% during the war at the Clairton Coke Works and 53% at Duquesne Smelting, but only 16% at the Homestead Works and 15% at Edgar Thomson in Braddock. Expansion of the mills worsened the already serious housing shortage, but large scale public housing projects started by Roosevelt during the depression were just coming on line as the war began. Seven public housing projects were constructed in Pittsburgh, including Aliquippa Terrace and Bedford Dwellings, and other projects were built in Duquesne, Clairton, Aliquippa, McKeesport, and North Braddock. Many of these started as all-white or integrated facilities, but after the war white families found it much easier to move out to the rapidly expanding suburbs. Blacks, however, were trapped by residential segregation patterns, and so the public housing projects gradually became black enclaves.[35]

In 1941, President Roosevelt established a Committee on Fair Employment Practices in response to A. Philip Randolph's threat to stage a march on Washington to protest job discrimination. In 1942 a group in Pittsburgh called the Housewives Cooperative Guild joined with the Urban League to demand that Bell Telephone open up operator and stenographer jobs to black women. In response to mounting complaints of discrimination around the nation, Roosevelt issued an executive order in 1943 establishing a Fair Employment Practices Committee that opened an office in Pittsburgh in 1945. At the Dravo shipyards where 1,700 blacks and 2,184 women were among the wartime employees, blacks protested their exclusive use as power brush operators exposed to thick dust and scale and the exclusion of black women from production work above the level of cleaner or laborer.[36]

Even in the mills where blacks were becoming significant factors numerically, they were often restricted by lines of progression to certain jobs or departments in the plant and excluded by foremen and sometimes their fellow white employees from access to the more skilled craneman or maintenance jobs. In production departments such as rolling mills, blast furnaces, open hearths and Bessemers, they were often restricted to the labor gang. Black workers held short wildcat strikes over being excluded from promotions at Clairton in 1943 and 1944, as well as at J&L's Aliquippa and Pittsburgh Works during the same period. Phil Murray insisted on integrated union gatherings, even in the South, and attempted to respond to the concerns of the black steelworkers by appointing a black SWOC organizer, Boyd Wilson, as his personal representative and non-voting member of the union's executive board. Wilson intervened in several plant disputes over promotion and in community disputes over access to housing. The union's Civil Rights Committee sponsored a conference on racial equality for the executive board and staff representatives of the union at Penn State in 1948, but Wilson's urgings for a union-wide anti-discrimination education campaign never materialized.[37]

Labor at War

Following the Nazi attack on Russia and especially once the Japanese attacked Pearl Harbor five-and-a-half months later, the leadership of organized labor was almost completely united behind the war effort. The lone exception was John L. Lewis. In September 1941, before the entry of the U.S. into the war, he ordered a strike against the captive mines of the seven major steel companies. Germany was triumphantly on the march and German U-boats were harassing American shipping. While 95% of the coal miners in the captive mines paid dues to the UMWA, Lewis wanted to secure the union shop before a declaration of war froze labor conditions. Despite intense pressure from FDR, Lewis refused to back down, telling the president: "If you would use the power of the state to restrain me as an agent of labor, then, sir, I submit, that you should use that same power to restrain my adversary who is an agent of capital. My adversary is a rich man named Morgan, who lives in New York." Roosevelt replied in a radio address: "…labor as a whole knows that a small minority is a menace to the true cause of labor itself, as well as for the nation as a whole…"[38]

After several postponements to allow negotiations, a vote of the National Defense Mediation Board went 9-2 against Lewis with only Murray and Thomas Kennedy voting for the union shop – the two AFL representatives on the board voted in the negative on the grounds that the imposition of the union shop by the government was undemocratic. On Saturday, November 15, two days before the opening of the CIO convention, Lewis ordered the miners out. The Roosevelt administration made threatening noises, but Lewis remained unfazed, responding: "If the soldiers come, the miners will remain peacefully in their homes, conscious of the fact that bayonets in coal mines will not produce coal." Roosevelt capitulated by establishing an arbitration board that everyone knew would rule for the union shop. Sixteen days later, the mineworkers got the union shop and returned to work. The date was December 7, 1941, and the nation hardly noticed the mineworker victory in the face of the stunning Japanese attack on Pearl Harbor.[39]

Lewis quickly proclaimed: "When the nation is attacked, every American must rally to its defense." However on January 17, 1942, Lewis dropped a bombshell on his two former mineworker officials, writing Phil Murray of the CIO and William Green of the AFL calling for the unification of the two federations in the name of national unity and the war effort. Opposition to the gambit was led by Murray, who justifiably felt undercut by Lewis and by the Communists who stood to see several left-wing led unions reverting to the AFL which held prior jurisdiction. While Mrs. Roosevelt termed the proposal "grand," the President saw it as an attempt to reassert Lewis's leadership and turn labor against him by undercutting his two closest allies, Murray and Hillman. Roosevelt's response was to establish a joint AFL and CIO consultation committee that did not include Lewis. The CIO's rejection of Lewis's unity proposal made a complete break with both Murray and the CIO inevitable. The hatred between Roosevelt and Lewis intensified and became almost obsessive on both sides.[40]

Lewis's anger led him to expand the organizing efforts of his catch-all District 50, headed by his daughter Kathryn. He launched an abortive attempt to unionize dairy farmers and ventured beyond mine construction projects to challenge the AFL building trades. He instructed UMWA Treasurer Tom Kennedy to write the CIO requesting that the UMWA's $30,000 monthly per-capita dues payment to the CIO be deducted from the CIO's debt to the mineworkers' union. Murray did not accept this arrangement and his refusal provided the basis for his expulsion from the mineworker organization he had served for over thirty years. On May 25, 1942, Lewis convened a three-day UMWA Policy Committee meeting in the basement of the union's Washington office that was chock-full of mementos and the trophies of John L.'s battles and triumphs. On the first day, Murray spoke to the hostile group. "I have loyally supported the president of the international union from the day I was a boy, and I should like to be privileged to do so as long as I live." On the second day, Lewis justified his unity proposal to the AFL, despite his earlier opposition to such a move, on the grounds that the two organizations were presently of equal strength and out of consideration for the demands of wartime unity. He then proceeded to present an itemized bill in excess of $7 million from the UMWA to the CIO for a decade of organizing costs. He angrily attacked Murray for refusing to begin paying down the CIO's debt by waiving the UMWA dues payments and for comparing Lewis's bolt-out-of-the-blue proposal to the Pearl Harbor surprise attack. Accompanied by the angry boos and curses of the committee, he accused Murray of calling him a Jap. Lewis said: "I am not a Jap, and I am as good an American as my former friend, Phil Murray." Murray, extremely distraught, responded that he had never sought the position of CIO president and had done his best in the job. On the third day of the grilling, as charges were being formally pressed against him, Murray asked to be excused to attend a CIO meeting. Lewis then raised the issue of Murray's acceptance of a paid position with the United Steelworkers Union a few days before, which Murray admitted. Lewis then dismissed the man who had served him so long and expelled Murray from the mineworkers union by executive order for "just and sufficient cause."[41]

David McDonald, who accompanied Murray to the showdown, testified that Lewis actually cocked his fist as Murray rose to deny Lewis's charges. "All I could think was, I hope we get out of here in one piece. These were our friends, people we had worked with through the bad years, people with whom we shared a past and – we thought – a future. They were about to eat us alive..." Pat Fagan reacted: "I was sick from what they did to Murray. It was a cruel thing; as cruel as you've ever heard of."[42] John Brophy, who knew both men intimately, wrote:

> Murray had been for many years the most important individual among Lewis's
> supporters. His great talent as a negotiator had been indispensable to Lewis. Both
> in dealings with the coal operators and in the early settlements of the CIO years,
> Murray often did the hard work of negotiation with Lewis coming in at the end to
> make a speech and affix his signature to the agreement. Further, Murray was

invaluable to Lewis in relations with people. He could soften the impact of Lewis's ultimatums and lead men to cooperate who might otherwise have been alienated by Lewis's driving. The two men were never friends in any real sense, and I know that Murray was often unhappy about his relation with Lewis, but swallowed his resentment in the interest of the union.[43]

In September 1942, at the UMWA convention, Lewis, who had just suffered the loss of his wife, gave a powerful, raging, angry performance ending: "...if you do not have enough pride and self-respect yourself for your own officers to sustain them in the positions they take as affecting the public questions in this country on matters affecting labor, then don't expect anyone else to have any confidence and do not expect me to carry out the rabbit policy, because, on my honor, there is no rabbit in me." The convention voted 2,867 to 5 to support John L. Lewis; thus, the mineworkers quit the Congress of Industrial Organizations that they had been so instrumental in creating. Lewis's wrath clearly was to be reckoned with. Years earlier, Lewis had offered Fagan to put District 5 into receivership and then appoint him director, so he would no longer have to run for election. Fagan recalled that he told Lewis: "I don't want to have anything to do with an organization that doesn't have autonomy and practice democracy and be responsible to the membership of the organization...I'd sooner go back to the mine and be a miner....(besides) You know someday you'll destroy me and you'll tell me I'm out. And I have no recourse." After the split with Murray, Lewis put the power and resources of the organization behind a rival candidate, and in 1943 Fagan was defeated as director of UMWA District 5.[44]

In early 1943, anthracite miners in eastern Pennsylvania went on an unsanctioned wildcat strike over rapidly rising prices for food and necessities while their wages had been frozen. Calling the strike unauthorized, Lewis, however, announced his determination to obtain a "wholesome wage increase" when coal contracts expired on April 30. When he entered into negotiations with operators, he demanded a $2 a day wage increase and, most importantly, "portal-to-portal pay." Miners were only paid for the time they spent at the face mining coal, while the one to two hour round trip from the entry of the mine to the face was uncompensated. On April 29, as President and Commander-in-Chief, Roosevelt threatened Lewis and ordered the mineworkers to stay on the job. On May 1, 500,000 coal miners laid down their tools for *their* president in defiance of *the* president. Lewis was widely denounced as a traitor and portrayed in the press as stabbing the soldier in the back. Schoolboys picketed his Alexandria home with signs reading "John L. Lewis – Hitler's helper." Roosevelt seized the mines, and American flags were flown over the mine entries. While labor officials, especially left-wingers like Harry Bridges, vilified Lewis, thousands of workers wrote Lewis expressing their support. When Roosevelt announced a major radio address, Lewis upstaged him by announcing minutes before the president's address a two-week truce and the miners' return to work. Attacks on Lewis only strengthened the miners' resolve. Since the government had seized the mines, Lewis was now negotiating with Secretary of the Interior Harold Ickes, whom he trusted, rather than the coal operators. Despite hard negotiating, however, no agreement was reached and Lewis again pulled the half-million miners out of the pits.[45]

Back-and-forth went the struggle with the miners' discipline giving Lewis great tactical flexibility. Up until this point, ample coal stockpiles meant war production had not been actually jeopardized. The coal operators who were increasingly uncomfortable with the government seizure of the mines began to crack. The Illinois coal operators approved an allowance for portal-to-portal travel and a package that actually raised wages by $3.00 a day. When the National War Labor

Board rejected that agreement as inflationary, the miners struck again on November 1 for the fourth general strike in a year. This time an agreement was reached that Lewis signed and miners returned to work. By 1945 Lewis had achieved portal-to-portal pay in both the bituminous and anthracite fields. Lewis won the most bitter and controversial battle of his career thanks to the unyielding discipline and devotion of the nation's coal miners.[46]

During the war, Phil Murray, in the role of the responsible patriotic labor statesman, presided over the expansion of the CIO. Though Murray assumed power reluctantly, his administrative and negotiating abilities, his long experience in the struggle to establish industrial unionism, and his determination to build and solidify the institutional framework of the labor movement made him the most important labor leader of the 1940s. If Lewis was labor's Old Testament prophet and military leader, Murray aspired to be its Christian ruler, slow to anger, but with a toughness disguised by a gentle demeanor. By 1944 Murray held a power and authority in the CIO greater than Lewis had ever known. Murray's humble bearing and genuine affection for ordinary workers raised him in the eyes of his loyalists. As the great journalist, Murray Kempton wrote of him: "It was Murray's special quality to touch the love and not the fears of men."[47]

Phil Murray supported Franklin Roosevelt out of patriotic attachment to the flag and the belief that the industrial union movement had a unique opportunity during wartime to restructure the American economy in a fundamental way so as to guarantee the long-range integration of organized labor into the very structure of the economic system. The need for wartime planning and the collective effort inherent in the total mobilization of society for war provided an opening for organized labor to gain a permanent voice in the country's industrial organization. In addition, the war presented itself as an opportunity to extend the democratic liberalism of the New Deal to a Europe plagued by depression and war. Ironically, in post-war Europe the Catholic corporatist vision of society dovetailed sufficiently with social democratic ideas to embrace tri-partite (labor-management-government) structures and in Germany even the co-determination of labor and management. These social partnership ideals have taken root in the European Union to a degree that Murray could only have dreamed of for his own country.[48]

An aggressive organizing drive in 1941 mobilized over 2.4 million workers in over four thousand strikes with more than two-thirds of them conducted under the banner of the CIO. During the war, worker unrest was fueled by inflation and lagging wages, while labor shortages gave workers relative impunity from punishment. With union leaders supporting production and stability, workers felt less need for the protection of the unions and increased their criticism of union leadership. Dues payments dropped, requiring embarrassing dues picket lines to enforce collection. While the USWA had gained exclusive bargaining rights, dues payments ran at about seventy percent and sometimes dues pickets had to exercise considerable pressure and even muscle to extract workers' dues. David McDonald, the union's secretary-treasurer, acknowledged: "About one-fifth of the workers were rabidly pro-union, about five percent were strongly anti-union and the remaining three-fourths really didn't give much of a damn one way or the other."[49]

Since both the CIO leadership and the Communists supported the no-strike pledge, the numerous wartime work stoppages, with the exception of coal, were local, short-lived, unsanctioned wildcats. This marked a sharp difference with the ideological strikes of World War I where a range of socialist and radical organizations and many rank-and-file workers were opposed to the war on principle. The establishment of the National War Labor Board shaped American industrial practice by setting industry-wide wage patterns and establishing arbitration as the prime conflict resolution mechanism and thereby serving as an instrument for the enforcement of the no-strike pledge. Confronted by worker restlessness and the example of John L. Lewis demanding higher wages and unafraid to strike during wartime, Murray and Hillman were able to obtain union security clauses and the dues check-off from the War Labor Board in 1942. Blocked in terms of wage increases by the Board, unions focused on expanding paid vacations and benefits. Maintenance of membership dues, available to any union respecting the no-strike pledge, dramatically increased the size and financial stability of the industrial unions. USWA membership almost doubled from 1941-1945, while membership in the UE tripled.[50]

The leftwing UE was especially energetic in support of the war effort. Incentive systems, overtime, speed-up, and labor-management production committees were all embraced. The incentive systems became a major area of conflict in the Westinghouse plants during the 1950s. In June 1944, the newspapers reported on a mass meeting in East Pittsburgh where thousands of Westinghouse Electric workers led by UE 601 president Tom Fitzpatrick took an unconditional pledge "that we will not strike or interrupt production....We pledge to the American boys and girls in the armed forces that we will not violate their faith in us. We pledge to our Commander-in-Chief, President Roosevelt, and to General Eisenhower, our full and unqualified support in this struggle for victory."[51]

The consequences of this reliance on governmental intervention and the loosening of the ties between union leadership and the rank-and-file were long term. Government policy increasingly became the crucial arena of political activity rather than the shop floor. The tri-partite model of labor-management-government participation took hold under the Allied occupation of Germany where the power of the traditional industrial ruling class was sharply curtailed. In the United States, on the other hand, the centralization of economic and political power in an emerging military-industrial alliance inexorably pushed labor to the sidelines. The government's planning and coordinating activities did not introduce a new social order, rather they helped cement corporate control over the publicly financed production apparatus created by war. The military-dominated production system most benefited corporations, including Westinghouse and U.S. Steel, with which the military had long cooperated.[52]

As the war effort began to appear victorious, the combined effects of price rises, housing shortages, unresolved wage inequalities and restrictions on premium pay stimulated worker restlessness. In 1944-45 more strikes took place and more workers stopped work than anytime since 1919, and more than half of the work stoppages took place in CIO union facilities. AFL unions which had historically been wary of governmental regulation were better able to respond to worker restlessness than unions in the CIO, which had allied themselves so closely to the Roosevelt administration's wage and production policies. Fearing the rising anti-labor sentiment among the electorate and Congress, the CIO stuck to its no-strike pledge and became more deeply enmeshed in the grievance arbitration mechanisms of the War Labor Board. These effectively shifted disputes from the immediacy of the shop floor to the arena of contractual interpretation where staff men, lawyers, and the values of orderly procedure were dominant. In such an arena, there was little consideration for the democratic rights of the shop floor militant or rebel leader.[53]

As the war ended, there was both elation and anxiety about how to return American society and the City of Pittsburgh to peacetime normalcy after such an enormous mobilization. With memories still vivid of the upheavals and repression that followed World War I, both labor and management looked ahead with concern. Workers in the plants faced inflation pressures and saw job reductions looming. For most of the soldiers and the girls they left behind, however, there was only elation and a sense of profound relief. Papers reported on the announcement of victory in Europe: "Girls began to fall upon any soldier caught in the open with his uniform." Jim Branagan from Mt. Washington was home on leave and he "could hardly walk across the Smithfield Bridge because of repeated amorous ambushes."[54]

Dave Lawrence and Richard King Mellon

David Lawrence spent the war years back home in Pittsburgh. While acquitted of corruption charges, the political wars had taken their toll. Democratic reverses, his bitter feud with former state Attorney General Charles Margiotti and the falling out with former mentor Joseph Guffey had exposed his vulnerability as Guffey was reelected to the U.S. Senate despite Lawrence's opposition. Named to the Democratic National Committee, Lawrence gave up his state party chairmanship and returned home to spend more time with his family than he had ever done before. On April 19, 1942, his two teenaged sons, both enrolled at Central Catholic High School, took their father's car for a joyride and were killed as back seat passengers when a teen friend lost control of the vehicle attempting to pass a car while descending a long hill on Route 19 north of Pittsburgh. The loss devastated Lawrence and his wife, Alyce. Lawrence threw himself into political work to dull the pain. At the Democratic convention in 1944, Lawrence abandoned Henry Wallace, whom he had helped obtain the party's vice-presidential nomination in 1940, and switched his support to Harry Truman, despite support for Wallace by Phil Murray, Sidney Hillman, and other labor delegates, especially those on the left. Truman met with Murray and Hillman on successive days before the 1944 Democratic Convention. They told Truman that they supported Wallace, could accept Truman, but were adamantly opposed to James Byrne, whom they considered anti-labor. In the 1944 election, Lawrence was instrumental in carrying Pennsylvania for Roosevelt and Truman.[55]

In 1941, Cornelius Scully, Lawrence's hand-picked candidate for Pittsburgh mayor, barely won re-election by 3,162 votes despite a Democratic registration edge of 81,000. In 1945, Lawrence was prevailed upon by party leaders to drop his preferred role of behind-the-scene manager and become a candidate for mayor. Against Lawrence's loyal organization and large party registration edge, the Republicans fielded a strong candidate, Robert Waddell. From 1922-1932, Waddell had been head football coach at Carnegie Tech in the glory days when Tech defeated Pitt before upwards of 50,000 fans four times and Notre Dame and Georgia Tech twice each. Lawrence in his campaign combined careful and meticulous organizational work in the usual church, school and union hall venues with a strong call for the rehabilitation of Pittsburgh's aging and crumbling infrastructure. His call for flood control, smoke control, a reconstructed highway system, and the redevelopment of the downtown Triangle, including a park at the Point, proved very attractive to business and civic leaders. In April 1945, in the midst of the mayoral campaign, Lawrence issued his call for the renewal of Pittsburgh in cooperation with the business leadership of the Allegheny Conference. It was significant that only one of the seven points in his electoral program reflected the New Deal agenda of aid for the poor and homeless. In the long run, this seemingly odd alliance condemned the Republican Party to irrelevance as the partnership subsumed the local Democratic Party to the corporate interest under what historian Roy Lubove described as a "reverse welfare state."[56]

When Lawrence launched his political program for downtown renewal, he was reflecting a growing consensus among professional planners, and the business and commercial interests that

Pittsburgh either had to renew or die. Corporate interests led by Richard King Mellon, driven by the depreciation of downtown real estate values and horrific environmental conditions resulting from 80 years of unregulated industrial production compounded by the pell-mell expansion of the war effort, demanded change. The key elements of what became known as the Pittsburgh Renaissance had been discussed at length for 25 years through the business-dominated Citizens Committee on City Planning that became the Pittsburgh Regional Planning Commission, that itself evolved into the technical and planning arm of the Allegheny Conference on Community Development. These proposals were crystallized in a 1939 report on Pittsburgh submitted by Robert Moses, national planning guru, which sat unimplemented because of the war. They included a park at the Point; three arterial highways defining the sides of the Golden Triangle, with two new bridges to replace those directly at the Point and one of those requiring a new tunnel under Duquesne Heights; plus flood control and smoke control projects. All these major projects demanded massive new public expenditures and expanded public powers. The large corporations that dominated Pittsburgh could no longer tolerate the conditions they had created and that depression and war had exacerbated. U.S. Steel, Westinghouse, and Alcoa were even making preliminary plans to leave the flood-prone, smoke-choked conglomeration at the Forks of the Ohio altogether.[57]

The vehicle for elite business involvement in urban redevelopment was the Allegheny Conference on Community Development, launched at a luncheon on May 24, 1943 in Henry Clay Frick's downtown hotel, the William Penn. The organization was descended from but was also clearly differentiated itself from earlier planning efforts by the personal involvement of key Pittsburgh business and university leaders. The person who brought them to the table was the undisputed leader of the third generation of the Mellon family interests, Richard King Mellon. R.K. and Democratic Mayor Dave Lawrence, each a clear ruler in his own sphere, created the alliance that harnessed public power and investment to private business ends. As Roy Lubove noted: "The irony of the environmental change process in 20ᵗʰ Century Pittsburgh was not that it hinged on constructive public intervention, but that use of public resources was so closely identified with the corporate welfare."[58]

After the deaths of Andrew W. and Richard B. Mellon in the 1930s, serious questions arose about the Mellon family's ability or even will to control and coordinate the family's vast wealth that was concentrated in the "crown jewels" of Mellon Bank, Gulf Oil, Alcoa, Koppers, and Carborundum, but whose tentacles reached into hundreds of corporate boardrooms and foundations. The two key partners in the second generation, A.W. and R.B., unlike the patriarch, old Judge Thomas Mellon, married late and bred sparingly. Andrew's only son Paul had little taste for banking even though he was the largest stockholder in the bank. Like many of the younger family members, he also had little interest in Pittsburgh. It fell to R.B.'s son, Richard King Mellon, or R.K., to assume the dominant role in overseeing the family's fortune, as well as guiding the evolution of the city that A.W. and R.B. once presided over as their personal fiefdom. Andrew's daughter Ailsa married David Bruce whose interests lay in diplomacy and foreign affairs. He served as ambassador to France, England, and West Germany, and, after his divorce from the Mellon heiress, he was the negotiator with Henry Kissinger of the Paris Peace Accord that brought an end to American involvement in Vietnam. Sarah Mellon, R.K.'s sister, married Pittsburgh business man Alan Scaife, whose only son Richard became a major funder of conservative, right-wing elements in the Republican Party and beyond. William Larimer Mellon's daughter Rachel married John F. Walton, who remained involved to a degree in Gulf Oil, but the family's direct hold on the patrimonial empire was attenuating.[59]

Richard King Mellon was raised in his father's 65-room, eleven-bath, mansion at 6500 Penn Avenue. He absorbed R.B.'s focus on the Pittsburgh base of the family fortune while Andrew was off running American capitalism from Washington. He cut his teeth on the banking end of the family's business empire, taking over a score of Western Pennsylvania banks in 1929 under a holding company called Mellbank. Andrew assigned a Kansas banker named Frank Denton to assist him, and Denton eventually became the operations man at Mellon Bank. R.K.'s obsession was the Rolling Rock Club, a 200 acre, 2,000 member club grouping Mellon friends and associates. The club was at the center of 18,000 acres of woodland and pasture assembled by R. B. Mellon and his son. Scattered throughout this vast seigniorial domain by the mid-1960s were the substantial homes of various branches of the Mellon family, plus the officers and directors of Mellon Bank including the chairmen of Gulf Oil, J&L Steel, Fisher Scientific, Duquesne Light, Koppers, H.J. Heinz, Alcoa, Consolidation Coal, Westinghouse Electric, U.S. Steel, and Mine Safety Appliances. Eleven miles north of these holdings was a second vast Mellon property that R.K. made into a private wildlife sanctuary, home to various exotic animals that provided sport for wealthy hunters. At the Club, the local gentry could gather with high-powered guests, golf, fish, hunt, ride with the foxhounds, and witness the famous annual steeplechase.[60]

R.K.'s sense of duty to Pittsburgh was atypical. Paul Mellon, like most of the Mellons of the third and fourth generation, felt little responsibility for the source of their fortunes. In this they were like Carnegie and Frick, who took their immense wealth with them and rarely looked back. Andrew Mellon's sole son, Paul, resented the political attacks launched against his father by the New Deal reformers. He demonstrated less interest in defending or expanding his patrimony than he did in living a life of style and taste. Riding to the hunt in Virginia or England, breeding and racing horses, collecting rare books and British painters of the eighteenth and nineteenth centuries, he maintained five elegant homes "to accord with his splendid means and civilized tastes." His main work was as president of the National Gallery of Art and manager of the family's foundations. He bore up nobly under the strain of dispensing money, however. "Giving large sums of money away nowadays is a soul-searching problem. You can cause as much damage with it as you may do good." Joining his brother-in-law in England during World War II, he was involved with David Bruce in the Office of Special Services, the forerunner of the CIA with "Wild Bill" Donovan, David Rockefeller, and Allen Dulles.[61]

In the opening days of his administration, Lawrence made it abundantly clear he would work with any group interested in the welfare of the city and would challenge any group no matter their politics if they acted against the city's interest. At the dawn of the new year of 1946, he would have ample opportunity to demonstrate independence from his union supporters as well as his willingness, even eagerness, to collaborate with the corporate establishment.[62]

Controlling Floods and Killer Smog

When Mayor Lawrence took office, he wasted no time demonstrating his seriousness of purpose. His passion for hard work, order, and organization was complemented by his experience on the macro-level of state and national politics, as well as on the micro-level of neighborhood concerns, the ward and committee levels of the party, the local dynamics of craft and industrial union politics.

He was not a political theorist or visionary; he was a doer, a man of action. His administration was generally competent and very loyal. Loyalty that extended to the grassroots levels of the party meant, unlike many of his mayoral successors, including his predecessor, Cornelius Scully, Lawrence had little trouble dominating a council that had displayed considerable independence in the past. Lawrence held closed-door meetings with councilmen and department heads where discussion and debate were lively. Once a decision was reached, however, a united front was expected and the public vote was pro-forma. This power provided Lawrence credibility in his alliance with R. K. Mellon, who exercised a comparable hold over the local corporate elite. Each had trusted aides that worked closely on the Renaissance: for Mellon, they were Adolph Schmidt and Arthur Van Buskirk; for Lawrence, they were Jack Robin and Jimmy Kirk.[63]

The partnership enlisted a solid team including Paul Martin, a civil engineer, who became head of Allegheny County Planning; Wallace Richards, the visionary who headed the Pittsburgh Regional Planning Association; Leslie Reese, financial expert with the Pennsylvania Economy League; Fred Bigger, head of City Planning; Theodore Hazlett, Allegheny Conference lawyer; and Anne Alpern, the City Solicitor. Given the recent disaster in 1936, flood control was essential. To entice corporations and businesses to stay downtown, Lawrence joined with the Pittsburgh Chamber of Commerce to lobby both Republicans and Democrats in Congress for major flood control investments. Work began on the Conemaugh Dam in 1949; and by 1953, eight of nine planned reservoirs, most in the Allegheny watershed, were completed. This assurance of flood protection prompted Heinz and J&L to expand, and Equitable Life Assurance to finance the construction of Gateway Center.[64]

Gateway Center, where nine of the largest corporations in Pittsburgh were induced to commit to twenty-year leases, was the "most dramatic expression of the reverse welfare state in Pittsburgh." The powerful Mellon-Lawrence alliance swept all before them. On the evening of March 22, 1946, Mayor Lawrence, accompanied by his executive secretary, Jack Robin, and political ally State Senator Joe Barr, gathered on the roof of the Pittsburgh Press Building to watch a spectacular fire that was consuming the railroad warehouse district at the Point. Lawrence must have felt some pangs of memory as he watched the jumble of sheds and overpasses that dominated the old First Ward neighborhood where he had been born and raised be reduced to rubble. The venerable Fort Pitt Blockhouse, survivor of the Native American siege of 1763 and the dismantlement of the fort, survived again. The three men were gleeful, however, in the realization that the serendipitous conflagration opened the way for the massive redevelopment of the Point that swiftly followed. The city moved to establish an Urban Redevelopment Authority that could exercise public power through eminent domain to acquire large numbers of private properties, consolidate them to create extensive development sites and then sell them to private developers in the name of the public good. The same public powers were invoked on behalf of the expansion of the J&L mill on the South Side where the construction of six new open-hearth furnaces required the demolition of more than sixty workers' homes and small businesses.[65]

The bi-partisan Lawrence-Mellon alliance pushed a series of bills through the Pennsylvania legislature called the "Pittsburgh Package." Among other things, these bills established a Parking Authority, a city department of parks and recreation, the extension of smoke control legislation and the completion of the Penn-Lincoln Parkway, that became known as the Parkway East. Smoke control plans provoked the opposition of the still powerful Pennsylvania Railroad, until one of its board members, R. K. Mellon, personally and forcefully intervened with the Pennsylvania Railroad's president Martin Clements. Smoke Control legislation greatly accelerated the transition from steam to diesel locomotives. By January 1953, diesels accounted for 79% of all locomotives in Allegheny County; by 1958, steam engines had vanished from the scene. More seriously for Mayor Lawrence, the imposition of strict smoke controls on homeowners' use of coal provoked grassroots political opposition. Eddie Leonard, a tough-talking officer in the AFL Plasterers' Local 31, who had served as secretary of the Building Trades Council in the early 1930s, was supported to fill "labor's seat" on Pittsburgh's City Council in 1938. When Lawrence proposed smoke control, Leonard opposed the regulations against the use of bituminous coal in home furnaces as a hardship on the poor that served the interests of the wealthy who could afford smoke control. To the consternation of party loyalists, Leonard declared his intention to challenge Lawrence in the 1949 Democratic Primary because the mayor "has become a valuable servant of the financial and industrial dynasty that has dominated the economy and political life of the community for three generations." Lawrence defeated Leonard, 75,838 to 53,205, in the closest election he ever faced as Pittsburgh's mayor.[66]

Pittsburgh's Smoke Control legislation was passed in 1941, but implementation was delayed until war's end. Regulations on homeowners were further delayed a year; but by the late 1940s, there was a dramatic *visible* improvement in Pittsburgh's air. While many dangerous, cancer-causing, gaseous chemicals escaped regulation, particulate smoke and sulfur emissions caused by burning local bituminous coal dropped dramatically. Homeowners and businesses switched first to "smokeless" coal and subsequently to natural gas as increased supplies became available. In the first year after the new regulations, the city experienced 39% more sunshine and as Allegheny County extended smoke control to the industrial valleys radiating out from the Point, "heavy" smoke declined by 98% from 1946 to 1954. In 1957, the city's program was merged into the County Health Department whose standards and enforcement were weaker.[67]

While the local air looked much better cleansed of the soot spewed in particulate form from inefficient fireplaces, furnaces, boilers, and heavily worn mechanical equipment, air quality was still extremely bad because of all the gaseous fumes that mixed with the air in a noxious brew. The urgency of toxic emissions control was dramatically illustrated by the air pollution disaster that occurred in Donora, a mill town on the Monongahela southeast of Pittsburgh, in late October, 1948. A few days before Halloween, a heavy fog blanketed the entire region as a still blanket of cold air trapped the gases from coal and coke furnaces, and the metal fumes from the town's zinc plant. Cars and trucks at first used headlights, but it soon became impossible to see the street. On Friday afternoon, the town's annual Halloween parade took place in a thick haze. On Saturday, the annual football game between Donora and Monessen was held even though spectators and players often lost sight of the ball. Donora's star tight end was called from the public address system to go home immediately, because his father who worked in the mill had collapsed. In Donora on Saturday, October 30, seventeen people died in twelve hours, hundreds were hospitalized, and thousands were left gasping for breath. While most local workers and residents recognized the role that the town's Zinc Works played in creating the deadly smog, a community fearful of losing jobs did not confront powerful corporate interests that marshaled lawyers, managers and retained experts to emphasize the role of weather and the valley terrain surrounded by 400 foot cliffs to explain the catastrophe.[68]

The Donora Zinc Works was built by American Steel & Wire Company, a U.S. Steel subsidiary. The zinc smelter produced molten zinc for the coating of sheet and wire steel products, plus liquid sulfuric acid that was sold to the corporation's by-product plant downriver at Clairton. Local residents and farmers had attempted unsuccessfully to bring legal action against the smelter on the basis of health concerns and damage to crops, orchards, livestock, and topsoil as well as the impact of toxic chemicals on houses and other real estate in Donora and neighboring Webster for nearly thirty years. Thomas Bell in his novel *Out of This Furnace* described the site where he had worked for a time in the 1930s: [69]

> Freshly charged, the zinc smelting furnaces, crawling with thousands of small flames, yellow, blue, green, filled the valley with smoke. Acrid and poisonous, worse than anything a steel mill belched forth, it penetrated everywhere, making automobile headlights necessary in Webster's streets, setting the river-boat pilots to cursing God, and destroying every living thing on the hills. [70]

By Friday, October 29, residents were crowding into local hospitals and fire department volunteers were administering oxygen to those unable to breathe. By noon on Saturday, eleven people had died and the density of the smog made further evacuation of the town impossible. On that day, Walter Winchell broke the news about the evolving disaster on his national radio broadcast. It was only after midnight early on Sunday morning, however, that U.S. Steel reacted by shutting down the smelter. Rather than the decision coming from the line production management, the order came down from Roger Blough, the corporation's general counsel. By the time the order came, atmospheric conditions were lifting and the worst was over. By midday Sunday, rains had dispersed the killer smog. The final death toll included twenty who died immediately, plus fifty people more than would be statistically expected died in the following month, and Devra Davis, a noted epidemiologist who grew up in Donora, estimates that thousands died prematurely over the next decade. [71]

State and federal response was weak and seemed inclined toward blaming an "atmospheric freak," rather than issuing any conclusions that pointed toward the mighty steel corporation, its operating procedures or its emergency response failures. The Donora Council made up of union members created their own investigation and accepted a $10,000 grant from USWA and CIO president Phillip Murray for an "independent and unbiased" study of the disaster. The grant was used to conduct a health effects study of the area, while the state tried to develop a system of area air sampling. Under-reporting of illness, by employees of the Zinc Works and their families worried about their jobs, helped mask the central issue which was the exposure of workers, families, and an entire community to extremely toxic chemicals in both the short and long term. The steel corporation moved swiftly to manage the crisis through the Industrial Hygiene Foundation, a consortium of manufacturers who sponsored research through Mellon Institute. The company denied responsibility for the smog and proposed a study of the health effects of the event that promised to be costly, contentious and time consuming. The focus on health effects rather than on pollution sources allowed cautious bureaucrats at the U.S. Public Health Service to avoid calling for regulation of the production or emission of toxic substances. The focus on weather and topography pushed researchers to concentrate on atmospheric conditions that might indicate when zinc production might be curtailed to avoid a recurrence of the catastrophe. The eroded hillsides and stripped vegetation downwind from the Zinc Works were largely ignored. As the company asserted, the smog was ultimately judged an "act of God." The Zinc Works reopened until a severe drop in metal prices in 1957 caused the closing of the facility. [72]

Strikes and Opportunities

1946 witnessed the greatest number of workdays lost to strikes in U.S. history. Wartime inflation undermined attempted price controls while wage controls, given corporate support and union acquiescence, were more effectively applied. The specter of the post-World War I upheavals of 1919 and the subsequent suppression of unions weighed heavily on the minds of men like Phil Murray and John L. Lewis. These concerns were mixed with those raised by the transition from a war economy to a peacetime one. Massive strikes in steel, auto, electrical, glass, aluminum, coal and other industries demonstrated the hunger of a working class who had gone from depression to war and now yearned for a family wage and economic security. In fact, the expansion of worker political power on both the national and grassroots level spared the country the trauma of a 1919 style social crisis. The 1946 strikes provided a breather to an economy in transition while the substantial pay increases won in 1946 helped fuel a peacetime building boom and the consumer economy.

In November 1945, 180,000 autoworkers struck General Motors; in January 1946, they were joined by 500,000 steelworkers and eventually another 250,000 fabricating workers, 200,000 electrical workers, and 150,000 packinghouse workers. Unlike the bitter clashes of the past, the strikes were disciplined and mostly peaceful as the vast majority of companies did not attempt to run plants or cross picket lines. While Murray was the head of the CIO, he was primarily occupied with the USWA struggle, while the Communist-led UE and the anti-Communist-led UAW vied with each other in militancy. In the Monongahela Valley, journalist Art Preis described "the plants sprawled lifeless" with strikers controlling access to the mills huddled by "friendly fires meant to warm and comfort pickets in the long freezing vigil of the near-zero night." Murray's assistant David McDonald felt the corporations were resigned to eventually cede on the 18.5 cent hourly wage increase endorsed by a presidential panel. The steel companies' acceptance of the wage increase was facilitated by the union's tacit support for a hike in steel prices.[73] McDonald also sensed there was something very different about the choreographed and institutionalized struggle of 1946 from the spontaneous wildcat strikes of the war years, or the earlier bitter battles for recognition:

> There was an undercurrent to this strike I'd never sensed before. No one was really very angry, and I had the feeling from the beginning that the steel industry...simply wanted a breather it could blame on us while its customers used up some of the swollen inventories. The feeling was by no means one-sided. Steelworkers who had been at it seven days a week for almost four years and had accumulated overtime savings they couldn't use during the war didn't object to a few weeks away from the mills. So the 1946 shutdown was more a vacation than a strike.[74]

The 1946 strike wave almost swamped the Pittsburgh Pirates baseball club, however. During the war, the government imposed a wage-freeze and the team saw 35 of its players serve in the military. The players wanted more money like most of the rest of the nation. On June 5, 1946, the team narrowly rejected a strike called by the American Baseball Guild. Two nights later, a majority of the team voted to strike; but the strike action failed to garner three-fourths of voters, a condition the players had agreed to prior to the vote. That year the team was purchased by a conglomerate that included Indianapolis banker Frank McKinney, Columbus real estate executive and horse breeder John Galbreath, and singer Bing Crosby. The following year, Pirates' hopes soared as the team acquired Hank Greenberg, who had led the American league in homers the previous season, to supplement the power hitting of a young star from Arkansas, Ralph Kiner. Kiner, back from a three-year stint with the Navy Air Corps, hit 23 homeruns that first year and then 51 in 1947 to tie as the league leader. Kiner's towering line-drive homers were announced over the radio by Rosey Rosewell, the Pirates' radio announcer, with descriptions that became his trademark. "Raise the window, Aunt Minnie, here she comes…right into your petunia patch." While the Pirates never finished higher than fourth in the post-war 1940s, Ralph Kiner's 40 homers in 1948 and 54 in 1949 brought fans into the ballpark. Leading the league in homeruns for seven consecutive years, Kiner was a star. He drove a Cadillac, saying that Fords were for singles hitters. He dated Elizabeth Taylor, hosted a TV show and married tennis pro Nancy Chafee.[75]

The war years had been even tougher on the Steelers than the Pirates. In 1942, the Steelers put together their first winning season behind the running of "Bullet" Bill Dudley. By the following season the war had depleted the ranks of all professional sports teams. To survive the dearth of talent and decline of interest, the Steelers merged with the Philadelphia Eagles in 1943 to form the Steagles and with the Chicago Cardinals to form the Card-Pitts in 1944. The odd-couplings lost three-fourths of their games. Hope flared during the 1946 and 1947 seasons when the great former Pitt coach Jock Sutherland took over the team as coach. Jock was the epitome of a new breed of football coaches who made a science out of football with playbooks, game films, classroom sessions, and a chalkboard on the sidelines. In 1947 he led the team to an 8-4 record, their best ever with a great tight end, Elbie Nickel, and Bill Dudley, back from the war, at halfback. That year the Steelers tied the Eagles for the Eastern Conference Championship. In the week before the playoff, however, the players struck for more money. Sutherland stood firm, but the distracted team lost the game. Shortly after the team lost in the playoffs, Sutherland died from a brain tumor. After his departure, the Steelers only had one winning season (1949) before the arrival of Buddy Parker as coach late in the following decade.[76]

The G.I. Bill provided working-class veterans hardened in depression and war an opportunity for technical and academic education that reduced short-term unemployment while greatly increasing the adaptability of the labor force and the stability of the economy. As long as they could gain admittance, veterans could attend the school of their choice with tuition, books, and a stipend paid by the government. Local universities prospered and expanded. The University of Pittsburgh had to open the Ellsworth Center in the fall of 1947 to absorb 2,500 students, most veterans, for the first two years of their university experience. Finally, unlike World War I, where the post-war U.S. military was rapidly reduced to a small percentage of its wartime status and the nation turned resolutely inward, the vast wartime military-industrial complex was not dismantled with the cessation of hostilities. The need for the United States to assist European reconstruction, the opportunities for economic and military expansion into the space created by the disintegration of the British and French colonial empires, plus the intensifying Cold War between the U.S. and its erstwhile Soviet ally, provided the rationale and the opportunity for a vastly expanded global business and military presence.[77]

While the nationwide strikes in steel, auto, and the electrical industry were beyond Lawrence's control or influence, he was confronted with a local labor crisis that elevated him in the public's mind from a backstage city boss to an acclaimed civic statesman. From February through October 1946, the city was faced with an electrical power strike. The shutdown of a city's power supply with the dramatic consequences such a shutdown entails in a complex urban environment catapulted this relatively small strike, in terms of the numbers of workers involved, into the national limelight and indelibly shaped the image of David Lawrence in the consciousness of Pittsburgh. Furthermore, since the strike was called by a former company, but increasingly independent union headed by George Mueller, it was sanctioned by neither the AFL nor CIO. As the first strike deadline approached, Lawrence gave a radio address appealing to the Duquesne Light workers. "I have championed the cause of labor all my life....But my first duty, and my only duty, is to all the people of this city." Failing to convince the light company's workers, he appealed to President Harry Truman to seize the company but the president refused. After Pittsburgh spent nearly twenty hours with curtailed electricity, Mueller suspended the strike and negotiations continued in thirty sessions through the summer into the fall without agreement.[78]

Lawrence became involved in a number of other local labor disputes that record strike year, mediating a hotel employees' strike, a brewery workers' strike and participating in a rally with Phil Murray for striking Westinghouse electrical workers. As fall approached, however, the mayor attempted to pressure Mueller and Duquesne Light chairman, Pressley McCance, to reach a settlement with a warning: "The public utilities live by the sufferance of the public...if the terms of that grant are violated, if service is not continuous, the people through their government will act." A court-ordered five-day injunction issued one minute before the strike deadline averted a shutdown while increasing the drama. On September 25, Mueller ordered his members to strike. The city was plunged in darkness, streetcars stopped, elevators were inoperative. Many businesses, stores, and restaurants closed. Some office workers walked or hitch-hiked to town and climbed stairs to work. Low levels of power were maintained by management, but strict conservation measures were applied. *Fortune* magazine described the scene: "Night travelers to Pittsburgh had the unnerving experience of coming into a city illuminated largely by candles. And the further they went into the dimmed-out city, the deeper grew the sense of having strayed into some darker century." [79]

On September 26, a three judge panel met to hear the city's request for a permanent injunction. Mueller termed the injunction a scrap of paper and the judges stunned everyone by sentencing Mueller to a year in prison for contempt of court. Reacting to the injunction and the labor leader's arrest, many unionists now rallied to Mueller's support and sympathy strikes erupted. The United Electrical Workers were conspicuous in their support for Mueller. Father Rice was heartily booed trying to calm thousands of union supporters who chanted "We want Mueller" and "Free Mueller." Lawrence was bitterly criticized for seeking an injunction to end the strike.[80]

Lawrence now had to decide whether to escalate the conflict and arrest more of the striking union's workers. Mueller's arrest provoked a wave of sympathy walkouts including 6,000 steelworkers at the J&L plant in Pittsburgh, 4,500 workers at the Westinghouse Airbrake, and a partial walkout involving 4,800 Westinghouse Electric workers in the satellite facilities in Trafford, Lawrenceville, and Homewood. Sympathy strikes added to the numbers of workers already out of work because of power shortages. Instead, the mayor decided to ask the court to lift the injunction and free Mueller so negotiations could be resumed. Upon his release, Mueller was hoisted to the shoulders of triumphant supporters as he left City Hall. In East Pittsburgh, a major meeting called to demand Mueller's release turned into a rally where Tom Fitzpatrick, president of UE District 6, promoted a possible third party presidential run by Henry Wallace while John Metcalfe, president of UE 601, urged municipal ownership of utilities. [81]

By mid-October, with electrical power available at minimum levels and trolley lines disrupted by roving pickets, Mueller's intransigence began to undermine rank-and-file support and union solidarity began to wane. A shooting that damaged a Duquesne Light generator helped shift public feeling against Mueller and he agreed to submit a proposal for binding arbitration to a union vote.

On October 21, twenty-seven days into the strike, the workers voted to accept arbitration 1,197-797. In a photo that became iconic, an exhausted Lawrence was pictured asleep slumped over his desk during the crisis. He became a national hero and voice of reason for holding the interests of the city over that of his party and its labor allies. The Duquesne Light strike defined Lawrence as a statesman and marked him as a leader with whom corporate interests could deal. In a presentiment of things to come, Lawrence received a request to appear before the House Un-American Activities Committee to testify about Communist influence in the light strike. Lawrence declined, replying: "…It is my belief that I could serve no useful purpose there. This strike is disastrous in its effects and in my opinion has been unnecessary because arbitration is possible, but I have no reason to believe that any communistic influences are influential in it."[82]

A surprising conclusion to the episode was the incorporation of the Duquesne Light workers into the AFL's IBEW. This achievement was largely due to the efforts of the union's organizer, Andy Johnson. Father Rice, who was deeply involved in trying to bring the strike to a peaceful conclusion, wrote about Johnson: "(He) is a tremendous worker, a very personable fellow and very, very clever. Johnson's opponents never are blessed with a whole lot of full nights of sleep."[83] For his part, Johnson recalled:

> We were able to get some of the guys who had been leaders in the independent union that were disenchanted with the conduct of Mueller. He was really starting to lord it over them….Mueller, when he saw the handwriting on the wall, came over and wanted to know if he threw his influence to the IBEW, what would we do for him. I told him that if the people wanted him, then he could have a position with us. We could not guarantee him a position. But along comes the Utility Workers Union, and they did guarantee him that they would give him a spot if he threw his influence to them. And he did throw his influence to them. They lost, but they kept him on….Last I heard, he was feeding animals out at the zoo under the terms of an agreement with the CIO organization."[84]

Individual Paths

While the post-war strike wave provoked a degree of anti-union resentment, improvements in the living standards of the working classes also fueled a spirit of optimism and gave people a sense of new possibilities. In the cultural realm, the Pittsburgh region provided models of an individualism based on hard work and truthfulness to one's own vision. The archetypal interpreter of a certain small town decency, willing to stand up against the rich and powerful, was Jimmy Stewart from Indiana, northeast of Pittsburgh. It was noted in his obituary that if John Wayne became the cinematic symbol of the American at war, Jimmy Stewart came to epitomize an America at peace. He was nominated for an Academy Award in 1939 for his portrayal of a decent and determined, if highly innocent, congressman, *Mr. Smith Goes to Washington*. When he won an Academy Award in 1941 playing opposite Katherine Hepburn in *The Philadelphia Story*, he sent his Oscar home where it was displayed for years in the window of his family's hardware store on Philadelphia Street, the town of Indiana's main drag. During the war, Stewart joined the Air Force and flew 20 missions over Germany, becoming a full colonel. After the war, he starred in the film that became a part of many American families' Christmas rituals, *It's a Wonderful Life*. Despite an angel character and wry humor, the film depicts stark class struggle between a small town financial institution, serving a hard-strapped community during the depression, and the greed and ruthlessness of the town's powerful banker, real estate speculator, and richest man. Decency triumphs in the end, of course; but the film's power comes from its depiction of the struggle of good versus evil. A lifelong conservative Republican, Stewart was one of the first actors to work for a percentage of a film's profits, an arrangement that made him a multi-millionaire.[85]

Another rugged individualist, also from the same town of Indiana, the writer Edward Abbey, was in some metaphysical or political sense almost the anti-Stewart. Born in 1927, nineteen years after the town's celebrated actor, Abbey described Indiana as a "town set in the cup of the green hills. In the Alleghenies. A town of trees, two-story houses, red-brick hardware stores, church steeples, the clock tower on the county courthouse, and over all the thin blue haze – partly dust, partly smoke, but mostly moisture – that veils the Appalachian world most of the time. The diaphanous veil that conceals nothing." He was the son of a radical, socialist, anarchist, working-class father, who took Walt Whitman's saying "resist much, obey little" to heart, and a talented musician mother, whose love of Chopin and classical music stayed with her wilderness-loving son. At the age of nine, Ed Abbey settled with his family on a farm that he called the "Old Lonesome Briar Patch" in Home, near Crooked Creek just north of Indiana. In the summer of 1944, after his junior year at Indiana High School, expecting to be drafted, he hitch-hiked west to the Rocky Mountains, developing a life-long love of the West, especially empty places where there were few people. He spent two years following graduation in the army, one year of college at Indiana State Teachers College (now IUP), and then he moved to New Mexico. He went on to write dozens of books including *Desert Solitaire*, often included on lists of the finest American nature writing, and *The Monkey Wrench Gang* about environmental saboteurs resisting environmental destruction. While most of his books grew out of his experiences as a forest ranger, and many concern the desert Southwest where his books are well known, perhaps his finest book is *Fool's Progress* where Abbey tells the tale of the misanthrope's final return to Appalachia and the Indiana home of his childhood. While he thinly disguised Indiana in the novel as Shawnee, West Virginia, he freely used the names of his family, friends and neighbors from hometown Indiana, as well as descriptions of the terrain around the actual and mythical Home, Pennsylvania.[86]

In the post-war era, the best-known novel about the Pittsburgh area was Marcia Davenport's *Valley of Decision*. Interestingly, today that distinction probably belongs to Thomas Bell's *Out of This Furnace*, which languished in obscurity after its publication in 1941 until rediscovered by David Demarest, professor of English at Carnegie Mellon University, and published by the University of Pittsburgh Press in 1976. Unlike Bell's novel, which was deeply rooted in his own family's working-class experience, Davenport's novel is sympathetic to management and tells a completely fictional story of a mill-owning family on Pittsburgh's North Side. Like *Out of This Furnace*, *The Valley of Decision* follows the path of multiple generations of a single family, though here it is the story of self-made men with a right to ownership rooted in their having built up a foundry operation through their own determination and ingenuity. It features an upstairs-downstairs romance between a house maid and the young son of the mill owner, whose relationship is threatened when members of her family, all workers in the mill, go on strike against his father. The strength of the novel comes from the excellent descriptions of Pittsburgh's North Side and of the accurate portrayals of the workings of a mid-sized industrial facility. The fame of the book was greatly augmented by a movie made in 1945, starring Gregory Peck and Greer Garson, nominated for an academy award for her performance. In a 1988 *Introduction* to a new edition of her work, Davenport credited Phil Murray for an astonishing level of support and personal interest in her project. "For it was Philip Murray who persuaded union bosses and shop foremen to let him bring me into the mills, something which I believe was unprecedented....So there is no place in *The Valley of Decision* where I describe a process in the making of steel which I did not witness myself, standing on a gallery with Philip Murray and one or two other men to explain every detail of what I saw."[87]

An even more famous cultural icon, Andrew Warhola, was born in 1928 in Pittsburgh's Soho district to Ruthenian or Carpatho-Rusyn parents from the Carpathian Mountains in the far northeast of today's Slovakia. Andy's father worked for Eichleay Engineering moving houses and was intensely religious, attending St. John Chrysostom Byzantine Catholic Church on Saline Street in Four Mile Run, a part of the Greenfield neighborhood. He died when Andy was thirteen. The iconography of the Byzantine tradition certainly influenced both the form and the content of his son Andrew's vision. The family was very poor, but his mother was artistic, loved cats as subjects, and taught the young Andy to draw. Andy was sickly, a "mother's boy," who preferred the company of girls. Because of recurrent illnesses, he spent a lot of time at home, where he made collages, lifted print from paper using wax, colored pictures and cut paper dolls. Movies were his passion. He loved Shirley Temple and developed his "dream America" from the cinema. He was also drawn to disasters, accidents, and suicides. He attended art classes in the Music Hall at the Carnegie Museum during the war, went to Schenley High School and was accepted at Carnegie Tech on the basis of his manifest artistic talent. He had a difficult time there initially. Painfully shy, he suffered in English classes with his *Pittsburghese* speech: "yunz"or "yinz" for you plural (the Northern equivalent of the Southern "y'all"); "ats" for that is, "n'at" for and that, etc. A fellow student remarked: "Andy wore his peasant heritage like a badge of honor. His use of working-class vernacular was part of it."[88]

At Carnegie Tech, Warhola absorbed his teachers' emphasis on commercial design, since the school taught that fine art and commercial art were essentially the same. He loved dance and the Pittsburgh Symphony, which was becoming one of the world's premier orchestras under the direction of William Steinberg. In his senior year, he caused a scandal with a painting of a little boy with his finger stuck defiantly in his nose entitled: "The Broad Gave Me My Face, but I Can Pick My Own Nose." In June 1949, despite his mother's predictions of disaster, he left for New York and there became Warhol. He plunged into the fashion magazine publishing world, where his ability was quickly recognized and his eccentricities appreciated. He was a workaholic who delivered several versions of each assignment, a practice that publishers greatly appreciated. In 1952 his mother joined him in his New York apartment. For ten years, he worked his way to the top of the fashion and commercial art business. In 1962 he catapulted into the limelight, the guru of "pop art" with his soup cans, dollar bills, Coke bottles, and images of Marilyn Monroe, and set his mark on the world cultural scene. Warhol gave cryptic interviews to journalists, like Bob Dylan did, during the same period in New York. However, at times he let it all hang out: "I just like to see things used and re-used. It appeals to my American sense of thrift," and "Why should I be original? Why can't I be non-original?"[89]

Labor, Communism, and the Democrats

The immediate post-World War II era brought to a head the long smoldering issue of Communism in American society and particularly inside the labor movement. The 1930s had effected a profound shift in Pittsburgh's politics as the previously tiny, marginalized Democratic

Party, lifted to a significant degree by the rising tide of the labor movement, arose out of the depths of the Great Depression to achieve majority status. During this political shift, the Communist Party played a significant but limited role in the broader liberal, labor, populist, left movement of the 1930s that arose out of the crisis of capitalism by providing dedicated union organizers and active political cadres influencing a wide range of professions. Wounded by its policy shifts before the war, the CP's super-patriotism and contribution to the war effort, in accord with the leadership of the CIO, brought the party's numbers at war's end to perhaps several hundred thousand nationwide and several thousand in the Pittsburgh region. While the actual numbers of Communists were never great, the numbers masked the party's real strength and influence since the party recruited dedicated and committed activists rather than attempting to develop a broad mass organization. Aside from their presence in the labor movement, they operated through an interconnected web of various interest groups promoting racial justice, peace, and opposition to the expansion of capitalism and the American military abroad. Through front and allied organizations they achieved a much wider influence and public presence among many who shared parallel concerns but were often unaware of the party's presence or role.

Despite its growing numbers and the respectability achieved by war's end, the second half of the decade of the 1940s witnessed the crushing of the American Communist Party. This occurred at least in part as a result of the intensification of the Cold War and the domestic party's adherence to an aggressive international line laid down by Stalin. Where the red threat had been a staple of right-wing and business propaganda going all the way back to the railroad riots of 1877 and especially to the red summer of 1919, the anti-communism of the 1930s operated in a climate of rising union power when capitalism was on the defensive. The anti-communism of members of the business class like Tom Girdler during the depression could be dismissed by liberals and labor leaders as anti-democratic rantings and exaggerated propaganda. While Catholic anti-Communists with ties to the labor movement, like Father Rice, were active as early as 1937, his attacks made little headway among liberals who sympathized with the Republican forces in Spain and with the United Front government in France. It was the Hitler-Stalin pact that marked the movement of liberal Democrats toward militant anti-Communism. What characterized the late 1940s was not the anti-Communism of the right though it certainly grew more virulent. What marked the "tragic purge" and provided its muscle was the ardor and personal knowledge of liberal and trade union activists whose attacks were more focused and effective for being based on experience rather than ideology.[90]

Looking back it is hard to appreciate how vulnerable both the Democrats and the union movement felt at the war's end in 1945. In 1928 the Republicans exercised a near dictatorship over state politics controlling all 36 House of Representative seats in Congress. Unlike more recent Pennsylvania history, it was not simply a question of Republican dominance over suburbs, small town, and rural areas. Unlike most northern states where the Democratic Party maintained control over the more populous urban areas in Republican-controlled states, in Pennsylvania, Republican machine control of both Pittsburgh and Philadelphia rendered the party total control over state politics before the New Deal breakthrough. By 1936, at the high water mark of the Democratic surge, Democrats captured 27 of 34 Congressional seats. During the "Roosevelt recession" of 1938, the Republicans regained the majority (19-15), but a genuine two-party system seemed established through four election cycles (1938-1944). However, Roosevelt's victory in 1944 was a narrow one; and in 1946, without the Roosevelt magic and with middle-class public opinion recoiling from massive labor unrest, the Republicans won 28 out of Pennsylvania's 33 Congressional House seats.

Republicans, in the 1946 election, made sweeping gains pounding on anti-Communist themes. At the Pennsylvania Republican convention held in Pittsburgh in September before the election, the party platform charged that "the insidious poison of communism has been injected into the blood and sinew of the Democratic Party." Liberals feared a repeat of the postwar "return to normalcy" of the 1920s. In a climate of mounting reaction and international tension with the Soviet Union, the anti-communist enthusiasm of the Democrats and the CIO was perceived as a question of political survival.[91]

The concerns of many labor leaders paralleled that of the Democrats. The strikes and upheavals of 1919 had been followed by sustained attacks on the labor movement. Labor leaders of Murray's generation had endured the effects of the 1919 defeat during more than a decade of bitter union retreat. While concerns about reds in 1919 had been more theoretical than real, an expansionist Soviet Union with a global revolutionary mission, plus a small but tightly organized domestic Communist Party with a significant but not easily calculable presence in the labor movement, gave the red scare of the 1940s more weight and credibility. After all, Marxist ideology identified the industrial working class as the agent of revolutionary transformation. Industrial unionism was the heart of the matter and the CIO was for many (Communists, as well as their opponents) the main source of hope that the progressive social agenda of the New Deal could be extended and strengthened into the future. In Pennsylvania's industrial union movement, struggles between Communist and non-Communist activists had a long history going back to the early 1920s. In the late 1940s, these divisions deepened and approximated the bitterness of the NMU-UMWA struggles of 1929-1932, but on a much larger and more consequential scale. In addition, World War II had taken many rank-and-file activists who had built the unions during the 1930s off to war. The new generation of workers, many of them returning young veterans without the previous generation's deep commitment to unions (or the Communist Party for that matter), were primarily concerned about a family, a house, and a decent standard of living. Fear of corporate political power had dissipated substantially while at the same time increased prosperity softened the desire to totally transform society.[92]

In Pittsburgh the main Communist labor strongholds were in the UE electrical worker locals of the Turtle Creek Valley, the Hotel and Restaurant Union local that in the late 1930s held Lenin birthday celebrations at Frick's downtown William Penn Hotel, some steel and aluminum worker locals, and a few scattered UMWA locals in the old radical strongholds of Washington County, the Allegheny Valley, and around Johnstown. In 1945 the national Communist Party leadership decided to develop a "steel concentration" and modest inroads were made in U.S. Steel's Mon Valley plants, Crucible Steel in Lawrenceville, and the J&L locals in Pittsburgh and Aliquippa. This effort remained embryonic given the strongly anti-Communist administration of the USWA under Murray and was buttressed by mounting anti-Communist sentiment in the country at large. By 1948 when Communist Party organizer Steve Nelson arrived in town to assist the Progressive Party campaign, he estimated only three hundred hard-core party members remained in and around Pittsburgh.[93]

During the 1946 strike wave, the issue of communism was not at the forefront, since some of the most actively anti-Communist unions, including Reuther's autoworkers and Murray's steelworkers, were on strike. The dramatic events in Pittsburgh connected to the Duquesne Light strike were hard to pin on Communists, since they played virtually no role in it. The electrical workers' national strike, however, continued the longest at Westinghouse where 65,000 workers struck, including 18,000 in the East Pittsburgh plant alone. A constant drumbeat of attack on the reds at Westinghouse appeared in a newspaper column in the *Wilkinsburg Gazette* written by Congressman John McDowell, an energetic member of the House Un-American Activities Committee (HUAC). He constantly excoriated reds at the East Pittsburgh plant, especially the president of UE 601, Tom Fitzpatrick, who he described as the "current Commissar of the comrades who hold Local 601 in bondage." McDowell, who was also known to make anti-Jewish comments, was defeated in 1948, thanks to the efforts of the UE, by liberal Harry Davenport. One of Davenport's key supporters was Tom Quinn, a young, skilled, thoughtful welder and shop floor activist, who was the chairman of Local 601's legislative committee and who ran on the Progressive ticket for state representative that year.[94]

The great electrical equipment complex in East Pittsburgh was a very different work environment than the giant steel mills just over the ridge in the Mon Valley. In steel, machinery dominated; workers were dwarfed by the physical process. By contrast, in the vast buildings of the Electric Valley, where generators, turbines and motors were machined, fabricated, and assembled, many hundreds of workers toiled in close proximity. These open workshops provided rich opportunity for a vigorous system of shop floor politics and activism. Veteran shop floor politicians who rose up through the ranks became expert interpreters and enforcers of the contract and past practices. Promotions, job assignments, pay systems, safety issues, discrimination against women and blacks were regulated by negotiation and, if necessary, vigorously contested under the union regime. Short sit-down strikes could erupt if workers felt that some company action went over the line. Union representatives negotiated settlements. The power of the foreman to harass or play favorites was sharply curtailed. Contested and lively union elections provided representatives with real status and protection from company harassment. The sectional and especially divisional stewards were important leaders with their own nucleus of supporters. They were expected to be militant and aggressive defenders of the members' interests. While the business agent ran the union office and the president represented the union in public forums, the chief steward ran the in-plant organization of the union. Being a steward in such a context, where every move was watched and gauged by one's constituency on issues directly relevant to daily work life and how workers earned their daily bread, was as close to an experience of pure democracy as citizen workers might ever experience.[95]

Aside from the sprawling main complex of large assembly buildings and machine shops in East Pittsburgh and Turtle Creek, there were a half-dozen smaller satellite plants, including a foundry in Trafford, a service center in Homewood, and the Nuttal precision gear plant in Lawrenceville. Croatian, Serbian, German, Italian, Irish, and other fraternal societies provided both refuge from Prohibition and also meeting places for union activists. The local Communist Party group met at the Croatian Club for many years. Most ethnic groups had a range of political factions, though some like the Polish, Italian, and Irish tended to be strongly anti-Communist. The valley fostered a rich radical stew seasoned by second and even third generation activists from socialist, anarcho-syndicalist, and communist traditions. The two Fitzpatrick brothers came to symbolize the intense political splits occurring in the Electric Valley that even divided families. Mike, the elder brother, had been an IWW activist and deeply resented the undemocratic imposition of party mandates on local union policy. He joined the anti-Communist forces at a critical juncture, when his younger brother emerged as a key leader of the left-wing forces and was becoming the focus of fierce right-wing attacks.[96]

While the anti-Communist faction inside the union won the union elections of December 1941, the left-wing group quickly recovered, regaining power in 1942 and maintaining it throughout the war years. Internal divisions reemerged in 1945 with the formation of the Rank-and-File caucus that became the nucleus of what would become the IUE. Among the candidates, however, on this initial Rank-and-File slate were men who later became left-leaning leaders of the Progressive group, including Porter Mechling and Tom Quinn. Father Rice, appointed the Pittsburgh area rent control director by President Roosevelt through the direct personal request of Phil Murray, re-entered the scene as an advisor to the right-wing opposition. Most members of the Rank-and-File were younger, lower seniority workers concentrated in the less-skilled production areas of the plant. While Catholics were the largest component, they were by no means exclusively so. The Rank-and-File group in fact had no common ideological point of reference other than anti-communism. Most were dedicated trade unionists and were not right-wing in a traditional sense, in that they supported the general philosophy and politics of the New Deal; but certainly some took advantage of the shifting political sands to run for union office and this earned them the epithet of opportunist from the older founders of the union.[97]

In 1947 the Republican Congress with help from Southern Democrats passed the Taft-Hartley Act over President Truman's veto with the intent to severely restrict union power. The act allowed states to ban union shops and pass so-called "right-to-work" laws, made unions liable to charges of unfair labor practices, and included a requirement that union officials sign an affidavit they were not members of the Communist Party. Refusal to swear such an oath by union officers removed the union from certification by the National Labor Relations Board and opened the union to raiding by other organizations. While Murray and other labor leaders initially resisted the requirement, and while John L. Lewis successfully defied it, pressure steadily mounted to use the requirement as a tool to purge the labor movement. That same year, the CIO's Pennsylvania Industrial Union convention, led by anti-Communist UE leader Harry Block from Philadelphia, passed a resolution excluding Communists, Nazis and members of the Klan from holding state office.[98]

At the very same time that conservative, right-wing forces in the United States were stepping up their attacks on the labor movement, the international Communist movement, now in control of six East-bloc nations and with strong Communist parties in France and Italy vying for power, was redefining its strategy. The new Communist International met in September 1947 and called for aggressive political action against social democrats and liberals who they denounced as supporters of western imperialism. As these positions became known and debated in the American party, a consensus grew that the Communists should separate from the Democrats and actively promote the creation of a third party. On December 20, 1947, Henry Wallace, with strong Communist support, announced his candidacy for the presidency. In January 1948, the CIO executive board condemned the third-party effort and endorsed George C. Marshall's plan to provide aid to rebuild Western Europe. Phil Murray urged union support of the Marshall Plan on humanitarian grounds. "The Marshall idea is to give money or food or economic aid to the devastated countries…, a means to feed the hungry and clothe the naked and shelter the homeless and give medicine to the sick." The left-wing minority in response attempted to assert union political autonomy and block CIO financial support for the Truman campaign.[99]

The Tragic Purge

The tipping point for all-out CIO attack on the left-wing unions came when most of their leaders endorsed Henry Wallace for President of the United States under the Progressive Party banner. With Truman facing a separatist Dixiecrat secession from the party on his right over Civil Rights, a split on his left seemed certain to ensure his defeat and confirm a hard turn to the right in domestic politics. Murray who had been loathe to split the CIO now moved decisively and, as Father Rice wrote to a friend, "set his face against The Brethren." He actively supported the national UE Members for Democratic Action (allied with the liberal anti-Communist Americans for Democratic Action) led by Harry Block, UE District 2 director and Pennsylvania CIO leader. He also began to provide active support to Father Rice in his campaign to change the leadership of the UE in the Pittsburgh area. Len DeCaux was cut from the *CIO News* by Murray and joined the swelling ranks of former activists who were cut off and looking for work in a world increasingly afraid to be associated with them. DeCaux wrote about people in his position. "The company was not inspiring – people worried about family future, political persecution, where the next paycheck was coming from, feeling they must look out for themselves. No joy of battle, no hope or plans for a comeback."[100]

The Wallace campaign also pushed Murray to cut his ties with Lee Pressman. Pressman had faithfully served Phil Murray as both SWOC and CIO general counsel. He brilliantly pursued the Labor Board charges against the Little Steel companies that successfully forced them into the CIO on the eve of World War II. Murray in turn had protected Pressman and sustained him in a very visible and prestigious position inside the organization. Once the Communist Party switched to support of the war, Pressman abandoned John L. Lewis, suppressed his class war instincts, and directed his efforts toward all-out support of the war effort, including cutting premium pay, supporting incentive plans and the speed-up. He maintained his position in the first two years following the war's end working to moderate and deflect growing anti-Communist pressures inside the labor federation while attempting to counter the intensifying external rightwing reaction against unionism itself. He tried to straddle the growing left-liberal division within the labor movement by creating formulations of artful ambiguity to cover deep divisions. His intellectual gymnastics reached their peak at the 1947 CIO Convention when he managed to write a resolution that endorsed the Marshall Plan, providing economic aid to Western Europe to resist the threat of Communist takeovers, without mentioning its name.[101]

While not formally a party member for most of his labor career, Pressman admired the Soviet Union and did not shrink from the ruthlessness of Lenin or Stalin. In an incident during Pressman's time in Pittsburgh, a friend, J.B.S. Hardman, who had been a teacher in Russia, wondered about Lenin. "Had there come a time, while he was signing the decrees ordering this man's death and that man's imprisonment, when he asked himself if the killing would ever stop?" Hardman noted the real shock on the Pressman's "hard young face." "Do you mean, J.B.," he said at last, "that you reject the terror?" Pressman's sharp legal mind and honed political instinct misjudged the tenor of the times in 1948. His decision to back Wallace's disastrous presidential campaign and to run himself for Congress, he described as a "miscalculation." In early 1948, the CIO executive board rejected the Wallace candidacy, despite support for the third party effort from eleven left-wing board members. Murray drew a line in the sand and three days later Pressman resigned. Murray Kempton observed: "For the first time in his public life, he (Pressman) displayed an emotion besides anger or cool indifference; he was crying and it could not have been entirely because he had lost his shield." Phil Murray was on his part so overcome with emotion that he would not step outside for a news picture.[102]

The Progressive Party initially stimulated real enthusiasm on the left. Its hopes for establishing a credible third party alternative by capturing 10% of the vote were undercut by Truman's stand against Taft-Hartley, his support for Civil Rights legislation and his support for Israel. These actions greatly reduced the Progressive Party's appeal among labor, blacks, and Jews – all critical constituencies for a left alternative. In addition, the imposition of an Iron Curtain across Central Europe was given dramatic demonstration in June 1948 as Stalin began the blockade of West Berlin, jointly administered by the Russians with American, British, and French zones, even though it lay 125 miles behind the military frontier between East and West Germany. Blocked by the Russians from using overland routes, the Americans and British began a dramatic airlift to supply West Berlin. Stalin's actions intensified the Cold War, strengthened Truman's candidacy, and steeled Murray's determination to move against the Communists in the labor movement.[103]

The importance of the struggle in Pittsburgh was recognized by all sides. Father Rice who had been pushing Murray to move against the Communist leadership of the UE for years, threw himself wholeheartedly into the struggle for control of UE 601. If the union was going to be purged of its Communist leadership from within as Rice had always wanted, then control of this Local 601's convention delegates was especially important. With financial assistance from Murray, he supported an anti-Communist UE activist, John Duffy, to staff the struggle. Rice enjoyed support among the pastors of the Turtle Creek, wrote a weekly column in the *Pittsburgh Catholic*, and had a weekly radio program. He also exchanged information on Communist activities with FBI agents who stopped by the House of Hospitality to "volunteer" or play ping-pong with the residents. He later publicly regretted these contacts but confessed to an enduring New Deal-based optimism about the reformability of the American system and its potential for good.[104]

The Communists responded to the threat in Pittsburgh with organizers from the national office, most notably Steve Nelson. Nelson, who was born Stjepan Mesaros in Croatia, immigrated to the United States in 1920 at the age of 17. Like many immigrants he held numerous jobs – in a slaughterhouse, as a carpenter, in a forge shop. Attracted first to the socialism of the Socialist Labor Party, he became converted to the Communist movement in 1923, because the party seemed to him committed to actually doing something about revolutionary change, not just talking about it. Shortly afterward, he moved to Pittsburgh where he became active with the Party's newspaper in the Turtle Creek Valley, the *Westinghouse Worker*, and with a party group at the Heinz plant. He met veterans of the Westinghouse strikes, including Fred Merrick and Communist leaders like Mother Bloor and William Z. Foster. He married a young Communist activist, Margaret Yaeger, who at 11 years of age had served lemonade to the 1916 Westinghouse strikers. Together they began a long dedicated organizing career that took them to Detroit, the anthracite coal fields of eastern Pennsylvania for a long stretch, with two years in Germany and Czechoslovakia just prior to Hitler's takeover, and then some years in California. In the summer of 1948, Nelson arrived back in Pittsburgh with his wife and two children.[105]

Nelson quickly grasped that the Progressive base was shrinking in Pittsburgh. With the Progressive Party collapse, anti-Communist repression was picking up force. Many Communist Party activists began to lose their jobs. Nelson estimated the number in the Pittsburgh area at over one hundred. An anti-Communist riot outside the Carnegie Library on Pittsburgh's North Side showed him how dangerous the climate was becoming. Nelson was chairing a meeting of several hundred party members and supporters to hear CP secretary Henry Winston speak about his trial under the Smith Act, when protestors numbering several thousand surrounded the building. Led by right-wing forces from UE 601, Catholic War Vets, American Legionaires, and others carrying signs that read "Uncle Sam's Vets vs. Stalin's Stooges," the demonstration degenerated into a mob supported by the police. People leaving the meeting were pushed and shoved, punches were thrown and a trolley window smashed.[106]

Liberal Democratic forces, which constituted the right-wing inside the union movements, were agitated by the news of the tightening Communist hold over eastern and central Europe. The Soviet occupation of eastern Poland in 1939 and subsequent annexation of the Baltic States deeply alienated the Polish and Lithuanian communities. The Soviet-engineered coup in Czechoslovakia brought the Communists to power in 1948 and increasing reports of Communist persecution of the Catholic Church in Croatia, Slovakia, Ukraine and Poland stimulated fierce anti-Communist feeling among ethnic groups that were very significant among the Western Pennsylvania working class. The two most famous of the eastern European prelate martyr/heroes were Croatian Archbishop Aloysius Stepinac and Hungarian Joseph Cardinal Mindszenty, who were imprisoned for their resistance to the Soviet-backed regimes. Ukrainian Catholic clergy who recognized the Pope were persecuted unless they renounced Rome and joined an Orthodox Church closely controlled by the Russian state. In the fall of 1948, the Italian community in Pittsburgh was also profoundly agitated by the possibility of a Communist victory in Italy's elections where the Communist Party was narrowly defeated.[107]

Religious persecution, plus the suppression of independent political parties and civil liberties by the Soviet occupiers of eastern and central Europe, handed anti-Communist labor leaders powerful weapons in their struggle with domestic leftists. Catholics, because of the international nature of their church, were often more deeply aware and concerned with areas of the world beyond the interest of the mainstream. This was especially true in regard to the intensely Catholic regions of central and eastern Europe. Both Catholicism and Communism had pretensions to universality. Catholics, who had been very critical of capitalism (especially the Pittsburgh variety) in the 1920s and 30s, dominated as it was by an anti-Catholic Presbyterian elite, were now confronted by a seemingly greater evil. The apocalyptic aspect of the struggle was enhanced by Communist expansion and the threat of nuclear annihilation. In September 1948, Mao Tse-tung proclaimed the People's Republic of China.

Then in September 1949, the Soviet Union tested an atomic bomb. Devotion to Our Lady of Fatima, who Catholics believed had appeared to three peasant children in Portugal, was widely promoted, in part because one of the prophecies she reportedly imparted to the children dealt with the ultimate conversion of Russia. Since the Catholic working-class constituency was essential for both the survival of the Democratic Party and the industrial union movement, mounting anti-Communist sentiment among important segments of blue collar workers could be ignored by neither. Furthermore, the fervor displayed in the anti-Communist crusade permitted Catholic labor and political leaders to seize the American flag out of the hands of the corporate establishment. Finally, the post-World War II baby boom and the improved standard of living brought by unionization and the G.I. Bill fueled a phenomenal growth in Catholic parishes, schools, and institutions. In comparison with the fate of their co-religionists behind the Iron Curtain, the Catholic position in a New Deal-reformed American capitalist society did not appear so bad.[108]

A key battle for the control of the UE became the August elections to the 1949 UE Convention that directly preceded the split in the CIO. Rice, in the most controversial action of his career, collaborated with the House Un-American Activities Committee (HUAC) to stage a hearing where four left-wing leaders and four right-wing leaders of UE 601 were called to Washington to testify. The entire affair was a set-up to influence the election in East Pittsburgh. The four right-wing leaders were gently handled, while the left-wing leaders were grilled mercilessly. Tom Quinn was not formally a Communist, but he had friends who were, who he respected and with whom he shared many views on working-class politics. In his testimony, he associated himself with Tom Fitzpatrick and Frank Panzino who had asserted the protection of the First and Fifth Amendments. He said that "the political beliefs, opinions and associations of the American people can be held secret if they so desire….I don't feel I am hiding behind the Constitution, but in this case standing before it, defending it, as small as I am." Despite being accused of nothing explicitly, except helping Negro girls in the plant who had experienced discrimination, Quinn would spend the next decade defending his honor and his freedom. His bitterest moment came when he confronted his old friend, the man he had worked so hard to elect, Congressman Harry Davenport of McKeesport, on the morning of his testimony, for some statement of support and received the legislator's cold brush-off: "You fellows have to clear yourselves."[109]

While the anti-Communist rank-and-file group won seven out of the nine delegate positions, Fitzpatrick and Panzino were elected despite screaming front page headlines in the Pittsburgh papers about their refusal to testify: "Fitzpatrick Silent on Reds in UE" (*Pittsburgh Press*). Tom Quinn won his election as a delegate to District 6 Council. Despite the right's delegate victory in East Pittsburgh, the left-wing forces maintained control of the national union at the convention by a three-to-two margin. The stage was set thereby for the expulsion of the UE and ten other left-wing unions at the CIO Convention in November.[110]

Steel Strike and CIO Split

The end of 1949 marked the decisive moment in Phil Murray's leadership of the American labor movement. During these months, he moved forcefully against the Communist-led labor unions, while at the same time leading a long and difficult negotiation and strike action against the steel industry. He managed to assert the centrality of class struggle in labor's relationship with capitalism (despite talk of partnership, relations remained deeply adversarial), while purging the significant faction of the organization that held class warfare or revolutionary goals. Charting a middle course, he rejected the cooperative labor-capital models of such intellectual advisors as Clint Golden and Harold Ruttenberg as good in the ideal, but impractical, in light of the deep anti-labor sentiment of business leaders. He also rejected the left revolutionary alternative as at once hopelessly impractical, given the deepening international crisis between the West and East and, morally repugnant, given Communism's anti-religious and anti-democratic tendencies. In the end, he chose to preserve unions as defensive structures protecting workers' rights on one hand, while aggressively demanding a share in the economic expansion of the capitalist system. He did this, however, without challenging the nature of the system or its increasingly aggressive role on the world stage. His course set the direction for the American labor movement for the next three decades.

While Murray's battles on the left are well documented, he had also long resisted completely embracing labor-management cooperation, especially the idea that unions should be engaged in employee involvement or in productivity gains-sharing proposals advocated by his staff members, Clint Golden, Joseph Scanlon, and Harold Ruttenberg. The goal of setting uniform standards and wages across an industry, pattern bargaining, was deeply engrained in Phil Murray's experience from bitter battles in coal and remained a consistent CIO goal in steel, auto, and other industries. This union strategy aims to take wages out of competition among businesses and is enshrined as a legal principle in Quebec and many European countries, where wage and benefit levels are set by negotiations between lead unions and companies and then extended by law throughout a particular industry. Both Murray and Brophy supported the idea of industrial councils and national planning, where the unions would share in decision-making power on matters of industry-wide and national importance, but business leadership was adamantly opposed. Phil Murray would most likely feel quite comfortable with present day European Union, tripartite, social-democratic labor relations practices.[111]

In 1945 and 1946, Ruttenberg engaged Murray in a long internal debate about the future of labor-management relations once the forced cooperation of the war effort ended. He argued wholeheartedly that Murray should use his great power to bring "the union and its members into participation in the management of their enterprises in which their livelihoods are intertwined." Ruttenberg and Golden both saw labor-management cooperation and worker participation as key to the survival of both unions and capitalism. Both left the union in the wake of the 1946 steel strike, Golden to teach at Harvard and Ruttenberg to practice his cooperative ideas from the management side as a vice-president of Portsmouth Steel Co. Murray had advocated worker participation ideas in the book he wrote with Morris Cooke. Ruttenberg argued that smaller firms needed relief from the USWA pattern and should be permitted to link wage and benefit increases to productivity. In the end, Murray's class consciousness made him feel much more comfortable with the egalitarian impulse behind pattern bargaining. Ruttenberg discerned in Murray a deeply felt antagonism toward the ruling class that was rooted in a religious sense of moral superiority based on his mission "to see that the workers and their families received their just due." So while Murray "set his face against the Brethren" and systematically purged the CIO of twenty-percent of its leftwing-led membership, he also nurtured an intense class consciousness and embraced labor's adversarial role inside capitalism – rejecting the company-union cooperative model proposed by some of his staff and which took hold in post-war Japan a decade later.[112]

While Ruttenberg was deeply disappointed Murray did not take up his worker participation crusade, he recognized that very few managers had expressed the slightest interest in worker participation. He reported Murray's retort: "Harold, I haven't found any of the steel moguls expressing any interest in sharing the management of their mills beyond the strict terms of our contracts. So the hell with them. They defend their management-prerogatives clause with a vengeance. We'll stick to our wage and benefits agenda, and contract after contract, we'll win gains for our members way beyond their expectations." Additionally, Murray told him: "If there is one thing that we have won and accomplished, it is our moral right to exist. We are recognized as well by law for having the moral right and obligation to promote the welfare of our people. This is our strength. No one can take it away from us."[113]

The 1949 CIO Convention opened in Cleveland on October 31, 1949. Murray, one month into a nationwide steel strike, responded in his opening speech to attacks from the Communist press accusing him of the betrayal of the principles of Franklin D. Roosevelt, as well as the betrayal of the working class on behalf of Wall Street. Murray attacked his critics: "Leaders of unions who wish to be judged as responsible men have accused your president of subservience to corporate interests; of selling out the interests of the American workers; of race baiting; of company unionism; of repudiation of the democratic principles to which your President, through all the years of his life, has remained steadfastly loyal." On the second day of the convention, the UE, failing to receive a commitment from Murray to end raiding of the UE by CIO affiliates, refused to pay their per-capita dues and consequently refused to take their seats at the convention. This prompted convention action to expel the UE and issue a charter to the International Union of Electrical, Radio and Machine Workers (CIO) headed by James Carey. With the powerful UE quitting before they could be expelled, the remaining, smaller, left-wing unions were left with few defenses.[114]

Immediately following the convention, the now totally non-Communist CIO executive board ordered hearings to be held on the ten CIO unions that consistently followed the Communist Party line, including two large organizations: the International Longshoremen's and Warehousemen's Union and the militant Mine, Mill and Smelter Workers International Union. The Longshoremen's Harry Bridges refused to quit and demanded to be kicked-out. He conducted a vigorous defense before what everyone acknowledged as a "kangaroo court," whose verdict was set before the hearing. By the mid-1950s, unions claiming more than a million members, a quarter of the CIO's membership, had been excised from the organization.[115]

While the major drama of the left-wing union expulsions was occurring in Cleveland, Phil Murray was a month deep into a national steel strike for health insurance and pensions. Murray, with Walter Reuther of the autoworkers, the United Rubber Workers, and others were advancing CIO contract demands on these issues. In September the United Autoworkers won a company-funded pension plan from Ford with a defined-benefit reflecting years of service. After the steel industry turned down the recommendations of a fact-finding board named by President Truman supported union pension and benefit demands, Murray ordered the mills shut down on October 1, 1949. At the end of the third week of the strike, Bethlehem Steel broke ranks with U.S. Steel's leadership of negotiations and agreed to grant pensions and benefits. When Murray mounted the platform at the Cleveland CIO Convention to launch his attack on the left-led unions, he was at the peak of his power and prestige. David McDonald, his longtime secretary and also the secretary-treasurer of the USWA, grasped the historical significance of the moment perhaps clearer than Murray, who was so deeply burdened with historical memory and philosophical anguish. McDonald saw the future of the institutionalized labor relations that he came to epitomize:

> We were no longer fighting a class war with management. Labor's purpose and function had generally been accepted by the American business community, and we were ready to go on to bigger and better things for the American workingman – things that would be delayed and perhaps be lost completely if we were to tolerate any longer the hate tactics of the Communists. This point couldn't have been better dramatized than the breakthrough in pensions and insurance with the steel companies just before the Communist expulsion took place.[116]

Breakthroughs in securing company-funded benefits and pensions undoubtedly represented important working-class advances. Union gains in manufacturing trickled down and spread out to many other workers, including managers and service, technical and professional workers. A strong middle class emerged in the Pittsburgh region based on union wages and benefits that largely became the standard for many non-union employees. These victories were real but limited, however. The inability of the CIO to gain sufficient political backing for an expanded Social Security program that would provide medical benefits and pensions for all forced the unions to settle for coverage for their members through employer-based plans. Linking pensions and health care to employment became increasingly problematic to labor, industry, and the government as the century wore on and an American industry in decline was saddled with shrinking employment and ballooning health and pension costs. In addition, the purging of the left-led industrial unions weakened labor, both in numbers, but perhaps more dangerously in critical spirit. With organized labor increasingly institutionalized as a junior partner in American capitalism, the system could insulate itself from critical evaluation as long as it provided the goods that workers were increasingly coming to expect.

Notes Chapter 11

[1]Ronald W. Schatz, *The Electrical Workers: A History of Labor at General Electric and Westinghouse, 1923-1960* (Urbana and Chicago: University of Illinois, 1983), 83-92.

[2]Ronald L. Fillippelli and Mark McColloch, *Cold War in the Working Class: The Rise and Decline of the United Electrical Workers* (Albany: State University of New York Press, 1995), 30-32.

[3]Schatz, *The Electrical Workers*, 93-99.

[4]Shatz, *The Electrical Workers*, 63-64; Filipelli and McColloch, *Cold War in the Working Class*, 39-41.

[5]Filipelli and McColloch, *Cold War in the Working Class*, 44-57.

[6]Filippelli and McColloch, *Cold War in the Working Class.*

[7]Filippelli and McColloch, *Cold War in the Working Class*, 6-10.

[8]Charles Owen Rice, *Fighter With a Heart: Charles Owen Rice, Pittsburgh Labor Priest*, ed. Charles McCollester (Pittsburgh: University of Pittsburgh Press, 1996), 64.

[9]Filippelli and McColloch, *Cold War in the Working Class*, 55-60.; Saul Alinsky, *John L. Lewis: An Unauthorized Biography* (New York: G.P. Putnam's Sons, 1949), 206.

[10]Alinsky, *John L. Lewis*, 206.

[11]Alinsky, *John L. Lewis*, 225-237.

[12]*Pittsburgh Press*, September 13, 1946; *Pittsburgh Sun-Telegraph*, July 24, 1942; *Pittsburgh Press*, December 20, 1940; *Pittsburgh Sun-Telegraph*, May 9, 1943.

[13]"Launching LSTs: Pittsburgh shipbuilders produced workhorse of the Navy," *Pittsburgh Tribune Review, Focus*, August 12, 2001.

[14]*Pittsburgh Post-Gazette*, June 24, 1943; July 3, 1944.

[15]*Pittsburgh Post-Gazette*, March 10, 1944; *Pittsburgh Sun-Times*, August 10, 1959, *Pittsburgh Post-Gazette*, December 20, 2007.

[16] David Love, *Frank Bolden: The Man Behind the Words*, A Multi-Cultural Initiative Film, 2001.

[17]Love, *Frank Bolde.*

[18] WQED documentary film, *Fly Boys: Western Pennsylvania's Tuskegee Airmen*, WQED Mutimedia, 2008.

[19]*Pittsburgh in the Nation's Crisis*, 1-5.

[20]William Serrin, *Homestead: The Glory and the Tragedy of an American Steel Town* (New York: Random House, 1992), 222; *Pittsburgh in the Nation's Crisis*, 5.

[21]Kenneth Warren, *Big Steel: The First Century of the United States Steel Corporation, 1901-2001* (Pittsburgh: University of Pittsburgh Press, 2001), 193-195; Frank C. Harper, *Men and Women of Wartime Pittsburgh and Environs: A War-Production Epic*, (Pittsburgh, 1945), 23.

[22]Serrin, *Homestead*, 116-120.

[23] Ed Sninsky, "Boyhood in the Final Years of Lower Homestead," *Portal to the Past: Homestead & Mifflin Township Historical Society*, December, 2005, 5(12).

[24]Warren, *Big Steel*, 196-197; Harper, *Men and Women of Wartime Pittsburgh*, 18-19, 34.

[25]*Post-Gazette*, May 6, 1943.

[26]David H. Wollman and Donald R. Inman, *Portraits in Steel: An Illustrated History of Jones & Laughlin Steel Corporation* (Kent, Ohio: The Kent State University Press, 1999), 121-129.

[27]Butler County Historical Society, "Bantam Car/Jeep," <www.butlercountyhistoricalsociety-pa.org/bantam.html>.

[28]Harper, *Men and Women of Wartime Pittsburgh and Environs*, 103-111.

[29]Harper, *Men and Women of Wartime Pittsburgh and Environs*. 121-139; *Post-Gazette*, February 11, 1943; "Launching LSTs: Pittsburgh shipbuilders produced workhorse of the Navy," *Pittsburgh Tribune Review, Focus*, August 12, 2001; Julia Love, *Women in the Wings: Pittsburgh's World War II Workers*, Documentary video, Carnegie Library of Pittsburgh.

[30]Harper, *Men and Women of Wartime Pittsburgh and Environs*, 73-89; David O. Woodbury, *Battlefronts of Industry: Westinghouse in World War II* (New York: John Wiley, 1948), 161-175.

[31]*Sun-Telegraph*, April 25, 1943.

[32]Westinghouse Electric Corporation, *History for Heavy Shop Activities*, Gear Department (June 30, 1945), 26. Heinz History Center Archives, Box 209, Folder 1.

[33]Harper, *Men and Women of Wartime Pittsburgh and Environs*, 91-101, 199.

[34]Schatz, *The Electrical Workers*, 30-33; 120-121; Amalgamated Transit Union Staff, *ATU 100 Years: A History of the Amalgamated Transit Union*, (Amalgamated Transit Union, 1992).

[35]Dennis C. Dickerson, *Out of the Crucible: Black Steelworkers in Western Pennsylvania, 1875-1980* (Albany: State University of New York Press, 1986), 151-159.

[36]Merle E. Reed, "Black Workers, Defense Industries, and Federal Agencies in Pennsylvania, 1941-1945," *Labor History*, 27 (June 1986), 356-384.

[37]Dickerson, *Out of the Crucible*, 164-172; David McDonald, *Union Man* (New York: E.P. Dutton & Co., 1969), 201.

[38]Alinsky, *John L. Lewis*, 238-241.

[39]Alinsky, *John L. Lewis*, 242-247.

[40]Alinsky, *John L. Lewis*, 249-254.

[41]Alinsky, *John L. Lewis*, 254-271.

[42]McDonald, *Union Man*, 161; Pat Fagan, *Interview* by Alice Hoffman, (September 24, 1968).

[43]John Brophy, *A Miner's Life* (Madison and Milwaukee: The University of Wisconsin Press, 1964), 288.

[44]Alinsky, *John L. Lewis*, 273-275; Pat Fagan, *Interview*, by Alice Hoffman, October 8, 1968.

[45]Alinsky, *John L. Lewis*, 281-286, 300-307.

[46]Alinsky, *John L. Lewis*, 318-324.

[47]Murray Kempton, *Part of Our Time: Some Ruins and Monuments of the Thirties* (New York: Modern Library, 1998), 79, 93.

[48]Nelson Lichtenstein, *Labor's War at Home: The CIO in World War II* (Cambridge: Cambridge University Press, 1982), 40-43.

[49]Lichtenstein, *Labor's War at Home*, 44-75.

[50]Lichtenstein, *Labor's War at Home*, 76-81.

[51]*Sun-Telegraph*, June 8, 1944.

[52]Lichtenstein, *Labor's War at Home*, 82-83; 89-95.

[53]Lichtenstein, *Labor's War at Home*, 178-181.

[54]*Post-Gazette*, May 8, 1945.

[55]Michael P. Weber, *Don't Call Me Boss: David L. Lawrence, Pittsburgh's Renaissance Mayor*, (Pittsburgh: University of Pittsburgh Press, 1988), 156-162; 181-187; Merle Miller, *Plain Speaking: An Oral Biography of Harry Truman*, (New York: G.P. Putnam's Sons, 1973).

[56]Weber, *Don't Call Me Boss*, 187-196; Roy Lubove, *Twentieth-Century Pittsburgh: Government, Business, and Environmental Change* (Pittsburgh: University of Pittsburgh Press, 1995), 106.

[57]Lubove, *Twentieth-Century Pittsburgh*, 106-108.

[58]Lubove, *Twentieth-Century Pittsburgh*, 108-112.

[59]Charles J.V. Murphy, *The Mellons of Pittsburgh* (Fortune Magazine reprint of three-part series in October, November, December issues, 1967), 24.

[60]Murphy, *The Mellons of Pittsburgh*, 17-22; In more recent times, Vice-President Dick Cheney visited the preserve several times and indulged his passion for shooting birds on one occasion by killing 70 stocked pheasants and a large number of mallard ducks in a single day's "hunt." In total 417 pheasants were killed by the ten "hunters" in Cheney's group. *Pittsburgh Post-Gazette*, December 9, 2003. A radio report mentioned that the birds were then freeze dried and packaged for Republican fundraisers. Wayne Pacelle, a senior vice president of the Humane Society, stated: "This wasn't a hunting ground. It was an open-air abattoir."

[61]Murphy, *The Mellons of Pittsburgh*, 28-33; William S. Hoffman, *Paul Mellon: Portrait of an Oil Baron* (Chicago: Follett Publishing, 1974), 112.

[62]Weber, *Don't Call Me Boss*, 218.

[63]Weber, *Don't Call Me Boss*, 232-238.

[64]Weber, *Don't Call Me Boss*, 238-239.

[65]Lubove, *Twentieth-Century Pittsburgh*, 122-123; Weber, *Don't Call Me Boss*, 255-264.

[66]Sherie R. Mershon and Joel A. Tarr, "Strategies for Clean Air: The Pittsburgh and Allegheny Smoke Control Movements, 1940-1960," *Devastation and Renewal: An Environmental History of Pittsburgh and its Region* (Pittsburgh, University of Pittsburgh Press, 2003), 163-169: Michael Weber, *Don't Call Me Boss*, 248-252.

[67]Weber, *Don't Call Me Boss*, 240-247; Charles O. Jones, *Clean Air: The Policies and Politics of Pollution Control* (Pittsburgh, University of Pittsburgh Press, 1978), 42-49. Jones calls the Pittsburgh approach an example of "disjointed incrementalism."

[68]Lynne Page Snyder, "Revisiting Donora, Pennsylvania's 1948 Air Pollution Disaster," *Devastation and Renewal: An Environmental History of Pittsburgh and Its Region* (Pittsburgh, University of Pittsburgh Press, 2003), 129-130; A more extensive account of Donora and the struggle between the public health community and powerful corporate interests over the response to the murderous effects of environmental pollution can be found in Devra Davis, *When Smoke Ran Like Water: Tales of Environmental Deception and the Battle Against Pollution*, (New York: Basic Books, 2002).

[69]Snyder, "Revisiting Donora, Pennsylvania's 1948 Air Pollution Disaster," 129-131; Davis, *When Smoke Ran Like Water*, 5-16.

[70]Thomas Bell, *Out of This Furnace*, (Pittsburgh, University of Pittsburgh Press, 1976), 356-357.

[71]Snyder, "Revisiting Donora, Pennsylvania's 1948 Air Pollution Disaster," 132-133; Davis, *When Smoke Ran Like Water*, 15-30.

[72]Snyder, "Revisiting Donora, Pennsylvania's 1948 Air Pollution Disaster," 135-144.

[73] John Hoerr, *And the Wolf Finally Came: The Decline of the American Steel Industry*, (Pittsburgh: University of Pittsburgh Press, 1988), 106.

[74]McDonald, *Union Man*, 178.

[75] John McCollister, *The Bucs!: The Story of the Pittsburgh Pirates* (Lenexa Kansas: Addax Publishing Group, 1998), 122-133; Richard F. Peterson, "Rinky Dinks and the Single Wing," *Pittsburgh Sports: Stories from the Steel City*, ed. Randy Roberts, (Pittsburgh: University of Pittsburgh Press, 2000), 31; Jim Reisler, *The Best Game Ever: Pirates vs. Yankees, October 13, 1960*, (New York, DaCapo Press), 140-144.

[76] Abby Mendelson, *The Pittsburgh Steelers: The Official Team History* (Dallas: Taylor Trade Press. 1996), 33-35; 131-133; Dan Rooney (as told to Andrew E. Masich and David F. Halaas), *My 75 Years with the Pittsburgh Steelers and the NFL*, (New York: Da Capo Press, 2007), 31, 36-37.

[77] James A. Kehl, "Peace Dividend: The Ellsworth Center Experience," *Pittsburgh Post-Gazette*, September 30, 2007.

[78] Weber, *Don't Call Me Boss*, 218-222; Rice, *Fighter With a Heart*, 71-75.

[79] *Fortune*, February, 1947, 69.

[80] Weber, *Don't Call Me Boss*, 223-224.

[81] *Pittsburgh Press*, September 26, 27, 1946.

[82] Weber, *Don't Call Me Boss*, 225-226.

[83] Rice, *Fighter With a Heart*, 76.

[84] Andy Johnson, *Interview* by Charles McCollester, (November 20, 1990).

[85] Marilyn Uricchio, "Jimmy Stewart, 89: A Wonderful Life," *Pittsburgh Post-Gazette*, July 3, 1997: reprinted in *Pittsburgh Lives: Men and Women Who Shaped Our City*, ed. David M. Schribman and Angelika Kane (Chicago: Triumph Books, 2006), 171-175.

[86] James M. Cahalan, *Edward Abbey, A Life*, (Tucson: University of Arizona Press, 2001), 3-51.

[87] Marcia Davenport, *The Valley of Decision*, (Pittsburgh: University of Pittsburgh Press, 1989), viii; David R. Demarest, Jr., *From These Hills, From These Valleys: Selected Fiction About Western Pennsylvania*, (Pittsburgh: University of Pittsburgh Press, 1976), 84. Aside from his friendship over many years, I am indebted to David Demarest for his comments on Davenport's novel that introduces an excerpt from the book in this collection. Ironically, it is he who judges Davenport's novel to be the "best-known single novel about the Pittsburgh region" in the very year that he succeeded in getting Bell's great novel reissued.

[88] Jane Daggett Dillenberger, *The Religious Art of Andy Warhol* (New York: Continuum, 1998), 17-25; Victor Bockris, *The Life and Death of Andy Warhol* (New York: Bantam Books, 1989), 6-38.

[89] Bockris, *The Life and Death of Andy Warhol*, 41-100; David Bourdon, "Warhol Interviews Bourdon, 1962-63," in *I'll Be Your Mirror: The Selected Andy Warhol Interviews*, ed. Kenneth Goldsmith (New York: Da Capo Press, 2004).

[90] The subject of the anti-Communist crusade in Pittsburgh has long deeply interested the present author. As a Chief Steward of UE 610 and a friend of Msgr. Rice for the last three decades of his long and extraordinary life, the meaning and consequences of this period have been often on my mind. Two recent books shed new light on this issue and I am indebted to both. The first is *Harry Tom and Father Rice*, by John Hoerr which I had the honor of reading in manuscript form. The second, *Cold War at Home: The Red Scare in Pennsylvania, 1945-1960* by Philip Jenkins published in 1999, only came to my attention while writing this chapter. Both books provide new and balanced analysis of the crisis of unionism and the Democratic Party during this period that has proved valuable. Hoerr's book is a powerful evocation of the terrible personal toll that the period exacted on many innocent and some not so "innocent" people.

[91] Philip Jenkins, *The Cold War at Home: The Red Scare in Pennsylvania, 1945-1960* (Chapel Hill: University of North Carolina Press, 1999), 50.

[92] Harry A. Levenstein, *Communism, Anticommunism and the CIO* (Westport, Connecticut: Greenwood Press, 1981), 184-190.

[93] Jenkins, *Cold War at Home*, 100-101; Steve Nelson, James R. Barrett, Rob Ruck, *Steve Nelson, American Radical* (Pittsburgh: University of Pittsburgh Press, 1981), 299.

[94] Jenkins, *Cold War at Home*, 106-107.

[95] John Hoerr, *Harry, Tom, and Father Rice: Accusation and Betrayal in America's Cold War* (Pittsburgh: University of Pittsburgh Press, 2005), 71; The author experienced UE shop floor democracy first hand as a UE 610 third-shift and second-shift machine shop steward, then chief steward at the Union Switch & Signal plant in Swissvale between 1979 and 1986.

[96] Schatz, *The Electrical Workers*, 189-190.

[97] Schatz, *The Electrical Workers*, 194-195.

[98] Schatz, *The Electrical Workers*, 181.

[99] Robert H. Zeiger, *The CIO, 1935-1955* (Chapel Hill: The University of North Carolina Press, 1995), 264-270.

[100] Schatz, *The Electrical Workers*, 178-179; Rice, *Fighter With a Heart*, 68; Len De Caux, *Labor Radical: From the Wobblies to the CIO, A Personal History* (Boston: Beacon Press, 1970), 482.

[101] Kempton, *Part of Our Time*, 94.

[102] Kempton, *Part of Our Time*, 80, 96; Gil Gall, *Pursuing Justice: Lee Pressman, the New Deal, and the CIO* (Albany, State University of New York Press, 1999), 230-233.

[103] Nelson, Barrett, & Ruck, *Steve Nelson*, 301.

[104] Rice, *Fighter With a Heart*, 96-106.

[105]Nelson et al., *Steve Nelson*, 21-28.

[106]Nelson et al., *Steve Nelson*, 303-304.

[107] Jenkins, *Cold War at Home*, 144-149; 172-173; Schatz, *The Electrical Workers*, 182-183.

[108]Jenkins, *Cold War at Home*, 170-172.

[109]Schatz, *The Electrical Workers*, 202; Hoerr, *Harry, Tom, and Father Rice*, 152-161.

[110]Hoerr, *Harry, Tom, and Father Rice*, 163-167.

[111]Brophy, *A Miner's Life*, 299-300.

[112]Harold J. Ruttenberg, *My Life in Steel: From CIO to CEO* (Tarentum: Word Association Publishers, 2001), 72-83; Hoerr, *And the Wolf Finally Came*, 262-288.

[113]Ruttenberg, *My Life in Steel*, 81-84.

[114]Levenstein, *Communism, Anticommunism and the CIO*, 298-302.

[115]McDonald, *Union Man*, 211; *CIO, 1935-1955: Industrial Democracy in Action* (Washington D.C.: Industrial Union Department, AFL-CIO, 1955), 2nd edition. 61-62.

[116]McDonald, *Union Man*, 211.

Chapter Twelve

The Flowering of the Mill Town

After the deprivation of the Great Depression, the enormous sacrifices of the Second World War, and the bitter union divisions that followed, the Pittsburgh working-class experienced a dramatic increase in prosperity and social well-being during the 1950s. While political dissent was suppressed and the black community remained marginalized despite substantial achievements, the period witnessed an explosion of activity and energy that was truly extraordinary. The post-World War II economic prosperity in Pittsburgh was driven by union wages and the G.I. Bill. Union wage increases as a result of the 1946 strike and in subsequent labor contracts to millions of industrial and craft workers stimulated the consumer economy and helped redirect military production toward acute human and material infrastructure needs.

Prosperity and its Perils

With the gains of the 1940s and 1950s, industrial workers for the first time had significant disposable income. The working class won improvements for many beyond their ranks as advances in wages, pensions and health insurance, sick days and vacations helped define a middle-class standard of living. The rising prosperity of the industrial worker created opportunity for diverse small businesses, stimulated improvements to residential and commercial real estate, and spurred consumer goods production. Tax policy under Roosevelt hit the rich with a progressive income tax that made enormous governmental spending for both war and peace possible.

The G.I. Bill, by providing generous opportunities to veterans for education and training, enriched society as a whole by developing the human capital necessary to adapt to a changing labor market. The G.I. Bill also acted as a social shock absorber, substituting subsidized education for unemployment. Institutions of higher learning expanded greatly but also had their elitist pretensions challenged. Classrooms were democratized as huge numbers of the working classes had an opportunity for higher education for the first time. Far from being a drag on educational standards, educators unanimously agreed that veterans actually raised standards and undermined ingrained prejudices about low-income students, married, and older students. Students who had fought on Omaha Beach or Tarawa, who had been part of the liberation of Paris or of a Nazi concentration camp not surprisingly added a great deal to the educational experience of newly minted high school students.

Of course the benefits of union wages and the educational opportunities for wartime service did not extend equally to everyone. Black veterans began to push against the historic barriers erected against them in education with more success than in housing. While black veterans embraced educational benefits at the same levels as their white counterparts, most directed their efforts toward vocational training, though historically black colleges experienced a boom in enrollments as well. Home loans showed the greatest racial disparity, since the Veterans Administration was not allowed to make loans directly as the Roosevelt administration had intended and could only act as the guarantor of the loans. Banks and other local financial institutions were free to preserve the existing patterns of racial exclusion and did so. Furthermore, the exclusion of war workers from the program's benefits meant that women were largely left outside the G.I. Bill's direct impact. Women were expected to return to the home and most did or were forced to do so. The positive impact for women came through the expansion of the middle class and especially in the next generation for the children of the G.I. Bill veterans, as the possibility of a college education became a possibility for both male and female children.[1]

Internationally, business growth accompanied the expansion of American military power. Containment of Soviet power, and the instabilities engendered by nationalist struggles against the weakened colonial powers of Europe, provided the justification for a permanently enlarged military establishment. While military production slackened from the extraordinary wartime levels, it never faded away like it had after World War I. The treatment of the veteran after the Second World War also stood in sharp contrast to the deferral of the World War I veterans' bonus and the brutal suppression of the Bonus Army on the streets of the nation's capitol. Franklin D. Roosevelt strongly supported expansive new veterans' benefits in his final campaign for the presidency, seeing them as an initial step toward establishing a broader employment, training, disability, and housing program for all Americans. While his dream was never realized in the postwar Republican-controlled Congress, the G.I. Bill had an enormous ripple effect, reaching further and deeper into American life than anyone expected. The G.I. Bill generated two million new homes in 1950 alone, 85 percent of them single-family houses, most in new developments that spawned new schools and the material infrastructure to support the burgeoning new communities. The "baby boom" peaked in 1957 with 4.3 million births, a rate 50 percent above 1939 and double the birth rate of 2001. While this growth was served by the market, it was driven by federal government policy.[2]

In Pittsburgh, the post-war rise in industrial wages was mirrored by contract improvements won by union building trades in the course of the massive construction projects of the Pittsburgh "Renaissance." Construction work was plentiful, union apprenticeship programs expanded and training facilities were improved. On May 18, 1950, a one-ton wrecking ball smashed into a 103 year-old red brick warehouse amidst the tangle of dilapidated industrial and commercial buildings that covered the Point. In attendance was a crowd of 2,000 including school children, the Carnegie

Tech band and the University of Pittsburgh ROTC band. Over the next decade, Gateway Center emerged, a corporate office park on what had been at the turn of the century, a hub of the city's social and cultural life. In those days, three giant structures, Exposition Hall, Mechanical Hall, and the Music Hall, had brought masses of people to the Point. The adjacent warehouse and transportation activity there helped support a network of small businesses, but the whole area suffered greatly during the 1936 flood when water reached the second story of some buildings. While much of the district was deteriorated, over eighty buildings occupied the site and many still housed viable and some even thriving businesses. Among them was the elegant Mayflower Hotel, built in 1895 as the Lincoln Hotel, that boasted a rooftop restaurant and a popular basement lounge, the Bradford Grill. The idea of condemning viable private businesses made many people uncomfortable, but the array of forces supporting the development was overwhelming. The Urban Redevelopment Authority with eminent domain powers was established to carry out development projects in the city.[3]

Gateway Center took shape as a vast corporate headquarters park with three twenty to twenty-four story cruciform, stainless steel buildings. These were flanked by a new state office building and a Hilton Hotel. The historian of Pittsburgh planning, Roy Lubove, wrote that the central business district "is being transformed into an enormous filing cabinet, which operates between the hours of 9-5. The expressionless stainless-steel facades of the Gateway offices towered over fenced-in grass and walks: no shops, no entertainment, no restaurants of note, no nightlife." Two more skyscrapers were constructed further uptown. The stainless steel U.S. Steel-Mellon Bank Building was squeezed between the stately classical Mellon Bank headquarters and the flamboyant Flemish-Gothic Union Trust building. The Alcoa building, a distinctive, aluminum-clad building facing Mellon Square was erected on the former site of the popular Nixon Theater. Lawrence and the URA, with the support of Phil Murray, assisted in the expansion of the J&L mill into a steelworker neighborhood in the South Side. Sixty-one working-class houses and several small shops were condemned to facilitate the building of six new open hearth furnaces. Later, J&L took over the Hazelwood community of Scotch Bottoms to expand their Coke operations on the north side of the river. The courts upheld URA eminent domain actions under the theory that individual interests must give way to the common good. In Pittsburgh the corporate agenda went a long way toward defining the common good.[4]

A dramatic example of urban renewal that ignored the concerns and needs of poor people was the Civic Arena project that eradicated the teeming Lower Hill District to erect a civic auditorium with a retractable roof meant to house the Civic Light Opera, a pet project of J. Edgar Kaufmann. While the Lower Hill was the poorest section of the city, it was also the heart and soul of black cultural and commercial life. Demolition began in 1956 and displaced 1,551, mostly black, families and 413 businesses. Where the area had been a locale where white money entered the black community, the vast expanse of concrete roads and parking lots around the new arena now isolated the Upper Hill community from the downtown. In addition, the acoustics of the hall were poor and the retractable roof expensive to operate and maintain. On the North Side, a major urban renewal disaster ripped the heart out of downtown Old Allegheny to put in the Allegheny Center Mall surrounded by a wide circle of concrete roadway. Among the jewels sacrificed to this box mall perched over a massive parking garage was the old Allegheny City Market House. This Romanesque stone-arched structure had been built in 1863 and was one of the finest 19th Century market buildings in the country. Its completely undistinguished successor floundered, never able to compete with suburban shopping malls.[5]

The Pittsburgh renaissance was a bonanza for the construction unions, however. In addition to all the downtown construction, hospital and university expansion in Oakland, the building of the Parkway East, the construction of the Fort Duquesne Bridge and Fort Pitt Bridge and Tunnel provided a seemingly endless flow of well-paid jobs. The massive construction projects helped strengthen the unionized trades as their extensive network of union training centers expanded to keep up with the evolution of construction techniques. Technological change was impacting the way the trades did their work. For the ironworkers who erected the high iron, cranes were steadily getting bigger and with more stable hydraulic supports could reach much higher than the stiff-legged derricks used previously, that were only able to reach two floors at a time. In the mid-1950s, high tensile bolts began replacing rivets in construction. For generations, four man rivet crews composed of the heater, the catcher, the riveter and the bucker-up were essential to the trade.[6] Electrical systems became more complex as the load requirements steadily increased. Union electrician Irv Grunebach cited the union training programs as the main draw that the unions exercised on him as a young worker for a non-union company in the late 1940s.

> It was just remarkable, the education and training the union people had over us non-union people in the field, because we weren't trained. We just learned from our mistakes. Here with the union, we had experience, we had knowledge, we had history, we had education. This was all coming from the union….I came from a non-union outfit where there were no safety standards, nothing, no regulation whatsoever – not on ladders, not on height, not on equipment. Bad equipment, tools, you had to use what you had, no matter what it was. The union set standards where your tools had to be safe. This was before OSHA….As electricians, we all felt that we had to be just a bit safer than any other trade, because this electricity could hit you and the next thing you know you're either dead or laying in the hospital for quite a few years.[7]

Out in the mill towns as well, there was an explosion of economic opportunity as increased industrial wages spilled over into the community. While young mill workers used their newly achieved affluence to climb up out of the industrial valleys and move to newly expanded suburbs like Penn Hills, West Mifflin, and White Oak, the old river towns flourished with packed bars and restaurants that operated around the clock all year long to accommodate the mill workers. Newly won pensions and Social Security checks gave independence and a measure of prosperity to the retirees who stayed in the old neighborhoods. The bustling commercial districts of the mill towns remained the shopping districts for many suburbanites until the 1960s brought major new shopping centers like the Monroeville Mall. The mills had materially helped win the wars and, with the cold war settling in, military expenditure was becoming a quasi-permanent feature of national life. Why wouldn't the mills be there forever? In Homestead there were three theaters, including the beautiful Leona that booked national stage acts and first-run movies. Along Eighth Avenue there were five furniture, seven appliance, and five "five-and-dime" stores: Woolworth, Newberry, Grants, McCrory, and Wheelwright. When the shift changes occurred at the mill, the streets were flooded with people and this street life continued virtually around the clock. Many workers who worked the "graveyard" night shift started their after-work drinking at 7 a.m. The dust, grit, and pollution was accepted and even celebrated as the price of prosperity.[8]

Author John Hoerr, who came of age in the McKeesport of the late 1940s, described the Mon Valley on the verge of its period of greatest prosperity:

In 1948, 718 retail establishments in McKeesport grossed $73 million, a large sum in the pre-Korean war period of low inflation. Braddock's 319 businesses brought in $32 million that year. Homestead ranked third with $21 million…. McKeesport had four movie houses, offering productions that ranged from Busby Berkeley musicals and other first-run films, which were shown in the elaborately ornate Memorial Theater, to Saturday morning serials featuring the evil Fu Man Chu, which were viewed by foot-pounding kids in the shabby Capital. Braddock had two or three movie houses, and Stahl's Theater in Homestead was said to be the first $1 million movie theater in the nation.

All kinds of sports were popular, but high school football was the focus of attention. The Saturday afternoon or Friday night game was the big event of the week for the entire town. Huge crowds packed McKeesport's football field on a hill overlooking downtown, and the roar of fans resounded for miles around. After the game, we walked down the hill, exhilarated by the cool night air, as cars filled with chanting kids went skidding down the brick streets. There were soda fountains and ice cream parlors with juke boxes in those days, and we would pile into the booths and talk about the game, as we sipped cokes and milk shakes and kept an eye peeled for girls.[9]

Not only business prospered. Churches were nearly as numerous as saloons in the steel towns. Since the industrial working class was predominantly Catholic and large families still the norm, prosperity fueled the rapid expansion of the Catholic school system. Solidly constructed schools, convents, rectories, and elaborate social halls were constructed. The Orthodox and African-American communities also erected institutional expressions of their relative prosperity. The churches were the incubators of family life, but the mill towns still retained their "wide open" and anything-goes quality. Down by the mill along Sixth Street in Homestead, the red light district offered drugs and available women. Nearly every mill town had a red light district. Homestead's was well known as were those in Steubenville and Wheeling. Perhaps the most famous of all the prostitution districts was Brick Alley in McKeesport. Like many of the red light districts, the women who worked in the houses along one side of Brick Alley a couple of blocks up from the Youghiogheny River were mostly black. By the 1960s, white high school students would drive down the alley on prom night with their dates to the catcalls of the women. Many young working-class men were initiated to the mysteries of life in these establishments.[10]

In Pittsburgh itself, corporate redevelopment goals drove the agenda for the Democratic administration of David Lawrence during the decade of the 1950s. While Lawrence had worked hard for the social and labor reforms of Pennsylvania's "Little New Deal" in the 1930s, social concerns were never a significant part of any Lawrence campaign after the war. Redevelopment improved the environmental and physical infrastructure of the city and provided employment. Political campaigns were targeted toward "finishing the job." Maintaining the effort and sustaining the vision of renewal generated widespread support. A major social problem was emerging, however. While skilled craft workers and the industrial working class were experiencing rising prosperity, the black community was falling behind. While black industrial workers were sharing in the union-driven wage increases and some blacks achieved decent public sector employment through political influence, African-Americans remained largely employed in low-paying jobs such as janitors and cleaning ladies. The exclusion of blacks from most of the construction craft unions meant they were largely unaffected by the building and construction boom with the exception of dangerous and low-pay demolition work. Douglas Anderson, trained as an electrician in the Navy during World War II, attempted unsuccessfully to enter IBEW Local 5 in the 1940s and again in the 1950s. He was finally admitted as the first black electrician in the local in the mid-1960s. Furthermore, since urban renewal projects targeted the poor and rundown areas where blacks lived, while restrictive residential housing practices blocked the movement of blacks into white neighborhoods, social pressures on the black community steadily increased. In 1957, Robert R. Lavelle sued the Greater Pittsburgh Multi-List for their exclusion of black realtors, thereby keeping blacks within tightly defined areas. It took ten years, but in 1967 Lavelle's suit in federal court was settled favorably opening the way for black realtors nationwide.[11]

August Wilson, one of America's greatest playwrights, growing up in the Hill District during the 1950s, a period that he treated in his play *Fences*, reflected on the differing fates of the children of the immigrants who passed through the Hill on their way to better neighborhoods and the members of the largely marginalized black community who remained.

> Near the turn of the century, the destitute of Europe sprang on the city with tenacious claws and an honest and solid dream. The city devoured them. They swelled its belly until it burst into a thousand furnaces and sewing machines, a thousand butcher shops and baker's ovens, a thousand churches and hospitals and funeral parlors and moneylenders. The city grew. It nourished itself and offered each man a partnership limited only by his talent, his guile, and his willingness for hard work. For the immigrants of Europe, a dream dared and won true.
>
> The descendants of African slaves were offered no such welcome or participation....The city rejected them, and they fled and settled along the riverbanks and under bridges in shallow, ramshackle houses made of sticks and tar-paper. They collected rags and wood. They sold the use of their muscles and their bodies. They cleaned houses and washed clothes, they shined shoes, and in quiet desperation and vengeful pride, they stole and lived in pursuit of their own dream: That they could breathe free, finally and stand to meet life with the force of dignity and whatever eloquence the heart could call upon.[12]

The New Political Order

Mayor David Lawrence was certainly aware of the mounting racial tensions. In 1946 he sponsored an interracial, inter-denominational Civic Unity Council to discuss ways to reduce racial tensions. When K. Leroy Irvis, secretary of the Urban League, picketed downtown department stores because of their refusal to hire black sales personnel, he received a telephone call from the mayor accusing him of "giving Pittsburgh a black eye." Irvis responded: "Pittsburgh already had a black eye and that he was only trying to see that it doesn't get worse." Lawrence brokered meetings where stores agreed to halt their discriminatory policies. After Communist-led efforts to integrate the Highland Park pool provoked violence in 1949, he was pushed to enforce the integration of the city pools when more sustained efforts were initiated by black Presbyterian minister Leroy Patrick of the NAACP with Alexander Allen from the Urban League, who faced angry crowds in the summer of 1951. "While lifeguards sat idly by, a gang of a hundred white teenagers ejected Allen from the pool, hurling racial slurs at him." Patrick organized small groups of blacks and whites including children to swim in traditionally all-white pools. When he entered Highland Park Pool for the first time, fearful of the consequences and not knowing how to swim, the whites all left the pool shouting epithets and claiming that the water had been made dirty. A suit was filed by the NAACP, police protection was provided, and ultimately the pool was integrated. The mayor supported the creation of a Fair Employment Practices Commission that evolved into the city's Commission on Human Relations in 1955. In 1959, six months before his inauguration as governor, he signed a Fair Housing Bill into law, only the second such legislation in the nation. Despite these efforts, progress was painfully slow as white resistance was widespread. On the state level, the long struggle of Homer S. Brown, Pittsburgh's first black legislator elected in 1934, finally came to fruition in 1955 when Governor George leader signed the Pennsylvania Fair Employment Practices Act into law. Then Judge Homer Brown was named to the commission established to enforce the law, and later, during the administration of Governor David L. Lawrence, its jurisdiction was extended to education and housing and renamed the Pennsylvania Human Relations Commission.[13]

The organizing of picket lines at the downtown stores gained national attention, but also cost K. Leroy Irvis his position at the Urban League. Irvis grew up in Albany, New York and earned a college degree and then a master's at the State College of New York. Despite graduating summa cum laude, he was unable to land a teaching job. Pittsburgh's Daisy Lampkin, called the "soul of the NAACP," found him a teaching job in Baltimore where he lived in the home of Thurgood Marshall, NAACP lawyer and future Supreme Court justice. After the war, it was Daisy Lampkin who got him a position with the Pittsburgh Urban League. In 1951, he entered Pitt Law School and became the first black law clerk in the city. In 1957 he was appointed an Assistant District Attorney and in 1958, Mayor Lawrence asked him to run for the Pennsylvania Legislature as a representative of the Hill District. He served for 30 years in the House of Representatives and was the only man other than Benjamin Franklin to be elected the Speaker of the House by acclamation. From his father he had inherited a love of books and learning, and from his mother a sense of the importance of emotions and artistic expression. When he retired, he was probably the most respected politician in the state of Pennsylvania.[14]

In one of the most controversial acts of his mayoral career, Lawrence supported the imposition of a wage tax. The city's massive redevelopment projects required significant government funding. Historically, Lawrence had long opposed a wage tax since state law mandated a flat or uniform rate that he characterized as a "soak the poor" tax. However, when other options proved even more unpalatable, the mayor decided to levy an earned income tax on residents that spared commuters who worked in, but lived outside the city. Labor unions expressed the most vigorous opposition to a tax that was widely seen as regressive. This action would have long-range negative impact as the city's population declined and grew poorer while the percentage of commuters working downtown and in Oakland's university and hospital district steadily increased over the years. Lawrence signed the bill stating:

> I am under no illusion that we have acted to achieve a momentary popularity....But
> I am sure that the council and the mayor have acted to protect the best interests of
> Pittsburgh and its people and that in the end such forthright action is what citizens
> desire from their public officials. The politician with no sense of responsibility is
> the worst enemy of democratic government.[15]

Lawrence's most glaring weakness as a mayor was his tolerance of the system of influence-peddling and petty corruption that was the heart and soul of ward politics. Loyalty was the coin of the realm. Many sins were tolerated in its name. The numbers racket operated city-wide; illegal gambling clubs proliferated, especially in East Liberty. Slot machines were important sources of revenue for bars all over the city. Selective enforcement of the law was a primary political tool. Ward politicians had great influence over the hiring of police, firefighters, and city maintenance crews. All were expected to contribute in some fashion at election time. City work crews routinely did favors for ward politicians and their allies. While Lawrence periodically launched campaigns against corruption, little concrete action was taken and operations continued as usual. In 1950, the mayor supported an ordinance prohibiting police officers from holding office or being campaign managers. During the 1950s, while Sam and Tony Grosso were taking over the numbers racket in Western Pennsylvania, Ray Sprigle, investigative reporter for the *Pittsburgh Press,* wrote: "Racket bosses elect and finance aldermen and constables. The ward chairmen then maintain and protect the operation of the racket bosses in their wards through control of the police department and police inspectors." Obviously, Lawrence's ambiguity toward corruption was explained by the fact that any serious cleanup would have to take on the very system of loyalty and rewards Lawrence had built and had brought the Democrats to power.[16]

As the electoral advantage began to run toward the Democrats and away from the Republicans in the city and the mill towns, powerful Republican ward chairmen switched and became Democrats to retain power. It is hardly surprising that many of the blatant voting irregularities practiced for years under the old corrupt Republican machine persisted under the new order. A veteran Hill politician, Lewis "Hop" Hendricks, remembered elections there during the 1940s and 50s. "A lot of whites had moved from there to the South Hills. I was surprised when I went to the polls to see deputy sheriffs and road crews voting, people who'd come back from the South Hills or wherever to vote. I discovered that I lived in a district where nobody ever died. More people voted than were on the books. And people were convinced that the paper ballot box that sat on the table had a hole in the bottom so your ballot would fall to the basement and be changed."[17]

During the 1950s, David Lawrence solidified his dominance of Pittsburgh politics while maintaining his stature as a major player on both state and national levels as well. For a decade, all three Pittsburgh newspapers gave him their endorsements. The CIO industrial unions were solidly behind him, especially after he supported the respected union leader, Pat Fagan, for city council. Fagan would come to serve as president of Pittsburgh City Council at the end of an amazing union and political career. The AFL craft unions fell in line politically after the defeat of Eddie Leonard's mayoral challenge in 1949 as they began to experience the benefits of the mayor's ambitious redevelopment plans. Democratic majorities increased with each election and the GOP began to wither as a viable party to the point where they resembled Pittsburgh's Democrats at the beginning of the century. Increasingly, they found it difficult to find candidates to run for office. The *coup de grace* was administered by Richard King Mellon's public endorsement of the mayor's renaissance efforts. *Fortune* and *Time* magazines hailed him as one of the nation's outstanding municipal managers. In 1954 Lawrence helped engineer the victory of Democrat George Leader as governor of Pennsylvania.[18]

Lawrence continued to play an important role in national Democratic politics as well. Having played a major role in dumping Henry Wallace in favor of Truman as Roosevelt's running mate in 1944, he and the president remained close politically. In 1952 with Truman not a candidate and the party deeply split, Lawrence successfully organized party support for Illinois Governor Adlai Stevenson, who he greatly admired. He repeated his strong organizational support for Stevenson in

1956 against the popular Republican incumbent, Dwight D. Eisenhower. In a political deal to obtain the support of rival candidate, Senator Estes Kefauver, for Stevenson, Lawrence supported Kefauver's nomination for vice-president against an ambitious young upstart senator from Massachusetts, John F. Kennedy. An axiom of Lawrence's political career had been that a Catholic could not be elected nationally or even statewide. Events would conspire to change his opinion on both accounts.[19]

In 1958, Pennsylvania Democrats were optimistic about victory in the governor's race because of increasing party registration numbers statewide; however, support was split between five candidates. After intense maneuvering, George Leader, who was leaving the governor's mansion to run for the U.S. Senate, began to push a sixth candidate, David Lawrence. Lawrence was supporting Allegheny County Controller, James Knox, but he came to be seen as the only candidate who could unite all the party factions while receiving labor and independent support. Furthermore, his strong personal support for Israel, generated through several visits there, made him popular among Jewish voters in the urban centers. Lawrence campaigned vigorously statewide visiting all sixty-seven counties. In Pittsburgh, one of his campaign workers was Molly Yard, a progressive activist who later became the head of the National Organization of Women. His Republican opponent, Arthur McGonigle, a millionaire from Reading attacked "Boss" Lawrence as a front for corruption and the rackets. In response, Lawrence spoke extensively before chambers of commerce, business, and professional groups all over the state stressing cooperation, revitalization, and a business-like administration. While Lawrence won by a 76,000 vote margin, George Leader was defeated by Republican Hugh Scott for the Senate. On January 20, 1959, David L. Lawrence was installed as the state's oldest and first Roman Catholic governor. At his first press conference, Duke Kaminsky, a sarcastic reporter from the *Philadelphia Inquirer* asked what "boss Lawrence" was going to do now? Lawrence turned on him saying: "Now let's get things straight right now. I am not a boss, and have never been a boss, and if that term is ever used again in my presence, you'll never be at another news conference."[20]

In the presidential campaign of 1960, Dave Lawrence played a pivotal role. Deeply tied emotionally to Adlai Stevenson and still skeptical of the ability of a Catholic to win the presidency, Lawrence remained uncommitted as Kennedy entered the Democratic Convention with the most primary votes, but not sufficient to secure the nomination. Facing strong grassroots pressure from the Kennedy forces within the Pennsylvania delegation, Lawrence endorsed Kennedy at the last moment allowing him to win on the first ballot at the convention. Lawrence then played a key role in securing the vice-presidential nomination for Lyndon B. Johnson. Ever the consummate practical politician, Lawrence pressed Johnson on Kennedy as the only running mate that added materially to his candidacy. In the end, it is likely that Johnson's addition made Kennedy's extremely narrow margin of victory possible. Lawrence's key role in the selection was highlighted when he was chosen to nominate Johnson for vice-president. Kennedy's candidacy energized the party as his election motorcade drew crowds estimated at a million people across the state.[21]

McCarthyism in Pittsburgh

In February 1950, Joseph McCarthy, the Republican junior senator from Wisconsin, gave an inflammatory Lincoln Day speech to the Ohio County Women's Club in Wheeling, West Virginia. There he waved a list of what he claimed were 205 people "known to the Secretary of State as being members of the Communist Party and are still working and shaping the policy of the State

Department." He had, in fact, no list of any sort; his speech a pastiche of Republican attacks on the Truman administration's softness on Communism. McCarthy at 41 was a heavy drinker who had been accused of taking bribes from companies and money from a lobbyist. He was riding on the coattails of Richard Nixon, who was gaining national prominence for his pursuit of Alger Hiss, accused and eventually convicted of passing large amounts of classified information and secret codes to the Russians. In Wheeling McCarthy simply paraphrased a Nixon speech given several weeks earlier. "One thing to remember in discussing the Communists is that we are not dealing with spies who get thirty pieces of silver to steal the blueprints of a new weapon. We are dealing with a far more sinister type of activity because it permits the enemy to guide and shape our policy." The accusation that there were traitors interwoven throughout the fabric of American life up into the highest levels of government became McCarthy's stock in trade. McCarthy got substantial support from a group of powerful right-wing newspaper publishers known as the China Lobby who were castigating Truman for the loss of China to the Communists.[22]

At the same time McCarthy was making the accusations in Wheeling that were picked up two days later by the *New York Times*, Matt Cvetic, an informant for the FBI and member of the local Communist Party since 1943, surfaced in Pittsburgh to corroborate J. Edgar Hoover's pronouncement that there were 2,876 Communists in Pennsylvania. Cvetic fed a media frenzy as he appeared as a witness in at least sixty-three hearings and named over five hundred people as members of the Party. All three Pittsburgh papers, the *Pittsburgh Press*, the *Post-Gazette*, and the *Pittsburgh Sun-Telegraph* published names, addresses and employers of the accused. The *Pittsburgh Press* had established something of a precedent when it printed the names and addresses of those signing Wallace for President petitions in 1948. An estimated one hundred people around Pittsburgh lost their jobs as a result. Many more suffered prolonged fear and anxiety. Some faced ostracism. Nick Lazari and George Nichols, officers in the hotel and restaurant union, were forced to resign their positions. In steel, Elmer Kish at Homestead, Tony Salopek at Duquesne, and Alex Staber at J&L were driven from union office.[23]

The anti-Communist drive in Pittsburgh gathered steam as war broke out and left-wing dissent became more plausibly equated with treason. On the last weekend in June, 1950, North Korean forces launched an all-out offensive against South Korea. Since the small American force in the south was there as a representative of the United Nations charged with supervising elections on Korea's future, the United Nations Security Council in a session boycotted by Russia condemned the attack and Truman committed armed support to the collapsing South Korean resistance. In a precedent-setting move, Truman did not ask Congress to declare war, but treated the conflict that eventually produced more than 100,000 U.N. casualties as a "police action under the United Nations." General Douglas MacArthur flew into Korea; and, witnessing the collapse of the South Korean army, he immediately requested American troops. The initial deployment of two Army divisions from Japan failed to break the North Korean momentum, however. After six weeks of retreat, the combined American and South Korean forces stiffened and established a 120-mile arc around the southern port of Pusan. The draft was instituted to raise 600,000 men as soon as possible. Artillery arrived and the troops dug in as U.N. contingents of soldiers arrived from Britain, France, Turkey, Australia, Holland, and the Philippines. On September 15, 1950, MacArthur, in the most brilliant military move of his checkered career, launched an amphibious attack behind enemy lines at Inchon west of Seoul and moved on the capital cutting off the retreat of the North's army. By October 1, the North Korean army was all but destroyed with nearly half becoming U.N. prisoners of war.[24]

At this point, General MacArthur overstepped his bounds and snatched defeat from the jaws of victory. In the press and in a message to the Veterans of Foreign Wars, he called for an aggressive strategy toward both North Korea and China. Truman, increasingly concerned about his commander's ego, flew to confer with him on Wake Island. There, Truman heard MacArthur downplay the danger from China, vastly underestimating the numbers of men China was capable of committing to the struggle. He bragged he would "have the boys home by Christmas." After feeding his troops a Thanksgiving dinner, McArthur, ignoring Chinese warnings, launched his offensive against the North without even providing winter clothing for his troops. In response, the Chinese struck with 33 divisions, 300,000 men. The United Nations forces were overwhelmed by a "bottomless well" of manpower. In bitter and heroic combat, the U.N. forces were forced to retreat to escape annihilation. The 1st Marine Division that had penetrated far into the north was forced to fight a desperate retreat. Their commander told them: "The enemy is in front of us, behind us, to the left of us, and to the right of us. They won't escape this time." Unwilling to attack China and drop 30 to 50 atomic bombs on Manchuria, as MacArthur wanted, Truman had to settle on a long and costly stalemate. Seoul was lost and then retaken. After nine bloody months, the two great armies faced each other across the 38th Parallel; and there they remained until the war ended on July 27, 1953, with a cost of 54,246 American casualties. Over 30,000 recruits from Allegheny County served in the "police action." Five men from the Pittsburgh region, Marines George Ramer and John D. Kelly and three Army infantrymen, Reginald Desiderio, Raymond Harvey and Don F. Porter, were awarded the Congressional Medal of Honor.[25]

The involvement of U.S. troops in a bloody confrontation with the forces of international Communism had a powerful impact on the already intense domestic debate about loyalty and treason. The most spectacular or, more exactly, theatrical exemplar of the anti-Communist crusader in Pittsburgh was Judge Michael Angelo Musmanno. A man of considerable talent and unlimited ambition, Musmanno was a candidate for Lieutenant Governor in 1950. An admirer of Mussolini while he was a law student during the early 1920s in Italy, he made his name later in the decade as an attorney representing Pennsylvania miners resisting eviction notices during strikes and then as a legislator seeking the abolition of the hated Coal and Iron Police. He served on the defense team for Sacco and Vanzetti. He was a major figure in the Italian-American world. Like Father Rice, but more extreme and mercurial, his support for labor was directly linked to his fervent anti-Communism. When Musmanno ran for the legislature in 1928, he asserted "the two most important planks of my platform were: the abolition of the Coal and Iron Police and dissolution of the Communist Party." In 1932 he was elected judge of the Court of Common Pleas. During World War II, he served in the Navy as Military Governor in southern Italy and was a judge at the Nuremberg War Crimes Tribunal. [26]

His theatrical displays of anti-Communist fervor began in March of 1950 with his refusal to swear in Alice Roth as a Grand Juror in Allegheny County because he recognized her as the secretary of the East Pittsburgh branch of the Communist Party. When Musmanno summoned Matt Cvetic to identify her as a Communist, Roth pointed at Cvetic saying: "There's a rat in this room." Musmanno dismissed her asking: "Should I not disqualify a grand juror who intended, in conspiracy with others, to destroy by force and violence, the government itself." Never an admirer of Musmanno, Mayor David Lawrence came to the defense of Allegheny County Assistant District Attorney Marjorie Matson when she publicly criticized Musmanno's actions and "the wave of hysteria which has swept this community as a result of the disclosures made by Matt Cvetic." Lawrence testified in her defense, calling her "thoroughly American and a mighty good Democrat," at hearings engineered by his old enemy, state Attorney General Charles Margiotti. When Chatham College composer-in residence Roy Harris was attacked for his staging of his symphony written in 1943 dedicated to the Russian people's heroic resistance to the Nazi invasion, Lawrence announced he would attend the concert despite threats by Musmanno and the Veterans of Foreign Wars that they would picket the event.[27]

Three days before a bitterly contested April 1950 election between the UE and the newly constituted IUE, Musmanno appeared at the plant gate of Westinghouse Electric to lend his weight to the struggle against Communists in the electrical workers union. Dressed in his naval officer uniform, he was accompanied by a unit of the Pennsylvania National Guard parading with flags and bayonets. The plant's union employment had shrunk to approximately half its wartime high of over 22,000. The firm had already begun transferring work out of East Pittsburgh to new smaller factories in the Midwest and South. While anti-Communist sentiment was clearly on the rise and the collapse of the Progressive Party had weakened the leftwing, cutbacks in employment probably helped the UE vote to some degree because its base was among the more skilled and higher seniority workers. Activists formed during the depression struggles tended to be more sympathetic to the UE, while the newly returned veterans tended to be more susceptible to the IUE's appeals to patriotism and national security.[28]

The showdown between the two organizations was hotly contested. IUE appeals focused on Communism and patriotism with a pamphlet entitled "Your Government Speaks Out for IUE-CIO" with a picture of President Truman on its cover. The anti-religious nature of the Soviet regime provided a powerful motivator for the churches. One major Catholic parish in the valley urged their parishioners to vote against the UE. "The leaders of the International UE support the attackers and persecutors of Archbishop Stepinac, Cardinal Mindzenty, and the heroic priests and nuns and Catholic people behind the Iron Curtain. The people over there cannot vote against Communism, you still can." The UE for its part charged that a Catholic conspiracy led by Father Rice was attempting to take over the local on behalf of a company-dominated union. UE leaflets stressed their organization's ability to effectively represent the workers and achieve wage gains. One leaflet festooned with pictures of clothing, appliances and groceries proclaimed: "Red-Baiting Won't Buy This! UE Contract Gains Will! Red-Baiting is Not Legal Currency! The Grocer Only Takes Cash!"[29]

After the first election produced a narrow IUE victory of 100 votes (5,763 to 5, 663) with "No Union" winning 170 votes, the NLRB held a run-off election in June 1950, where the IUE won 5,964 to 5,705. Thus ended more than seven months of intense political struggle as continuous political warfare roiled the Turtle Creek Valley with parades, rallies, constant barrages of leaflets and pamphlets, letters to the homes, buttons, billboards, posters in bars, stores and on telephone poles, loudspeaker-trucks cruising the valley projecting angry accusations. Following raids by other unions on the UE during the 1950s, the workers at Westinghouse nationwide were divided into three unions, the IUE, UE, and IBEW, with the UE representing only 20% of Westinghouse production workers. One of the many casualties of the intense political struggle was Congressman Harry Davenport, who grew up in McKeesport and whose district included parts of Pittsburgh and its eastern suburbs. After his failure to provide any measure of comfort when his former friend and political ally, Tom Quinn, was dragged before HUAC, Davenport collapsed under pressure from Democratic Party chairman David Lawrence, and appeared at an IUE rally to pronounce: "The UE is controlled by the puppets of Moscow." From a liberal critic of HUAC who had introduced a resolution to abolish the committee, Davenport, according to his nephew and historian, John Hoerr, "was a shrunken political figure. He had turned himself inside out in accommodating to the political climate, compromising deeply held beliefs, including freedom of speech and association that he had once held inviolate." With the collapse of the UE's well-oiled political machine, Davenport went down to defeat in the fall election as voter turnout in his district dropped from 71 percent in 1948 to 59 percent in 1950.[30]

On the afternoon of July 19, 1950, Musmanno, accompanied by two Pittsburgh detectives, crossed Grant Street from the Allegheny County Courthouse to the Bakewell Building, climbed to the fourth floor and entered the headquarters of the Communist Party in Pittsburgh. There he observed: "A large map of the Soviet empire dominated the locale while from a hundred angles the eyes of Joseph Stalin pierced me with their metallic gaze over his ambushing mustaches....A map of Korea on one wall spectacularly announced the smashing advance of the North Korean Communists while depicting the 'headlong retreat of American troops.'" He verbally confronted two Communist Party leaders, Jim Dolsen and Andrew Onda, concerning the nature of American democracy and the Soviet system. He then went on a shopping spree purchasing a raft of books and pamphlets that he would eventually employ to demonstrate Communist support for violent revolution.[31]

The focus of Judge Musmanno's anti-Communist crusade was Steve Nelson, chairman of the Communist Party of Western Pennsylvania. Musmanno was convinced Nelson had been involved in obtaining atomic bomb secrets through a friendship with Robert Oppenheimer's wife while Nelson lived in Los Angeles in the mid-forties. For Musmanno, Nelson was the "arch traitor, Lenin disciple and American-hater." Nelson was without a doubt an intelligent and resourceful, militant organizer. He knew Pittsburgh and bought the center house of a triplex in the Hill District where his family was somewhat shielded from attack by the majority black community. He had been a battle-tested officer for the Republic in the Spanish Civil War. Inside Communist Party ranks, he advocated for a more independent American national policy with less adherence to the Russian party line. "The concept that we couldn't promote a Soviet model of communism in the United States had begun to register, but nobody had the guts to stand up and say it in so many words." Nelson saw, but was unable to change the rigid sectarianism that the party adopted in response to wholesale attack.[32]

Nelson's trial began on January 8, 1951, and continued through April 19, 1951, when *I was a Communist for the FBI* opened with a gala at the Stanley Theater in the presence of Mayor Lawrence and other dignitaries including Pittsburgh's own Matt Cvetic. In the movie version, the short fat and rather mousy Cvetic was transformed into a square-jawed six-footer who lived in constant danger from his ruthless comrades. In the lurid and overheated fictional account, Steve Nelson, identified by name, killed a man. A month later in May, Nelson was seriously injured in a car accident traveling with his family near Philadelphia and spent two months in the hospital with four broken ribs, a dislocated arm, a broken leg and kneecap. On a hot August day, in a cramped Philadelphia apartment of a friend who had taken him in during his recovery, Nelson was personally confronted by Musmanno, accompanied by two Philadelphia detectives, who came "to see how soon you were coming back for your trial." He was ordered to appear for trial on sedition in Pittsburgh the following month. Nelson, after more than twenty solicitations, failed to find any lawyer willing to represent him given the attack Musmanno launched against local progressive attorney, Hy Schlesinger – arrested and held in contempt of Musmanno's court basically because of the politics of the people he defended. Without counsel and on crutches, Nelson asked for a postponement because of his medical condition. He was then ordered by Judge Harry Montgomery to undergo a medical exam by the head doctor for U.S. Steel (presumably to thereby remove all possible taint of liberal sympathy). While undergoing tests in the hospital, Nelson charged that he was threatened by a gunman who claimed his brother had been killed in Korea. Despite his physical condition he was declared fit for trial.[33]

Steve Nelson, the Croatia-born Stjepan Mesaros, was a veteran of struggle, a warrior for an internationalist cause. An ideologue like Musmanno, he wore his loyalties on his sleeve. In a memoir published in 1980, Nelson described his attitude at the time:

> I accepted Stalin's argument that the class struggle continues under socialism and that "class enemies must be decisively confronted and eliminated. The idea of converting people who disagreed was lost in the shuffle. We allowed ourselves to take this concept of "class struggle" and pervert its meaning until we reached the point where anyone who disagreed with the position of the Party could be labeled an enemy of socialism. The concept of democratic centralism, forged in the underground, war and counter-revolution, allowed for little flexibility or dissent....These mistakes had tragic consequences. But I didn't see this when I was in the Soviet Union in the early 1930s. Then I felt that I was in the midst of a vast, almost noble undertaking that required total effort, total support.[34]

When his sedition trial resumed on December 19, 1951, Nelson acted as his own attorney and conducted cross-examinations of the prosecution's witnesses. Musmanno's nephew served as the state prosecutor and the second witness he called in the trial was Judge Musmanno himself. For days, Nelson and Musmanno sparred intellectually. Next, Nelson confronted Matt Cvetic whose testimony against him covered a Communist Party Convention in old Andy Carnegie's Allegheny Library. Cvetic quoted Nelson as saying: "Now that we have the A-bomb, they won't be in such a goddamn hurry to start a war." Nelson grilled Cvetic for two days about his movie contract and the magazine articles and radio serial that were spin-offs from *I was a Communist for the FBI* – and then grilled him about workers he had "fingered." In July Nelson was sentenced to 20 years and conveyed to the Blawnox workhouse where he quickly became a spokesperson for inmate grievances. These activities earned him repeated confinements in the "Hole" where prisoners were kept naked and conditions were bestial. He was released from jail in 1953 as a result of federal appeals and, in April 1956, the Supreme Court ruled that states had no power to try individuals for sedition. [35]

While Nelson remained free of prison, he eventually quit the Communist Party that he had faithfully supported through such difficult times. Already critical of party leadership for its slavish subservience to the Soviet line and the "failure to base our approach to the American people on their very real commitment to democratic values," Nelson was horrified by the revelation of Stalin's crimes. At a tense plenum meeting of the National Committee of the Communist Party in New York in April 1956, Nelson was elected to chair the meeting where delegates were read the entire text of Nikita Krushchev's famous speech. It included detailed confirmation of Stalin's murderous ways, not only toward his supposed class enemies but also to the leadership cadres of the party. "Of the 1,996 delegates to the 1934 Seventeenth Congress of the Soviet Party, 1,108, including many members of the Central Committee, were arrested, and many of them executed by 1936....An entire generation of leadership – the cream of the Bolsheviks, the men and women who made the Revolution – was wiped out....The words of the speech were like bullets, and each found its place in the hearts of the veteran Communists."[36]

Nelson's experience with McCarthyism was bitter, but the witch hunt had strengthened his resolve. Before he quit the Party, he was an unapologetic Communist who saw the prosecutorial zeal of his enemies as an illustration of the flawed nature of the American justice system. Subsequently, discovering the even more extreme injustices practiced in Russia undermined his resolve. He became angry with himself and others who had been "so blind in our adherence to Soviet policy and so mechanical in our application of Marxism." He faced the angry feelings of betrayal that his 14 year old daughter felt from all the years of attacks and insults the family had suffered in the belief they were faithful to a noble cause. The disarray felt by the remaining Party faithful was further accentuated in June 1956 by the rising of industrial workers in Poznan, Poland, crushed when the police and army fired on demonstrators killing more than seventy. This was followed shortly after in October by the bloody uprising in Hungary, suppressed in turn by a massive Soviet military invasion. When the Communist Party old guard, united behind William Z. Foster, the aging 1919 strike leader, refused to question the standard verities, Nelson resigned and left Pittsburgh to try to start a new life with his family. In the 1960s, he and Father Rice reconciled and when Nelson died in 1993, Rice called him "an honorable antagonist."[37]

Tom Quinn's situation was very different and he came to epitomize those who worked beside but were not formally Communists, and whose friendships and personal loyalties did not permit their collaboration with the witch-hunters. After the UE's narrow defeat inside Local 601, Quinn continued working as a welder and tried to keep the old UE organization intact under the new regime. However, in February 1951, he was convicted of contempt of Congress and sentenced to six months in prison. Jailed overnight before he was released on bail, he and his family faced four years of appeals and the constant threat of imprisonment. In November 1953, the Senate Internal Security Subcommittee came to Pittsburgh and Quinn was again summoned to testify and again faced accusations from Matt Cvetic that he had been a member of the Party. A month following the hearing, Quinn left the Westinghouse plant early on New Year's Eve when most of the men were partying and was fired for time card falsification. John Vento, an IUE steward, asserted that "Westinghouse set him up and fired him on a phony issue." The UE hired him a few days later as an international staff representative. Throughout his ordeal, Quinn received full support from his wife, family, and union. As many as a dozen men were fired by Westinghouse for taking the Fifth Amendment during hearings.[38]

The UE was decimated by the attacks of the 1950s. From more than 500,000 members in the mid-1940s, the union's membership fell to 203,000 in 1953 and 58,000 in 1960. The Communist Party, itself shrunk to barely 5,000 members, urged the UE to dissolve and rejoin the CIO. Matles and most of the UE leadership strongly rejected this option as suicidal. In late 1954, McCarthy was brought down and censured in the Senate after he overreached and attacked U.S. Army leadership. In 1955 the U.S. Supreme Court handed down its decision in Quinn vs. the United States. The justices ruled that Tom Quinn had properly invoked his Fifth Amendment rights and dismissed the criminal complaint against him. HUAC kept up the hunt for subversives, however; and in 1959 a panel came to Pittsburgh to investigate the UE. Tom Quinn, now UE staff organizer, was summoned to testify. Angrily calling old and stale accusations by Cvetic and Mazzei lies, Quinn, exasperated after being threatened again with contempt of Congress, was pressed hard as to whether he was ever a member of the Communist Party while an employee of Westinghouse. Quinn replied in a "rousing baritone" that "I am not now, and never was, a member of the Communist Party." When Quinn was threatened again with contempt for the angry tone of his answers, he assured the panel: "I don't

385

have contempt for Congress, just contempt of this committee. Make that clear." Since the only witnesses who claimed Quinn was a Communist were the now discredited Matt Cvetic and Joseph Mazzei, the long ordeal of Tom Quinn was over. In the early 1970s, he left the staff of the UE and quickly became a highly respected state mediator, eventually named by Republican Governor Thornberg to head the Pennsylvania Department of Mediation.[39]

In 1955-56, the now seriously divided electrical workers went on strike against Westinghouse over issues involving incentive pay and seniority issues concerning bumping rights, especially during layoffs. The corporation was determined to increase output while at the same time lowering incentive rates through expanded use of time-studies. The IUE and UE were generally united in their resistance to the corporation's demands, and they were joined on strike by units represented by the IBEW and the International Association of Machinists (IAM). While the latter two organizations reached an agreement after three months, agreement between Westinghouse and the IUE and UE came only after a long winter strike of 154 days. Significant wage gains were achieved at the cost of some compromise on allowing time-studies on incentive rates, especially in plants represented by the IUE like East Pittsburgh. Westinghouse, meanwhile, was embarking on a major program of decentralization and used the threat of moving sections of its East Pittsburgh operations to exact concessions from the union's leadership. While future debates in Pittsburgh about "Who Killed Westinghouse?" would focus on management decisions made in the 1960s and 1970s, the decentralization of manufacturing, spurred at least in part by a desire to reduce union power, preceded and helped justify the sprawling organizational complexity that was often cited as a key factor in the company's decline. Huge layoffs in 1958-59 further eroded the ability of the union to resist company programs. Paul Charmichael, IUE Local 601's president at the end of the decade, described the union's position: "The company provides the jobs and it is our job to eliminate trouble and yet assure the best working conditions for the men we represent."[40]

Culture and Sport

The rising prosperity of the unionized working class and the resulting disposable income stimulated the proliferation of cultural and athletic activities in the Pittsburgh region. The black community, whose employment opportunities were restricted and whose geographical dispersion was blocked by restrictive housing patterns, played a role in Pittsburgh's sports and cultural life of the 1950s out of proportion to their numbers. Black cultural influence spread out from the Hill, Homewood, the North Side, Beltzhoover, Braddock and Homestead. The Hill District was the crossroads of the world as far as jazz was concerned, as its position between New York and Chicago and its intense local jazz scene attracted nearly all the Jazz greats to pass through town and interact with local talent. On the level of popular culture, a radio disk jockey named Porky Chedwick helped make Pittsburgh a key location for the breakthrough of "race music," rhythm and blues, and what became known as rock and roll. In sports, black athletes were becoming stars for the Steelers; and a young right fielder from Puerto Rico, Roberto Clemente, was beginning a career that redefined the standard of greatness for outfielders.

Pittsburgh gained a reputation as jazz's "piano city" due to the contributions of Earl "Fatha" Hines, Mary Lou Williams, Billy Strayhorn, Errol Garner, and Ahmed Jamal. Earl Hines, a major force in shaping jazz piano, was born in Duquesne in 1903 and attended Schenley High School in Pittsburgh. He moved to Chicago and in 1926 joined forces with Louis Armstrong, recording classics like "St. James Infirmary," "Muggles," "It's Tight Like That," featuring Armstrong trumpet solos and Hines' piano. They created the central characteristic of modern jazz, the long instrumental sorties by individual soloists. During World War II, the Hines band featured be-bop originators, Charlie Parker and Dizzy Gillespie. In 1938, at the age of 23, pianist Billy Strayhorn met Duke Ellington who was performing at Pittsburgh's Stanley Theater. For the next 29 years, Strayhorn served as Ellington's co-writer and collaborator helping Ellington compose orchestral suites, theatrical works and movie scores. Strayhorn, who was gay, stayed out of the limelight that Ellington relished. He was the composer of the Duke's theme, "Take the A Train," and many other works including his own subtle and complex signature piece "Lush Life," which begins "I used to visit all the very gay places, Those come what may places, Where one relaxes on the axis of the wheel of life." Mary Lou Williams was born in Atlanta but moved to Pittsburgh when she was three years old. At the age of ten she was recognized as a prodigy. "I used to play for the Mellons, you know the very rich people. Their chauffeur would come by and get me off the sidewalk to play at their parties. I was known as "the little piano girl."[41]

Mary Lou Williams worked with many big bands including Count Basie in Kansas City, but in 1942 she returned to Pittsburgh and formed a band with Art Blakey. When Williams eventually split to pursue a solo career, Blakey teamed up with fellow Pittsburghers to form the original be-bop orchestra. Blakey switched to drums when the band was joined by the young Errol Garner. In the early 1950s, Blakey went to Africa for two years, became a Muslim, and returned in 1953 to form the transformative group *The Jazz Messengers*. Mary Lou Williams, on the other hand, converted to Catholicism in 1957, was the recipient of six honorary doctoral degrees, including ones from Fordham University in New York and Loyola University of New Orleans. She taught music at Duke University near the end of her career. Another local jazzman was the "man with the golden horn," Roy Eldridge, considered the greatest of the Swing trumpeters and the link between Louis Armstrong and Dizzy Gillespie. He worked in Pittsburgh through the 1930s and during the 1940s was a soloist and singer, first for Gene Krupa, and later Artie Shaw. Like many black jazz players he went to Paris in the 1950s. Billy Eckstine was a trombonist who became one of the most successful vocalists in the history of Jazz. Born and raised in East liberty, he graduated from Peabody High School. In the late 40s and early 50s, he had 11 gold records including "When Fools Rush In," "Blue Moon," and "Body and Soul." Errol Garner, born in 1921, became one of Pittsburgh's most popular artists. Never able to read or write music, he became an international star beginning with an appearance at the 1948 Paris Jazz Festival. Another great Pittsburgh pianist was Ahmad Jamal, who, like many local artists, first developed his musical talents at Westinghouse High School, in his case, during World War II. Two Pittsburghers, Kenny Clark on drums and Ray Brown on bass, formed half of the Modern Jazz Quartet. Ray Brown was born in Pittsburgh in 1926, played with Dizzy Gillespie in the late 1940s and married Ella Fitzgerald. George Benson, born in the Hill in 1943, sang on the street corners in the late 1940s, had a record contract in his teens and developed into a guitar virtuoso and singer in the 1960s.[42]

Pittsburgh jazz had three major temples. The Crawford Grill, which had been the central location for jazz since the 1930s, was forced by the construction of the Civic Arena to move further up Wylie Avenue in the mid-50s. In 1953, its major rival, the Hurricane, was opened by Birdie Dunlap on Wylie Avenue. You might see Sarah Vaughan, Nancy Wilson, or Duke Ellington there or at the Crawford Grill having breakfast after a downtown concert followed by an all night session at the Musicians Club. The clubs brought white money to the Hill and a good time was had by all.

Lady that she was, Birdie Dunlop explained: "I never had a bouncer. I threw them out myself. Bobby Layne, the Steeler quarterback, used to bring the whole football team up. His buddy was Ernie Stautner, but he really loved his black players – Big Daddy Lipscomb, John Henry Johnson, and John Nisby. He loved the music; he loved to drink; and he loved the Hurricane. He'd drop a $200 tip into the end of someone's horn. Then he'd get up on stage and pretend that he was playing himself."[43]

The hub of Pittsburgh's jazz scene was the private social hall of Local 471 of the Musicians' Union. From early in the 20th Century until the black local union's tragic fusion with the white Local 60 in 1965, the Pittsburgh Musicians Club was the center of music creativity, where "musicians gathered to show off, learn the newest techniques and material, and get hired." Any black musician that did any work around the city had to belong to Local 471. As jazz trombonist and music historian Dr. Nelson Harrison remembers: "When the big names came to town they'd always have to test themselves against the locals." When Stan Getz came in one time, he was given a run for his money by a teenage Ahmad Jamal. Musicians' Union historian and trumpet player Chuck Austin observed that "we used to take it for granted when we would walk in and Duke Ellington would be hanging out with Frank Sinatra and maybe Nat King Cole....It's difficult to fully describe the environment at the Club: This place was the site of some of the most profound interaction between many of the greatest musicians." The union was the working musicians' vehicle and the Club was its expression. Harrison remembers; "Guys were serious about the union...they'd want to see your paid-up dues card. If you had a card that wasn't paid up, get off the bandstand! They'd throw you off the stage! And if you didn't like it, they'd open their jacket to let you know they were serious." Forced to move by the construction of the Civic Arena, the Club migrated to Centre Avenue and then to Homewood, before it was disbanded as part of the merger of the black and white locals in 1965.[44]

While the Hill was becoming increasingly black, whites of many nationalities still lived there, owned businesses, and frequented the neighborhood. One of them, Sophie Masloff, growing up in the 40s and 50s on a Romanian Orthodox Jewish street in the Hill, got a job with the city, worked very diligently to understand the workings of government, and in time rose to become the first female and the first Jewish mayor of Pittsburgh.[45]

Also on those Hill District streets during the 1950s was August Wilson, an intense young man who would go on to become one of America's greatest playwrights. Son of a German baker, Frederick Kittel, and a black woman, Daisy Wilson, he was the fifth of seven children. Raised by an intensely religious Catholic mother who attended St. Benedict the Moor Church, Wilson adopted her name and deeply affirmed his African-American culture. His mother strongly emphasized education and August's proudest possession was his Carnegie Library card. When a teacher doubted that an article he had written on Napoleon was his, he quit school and spent his days at the library. "I dropped out of school, but I didn't drop out of life. I would leave the house each morning and go to the main branch of the Carnegie Library in Oakland, where they had all the books in the world....I felt suddenly liberated from the constraints of a prearranged curriculum that labored through one book in eight months." With friends including poet Rob Penny and Sala Udin, later a Pittsburgh City Councilman representing the Hill District, he listened and learned on the streets. "When I was 20, I went down onto Centre Avenue to learn from the community how to become a man." His ear for language, his deep appreciation for the culture and traditions of the Hill provided the basis for a monumental cycle of ten plays covering the ten decades of the 20th Century that earned him two Pulitzer prizes, a couple of dozen honorary doctorates, and many other awards. [46]

At the very same time Wilson was haunting the Oakland Carnegie Library, a young middle-class white girl was frequenting the Homewood Carnegie Library. While the body of her work was less Pittsburgh-centric than August Wilson's, Annie Dillard also won a Pulitzer Prize and wrote *An American Childhood,* a book about her growing up in Pittsburgh's East End. While her upbringing was more prosaic than Wilson's hustle on Centre Avenue, she shared his love of the word and the life of the imagination that the word unlocked. "The actual world is a kind of tedious plane where dwells, and goes to school the body, the boring body which houses the eyes to read the books and houses the heart the books enflame." [47]

While the jazz scene was attracting whites and big names to the Hill, a white disc jockey was helping to bring black rhythm and blues to the white working class kids who had more time and more money than their Depression era parents could ever imagine. In 1948, a young white guy named Porky Chedwick got a job doing a five-minute sports show on WHOD, a local radio station that promoted a wide variety of ethnic music as "The Station of the Nations" situated in the rear of a candy store in Homestead. He was the first white DJ in the east to present a program of black music called the "Masterful Rhythm, Blues and Jazz Show." Porky said: "I was mainly looking for the gospel sound and down-home rhythm and blues – the songs which spoke of the problems of poor people – that was *my* music." Within a year, he was introducing working-class kids to "race music" he picked up from Sonny Man Jackson's record store in Homestead. He had been preceded by black female DJ Mary Dee who played black rhythm-and-blues when WHOD was up in the Hill. As "Pork the Tork, Your Platter-Pushin' Papa, the Daddio of the Radio," Chedwick spread the gospel of what became rock and roll. In 1950 the station changed its call letters to WAMO (the last three call letters standing for the Allegheny, Monongahela, Ohio). Rather than playing exclusively new releases like the other stations, Porky was the very first to develop an "oldies but goodies" format that he called "dusty discs." While he played new songs that he considered a "breaker," he also liked to play the B-sides of records and mix in little known, older, and often considerably raunchier black songs that previously had never been aired. In 1954, when mainstream jocks were playing McGuire Sisters' cover of "Sincerely," Porky was playing the original by the Moonglows, along with other black music that became Pittsburgh classics like "Sixty-Minute Man" ("I rock 'em, roll 'em, all night long, I'm a sixty minute man"). He was accused of promoting drug use, rebellion, and juvenile delinquency; but he was not charged with taking gifts or payola to promote records. Porky remarked: "I made a million dollars but I never saw it."[48]

Porky Chedwick helped promote integrated groups like the Marcels ("Blue Moon") from the North Side, local white groups influenced by black vocal groups like the Smoothtones, Jimmy Beaumont and the Skyliners from the Carrick neighborhood ("Since I Don't Have You," "Earth Angel," "In the Still of the Night"), and the Dell-Vikings, an integrated group that worked together at the Nike missile site in Oakdale and had national smash hits like "Come Go With Me" and "Whispering Bells." Canonsburg, southwest of Pittsburgh, produced the Four Coins and Perry Como, who was one of the most successful mainline singers of the 1950s. Young people flocked to great dance halls like the Palisades in McKeesport, the White Elephant in White Oak, and the Danceland in Westview Park. At these venues and many others, DJs like Porky Chedwick and "Mad Mike" Metrovich stoked a rich and distinctive working-class musical culture. The popularity of this Pittsburgh sound was demonstrated in 1961 when 10,000 teens crowded the streets in front of the

Stanley Theater downtown where Porky was broadcasting. When police estimated that 50,000 more were tying up traffic to the downtown in an attempt to get there, Mayor Joe Barr had to intervene and ask Porky to suspend the broadcast.[49]

Perhaps even more fundamental to Pittsburgh's working-class life than the music that streamed from car radios and wafted through its clubs, sock hops and dance halls was the sports culture, already deeply rooted, that flowered in the baby-boom expansion of the 1950s. Little league baseball, Pop Warner football, basketball leagues, industrial league softball, bowling, wrestling, boxing, and hockey played out in big arenas and back lots. The region expressed itself in physicality, respected toughness and a fighting spirit. Hockey enjoyed a period of glory from the 1930s until the Pittsburgh Hornets lost their Duquesne Gardens rink to the wrecking ball in 1956. An entry in the American Hockey League, the Hornets won the Calder Cup in 1952 as the premier minor league team. Hockey only returned to Pittsburgh with the Penguins in 1967. The Duquesne Gardens had also been the birthplace of the Ice Capades. Organized by John H. Harris, these extravaganzas featured up to 150 young women skaters in both elaborate and sometimes scanty attire. Wrestling was big in Pittsburgh, and the legendary Bruno Sanmartino began his career here in the late 1950s, becoming World Wrestling Federation champion several times in the 1960s and 1970s, when wrestlers commanded more respect as professionals than entertainers.[50]

The courts at Mellon Park on Fifth Avenue, part of old R. B. Mellon's estate, became the hottest venue for basketball in Pittsburgh during the 1950s. While professional basketball never took hold in Pittsburgh, high school and college games were intensely followed. Those asphalt courts produced Charlie Cooper, who went from Westinghouse High to Duquesne University to the Boston Celtics, one of the first group of three black players to break into the National Basketball Association. Those courts also produced Ed Fleming, who graduated from Westinghouse to play at Niagara; Jack Twyman, who went from Central Catholic to Cincinnati; and perhaps the greatest of all, Maurice Stokes, who graduated from St. Francis College. The Duquesne University Dukes with All-American players like Dick Ricketts and Si Green won the National Invitation Tournament, which was the big venue in 1955. In that NIT contest, Stokes, who came from Rankin and led Westinghouse High to back-to-back city championships, won the most valuable player award for the tournament despite playing for the fourth place St. Francis team. Stokes went on to become the National Basketball Association Rookie of the Year in 1956 for a Rochester Royals team that included three Pittsburgh starters: Stokes, Fleming and Twyman. After the Royals moved their franchise to Cincinnati, Stokes, who Bob Cousy of the Boston Celtics called the "first great, athletic power forward" to play the game, was injured in a contest in Minneapolis and then collapsed three days later and remained permanently paralyzed. He won a workers' compensation claim and teammate Jack Twyman became his guardian. The story of the friendship between the black and white basketball stars from Pittsburgh became a Hollywood movie called "Maurie." Jack O'Malley, who played on those same courts a few years later, and knew all of the men who played there, went on to star for St. Francis and signed as a free agent for the Detroit Pistons but decided to become a priest. He went on to join Monsignor Charles Owen Rice in the 1960s as an activist for peace and social justice and became Pittsburgh's best known labor priest in the succeeding generation and a chaplain to the Pennsylvania AFL-CIO.[51]

The 1950s saw the rise of football as a sport capable of challenging the dominance of baseball as the national pastime. Friday night football games packed stadiums and fed fierce rivalries among teams. Vigorous high school programs fed collegiate programs which in turn fed the professional game. For 25 years from 1946 to 1966, Westinghouse High School won nearly every city title even as the complexion of its players changed from mostly white to virtually all black. Steel towns like Aliquippa, McKeesport, Homestead, and Duquesne had powerhouse programs that produced top level players. Leon Hart, who came out of the Turtle Creek Valley, was only the second lineman to win the Heisman trophy, which he did in 1949 at Notre Dame. Another Pro Hall of Famer, "Iron Mike" Ditka, graduated from Aliquippa High School in 1957. Dan Rooney of the Steelers explains the regional obsession with football. "The hard-working people, many of immigrant stock, adopted the game and made it their own. The sport that evolved in Western Pennsylvania bore little resemblance to the high-brow college game that came from Princeton and Yale at the end of the 19th Century. Western Pennsylvania-style football was physically tough, straight-ahead, and hard-hitting, reflecting the often brutal and sometimes violent realities of work in the steel mills and coal mines."[52]

The Steelers in the 1950s, despite a decided lack of pizzazz for most of the decade, developed a loyal working-class following based on tough defensive football. As a fan remarked: "Winning was not a concern of ours. It was how hard they played. Ernie Stautner, Jack Butler – those incredible hits made your week." Tackle Ernie Stautner, the last Steeler to play both offense and defense, made football's Hall of Fame, while defensive back Jack Butler, All-Pro from 1951-1959, holds the Steeler record of four interceptions in a single game. The culture of the Steelers established itself as "hard-nosed, hard-working, dirty, unkempt and tough." The Steelers had some talented quarterbacks with Jim Fink in 1952 throwing for 2,307 yards, local boy Ted Marchibroda in the mid-50s, and especially Bobby Layne, who joined the team in 1958 and led it to successive winning seasons (their only such in the decade). Layne was as famous for his exploits off the field as he was for those on it, for his ability "to soar with the eagles after hooting with the owls." Jack Butler said of Layne: "He was a smart ballplayer. Win at all costs. There was no in between, no gray area. He played one way – all out." Art Rooney respected character and loved characters. When it was time to renegotiate his contract, Layne signed the blank contract, handed it to the chief. "You fill in the rest. I trust you." Rooney gave Layne a larger amount than he would have asked for himself.[53]

The most famous football products of the hills of Western Pennsylvania have been its great quarterbacks. After the war, there was Johnny Lujack from Connellsville, winner of the Heisman trophy while leading Notre Dame to the national championship in 1946 and 1947, who went on to play for the Chicago Bears. In the 1950s, there were Youngwood's George Blanda, who was a Hall of Fame player for the Bears, Oilers, and Raiders; Rochester's Vito "Babe" Parilli, third in voting for the Heisman in 1951, who played for the Packers, Patriots, and Jets; and Ted Marchibroda, of Franklin High School, who led the Steelers for three years. Willie Thrower, the first black quarterback to play in the Big Ten for Michigan State, and in the National Football League for the Chicago Bears, was a star quarterback for two time WPIAL Class AA champion New Kensington. The New Kensington team turned down a chance to play in a prep game before the 1947 Orange Bowl because its sponsors objected to the color of its quarterback. His brief chance in the pros came on October 18, 1953, when he completed three of eight passes for 27 yards, but was removed by Bears coach, George Halas, in favor of starter George Blanda. Later, in the decades that followed, quarterbacks like Joe Namath (Beaver Falls), Joe Montana (Ringgold), Jim Kelly (Brady's Bend), and Oakland Central Catholic's own Dan Marino would bring fame to Western Pennsylvania football. Perhaps the greatest of all was the one that slipped through the hands of the Pittsburgh Steelers, Mt. Washington's Johnny Unitas. [54]

John Constantine Unitas, born in the Brookline neighborhood of Phil Murray and Pat Fagan in 1933, was the son of a Lithuanian coal delivery driver who died when he was only five. Forced by economic circumstances, his mother took her three children to a small two-bedroom house on unpaved William Street, a twisting road that cut a precarious path down the face of Mt. Washington. After his father's death, John and his older brother helped to keep their father's delivery business going. His mother worked multiple jobs to keep food on the table and she drilled into her children both stoicism and an intense work ethic with sayings like: "If you have to clean toilets for a living make them shine," "If you have a 'need,' we'll talk about it. But if it's only a "want" don't bring it up." From his mother, John absorbed an intense Catholicism that led him to mass on game day throughout his career. Unitas began his football career playing for little St. Justin's High School on Mt. Washington. It had barely 250 students, while the Catholic League superpowers were North Catholic with 1,000 students and Central Catholic in Oakland with 1,200. In John's junior year, North Catholic won the Catholic League championship, but Unitas beat out North Catholic's quarterback, Dan Rooney, for All-Catholic first-team honors. Notre Dame invited him on a recruiting visit to campus; but less than 140 pounds at the time, he got no offer. Bow-legged, downright skinny, with long arms and legs and exceptionally big hands, Unitas could throw the ball with authority. Unitas starred for a relatively weak Louisville program; and in 1955, in the ninth round, the 102nd pick, the Pittsburgh Steelers selected John Unitas. They signed him for $5,500. [55]

Unitas was kept on the team through the exhibition season with little chance to play, except in one remarkable scrimmage game in the mud when he put on a dazzling passing display. The Steelers under Coach Keisling were a conservative, hard-running team and Unitas got the axe despite having impressed some of the younger members of the Rooney family. After the cut, he had to hitch-hike back to Pittsburgh from St. Bonaventure's in Olean, New York, where the Steelers then trained. He got work as a Carpenters' Union pile-driver by day and played quarterback for the semi-pro Bloomfield Rams, starting at $6 a game. The Rams practiced at Deans Field under the Bloomfield Bridge and played their home games at Arsenal Park. Unitas led the team to an undefeated season against tough regional semi-pro teams like the Arnold Athletic Club and the Nanty-Glo Blackhawks, a team composed mostly of tough coal miners. As a college graduate who had had a tryout with the Steelers, he became a target for opposing teams. In 1955 Unitas got an invitation to try out for the struggling Baltimore Colts. Unitas went on to become one of the greatest quarterbacks in the history of the game with ten straight years in the Pro Bowl. But the game of games was the 1958 championship where Unitas led the Colts to a thrilling overtime win against the New York Giants in a game that saw twelve players who would enter professional football's Hall of Fame perform. With 349 yards passing, the performance of St. Justin's John Unitas in the dramatic victory before a huge television audience captured the imagination of the country and pushed professional football into serious contention with baseball as the nation's most popular sport. Unitas, as the game's most valuable player, was awarded a Chevrolet Corvette by *Sport* magazine. He traded it in for a station wagon. [56]

Stabilization in Steel

Phil Murray, approaching the 1952 labor negotiations, was worn and weary. Survivor of a succession of heart attacks, he had been at or near the center of the union movement for four decades. Rising to leadership in the Pittsburgh district of the mineworkers, hardened by the terrible labor struggles that followed World War I, administrator and negotiator during labor's astonishing rise to national power and influence, pilot of the labor movement during the massive mobilization of World War II and through the bitter purges that followed, he could contemplate the past with some satisfaction while viewing the future with a measure of anxiety. The union he headed had dramatically improved workers living standards, but the top-down command structure inherited from the Mineworkers was revealing its limitations. Aware of his increasing frailty and certain mortality, Murray began to worry about his successor. While succession to the presidency of the Congress of Industrial Organizations would be largely beyond his control, he grew increasingly concerned about the organization where he exercised near complete control, the United Steelworkers of America. His concern over succession was shared with even greater acuity by the man he had installed as Secretary-Treasurer, David J. McDonald.

While Phil Murray himself had risen to the top through a long term apprenticeship to John L. Lewis, he had worked as a miner, exercised elected leadership as a local and district president before serving Lewis as vice-president of the UMWA and the CIO. Dave McDonald, on the other hand, had always been a staff man even as he progressed from Murray's personal secretary to his diligent apprentice. Born in 1902 in the Hazelwood section of Pittsburgh, McDonald claimed a union pedigree through a steelworker father and maternal uncles, one of whom he claimed rather dubiously had been wounded in the Homestead strike and another, an ironworker, had been "knocked from a scaffolding to his death in the Monongahela by a runaway crane dangling a steel girder." His father was badly burned in an accident at the J&L mill. Young Dave set his sights on a white collar job and for two years hiked across the hot metal bridge to Holy Cross High School on the South Side to attend commercial courses in typing, shorthand, and bookkeeping. He worked short stints in the offices of J&L and later National Tube while the family moved up the hill to Greenfield. There, at St. Rosalia's, McDonald played tackle on the football team and picked up an interest in the theater. "I enjoyed acting and I was good at it."[57]

In 1920 McDonald took a typist job in the office of Wheeling Steel in downtown Pittsburgh. In 1923, he heard that Phil Murray, Vice-president of the United Mine Workers, was looking for a male secretary. Interviewed by Murray in the downtown office of UMWA District 5 President Pat Fagan, McDonald described the man he would work for over the next thirty years. "Phil Murray was thirty-eight then, a handsome, dignified, impeccably dressed man, with a shock of black hair that bent over rigidly horizontal eyebrows." Murray liked McDonald's Catholicism and his attitude toward education and hired him. He took his young secretary to New York two days later for a meeting with John L. Lewis. That first night in New York, he was among the crowd of 80,000 who saw Jack Dempsey knock out Luis Firpo from Argentina, the "Wild Bull of the Pampas," in the second round of a title fight at the Polo Grounds. The following day, he accompanied Murray and Lewis to Wilkes-Barre for a speech celebrating the anthracite strike settlement. Dave McDonald was playing in the big leagues and was determined to stay there.[58]

Over the thirty years that followed, McDonald proved his worth to Murray, the consummate contract negotiator, as secretary and administrator. McDonald also honed his skills as a bureaucratic in-fighter dedicated to inculcating union staff loyalty to the future top man. When Clint Golden left the vice-presidency for Harvard in 1946, a formidable rival was removed. Shortly afterward, when Michael Harris, a popular district director was nominated by several locals to run against McDonald for Secretary-Treasurer, McDonald moved swiftly and forcefully to deny him the nomination on the basis that his dues had not been paid in a timely manner. Harris then quit the union to take a government job obtained with Golden's assistance. McDonald worked assiduously using his position to secure the loyalty of key staff and directors.[59]

The talented director of the union's research department, Otis Brubaker, with a doctorate from Stanford, revealed the crass aspect of McDonald's methods. It happened that the general counsel of U.S. Steel, Roger Blough, was impressed by Brubaker's obvious talents. Inviting Brubaker to lunch at Pittsburgh's exclusive Duquesne Club, Blough offered to double his salary if Brubaker would switch sides. Brubaker refused and immediately reported the offer to Phil Murray, who deeply appreciated his principled position. A few hours later, McDonald, who Brubaker believed was contacted by the corporation directly, summoned the researcher into his office, called him a "God-damned fool" and advised "how I shouldn't be contemptuous about the power of money. He had long since discovered that most people could be bought for money and that he could buy and sell most of the people who worked for the union. And then he came with a real gem – for him at least – 'I never could quite trust anyone I couldn't buy.' At this stage, I really laughed....I should think, I said, that the last person on earth you could trust is somebody you could buy, because he's for sale to the next guy who'll pay a little more. I don't think that quite got through." Brubaker continued: "This judicious use of the union's money can and did build a very strong machine of people who owed a lot to him, and therefore were loyal in their own way."[60]

McDonald used Murray's serious health crises in 1941, 1948 and 1951 and his absorption in the political crisis of the CIO to build and consolidate organizational influence. Murray had long had misgivings about McDonald's personal and class loyalties. These doubts crystallized in 1951 when he was told that McDonald had revised Murray's obituary. Murray reportedly exploded: "See what the dirty son of a bitch has done to me. He's got me buried." In early January 1952, after extending the steel contract beyond its expiration date in response to a request from President Truman, Murray convened a special two-day union leadership conference in Atlantic City to explain the action he had taken in consideration of the increasingly dangerous Korean War situation. Murray used the occasion to launch an attack on McDonald, making it clear that his secretary's days as a power in the union were numbered, and called for greater accountability of the union's leadership to the members. Addressing the delegates, he asserted that "whatever life I have got shall be dedicated to bringing this organization closer to you. There is going to be no money used out of the treasury of this organization to buy the friendship of anybody in this union, to promote any man to any office in this organization and you are going to help the officers of your union, when a Convention comes around, to see to it that you have the kind of constitution that will permit you, the owners of this organization, to play a part in the operation of its affairs. That is the principle to which we adhere, and the bigger you get and the more responsibilities you assume, the closer you must live with the people who pay the taxes."[61]

At the Executive Board meeting before the May 1952 Philadelphia Convention, Murray moved to consolidate power in his own hands and strip the Secretary-Treasurer of many of the prerogatives he had accumulated. Looking to the future, he removed the election machinery from the office of the Secretary-Treasurer and set up a mechanism to allow the counting of ballots by an outside agency. Refusing to take Murray on, McDonald sat in silence while he was publicly disgraced and stripped of many powers and privileges. Abandoned by his retainers, he appeared a lonely and weak figure; but he was biding his time. In response to a query by a supporter as to why he had not fought back and gained thereby some respect from the union's board, McDonald confided: "Murray's not going to live....That's the reason why I took it. I'll inherit everything."[62]

Murray had other major concerns that took precedence over his Secretary-Treasurer. There was a steel contract to achieve and a presidential election to win. Once Murray postponed the strike, hearings were held before the federal Wage Stabilization Board; and in April 1952, the board issued a report that accepted a number of union bargaining positions. The steel industry rejected the findings, however, angering the president. Truman shocked the nation by seizing the mills in the name of national defense while refusing to use his Taft-Hartley injunction power against the union. Murray was ecstatic and the workers remained on the job. The steel industry immediately challenged the constitutionality of the presidential action; and on June 2, 1952, the Supreme Court declared the president's seizure of the mills unconstitutional. Murray immediately ordered the mills shutdown. On July 24, Truman called Murray and Benjamin Fairless of U.S. Steel to the White House and left them to settle the strike, which they did in short order. An important contract clause maintained against company-attack was Section 2-B. This past-practice agreement first won from U.S. Steel in 1947 accorded the union vastly expanded monitoring and negotiating power at the shop floor level. Improvements workers could see, smell, and taste in the experience of their daily lives, greatly strengthened their loyalty to the union at the grassroots level.[63]

Murray shifted his attention to the presidential election. His strategy since the 1930s had relied on using ties to a friendly government to wrest concessions from industry. With the growing possibility of a Republican president, that strategy was revealing its limitations. Despite declining health, Murray threw himself into the 1952 campaign for Adlai Stevenson warning workers of the "raw deal" that would replace Truman's Fair Deal if the Republicans regained control of the federal government after 20 years out of power. The immense popularity of Dwight David Eisenhower was not to be denied, however, as he won the election by 6.5 million votes. Exhausted and depressed, Murray stopped in San Francisco to give a speech to the steel union's western district before continuing on to Los Angeles to address the convention of the CIO. Before he left Pittsburgh, he confided in several staff members that he was determined to replace McDonald for using the wealth and power of the union for selfish purposes. In his final speech, Murray was rambling and conversational. In the words of one staffer, he "opened his heart and revealed the depth of feeling he held for the men of the mills." Murray said: "I take it that all of you feel, as I feel and believe, that it is the primary function of the trade union movement to feel the pulse-beats of the people; to live close to the people and understand their problems; and then use the constructive, intelligent strength of the organization to promote the well-being of the members of the union and their families."[64]

Murray collapsed that night while his wife lay asleep in bed. His death was discovered when he didn't respond to a hotel call at 6:30 a.m. to attend Sunday mass before catching the train for Los Angeles. Alerted by a subordinate, Dave McDonald rushed to Liz Murray's side and got permission to take over the funeral arrangements. He worked the phone all day, chartering a plane for himself and union leaders and ensuring that a large crowd would be on hand to meet him when he arrived in Pittsburgh. By seeming coincidence, his plane landed at the same time that Murray's body arrived in Pittsburgh, having been flown to Chicago and transferred to a train for Pittsburgh, so only a handful of staff went to the train station for the arrival of the body. Steelworker education director, Emery Bacon, described the scene at the airport. "I myself was terribly devoted to Murray but I did go to the airport…mainly for the spectacle that was involved in seeing this flight come in – all of us sitting in the Ambassadors Club and getting reports on the progress of the chartered McDonald flight across the continent…seeing all the people who would gather out there to welcome the new emperor and the retinue that would get off the plane and get into the limousines that were lined up. We did not go up and shake hands with David or greet him. We were sick, really sick, but we did watch what happened."[65]

Murray's funeral at St. Paul's Cathedral in Pittsburgh was befitting a head of state. The large church was packed and thousands stood outside during the service. In the mills, hundreds of thousands stood for a minute of silence in Murray's honor. McDonald, meanwhile, worked feverishly to consolidate his power. The only possible alternative to his ascension to the throne was the vice-president, James Thimmes, who was the first actual steelworker to rise to a top officer's position in the union. He had authored the resolution that folded the old Amalgamated Association into the CIO's Steel Workers Organizing Committee in 1936 at its Canonsburg Convention. McDonald offered him a vice-presidency of the CIO along with the retention of his USWA position and Thimmes accepted. On November 15, the USWA's Executive Board anointed McDonald as Murray's successor. Appearing before the press assembled at the William Penn Hotel, the new president declared: "I shall miss Philip Murray as much, if not more, than any man would. I hope that almighty God will give me the wisdom to carry on." McDonald chose as his successor as Secretary-Treasurer, I. W. Abel, a quietly competent, but little known district director from Canton, Ohio, who had worked at a number of steel companies and negotiated the first contract with Timken Roller Bearing Co. in 1937. In time, Abe, as he was known, would become a focus of internal opposition to McDonald's rule.[66]

David J. McDonald adopted a radically different lifestyle from Phil Murray, who rode the trolley to work from Brookline and until his death sought relaxation talking with old miner friends on the porch of Aunt Jane, his wife's sister-in-law, in the mining community of Hazelkirk, not far from where he met and married Liz Lavery, his wife of 42 years. Unlike Murray, Dave loved the limelight and always surrounded himself with a phalanx of retainers. He bought a house in the wealthy Pittsburgh suburb of Mt. Lebanon and a second one in Palm Springs, California. He adopted a hands-off management style that allowed his district directors to run their own fiefdoms with little interference as long as they were loyal and did not bother him. He wore Brooks Brother's suits, traveled in chauffeured limousines, and reveled in the company of the rich and powerful. The press by and large loved him because he was a show, and he knew how to feed them. They referred to him as a "labor statesman" as well as a "union businessman," and he considered both terms to be compliments. At the end of the 1952 negotiations, Ben Fairless had invited Murray to go on a joint tour of the steel corporation's mills. The invitation was extended to McDonald in the presence of Richard King Mellon on Christmas Eve in Fairless's corporate office shortly after Murray's demise. McDonald performed his role with gusto, explaining the tour "demonstrated to hundreds of thousands of union members that Fairless didn't have horns and to management across the nation that I could talk in complete sentences and didn't carry bombs in my suitcase." While McDonald began the tour in his usual style in a limousine, Vin Sweeney, the union's public relations man, pointed out this was making a bad impression on the workers. From then on, the labor statesman toured by bus.[67]

A year after McDonald ascended to the presidency, a huge party was thrown for him in Pittsburgh. Mayor Lawrence declared November 28, 1953, David J. McDonald Day. The entire downtown was lit up in his honor as 3,000 business and labor leaders gathered in the "Day for Dave" dinners. At the main dinner affair, Ben Fairless proclaimed that labor and management were "inseparably bound together in a state of economic matrimony." Several months later, a fawning biography called *Man of Steel* was published that hailed McDonald as the "master mason of the pedestal that lifted the richly-gifted elder statesman, Murray, into the high public position that he won and held." Breathless prose wafted like incense throughout. "He looked more like a college football coach, big, broad shouldered, blue-eyed, handsome with silver-white hair. Unlike the old-style labor leaders who thought the members wanted them to put up a 'poor front,' this man of steel dresses to fit the occasion and in keeping with the growing prestige of labor." In general, the biography was greeted with either laughter or embarrassment. McDonald cultivated many outside interests and the day-to-day running of the union was gradually turned over to the union's general counsel, Arthur Goldberg. The talented lawyer initially regarded McDonald with "distrust and dismay," but ultimately came to accept his own increasingly central role in the union, filling the vacuum created by the president's varied social activities.[68]

Surrounded by his coterie of well-paid attendants, Dave came to specialize in dramatic entrances. He kept the headquarters staff under tight reins through his personal secretary, Howard Hague, and an ex-FBI man, Robert Maheu, who allegedly tapped phones and employed blackmail to impose control. When Vice President James Thimmes died, McDonald announced his intention to name Hague as VP, but was fiercely opposed by Joe Molony, director of the New York district that included Buffalo and Lackawanna. McDonald rammed through Hague's interim appointment over the strong objections of ten members of the union's International Executive Board. Meeting privately with Molony after the tumultuous and acrimonious board meeting, McDonald told him: "If you were in the United Mine Workers, you'd be dead by now." Molony replied: "You silly son of a bitch, first of all, this is not the United Mine Workers of America and I don't like people to threaten me, and don't you ever try it again." Under intense pressure from McDonald, the rebel directors began to cave, but Molony decided to run against Hague. For the first time, a serious challenge was mounted to the leadership of the union. Under severe staff pressure, Hague garnered the nomination of 1,527 locals to 540 for Molony. Molony's campaign, which was subjected to threats and acts of violence including a beating of Molony himself, convened a Rank and File Conference in Cleveland where they urged the formation of a staff union and open elections with independent tellers. Molony and his supporters were often blocked from addressing union meetings and held gatherings in local taverns. Hague defeated Molony 400,017 to 184,542. Despite suspicion of widespread vote tampering, Molony declined to contest the count. What testified to the fundamental health of the union was not the shenanigans of McDonald and his supporters, but the fact that Molony and other rebel directors survived politically in the aftermath of the contest as elected leaders with secure bases in their own locals and districts.[69]

McDonald had little interest in conflict with the corporations. In 1954 there was a 12-hour strike. In 1956 the union for the first time entered into industry-wide bargaining negotiations. McDonald assumed the chairmanship of all the negotiating committees at the six biggest companies. The union had always striven for industry-wide wage uniformity and it made sense for U.S. Steel, especially, to control the rate of wage rise and spread the cost evenly across the competitors. Previously, an agreement was reached with U.S. Steel that then set a pattern for negotiations with other companies. McDonald was at his best in these sorts of multi-faceted negotiations and after a four-week walkout, the union arguably won the best contract it ever achieved. Besides a significant annual wage increase, the union won a cost-of-living allowance, the establishment of a Supplemental Unemployment Benefit that cushioned the effect of economic cycles on steelworkers by guaranteeing them 80 percent of their salary when laid-off, rather than the 60 percent provided by governmental unemployment benefits. They also secured the long-sought union shop provision.[70]

McDonald played a major role in the reuniting of the AFL and the CIO by using John L. Lewis and undercutting Walter Reuther. While two members of the old Mineworker triumvirate of John L. Lewis, Phillip Murray, and William Green that had played such a dominant role in national union politics were now dead, John L. Lewis remained, defiant and isolated, undisputed king of a shrinking domain. Lewis led his last great strike in 1949 in defense of the Miners' health, welfare, and pension funds. It was finally settled in early 1950 through extensive wildcat strikes by miners that turned into a national shutdown in "defiance" of Lewis's order to return to work. Lewis, under criminal and civil contempt of court charges, faced with a Taft-Hartley injunction and Truman's threat to seize the mines, had to rely on the miners' "disobedience" of his orders to return to work to win the contract. Following the settlement, Lewis tried to maintain a position of national prominence by brokering a reunion of the AFL and CIO, but neither of the new leaders, George Meany or Walter Reuther, wanted to let the old lion of labor back into the top leadership circles of the labor movement. As the demand for coal shrunk with the expansion of oil, natural gas, hydroelectric production, and the beginnings of nuclear power generation, operators sought to protect profits by reducing labor costs. They did this by mechanization in the large and mid-sized union mines, but small non-union operations began to proliferate as well. Also, largely non-union strip-mining operations accounted for one-quarter of the annual output of coal by the mid 1950s. All these factors reduced the number of miners along with John L. Lewis's power and prestige. Mining employment dropped by about 300,000 and young workers bore the brunt of the reductions. Furthermore, the unionized sector of the industry was interested in solving the industry's problems in a less confrontational and businesslike way. George Love, a Pennsylvania blue blood with a Princeton degree, became the force behind the consolidation of the industry. In 1945 he had merged three of the largest companies including most of the old Mellon and Frick properties into Consolidation Coal or Consol, the world's largest producer of bituminous coal. In 1950 he was the driving force behind the organization of the Bituminous Coal Operators Association that accounted for fifty percent of all coal production in the country. By the late 1950s a relative peace was settling over the historically tumultuous coal industry based on economic necessity, not interclass love."[71]

On December 5, 1955, the Congress of Industrial Organizations, now led by Walter Reuther of the United Auto Workers, merged with the American Federation of Labor, headed by a crusty, blunt talking plumber named George Meany. While the joining of the two rival labor federations received extensive press coverage (including banner headlines in the *New York Times* for most of the unification convention), there was little doubt the act was one of stabilization and consolidation, not inspiration and growth. The healing of the split between the two great labor federations that had occurred 20 years earlier with such drama and national resonance among the working class inspired little interest or enthusiasm among the rank and file. Two years earlier, Daniel Bell, labor reporter for the business magazine *Fortune* wrote of "the decline of unionism as a moral vocation….Where there has not been outright spoliation, one finds among union leaders an appalling arrogance and high-handedness in their relation to the rank and file, which derives from the corruption of power." While this judgment was perhaps overly severe and ignored a lot of democratic stirring at the local union level, there was an uncomfortable element of truth in the observation.[72]

Dave McDonald acted as the unlikely midwife and his counsel, Arthur Goldberg, the draftsman of the reunited labor federation. Whatever his other limitations, McDonald was highly skilled at political maneuver. It was McDonald's highly publicized meetings with John L. Lewis and the Teamsters President Dave Beck, plus threats to withdraw USWA per capita payments to the industrial union federation, that drove the CIO into the arms of the AFL. The centralized union structure of the Steelworkers had evolved to deal effectively with the powerful steel industry dominated for most of the century by U.S. Steel. The auto union, on the other hand, had emerged from the 1930s with a strong tradition of factionalism and internal dissent. The UAW, bargaining with the newer and more technologically advanced auto companies, had raised autoworkers' wages and benefits somewhat above the steelworkers. The diverse character of the two large unions reinforced divergent leadership styles. McDonald and Reuther heartily detested one another and since their two unions constituted 60 percent of the members of the industrial federation, their personal relationship mattered. McDonald referred to Reuther as "that no good, red-headed socialist bastard," while Reuther's people saw McDonald as a "boozy, self-inflated fraud." John L. Lewis, ever the consummate wordsmith, referred to the Reuther-led CIO as "a federated group dominated by intellectual inebriates in frantic pursuit of the butterflies of their own delusions."[73]

The CIO's problems went deeper than personality conflicts, however. By 1950, after the CIO had expelled a quarter of its members and was engaged in divisive raids on left-wing unions, the AFL legitimately claimed twice the membership of the CIO. While Reuther called for expansion and organizing, the CIO focused mostly on recalcitrant industrial sectors like textiles and petrochemicals, while ignoring public sector workers, and especially women and blacks who occupied the lowest rungs in the growing clerical and service sectors of the society. In fact, the AFL unions, especially the Teamsters, despite its reputation for criminal connections and corruption, had made modest but greater progress in those sectors than the CIO. Increasingly, the CIO had become a lobbying and public relations operation. The industrial federation's final convention immediately preceded the combined reunification convention that opened in New York on December 5, 1955. Only Mike Quill of the Transit Workers Union denounced the merger and called the constitution of the combined organization "a license for inter-union warfare; a license for racketeering; a license for discrimination against minority groups."[74]

In fact, it was the inability of unions to reach out to blacks and women that severely limited the growth of organized labor. The position of African-Americans inside the unions and in the greater society emerged in the 1960s as a major challenge. Due in significant measure to the gains made by industrial unions, blacks had seen their incomes rise from 40 to 60 percent of whites in the 20 years of the independent CIO's existence. While the new AFL-CIO constitution asserted that "all workers whatever their race, color, creed or national origin are entitled to a share in the full benefits of trade union organization," the lack of any enforcement mechanism to secure minority rights reduced the impact of such principles in an organization that jealously defended individual union autonomy. If the position of blacks inside, as well as outside, the labor movement was ignored, the status of women workers received even less attention than that given to minorities. Women who had made such significant contributions to the war effort were expected to return to home and family once the mobilization was over. When *Steel Labor* featured "Women of Steel" on its cover in 1951, it was not the welders, riveters, and machine operators of the war years, but housewives shown shopping, canning, and baking pies for their happy children. The fact that the Communist-led unions had been the most aggressive in their advocacy of expanded rights for blacks and women helped undercut support for advances in these areas once they were expelled. The inability to achieve national health care, pension, and unemployment coverage for everyone isolated unionized workers from the low-pay and benefit-poor workers in the south and in the service sector. [75]

While McDonald was playing an important role in the national arena, a second challenge to his increasingly high-handed regime came not from the union's district leadership, but arose spontaneously out of a rank and file revolt during the course of the 1956 convention in Los Angeles. The rebellion caught McDonald completely by surprise with some justification, since he had just negotiated a very favorable contract. Rank and file convention ferment began with a revolt by Canadian union members against an administration proposal to eliminate the elected position of national director for Canada and make the post an appointed one. A forceful protest against the proposal by the Canadian delegates with a vigorous lobbying effort in the hallways and reception rooms caused the first rejection of a leadership proposal by convention delegates in the union's history. With the convention pot now stirred, a more dangerous revolt was ignited by a proposed dues increase from three to five dollars a month that followed on the heels of a substantial wage increase voted by the convention for the union's top officers. The convention split bitterly over the issue; and after a tumultuous debate, the proposal was declared passed without a roll call vote. Delegates who were opposed to the proposal returned to their locals with an issue guaranteed to stir membership discontent.[76]

While the dues increase provided the hot issue, a rebellion was brewing that envisioned nothing less than a change of union leadership. Despite wild accusations by McDonald, the rebels were not ideologues with a radical ambition to restructure the union, let alone overthrow the existing social order. The revolt against McDonald was centered in the International's backyard in Western Pennsylvania and fundamentally involved the right to challenge the leadership through the electoral instruments of the union's own making. Fifty delegates met in the back room of Leonard's Cafe in McKeesport and formed the Dues Protest Committee with Donald Rarick of the Mon Valley's Irvin Works as chairman. Other key leaders included Frank O'Brien from the Hazelwood J&L plant, where McDonald's father had worked; Nick Mamula, president of J&L's Aliquippa Works, the union's second largest local; and Anthony Tomko, from the McKeesport Tube Works local. Any rebellion from below faced formidable obstacles to uniting disparate and far-flung local unions against a strong centralized administration. A call by the rebels for a special convention to reconsider the dues increase picked up considerable steam when Gary, Indiana's Local 1014, the largest in the union, endorsed the petition. When USWA General Counsel Goldberg ruled the petition unconstitutional and dissident directors Bill Hart and Joe Molony declined to lead the revolt, Rarick decided to run against McDonald for president. Rarick succeeded in gaining the nomination of 91 locals versus 1,905 for the incumbent. McDonald pulled out all the stops, mobilizing the staff, printing an edition of Steel Labor immediately prior to the election characterized as a "sustained hymn of praise for McDonald," and reportedly combined threats and bribe offers to Rarick in an unsuccessful effort to get him to withdraw. Despite widespread charges of vote fraud and ballot tampering, Rarick, a virtual unknown, received over a third of the votes by the official tally, 404,172 for McDonald and 223,516 for the challenger.[77]

Appeals by Rarick to Senator McClellan's Select Committee on Improper Activities in the Labor or Management Field were eventually denied by its Chief Counsel Robert F. Kennedy, who perhaps was sensitive to the importance of the USWA's support for his brother's political ambitions. The rebels, however, demonstrated their support at the local level as Rarick won the presidency of his Irvin Works local; O'Brien, the presidency of the Hazelwood local; Tony Tomko won the presidency in McKeesport; Mamula was re-elected president in Aliquippa; and Thomas Flaherty, another rebel, won in the Fontana, California local. Without a doubt, the greatest achievement of the rebellion was the re-energizing of rank-and-file democracy at the local level. Despite widespread dislike of McDonald, the exercise of the democratic process strengthened the union and helped secure membership solidarity when it was tested in the great strike that ended the decade of the 1950s.[78]

At the 1958 union convention, McDonald took no chances on a repeat performance by the dissidents. He made his entry into the convention with upraised arms from behind parted curtains as the band played a football fight song. He invoked the spirit of Phil Murray and thundered from the podium that he would "not permit the enemies from within to destroy this union of yours." His blistering speech, improbably accusing the rebels of harboring Communists, Trotskyites, agents of the companies and the National Association of Manufacturers, ended with a dramatic call: "Rise up, you strong men of steel, rise up united, strong men of steel, and show America, show those who hate you and show all the people of the world the real tough metal of which you are made." At this point, the doors to the hall crashed open and a large group of McDonald supporters snake-danced down the aisle carrying a casket marked "DPC." The remainder of the first day was taken up by oratorical hymns to the president's leadership. [79]

On the second day of the convention, Frank O'Brien, one of the most respected of the dues protesters, rose to protest the characterization of the rebels as union-wreckers. Mike Zahorsky from Mamula's Aliquippa local defended the members' "God-given right to express opinions" as good for the union. When Rarick rose to speak, he was constantly interrupted; but McDonald, aware of Rarick's weakness as a public speaker, expressed repeated solicitude that he be heard and offered his "personal protection." While Rarick was speaking, however, a scurrilous pamphlet entitled "Mask of Deceit" was circulated to every delegate warning them of the dues protesters insidious goals. Sections of the pamphlet were titled: Gangster Alliance, Terror Reign, Big Lie, Management Collusion, etc. Over the course of the day, proposals to elect staff men, to number election ballots, and to reintroduce the issue of the dues increase were shouted down and then defeated. O'Brien, Mamula, and Rarick remained defiant and defended themselves repeatedly at the convention despite an attack on them by Joe Molony himself, who opposed this rebellion and initiated a resolution to have the locals try those "who under the guise of protesting a dues increase in fact are seeking to undermine the union as an institution." As perhaps Molony anticipated, the charges of "dual unionism" were not upheld by the locals; and with the revolt effectively suppressed, McDonald even invited Rarick to serve on the 1959 U.S. Steel negotiating committee. In the 1960 local elections, Rarick, O'Brien, Mamula, and Tomko were all re-elected to lead their locals. A measure of union democracy survived at the grassroots.[80]

Complacency and Crisis

While Dave McDonald's reign inside of the USWA epitomized the institutionalization of big labor inside the capitalist system and revealed the limitations of its top-down management style, the complacency and over-confidence of the steel industry also ignored the approach, in the words of the foremost steel historian, Kenneth Warren, of "a period of unprecedented troubles." Corporate complacency was to a degree comprehensible. The post-World War II expansion of American power opened global markets to U.S. production. In 1945, American production of 80 million tons of raw steel, down from its 1944 record high, amounted to an estimated 62.4 percent of total world production. In 1950, as Western European production recovered, the U.S. share fell to 46.6 percent even though its total production continued to increase. From its peak production of 95.5 million tons at the height of World War II, yearly production reached 147.6 million tons a year prior to the 1959 strike. Despite increased production and solid profitability, the leadership of the U.S. steel industry resembled an ostrich with its head buried in the sand in its failure to take account of the rapid technological advances that were transforming the industry and invigorating its competitors. Warren wrote of this period that American steel companies were afflicted with "overweening self-confidence combined with an incapacity to recognize that there were innovators, good practical steel men, and expansion-minded companies elsewhere in the world." By 1960 the United States produced only 26 percent of the world's steel, a lower percentage than any time since the 1870s, at the very dawn of the age of steel.[81]

The steady increase of American steel capacity following the war and through the decade of the 1950s was due to three fundamental factors: first, the permanent war economy stimulated by the Korean War and sustained by Cold War competition with the Soviet Union; second, the explosive demand for consumer goods fed by the broad growth of the middle class; and finally, the burgeoning automobile culture that spawned suburban sprawl and drove the enormous infrastructure investments necessitated by residential expansion beyond the confines of the urban centers and the crowded industrial valleys. The overwhelming bulk of this growth in steel production was achieved by expansion at existing mill sites which preserved old patterns of production and distribution. Less than five percent of the new production came from greenfield plants. While growth declined in heavy plate production and rail, it increased rapidly in construction materials like structural beams, reinforcing rods, and especially in the light, flat-rolled products that supplied the mass consumer market. U.S. Steel's strength, however, was in product lines that were growing slowly or not at all. In addition, southern and western markets were expanding faster than the northeast and mid-west regions served by the Pittsburgh region. The raw steel-making capacity of U.S. Steel in the Pittsburgh district remained essentially flat from 1945 to 1959 at 12 million tons. The Chicago region regained its dominance in steel, an achievement that was strengthened by the opening of the St. Lawrence Seaway in 1959. An increased reliance on foreign sources of high-grade iron ore led U.S. Steel to make its one concession to the shifting global realities when it opened its sole 1950s greenfield plant, the Fairless Works, on the east coast where it could be supplied by newly acquired sources of ore in Venezuela. However, massive postwar investments in taconite ore production in Minnesota and the opening of Canadian mines tied the corporation to expensive sources while other countries had access to much cheaper ores increasingly available by ship on the international market. Japan, especially, and to a lesser extent Europe, was building new mills at large efficient coastal facilities serviced by ships to target expanding global markets. Already by 1960, 11 percent of the world's output of steel was being shipped across national boundaries. Despite these warning signs, corporate confidence was sustained by healthy profit levels during the 1950s.[82]

The complacency that reigned at U.S. Steel was revealed most starkly in its attitude toward technological innovation. By the late 1950s, Japan was building blast furnaces that were bigger and more efficient than their American rivals. In 1952 the basic oxygen furnace was introduced in Austria, while the new U.S. Steel Fairless Works that also opened in 1952 employed the open hearth technology. In the 1950s, U.S. industry installed 40 million tons of new melt capacity, all of which was obsolete when built, but which needed to be maintained to recoup the huge capital investments that had been expended. McLouth Steel in Detroit installed an oxygen converter in 1954 and J&L's Aliquippa works installed the country's second one in 1957. A similar situation involved the adoption of continuous casting technology, which despite the United States having done much of the research and development on the process was slow in its application in the nation's mills. This process involved pouring the molten steel into a mold that directed the cooling metal through rollers to produce a semi-finished slab that could go directly to the finishing mills, thus eliminating the primary mills and soaking pits involved in traditional ingot production. These new processes represented the biggest improvements in steelmaking since the introduction of the Bessemer furnace and the open-hearth furnaces installed by Carnegie at his Edgar Thomson works in the 1870s. Ironically, a continuous caster was installed in Braddock only in 1986 as part of the settlement of a six-month strike with the USWA.[83]

A sense of crisis was deepening in the country during the late 1950s. Racial tensions were stimulating black militancy and broad challenges to patterns of segregation and discrimination that were blatant and obvious in the south, but no less real in northern cities such as Pittsburgh. The Cold War, which had focused on enemies both real and imagined within, was now increasingly being expressed as a global competition in technology and productive capacity. At the end of the decade, the steel industry underwent a sustained strike that seemed to be simply the continuation of the pattern of ritualized labor-management struggles that had followed World War II, but which marked a watershed in labor relations and marked the end of an era. Ahead lay a new decade when the issues of racism, war, and economic justice would take on a new urgency and generate a level of internal social conflict not seen inside the country since the 1930s.

In September 1957, at the opening of the school year, the country witnessed a flaring of mob violence against the integration of the public schools in Little Rock, Arkansas. A 14 year-old black girl had nearly been lynched in the initial attempt at integration. In 1954 the U.S. Supreme Court had struck down the "separate but equal" legal doctrine that underpinned legal racial segregation. Governor Orval Faubus openly defied a federal court injunction and seemingly encouraged acts of defiant resistance. In response, President Eisenhower, who had vacillated and remained silent throughout the building crisis, dispatched 1,000 paratroopers from the 101st Airborne Division to Little Rock. For the former five-star general, the issue was no longer racial integration, but insurrection. This was the first time federal troops had been dispatched to the South since their withdrawal in 1877. The president was widely criticized for following inaction with over-reaction. These events damaged Eisenhower's prestige; but on October 4, the Soviet Union launched Sputnik, the first man-made satellite to reach earth orbit and the United States was in the middle of a full-blown political crisis.[84]

The launching of an artificial satellite by the Soviets caused deep consternation in the United States. Ironically, Sputnik helped undermine one of the basic premises of McCarthyism. Russian technological accomplishment could no longer be blamed on internal betrayal. The Russians had not copied us or stolen our secrets; they had surged ahead of us on their own power. Nikita Khrushchev, the Soviet premier, had consolidated his power after his momentous denunciation of Stalin's crimes by displacing many of his rivals within the Soviet system. Unlike his predecessor, however, he did not execute those he perceived as resistant to his rule, he demoted them. He had staked much of his prestige and power behind the Russian development of Inter-Continental Ballistic Missiles (ICBMs). American U-2 spy planes that could traverse Soviet territory beyond the reach of Russian planes or guns at 70,000 feet were a security threat and a major irritant. On October 4, the Soviets launched Sputnik and, thereby, in the eyes of the world, leapfrogged over the Americans in terms of technological accomplishment. They now had a surveillance vehicle that trumped the Americans, demonstrated their prowess in rocketry and their potential ability to reach American targets from

Soviet missile sites. This event, more than any other, led Americans to question the nation's political leadership and opened an opportunity for a younger and more hopeful generation of politicians. Anxieties stimulated by Cold War security concerns had been revealed the preceding year in Pittsburgh, January 31, 1956, when a B-25 airplane swooped down low over the Homestead High Level Bridge, ditched, floated, and then sank into the Monongahela opposite the neighborhood of Hazelwood. Trains and roads were closed, police and federal agents sealed the area and great secrecy was imposed. These measures led to widespread speculation that the plane carried chemical or nuclear material. At least one crewman died. Despite the testimony of local kids who had little difficulty avoiding the security cordons and watched the removal of the plane, the question of whether the plane was raised from the muddy waters became a subject of great rumor and speculation for 50 more years.[85]

Nikita Khrushchev, himself, visited Homestead on September 25, 1959. After a stop in Washington to meet with President Eisenhower, the Soviet Premier went on a tour of America with three requests. He wanted to visit Disneyland, an Iowa farm, and Mesta Machine in West Homestead. While in California, he had his trip to Disneyland cancelled for security reasons. He held a friendly meeting with Harry Bridges of the Longshoremen's Union but was snubbed by AFL-CIO president George Meany and rudely lectured to by Walter Reuther. After visiting a large farm in Iowa where he enjoyed himself immensely and began receiving more sympathetic press coverage, he arrived in Pittsburgh on September 23, 1959. After stopping on Mt. Washington for a nighttime view of the city, he traveled the next morning out to Homestead. What his thoughts were on that brilliant autumn day in the middle of the longest steel strike in American history as he passed over the Homestead High Level Bridge and stared down at the silent mill – whether he was impressed by either the power or the freedom of the American worker – was not recorded. Coming off the bridge, waving to the crowds from his open convertible, he passed Chiodo's tavern and the Steel Workers Organizing Committee's granite obelisk honoring the Homestead strikers who died on July 6, 1892 that had been dedicated in 1942. Turning right, he proceeded to the great Mesta Machine plant, ironically a non-union facility still working despite the steel strike. Inside the plant, despite cordons of security, Khrushchev talked to one of the workers, Dmitri Zastupenevich, in Russian and was offered a cigar by a clerk, Kenneth Jackey. Touched by the gesture, the Soviet Premier stripped off his wristwatch and gave it to the worker. [86]

The 1959 Steel Strike

The 1959 steel strike lasted 116 days and had profound implications for both the union and the industry though most observers simply saw it as the sixth and final strike in a series of work stoppages in steel after World War II that had become almost ritualistic. The significance of the strike as an exercise in deepening rank-and-file commitment to the union has been brilliantly analyzed in a book by Jack Metzgar, *Striking Steel*. Partially a memoir of the relationship of a youth and his steelworker father during the long work stoppage in Johnstown, the book also examines what the strike and the union meant to working conditions on the shop floor and in an improved standard of living for both their family and the community in which they lived. From the time that Metzgar's dad joined the union in 1936 up to 1959, steelworkers *real* wages increased 110 percent, with most of that increase coming after the war. The family owned a car, refrigerator, and television set. They also had life, health, and disability insurance, supplemental unemployment benefits, and the promise of a pension to supplement Social Security. The union had brought a significant measure of dignity and freedom to workers lives, and they were fully prepared to sacrifice to maintain them.

The perception and remembrance of the 1950s as a time of repressive conformism and spiritless materialism might relate to the middle-class organization man, the white-collar professional and management worker of the time. It did not relate to us. All the discretion that the foreman and the company were losing was flowing right into our home. There were choices. There were prospects. There were possibilities. Few of these had been there before. Now they were. And because they came slowly, year by year, contract by contract, strike by bitter strike, they gave a lilting, liberating feeling to life – a sense that no matter what was wrong today, it could be changed, it could get better – in fact, by the late 1950s, that it was quite likely that it *would* get better. Hang in there. Stick with it. These moral injunctions to daily fortitude made so much sense then when there were so many visible payoffs for doing so. And as my father would find out, my mother, my sister and I – like nearly everybody else in American society – were learning to tolerate less and less repression from anybody or anything, including him. If what we lived through in the 1950s was not liberation, then liberation never happens in real lives.[87]

Representing the steel industry in negotiations was U.S. Steel Chairman Roger Blough, a cold and humorless corporate lawyer who had risen through the industry's financial side and his labor relations chief, R. Conrad Cooper, a fiercely competitive former University of Minnesota football star. Interpreting rank-and-file discontent as a sign of union disunity, the corporation was looking for a fight with a recession slowing demand for steel and a decade of high profits filling their war chest. The total value of U.S. Steel common stock had risen from $500 million to $5 billion over the decade. The U.S. industry was actually in trouble for poor investment decisions and leadership complacency, but Blough saw an opportunity to weaken the union and solve the industry's long-range problems on the backs of the workers. The company opened negotiations demanding a wage and benefit freeze and the liquidation of the cost-of-living allowance. For his part McDonald believed the union's members were "generally fat and comfortable and had little stomach for a strike." However, a month before the strike contract expiration, the company demanded eight basic changes in what workers regarded as the "workplace rule of law." The first seven of these proposals targeted work schedules, seniority, vacation scheduling, and management's right to set incentives and work standards. These demands were advanced to push the union into a strike, while the real company target was the eighth demand – the elimination of Section 2-B, the major control the local union at the shop floor level exercised on the imposition of management rights.[88]

When the company revealed its real point of attack, McDonald was elated. "The industry negotiators…had done us a favor, handed us an issue. I couldn't have written the script better myself." McDonald was right. The company had attacked the most important tool that workers possessed to regulate matters at the point of production. Section 2-B, for workers and their immediate shop floor representatives like Jack Metzgar's union steward father, was a tremendous source of daily power, control, and dignity on the job. For the company, the section was an onerous restriction on management rights, an invitation to featherbedding, and the source of those "rigid work rules" that were rendering American industry uncompetitive. The oncoming struggle had become a test of wills and the relative willingness of both sides to sacrifice.[89]

On July 15, 1959, 500,000 steelworkers went on strike when David J. McDonald told the Associated Press "We're on strike." Despite McDonald's lack of popularity in many quarters of the union, there was no crack in rank-and-file solidarity, no thought of crossing the picket line, and the companies made no effort to try. Below McDonald, the union had developed into a complex organization with strong regional leaders, 1,200 staff representatives and in nearly every local union, officers and grievance men who were tough, elected representatives who had earned the respect of their constituency. The demand by the steel corporation for unrestrained shop floor control galvanized the union base. The dues protesters lined up for battle with the corporations behind their leadership without a peep of complaint. Some union activists had been sharply critical of the rebels for publicly demonstrating division and dissension within the union, thereby raising the hopes of corporate leadership that they could take McDonald on and weaken the union. Joe Periello, a union militant at Aliquippa, blamed the dues protesters for the strike. "They almost killed us – almost destroyed the union." He had a point. Unity was the source of union power. As veteran activist, A. J. Muste wrote in the 1920s, a union is an uneasy combination of an army, with discipline required to take on powerful foes; while at the same time, it is also a town meeting that relies on the voluntary adherence of its members rooted in the conviction that they have both a stake and a voice in the organization. The strength of the union in 1959 came from the uneasy balance that had been maintained through the combination of struggle and solidarity.[90] Jack Metzgar's father, Johnny Metzgar, disliked McDonald and allied himself with the protesters, however:

> For my father, democracy in the union was not a primary value, and there definitely was a danger in having too much of it. Usually, indeed almost always good union members followed their leaders – from McDonald to the lowest level of griever – without questioning or carping. But there needed to be a time for questioning and carping, not for the sake of some principle, but because such a time was necessary to inform and correct leaders and to be informed and corrected by them. More than that, such a time and such a process was necessary for achieving unity and discipline – that is, for *being* a union. Without that outlet, the union would eventually either burst apart like a balloon with to much air or shrivel for the lack of it.[91]

The 1959 strike established that there would be no backward steps and successfully defended all the principles the union had won in the previous 20 years. There would be no steel strike of any kind for a quarter of a century afterward, and there would never be another nationwide steel strike again. Avoiding a strike became the primary goal of every negotiation from then until 1973 when the steelworkers gave up the right to strike for a period of time in an attempt to deal with the deepening crisis of the industry.[92]

At the center of the 1959 conflict was Section 2-B of the steel contract, "Local Working Conditions." Called the "best past-practice clause an American union ever got in its contract," the clause, won in 1947, affirmed that none of the well-established ways of doing things in any given workplace could be changed without negotiation with the union, or if "the basis for the existence of the local working condition is changed or eliminated, thereby making it unnecessary to continue such local working condition" (for example by technological change). A 1953 arbitration decision by Sylvester Garrett determined that changes to work crews could not be made by arbitrary decision or by time-study men who argued that fewer men could do the job. Crew sizes could only be cut if there was improved technology that reduced the need for the men, not by devising incentive systems that drove the existing crew to work harder or faster. The clause gave the union the power to take company changes to arbitration, and in 1960 the U.S. Supreme Court ruled in what became known as the *Steelworkers Trilogy* that arbitrators had the final word in such disputes. In short, management had to negotiate with workers, not simply boss them. The clause encouraged investment in new technology, because productivity increases could only be achieved through technological change, not speed-up.[93]

For workers, Section 2-B was a powerful tool to regulate the pace of work and control an incentive system that tried to push men as fast as physically able. Sticking together, recognizing the need to give a fair day's work so as to not price yourself out of a job, but also to pace oneself, so as to not work yourself or your neighbor out of a job by destroying one's health, this ethic was the basis for working class life. The union became the instrument on the shop floor for the "blue collar ethic." This ethic much heralded by advertising agencies promoting the Pittsburgh region or its sports teams is based on notions about hard work and team effort which are true as far as they go, but the real thing in its day was a collective understanding about the relationship between hard work and the good life in a community based on mutuality and respect.[94]

The 1959 strike ended in virtually a complete victory for the union. The working-class communities held together for 116 payless days, outlasted the companies, supported one another, and defended a way of life. Foreign imports of steel increased during the strike, though they had yet to become a serious threat. The recession that followed the strike meant that many workers were laid-off. For them and their families, the hard times continued. New competition for steel from plastics and aluminum were eating away at steel's consumer markets. The conservative investment strategies of the 1950s became an albatross around the steel industry's neck in the 1970s and helped bring on the collapse of the 1980s. For the Pittsburgh corporate establishment, the union victory helped harden historically strong anti-union attitudes. In 1960, with black students sitting-in southern lunch counters, and a young charismatic president issuing a challenge to a new generation, the tough solidarity of the 116 day strike faded from memory. The popular media hardly noticed it anyway as they directed more attention to cheating on a game show than they did trying to understand the meaning of a disciplined and non-violent shutdown of a major industry by a half-million of its citizens. When an entire new generation began to rebel in the search for a better society, they regarded the union movement as a conservative obstacle. Precious few of those radical middle-class kids with working-class roots realized on whose shoulders they stood.[95]

Changing Images, New Stirrings

While Pittsburgh in the 1950s reached a high plateau of growth and prosperity and much of its working-class population was beginning to relax a bit and enjoy the fruits of the heroic efforts of the previous two decades, there were stirrings of new consciousness, as well as new developments whose significance would only be realized in time. The importance of the city's universities in the future of the city was signaled by the achievements of medical research at the University of Pittsburgh and new computing science at Carnegie Tech. Just west of Pittsburgh, the world's first nuclear power plant was erected stimulating new concerns about the long term poisoning of the planet. The cleansing of the sooty skies opened the city to the photographer's eye in a manner heretofore impossible. As working class people made solid economic gains, they, and especially their children, began to fill up the middle class with people of diverse professional vocations and strong educational interests.

At the initiative of Paul Mellon, the University of Pittsburgh founded a school of public health associated with its Medical Center to respond to Pennsylvania's low public health ranking among the states (42 among the then 48 states) and its manifest weakness in industrial hygiene and environmental health. The new school contributed to the strengthening of the School of Medicine, where, in 1947, a young epidemiologist named Jonas Salk was hired. He became the focus of one of the most dramatic stories in the history of medicine. Poliomyelitis – infantile paralysis – was an infectious and contagious disease that primarily infected young children under five years of age. In 1952 polio killed more American children than any other contagious disease. Out of 57,000 cases, 21,269 were fatal and those that survived were permanently and dreadfully paralyzed. The hysteria around polio was contemporary with and paralleled the Red Scare. There was danger in our midst. The *March of Dimes* campaign mobilized millions of school children as fundraisers to find a cure. Attendance dropped by half at Forbes Field (1951-1954), though poor play by the Pirates contributed. Swimming pools were deserted, while drive-in theaters boomed.[96]

Jonas Salk, who had begun his work at Pitt on influenza, increasingly concentrated on polio. In 1949 three Harvard doctors discovered how to grow live polio virus in test tubes. The lead doctor, John Enders, received the Nobel Prize for medicine, but refused to accept it until his two colleagues were included. This selflessness would stand in stark contrast to Salk's subsequent behavior. Salk was given a large grant through the *March of Dimes* campaign (to which an estimated one hundred million Americans contributed) to identify the main strains of the virus, a key step in developing an effective vaccine. Harry Weaver of the National Foundation for Infantile Paralysis wrote of Salk: "There was nobody like him in those days….Everything was on a small scale….He thought big. He wanted lots of space, was perfectly comfortable with the idea of using hundreds of monkeys, and running dozens of experiments at a time….He wanted to leap, not crawl." He assembled a talented staff of research scientists, the senior of whom was James Youngner. In an interview before a dinner at Mellon Institute on May 12, 1952, Salk announced he would soon begin tests of a polio vaccine on human beings. John Troan, science reporter for *The Pittsburgh Press* in a story that got worldwide attention, announced the exciting possibility of a vaccine. Salk defied normal medical protocol by crediting himself as the main author, while relegating his collaborators to a separate group. On March 23, 1953, Salk and his associates published a long article on his vaccine that employed an inactivated rather than live virus, in the *Journal of the American Medical Association*. However, two days before the article's publication, Salk broke the news about his vaccine in a prime-time CBS radio broadcast. Salk became a national hero; and, despite Pitt's efforts to name it the "Pitt Vaccine," it became universally known as the Salk Vaccine. Salk, who proved to be very media savvy, partnered with the *Press's* Troan, who became the conduit for national articles hailing him as the "great benefactor for mankind."[97]

To be fair, at least part of Salk's motive for the media campaign was to gain acceptance among the public for mass inoculations. The fact that his vaccine used "dead' or inactivated virus reassured parents. In the spring and summer of 1954, in the largest field test in American history begun at the Arsenal Elementary School in Lawrenceville, more than 1.8 million children, grades one through three in twelve states, were inoculated. Following the grandly staged media announcement of the trial's success before 500 doctors and scientists and hordes of newsmen, Salk was treated as a superstar. In his remarks he failed to mention the work of Dr. Youngner or the rest of his staff, an omission that caused deeply wounded feelings. By 1960 Allegheny County's mass inoculation program made Pittsburgh the first American city to eradicate polio. The American Medical Association disliked

Salk's program of free mass vaccinations which in their opinion smacked of socialized medicine. In the 1960s, the orally administered "live virus" vaccine of Dr. Albert Sabin supplanted the Salk vaccine because of its relative ease of administration. Salk in a dispute with the Pitt's Chancellor Litchfield over control of a proposed Institute for Experimental Medicine left for San Diego in 1960. Pitt benefited greatly from Salk's presence. Its medical school's external funding swelled from almost nothing to the highest of any medical school in the nation laying the foundation for important medical achievements to come. Best of all, by 1965, as reported by the National Foundation for Infantile Paralysis, the terrifying scourge had all but disappeared. "The fear-haunted days and nights that patients endured, the frantic rush of teams of doctors and nurses to areas savagely hit by this plague, the shuttered schools and churches and theaters, the barricaded beaches, the mounting polio casualty lists – those horrors and terrors belong to the past."[98]

While Pitt and Pittsburgh basked in the positive attention and Mayor Lawrence cited the vaccine as "a prideful example of Pittsburgh's ever-growing importance as a center of medical care and research," there were other stirrings over in the basements of Carnegie Tech that in the long run would impact the world even more profoundly. Professor Herbert Simon, interested in finding ways of simulating human thinking in decision-making and problem-solving processes, began using the computer as a tool in 1954. Simon who won the Nobel Prize for Economics in 1978 was a wide-ranging thinker in many fields: economics, philosophy, psychology, computer science and artificial intelligence among them. He convinced the administration at Tech to hire Allen Newell from the Rand Corporation to assist a growing number of professors who recognized the computer's educational and research potential. Over Christmas break in 1955, Simon, Newell, and programmer J. C. Shaw created a computer program, Logic Theorist, which could discover proofs of geometric theorems. This marked the beginnings of what became known as artificial intelligence. Purchasing an IBM 650 digital machine, Carnegie Tech became the first school in the world to install a computer for research and teaching purposes. The 650 was a vacuum tube machine and it soon was pressed into service 24 hours a day to accommodate the stream of researchers. It got to the point where people had to stand in line all through the night on Sunday to sign for computer time during the following week. Alan Bond, an early Carnegie Tech researcher in the field, explained the attraction: "For once, man could communicate with a very responsive and tireless information processing system. In computer science, more than any other field, one could do massive, complicated, energy consuming tasks by specifying understandable and simple steps." In 1960, the university invested in a G-20 computer from Bendix that came with primitive software. Tech researchers rewrote the entire operating system, and the computer age was launched.[99]

In 1957, west of Pittsburgh, just down the Ohio from the sprawling J&L plant in Aliquippa, the first commercial nuclear power plant was brought on line. The Pittsburgh region which had been so central to the modern steel industry, to oil and gas production and refining, to glass and aluminum production, added another major first to its list of achievements. The sleepy little farming village of Shippingport got its name because of its early role shipping farm produce on the river. It had one industry, a gravel pit employing ten workers. Duquesne Light had purchased a large piece of land in the borough 30 years earlier with the intention of building a coal-fired facility that never materialized. When the Atomic Energy Commission (AEC) put out a bid to build the reactor, Duquesne Light's bid was chosen over nine competitors. The Ohio River provided ample water to cool the reactor, excellent rail connections were close, the Greater Pittsburgh Airport was only 25 miles distant, and Westinghouse Electric which would design and build the reactor was nearby. For

Duquesne Light, the reactor provided a means to meet increased power demands without increasing sulfur dioxide emissions that were becoming a growing political concern as Pittsburgh and surrounding areas were introducing stricter smoke control regulations.[100]

The region also had all the skilled crafts required to construct a complex new facility that was radically different than any power plant previously put on line. Ironworkers, the cement trades, carpenters, laborers, and teamsters were critical to the plant in the construction phase. The steamfitters, insulators, electricians, and painters were central to the operational aspect of the plant, along with sheet metal workers and millwrights engaged in turbine rebuilds. Insulator Bill Yund worked on several nuclear plants. "Insulation and painting/sealing play a higher role in a nuke than in conventional plants because of the need to reduce contamination levels and waste as well as maximize thermal efficiency. Keeping the place dust free and easily cleanable is a priority also." Very high tech materials and procedures were pioneered at the plant requiring workers to adapt their methods and practices. Work rules were very strict with background checks and monitoring stations. Radiation badges were worn at all times. When the plant was shutdown for maintenance, laborers in full body suits had to come in and decontaminate the plant before other trades were allowed in. They had to wipe down floors, walls, beams and equipment. Ed Hribar of Laborers Local 833, who worked on the construction of the Beaver Valley reactors 1 and 2 and did maintenance work at Shippingport, remembered how strange the plant was the first time he entered. "It was spooky. We'd all seen spooky movies about nuclear radiation."[101]

The place was wide open to visitors – foreign and domestic. School groups and community organizations trooped through the facility marveling at its cleanliness. Technician Mike Coppula remembers, "We wanted to let the people know that the plant was safe." Hyman Rickover, the Navy Admiral who had overseen the development of the nation's first nuclear submarine, the USS Nautilus, supervised the Shippingport project. An extremely short, barely five foot tall, and intense man, Rickover could be an intimidating figure. Joe Zagorski who became the plant manager said, "He scared the hell out of you." He tested employees' endurance under pressure by cutting the front legs off of chairs and making them sit, struggling to keep their balance, while he shouted questions at them about plant procedures. Contractors kept a spotter on the roof of the facility to warn everyone when Rickover's helicopter swooped in on the plant. They would run in and yell: "Here he comes." After 25 years, the Shippingport facility was closed and replaced by two Beaver Valley Nuclear Power Plant units. In interviews conducted by reporter Bob Bauder on the fiftieth anniversary of the plant's opening, all of the former plant workers declared their firm belief in the safety of nuclear power.[102]

George Rommler, member of Steamfitters' Local 449, worked for Dravo Corporation, which acted as the prime contractor for the reactor itself. He remembers that a flaw was discovered on the inside of a weld on a 15" primary loop pipe that carried 700 degree superheated radioactive water at over 2,000 pounds pressure from the reactor to the heat exchangers that created the clean steam to turn the turbines. Any imperfection that might create a hot spot had to be repaired. The AEC called in a union steamfitter from Georgia who was a four foot tall midget. He crawled into the pipe through a valve into a 60 degree fitting to successfully make the repair. Rommler distrusted radioactivity and when they brought in the uranium rods, he moved on to another job. "When it gets hot, I want to leave."[103]

Not everyone was sanguine about the potential of the nuclear age. In October 1960, while Pittsburgh was fixated on the Pirates World Series appearance and the presidential election, Rachel

Carson wrote a new preface to her 1950 best-selling book, *The Sea Around Us*. That beautifully written book, named the "outstanding book of the year" by the *New York Times*, had remained on the best seller list for 86 weeks and won the prestigious National Book Award. Born in 1911, Carson grew up in a farmhouse on a rise above the Allegheny River in Springdale, near the spot where James Audubon, nearly a century before, shot the pair of passenger pigeons he used as models for his classic portrait of the doomed species. The extinction of that once prolific bird whose massive flocks had darkened the sky in bygone days occurred before Rachel's birth, but she was acutely aware from childhood of the systematic deterioration of the natural world that was occurring around her. As she grew up, she collected insects and identified birds in the woods around her; but also watched the once pristine Allegheny below her family's house become increasingly remote with the construction of two coal-fired power plants fed by nearby mines and the extension of the squalid homes of the immigrant workers along the river's border. The Harwick mine, barely a mile distant, had exploded eight years before her birth in the worst coal-mining accident in the history of Allegheny County. Her father worked at the same mine as an electrician for a time in her youth. Rachel escaped the industrial ravages on her beloved Springdale in the mid-1930s, getting a degree in biology from the Pennsylvania College for Women (now Chatham College) and then taking a job with the U.S. Bureau of Fisheries. She spent much of the rest of her life near the ocean observing its character and its creatures. In 1941 she wrote her first book, *Under the Sea Wind*, which attracted little notice in the shadow of the gathering storms of war.[104]

In 1960, when she penned the new introduction to *The Sea Around Us*, she was deeply engrossed in the work that would change the world, *Silent Spring*, about the threat posed by pesticides and other toxic chemical on birds and ultimately on life itself. With her eyes intently focused on the natural world, Carson made very few references to the workers, however, who toiled in the chemical and atomic industries and suffered the most direct human contact with these substances. Despite her blindness toward the producers, her warning voice inspired others, like Tony Mazzocchi of the Oil, Chemical and Atomic Workers, to tear down the factory fence that separated the scientists from the workers and their communities. Under his leadership, a union for the first time in the United States attempted to systematically ally with environmentalists.[105] With the backdrop of the Cold War, extensive nuclear testing, commercial nuclear power development, and rising radioactivity levels on land and sea, Rachel Carson addressed the danger posed by nuclear waste. She was deeply concerned by the dumping of nuclear waste into the oceans.

> Although man's record as a steward of the natural resources of the earth has been a discouraging one, there has been a certain comfort in the belief that the sea, at least, was inviolate, beyond man's ability to change and despoil. But this belief, unfortunately, has proved to be naive. In unlocking the secrets of the atom, modern man has found himself confronted with a frightening problem – what to do with the most dangerous materials that have ever existed in all the earth's history, the by-products of atomic fission. The stark problem that faces him is whether he can dispose of these lethal substances without rendering the earth uninhabitable....It is known that plants and animals of the sea pick up and concentrate radiochemicals...for the tiny organisms are eaten by larger ones and so on up the food chain to man. By such a process tuna over a million square miles surrounding the Bikini bomb test developed a degree of radioactivity enormously higher than that of the sea water....The truth is that disposal has proceeded far more rapidly than our knowledge justifies.

To dispose first and investigate later is an invitation to disaster, for once radioactive elements have been deposited at sea they are irretrievable. The mistakes that are made now are made for all time.

It is a curious situation that the sea, from which life first arose, should now be threatened by the activities of one form of that life. But the sea, though changed in a sinister way, will continue to exist; the threat is rather to life itself.[106]

Clearly the world was changing and muscular Pittsburgh was also. But like Rachel Carson's ocean, portentous shifts were occurring under the surface that only a few people recognized, because the changes that were occurring in front of people's eyes in their own daily lives and experience were both dramatic and distracting. The new medium of television was steadily invading homes and impacting how the masses understood the world and society. In the early 1950s, KDKA TV, which first went on air as WDTV, pioneered local news programming. Its first regular program was a local news program called "Pitt Parade" which was a five to ten minute collage of local events. Edited film clips, combining some hard news with mostly soft human-interest footage, were spliced into a segment with a voice-over narration. In 1954, a gentle unassuming man named Fred Rogers became program director for WQED, the first community-sponsored television station in the United States. From 1954 to 1961, he and Josey Carey produced and performed in *The Children's Corner* that was picked up nationally by NBC. In the 1960s, this evolved into one of Pittsburgh's best known products *Mister Rogers' Neighborhood*.[107]

Pioneer in radio and television, Pittsburgh had also always been a great location for photography. There is the dramatic terrain where three rivers meet in a natural amphitheater bordered by cliffs and slopes. The ravages of water on the ancient plateau created a complex geography with thousands of unique vantage points on the city and its neighborhoods. For more than a century, there was the added drama of the industrial landscape with its flames, sparks, and billowing smoke. Finally, there are the people, their faces tempered in furnaces, tested in struggle; people of the hills, the slopes, the ridges and the flats; people from a hundred tribes and places. Photographers captured the gnarled hands, the seared faces of the workers as well as the lovely legs of Pittsburgh gals shaped by climbing steps and mounting streets. Many photographers did notable work here: Benjamin Dabbs, who did the portraits of the city's rich and famous, captured the burning of the Pinkerton barges at the great Homestead battle; Lewis Hine, the "reformer with a camera," whose documentation of child labor, factory conditions, and immigrant life illustrated the *Pittsburgh Survey*; Charles "Teenie" Harris who chronicled African-American life in Pittsburgh for 40 years as a cameraman for the *Pittsburgh Courier*; Luke Swank, hired as the University of Pittsburgh's official photographer in 1935, extensively documented the mills and the neighborhoods of the area.[108]

The 1950s saw an extraordinary extension of the photo-documentation of the city. Margaret Bourke-White, staff reporter for *Fortune* and *Life*, who had photographed Pittsburgh in 1935-36, returned to the city in the early 1950s to do a striking series of aerial photos. While there was still plenty of smoke and fire left in the old town, the deadly thick pall of smog had largely lifted and the city more clearly revealed its muscle and contours. Between 1950 and 1954, Roy Stryker, who had headed the remarkable Farm Security Administration documentary photo survey of rural life during the 1930s, assembled a team to document the city's renaissance. His team of photographers included Esther Bubley; Harold Corsini; Richard Saunders, a black cameraman from Bermuda hired to document a lower Hill District slated for demolition; and especially Clyde Hare, who produced some of the finest construction and industrial images ever taken. When Hare arrived on the scene in 1950, he recalled: "Everything was in shambles. Everywhere you looked, something big was coming down or going up, and the earth shook from the pile driving." Together the team produced more than fourteen thousand images of a city in transition.[109]

Later in the '50s, perhaps the most impressive photographic interpretation of any American city was undertaken by W. Eugene Smith, who was contracted for three weeks work by Stefan Lorant to shoot a series of contemporary images of the city for his classic *Pittsburgh: The Story of an American City*. Smith, an intense artist whose life was in turmoil, stayed in the city for a full year and returned often over the next two years with a vision of creating a great work of art that would express the soul of the great industrial city. That his intentions vastly outstripped the assignment he had accepted for Lorant was indicated by the fact that he arrived in Pittsburgh with twenty pieces of luggage, a record player, and hundreds of books and records. Lorant, whose project was funded by the Allegheny Conference to showcase its renaissance, ultimately got 100 images acceptable for his purposes. Obsessed with the city and his vision of interpretation, Smith labored countless hours producing more than 10,000 negatives, many of which he developed himself, for a book that he was never able to complete. His goal as expressed in a successful grant application to the Guggenheim Foundation was profoundly ambitious. [110]

> I would search civic pride and civic shame; specific problems and specific interests –
> at odds, at cooperation, at due process; government, business, management, worker,
> as qualified through the infinite mixtures and the rewards and the stresses of being
> of this place at this time. I would give the taste of its very breathing – at work, at
> humdrum, at learning, at worship, at play, at growth (and the decay which is
> simultaneous with growth in every living thing). My intention of a result – health,
> sustenance, talent, and the variables of fate be willing) – a strong example of an
> individual and functioning city.[111]

Smith, who believed in the social responsibility of the photographer, displayed an unusual compassion for his subjects. In his Pittsburgh photos, published finally in 2001 as *Dream Street*, on the occasion of a comprehensive exhibition of his efforts at the Carnegie Museum of Art, the grit and integrity of the city are displayed with a stark and terrible beauty. While Stryker's team meticulously documented with cool detachment the city's transformation for a corporate client, Smith's goal, to which he nearly sacrificed his career, was to penetrate the soul of the city, to portray it as a living entity. Smith's Pittsburgh is no gleaming corporate embodiment of progress, but a complex, tormented being where volcanic forces lurk beneath the placid public relations facade celebrated by Lorant. It was he who called Pittsburgh "the man-breaking city." Pittsburgh in the 1950s could certainly still be a tough place, with hard, dangerous work, and sub-standard housing commonplace, but the irony of the matter is that it had by then become a much better place for the working class than it was for example in 1900 or 1930. However, better than anyone, W. Eugene Smith's work captured the dynamic tension between the classes and portrayed the dramatic intensity of the city.[112]

On Top of the World

Pittsburgh in 1960 was on top of the world. Muscular and prosperous, diverse and yet increasingly united socially, the consolidation of unionism and the gradual acceptance of at least part of Roosevelt's vision of a social contract, by-and-large, had survived eight years of Republican administration and created a strong, viable, working middle class. With an Irish Catholic capturing the Democratic nomination for the presidency and a Pittsburgher occupying the Governor's mansion in Harrisburg, the struggle for assimilation of the once despised immigrant masses seemed assured. While a dangerous complacency reigned among both corporate management and organized labor about the long-term implications of the nation's military and economic hegemony over more than half the world, the times were very good. Not all problems were solved certainly. Urban renewal for the black community had brought displacement, and the significant obstacles placed on blacks in terms of their residential, commercial, and employment opportunity increased racial tensions. The Soviet presence in space and the threat of nuclear war hovered ominously in the background, but working-class life at the neighborhood level had never been better. The euphoria, the feeling of hopefulness and accomplishment, would be stoked by "the best game ever," the seventh game of the 1960 World Series. The tough Pirates faced the mighty pin-striped Yankees in a series and played a final game best described as improbable. The election of John F. Kennedy some three weeks later was frosting on the cake for many.[113]

The Pirates were tied at the end of six games with the Yankees through guile and persistence, two admirable blue-collar traits. In their three wins, the Yanks had out scored the Bucs 38-3; while the Pirates had won three games scoring only 14 runs. Kennedy and Nixon were preparing for their third televised debate. Three days before that seventh game, a campaigning John F. Kennedy responded to an uproarious greeting at Pittsburgh's Syria Mosque by cautioning the crowd: "I am NOT Roberto Clemente." When the Pirates returned to Pittsburgh from New York leading the Series 3-2, 15,000 fans met them at the Airport. It was noted that when the Yankees had returned to New York for the third game, they had been met only by wives and family. Sportswriters characterized the game as class struggle: the scrappy, blue-collar, lunch-pail-toting underdogs vs. the patrician, pin-striped, corporate elite. The rapid expansion of television was transforming both sports and presidential elections. From 4 million sets in 1950, by the 1960 World Series and presidential election, 60 million Americans owned TV sets.[114]

The 1950s had been a tough decade for the Pirates. In 1952 they lost 112 games and in 1954, they finished 54 ½ games behind the league-leading Brooklyn Dodgers. In 1954, with former Dodger Branch Rickey as General Manager, the team hired its first black player, Curt Roberts, who played second base brilliantly, but was a consistently weak hitter. In 1954, they signed a 19-year-old second baseman named Bill Mazeroski. Mazeroski, like Honus Wagner, was a local coal miner's son. His father had a major league opportunity crushed along with his foot in a coal mine accident. He drilled his son in athletics, the way up and out of the coal patch. Despite basketball scholarship offerings by Ohio State, WVU, and Duquesne, he signed with the Pirates, played briefly in the minors at Williamsport, then in the Pacific Coast League, finally playing a winter season in the tough, competitive Dominican Republic League before joining the Pirates. "That (winter) season made a man out of me, both on and off the field....I knew after playing there that no matter what happened on the field, no matter how much you were booed or cursed, no matter how silly you felt for striking out, the world went on the same as always."[115]

In 1955 a flashy 20-year-old Puerto-Rican, Roberto Clemente, joined the club and Pirates broadcaster Bob Prince encouraged fans to chant "Arriba! Arriba!" Clemente, an exciting player whose raw talent was obvious to most, was moody, unpredictable, and quick to react to any perceived affront. While the team finished last again in 1956, two solid pitchers, Vernon Law and Bob Friend, began to emerge and Elroy Face was developing into the finest reliever in the game. Dick

Groat, born in Wilkinsburg and a star in several sports at Swissvale High School, was an All-American basketball player at Duke before he joined the club in 1952. Despite an expanding stable of young talent, the Pirates were mired in last place in 1957, when the team brought former Pirates second baseman Danny Murtaugh in to manage the team. In 1958 the team surged to second-place with Frank Thomas, Ralph Kiner's replacement at first base, hitting 35 homeruns; Bob Skinner leading the team in batting; Bob Friend winning 22 games; and Elroy Face leading all big league relievers with 20 saves. In 1959, despite great hopes, the team had a mediocre year. Perhaps symbolically for that year, pitcher Harvey Haddix pitched a perfect game for 12 innings only to lose the game in the 13th. Face, however, won 18 straight games in relief.[116]

1960 was a watershed year. While the Pirates were marching through the season to win the National League pennant by seven games over the Milwaukee Braves, a graceful and charismatic Catholic senator from Massachusetts was simultaneously marching though a series of brilliant primary victories to lead in delegates for the Democratic nomination for the presidency. Pittsburgh's own Dave Lawrence played kingmaker with Chicago's Richard Daley, as Kennedy, who had won the most primaries, needed Pennsylvania's delegates to win the nomination. As Pennsylvania's first Catholic Governor, Lawrence could hardly deny that times had changed and if a Catholic could win in Pennsylvania, then who was he to say it could not happen nationally. Kennedy stirred the imagination of youth with a message of hope and challenged their aspirations with an inspirational call to service. His opponent in the elections, Vice-President Richard Nixon, had built his career on Cold War anti-Communism, playing to the fears and anxieties of the American people. In their first televised debate on September 26, Nixon's "five-o'clock shadow" and darker vision of the world stood in sharp contrast to Kennedy's confidence and hopeful, dynamic presence. Kennedy struck a deep chord in the industrial working class with his Catholic background and an oratorical style reminiscent of Franklin Roosevelt.[117]

The 1960 Pirates also seemed like something whose time had come. Roberto Clemente, who batted .314 and led the team in RBIs, was the most exciting player in baseball with sure hands and extraordinary speed and grace in the field. He played with a fierce intensity or what was described as a "beautiful fury." A man deeply proud of his heritage, Clemente saw himself as a symbol of Puerto Rico and all of Latin America. Often temperamental and prickly, Clemente won Pittsburgh over by a work ethic that struck a deep chord.

> This is something that from the first day, I said to myself: 'I am the minority group.
> I am from the poor people. I represent the poor people. I represent the common
> people of America. So I am going to be treated as a human being. I don't want to be
> treated like a Puerto Rican, or a black, or nothing like that. I want to be treated like
> any person that comes for a job.' Every person who comes for a job, no matter what
> type of race or color he is, if he does the job he should be treated like whites.[118]

Team captain and hometown boy, Dick Groat led the league in batting with a .325 average and was named the league's Most Valuable Player. Vernon Law, a deacon in the Mormon Church, posted a 20-9 record and won the Cy Young Award. Bob Friend won 18 games, and Elroy Face remained a premier reliever. The Bucs added another key pitcher in May when they purchased Wilber "Vinegar Bend" Mizell from the St. Louis Cardinals.

On their side, the Yankees fielded one of their greatest teams with All-Stars Mickey Mantle, Roger Maris, Yogi Berra, Tony Kubek, Bobby Richardson, Bill Skowron and Elston Howard in a lineup that was compared to the legendary 1927 "Murderers' Row" Yankees, who had crushed the

Pirates in Pittsburgh's last World Series appearance 33 years earlier. Thirty-five World Series contests have gone seven games, but only one was decided by a homerun on the final pitch. To the delight of the Forbes Field crowd, the Pirates jumped out to a 4-0 lead; but the Yankees came roaring back to go ahead 7-5 until back-up catcher Hal Smith's homerun put the Bucs ahead 9-7 at the end of eight innings. In the top of the amazing ninth, the Yankees scored twice to tie the game. In the bottom of the ninth, Pirate second baseman, Bill Mazeroski, connected with Yankee reliever Ralph Terry's second pitch and sent the ball 400 feet over the left-centerfield wall. Pittsburgh celebrated with abandon. Neighborhoods erupted in celebration with thousands of fans swamping the Golden Triangle and Oakland. By evening an estimated three hundred thousand fans were celebrating in downtown streets. The celebration, though ecstatic and at times rowdy, was amazingly civil with few arrests or incidents. The *Post-Gazette* headlined: "Crowds Yell, Firecrackers Boom, Air Raid Sirens Shriek, Confetti Rains, Church Bells Ring – Our Town Goes Wild Over Pirate Victory."[119]

And so it was in the fall of 1960. Never before or since would Pittsburgh be more prosperous and hopeful. A bit more than two centuries after General Forbes and his army arrived upon the burning embers of Fort Duquesne, the city and its region basked in the glow of prodigious success. Its workers and industries had produced incalculable volumes of coal, iron, steel, and glass. Its inventors and laborers had been the first to refine oil, manufacture aluminum, and create some of the primary mechanisms of electrical generation and distribution. In a stupendous effort, its mills and factories had been the arsenal of democracy, providing much of the muscle that made the United States of America the world's most powerful nation. But if Pittsburgh has a tradition of production, it also has a tradition of struggle: whiskey rebels, cordwainer conspirators, cotton mill rioters, anti-slavery militants, and especially the generations of union organizers who fought for an organizational voice, due process and justice in the workplace, along with all those since the founding of the city who defended civil liberties and human rights in the community and in the streets. Production and struggle – the point of Pittsburgh.

The city's greatness in 1960 was far from over. For 20 more years through the long, demoralizing Vietnam War, Pittsburgh's mines and mills remained significant factors in the calculus of national power. In sports, an "immaculate reception" on a football gridiron would come to rival the magic of that homerun by a coal miner's son on that splendid fall day in 1960. But still, when the blue-collar Pirates defeated the pin-striped, corporate Yankees and the dashing young president articulated a vision of responsibility toward the poor and of service for world peace, Pittsburgh rested with pride on a unique history of production and struggle that helped shaped the course of the nation and the world.

Notes Chapter 12

[1] Edward Humes, *Over Here: How the G.I. Bill Transformed the American Dream* (Orlando: Harcourt Books, 2006), 125-126; 195-214; 220-228.

[2] Humes, *Over Here,* 17-23; 100-102.

[3] Clarke M. Thomas, *Witness to the Fifties: The Pittsburgh Photographic Library, 1950-1953,* eds. Constance B. Schulz and Steven W. Plattner, (Pittsburgh: University of Pittsburgh Press, 1999), 38-58; Michael P. Weber, *Don't Call Me Boss: David L. Lawrence* (Pittsburgh: University of Pittsburgh Press, 1988), 256-257.

[4] Thomas, *Witness to the Fifties,* 60; Roy Lubove, *Twentieth-Century Pittsburgh* (Pittsburgh, University of Pittsburgh, 1995), 139-140.

[5] Lubove, *Twentieth-Century Pittsburgh,* 128-132.

[6] Bill Sullivan, *Interview* by Charles McCollester, May 22, 2008. Bill became a Business Agent of Iron Workers Local 3 in 1965 and First General Vice President of the Iron Workers International Union in 1975.

[7] Irv Grunebach, Interview by Charles McCollester (May 7, 1991).

[8] William Serrin, *Homestead: The Glory and Tragedy of an American Steel Town* (New York: Random House, 1992).; Judith Modell, *A Town Without Steel: Envisioning Homestead,* (Pittsburgh: University of Pittsburgh Press, 1998), 26-35.

[9] John Hoerr, *And the Wolf Finally Came: The Decline of the American Steel Industry* (Pittsburgh: University of Pittsburgh Press, 1988), 188-189.

[10] Modell, *A Town Without Steel,* 32-33, 237-242.

[11] Weber, *Don't Call Me Boss,* 277-278; Douglas Anderson, *Interview* by Charles McCollester, 1992; Chris Moore and Minette Seate, *Torchbearers,* WQED TV, 2006.

[12] August Wilson, *Three Plays,* (Pittsburgh: University of Pittsburgh Press, 1991), 103.

[13] Weber, *Don't Call Me Boss,* 279-282; Steve Nelson, James R. Barrett, Rob Ruck, *Steve Nelson: American Radical* (Pittsburgh: University of Pittsburgh Press, 1981), 315-316; Clarke M. Thomas, *Front-Page Pittsburgh: Two Hundred Years of the Post-Gazette* (Pittsburgh: University of Pittsburgh Press, 2005), 212; Ervin Dyer, "Reverend LeRoy Patrick: Bona-Fide Hero of Civil Rights Movement," *Pittsburgh Post-Gazette,* January 13, 2006. Reprinted in *Pittsburgh Live: Men and Women Who Shaped Our City,* eds. David M. Shribman and Angelika Kane (Chicago: Triumph Books, 2006), 26-28; Chris Moore and Minette Seate, *Torchbearers,* WQED TV, 2006; Eric Ledell Smith & Kenneth Wolensky, "A Novel Public Policy: Pennsylvania's Fair Employment Practices Act of 1955," *Pennsylvania History,* v. 69, n. 4, (Autumn, 2002), 489-523.

[14] Robert Hill, *K. Leroy Irvis: The Lion of Pennsylvania,* (University of Pittsburgh, 2004), Documentary Video.

[15] Weber, *Don't Call Me Boss,* 289.

[16] Weber, *Don't Call Me Boss,* 293-310.

[17] Clarke M. Thomas, *Fortunes and Misfortunes: Pittsburgh and Allegheny County Politics, 1930-1995.* (Pittsburgh: Institute of Politics, 1998), 38-39.

[18] Weber, *Don't Call Me Boss,* 317-318.

[19] Weber, *Don't Call Me Boss,* 330-338.

[20] Weber, *Don't Call Me Boss,* 340-350.

[21] Weber, *Don't Call Me Boss,* 360-365.

[22] William Manchester, *The Glory and the Dream: A Narrative History of America, 1932-1972* (Boston: Little, Brown, and Company 1973), I:636-645.

[23] David Caute, *The Great Fear: The Anti-Communist Purge Under Truman and Eisenhower* (New York: Simon and Schuster, 1978), 216-217; Nelson et al., *Steve Nelson,* 310.

[24] Manchester, *The Glory and the Dream,* 652-664.

[25] Manchester, *The Glory and the Dream,* 664-679; *Hall of Valor,* Soldiers and Sailors Museum, Pittsburgh.

[26] Michael A. Musmanno, *Across the Street from the Courthouse* (Philadelphia: Dorrance & Company, 1954), 25; 73-74; His extensive involvement in the Sacco and Vanzetti case is recounted in Michael A. Musmanno, *Verdict!: The Adventures of the Young Lawyer in the Brown Suit* (Garden City, NY: Doubleday & Company, 1958), 267-323.

[27] Musmanno, *Across the Street from the Courthouse,* 37-46; Weber, *Don't Call Me Boss,* 284-286.

[28] Ronald W. Schatz, *The Electrical Workers: A History of Labor at General Electric and Westinghouse, 1923-1960* (Urbana and Chicago: University of Illinois Press, 1983), 199-202.

[29] Schatz, *The Electrical Workers.*

[30] John P. Hoerr, *Harry, Tom and Father Rice* (Pittsburgh: University of Pittsburgh Press, 2005), 184-200.

[31] Musmanno, *Across the Street from the Courthouse,* 38-55.

[32] Musmanno, *Across the Street from the Courthouse,* 75-78; Nelson et al., *Steve Nelson,* 275-278.

[33] Nelson et al., *Steve Nelson,* 319-326.

[34] Nelson et al., *Steve Nelson,* 136.

[35] Nelson et al., *Steve Nelson,* 329-340; 370.

[36]Nelson et al., *Steve Nelson*, 383-388.

[37]Nelson et al., *Steve Nelson*, 387-398; Charles Owen Rice, *Fighter With a Heart: Charles Owen Rice, Pittsburgh Labor Priest*, ed. Charles McCollester (Pittsburgh: University of Pittsburgh Press, 1996), 228-229.

[38]Hoerr, *Harry, Tom, and Father Rice*, 217-227; One of the points of pride in the present author's life is that he was the only person invited to speak at memorial services for both Tom Quinn and Monsignor Rice.

[39]Hoerr, *Harry, Tom, and Father Rice*, 235-239.

[40]Ronald L. Filipelli and Mark D. McColloch, *Cold War in the Working Class: The Rise and Decline of the United Electrical Workers* (Albany: State University of New York Press, 1995), 161-165; Mark McColloch, "The Shop-Floor Dimension of Union Rivalry: The Case of Westinghouse in the 1950s," in *The CIO's Left-Led Unions*, ed. Steve Rosswurm (New Brunswick, NJ: Rutgers University Press, 1992), 191-198; "Who killed Westinghouse?," *Pittsburgh Post-Gazette*, March 1-7, 1998.

[41]Frank Joseph, "We Got Jazz," *Pittsburgh Magazine*, October, 1979, 32-33; Billy Strayhorn, *Billy Strayhorn: Lush Life*, Audio CD, (New York: Blue Note Records, January 23, 2007). See Robert Levi in the liner notes for this tribute CD.

[42]Joseph, "We Got Jazz," 34-52; Ernie Hoffman, "Billy Eckstine, 78: Jazz Vocalist and Trombonist," *Pittsburgh Post-Gazette*, March 9, 1993; reprinted in *Pittsburgh Lives: Men and Women Who Shaped Our City*, ed. David M. Schribman and Angelika Kane (Chicago: Triumph Books, 2006), 151-153.

[43]*Pittsburgh Post-Gazette*, March 23, 1990.

[44]Hill Jordan, "Card-carrying Embers," *Pittsburgh City Paper*, August 8 – 15, 2001.

[45]Barbara Burstin, *A Jewish legacy: Pittsburgh*, Documentary film (Carnegie Library of Pittsburgh).

[46]Christopher Rawson, "August Wilson, 60: Playwright Who Chronicled Black Experience," *Pittsburgh Post-Gazette*, October 3, 2005; reprinted in *Pittsburgh Lives: Men and Women Who Shaped Our City*, ed. David M. Schribman and Angelika Kane (Chicago: Triumph Books, 2006), 181-188.

[47]Annie Dillard, *An American Childhood*, (New York: Harper & Row Publishers, 1987), 120-121.

[48]Ed Masley, "Oldie but Goodie," *Pittsburgh Post-Gazette*, April 10, 1998; Ed Weigle, "Porky Chedwick: Radio's Most Ignored Pioneer," <www.oldradio.com/archives/stations/porky.htm>.

[49]I am grateful to Cal Schuchman, D.J. and member of the Pittsburgh Old Record Collectors Club for much of this information and sources; Dave Goodrich, "Hitsburgh: It wasn't Detroit, but they were really rockin' in Pittsburgh," *In Pittsburgh*, October 11-October 17, 1989; Ed Weigle, "Porky Chedwick: Radio's Most Ignored Pioneer," <www.oldradio.com/archives/stations/porky.htm>.

[50] Information gathered from the John Heinz Regional History Center Sports Museum; Brian Palmer, "Professional wrestling isn't what it used to be," *The Pitt News*, February 3, 2005.
Chuck Martoni, Dean of Students at Boyce Campus of the Community College of Allegheny County and Allegheny County Councilman, who wrestled against Sanmartino as "The Masked Marvel," asserts that Sanmartino regularly sold out New York's Madison Square Garden.

[51] Bob Carter, "Stokes' life a tale of tragedy and friendship," *ESPN Classic*, <HTTP://espn.go.com/classic/biography/s/stokes_maurice.html>; Fr. Jack O'Malley, *Interview*, February 13, 2008.

[52]Richard F. Peterson, "Rinky Dinks and the Single Wing," in *Pittsburgh Sports: Stories from the Steel City*, ed. Randy Roberts (Pittsburgh: University of Pittsburgh Press, 2000), 40-42; John Heinz Regional History Sports Museum; Dan Rooney, as told to Andrew E. Masich and David F. Halas, *My 75 Years with the Pittsburgh Steelers and the NFL*, (New York: Da Capo Press, 2007). 39.

[53]Abby Mendelson, *The Pittsburgh Steelers: The Official Team History*, (Lanham, MD: Taylor Trade Publishing, 2005), 35-46; Dan Rooney, *My 75 years with the Pittsburgh Steelers and the NFL*, 82.

[54]John Heinz Regional History Sports Museum; Chuck Finder, "Willie Thrower, 71: Opened Door for Black Quarterbacks." *Pittsburgh Post-Gazette*, February 24, 2002; reprinted in *Pittsburgh Lives: Men and Women Who Shaped Our City*, ed. David M. Schribman and Angelika Kane (Chicago: Triumph Books, 2006), 116-118.

[55]Tom Callahan, *Johnny U: The Life and Times of John Unitas*, (New York: Crown Publishers, 2006), 9-27; Dan Rooney, *My 75 years with the Pittsburgh Steelers and the NFL*, 61; The author's "first contact" with Pittsburgh, literally, was as a second string fullback for Aquinas Institute of Rochester N.Y. in a game against North Catholic of Pittsburgh in 1959. North Catholic handed Aquinas its only defeat that year.

[56]Callahan, *Johnny U*, 50-62, 151-175.

[57]David J. McDonald, *Union Man: The Life of a Labor Statesman* (New York: E.P. Dutton & Co., 1969), 21-29; McDonald claims that his Uncle Jack Kelly had a leg broken by a club-swinging Pinkerton during the Homestead battle, which seems unlikely given that the Pinkertons never successfully disembarked from their barges until their surrender.

[58]McDonald, *Union Man*, 31-38.

[59]John Herling, *Right to Challenge: People and Power in the Steelworkers Union* (New York, Harper & Row, 1972), 9-11.

[60]Herling, *Right to Challenge*, 11-14.

[61]Herling, *Right to Challenge*, 16-17.

418

[62]Herling, *Right to Challenge*, 18-19; Serrin, *Homestead*, 255-256.

[63]Serrin, *Homestead*, 252-253; Jack Metzgar, *Striking Steel Solidarity Remembered* (Philadelphia: Temple University Press, 2000), 103.

[64]*Steel Labor*, December 1952.

[65]Herling, *Right to Challenge*, 20.

[66]Serrin, *Homestead*, 260-261; *Steel Labor*, December, 1952.

[67]Serrin, *Homestead*, 263-273; John Chamberlain, "Phil Murray: The CIO boss was soft-spoken and humble, but tough in a pinch," *Life Magazine*, February 11, 1946 (reprinted in *Steel Labor*, December, 1952); McDonald, *Union Man*, 232-236.

[68]Herling, *Right to Challenge*, 24-26; George Kelly and Edwin Beachler, *Man of Steel: The Story of David J. McDonald*. (New York: North American Book Co., 1954), 123-130.

[69]Herling, *Right to Challenge*, 33-40.

[70]Metzgar, *Striking Steel*, 165; Hoerr, *And the Wolf Finally Came*, 229-231.

[71]Melvyn Dubofsky and Warren Van Tine, *John L. Lewis: A Biography* (New York: Quadrangle/The New York Times Book Co., 1977), 282-501.

[72]Serrin, *Homestead*, 276.

[73]Robert H. Zieger, *The CIO, 1935-1955* (Chapel Hill & London: The University of North Carolina Press, 1995), 334-337.

[74]Zieger, *The CIO*, 355-370.

[75]Zieger, *The CIO*, 362-363; 374-376; John Hinshaw, *Steel and Steelworkers: Race and Class in Twentieth-Century Pittsburgh* (Albany: State University of New York Press, 2002), 156-159.

[76]Herling, *Right to Challenge*, 45-48.

[77]Herling, *Right to Challenge*, 48-53; Hoerr, *And the Wolf Finally Came*, 250-254. John Herling mistakenly placed Frank O'Brien in the Homestead local, an error copied by William Serrin and Jack Metzgar. O'Brien became the president of the J&L Hazelwood local and was subsequently elected as a state representative while a local union officer. During the plant shutdown struggles of the 1980s, he became the chair of the Steel Valley Authority, a grassroots public entity that advocated the seizure of closed mills by eminent domain. The present author was an organizer of the SVA and succeeded Frank O'Brien as its chair.

[78]Herling, *Right to Challenge*, 56-58.

[79]Herling, *Right to Challenge*, 59-60.

[80]Herling, *Right to Challenge*, 61-69; Steelworkers Committee to Sponsor Truth, *The Mask of Deceit: Expose of the Goals and Techniques of the Dues Protest Committee (DPC) Leaders* (undated). This document was signed by seven local union presidents; Metzgar, *Striking Steel*, 162.

[81]Kenneth Warren, *Big Steel: The First Century of the United States Steel Corporation* (Pittsburgh, University of Pittsburgh Press, 2001), 215.

[82]Warren, *Big Steel*, 215-223; Hoerr, *And the Wolf Finally Came*, 93-94.

[83]Warren, *Big Steel*, 245-258, 341.

[84]Matthew Brzezinski, *Red Moon Rising: Sputnik and the Hidden Rivalries that Ignited the Space Age* (New York: Times Books, 2007), 138-140.

[85]Brzezinski, *Red Moon Rising*, 152-160; the Heinz History Center carried on highly advertised searches for the B-25 airplane and the classified records of the event in 2002, but the plane's carcass was officially found.

[86]Serrin, *Homestead*, 293-295.

[87]Metzgar, *Striking Steel*, 39.

[88]McDonald, *Union Man*, 264-267; Metzgar, *Striking Steel*, 64-65.

[89]McDonald, *Union Man*, 267;

[90]A.J. Muste, "Factional fights in Trade Unions," *American Labor Dynamics*, ed. J.B.S. Hardman, (New York: Harcourt, Brace & Co., 1928), 332-33; Metzgar, *Striking Steel*, 161-163.

[91]Metzgar, *Striking Steel*, 163.

[92]Metzgar, *Striking Steel*, 91-92.

[93]Metzgar, *Striking Steel*, 91-111.

[94]Metzgar, *Striking Steel*, 111-117.

[95]Jack Metzgar's poignant remembrance of his own relationship with his father as he came of age as a 1960s radical is in *Striking Steel*, 181-201.

[96]Robert C. Alberts, *Pitt: The Story of the University of Pittsburgh, 1787-1987*. (Pittsburgh: University of Pittsburgh Press, 1986), 204-211; Marc Selvaggio, "The Making of Jonas Salk," *Pittsburgh Magazine* (June, 1984), 44.

[97]Alberts, *Pitt*, 212-216; Selvaggio, "The Making of Jonas Salk," 45.

[98]Alberts, *Pitt*, 217-218; Selvaggio, "The Making of Jonas Salk," 47-50; Douglas Heuk, "Salk's regrets are few," *Pittsburgh Post-Gazette*, November 27, 1994.

[99]Information for this paragraph comes from the *Fifty Years of Computer Science* historical exhibit in Carnegie Mellon University's Newell-Simon Hall; Byron Spice, "Herbert A. Simon, 84: Nobel Prize Winner," *Pittsburgh Post-Gazette*, February 10, 2001 reprinted in *Pittsburgh Lives: Men and Women Who Shaped Our City*, ed. David M. Schribman and Angelika Kane, (Chicago: Triumph Books, 2006), 7-10.

[100]Bob Bauder, "On Cloud Nine, Cats Down in D.C. Flipped Over Beaver County Site," *The Beaver County Times*, December 16, 2007, C-2.

[101] Bill Yund, the artistic collaborator on this book, who worked on maintenance jobs at Shippingport and in the construction phase of the Beaver Valley I and II nuclear plants, provided information; Ed Hribar, *Interview*, June 14, 2008 by Charles McCollester. Mr. Hribar was elected Business Manager of Laborers Local 833 in 1965.

[102]Bob Bauder, "Radioactive, Man! Shippingport Workers Had It Made in the Shade," *The Beaver County Times*, December 16, 2007, C 14-15.

[103]George Rommler, *Interview*, June 21, 2008 by Charles McCollester.

[104]Linda Lear, *Rachel Carson: Witness for Nature* (New York: Henry Holt and Company, 1997), 7-53.

[105]Les Leopold, *The Man Who Hated Work and Loved Labor: The Life and Times of Tony Mazzocchi*, (White River Junction, Vermont: Chelsea Green Publishing Company, 2007), 224-231.

[106]Rachel Carson, *The Sea Around Us* (Oxford: Oxford University Press, 1951).

[107]Lynn Boyd Hines, *Broadcasting the Local News: The Early Years of Pittsburgh's KDKA-TV*, (University Park: Penn State Press, 1995), 35-60; Mark Collins and Margaret Mary Kimmel, *Mister Rogers' Neighborhood* (Pittsburgh: University of Pittsburgh Press, 1996).

[108]Charlee Brodsky and Linda-Benedict Jones, "Lost and Found: Pittsburgh's Photographic History," *Pittsburgh Revealed: Photographs Since 1850* (Pittsburgh: Carnegie Museum of Art, 1997), 146-154.

[109]Constance B. Schulz, "The Pittsburgh Photographic Library," *Witness to the Fifties: The Pittsburgh Photographic Library, 1950-1953*, eds. Constance B. Schulz and Steven W. Plattner, (Pittsburgh: University of Pittsburgh Press, 1999), 3-26; *Clyde Hare's Pittsburgh*, Photographs by Clyde Hare, text by Alan Van Dine, (Pittsburgh: Pittsburgh History & Landmarks Foundation, 1994), 11.

[110]Sam Stephenson, "W. Eugene Smith and Pittsburgh," in *Dream Street: W. Eugene Smith's Pittsburgh Project*, ed. Sam Stephenson, (New York: W.W. Norton & Company, 2001), 17-22.

[111]Stephenson, *Dream Street*, 48.

[112]Alan Tractenberg, "Man-breaking City: W. Eugene Smith's Pittsburgh," in *Dream Street: W. Eugene Smith's Pittsburgh Project*, ed. Sam Stephenson, (New York: W.W. Norton & Company, 2001), 163-167.

[113]Jim Reisler, *The Best Game Ever: Pirates vs. Yankees, October 13, 1960*, (Cambridge: Carroll & Graf Publishers, 2007).

[114]Reisler, *The Best Game Ever*, xvii-xix.

[115]Reisler, *The Best game Ever*, 177.

[116]John McCollister, *The Bucs!: The Story of the Pittsburgh Pirates* (Lenexa: Addax Publishing, 1998), 142-154.

[117]Theodore H. White, *The Making of the President 1960* (New York: Atheneum Publishers, 1962), 160-161.

[118]David Maraniss, *Clemente: The Passion and Grace of Baseball's Last Hero*, (New York: Simon & Schuster, 2006), 5, 71.

[119]Reisler, *The Best Game Ever*, 201-236; McCollister, *The Bucs*, 160-163.

BATTLE OF HOMESTEAD FOUNDATION

The Point of Pittsburgh Book Project Committee

Co-Chairs:
Paul Quarantillo, Laborers District Council
Leo Gerard and Jim English, United Steelworkers
William George & Richard Bloomingdale, Pennsylvania AFL-CIO
Scott Malley, Ironworkers Local 3
Michael Dunleavy, International Brotherhood of Electrical Workers, Local 5
Cindy Spielman, Pennsylvania Center for the Study of Labor Relations, IUP

Committee Members:
Robert J. Lavely & Linda R. Jack, Westmoreland County Labor Council
Jack Shea, Allegheny County Labor Council
Jack Brooks, Greater Pennsylvania Regional Council of Carpenters
Thomas G. Bigley, Plumbers Local 27
Kenneth Greiner, Sheet Metal Workers Local 12
Patrick J. McMahon, Amalgamated Transit Union Local 85
Rosemary Trump, Trump Fund, Pittsburgh Foundation
James Kunz, International Union of Operating Engineers Local 66
Joni Rabinowitz & John Haer
John DeFazio, United Steelworkers, District 10
Kenneth Broadbent & Joseph Little, Steamfitters Local 449
James Testerman, Michael Crossey, Gerard Oleksiak, Pennsylvania State Educational Association
John Conroy, Insulators Local 2
Mike Stout, Steel Valley Printers, Inc.
Mike Healey, Healey & Hornack, P.C.

Supporters:
Don Dunleavy; Lynn R. Williams; Jerry Starr; Nancy Bernstein

Community College of Allegheny County; Christopher Mark; Russell Gibbons; Paul Laxton;
Ann and Ike Gittlen; Joseph J. Pass, Jubelirer, Pass & Intrieri, P.C.; Drs. John and Rose Delaney;
Gregory F. Stephens

Ronald Demicheli, AFGE; Norm Koehler; William Cagney, Stationary Engineers; Fr. Garrett Dorsey;
James Watta & Dreama Van Cise; John Tarka, Pittsburgh Federation of Teachers; IBEW Local 29;
Kenneth C. Wolensky; Steffi Domike & Hilary Chiz; Fr. Bernard Survil; Mark J. Duffy; Donna Puleio
Spadero; Bill Buckley; Graphic Communications Conference/Teamsters Local 24M; John and Joanne
Hoerr; Marcus Rediker & Wendy Z. Goldman; Jim Kelly; John Stephen & Jennifer Thoma; Nick Coles;
Pat & Cathy Fagan; Patrick M. Fagan; Sylvia Wilson; Senator James Ferlo; Charles & Marianne
Martoni; Raymond Martin; Jacob & Stephanie Birnberg; Ernest B. Orsatti, Esquire; Bette McDevitt;
Pittsburgh Raging Grannies; Judith A. Ruszkowski & Ken Regal; Marie Malagreca; Jane Becker; Edith
Bell, Womens' International League for Peace and Freedom; Anne Feeney; Teamsters Local 249;
Stember Feinstein Doyle & Payne, LLC; Jim Seguin, Erica Peiffer, Bill Judson, Center for Documentary
Production and Study, Robert Morris University; Elaine Kuhar; John G. Oesterle; Maria McCollester;
Joyce Rothermel & Michael Drohan, Kathleen Werner, Nick Molnar

Bibliography
(Works Consulted)

General History and Arts

History:

Foner, Philip S. *History of the Labor Movement in the United States.* New York: International Publishers, Volumes I-IX, 1964-1991. No other history contains such wealth of detail—Volumes I, II, IV, and VIII are most relevant to Pittsburgh's labor history.
>> Volume I- *From Colonial Times to the Founding of the American Federation of Labor* (1947)
>> Volume II- *From the Founding of the American Federation of Labor to the Emergence of American Imperialism* (1955)
>> Volume IV-*Industrial Workers of the World, 1905-1917* (1965)
>> Volume VIII-*Post War Struggles, 1918-1920* (1988)

Harper, Frank C. *Pittsburgh of Today: Its Resources and People.* Vol. 1. (Pittsburgh: The American Historical Society, 1931).

Hays, Samuel P., ed. *City at the Point: Essays on the Social History of Pittsburgh.* Pittsburgh: University of Pittsburgh Press, 1989.

Lorant, Stefan. *Pittsburgh: The Story of an American City.* Garden City: Doubleday & Company, Inc., 1964. Includes: Seidenberg, Mel, Lois Mulkearn and James W. Hess. "Two Hundred Years of Pittsburgh History: A Chronology of Events Complied." *Pittsburgh, the Story of an American City.*

Smith, Helene and George Swetnam. *A Guidebook to Historic Western Pennsylvania.* Pittsburgh: University of Pittsburgh Press, 1991.

Vexler, Robert I. *Pittsburgh: A Chronological & Documentary History, 1682-1976.* New York: Oceana Publications, 1977.

Arts:

Evert, Marilyn. *Discovering Pittsburgh's Sculpture.* Pittsburgh: University of Pittsburgh Press, 1983.

Irvin, George. *The Art of Robert Griffing: His Journey into the Eastern Frontier.* Gibsonia, PA: East/West Visions, 2000.

Kidney, Walter C. *Landmark Architecture of Allegheny Country.* Pittsburgh: Pittsburgh History and Landmark Foundation, 1985.

Kidney, Walter C. *Pittsburgh's Bridges: Architecture and Engineering.* Pittsburgh: Pittsburgh History & Landmarks Foundation, 1999.

Pittsburgh Revealed: Photographs Since 1850. Pittsburgh: Carnegie Museum of Art, 1999.

Van Trump, James D. *Life and Architecture in Pittsburgh.* Pittsburgh: Pittsburgh History & Landmarks Foundation, 1983.

Sources by Chapters:
To encourage the readers' investigation into particular periods of Pittsburgh history, sources are arranged by chapter.

Chapter 1 Land and Waters

Cate, Addison and Louis Heyman. "Regional Geological Setting of Western Pennsylvania." *Geology of the Pittsburgh Area.* Edited by W. Wagner. Harrisburg, PA Geological Survey, 1970.

Dunbar, Carl. *Historical Geology.* New York: John Wiley & Sons, 1949.

Eavenson, Howard. *The Pittsburgh Coal Bed – Its Early History and Development.* Transactions of the American Institute of Mining and Metallurgical Engineers, Coal Division. New York, 1938.

Hadley, Trevor. "Deep Waters Run Still." *Pittsburgh Magazine*, March 1989.

Harper, Frank C. *Pittsburgh of Today: Its Resources and People.* Vol. 1. Pittsburgh: The American Historical Society, 1931.

Harper, John A. "Lake Monongahela: Anatomy of an Immense Ice Age Pond." In *Pennsylvania Geology*, v.32, n.1. Spring, 2002.

Harper, John A. "Of Ice and Waters Flowing: The Formation of Pittsburgh's Three Rivers." *Pennsylvania Geology*, v.28, n.3,4. Fall/Winter, 1997.

Jennings, O.E. "When Pittsburgh Was a Lake." *Carnegie Magazine*, 1959.

Leighton, Henry. "Useful Minerals of the Pittsburgh Region." *Geology of Pittsburgh and Environs.* Pittsburgh, 1915.

Norris, James. "The Monongahela River." *Western Pennsylvania Historical Magazine*, July 1923.

Schmidt, Earl R. and D.B. Schmidt, eds. *Pittsburgh Regional Ecology.* Pittsburgh: Vulcan Press, 1971.

Spackman, William and Alan Davis. "Origin, Characteristics and Properties of Pennsylvania Coal." *Pennsylvania Coal:*

Resources, Technology, and Utilization. Harrisburg: The Pennsylvania Academy of Science Publication, 1983.

Wagner, W.R. and W.S. Lytle. *Geology of Pennsylvania's Oil and Gas*. Harrisburg: Commonwealth of Pennsylvania Department of Environmental Resources, 1968.

Chapter 2 Natives at the Forks: 14,000 BC-1740

Adovasio, J.M. and Jake Page. *The First Americans: In Pursuit of Archaeology's Greatest Mystery*. New York: Random House, Inc., 2002.

Anderson, Fred. *The Crucible of War: The Seven Years' War and the Fate of an Empire in British North*. New York: Vintage, 2000.

Borkowski, Joseph. "Historical Background." *Miscellaneous History of Lawrenceville*. Pittsburgh: Lawrenceville Historical Society, 1989.

Butler, William. "The Archeology of McKees Rocks Late Prehistoric Village Site." *Pennsylvania Archeologist*.

De Tocqueville, Alexis. "America Visited." *Democracy In America*. Vol. 1. Edited by Edith I. Coombs. New York, Book League of America, 1900.

Diamond, Jared. "The Arrow of Disease." In *Discover*, October 1992.

Diamond, Jared. *Guns, Germs, and Steel: The Fates of Human Societies*. New York and London: W.W. Norton & Company, 1999.

Dowd, Gregory Evans. *A Spiritual Resistance: The North American Indian Struggle for Unity 1745-1815*. Baltimore and London: The John Hopkins University Press, 1991.

Dragoo, Don. *Mounds for the Dead*. Pittsburgh: Annals of the Carnegie Museum, 1963.

Eccles, W.J. *The Canadian Frontier*. Albuquerque: University of New Mexico Press, 1983.

Fitting, James. "Regional Cultural Development, 300 B.C. to A.D. 1000." *Handbook of North American Indians*. Vol. 15. Washington, D.C.: Smithsonian Institute, 1978.

Gilday, John. "The Pigeons of Meadowcroft." *Carnegie Magazine*, 1977.

Heckewelder, John. *History, Manners, and Customs of the Indian Nations Who Once Inhabited Pennsylvania and the Neighboring States*. New York: Arno Press, 1971.

Hunt, George. *The Wars of the Iroquois: A Study of Intertribal Trade Relations*. Madison: The University of Wisconsin Press, 1960.

Jennings, Francis. *The Ambiguous Iroquois Empire*. New York: W.W. Norton & Company, 1984.

Johansen, Bruce E. *Forgotten Founders: How the American Indian Helped Shape Democracy*. Boston: The Harvard Common Press, 1982.

Kennedy, Roger. *Hidden Cities: The Discovery and Loss of North American Civilization*. New York, Penguin Books, 1994.

Klein, Herbert. "The Current Debate About the Origins of the Paleoindians of America." *Journal of Social History*, 2003.

Kraft, Herbert. *The Lenape: Archaeology, History, and Ethnography*. Newark: New Jersey Historical Society, 1986.

Lankford, John, ed. *Captain John Smith's America*. New York: Harper, 1967.

Mann, Charles. "1491." *The Atlantic Monthly*, 2002.

Martin, Calvin. *Keepers of the Game: Indian-Animal Relationships and the Fur Trade*. Los Angeles: University of California Press, 1978.

Mayer-Oakes, William. *Prehistory of the Upper Ohio Valley: An Introductory Archeological Study*. Pittsburgh: Annals of Carnegie Museum, 1995.

Palowitch, Barbara. "The Meadowcroft Dig." *Carnegie Magazine*, 1977.

Pointing, Clive. *A Green History of the World*. New York: Penguin Books, 1992.

Veech, James. *The Monongahela of Old: Historical Sketches of South-Western Pennsylvania to the Year 1800*. Pittsburgh: Private Distribution. 1892.

Wallace, Anthony F.C. *The Death and Rebirth of the Seneca*. New York: Vintage Books, 1972.

Wallace, Paul A. *Indians of Pennsylvania*. Harrisburg: The Pennsylvania Historical and Museum Commission, 1975.

Wallace, Paul A. *Indian Paths of Pennsylvania*. Harrisburg: Pennsylvania Historical and Museum Commission, 1987.

Wallace, Paul A., ed. *The Travels of John Heckewelder in Frontier America*. Pittsburgh: University of Pittsburgh, 1985.

Weslager, C.A. *The Delaware Indians: A History*. New Brunswick: Rutgers University Press, 1996.

Witthoft, John. *The American Indian as Hunter*. Harrisburg: Pennsylvania Historical and Museum Commission, 1990.

Woodward, Susan and Jerry McDonald. *Indian Mounds of the Middle Ohio Valley: A Guide to Adena and Hopewell Sites*. Blackburg: The McDonald & Woodward Publishing Company, 1986.

Zeisberger, David. *David Zeisberger's History of the Northern American Indians*. Lewisburg: Wennawoods Publishing, 1999.

Chapter 3 Invasion and Resistance: 1741-1790

Alberts, Robert C. "Braddock's Alumni." *American Heritage.* February, 1961.

Anderson, Fred, ed. *George Washington Remembers: Reflections on the French and Indian War.* New York: Rowman & Littlefield Publishers, 2004.

Anderson, Fred. *The Crucible of War: The Seven Years' War and the Fate of Empire in British North.* New York: Vintage, 2000.

Bearer, Bob. *Leading by Example: Partisan Fighters & Leaders of New France.* Westminster: Heritage Books, Inc., 2002.

Brown, Parker B. "The Historical Accuracy of the Captivity Narrative of Doctor John Knight." *Western Pennsylvania Historical Magazine.* January, 1987.

Buck Solon J. and Elizabeth Hawthorn Buck. *The Planting of Civilization in Western Pennsylvania.* Pittsburgh: University of Pittsburgh Press, 1979.

Cassell, Frank. "The Last Days of General Braddock: The March through Westmoreland and Allegheny Counties." *Westmoreland History,* September 2002.

Chapman, T.J. *The French in the Allegheny Valley.* Cleveland: W.W. Williams, 1887.

Colwell, David G. "The Causes and Accuracy of the Reputation of Simon Girty in American History," *Pittsburgh History,* Spring 1994.

Dahlinger, Charles W. "A Place of Great Historic Interest: Pittsburgh's First Burying Ground." In *Western Pennsylvania Historical Magazine,* October 1919.

Daudelin, Don. "Numbers and Tactics at Bushy Run." In *Western Pennsylvania Historical Magazine,* 1985.

Dowd, Gregory Evans. *A Spiritual Resistance: The North American Indian Struggle for Unity, 1745-1815.* Baltimore and London: The John Hopkins University Press, 1991.

Downes, Randolph C. *Council Fires on the Upper Ohio: A Narrative of Indian Affairs in the Upper Ohio Valley until 1795.* Pittsburgh: University of Pittsburgh Press, 1968.

Eccles, W.J. *The Canadian Frontier.* Albuquerque: University of New Mexico Press, 1983.

Eckert, Allan W. *That Dark and Bloody River.* New York: Bantam Books, 1995.

Eid, Leroy V. "A Kind of Running Fight: Indian Battlefields Tactics in the Eighteenth Century." In *Western Pennsylvania Historical Magazine,* April 1988.

Fellner, Felix. "Early Catholicity in Western Pennsylvania." *Catholic Pittsburgh's One Hundred Years.* Chicago: Loyola University Press, 1943.

Gallup, Andrew. *The Celeron Expedition to the Ohio Country: The Reports of Pierre-Joseph Celoron and Father Bonnechamps.* Bowie: Heritage Books, 1997.

Garbarino, Jr., William. *Along the Monongahela.* Midway: Midway Publishing, 2000.

Harper, Frank C. *Pittsburgh of Today: Its Resources and People.* Vol.1. Pittsburgh: The American Historical Society, 1931.

Kent, Donald H. *The French Invasion of Western Pennsylvania 1753.* Harrisburg: Pennsylvania Historical Museum and Commission, 1981.

Knight, John. "The Narrative of Dr. Knight." In *Loudon's Indian Narratives.* By Archibald Loudon. Lewisburg, Pennsylvania: Wennawinds Publishing, 1996.

Kopperman, Paul E. *Braddock at the Monongahela.* Pittsburgh: University of Pittsburgh, 2003.

Lambing, A. A. *Register of Fort Duquesne, 1754-1756.* Pittsburgh, The Catholic Historical Society of Western Pennsylvania, 1954.

Lankford, John, ed. *Captain John Smith's America.* New York: Harper, 1967.

McClure, Marie. *Captain Sam Brady, Indian Scout.* Beaver: Beaver Area Heritage Foundation, 1971.

Myers, James P. "Pennsylvania's Awakening: The Kittanning Raid of 1756," *Pennsylvania History,* 1999.

O'Meara, Walter. *Guns at the Fork.* Pittsburgh: University of Pittsburgh Press, 1979.

Quinion, Stephen. "The Old Indian Burying Ground," In *Western Pennsylvania Historical Magazine,* October 1920.

Richardson, James B. "Who Were Those Guys? The Destruction of Hanna's Town, Part II." In Western Pennsylvania History. Fall 2007.

Richter, Daniel K. *Facing East from Indian Country.* Cambridge: Harvard University Press, 2003.

Sayre, Gordon. *Les Sauvages Americans: Representations of Native Americans in French and English Colonial Literature.* Chapel Hill: North Carolina Press, 1997.

Sipe, C. Hale. *The Indian Chiefs of Pennsylvania.* Lewisburg: Wennawoods Publishing, 1995.

Sipe, C. Hale. *The Indian Wars of Pennsylvania.* Harrisburg: The Telegraph Press, 1929.

Smith, James. "Prisoner of the Caughnawagas." *Captured by the Indians.* Edited by Frederick Drimmer. New York: Dover, 1985.

Steinmet, Dillie. "Early History and Pioneer Settlement of Braddock's Field." *The Unwritten History of Braddock's Field (Pennsylvania).* Bowie: Heritage Books, Inc., 1999.

Wallace, Paul A. *Daniel Boone in Pennsylvania.* Harrisburg: PHMC, 1987.

Wallace, Paul A. *Conrad Weiser: Friend of Colonist and Mohawk*. Lewisburg: Wennawoods Publishing, 1996.

Ward, Matthew C. *Breaking the Back Country: The Seven Years War in Virginia and Pennsylvania, 1754-1765*. Pittsburgh: University of Pittsburgh Press, 2003.

Washington, George. *The Journal of Major George Washington*. Williamsburg: The Colonial Williamsburg Foundation, 1959.

Williams, Edward G. *Fort Pitt and the Revolution on the Western Frontier*. Pittsburgh: Historical Society of Western Pennsylvania, 1978.

Witthoft, John. *The American Indian as Hunter*. Harrisburg: Pennsylvania Historical Museum and Commission, 1990.

Chapter 4 Gateway to the Heartland: 1791-1850

Albig, W. Espy. "Early Development of Transportation on the Monongahela River." In *Western Pennsylvania Historical Magazine*, April 1919.

Baldwin, Leland D. *Pittsburgh: The Story of a City, 1750-1865*. Pittsburgh: University of Pittsburgh Press, 1970.

Baldwin, Leland D. *The Keelboat Age on Western Waters*. Pittsburgh: University of Pittsburgh Press, 1980.

Baldwin, Leland D. *Whiskey Rebels: The Story of a Frontier Uprising*. Pittsburgh: University of Pittsburgh Press, 1976.

Barcousky, Len. "Pittsburgh Almanack Mixes Practical, Poetic." *Pittsburgh Post-Gazette*. February 10, 2008.

Binder, Fredrick Moore. *Coal Age Empire; Pennsylvania Coal and its Utilization to 1860*. Harrisburg: Pennsylvania Historical and Museum Commission, 1974.

Brackenridge, Hugh Henry. *Famous Men & Women of Pittsburgh*. Pittsburgh: Pittsburgh History & Landmarks Foundation, 1981.

Brackenridge, Hugh Henry. "Incidents of the Insurrection." *A Hugh Henry Brackenridge Reader, 1770-1815*. Edited by Daniel Marder. Pittsburgh: University of Pittsburgh Press, 1970.

Brackenridge, Hugh Henry. "Thoughts on the Enfranchisement of the Negroes." *A Hugh Henry Brackenridge Reader, 1770-1815*. Edited by Daniel Marder. Pittsburgh: University of Pittsburgh Press, 1970.

Brackenridge, Hugh Henry. "The Trial of Mamachtaga, a Delaware Indian, the First Person Convicted of Murder West of the Allegheny Mountains, and Was Hanged for His Crime," In *Western Pennsylvania Historical Magazine*, January 1918.

Buck, Solon J. and Elizabeth Hawthorn Buck. *The Planting of Civilization in Western Pennsylvania*. Pittsburgh: University of Pittsburgh Press, 1979.

Calvert, Monte A. "The Allegheny City Cotton Mill Riot of 1848." In *Western Pennsylvania Historical Magazine*, April 1963.

Campbell, Paul E. "The First Bishop of Pittsburgh." In *Catholic Pittsburgh's One Hundred Years*. Chicago: Loyola University Press, 1943.

Clouse, Jerry A. *The Whiskey Rebellion: Southwestern Pennsylvania's Frontier People Test the American Constitution*. Harrisburg: Pennsylvania Historical and Museum Commission, 2000.

Commons, John R. and others, eds. *A Documentary History of American Industrial Society*. New York: Russell & Russell, 1958.

Cramer, Zadok. *The Navigator 1811: The Ohio River Collection*. Edited by Benjamin F. Klein. Cincinnati: Young and Klein, Inc., 1979.

Dahlinger, Charles W. "The Dawn of the Women's Movement." In *Western Pennsylvania Historical Magazine*, 1918.

Dickens, Charles. *American Notes: A Journey*. New York: International Publishing Corporation, 1985.

Donaldson, Mary Katherine. *Composition in Early Landscapes of the Ohio River Valley: Background and Components*. PhD. Thesis: University of Pittsburgh, 1971.

Doddridge, Joseph. *Notes on the Settlement and Indian Wars*. Edited by Special Collectors. Parsons: McClain Printing Company, 1912.

Dunaway, Wyland F. *A History of Pennsylvania*. Vol. 2. New York: Prentice-Hall, 1950.

Elkus, Leonore R., ed. *Famous Men & Women of Pittsburgh*. Pittsburgh: Pittsburgh History & Landmarks Foundation, 1981.

Foner, Philip S. *History of the Labor Movement in the United States*. Vol.1: *From Colonial Times to the Founding of the American Federation of Labor*. New York: International Publishers, 1962.

Fox, Arthur B. *Pittsburgh During the American Civil War, 1860-1865*. Chicora: Mechling Bookbindery, 2002.

Glasco, Laurence A., ed. *The WPA History of the Negro in Pittsburgh*. Pittsburgh: University of Pittsburgh Press, 2004.

Harbison, Francis R. *Flood Tides Along the Allegheny*. Pittsburgh: Francis R. Harbison, 1941.

Harper, Frank C. *Pittsburgh of Today: Its Resources and People*. Vol. 1. New York: The American Historical Society, 1931.

Harpster, John W., ed. *Pen Pictures of Early Western Pennsylvania*. Pittsburgh: University of Pittsburgh Press, 1938.

Harrison, William Henry. *Letters from William Henry Harrison, Western Pennsylvania Historical Magazine*, 1918.

Hersh, Burton. *The Mellon Family: A Fortune in History*. New York: William Morrow and Company, 1978.

Hoffert, Sylvia D. *Jane Grey Swisshelm: An Unconventional Life, 1815-1884*. Chapel Hill: The University of North Carolina Press, 2004.

Ilisevich, Robert D. and Carl Burkett, Jr. "The Canal Through Pittsburgh: Its Development and Physical Character." In *Western Pennsylvania Historical Magazine,* 1985.

Jackson, Donald. *Letters of the Lewis and Clark Expedition*. Vol. 1. Champaign: University of Illinois Press, 1979.

Jones, Samuel. *Pittsburgh: In the Year 1826*. New York: Arno Press, 1970.

Kidney, Walter C. *Landmark Architecture of Allegheny County*. Pittsburgh: Pittsburgh History and Landmark Foundation, 1999.

Kidney, Walter C. *Pittsburgh's Bridges: Architecture and Engineering*. Pittsburgh: Pittsburgh History and Landmarks Foundation, 1999.

Lamb, George H. *The Unwritten History of Braddock's Field (Pennsylvania)*. Bowie: Heritage Books, Inc., 1999.

Laws of the General Assembly of the Commonwealth of Pennsylvania Passed at the Session of 1848. Harrisburg, Pa: J.M.G. Lescure, 1848. "An Act to limit the hours of labor, and to prevent the employment, in factories, of children under twelve years of age."

Linaberger, James. "The Rolling Mill Riots of 1850." In *Western Pennsylvania Historical Magazine*, January 1964.

Long, E. John. "Johnny Appleseed in Pittsburgh." In *Western Pennsylvania Historical Magazine*. Vol. 13. 1930.

Lorant, Stefan. *Pittsburgh: The Story of an American City*. Garden City: Doubleday & Company, Inc., 1964.

Low, M. *A Guide to Audubon's Birds of America*. New Haven: William Reese Company & Donald Heald, 2002.

Madarasz, Anne. *Shattering Notions*. Pittsburgh: Historical Society of Western Pennsylvania, 1988.

Mass, Alfred A. "Brownsville's Steamboat Enterprise and Pittsburgh's Supply of General Jackson's Army." In *Pittsburgh History*, Spring 1994.

Michener, Carolee K. *Franklin: A Place in History*. Franklin: Franklin Bicentennial Committee, 1995.

Moulton, Gary E. *Journals of the Lewis and Clark Expedition*. Vol. II. Lincoln: University of Nebraska Press, 1987.

Patton, Benjamin. *The Factory Riots in Allegheny City: Judge Patton's Charge to the Jury*. Pittsburgh: January 20, 1849.

Penick, Jr., James. *American Heritage*. Vol. XXVII, 1975.

Pointing, Clive. *A Green History of the World*. New York: Penguin Books, 1992.

Pollan, Michael. *The Botany of Desire*. New York: Random House, 2001.

Price, Robert. *Johnny Appleseed: Man and Myth*. Bloomington: Indiana University Press, 1954.

Reiser, Catherine Elizabeth. *Pittsburgh's Commercial Development 1800-1850*. Harrisburg: Pennsylvania Historical and Museum Commission, 1951.

Rhodes, Richard. "John James Audobon: America's Rare Bird," *Smithsonian*, December 2004.

Rhodes, Richard. *John James Audobon: The Making of an American*. New York: Alfred Knopf, 2004.

Rishel, Joseph F. *Founding Families of Pittsburgh: The Evolution of a Regional Elite, 1760-1910*. Pittsburgh: University of Pittsburgh Press, 1990.

Rosenberg, Max. *The Building of Perry's Fleet on Lake Erie, 1812-1813*. Harrisburg: Pennsylvania Historical and Museum Commission, 1974.

Rush, Benjamin. "A Letter from a Citizen of Pennsylvania." In *Pen Pictures of Early Western Pennsylvania*. Edited by John W. Harpster. Pittsburgh: University of Pittsburgh Press, 1938.

Shank, William H. *The Amazing Pennsylvania Canals*, (170th Anniversary Edition). York: American Canal and Transportation Center, 2001.

Slaughter, Thomas P. *The Whiskey Rebellion: Frontier Epilogue to the American Revolution*. New York: Oxford University Press, 1986.

Stearns, Morton E. "Pittsburgh in the Mexican War." *Historical Society of Western Pennsylvania*, October 1924.

Sullivan, William A. "The Pittsburgh Working Men's Party." In *Western Pennsylvania Historical Magazine*, September 1951.

Swedenborg, Emanuel. *Heaven and Its Wonders and Hell: Things I Heard and Seen*. London: Swedenborg Society, 1966.

Swisshelm, Jane Grey. *Half a Century*. Chicago: Jansen, McClurg & Company, 1880.

Taft, Philip. *Organized Labor in American History*. New York: Harper & Row, 1964.

Thomas, Clarke M. *Front Page Pittsburgh: Two Hundred Years of the Post Gazette*. Pittsburgh: University of Pittsburgh Press, 2005.

Vardy, Steven B. "Louis Kossuth: A Celebrated, Disillusioned Hungarian Revolutionary's Visit to Pittsburgh in 1852." *Western Pennsylvania History,* Spring 2008.

Walters, Jr., Walter. *Albert Gallatin: Jeffersonian, Financier and Diplomat*. Pittsburgh: University of Pittsburgh Press, 1969.

Chapter 5 Civil War and Industrial Might: 1851-1875

Alberts, Robert C. "H.J. Heinz." In *Famous Men and Women of Pittsburgh*, ed. Leonore R. Elkus (Pittsburgh: Pittsburgh History and Landmarks Foundation, 1981)

Alberts, Robert C. *The Good Provider: H.J. Heinz and His 57 Varieties*. Boston: Houghton Mifflin Company, 1973.

Anonymous. "Western Pennsylvania and the Election of 1860." In *Western Pennsylvania Historical Magazine*, 1923.

Asbury, Herbert. *The Golden Flood: An Informal History of America's First Oil Field*. New York: Alfred A. Knopf, 1942.

Baldwin, Leland D. *Pittsburgh: The Story of a City, 1750-1865*. Pittsburgh: University of Pittsburgh Press, 1970.

Bates, Samuel. "The Fort Pitt Works." The Marital Deeds of Pennsylvania. Philadelphia: T.H. Davis & Co., 1876

Becer, Allan. "An Appalling Disaster: The Allegheny Arsenal and the Great Explosion of 1862." Paper present at The 26th Annual Duquesne University History Forum. Pittsburgh: 1993.

Blackett, R.J.M. "Freedom, or the Martyr's Grave: Black Pittsburgh's Aid to the Fugitive Slave." In *African Americans in Pennsylvania*. University Park: Pennsylvania State University Press, 1997.

Boucher, John Newton, ed. *A Century and a Half of Pittsburgh and Her People*. Vol. II. Pittsburgh: The Lewis Publishing Co., 1908.

The City Hall, Pittsburgh. Pittsburgh: Stevenson & Foster, 1874.

Coleman, John F. *The Disruption of the Pennsylvania Democracy 1848-1860*. Harrisburg: The Pennsylvania Historical and Museum Commission, 1975.

Cramer, J.H. "A President-Elect in Western Pennsylvania." In *Western Pennsylvania Historical Magazine*. Vol. 71, July 1947.

Delany, Martin. *Blake or the Huts of America*. Boston: Beacon Press, 1970.

Delany, Martin. *Martin Delany's Speeches*, West Virginia University Libraries, [database online]

Dahlinger, Charles W. "Abraham Lincoln in Pittsburgh and the Republican Party." In *Western Pennsylvania Historical Magazine*, October 1920.

Dahlinger, Charles W. "The Republic Party Originated in Pittsburgh." In *Western Pennsylvania Historical Magazine*, January 1921.

Davis, James J. *The Iron Puddler, My Life in the Rolling Mills and What Came of It*. New York: Grosset & Dunlap, 1922.

Donaldson, Mary Katherine. *Composition in Early Landscapes of the Ohio River Valley: Background and Components*. Dissertation: University of Pittsburgh, 1971.

Dubois, W.E. Burghardt. *John Brown*. New York: International Publishers, 1969.

Dyer, Ervin. "Noted Hill Abolitionist Forgotten No Longer." In *Pittsburgh Post Gazette*, 2004.

Elkus, Leonore R., ed. *Famous Men and Women of Pittsburgh*. Pittsburgh: Pittsburgh History and Landmarks Foundation, 1981.

Flexner, James Thomas. "The Dark World of David Gilmour Blyth." In *American Heritage Magazine*, 1962.

Foner, Philip S. *History of the Labor Movement in the United States*. Vol. I: *From Colonial Times to the Founding of the American Federation of Labor*. New York: International Publishers, 1962.

Fox, Arthur B. *Pittsburgh During the American Civil War 1860-1865*. Chicora, PA: Mechling Bookbindery, 2002.

Gancas, Ron. *Field of Freedom: United States Colored Troops for Southwestern Pennsylvania*. Pittsburgh: Soldiers & Sailors Memorial Hall and Museum Trust, Inc., 2004.

Glasco, Laurence A., ed. *The WPA History of the Negro in Pittsburgh*. Pittsburgh: University of Pittsburgh Press, 2004.

Grossman, Jonathan P. *William Sylvis, Pioneer of American Labor: A Study of the Labor Movement During the Era of the Civil War*. Cincinnati: The Sylvis Society, 1986.

Gugliotta, Angela. *"Hell With the Lid Taken Off: A Cultural History of Air Pollution – Pittsburgh."* Dissertation. Graduate Program in History: University of Notre Dame, 2004.

Hanchett, Catherine. "George Boyer Vashon, 1824-1878: Black Education, Poet, Fighter for Equal Rights," In *Western Pennsylvania Historical Magazine*, 1985.

Hodges, Jr., Fletcher. *Stephen Foster, Maker of American Songs*. Historical Pennsylvania Leafflet No. 3. Edited by Leonore R. Elkus. Harrisburg: Pennsylvania Historical and Museum Commission, 1977.

Hoffert, Sylvia D. *Jane Grey Swisshelm: An Unconventional Life, 1815-1884*. Chapel Hill: The University of North Carolina Press, 2004.

Hoffman, William S. *Paul Mellon: Portrait of an Oil Baron*. Chicago: Follett Publishing Company, 1974.

Holt, Michael Fitzgibbon. *Forging a Majority: The Formation of the Republican Party in Pittsburgh, 1848-1860*. Pittsburgh: University of Pittsburgh Press, 1990.

Kobus, Ken. *Supporting Documentation for the Clinton Furnace Historical Marker*. Harrisburg: Pennsylvania Historical and Museum Commission, 2002.

Koskoff, David E. *The Mellons: The Chronicle of America's Richest Family*. New York: Thomas Y. Crowell, 1978.

Leupp, Francis E. *George Westinghouse: His Life and Achievements*. Boston: Little, Brown and Company, 1918.

McBridge, Mary Ellen Leigh. "Jane Grey Swisshelm." In *Famous Men & Women of Pittsburgh*. Edited by Leonore R. Elkus. Pittsburgh: Pittsburgh History & Landmarks Foundation, 1981.

McCarthy, Bill. "One Month in the Summer of '63: Pittsburgh Prepares for the Civil War." *Pittsburgh History*, 1998.

Montgomery, David. *Beyond Equality: Labor and the Radical Republicans 1862-1872*. New York: Vintage Books, 1967.

Pinkowski, Edward. *John Siney: The Miners' Martyr*. Philadelphia: Sunshine Press, 1963.

Prout, Henry G. *A Life of George Westinghouse*. New York: Charles Scribner's Sons, 1922.

Rodman, Major T.J. "Testimony," *Report of the Joint Committee on the Conduct of War, 1864*. Port Huron: Antique Ordnance Publishers, 1980.

Rupp, Israel. "Early History of Western Pennsylvania." 1846.

Sanders, Meyer A. "Labor." In *Allegheny County: A Sesqui-Centennial Review, 1788...1938*. Edited by George E. Kelly. Pittsburgh: Allegheny Sesqui-Centennial Committee, 1938.

Smith, Eric Ledell. "The Pittsburgh Memorial: A Forgotten Document of Pittsburgh History." *Pittsburgh History*. Vol.8, no.3. 1997.

Switala, William J. *Underground Railroad in Pennsylvania*. Mechanicsburg: Stackpole Books, 2001.

Teilman, Herdis B. "Mary Cassatt." In *Famous Men and Women of Pittsburgh*. Edited by Leonore R. Elkus. Pittsburgh: Pittsburgh History and Landmarks Foundation, 1981.

Thomas, Clarke M. *Front Page Pittsburgh: Two Hundred Years of the Post Gazette*. Pittsburgh: University of Pittsburgh Press, 2005.

Wall, Joseph Frazier. *Andrew Carnegie*. Pittsburgh: University of Pittsburgh Press, 1989.

Wilkins, David G. *Paintings and Sculpture of the Duquesne Club*. Pittsburgh: Art and Library Committee of the Duquesne Club, 1986.

Williams, Edward G. "Pittsburgh, Birthplace of a Science." In *Western Pennsylvania Historical Magazine*. September, 1962.

Williams, Irene E. "The Operation of the Fugitive Slave Law in Western Pennsylvania from 1850-1860." In *Western Pennsylvania Historical Magazine*, July 1921.

Wollman, David H. and Donald R. Inman. *Portraits in Steel: An Illustrated History of Jones & Laughlin Steel Corporation*. Kent: The Kent State University Press, 1999.

Wudarczyk, James. "A Lost Landmark: A Study of the Fate of the Allegheny Arsenal." In *Western Pennsylvania Historical Magazine*. 1987.

Wudarczyk, James. *A Decision to Destroy: A Study of the Fate of the Allegheny Arsenal*. Notes and Documents Relating to Pittsburgh's Allegheny Arsenal. Pittsburgh: Carnegie Library, 1997.

Wudarczyk, James. *Pittsburgh's Forgotten Allegheny Arsenal*. Apollo: Closson Press, 1935.

Chapter 6 Dominance and Resistance: 1876-1894

Berkman, Alexander. *Prison Memoirs of an Anarchist*. Pittsburgh: Frontier Press, 1970.

Black, Bertram J. and Aubrey Mallach. *Population Trends in Pittsburgh and Allegheny County, 1840-1940*. Edited by Roy Lubove. New York: New Viewpoints, 1976.

Brashear, John A. *A Man Who Loved the Stars*. Pittsburgh: University of Pittsburgh Press, 1988.

Brecher, Jeremy. *Strike!*. Cambridge: South End Press, 1997.

Bridge, James H. *The Inside History of the Carnegie Steel Company*. New York: The Aldine Book Company, 1903.

Brignano, Mary and Hax McCullough. *The Search for Safety: A History of Railroad Signals and the People Who Made Them*. Pittsburgh: American Standard Inc., 1981.

Brody, David. *Steelworkers in America: The Nonunion Era*. New York: Harper & Row, 1969.

Brown, Mark. "Technology and the Homestead Works: 1879-1945." In *Canal History and Technology Proceedings*. Edited by Lance E. Metz. Easton: Canal History and Technology Press, 1992.

Bruce, Robert V. *1877: Year of Violence*. Chicago: Quadrangle Paperback, 1977.

Cheney, Margaret and Robert Uth. *Tesla: Master of Lighting*. New York: Barnes & Noble Books, 1999.

Clark, Joseph S. "The Railroad Struggle for Pittsburgh." *The Pennsylvania Magazine of History and Biography*. Philadelphia: Historical Society of Pennsylvania, 1924).

Cooper, Jerry M. "The Army of Strikebreaker-The Railroad Strikes of 1877 and 1894." *Labor History*, 1977.

Couvares, Francis G. *The Remaking of Pittsburgh: Class and Culture in an Industrializing City, 1877-1919*. Albany: State University of New York Press, 1984.

Demarest, Jr., David R., ed. *The River Ran Red: Homestead 1892*. Pittsburgh: University of Pittsburgh Press, 1992.

Demmler, Ralph H. *The First Century of an Institution: Reed Smith Shaw & McClay*. Pittsburgh, 1977.

Dickerson, Dennis C. *Out of the Crucible: Black Steelworkers in Western Pennsylvania, 1875-1980*. Albany: State University of New York Press, 1986.

Doctorow, E.L. *Ragtime*. New York: Random House, 1975.

Dreiser, Theodore. *A Book About Myself*. New York: Boni & Liveright, 1922.

Eastman, Crystal. "Work Accidents and the Law." *The Pittsburgh Survey*. New York: Russell Sage Foundation, 1910.

Fitch, John A. *The Steel Worker*. (The Pittsburgh Survey). Pittsburgh: University of Pittsburgh Press, 1989.

Floyd, Barbara, Richard Oram and Nola Skousen. "The City Built of Glass." *Labor's Heritage*. Vol. 2. 1990.

Fogelson, Robert M. *America's Armories: Architecture, Society, and Public Order*. Cambridge: Harvard University Press, 1989.

Foner, Eric. *Reconstruction: America's Unfinished Revolutions 1863-1877*. New York: Harper & Row Publishers, 1988.

Foner, Philip S. *History of the Labor Movement in the United States*. Vol. II: *From the Founding of the American Federation of Labor to the Emergence of American Imperialism*. New York: International Publishers, 1955.

Foner, Philip S. *The Great Labor Uprising of 1877*. New York: Monad Press, 1977.

Gage, Tom. "Hands-on, All-Over: Captain Bill Jones." *Pittsburgh History*, Winter, 1997-1998.

Glasco, Laurence. "Double Burden: The Black Experience in Pittsburgh." In *City at the Point: Essays on the Social History of Pittsburgh*. Edited by Samuel P. Hays. Pittsburgh: University of Pittsburgh Press, 1990.

Grant, John A. *Coxey's 38-Day March: Through the Alleghenies in Search of Economic Justice*. Pittsburgh: The Council of Alleghenies, 1999.

Green, James. *Death in the Haymarket*. New York: Pantheon, 2006.

Gutman, Herbert G. "The Buena Vista Affair, 1874-1875." *The Pennsylvania Magazine of History and Biography*, 1964.

Hersh, Burton. *The Mellon Family: A Fortune in History*. New York: William Morrow & Company Inc., 1978.

Hessen, Robert. *Steel Titan: The Life of Charles M. Schwab*. Pittsburgh: University of Pittsburgh Press, 1975.

James, Alfred P. "The First Convention of the American Federation of Labor, Pittsburgh Pennsylvania November 15-18, 1881." In *Western Pennsylvania Historical Magazine*, Vol. 6, no.4; Vol. 7, no.1; Vol.7, no.2.

Jones, Mary Harris. *The Autobiography of Mother Jones*. Chicago: Charles H. Kerr Publishing Company, 1977.

Kenny, Kevin. *Making Sense of the Molly Maguires*. New York: Oxford University Press, 1998.

Kellogg, Paul U. "Editor's Forward." In Byington, Margaret, *Homestead: The Households of Mill Town*. Pittsburgh: University of Pittsburgh Press, 1974.

Kidney, Walter C. *Landmark Architecture of Allegheny Country*. Pittsburgh: Pittsburgh History and Landmark Foundation, 1985.

Kobus, Ken and Jack Consoli. *The Pennsy in the Steel City*. The Pennsylvania Railroad Technical and Historical Society: Kutztown Publishing, 1996.

Krause, Paul. *Labor-Republicanism and 'Za Chlebom': Anglo-American and Slavic Solidarity in Homestead*. DeKlab: Northern Illinois University Press, 1986.

Krause, Paul. *The Battle of Homestead 1880-1892: Politics, Culture, and Steel*. Pittsburgh: University of Pittsburgh Press, 1992.

Kroeger, Brooke. *Nellie Bly: Daredevil, Reporter, Feminist*. New York: Times Books, 1994.

Latton, Harry B. "Steel Wonders." *The River Ran Red: Homestead 1892*. Edited by David R. Demarest, Jr. Pittsburgh: University of Pittsburgh Press, 1992.

Leupp, Francis E. *George Westinghouse: His Life and Achievements*. Boston: Little, Brown, and Company, 1918.

Martin, Edward Winslow and James Dabney McCabe. *The History of the Great Riots and of the Molly Maguires*. New York: Augustus M. Kelley Publishers, 1971.

Madarasz, Anne. *Shattering Notions*. Pittsburgh: Historical Society of Western Pennsylvania, 1988.

McAteer, Davitt. *Monongah: The Tragic Story of the Worst Industrial Accident in U.S. History*. Morgantown: West Virginia Press, 2007.

McCollester, Charles. "Pittsburgh's IBEW Local 5: The Formation of a Century-Old Electrical Craft Unions." In *Pittsburgh History*, 1996.

McCullough, David G. *The Johnstown Flood*. New York: Simon and Schuster, 1968.

McElroy, Hanice H., ed. *Our Hidden Heritage: Pennsylvania Women in History*. Washington, D.C.: American Association of University Women, 1983.

Miller, Donald L. and Richard E. Sharpless. *The Kingdom of Coal: Work, Enterprise, and Ethnic Communities in the Mine Fields*. Philadelphia, PA: University of Pennsylvania Press, 1985.

Musser, Charles, ed. *1877-The Grand Army of Starvation*, VHS. New York: American Social History Productions, 1984.

Nasaw, Andrew. *Andrew Carnegie*. New York: Penguin, 2006.

Norwood, Stephen H. *Strikebreaking & Intimidation: Mercenaries and Masculinity in Twentieth-Century America*. Chapel Hill: University of North Carolina Press, 2002.

O'Connor, Richard J. *Cinderheads and Iron Lungs: Window-Glass Craftsmen and the Transformation of Workers Control, 1880-1905*. Dissertation: University of Pittsburgh Press, 1991.

Palucka, Tim and Sherie Mershon. *The Engineers' Society of Western Pennsylvania: Celebrating 125 Year of Engineering*. Tartentum: Word Association Publishers, 2006.

Parton, Mary Field, ed. *The Autobiography of Mother Jones*. Chicago: Charles H. Kerr Publishing Company, 1977.

Pennsylvania Legislature. *Report of the Committee Appointed to Investigate the Railroad Riots in July, 1877*. Harrisburg: Lane S. Hart, 1878.

Pinkerton, Allan. *Strikers, Communists, Tramps, and Detectives*. New York: Arno Press & The New York Times, 1969.

Powderly, T.V. "The Homestead Strike." In *Pittsburgh*. Edited by Roy Lubove. New York: New Viewpoints, 1976.

Prout, Henry G. *A Life of George Westinghouse*. New York: Charles Scribner's Sons, 1922.

Pulay, Emoke. "The Shots Fired at Morewood." *The Connelsville Courier*, April 10, 1891.

Rinehart, Mary Roberts. *My Story,* quoted in David R. Demarest Jr., *From These Hills, From These Valleys.* Pittsburgh: Pittsburgh University Press, 1976.

Rishel, Joseph F. *The Spirit That Gives Life: The History of Duquesne University, 1876-1996.* Pittsburgh: Duquesne University Press, 1997.

Robertson, Raymond J. *Ironworkers 100ᵗʰ Anniversary, 1896-1996: A History of the Ironworkers Union.* The Ironworkers Union, 1996.

Sanders, Meyer A. "Labor." In *Allegheny County, A Sesqui-Centennial Review, 1788…1938.* Edited by George E. Kelly. Pittsburgh: Allegheny County Sesqui-Centennial Committee, 1938.

Schmidt, E.R., ed. *Pittsburgh Regional Ecology.* California, PA: Vulcan Press, 1971.

Smith, Robert Michael. *From Blackjacks to Briefcases.* Athens: Ohio University Press, 2003.

Standiford, Les. *Meet You in Hell: Andrew Carnegie, Henry Clay Frick, and the Bitter Partnership That Transformed America.* New York: Crown Publishers, 2005.

Stoughton, Bradley. *The Metallurgy of Iron and Steel,* 4ᵗʰ ed. New York: McGraw Hill Book Company, 1934.

Steffens, Lincoln. *The Shame of the Cities.* New York: Hill and Wang, 1957.

Taft, Philip. *The A.F. of L. in the Time of Gompers.* New York: Harper & Brothers, 1957.

Taft, Philip. *Organized Labor in American History.* New York: Harper Row, 1964.

Tarr, Joel A. "Infrastructure and City-Building in the Nineteenth and Twentieth." In *City at the Point: Essays on the Social History of Pittsburgh.* Edited by Samuel P. Hays. Pittsburgh: University of Pittsburgh Press, 1990.

Thomas, Clarke M. *Front-Page Pittsburgh: Two Hundred Years of the Post-Gazette.* Pittsburgh: University of Pittsburgh Press, 2005.

Trimble, William F. *High Frontiers: A History of Aeronautics in Pennsylvania.* Pittsburgh: University of Pittsburgh Press, 1982.

Trusilo, Sharon. "Amalgamated Association of Iron and Steel Workers." In *The River Ran Red: Homestead 1892.* Edited by David R. Demarest, Jr. Pittsburgh: University of Pittsburgh Press, 1992.

University of Pittsburgh Archives. "Labor Legacy." <http://www.library.pitt.edu/labor_legacy/>.

Wall, Joseph Frazier. *Andrew Carnegie.* Pittsburgh: University of Pittsburgh Press, 1989.

Warren, Kenneth. *Industrial Genius: The Working Life of Charles Michael Schwab.* Pittsburgh: University of Pittsburgh Press, 2007.

Warren, Kenneth. *Triumphant Capitalist: Henry Clay Frick and the Industrial Transformation of America.* Pittsburgh: University of Pittsburgh Press, 2000.

Westinghouse Electric Corporation. *George Westinghouse 1846-1914.* Wilmerding: George Westinghouse Museum Foundation, 1946.

Woodward, C. Vann. *Reunion & Reaction.* Garden City: Doubleday Anchor Books, 1956.

Chapter 7 The Triumph of Capital: 1895-1909

Abrams, Roger I. *The First World Series and the Baseball Fanatics of 1903.* Boston: Northeastern University Press, 2003.

Acheson, Edward. "A Pathfinder: Discovery, Invention, and Industry." *Educational Biographical Sketches of Eminent Investors.* New York: The Press Scrap Book, 1910.

Amalgamated Transit Union Staff. *ATU 100 Years: A History of the Amalgamated Transit Union.* Amalgamated Transit Union, 1992.

Asmonga, John and Linda Asmonga. *Comparison of the Harwick Miners Surnames.* Unpublished Manuscript, 1906.

Bolles, Albert S. *The Legal Relations Between the Employed and Their Employers in Pennsylvania Compared with the Relations Existing Between them in Other States.* Edited by the Bureau of Industrial Statistics. Harrisburg: W.M. Stanley Ray, 1901.

Bonk, Dan and Len Martin. "The First World Series & Its Pittsburgh Connections." In *Western Pennsylvania History.* Fall 2003.

Bridge, James H. *The Inside History of the Carnegie Steel Company.* New York: The Aldine Book Company, 1903.

Brooks, Robert R. *As Steel Goes,…: Unionism in a Basic Industry.* New Haven: Yale University Press, 1940.

Burstin, Barbara. *A Jewish Legacy: Pittsburgh.* Documentary video. Carnegie library of Pittsburgh.

Butler, Elizabeth Beardsley. *Women and the Trades: Pittsburgh, 1907-1908.* (Pittsburgh Survey) Pittsburgh: University of Pittsburgh Press, 1984.

Byington, Margaret. *Homestead: The Households of a Mill Town.* (Pittsburgh Survey) Pittsburgh: University of Pittsburgh Press, 1974.

Byrne, Kathleen and Richard Snyder. *Chrysalis: Willa Cather in Pittsburgh.* Pittsburgh: Historical Society of Western Pennsylvania, 1980.

Cannadine, David. *Mellon, An American Life.* New York, Vintage Books, 2008.

Carr, Charles C. *ALCOA: An American Enterprise.* New York: Rinehard & Company, Inc., 1952.

Casner, Nicholas. *Devastation and Renewal: An Environmental History of Pittsburgh and Its Regions.* Edited by Joel A. Tarr. Pittsburgh: University of Pittsburgh Press, 2003.

Commons, John R. & William M. Leiserson. "Wage-Earners of Pittsburgh." *Wage-Earning Pittsburgh* (The Pittsburgh Survey). New York: Survey Associates, 1914).

Dahlinger, Charles W. "Old Allegheny." In *Western Pennsylvania Historical Magazine,* 1918.

Department of Environmental Resources. *Annual Report on Mining Activities, 1991.* (Harrisburg: Commonwealth of Pennsylvania, 1991).

Department of Mines of Pennsylvania. *Report: Part II Bituminous 1904.* Harrisburg: Harrisburg Publishing Co., 1905.

Derickson, Alan. *Black Lung: Anatomy of a Public Health Disaster.* Ithaca: Cornell University Press, 1998.

Devine, Edward. "Pittsburgh the Year of the Survey." *The Pittsburgh District: Civic Frontage.* (Pittsburgh Survey) New York: Arno Press, 1974.

Doctorow, E.L. *Ragtime.* New York: Random House, 1975.

Dreiser, Theodore. *A Book About Myself.* New York: Boni & Liveright, 1922.

Dubofsky, Melvyn. *We Shall Be All: A History of the Industrial Workers of the World.* New York: New York Times Books, 1969.

Dvorchak, Robert. "Golf the way it's meant to be." *Pittsburgh Post-Gazette.* June 10, 2007.

Eastman, Crystal. *Work Accidents and the Law.* (The Pittsburgh Survey). New York: Russell Sage Foundation, 1910.

Eggert, Gerald G. *Steelmasters and Labor Reform, 1886-1923.* Pittsburgh: University of Pittsburgh Press, 1981.

Feldman, Jacob. *The Jewish Experience in Western Pennsylvania: A History, 1755-1945.* Pittsburgh: Historical Society of Western Pennsylvania, 1986.

Fenton, Edwin. *Carnegie Mellon, 1900-2000: A Centennial History.* Pittsburgh: Carnegie Mellon University Press, 2000.

Fitch, John A. *The Steel Workers.* Pittsburgh: University of Pittsburgh Press, 1989.

Fitzgerald, F.A., ed. *The International Engineer: Fifty Years of Progress: 1896-1946.* December, 1946.

Foner, Philip S. *History of the Labor Movement in the United States,* Vol. 4: *The Industrial Workers of the World, 1905-1917.* New York: International Publishers, 1965.

Greenwald, Maureen Weiner. "Women at Work Through the Eyes of Elizabeth Beardsley Butler and Lewis Wickes Hines," Introduction to Elizabeth Beardsley Butler, *Women and the Trades.* Pittsburgh: University of Pittsburgh Press, 1984.

Hageman, William. *Honus: The Life and Times of a Baseball Hero.* Chicago: Sagamore Publishing, 1996.

Haywood, Bill. *The Autobiography of Big Bill Haywood.* New York: International Publishers, 1974.

Hessen, Robert. *Steel Titan: The Life of Charles M. Schwab.* Pittsburgh: University of Pittsburgh Press, 1975.

Hoerr, John. *And the Wolf Finally Came: The Decline of the American Steel Industry.* Pittsburgh: University of Pittsburgh Press, 1988.

Jackson, Carlton. *The Dreadful Month.* Bowling Green, Ohio: Bowling Green State University Popular Press, 1982.

Kidney, Walter. *Landmark Architecture of Allegheny Country.* Pittsburgh: Pittsburgh History & Landmarks Foundation, 1985.

Kidney, Walter C. *Pittsburgh's Bridges: Architecture and Engineering.* Pittsburgh: Pittsburgh History and Landmark Foundation, 1999.

Koskoff, David E. *The Mellons: The Chronicle of America's Richest Family.* New York: Thomas Y. Crowell, 1978.

Leib, Frederick G. *The Pittsburgh Pirates.* Carbondale: Southern Illinois University Press, 2003.

Levinson, Edward. *Break Strikes!: The Technique of Pearl L. Bergoff.* New York: Robert M. McBride and Company, 1935.

Long, Haniel. *Pittsburgh Memoranda.* Pittsburgh: Brenton Books, 1990.

Lubove, Roy. *Twentieth-Century Pittsburgh: Government, Business, and Environmental Change.* Pittsburgh: University of Pittsburgh Press, 1995.

March, Alden. *A New History of the Spanish-American War.* Philadelphia: American Book & Bible House, 1899.

McCollister, John. *The Bucs!: The Story of the Pittsburgh Pirates.* Lenexa: Addax Publishing Group, 1998.

Mellon, William Larimer. *Judge Mellon's Son.* Pittsburgh: Private Printing, 1948.

Mine Safety and Health Administration. U.S. Department of Labor. "Mine Disasters." 2000.

Norwood, Stephen H. *Strikebreaking & Intimidation: Mercenaries and Masculinity in Twentieth-Century America.* Chapel Hill: University of North Carolina Press, 2002.

O'Connor, Harvey. *Mellon's Millions: The Biography of a Fortune; The Life and Times of Andrew W. Mellon.* New York: John Day Company, 1933.

O'Connor, Harvey. *Steel Dictator.* New York: The John Day Company, 1935.

Pittsburgh Professional Fire Fighters: 100th Anniversary. Pittsburgh Fire fighters, 1974.

Rice, Charles Owen. "Biddley Byes." In *Fighter with a Heart: Charles Owen Rice, Pittsburgh Labor Priest.* Edited by Charles McCollester. Pittsburgh: University of Pittsburgh Press, 1996.

Riffle, Denise. *Willa Cather: The Pittsburgh Years, 1896-1906.* Pittsburgh: University of Pittsburgh Press, 1993.

Robertson, Raymond J. *Ironworkers 100*[th] *Anniversary, 1896-1996: A History of the Ironworkers Union*. The Ironworkers Union, 1996.

Sanders, Meyer A. "Labor." In *Allegheny County, A Sesqui-Centennial Review, 1788…1938*. Edited by George E. Kelly. Pittsburgh: Allegheny County Sesqui-Centennial Committee, 1938.

Sanger, Martha Frick Symington. *Henry Clay Frick*. New York: Abbeville Press, 1998.

Schloetzer, Mattie. "Andrew Carnegie's Original Reproductions: The Hall of Architecture at 100." In *Western Pennsylvania History*. Fall 2007.

Schmidt, E.R., ed. *Pittsburgh Regional Ecology*. California PA: Vulcan Press, 1971.

Schreiner, Jr., Samuel A. *Henry Clay Frick: The Gospel of Greed*. New York: St. Martin's Press, 1995.

Seldes, George. *Witness to a Century*. New York: Ballantine Books, 1987.

Slavishak, Steward. "Artificial Limbs and Industrial Workers' Bodies in Turn-of-the-Century Pittsburgh." *Journal of Social History*, 2003.

Spencer, Ethel. *The Spencers of Amberson Avenue: A Turn-of-the-Century Memoir*. Edited by Michael P. Weber and Peter N. Stearns. Pittsburgh: University of Pittsburgh Press, 1984.

Tarr, Joel A. *Devastation and Renewal: An Environmental History of Pittsburgh and Its Regions*. Pittsburgh: University of Pittsburgh Press, 2003.

Tersak, Joseph and James Craig. "Pittsburgh, PA Police: 98 Years of Police Motorcycles." In *The Mounted Officer*. 2007.

Thaw, Harry K. *The Traitor*. Philadelphia: Dorrance and Company, 1926.

Thomas, Marlin S. *A Chapter in the Development of Local #66 I.U.O.E.* Pittsburgh: I.U.O.E., 1981.

Thompson, Craig. *Since Spindletop: A Human Story of Gulf's First Half-Century*. Pittsburgh: Gulf Oil Corporation, 1951.

U.S. Supreme Court, "Hunter v. City of Pittsburgh," ed. 207 U.S. 161 (1907).

Verity, C. William. "The Pioneers," *National Safety Congress* 1 (1972).

Vexler, Robert I. *Pittsburgh: A Chronological & Documentary History, 1682-1976*. New York: Oceana Publications, 1977.

Wall, Joseph Frazier. *Andrew Carnegie*. Pittsburgh: University of Pittsburgh Press, 1989.

Warren, Kenneth. *Charles Schwab: Industrial Genius*. Pittsburgh: University of Pittsburgh Press, 2007.

Warren, Kenneth. *Triumphant Capitalism*. Pittsburgh: University of Pittsburgh Press, 1996.

Wing, Frank E. "Thirty-Five Years of Typhoid," in *The Pittsburgh District: Civic Frontage*. New York: Arno Press, 1974.

Chapter 8 The Americanization of Labor: 1910-1919

Anonymous, "National Committee for Organizing Iron and Steel Workers." *The Bridgemen's Magazine*, October 1919.

Anonymous, "Stogy Makers and the IWW in Pittsburgh," *The Survey*, November 29, 1913.

Attaway, William. *Blood on the Forge*. New York: Monthly Review Press, 1987.

Benford, Jennie. "Sisters Anxious for the Ballot: Pittsburgh Suffragists." In *Pittsburgh Women's Suffrage Folder*. Carnegie Library, Western Pennsylvania Room.

Borland, J.R. "Coroner's Press Report, August 26, 1919." Tarentum: University of Pittsburgh Archives, 1919.

Braverman, Harry. *Labor and Monopoly Capital*. New York: Monthly Review Press, 1984.

Brewster, Freida Truhar. "A Personal View of the Early Left in Pittsburgh." In *The Western Pennsylvania Historical Magazine*, 69(4). October, 1966.

Brody, David. *Labor in Crisis: The Steel Strike of 1919*. Urbana: University of Illinois Press, 1987.

Brody, David. *Workers in Industrial American: Essays on the Twentieth Century Struggle*. New York: Oxford University Press, 1980.

Buni, Andrew. *Robert L. Vann of the Pittsburgh Courier: Politics and Black Journalism*. Pittsburgh, University of Pittsburgh Press, 1974.

Butler, Elizabeth Beardsley. *Women and the Trades: Pittsburgh, 1907-1908*. (Pittsburgh Survey) Pittsburgh: University of Pittsburgh Press, 1984.

Cassedy, James. "A Bond of Sympathy: The Life and Tragic Death of Fannie Sellins." In *Labor Heritage*, Vol. 8, no. 4, Winter 1992.

Connors, Michael. "Finding Private Enright." *Pittsburgh Post-Gazette*, November 11, 2007.

Coroner's Office. "Coroner's Jury Verdict (Fannie Sellins)." State of Pennsylvania, County of Allegheny, 1919.

Davies, Norman. *God's Playground: A History of Poland*, II. New York: Columbia University Press, 1982.

Dickerson, Dennis C. *Out of the Crucible: Black Steelworkers in Western Pennsylvania, 1875-1980*. Albany: State University of New York, 1986.

Draper, Theodore. *The Roots of American Communism*. New York: Viking Press, 1963.

Dubofsky, Melvin and Warren Van Tine. *John L. Lewis, A Biography*. New York: Quadrangle Books, 1977.

Fitch, John A. "A Strike for Freedom." *The Survey*, September 27, 1919.

Fitch, John A. "The Labor Policies of Unrestricted Capital." *The Survey*, April 6, 1912.

Fitch, John A. *The Steel Workers*. Pittsburgh: University of Pittsburgh Press, 1989.

Foley, William and Thomas Pierce. *History of the Great Westinghouse Strike*. Unpublished manuscript.

Foner, Philip S. *History of the Labor Movement in the United States*. Vol. 8. *Postwar Struggles, 1918-20*. New York: International Publishers, 1988.

Foner, Philip, S., ed. *Mother Jones Speaks: Collected Writings and Speeches*. New York: Monad Press, 1983.

Foster, William Z. *The Great Steel Strike and Its Lessons*. New York: B.W. Huebsch, Inc., 1920.

Gibbons, Russell W. "Dateline Homestead." In *The River Ran Red: Homestead 1892*. Edited by David R. Demarest, Jr. Pittsburgh: University of Pittsburgh Press, 1992.

Glasco, Laurence A. ed. *The WPA History of the Negro in Pittsburgh*. Pittsburgh: University of Pittsburgh Press, 2004.

Gompers, Samuel. *Seventy Years of Life in Labor.* New York: Cornell University, 1984.

Gottlieb, Peter. *Making Their Own Way, 1916-1930*. Urbana: University of Illinois Press, 1987.

Harper, Frank C. *Pittsburgh of Today: Its Resources and People*. Vol. 1&2. New York: Pennsylvania Historical Society, 1931.

Harrison, Shelby M. and Paul U. Kellogg, "The Westmoreland Strike." *The Survey*, 1911.

Hill, Charles. "Fighting the Twelve-Hour Day in the American Steel Industry." In *Labor History*, Vol. 15, Winter 1974.

Jones, Mary Harris. *The Autobiography of Mother Jones*. Chicago: Charles H. Kerr, 1977.

Kellogg, Paul U. "Westmoreland Strike Called Off." *The Survey*, July 29, 1911.

Kelly, George E., ed. *Allegheny County, A Sesqui-Centennial Review, 1788…1938*. Pittsburgh: Allegheny County Sesqui-Centennial Committee, 1938.

Kleppner, Paul. "Government, Parties, and Voters in Pittsburgh." In *City at the Point: Essays on the Social History of Pittsburgh*. Edited by Samuel P. Hays. Pittsburgh: University of Pittsburgh Press, 1989.

Koskoff, David E. *The Mellons: The Chronicle of America's Richest Family*. New York: Thomas Y. Crowell, 1978.

Legendary Ladies: A Guide to Where Women Made History in Pennsylvania: Greater Pittsburgh. Pennsylvania Commission for Women, <www.WomenMadeHistoryInPa.com>.

Leupp, Francis E. *George Westinghouse: His Life and Achievements*. Boston: Little, Brown, and Company, 1918.

Lunt, Richard D. *Law and Order vs. The Miners: West Virginia*. Hamden: CN, 1979.

Margolis, Jacob. "The Streets of Pittsburgh." *International Socialist Review*. Vol. 13, no.4, 1912.

McCollester, Charles. "Turtle Creek Fights Taylorism: The Westinghouse Strike of 1914." *Labor's Heritage*, Summer 1992.

McCormick, Charles H. *Seeing Reds: Federal Surveillance of Radicals in the Pittsburgh Mill District, 1917-1921*. Pittsburgh: University of Pittsburgh Press, 1997.

Meyerhuber, Jr., Carl I. *Less Than Forever: The Rise and Decline of Union Solidarity in Western Pennsylvania, 1914-1948*. London: Associated University Presses, 1987.

Michales, George. "The Westinghouse Strike." *The Survey*, August 1914.

Montgomery, David. *The Fall of the House of Labor: The Workplace, the State, and American Labor Activism, 1865-1925*. Cambridge: Cambridge University Press, 1987.

Murdock, Frank R. "Some Aspects of Pittsburgh's Industrial Contribution to the World War." *Western Pennsylvania Historical Magazine*, October 1921.

Norwood, Stephen H. *Mercenaries and Masculinity in Twentieth-Century America*. Chapel Hill: University of North Carolina, 2002.

O'Connor, Harvey. *Mellon's Millions: The Life and Times of Andrew W. Mellon*. New York: John Day Company, 1933.

O'Connor, Harvey. *Steel Dictator*. New York: The John Day Company, 1935.

Pittsburgh Professional Fire Fighters: 100th Anniversary. Pittsburgh Firefighters, 1974.

Robertson, Raymond J. *Ironworkers 100th Anniversary, 1896-1996: A History of the Ironworkers Union.* The Ironworkers Union, 1996.

Ruck, Rob. *Sandlot Seasons: Sport in Black Pittsburgh*. Urbana: University of Illinois Press, 1993.

Scoggs, William O. "Interstate Migration of Negro Population" *Trade Unionism and Labor Problems*. Edited by John R. Commons. New York: A.M. Kelley, 1920.

Smulls Legislative Handbook and Manual of the State of Pennsylvania, 1913.

Steuben, John. *Labor in Wartime*. New York: International Publishers, 1940.

Swetnam, George. "Pittsburgh's Determined Suffragettes." *Pittsburgh Press,* Nov. 4, 1956.

Taft, Philip. *Organized Labor in American History.* New York: Harper Row, 1964.

Tarbell, Ida M. *The Life of Elbert H. Gary: The Story of Steel*. New York: D. Appleton and Company, 1925.

The Interchurch World Movement Report. *The Steel Strike of 1919*. New York: Harcourt, Brace and Company, 1921.

The Interchurch World Movement, The Commission of Inquiry. *Public Opinion and the Steel Strike: Supplementary Reports of the Investigators to the Commission of Inquiry, the Interchurch World Movement*. New York: Harcourt, Brace, and Company, 1921, Reprinted in facsimile edition, New York: Arno Press, 1969.

Trimble, William F. *High Frontiers: A History of Aeronautics in Pennsylvania*. Pittsburgh: University of Pittsburgh Press, 1982.

Tuttle, William J. *Race Riot: Chicago in the Red Summer of 1919.* New York: Atheneum, 1970.

University of Pittsburgh Archives. Borland, J.R. *"Coroner's Press Report, August 26, 1919."* (Fannie Sellins); *Coroner's Jury Verdict.* State of Pennsylvania, County of Allegheny, 1919. (Fannie Sellins)

Voltz, Elizabeth. "Local Women Make Long Fight to Secure Privilege of Ballot and Share in Credit for Victory." In *Pittsburgh Women's Suffrage Folder,* Carnegie Library, Western Pennsylvania Room.

Vorse, Mary Heaton. *Men and Steel.* New York: Boni and Liveright Publishers, 1920.

Weinstein, James. *The Decline of Socialism in America, 1912-1925.* New York: Vintage, 1969.

White, Kenneth A. "Pittsburgh in the Great Epidemic of 1918," *The Western Pennsylvania Historical Magazine,* 1985.

Chapter 9 Mellons' Rule and Capital's Crash: 1920-1932

Abern, Martin. "Attack on the National Miners' Union Convention," *James P. Cannon and the Early Years of American Communism, Selected Writings and Speeches.* New York: Spartacist Publishing, 1992.

Alberts, Robert C. *Pitt, the Story of the University of Pittsburgh, 1787-1987.* Pittsburgh: University of Pittsburgh Press, 1986.

Amalgamated Transit Union Staff. *ATU 100 Years: A History of the Amalgamated Transit Union.* Amalgamated Transit Union, 1992.

Anonymous, "Pittsburgh's Broadcasting Pioneers," *The Literary Digest,* September 2, 1992.

Archer, Gleason Leonard. *The History of Radio.* New York: Arno Press, 1971.

Beik, Mildred Allen. *Remembering the Strike for Union in 1922-23.* University Park: The Pennsylvania State University Press, 1997.

Beik, Mildred Allen. *The Miners of Windber: The Struggles of New Immigrants for Unionization, 1890's-1930's.* University Park: The Pennsylvania State University Press, 1996.

Berstein, Irving. *The Lean Years: A History of the American Worker, 1920-1933.* Baltimore: Penguin Books, 1970.

Brophy, John. *A Miner's Life.* Madison: University of Wisconsin Press, 1964.

Cavanaugh, Jack. *Tunney: Boxing's Brainiest Champ and His Upset of the Great Jack Dempsey.* New York: Random House, 2006.

Cannadine, David. *Andrew Mellon.* New York: Vintage Book, 2006.

Cecil, Jeanne Svitesic. *Our Coal-Mining Community Heritage: Harmarville, PA.* Homestead: Steel Valley Printers, 2002.

Coode. Thomas H. and John D. Petrarulo. "The Odyssey of Pittsburgh's Father Cox." In *Western Pennsylvania Historical Magazine.* July 1972.

Davin, Eric Leif. "Blue Collar Democracy: Class War and Political Revolution in Western Pennsylvania, 1932-1937." In *Pennsylvania History.* Spring 2000.

Department of Environmental Resources. *Annual Report on Mining Activities, 1991.* Harrisburg: Commonwealth of Pennsylvania, 1991.

Dix, Keith. *What's a Coal Miner to Do?: The Mechanization of Coal Mining.* Pittsburgh: University of Pittsburgh Press, 1988.

Draper, Theodore. *American Communism and Soviet Russia.* New York: Viking Press, 1960.

Encyclopedia of Radio and TV Broadcasting

Fitzgerald, F.A., ed. *The International Engineer: Fifty Years of Progress: 1896-1946.* December, 1946.

Foster, W.Z. *History of the Communist Party of the United States.* New York: International Publishers, 1968.

Fox, Maier B. *United We Stand: The United Mine Workers of America, 1800-1990.* Washington D.C.: United Mine Workers of America, 1990.

Gilfillen, Lauren. *I Went to Pit College.* New York: The Literary Guild, 1934.

Heineman, Kenneth J. *A Catholic New Deal: Religion and Reform in Depression Pittsburgh.* University Park: Penn State Press, 1999.

Herr, E.M. "Pittsburgh and the Electrical Industry," *Pittsburgh and the Pittsburgh Spirit.* (Addresses at the Pittsburgh Chamber of Commerce, 1927-1928).

Hersch, Burton. *The Mellon Family: A Fortune in History.* New York: William Morrow and Company, 1978.

Jenkins, Philip. *Hoods and Shirts: The Extreme Right in Pennsylvania, 1925-1950.* Chapel Hill: University of North Carolina Press, 1997.

Kelly, George E., ed. *Allegheny County, A Sesqui-Centennial Review, 1788...1938.* Pittsburgh: Allegheny County Sesqui-Centennial Committee, 1938.

Kluppell, H.L. *Electrical Workers Journal.* 1920.

Koskoff, David E. *The Mellons: The Chronicle of America's Richest Family.* New York: Thomas Y. Crowell, 1978.

Love, Gilbert. "College Students Are Beating the Depression" *School and Society,* June 10, 1933 reprinted in David A. Shannon. *The Great Depression.* Saddle River, NJ: Pearson/Prentice Hall, 1961.

Marcus, Irwin, James Dougherty, and Eileen M. Cooper, "Irwin Marcus, Confrontation at Rossiter: The Coal Strike of 1927-28 and its Aftermath." In *Pennsylvania History,* Vol. 59, no.4, October 1992.

McCollester, Charles, ed. *Fighter With a Heart: Charles Owen Rice, Pittsburgh Labor Priest*. Pittsburgh: University of Pittsburgh, 1996.

McCollister, John. *The Bucs!: The Story of the Pittsburgh Pirates*. Lenexa: Addax Publishing Group, 1998.

Meyerhuber, Jr., Carl I. *Less Than Forever: The Rise and Decline of Union Solidarity in Western Pennsylvania, 1914-1948*. London: Associated University Presses, 1987.

Mosley, Leonard. *Power Play: Oil in the Middle East*. New York: Penguin, 1974

Nelson, Steve, James R. Barrett, & Rob Ruck. *American Radical*. Pittsburgh: University of Pittsburgh Press, 1981.

O'Connor, Harvey. *Steel Dictator*. New York: The John Day Company, 1935.

Rice, Grantland. *The Tumult and the Shouting*. New York: A.S. Barnes & Co., 1954.

Ricketts, Elizabeth C. *Our Battle for Industrial Freedom: Radical Politics in the Coal Fields of Pennsylvania, 1916-1926*. UMI Dissertation Information Service, 1996.

Rosenberg, David L. "Labor Lyceums a Forgotten, Rich Labor Heritage," Pennsylvania Labor History Journal. Vol. 27. December, 2005.

Rosenberg, David L. "The Re-formation of the Pittsburgh Chapter of the American Civil Liberties Union 1928-1930." Unpublished paper: Archives Service Center, University of Pittsburgh.

Sanders, Meyer A. "Labor." In *Allegheny County, A Sesqui-Centennial Review, 1788…1938*. Edited by George E. Kelly. Pittsburgh: Allegheny County Sesqui-Centennial Committee, 1938.

Seidenberg, Mel, Lois Mulkearn, and James W. Hess. "Two Hundred Years of Pittsburgh History; A Chronology of Events Complied." In Stefan Lorant's *Pittsburgh: The Story of an American City*. Garden City: Doubleday & Company, Inc., 1964.

"Smulls Legislative Handbook and Manual of the State of Pennsylvania," Harrisburg, 1913.

Stave, Bruce M. *The New Deal and the Law Hurrah, Pittsburgh Machine Politics*. Pittsburgh: University of Pittsburgh Press, 1970.

Thomas, Clarke M. *Fortunes and Misfortunes: Pittsburgh and Allegheny County Politics, 1930-1995*. Pittsburgh: Institute of Politics, 1998.

Thomas, Clarke M. *Front-Page Pittsburgh: Two Hundred Years of the Post-Gazette*. Pittsburgh: University of Pittsburgh Press, 2005.

Tunney, Gene. *A Man Must Fight*. New York: Houghton Mifflin Company, 1932.

Weber, Michael P. *Don't Call Me Boss: David L. Lawrence*. Pittsburgh: University of Pittsburgh Press, 1988.

Witt, Sally. "Father Cox and Pittsburgh in the 1940s." In *Pittsburgh History*. Summer, 1997.

Chapter 10 Labor's Rise: 1933-1940

Adamic, Louis. "My Friend Maxo Vanka" In *My America: 1928-38*. New York: Harpers, 1938.

Alberts, Robert C. *Pitt, the Story of the University of Pittsburgh, 1787-1987*. Pittsburgh: University of Pittsburgh Press, 1986.

Alinsky, Saul. *John L. Lewis: An Unauthorized Biography*. New York: G.P. Putnam's Sons, 1949.

Amalgamated Transit Union Staff. *ATU 100 Years: A History of the Amalgamated Transit Union*. Amalgamated Transit Union, 1992.

Bell, Thomas. *Out of This Furnace: A Novel of Immigrant Labor in America*. Pittsburgh: University of Pittsburgh Press, 1976.

Bernstein, Irving. *Turbulent Years: A History of the American Worker, 1933-1941*. Boston: Houghton Mifflin, 1971.

Betten, Neil. *Catholic Activism and the Industrial Worker*. Gainesville: University Presses of Flordia, 1976.

Bonosky, Philip. *Burning Valley*. Urbana and Chicago: University of Illinois Press, 1998.

Boyle, Harvey. *Pittsburgh Post Gazette*. In *Pittsburgh Sports: Stories from the Steel City*. Edited by Randy Roberts. Pittsburgh: University of Pittsburgh Press, 2000.

Brooks, Robert R. R. *As Steel Goes: Unionism in a Basic Industry*. New Haven: Yale University Press, 1940.

Brooks, Thomas R. *Clint: A Biography of a Labor Intellectual, Clinton S. Golden*. New York: Atheneum, 1978.

Burstein, Barbara. *A Jewish Legacy: Pittsburgh*. Video documentary. Carnegie Public Library.

Congress of Industrial Organizations. *CIO 1935-1948: Industrial Democracy in Action*. Washington: Industrial Union Department, AFL-CIO, 1955.

Cope, Myron. *Double Yoi!: A Revealing Memoir by the Broadcasting/Writer*. Sports Publishing, L.L.C., 2002.

Cortner, Richard C. *The Jones and Laughlin Case*. New York: Alfred A. Knopf, 1970.

Davin, Eric Leif. "Blue Collar Democracy: Class War and Political Revolution in Western Pennsylvania, 1932-1937." *Pennsylvania History*. Vol. 67, No. 2. Spring 2000.

Davin, Eric Leif. "The Littlest New Deal: How Democracy and the Union Came to Western Pennsylvania." Paper delivered at the Annual Meeting of the Organization of American Historians. Chicago. April 1992.

DeFord, Frank. "The Boxer and the Blonde." *Sports Illustrated*. June 17, 1985.

Demarest Jr., David R. "Afterword." In *Out of This Furnace: A Novel of Immigrant Labor in America* by Thomas Bell. Pittsburgh: University of Pittsburgh Press, 1976.

Demarest Jr., David R. *Maxo Vanka's Millvale Murals.* Millvale, PA: St. Nicholas Croatian Catholic Church, 1995.

Dubofsky, Melvyn. "Labor's Odd Couple: Philip Murray and John L. Lewis." In *Forging a Union of Steel: Philip Murray, SWOC and the United Steelworkers.* Edited by Paul F. Clark, Peter Gottlieb, and Donald Kennedy. Cornell: ILR Press, 1987.

Dubofsky, Melvyn and Warren Van Tine. *John L. Lewis: A Biography.* New York: Quadrangle/ New York Times, 1977.

Feldman, Jacob. *The Jewish Experience in Western Pennsylvania: A History 1755-1945.* Pittsburgh: The Historical Society of Western Pennsylvania, 1986.

Fitzgerald, F.A., ed. *The International Engineer: Fifty years of Progress: 1896-1946.* December, 1946.

Francis, Owen. "The Saga of Joe Magarac: Steelman, A steelworker takes his place beside Paul Bunyan." In *Scribner's Magazine.* November 193. Reprinted in the *Standard Dictionary of Folklore, Mythology and Legend,* Vol. 2. Edited by Maria Leach and Jerome Fried. New York, 1970.

Garrity, John A., ed. *Dictionary of American Biography,* Supplement Six, 1956-1960. New York: Charles Scribner's Sons, 1980.

Gensure, Kathy. "The PFT's Inception and Early Days – Reminiscences on a Time Gone By." Interview with Anne Leifer, Albert Fondy, and Joseph Zunic in *Pittsburgh Federation of Teachers' 50th Anniversary Book,* 1985.

Green, James. "Democracy Comes to 'Little Siberia,'" In *Labor's Heritage.* Vol.5, no.2, Summer, 1993.

Hoerr, John. *And the Wolf Finally Came.* Pittsburgh, University of Pittsburgh Press, 1988.

Jenkins, Philip. *Hoods and Shirts: The Extreme Right in Pennsylvania, 1925-1950.* Chapel Hill: University of North Carolina Press, 1997.

Joughin, Louis and Edmund M. Morgan. *The Legacy of Sacco and Vanzetti.* Princeton, NJ: Princeton University Press, 1948.

Klehr, Harvey. *The Heyday of American Communism: The Depression Decade.* New York: Basic Books, 1984.

Kocherzat, Steve and Charles McCollester. "NLRB v. Jones & Laughlin Supreme Court Ruling." *Aliquippa's Struggle and Labor Law Reform.* Homestead: Steel Valley Printers, 2000.

Koskoff, David E. *The Mellons: The Chronicle of America's Richest Family.* New York: Thomas Y. Crowell, 1978.

Leopold, David. *The Gift of Sympathy: The Art of Maxo Vanka.* Bucks County, PA: The James A Michner Museum, 2001.

Levenstein, Harvey A. *Communism, Anticommunism, and the CIO.* Westport: Greenwood Press, 1981.

Litsky, Frank. "John Woodruff, an Olympian, Dies at 92." In *New York Times,* November 1, 2007.

Lynd, Staughton. "The Possibility of Radicalism in the Early 1930's: The Case of Steel." *Radical America.* Vol. 6, no. 6, November-December 1972.

McCollister, John. *The Bucs!: The Story of the Pittsburgh Pirates.* Lenexa: Addax Publishing Group, 1998.

Meyerhuber, Jr., Carl I. *Less Than Forever: The Rise and Decline of Union Solidarity in Western Pennsylvania, 1914-1948.* Selinsgrove: Susquehanna University Press, 1987.

Minutes of the Organizational Meeting of the Steel Workers Organizing Committee of the Committee for the Industrial Organizations, June 17, 1936.

O'Connor, Harvey. *Steel Dictator.* New York: The John Day Company, 1935.

O'Toole, Andrew. *Sweet William: The Life of Billy Conn.* Urbana and Chicago: University of Illinois Press, 2008.

Otty, Harry. *Black Dynamite: Charles Duane Burley.* <http://cyberboxingzone.com/boxing/burley.htm>.

Pogue, Forrest C. *George C. Marshall: Education of a General (1880-1939).* New York: Viking Press, 196.

Pope, James Gray. "The Western Pennsylvania Coal Strike of 1933, Part I: Lawmaking from Below and the Revival of the United Mine Workers." *Labor History,* Vol. 44, no.1, 2003.

Pope, James Gray. "Worker Lawmaking, Sit-down Strikes, and the Shaping of American Industrial Relations, 1935-1958." *Law and History Review,* Vol. 24, Issue 1, Spring 2006.

Powers, George. *Cradle of Steel Unionism, Monongahela Valley, PA.* East Chicago, Indiana: Figueroa Printers, 1972.

Proceedings of the First Constitutional Convention of the Congress of Industrial Organizations. Pittsburgh: November 14 to 18, 1938.

Reutter, Clifford J. "The Puzzle of a Pittsburgh Steeler, Joe Magarac's Ethnic Identity." In *Western Pennsylvania Historical Magazine,* Vol. 63, No.1. January 1980.

Rice, Charles Owen. "America's Darkest Decade." In *Fighter with a Heart: Charles Owen Rice, Pittsburgh Labor Priest.* Edited by Charles McCollester. Pittsburgh: University of Pittsburgh Press, 1996.

Rooney, Dan. *Dan Rooney: My 75 Years with the Pittsburgh Steelers.* New York: Da Capo Press, 2007.

Rose, James D. *Duquesne and the Rise of Steel Unionism.* Urbana and Chicago: University of Illinois Press, 2001.

Ruck, Rob. "Art Rooney and the Pittsburgh Steelers;" "I Lived Baseball: Harold Tinker and the Pittsburgh Crawfords." In *Pittsburgh Sports: Stories from the Steel City.* Edited by Randy Roberts. Pittsburgh: University of Pittsburgh Press, 2000.

Ruck, Rob. *Sandlot Seasons: Sport in Black Pittsburgh.* Urbana: University of Illinois Press, 1987.

Sanders, Meyer A. "Labor." In *Allegheny County: A Sesqui-Centennial Review, 1788...1938*. Edited by George E. Kelly. Pittsburgh: Allegheny Sesqui-Centennial Committee, 1938.

Schott, Thomas E. "Pittsburgh Poison: The Waner Boys." In *Pittsburgh Sports: Stories from the Steel City*. Edited by Randy Roberts. Pittsburgh: University of Pittsburgh   Press, 2000.

Serrin, William. *Homestead: The Glory and the Tragedy of an American Steel Town*. New York: Random House, 1992.

Stave, Bruce M. *The New Deal and the Last Hurrah: Pittsburgh Machine Politics*. Pittsburgh: University of Pittsburgh Press, 1970.

Sweeney, Vincent D. *The United Steelworkers of America*. Pittsburgh: USWA, circa 1956.

Thomas, Clarke M. *Fortunes and Misfortunes: Pittsburgh and Allegheny County Politics, 1930-1995*. Pittsburgh: Institute of Politics, 1998.

Toker, Franklin. *Fallingwater Rising: Frank Lloyd Wright, E. J. Kaufman and America's Most Extraordinary House*. New York: Alfred A. Knopf, 2003.

Uchitelle, Louis. "The Richest of the Rich, Proud of a New Gilded Age." *New York Times*, July 15, 2007.

Weber, Michael P. *Don't Call Me Boss: David L. Lawrence, Pittsburgh's Renaissance Mayor*. Pittsburgh: University of Pittsburgh Press, 1988.

Wolensky, Kenneth C. "An Activist Government in Harrisburg: Governor George H. Earle III and Pennsylvania's 'Little New Deal.'" In *Pennsylvania Heritage*. Vol. 34, no.1. Winter 2008.

Wollman, David H. and Donald R. Inman. *Portraits in Steel: An Illustrated History of the Jones and Laughlin Steel Corporation*. Kent, Ohio: Kent State University Press, 1999.

Young, Jim. "Bitter Pill in Chocolate Town: The Sit-down Strike of 1937." *Pennsylvania Labor History Journal*. December 2005.

Yudkoff, Alvin. *Gene Kelly: A Life of Dance and Dreams*. New York: Back Stage Books, 1999.

Zeiger, Robert H. *The CIO: 1935-1955*. Chapel Hill: University of North Carolina Press, 1995.

Chapter 11 Victory and Division: 1941-1949

Alinsky, Saul. *John L. Lewis: An Unauthorized Biography*. New York: G.P. Putnam's Sons, 1949.

Bell, Thomas. *Out of This Furnace: A Novel of Immigrant Labor in America*. Pittsburgh: University of Pittsburgh Press, 1976.

Bockris, Victor. *The Life and Death of Andy Warhol*. New York: Bantam Books, 1998.

Brophy, John. *A Miner's Life*. Madison and Milwaukee: University of Wisconsin Press, 1964.

Butler County Historical Society. "Bantam Car/Jeep." (2008). Available from: <www.butlercountyhistoricalsociety-pa.org/bantam.html>.

Cahalan, James M. *Edward Abbey, A Life*. Tuscon, University of Arizona Press, 2001.

De Caux, Len. *Labor Radical: From the Wobblies to the CIO, A Personal History*. Boston: Beacon Press, 1970.

Dickerson, Dennis C. *Out of the Crucible: Black Steelworkers in Western Pennsylvania, 1875-1980*. Albany, NY: State University of New York Press, 1986.

Dillenberger, Jane Daggett. *The Religious Art of Andy Warhol*. New York: Continuum, 1998.

Fillippelli, Ronald L. and Mark McColloch. *Cold War in the Working Class: The Rise and Decline of the United Electrical Workers*. Albany, NY: State University of New York Press, 1995.

Gall, Gil. *Pursuing Justice: Lee Pressman, the New Deal, and the CIO*. Albany, NY: State University of New York, 1999.

Harper, Frank C. *Men and Women of Wartime Pittsburgh and Environs: A War-production Epic*. Pittsburgh, 1945.

Hoerr, John A. *Harry, Tom, and Father Rice: Accusation and Betrayal in America's Cold War*. Pittsburgh: University of Pittsburgh Press, 2005.

Hoffman, William S. *Paul Mellon: Portrait of an Oil Baron*. Chicago: Follett Publishing, 1974.

Humes, Edward. *Over Here: How the G.I. Bill Transformed the American Dream*. New York: Harcourt, 2006.

Industrial Union Department. *CIO, 1935-1955: Industrial Democracy in Action*. Washington D.C.: AFL-CIO, 1955. 2nd edition.

Jenkins, Philip. *The Cold War at Home: The Red Scare in Pennsylvania, 1945-1960*. Chapel Hill: University of North Caroline Press, 1999.

Jones, Charles O. *Clean Air: The Policies and Politics of Pollution Control*. Pittsburgh: University of Pittsburgh Press, 1978.

Kehl, James A. "Peace Dividend: The Ellsworth Center Experience." *Pittsburgh Post-Gazette*, September 30, 2007.

Kempton, Murray. *Part of Our Time: Some Ruins and Monuments of the Thirties*. New York: Modern Library, 1998.

Knox, James W. "The Birth of the LST." Georgetown, PA: Pennsylvania LST Association, 2000.

Levenstein, Harvey A. *Communism, Anticommunism, and the CIO*. Westport: Greenwood Press, 1981.

Lichtenstein, Nelson. *Labor's War at Home: The CIO in World War II*. Cambridge: Cambridge University Press, 1982.

Love, David. *Frank Bolden: The Man Behind the Words*. A Multi-Cultural Film, 2001.

Lubove, Roy. *Twentieth-Century Pittsburgh: Government, Business, and Environmental Change.* Pittsburgh: University of Pittsburgh Press, 1995.

McCollister, John. *The Bucs: The Story of the Pittsburgh Pirates.* Lenexa, KS: Addax Publishing Group, 1998.

McDonald, David J. *Union Man: The Life of a Labor Statesman.* New York: E.P. Dutton & Co., 1969.

Mendelson, Abby. *The Pittsburgh Steelers: The Official Team History.* Lanham, MD: Taylor Trade Press, 1996.

Mershon, Sherie R. and Joel A. Tarr. "Strategies for Clean Air: The Pittsburgh and Allegheny Smoke Control Movements, 1940-1960." *Devastation and Renewal: An Environmental History of Pittsburgh and its Region.* Pittsburgh, University of Pittsburgh Press, 2003.

Murphy, Charles J. V. "The Mellons of Pittsburgh." *Fortune Magazine*, October, November, December, 1967.

Nelson, Steve, James R. Barrett, and Rob Ruck. *Steve Nelson, American Radical.* Pittsburgh: University of Pittsburgh Press, 1981.

Reed, Merl E. "Black Workers, Defense Industries, and Federal Agencies in Pennsylvania, 1941-1945." *Labor History*, Vol. 27, June 1986.

Rice, Charles Owen. *Fighter with a Heart: Charles Owen Rice, Pittsburgh Labor Priest.* Edited by Charles McCollester. Pittsburgh: University of Pittsburgh Press, 1996.

Ruttenberg, Harold, J. *My Life in Steel: From CIO to CEO.* Tarentum: Word Association Publishers, 2001.

Schatz, Ronald W. The *Electrical Workers: A History of Labor at General Electric and Westinghouse, 1923-1960.* Urbana and Chicago: University of Illinois, 1983.

Serrin, William. *Homestead: The Glory and the Tragedy of an American Steel Town.* New York: Random House, 1992.

Sninsky, Ed. "Boyhood in the Final Years of Lower Homestead." In *Portal to the Past: Homestead & Mifflin Township Historical Society.* Volume 5, No. 12, December 2005.

Snyder, Lynne Page. "Revisiting Donora, Pennsylvania's 1948 Air Pollution Disaster." *Devastation and Renewal: An Environmental History of Pittsburgh and Its Region.* Pittsburgh: University of Pittsburgh Press, 2003.

Uricchio, Marilyn. "Jimmy Stewart: A Wonderful Life." *Pittsburgh Lives: Men and Women Who Shaped Our City.* Edited by David M. Schribman and Angelika Kane. Chicago: Triumph Books, 2006.

Warren, Kenneth. *Big Steel: The First Century of the United States Steel Corporation, 1901-2001.* Pittsburgh: University of Pittsburgh Press, 2001.

Weber, Michael P. *Don't Call Me Boss: David L. Lawrence, Pittsburgh's Renaissance Mayor.* Pittsburgh: University of Pittsburgh Press, 1988.

Westinghouse Electric Corporation. *History for Heavy Shop Activities.* Gear Department, June 30, 1945, 26. Heinz History Center Archives, Box 209, Folder 1.

Wollman, David H. and Donald R. Inman. *Portraits in Steel: An Illustrated History of the Jones and Laughlin Steel Corporation.* Kent, Ohio: Kent State University Press, 1999.

Woodbury, David O. *Battlefronts of Industry: Westinghouse in World War II.* New York: John Wiley, 1948.

WQED Documentary Films. Fly Boys: Western Pennsylvania's Tuskegee Airmen. WQED Multimedia, 2008.

Zeiger, Robert H. *The CIO: 1935-1955.* Chapel Hill: University of North Carolina Press, 1995.

Chapter 12 The Flowering of the Mill Town: 1950-1960

Alberts, Robert C. *Pitt: The Story of the University of Pittsburgh, 1787-1987.* Pittsburgh: University of Pittsburgh Press, 1986.

Bauder, Bob. "On Cloud Nine, Cats Down in D.C. Flipped Over Beaver County Site." *The Beaver County Times*, December 16, 2007.

Bauder, Bob. "Radioactive, Man! Shippingport Workers Had It Made in the Shade." *The Beaver County Times*, December 16, 2007.

Brodsky, Charlee and Linda-Benedict Jones. "Lost and Found: Pittsburgh's Photographic History." In *Pittsburgh Revealed: Photographs Since 1850.* Pittsburgh: Carnegie Museum of Art, 1997.

Brzezinski, Matthew. *Red Moon Rising: Sputnik and the Hidden Rivalries that Ignited the Space Age.* New York: Times Books, 2007.

Callahan, Tom. *Johnny U: The Life and Times of John Unitas.* New York: Crown Publishers, 2006.

Carson, Rachel. *The Sea Around Us.* Oxford: Oxford University Press, 1951.

Carter, Bob. "Stokes' life a tale of tragedy and friendship." *ESPN Classic.* Available from: <http://espn.go.com/classic/biography/s/stokes_maurice.html>.

Caute, David. *The Great Fear: The Anti-Communist Purge Under Truman and Eisenhower.* New York: Simon and Schuster, 1978.

Chamberlain, John. "Phil Murray: The CIO Boss Was Soft-spoken and Humble, but Tough in a Pinch." In *Life Magazine*, February 11, 1946.

Collins, Mark and Margaret Mary Kimmel. *Mister Roger's Neighborhood*. Pittsburgh: University of Pittsburgh Press, 1996.

Dubofsky, Melvyn and Warren Van Tine. *John L. Lewis: A Biography*. New York: Quadrangle/The New York Times Book Co., 1977.

Dryer, Ervin. "Reverend LeRoy Patrick: Bona-Fide Hero of Civil Rights Movement." *Pittsburgh Post-Gazette*, January 13, 2006. Reprinted in *Pittsburgh Live: Men and Women Who Shaped Our City*. Edited by David M. Shibman and Angelika Kane. Chicago: Triumph Books, 2006.

Filipelli, Ronald L. and Mark D. McColloch. *Cold War in the Working Class: The Rise and Decline of the United Electrical Workers*. Albany: State University of New York Press, 1995.

Finder, Chuck. "Willie Thrower, 71: Opened Door for Black Quarterbacks." *Pittsburgh Post-Gazette*, February 24, 2002. Reprinted in *Pittsburgh Lives: Men and Women Who Shaped Our City*. Edited by David M. Schribman and Angelika Kane. Chicago: Triumph Books, 2006.

Goodrich, Dave. "Hitsburgh: It Wasn't Detroit, but They Were Really Rockin' in Pittsburgh." *In Pittsburgh*. October 11-17, 1989.

Hare, Clyde. *Clyde Hare's Pittsburgh*. Photographs by Clyde Hare. Text by Alan Van Dine. Pittsburgh: Pittsburgh History & Landmarks Foundation, 1994.

Herling, John. *Right to Challenge: People and Power in the Steelworkers Union*. New York: Harper & Row, 1972.

Heuk, Douglas. "Salk's Regrets Are Few." *Pittsburgh Post Gazette*, November 27, 1994.

Hines, Lynn Boyd. *Broadcasting the Local News: The Early Years of Pittsburgh's KDKA-TV*. University Park: Penn State Press, 1995.

Hinshaw, John. *Steel and Steelworkers: Race and Class in Twentieth-Century Pittsburgh*. Albany: State University of New York Press, 2002.

Hoerr, John P. *And the Wolf Finally Came: The Decline of the American Steel Industry*. Pittsburgh: University of Pittsburgh Press, 1988.

Hoerr, John P. *Harry, Tom and Father Rice*. Pittsburgh: University of Pittsburgh Press, 2005.

Hoffman, Ernie. "Billy Eckstine, 78: Jazz Vocalist and Trombonist." *Pittsburgh Post-Gazette*, March 9, 1993.

Humes, Edward. *Over Here: How the G.I. Bill Transformed the American Dream*. Orlando: Harcourt Books, 2006.

Jordan, Hill. "Card-carrying Embers." *Pittsburgh City Paper*, August 8-15, 2001.

Joseph, Frank. "We Got Jazz." *Pittsburgh Magazine*, October 1979.

Kelly, George and Edwin Beachler. Man of Steel: The Story of David J. McDonald. New York: North American Book Co., 1954.

Lear, Linda. *Rachel Carson: Witness for Nature*. New York: Henry Holt and Company, 1997.

Lubove, Roy. *Twentieth-Century Pittsburgh*. Pittsburgh: University of Pittsburgh Press, 1995.

Manchester, William. *The Glory and the Dream: A Narrative History of America, 1932-1972*. Vol. I. Boston: Little, Brown and Company, 1973.

Maraniss, David. *Clemente: The Passion and Grace of Baseball's Last Hero*. New York: Simon & Schuster, 2006.

Masley, Ed. "Oldie but Goodie." *Pittsburgh Post-Gazette*. April 10, 1998.

Masich, Andrew E. and David F. Halas. *Dan Rooney: My 75 Years with the Pittsburgh Steelers and the NFL*. New York: Da Capo Press, 2007.

McCollister, John. *The Bucs: The Story of the Pittsburgh Pirates*. Lenexa, KS: Addax Publishing, 1998.

McColloch, Mark. "The Shop-Floor Dimension of Union Rivalry: The Case of Westinghouse in the 1950s." In *The CIO's Left-Led Unions*. Edited by Steve Rosswurm. New Brunswick, NJ: Rutgers University Press, 1992.

McDonald, David J. *Union Man: The Life of a Labor Statesman*. New York: E.P. Dutton & Co., 1969.

Mendelson, Abby. *The Pittsburgh Steelers: The Official Team History*. Lanham, MD: Taylor Trade Publishing, 2005.

Metzgar, Jack. *Striking Steel: Solidarity Remembered*. Philadelphia: Temple University Press, 2000.

Modell, Judith. *A Town Without Steel: Envisioning Homestead*. Pittsburgh: University of Pittsburgh Press, 1998.

Musmanno, Michael A. *Across the Street from the Courthouse*. Philadelphia: Dorrance & Company, 1954.

Musmanno, Michael A. *Verdict!: The Adventures of the Young Lawyer in the Brown Suit*. Garden City, NY: Doubleday & Company, 1958.

Nelson, Steve, James R. Barrett & Rob Ruck. *Steve Nelson: American Radical*. Pittsburgh: University of Pittsburgh Press, 2005.

Peterson, Richard F. "Rinky Dinks and the Single Wing." In *Pittsburgh Sports: Stories from the Steel City*. Edited by Randy Roberts. Pittsburgh: University of Pittsburgh Press, 2000.

Rawson, Christopher. "August Wilson, 60: Playwright Who Chronicled Black Experience." *Pittsburgh Post-Gazette*, October 3, 2005.

Reisler, Jim. *The Best Game Ever: Pirates vs. Yankees, October 13, 1960*. Cambridge: Carroll & Graf Publishers, 2007.

Rice, Charles Owen. *Fighter with a Heart: Charles Owen Rice, Pittsburgh Labor Priest*. Edited by Charles McCollester. Pittsburgh: University of Pittsburgh Press, 1996.

Schatz, Ronald W. *The Electrical Workers: A History of Labor at General Electric and Westinghouse, 1923-1960*. Urbana and Chicago: University of Illinois Press, 1983.

Schulz, Constance B. "The Pittsburgh Photographic Library." In *Witness to the Fifties: The Pittsburgh Photographic Library, 1950-1953*. Edited by Constance B. Schulz and Steven W. Plattner. Pittsburgh: University of Pittsburgh Press, 1999.

Selvaggio, Marc. "The Making of Jonas Salk." *Pittsburgh Magazine*, June 1984.

Serrin, William. *Homestead: The Glory and the Tragedy of an American Steel Town*. New York: Random House, 1992.

Shribman, David M. and Angelika Kane, eds. *Pittsburgh Lives: Men and Women Who Shaped Our City*. Chicago: Triumph Books, 2006.

Spice, Byron. "Herbert A Simon, 84: Nobel Prize Winner." *Pittsburgh Post-Gazette*, February 10, 2001. Reprinted in *Pittsburgh Lives: Men and Women Who Shaped Our City*. Edited by David M. Shribman and Angelika Kane. Chicago: Triumph Books, 2006.

Steelworkers Committee to Sponsor Truth. *The Mask of Deceit: Expose of the Goals and Techniques of the Dues Protest Committee (DPC) Leaders*. Undated.

Stephenson, Sam. "W. Eugene Smith and Pittsburgh." In *Dream Street: W. Eugene Smith's Pittsburgh Project*. Edited by Sam Stephenson. New York: W. W. Norton & Company, 2001.

Strayhorn, Billy. *Billy Strayhorn: Lush Life*. Audio CD. New York: Blue Note Records, January 23, 2007.

Thomas, Clarke M. *Fortunes and Misfortunes: Pittsburgh and Allegheny County Politics, 1930-1995*. Pittsburgh: Institute of Politics, 1998.

Thomas, Clarke M. *Front-Page Pittsburgh: Two Hundred Years of the Post-Gazette*. Pittsburgh: University of Pittsburgh Press, 2005.

Thomas, Clarke M. *Witness to the Fifties: The Pittsburgh Photographic Library, 1950-1953*. Edited by Constance B. Schulz and Steven W. Plattner. Pittsburgh: University of Pittsburgh Press, 1999.

Tractenber, Alan. "Man-breaking City: W. Eugene Smith's Pittsburgh." In *Dream Street: W. Eugene Smith's Pittsburgh Project*. Edited by Sam Stephenson. New York: W. W. Norton & Company, 2001.

Warren, Kenneth. *Big Steel: The First Century of the United States Corporation*. Pittsburgh: University of Pittsburgh Press, 2001.

Weber, Michael P. *Don't Call Me Boss: David L. Lawrence*. Pittsburgh: University of Pittsburgh Press, 1988.

Weigle, Ed. "Porky Chedwick: Radio's Most Ignored Pioneer." Available from: <www.oldradio.com/archives/stations/porky.htm>.

White, Theodore H. *The Making of the President 1960*. New York: Atheneum Publishers, 1962.

Wilson, August. *Three Plays*. Pittsburgh: University of Pittsburgh Press, 1991.

Zieger, Robert H. *The CIO, 1935-1955*. Chapel Hill & London: The University of North Carolina Press, 1995.

Newspapers and Magazines cited:
Pittsburgh Publications:

The Daily Post
In Pittsburgh
The Mystery
Pittsburgh Leader
Pittsburgh Chronicle Telegraph
Pittsburgh Commercial Gazette
Pittsburgh City Paper
Pittsburgh Daily Gazette
Pittsburgh Dispatch
Pittsburgh Gazette Times
Pittsburgh Post-Gazette
Pittsburgh Press
Pittsburgh Sun
Pittsburgh Sun-Telegraph

Regional Publications:
Amusement Park Annual
The Beaver County Times
Brownsville Herald
The Connellsville Courier
Homestead Daily Messenger
The Valley Daily News
Justice

National Publications:
American Manufacturer and Iron World
The Engineering and Mining Journal
Iron Age
Life Magazine
The Literary Digest
New York Times
Scientific American
The Survey
The World

Labor Publications:
The Amalgamated Journal
The Bridgemen's Magazine
The Electrical Worker Journal
Steel Labor

Interviews:
Branthoover, Bill. Interviewed by Charles McCollester. May 5, 1991.
Fagan, Patrick M. Interviewed by Charles McCollester. December, 2007.
Fay, Bob. Interviewed by Charles McCollester. Oct. 20, 1990.
Grunebach, Irv. Interviewed by Charles McCollester. May 7, 1991.
Hribar, Ed. Interviewed by Charles McCollester. June 14, 2008.
Johnson, Andy. Interviewed by Charles McCollester. November 27, 1990
O'Malley, Fr. Jack. Interviewed by Charles McCollester. February 13, 2008.
Rommler, George. Interviewed by Charles McCollester. June 21, 2008.
Sargent, Edward J. Interviewed by Charles McCollester. .Aug. 21, 1991.
Sullivan, Bill. Interviewed by Charles McCollester, May 30, 2008.

Interviews from the Alice Hoffman collection of oral interviews housed at the Labor Archives of The Pennsylvania State University relevant to Pittsburgh's history:
Atallah, Albert. Director District 8. Baltimore, Maryland. September 20, 1967.
Burke, Walter. Secretary-Treasurer, USWA. January, 1971; March 8, 1972; September 5, 1975
Fagan, Patrick T., President of the City Council of Pittsburgh; President of District 5 of the United Mine Workers of America: September 24, 1968; October 1, 1968; August 8, 1972.
Mullen, John. Former Mayor of Clairton, Pennsylvania. Fall, 1966.
Patterson, George. Staff Representative, District 33, USWA. October 21, 1967.
Zonarich, Nick. Director Department of Industrial Relations, AFL-CIO. May 19, 1966.

Index

456

ORDER COPIES DIRECT FROM PUBLISHER.

Retail price $75 for hard-cover and $50 for soft-cover. Copies may be ordered directly from the publisher and for the discounted price of $50 for hard-cover and $35 for soft-cover (plus shipping). Order from Steel Valley Printers, Homestead, Pa. at 412-461-5650 (fax-412-461-5653) quantity discounts are also available from the publisher.

Copies may also be ordered online at www.PointofPittsburgh.com. Half of all proceeds will be donated to labor education programs.

To arrange a Book-Signing or related public program, please e-mail us at: info@PointofPittsburgh.com. Book signings may be for Union Halls or other organizations.

Cover art is available as a 12 x 18 poster for $10 including postage.

Music inspired by the stories in the Point of Pittsburgh book, by Mike Stout is also available by calling Steel Valley Printers at 412-461-5650 (fax 412-461-5653) or online at www.PointofPittsburgh.com. Conact the publisher, Steel Valley Printers in Homestead, PA at 412-461-5650 for quantity discouts.

The Point of Pittsburgh

Production and Struggle at the Forks of the Ohio

BY **CHARLES MCCOLLESTER**

ILLUSTRATIONS BY **BILL YUND**

People's Pittsburgh 250 Edition (first edition)

BATTLE OF HOMESTEAD FOUNDATION

PITTSBURGH, PENNSYLVANIA

Published:	2008 Pittsburgh, Pennsylvania, U.S.A, Battle of Homestead Foundation
Copyright: Illustrations:	© 2008, Charles McCollester © 2008, Bill Yund
ISBN:	978-0-9818894-0-5 (cloth) 978-0-9818894-1-2 (softcover) All rights reserved.
	People's Pittsburgh 250 Edition Point of Pittsburgh Book Project P. O. Box 60104 Pittsburgh, PA 15211
Typesetting: Layout/Design:	Steel Valley Printers Lloyd Cunningham Jim Hohman
Cover Design:	Bill Yund
Printing:	Allegheny Commercial Printing Pittsburgh, Pennsylvania
For Information or Sales:	Steel Valley Printers, Inc. 107 East Eighth Avenue Homestead, Pennsylvania 15120 U. S. A.
	412-461-5650 412-461-5653 (fax)